Attachment Theory and the Psychoanalytic Process

Attachment Theory and the Psychoanalytic Process

Edited by

MAURICIO CORTINA

Washington School of Psychiatry and Institute for
Contemporary Psychotherapy and Psychoanalysis, Washington DC

and

MARIO MARRONE

Psychoanalyst, London

W
WHURR PUBLISHERS
LONDON AND PHILADELPHIA

© 2003 Whurr Publishers Ltd
First published 2003
by Whurr Publishers Ltd
19b Compton Terrace
London N1 2UN England and
325 Chestnut Street, Philadelphia PA 19106 USA

British Library Cataloguing in Publication Data

A catalogue record for this book
is available from the British Library.

ISBN 1 86156 287 X

Printed and bound in the UK by Athenaeum Press Ltd, Gateshead,
Tyne & Wear.

Dedications

To the memory of my father, who awakened me to the joys of the intellect, and my mother, who at 91 has maintained a contagious *joie de vivre*.
Mauricio Cortina

I wish to dedicate my work in this book to my analyst, Eric Rayner.
Mario Marrone

Contents

Contributors

Hugo Bleichmar, Professor of Psychoanalysis and Director of the Programme on Psychoanalytic Psychotherapy Training at the Comillas University (Madrid). President of Forum Society for Psychoanalytic Psychotherapy. Editor of *Aperturas Psicoanalíticas*. He has published widely in Spanish and – to a lesser degree in English – and has carried out studies on motivation and clinical and psychogenic aspects of depression. Member of the International Attachment Network.

K. Chase Stovall-McClough PhD, Currently employed by an Individual NRSA Award and conducting research at the Anxiety and Traumatic Stress Program, Weill Medical College of Cornell University in New York.

John F. Clarkin PhD, Professor of Clinical Psychology, Department of Psychiatry, Weill Medical College of Cornell University, and the Co-Director of the Personality Disorders Institute and Director of Psychology at the Cornell Medical Center. For the past 12 years, he has directed a large-scale clinical study of the effect of psychodynamic psychotherapy for patients with borderline personality disorder.

Mauricio Cortina, Psychiatrist. Faculty member and supervisor, Washington School of Psychiatry and Institute for Contemporary Psychotherapy and Psychoanalysis in Washington DC. Honorary member, Instituto de Mexicano de Psicoanalisis A.C. and member of the Instituto de Socio-Psicoanalisis A.C. in Mexico City. Assistant Professor, Department of Psychiatry, George Washington University. In private practice in Washington DC. Chair, Washington DC Chapter of the International Attachment Network.

Rafael Cristóbal, Psychiatrist, group analyst, developmental psychologist and psychoanalytic psychotherapist trained in Switzerland. Formerly

Medical Director of the Psychiatric Hospital and Professor of Psychopathology at the University of the Basque Country, he is now Professor of Developmental Psychology at the University of Mondragon (Spain). He is a founder member and Vice-Chair of the Spanish Chapter of the International Attachment Network.

Diana Diamond, Psychologist and psychoanalyst, she is Associate Professor in the Doctoral Program in Clinical Psychology at the City University of New York, and Adjunct Professor of Psychiatry at the New York Presbyterian Hospital – Weill Cornell Medical Center, where she is a senior fellow at the Personality Disorders Institute. She has co-authored several books, including *Affect and Attachment in the Family* (with Jeri Doane) and *Borderline Patients: Extending the Limits of Treatability* (with Koenigsberg, Kernberg, Stone, Appelbaum and Yeomans). She has published a number of articles in the areas of attachment theory, borderline personality and mental representation. She is on the editorial board of *Psychoanalytic Inquiry* and has edited a two-volume series on *Attachment Research and Psychoanalysis: Theoretical Considerations and Clinical Implications*. She is a psychoanalytic candidate at the New York University Postdoctoral Program in Psychoanalysis, and is in private practice in New York.

Nicola Diamond, Director of PhD Studies at Regent's College (City University, London) and psychoanalytic psychotherapist in private practice in London. She obtained her PhD in psychoanalysis at Kent University. She has lectured internationally. She has an interdisciplinary background and has been working in linking psychoanalysis with developmental psychology, the social sciences and philosophy. She is an associate member of the British Association of Psychotherapists (BAP) and founder member, and member of the Executive Committee, of the International Attachment Network.

Pamela A. Foelsch PhD, Clinical Assistant Professor of Psychology in Psychiatry at the Weill Cornell Medical School and Fellow in the Personality Disorders Institute at the Westchester Division of the NYPH. Dr Foelsch is a supervisor and trainer of Transference Focused Psychotherapy.

Mary Gales Shane, Psychiatrist and psychoanalyst, she is Assistant Clinical Professor, Department of Psychiatry, UCLA. Founding secretary of the Autonomous Psychoanalytic Institutes (AAPI). In private practice in Los Angeles California. She is co-author with Morton Shane and Estelle Shane of *Intimate Attachment. Towards a New Self Psychology*.

Sonia Gojman de Millán, Psychologist and psychoanalyst, she is Secretary General of the International Federation of Psychoanalytic Societies. She is training and supervisory analyst at the Instituto Mexicano de Psicoanalisis and a Training and supervisory analyst of the Seminario de Sociopsicoanalisis, A.C. (Semsoac). She is an AAI Trainer (in San Diego, California, and at the University of Berkeley, California). She directs the Attachment Research project of Mexican Indian Dyads and their Social Character. Active social character researcher in various community and inter-cultural projects since 1974. Member of the Social Character International Network. Dr Gojman de Millán was formerly a clinical professor and head of the Social Psychology Department of the Mexican National University (UNAM).

Tirril Harris, Divides her time between psychoanalytic psychotherapy in private practice in North London (registered with the British Association of Psychotherapists) and research in social psychiatry. She is a Senior Research Fellow at the Socio-Medical Research Group, St Thomas' Hospital, London. She has worked with Professor George Brown for a number of decades, producing *Social Origins of Depression* (1978), *Life Events and Illness* (1989) and *Where Inner and Outer Worlds Meet* (2000). Founder member, and member of the Executive Committee, of the International Attachment Network.

Bruno Intreccialagli, Psychiatrist, member of the Board of Directors of the Italian Association of Behavioral and Cognitive Therapies (SITCC), 1994–2000, and Director of Training in the same Association. Lecturer on Cognitive Psychotherapy in the APC School of Psychotherapy, Rome, Italy.

Luis J. Juri, Clinical psychologist and psychoanalytic psychotherapist, he is currently in private practice in the city of Rosario (Argentina). He has been Professor at the Faculty of Psychology of the National University of Rosario. He has published articles and books in Spanish and lectured widely in South America, Spain and the UK. He is a member of International Advisory Committee of the International Attachment Network.

Jean Knox, Psychiatrist and Jungian analyst in private practice in Oxford. She is a professional member of the Society of Analytic Psychology and editor of the *Journal of Analytical Psychology*. She has completed a PhD at the Psychoanalysis Unit, University College London, comparing psychodynamic and cognitive science models of the effect of emotion on memory. She is currently writing a book exploring the implications of research in attachment theory and developmental psychology for psychodynamic concepts such as archetypes and internal objects. She is a member of the Executive Committee of the International Attachment Network.

Hilary Levine PhD, Psychologist at Bellevue Hospital Center and a research assistant in the Personality Disorders Institute at New York Presbyterian Hospital, Westchester Division.

Kenneth N. Levy PhD, Assistant Professor, Department of Psychology, Hunter College and the Graduate School and University Center of the City University of New York; Adjunct Assistant Professor of Psychology in Psychiatry, Weill Medical College of Cornell University.

Giovanni Liotti, Psychiatrist, President of the Italian Association for Behavioral and Cognitive Therapies (SITCC). Teaches implications of attachment theory for cognitive psychotherapy at the APC School of Psychotherapy, Rome, Italy, and in the Postgraduate School of Clinical Psychology of the Salesian University, Rome, Italy. Founder and Past-President of the Roman Association for Research on the Psychopathology of the Attachment System (ARPAS).

Mario Marrone, Formerly a hospital psychiatrist in the National Health Service (UK), he is currently in full-time private practice as a psychoanalyst in London. He is an associate member of the British Psychoanalytical Society, member of the Institute of Group Analysis (London), and member of the London Centre for Psychotherapy. He is also External Supervisor and Training Analyst for CAPP (Centre for Attachment-based Psychoanalytic Psychotherapy, London). He had clinical supervision with John Bowlby for ten years. Founder member and international co-ordinator of the International Attachment Network.

Salvador Millán, Psychiatrist, a co-founder, and training and supervising analyst of the Seminario de Sociopsicoanalisis A.C. Mexico City. He co-directs with Sonia Gojman de Millán the Attachment Research Project of Mexican Indian Dyads and their Social Character. Active social character researcher in various community and inter-cultural projects since 1974.

Malcolm Pines, Psychiatrist, group analyst and psychoanalyst. Formerly a consultant psychotherapist at the Maudsley Hospital and Tavistock Clinic, he is now in private practice as a psychoanalyst in London. He is a founder member of the Institute of Group Analysis (London) and Group Analytic Society. He is Past President of the International Association of Group Psychotherapy and has published and lectured widely and internationally for many years. Honorary member of the International Attachment Network.

Estelle Shane, Psychiatrist and psychoanalyst, Autonomous Psychoanalytic Institute in Los Angeles, California. Clinical Faculty, Department of Adult and Child Psychiatry, University of California, Los Angeles.

Morton Shane, Psychiatrist and psychoanalyst, Clinical Professor, Department of Adult and Child Psychiatry, UCLA. Founding president of the Autonomous Psychoanalytic Institutes (AAPI). In private practice in Los Angeles, California. He is co-author with Estelle Shane and Mary Gales Shane of *Intimate Attachment. Towards a New Self Psychology*.

Doris Silverman, Psychologist and psychoanalyst, she is an adjunct clinical professor in the Postdoctoral Program in Psychoanalysis and Psychotherapy at NYU and is engaged in teaching and supervision. Training analyst fellow, teacher and supervisor at The Institute for Psychoanalytic Training and Research (IPTAR). Dr Silverman has written many articles on infant research with a particular focus on the attachment system, its relevance for psycho-analytic theories and its clinical implications.

June W. Sroufe, Clinical psychologist in private practice, focusing on intervention with children and their families. She is a certified trainer in the Adult Attachment Interview and has conducted research on assess-ment of family relationships and adolescent development.

Howard Steele, Senior Lecturer in Psychology at University College London, where he is also Director of the Attachment Research Unit. He is the Editor of the international journal *Attachment and Human Development* and has published widely on attachment processes across the life cycle and across generations. Honorary member of the International Attachment Network.

Miriam Steele, Child Psychotherapist, Senior Research Fellow at the Anna Freud Centre and Lecturer in Psychology at University College London (UCL). She convenes the Anna Freud Centre-UCL MSc Course in Psychoanalytic Developmental Psychology. Her research is concerned with attachment processes in high-risk adoption and foster care contexts, as well as in low-risk contexts.

Sandra Weiner, Her initial degree was in the Social Sciences. She has worked in education for many years. She is now in private practice as a psychoanalytic psychotherapist in London. She is Associate Member and member of the Professional Committee of the London Centre for Psychotherapy. Member of the International Attachment Network.

Frank E. Yeomans MD, PhD, Clinical Associate Professor of Psychiatry at the Weill Medical College of Cornell University and Senior Supervisor at the Personality Disorders Institute at the New York Presbyterian Hospital, Westchester Division. Dr Yeomans teaches and supervises Transference-Focused Psychotherapy in Quebec, the Netherlands, Switzerland and Germany.

Foreword

PHIL MOLLON

Attachment is a fundamental fact of human psychology – forming its imprint in the dimensions of neurobiology, subjective experience, and interpersonal behavior. The early attachment relationship relentlessly impacts upon many crucial developmental phenomena, such as subtle aspects of the maturation of the brain (the interpersonal *settings* of the brain's functioning), the capacity to regulate emotion and mood, the internal working models that organize the person's expectations and behavior in relation to others, as well as self-esteem and self-image. Basically it is the quality of early attachment that determines the quality of emotional life available to the later adult. These facts, so obvious once understood, were not recognized until Bowlby and subsequent clinicians and researchers began to provide and organize the relevant data.

In this timely book, Mauricio Cortina and Mario Marrone have gathered a rich collection of contributions demonstrating the crucial role of the attachment perspective in understanding and working with issues such as: transference; the therapeutic alliance; developmental history; defensive processes; cognitive science and models of the mind; traumatic memory; sexual disorders; borderline personality disorder; adult intimacy – and many other areas of key significance to both clinicians and researchers.

Why are these considerations of such importance? Quite simply, it is because attachment theory and associated research have evolved to a point where an appreciation of their clinical implications can now be considered essential for the effective and responsible practice of the well-informed psychotherapist or psychoanalyst.

Without some version of attachment theory, psychoanalysis is simply not grounded in developmental reality. The child's personality and its internal models of relationships are formed by the attachment experiences

xviii   Attachment Theory and the Psychoanalytic Process

provided by the environment. There is an absolute dependence on this early environment, which is often not fully reflected in many variants of psychoanalytic theorizing, where the instinctual drives and associated phantasies are implicitly still given primacy. This can result sometimes in a quite unbalanced technical stance in which reconstruction of developmental history (the history of the individual's attachments and development of internal working models) is eschewed in favor of a near exclusive emphasis upon interpreting the patient's activity in relationship to the analyst in the here-and-now. Such technique might be supported by an argument that the infantile state of mind is alive in the present, in the transference, and this is where is must be addressed. However, it seems possible that the neglect of developmental reconstruction might impede the patient's progress, because it may be only through understanding why the original defensive adaptations were felt to be necessary in the childhood environment that a person is able to relinquish these and find a more satisfying reconciliation with reality and an engagement with the opportunities available in adult relationships. It is often the potential awareness of the painful realities of parental neglect, lack of empathy, or malevolence, and the childhood *helplessness* in the face of these, that is defended against most vehemently by the adult patient in analysis – a denial of helplessness that seems to be mirrored in some versions of psychoanalytic theorizing that assume an exaggerated agency on the part of the child. Issues such as these are amongst the many important topics discussed by Marrone and Cortina in their introductory chapters.

Attachment theory is closely compatible with the self psychology originated by Heinz Kohut (Mollon, 2001). Interestingly, Kohut himself did not believe this to be the case. His own view of Bowlby's work was that it was a kind of social or interpersonal psychology, which he saw as distinct from the essentially internal focus of psychoanalysis. He considered psychoanalysis should be concerned with the attempt at *empathic* understanding of the analysand's complex mental states and their developmental origin – the observational focus being *within the analysand's mind* as empathically grasped by the analyst. By contrast, he saw attachment theory (and also the related work of Margaret Mahler) as based upon the investigation *from an external vantage point* of the interactions between child and caregiver. However, had he lived longer, I suspect that Kohut would have recognized how attachment theory, especially in its more recent developments, is highly compatible with many of his own formulations. He would surely have seen, for example, that the view of attachment as the dyadic regulation of affect (Sroufe, 1996) captures something very close to his concept of the selfobject.

Recent advances in understanding neurobiology within an attachment framework (Schore, 1994) powerfully validate Bowlby's and Kohut's emphasis upon the regulatory function of the caregiver. The recurrent interactional experiences within the main attachment relationships directly affect the developing brain, its states of emotional arousal, and its capacities to engage with the brains of others and to perceive the emotions of others. We now know that repeated interpersonal trauma in childhood may significantly impair brain development, as well as creating internal working models that make good relationships impossible – and that this is often the basis for borderline personality disorder (Allen, 2001), rather than constitutionally strong envy or aggression as postulated by some earlier psychoanalytic theories.

One of the refreshing features of attachment theory and its associated clinical practice is that it naturally draws upon, inspires, and interacts with, developmental research. It engages easily with other fields of human study. Fundamental psychoanalytic concerns, such as with the content and process of the unconscious mind and with strategies of defense, need not be in any way threatened by attachment theory – all that is good in psychoanalysis can be preserved. Moreover, psychoanalysts and psychotherapists who ground their work in an attachment framework need not fear that their practice will lack a firm scientific foundation – a real and legitimate worry in the climate of 'clinical governance' in Britain and the increased emphasis on 'evidence-based' interventions in the United States and Europe. I have no doubt that the healthy future of psychoanalysis lies in attachment theory and research – a direction illustrated by the excellent collection of papers in this book.

References

Allen JG (2001) Traumatic Relationships and Serious Mental Disorders. Chichester: Wiley.

Mollon P (2001) Releasing the Self. The Healing Legacy of Heinz Kohut. London: Whurr.

Schore AN (1994) Affect Regulation and the Origin of the Self. Hillsdale, NJ: Erlbaum.

Sroufe, L. A. (1996) Emotional Development. The Organization of Emotional Life in the Early Years. New York: Cambridge University Press.

Acknowledgements

Many deadlines came and went as we put this book together and it ended up being significantly longer than anticipated. Thanks to Louis Breger, Giovanni Liotti, Michael Maccoby, Alan and June Sroufe for commenting on some of the chapters of this book and making valuable suggestions, and to Philip Mollon for a perceptive and thoughtful Foreword. We also wish to express our gratitude to Sandra Weiner and Tirril Harris for their editorial assistance.

I (Mauricio Cortina) thank my wife, Barbara Lenkerd who read, critiqued and edited chapters that I authored alone and with Mario Marrone. She has been my secure base that has allowed me to explore, and at the same time a tough and loving critic of my work.

I (Mario Marrone) thank Jackie Levitsky for having introduced me to Mauricio Cortina. Working with Mauricio has been a great pleasure. It has also been a source of joy to discover how compatible our thinking is and the cooperation we were able to develop across the North Atlantic (a sentiment that Mauricio shares). By the way, what did people do before there was e-mail?

Mauricio has been the 'chief in command' of this operation and I am in debt for the meticulous care he has put into editing some chapters and producing what seems like a coherent book. My whole input into this book has taken the form of mutual collaboration with colleagues. I have also benefited from the intellectual support of Nicola Diamond, many of my friends and colleagues of our International Attachment Network, as well as from Patrick Casement, my current supervisor.

CHAPTER 1

Introduction: reclaiming Bowlby's contribution to psychoanalysis

MARIO MARRONE AND MAURICIO CORTINA

In the past decade clinicians have taken a growing interest in attachment theory and the rich and fruitful research agenda it has spawned. This volume, a collection of chapters written by an international group of clinicians and scholars, is an expression of this interest and excitement.[1] All the contributors to this volume integrate an expanding body of knowledge informed by attachment theory with new developments in psychoanalysis, neuroscience, developmental psychology and cognitive science. We hope this volume will help in validating the importance of attachment theory for contemporary psychoanalytic thinking.

We have organized the introduction in three parts:

- Part one consists of a summary of central concepts of attachment theory.
- In part two we address why the psychoanalytic community initially ignored Bowlby's work[2] while his work was being productively tested and developed by developmental psychologists and social psychologists.
- In part three we examine some of the reasons behind the dramatic change of opinion among many psychoanalysts and clinicians in favor of attachment theory. This change is particularly evident in the United States, although in many parts of Europe Bowlby's work still remains relatively unknown within the psychoanalytic community. We hope this book will contribute to attachment theory acquiring full citizens' rights around the world.

Part one: key points in attachment theory

Attachment theory was formulated in order to achieve greater coherence and accuracy in describing and explaining observations made in the clinical and empirical settings. Attachment theory was used by Bowlby as a

1

convenient term to include a wide range of theoretical postulates as well as clinical and empirical observations. There is more to attachment theory than just a theory of attachment ties across the life span. Bowlby developed a new theory of motivation that includes affects, cognitive appraisals, control systems and memory systems, developed and mobilized to support and sustain attachment ties. Bowlby also sketched an information processing approach toward understanding defensive processes to explain the psychological mechanisms that come into play when there is trauma or loss of these affectional ties or there is neglect or rejection by attachment figures. We now turn to these key concepts.

Attachment theory is a theory of normal developmental processes and of psychopathology

The heart of attachment theory consists in recognizing the critical importance of the attachment relationships and the secure base phenomena throughout development (Sroufe, 1996; Waters and Cummings, 2000; and June Sroufe, Chapter 9 in this volume). Ainsworth et al. (1978) observed that children use attachment figures as a base from which to explore their surroundings. Longitudinal research has shown that the freedom to explore the world, the ability to moderate impulses, to handle stress and change, and the capacity for establishing good peer relations or intimate relations all build on the foundation of a secure base with attachment figures (Sroufe, 1996; Thompson, 1999; Sroufe, Egeland and Carlson, 1999; Cassidy, 2001).

Developing a secure base in early childhood is a foundation for a sense of security. New developmental tasks build on this foundation and by middle school, peer relations, athletic and academic competence, competition and/or cooperation with siblings become new sources of security (or insecurity). During adolescence, identification with peer groups, incipient romantic relationships and physical appearance can become all-consuming issues. In early adulthood the selection of a vocation or career path, the capacity to develop intimate relations and the consolidation of identity take front and center as key developmental tasks (Erikson, 1950; Sroufe, 1990b; Waters and Cummings, 2000). Furthermore, all these developmental sources of security and insecurity are played out in the context of specific economic conditions, social institutions and belief systems (religious and secular) that define the limits and possibilities for development.

Our point is that, while Bowlby's theory is a base for understanding the origin of security and anxiety, to develop a broader view of the sources of security (or insecurity) in life we also need models of development envisioned by psychoanalytic pioneers such as Erik Erikson (1950),

Fromm and Maccoby (1970) and psychologists such as Bronfenbrenner (1979) who view development as the product of complex interactions between individuals within specific social, economic and cultural contexts (see Chapter 8 by Gojman and Millán in this volume and the special issue on contextualism and developmental psychopathology edited by Cicchetti and Nurcombe, 1998). New developmental tasks are constrained or enhanced by social sorrows. This broad perspective from which to look at the importance of attachment relationships was perfectly congenial to Bowlby (see below).

Bowlby's point of departure was based on observing young children's reactions to relatively brief separations from their attachment figures. The observation of the sequence of protest and anger, despair and detachment became the basis for developing attachment theory and reconceptualizing some of Freud's astute clinical observations made during the course of his career. Freud first encountered the problem of defense in his cases of hysteria. It was much later in 'Mourning and melancholia' that he tried to conceptualize loss and it was not until 'Inhibitions, symptoms and anxiety' that he came full circle to the problems of separation anxiety and attachment. As Bowlby noted, in 'Inhibitions, symptoms and anxiety' Freud had sketched a new route: 'Anxiety is the danger of losing the object, the pain of mourning the reaction to the actual loss of the object, and defense a mode of dealing with anxiety and pain' (Bowlby, 1973, p. 29). Freud, working retrospectively with clinical populations, had gone from defense, to loss and separation, to attachment, whereas Bowlby, looking at the same phenomena developmentally and prospectively, went in reverse order: from attachment, to separation and loss, and finally to defense. Indeed, the best way to understand Bowlby's trilogy on Attachment (1969), Separation (1973) and Loss (1980) is to see these three volumes as a development of this central insight.

Bowlby used the concept of *developmental pathways*, proposed by the biologist C.H. Waddington (1957), to understand normal and pathological development. He eschewed concepts of 'regression' and 'fixation' rooted in Freudian metapsychology and mechanistic conceptions of fixed developmental stages. From a developmental pathway perspective, human personality is viewed as a system that develops unceasingly along one or another of an array of possible and discrete pathways. Some pathways are optimal and promote resilience to future adversity in life. Other pathways are suboptimal and promote vulnerability to life stressors. Pathways are strongly influenced by the quality of interaction between the growing individual and his or her attachment figures within specific social and cultural contexts. The greatest deviance from an optimal pathway takes place when a child has been severely traumatized within attachment relationships, that is to say when sexual, emotional or physical abuse occurs. Abandonment, rejection, neglect and dysfunctional parenting are also common conditions promoting vulnerability. Bowlby's model of development is consistent with the emerging multidisciplinary field of developmental psychopathology that views normality and psychopathology together. Attachment theory has made important contributions to this exciting new field (Cicchetti, 1989; Sroufe, 1990a, 1997).

Attachment theory is a theory of motivation

Bowlby's revision of Freud's theory of motivation consisted of two parts. First, Bowlby, like many other major psychoanalytic innovators, rejected Freud's mechanistic tension-reduction concepts of libido and psychic energy. Second, Bowlby moved beyond Freud's dualistic theory of motivation (sexual versus self-preservative drives and in a later version, Eros versus the death instinct). Bowlby thought that attachment, caregiving and exploration were closely linked and functioned as separate motivational systems. Without minimizing the importance of sexuality and aggression, attachment theory helps us look at aggression and sexuality in perspective. For instance, in normal circumstances, anger and protest (aggression) serve an important adaptive function of preserving attachment ties. Bowlby (1988) regretted that he had not been able to address the relation between attachment and sexuality, but hoped that this important issue would be tackled in the future (see Chapters 18 and 19 in this volume for a discussion of attachment and sexuality in normal and pathological development).

However, by describing attachment as a *behavioral system*, Bowlby inadvertently contributed to the failure of many psychoanalysts to see that he was providing a new theory of *motivation* based on control theory and ethological concepts rather than on Freud's dated theory of drives based on atavistic impulses and psychic energy. While Bowlby often described attachment as a behavioral system, he also described attachment as an instinctive source of motivation, and the attachment relationship as an affectional tie. Of course, attachment is *all* the above, but we believe it is best conceptualized as a *motivational system*. The following remarks may clarify this point. Seeking protection from an attachment figure is monitored by felt security. Felt security or insecurity are organismic signals that evaluate whether internal and external conditions require the activation of the attachment system. To put it in Bowlby's terms, felt security is part of a goal-corrected control system that functions to elicit care in moments of distress. '*Seeking physical proximity to attachment figures (through behavior) is a means to achieve the goal of felt security*' (Sroufe and

Waters, 1977). Support for this view is based on the common observation that the need for physical proximity in young children will change from moment to moment according to conscious and unconscious appraisals of danger. Behaviors change. What remains constant is the felt need for security. Attachment behaviors also change dramatically through development.

What has been selected through evolution are not discrete behavioral systems, but functional adaptive systems (new phenotypes) such as the use of an attachment figure from which to explore the world and interpersonal motivational systems such as the attachment–caregiving system. New phenotypes (neophenotypes) are the product of complex gene–environmental interactions (coactions) that come together during the course of ontogenetic development (Cortina, 1996; Gottlieb, 1997). In other words, neophenotypes (based on developmental innovations) are the 'unit' of selection. This developmental unit comprises organismic signals (emotions), control systems, appraisal processes, memory and behavior systems. Behavioral systems are just one of the important components of this developmental matrix. For all these reasons, we believe it is better to think of attachment as being part of a developmental-motivational system than to think of it as being primarily a behavioral system.

As a motivational system, attachment has to be distinguished from its complement, the caregiving system (Heard and Lake, 1997). The attachment and the caregiving systems constitute the attachment relationship. Attachment also has to be distinguished from exploration and competence, from sexuality, from physiological needs, like hunger and thirst, and from what Lichtenberg (1989) calls the aversive (fight/flight) system, which attachment theory calls the fear system and which we refer to as the alarm system. Bleichmar (Chapter 16) conceptualizes the desire to be validated and recognized by the other as a separate person, yet simultaneously feel united and whole by this recognition as a separate motivational system – traditionally thought of as *normal* narcissism within psychoanalysis. Liotti and Intreccialagli (Chapter 15) describe several interpersonal motivational systems, including the attachment and caregiving systems, but they add a competitive or agonistic system and the cooperative system to their interpersonal set of motivational systems. We think that the need for affiliation to a social group *beyond* the attachment to family members is also a basic feature of the human condition. During 99 per cent of the history of our species, human societies were organized in the form of small bands of hunters and gatherers. Selective pressures at the group level may have led to the genetic fixation of behavioral adaptations such as cooperation and altruism.[3] Bowlby was very enthusiastic about the idea of affiliation to groups (personal communication with Mario Marrone) and thought that the idea was consistent with the evolutionary framework of attachment theory. A complementary discussion of motivation is to be found in the book Attachment and Intersubjectivity (Diamond and Marrone, 2003).

Depending on the appraisal of environmental conditions and inner states, motivational systems may be activated or deactivated sequentially. For instance, a state of felt security (that deactivates the attachment system) may activate exploration and play. Or a threat to the attachment system may activate the alarm (fight/flight) system. Some motivational systems may also be activated defensively. Exploration can be used to defend against the need for comfort (as in avoidant attachment strategies). The sexual system can be used defensively to defend against the threat of intimacy (see Chapters 16 and 19). It remains to be seen if future developmental, clinical or biological research will support some of these ideas in regard to distinct but interrelated motivational systems. For now, the best tested of these motivational systems has been the attachment system and the intimately associated caregiving, exploratory and alarm fight/flight systems.

In emphasizing attachment as a motivational system, we do not mean to imply that Ainsworth's or Bowlby's attention to behavior was misguided. Quite the contrary, attachment theory draws strength from behavioral observations made by ethologists of attachment behavior in nonhuman primates and by developmental psychologists of attachment behavior in humans. The Robertsons' observations on the effects of separation of young children from their parents (Robertson and Robertson, 1989) and the enormous wealth of naturalistic observations made by Ainsworth in Uganda and in Baltimore have also played an immense role in the development of attachment theory. However, the strength of attachment theory has always been to infer the meaning of any given behavior according to its relational, developmental and cultural context rather than assume that similar behaviors have similar meanings (regardless of context) or that attachment behaviors will remain unchanged throughout development.

Attachment theory is a relational theory of socio-psychological interactions

Bowlby clearly understood that attachment relationships do not exist in isolation and that parent–child relationships had to be seen as developing within the broader context of group and family dynamics (personal communication with Mario Marrone). Attachment theory reaffirms a movement from a one-person psychology to a multi-person psychology (Diamond, 1996, 1998; Cortina, 2000; Diamond and Marrone, 2003). There has been a misconception that attachment theory merely reflects a dyadic or *two-person psychology* model. Bowlby thought that dyadic relationships do not take place in a vacuum; they take place in a socio-cultural context. In discussions he held with Earl Hopper at the Institute of Group Analysis in London (Marrone, 1998, pp. 28–29), Bowlby made it clear that attachment theory was compatible with the socio-cultural school of psychoanalysis. Individuals can be understood only as part of an interactional web that involves families, social and cultural institutions as well as economic realities (Erikson, 1950; Fromm and Maccoby, 1970, Gojman and Millán, Chapter 8 in this volume). As Nicola Diamond (Chapter 17) notes, if individuals are conceived as discrete entities inhabiting their own private world, it is difficult to understand how they come to appropriate this world as internal working models of self and others.

Attachment theory is a theory of the encoding and representation of experience within different memory systems

Parent–child interactional patterns become internal structures (*internal working models* – IWMs) with organizing functions over the psychological, psychosomatic and psychosocial life of the individual. Bowlby's concept of internal working models is an alternative to concepts such as internal objects, introjection and internalization (see Cortina, Chapter 12). Building on Tulving's (1972) work on memory systems, Bowlby pointed out that memory could be stored *semantically* as general propositions about self and others (I am lovable, significant others are trustworthy) and *episodically* as memories of specific biographical episodes. Clinically, this distinction is very important. What a child is told about specific events or interactions ('I am only doing this for your own good') and the child's own experience of the event or interaction might be quite different. What a parent might label as 'good' may be based on his or her need for control. Hence, the child will experience 'being good' as oppressive. Because experience is encoded and stored semantically and episodically, some children grow up with two very different and contradictory IWMs: what they *actually* experienced (usually a weak IWM) and what they are told they *should* experience (usually a dominant IWM). Further developments in the field of cognitive science made it clear that experience is also stored at least at two levels: the subsymbolic level (procedural or implicit memory) and the symbolic levels (declarative or explicit memory). We now have to add to Bowlby's concept of IWM the idea that IWM can be encoded at subsymbolic (non-representational) levels and symbolic (representational) levels (see Chapters 12, 13, 15 and 17 for discussion of some clinical implications of these issues).

Attachment theory is a theory of anxiety

Bowlby supported the view that the main source of anxiety in childhood is the threat of losing an attachment figure. This view contrasts with Freud's first theory of anxiety, that understood anxiety as originating from the build-up of libido, but is consistent with Freud's (1926) signal theory of anxiety. In this second theory, anxiety is triggered whenever individuals assess a current situation as being reminiscent of a previous experience in which they felt helpless (a danger situation). In early childhood, the most common situation leading to a sense of danger and helplessness is an unexpected separation or loss of an attachment figure. This view, central to attachment theory, contrasts with the Kleinian view that the main source of anxiety is fundamentally internal and arises out of the threat posed by the death instinct and its derivatives. Bowlby's theory of anxiety has been usefully elaborated by Main (2000a, 2000b). Main makes a distinction between *fear with solution* observed within the *organized* (secure and insecure) patterns of attachment and *fear without solution* (that leads to a temporary breakdown of organization), and is observed within the *disorganized* patterns of attachment.

Attachment theory offers a good base from which to develop a general theory of affects and emotions

According to Bowlby, some of the strongest and most significant emotions are rooted in and linked to attachment-relevant events, such as the formation, break-up and renewal of attachment relationships as well as feeling sensitively or insensitively understood and responded to. Attachment figures have a major role to play in the early regulation of affects and arousal levels in young children and allow for the gradual expression of strong positive and negative emotions and the gradual capacity to engage in exploration of novel situations without becoming overstimulated (Sroufe, 1996). Cortina (Chapter 12), Bleichmar (Chapter 16) and Liotti and Intrecciagli (Chapter 15) note that some emotions are often associated with specific motivational systems such as the exploratory, sexual, alarm (fight/flight) systems, the need for intimacy (Bleichmar) or the agonistic or ranking system (Liotti and Intrecciagli). These different motivational systems *may or may not* be linked with the attachment and caregiving systems. But the emotional responses associated with the activation of these motivational systems serve the function of subjectively monitoring the goal-corrected aims inherent in each of these motivational systems. As Bleichmar and Cortina point out, emotions have an expressive as well as an inductive function that may promote intimacy (Bleichmar, Chapter 16) and communication (Cortina, Chapter 12) as well as 'contagious' qualities that produce a sense of merger with the other (Bleichmar, Chapter 16).

Attachment theory is a theory of defense

Attachment theory bases its theory of defense on well-established and commonly accepted psychoanalytic principles and observations. It proposes that unconscious defenses against anxiety and painful affects are rooted in interpersonal events and that defense mechanisms influence a person's interpersonal modes of relating. It also suggests that defense mechanisms and attachment strategies shape a person's character defenses, e.g. the way an individual regulates felt security and optimal proximity to significant others. In this respect, attachment theory bears a strong resemblance to Sullivan's interpersonal theory (for instance, Sullivan's concept of security operations; Cortina, 2001). Defensive processes operate at many levels. Defensive processes can skew internal working models toward rigid and inflexible models. Particularly in cases involving trauma, incompatible and contradictory IWM of attachment figures might remain segregated by defensive processes (Bowlby, 1980). Defensive processes involving trauma might also disrupt a sense of cohesive bodily self and of agency (Nicola Diamond, Chapter 17). Defensive processes may uncouple cognitive, emotional and motivational systems that are normally linked together (Cortina, Chapter 12).

Attachment theory is a theory of the self

Alan Sroufe (Sroufe and Waters, 1977; Sroufe, 1990b) has proposed an organizational model of the self in which the attachment relationship is seen as the most important organizer of early experience. The model holds the view that a person's capacity to view himself as a separate individual, with an optimal and realistic self-esteem, capable of maintaining a state of relative internal integration, self-regulation or cohesiveness, is normally based upon an optimal or secure attachment history (see Chapter 12 for further discussion of an integrative or holistic model of the self). Dissociative states of the self are – by and large – the result of early traumas in attachment relationships (see Chapters 15 and 17).

Attachment theory is a theory that explains the intergenerational transmission of attachment patterns

Parental functions are organized by the parent's own internal working models, which in turn were formed under the influence of their own parents' internal working models. There is now robust empirical support for this hypothesis (van IJzendoorn, 1995). For instance, one study using three-way comparison between infant and adult categories found a 65 per cent transmission of attachment patterns across three generations (Benoit and Parker, 1994; see also part three of this chapter).

Part two: why was Bowlby's contribution initially ignored or rejected?

From its inception, psychoanalysis lacked a good theory of normal development. This deficiency has hindered its efforts in developing a better understanding of the processes that lead to deviations from normal development as well as efforts to understand the self-righting potential that we support in the psychoanalytic process. Maladaptive developmental pathways provide the fertile ground from which psychopathology will flourish. The central subject matter of psychoanalysis has always been an understanding of demonic forces that haunt the human soul. It was Freud's great discovery that most of these demonic forces operated at unconscious levels. By shedding light and meaning into the dark recesses of the human mind, Freud hoped to liberate the human spirit from bondage. 'Where id was, there ego shall be' became the rallying cry and the *raison d'être* of the psychoanalytic movement. As Freud grappled with these demonic forces in his patients, he courageously tried to come to terms with his own demons. It was here that Freud got off to a bad start from which we are still trying to recover 100 years later.

In his self-analysis, Freud misconceived his need for affectional ties to his mother (and to attachment figures in general) as sexual in nature. Why this gross misconception? Freud was traumatized by catastrophic events in his early childhood. His mother was mourning the loss of her brother Julius, who died at age 20 from tuberculosis just before she gave birth to her second son, named after her deceased brother. Sigmund (the first born) was 2 years old when his infant brother Julius died from an intestinal infection. Six more babies followed before Sigmund was 10 years old. On top of that, Freud lost his nursemaid at age 2½ (she was caught stealing and sent to jail) and his father lost his business around this time and had to move his family from Freiberg to Vienna. As a consequence of this move Freud also lost his first playmates. Freud himself considered this move catastrophic for the family. The combination of the mother grieving fresh losses, the loss of his nursemaid, his mother having one baby after another and the collapse of his father's business must have combined to overwhelm little 'Sigi' with grief, fear and sadness (Breger, 2000). Freud's travel phobia, originating from this traumatic move from Freiberg to a poor ghetto in Vienna, lasted all his life.

In his excellent biography of Freud, Louis Breger (2000) makes the case that Freud defended himself from the impact of these early traumas by means of a brilliant but idiosyncratic interpretation of Oedipus Rex. Freud's interpretation of the oedipal myth served as a 'cover story' that concealed a hidden plot: the catastrophic events of his early childhood. By interpreting the child's tie to attachment figures as being sexual, Freud is able to make the little boy more adult-like, an erotic rival for his mother's affection rather than a dependent and vulnerable child. Throughout his career, Freud continued to confuse and conflate two very different motivational systems: the affectional tender feelings emanating from the attachment system, and the erotic feelings emanating from the sexual system. This was a veritable 'confusion of tongues' as Ferenczi (1933) put it. This confusion of tongues seriously limited Freud's clinical approach, as was noted by Ferenczi in his analysis with Freud:

> My own analysis could not be pursued deeply enough because my analyst (by his own admission of a narcissistic nature) with his strong determination to be healthy and his antipathy toward any weakness and abnormality, could not follow me into those depths (Ferenczi, 1932, p. 62).

Ferenczi's observations are consistent with Breger's interpretation. With the exception of a few charismatic friends and close confidants like Fleischl, Flies and Jung, whom he initially idealized and then rejected; Freud rarely allowed himself to feel vulnerable in intimate relationships. Instead he identified with towering intellectual figures like Leonardo da Vinci and with conquistadors and adventurers like Oedipus and Alexander the Great and Hannibal. The end result of this tortuous history is that Freud projected into children the psychopathology he observed in himself and in his adult patients. Consequently, children began to be seen as harboring incestuous and murderous impulses, a psychoanalytic version of the Augustinian doctrine of Man's inherent evilness.

Melanie Klein, an enormously influential figure in the psychoanalytic world, also experienced multiple losses and had depressive tendencies (see Grosskurth, 1987). Her tendency to dismiss the importance of the impact of real life events during development might have been an unconscious defense against her own pain. The developmental histories of Freud and Klein support Hamilton's (1985) contention that the main reason Bowlby's work was ignored stems from the fact that attachment theory specifically addresses issues of trauma, separation and loss. These memories engender enormous pain, fright and helplessness, and frequently become repressed or dissociated. With a few notable exceptions, the psychoanalytic community colluded for too long in ignoring the reality of the maltreatment and neglect of children. This has been reflected not only in theory, but also in the tendency to confine analytic explorations to the here-and-now, to the neglect of the patient's attachment history. Bowlby believed that an analyst who rigidly confines his work to the *here-and-now* invalidates the patient's account of negative experiences in childhood and leaves the patient alone to deal with his plight. Having sought therapy, and feeling left alone once again, the patient further withdraws into his shell. Bowlby thought that a patient is more likely to shut off from consciousness painful events of his past than to invent events that never happened (personal communication with Mario Marrone). See Cortina and Marrone (Chapter 2) for further discussion of this issue.

The tendency to conceptualize normal development based on clinical reconstructions with patients

The tendency of skewing normal development toward pathology has been ubiquitous in most psychoanalytic theorizing. This was probably unavoidable. Early pioneers had to build theory from somewhere and the only data at hand were their own personalities (Atwood and Stolorow, 1993) and clinical observations with patients, who of course, come to the consulting room with emotional troubles. Because the study of early development was basically made retrospectively with clinical populations, development was impregnated with language taken from psychopathology. The pathologizing of normality was most evident with early Kleinian thinking, even though Klein added a matricentric twist to Freud's patriarchal views that emphasized the rivalry between the father and son as a key to understanding neurosis. In order to maintain the attachment with mother, Klein's infant has to split the desire for care into a good mother/good object, and destructive and greedy impulses into a bad mother/bad object (the paranoid-schizoid position). It is only after the mothering figure can contain and 'metabolize' these destructive impulses that infants can integrate these split off imagoes (the depressive position) and achieve a sense of wholeness. Colwyn Trevarthen, a distinguished infant researcher, believes that the Kleinian retrospective view of infancy corresponds to that of a traumatized child. Research based on normal development does not validate this view of infancy (personal communication to Mario Marrone).

It is against this historical backdrop that we can begin to understand the utter incomprehension and hostility that was directed at Bowlby's contribution, particularly among his Kleinian colleagues. In the late 1950s Bowlby gave a brilliant series of papers to the British Psychoanalytic

Society which had a particularly negative reception from most of his colleagues (see Bretherton, 1991, pp. 17–18; Marrone, 1998, pp. 25–6).[4]

At the time Bowlby gave these papers it was an absolute requirement that authors declared their debt to Freud and trace connections between Freud's work and their own (Arden, 2001). It was unacceptable to disagree with Freud beyond certain limits without risking becoming a psychoanalytic pariah. Those who questioned established theory were considered to be 'in need of further analysis'. As Kernberg (1993) points out, by and large, the organization of psychoanalytic institutes has supported the establishment of party lines and has conspired against psychoanalytic programs becoming educational institutions that foster a spirit of free inquiry.[5]

What was Bowlby's response to this form of idolatry? Bowlby thought that Freud was a great explorer and innovator and that psychoanalysis was on to all the right questions. But he believed there was a huge gap between the brilliant clinical observations made by psychoanalysis and the theory that was used to explain these observations. He believed that the best way to honor Freud was to take a critical look at his work and build a better framework to address the clinical issues Freud had grappled with. Bowlby always considered himself a psychoanalyst and believed that his work was in keeping with the best psychoanalytic tradition. He was baffled when his psychoanalytic colleagues rejected his work as not being psychoanalytic.

Bowlby described himself as a 'plunger' who had dared to plunge into new territory in order to provide better explanations of clinical phenomena. He admitted to struggling to overcome his fears in order to take the bold steps toward a new theory, which involved areas like ethology and cybernetics, where he considered himself an amateur (comments made at University of Virginia conference in 1985). It was only later that his bold ideas found empirical support. Bowlby emphasized the enormous importance of this phase of exploration in his career. He pointed out that his ideas had not come out ready-made, like Athena emerging from the head of Zeus.

Bowlby's view of infancy and the nature of the infant's tie to his mother offered a radically different view from those of Freud and Klein. Like most contemporary models of development (Stern, 1985; Emde, 1988), Bowlby saw young children as being biologically prepared to interact with primary caregivers. Bowlby's 'adapted infant' does not possess the mental abilities to perform the complex defense mechanisms envisioned by Klein. The Kleinian school treated phantasies as if they were 'hard wired' (preformed) and needed only the experience of frustration to emerge in full form (the 'phantasmagoric infant'). Bowlby was very critical of this 'autonomous' view of phantasy, but he did not discard the concept of phantasy. He regarded phantasy as a way of making sense of interpersonal experience (personal communication with Mario Marrone) but insisted that it was necessary to pay close attention to actual events, which were the base from which phantasy was elaborated. Infants do not possess the elaborate capacity for imagination envisioned by Klein, which cannot be part of the developmental repertoire of infants until children are about 3 years old (see Chapters 12 and 13 in this volume for further discussion of these issues). The ethologically based model used by Bowlby to understand the nature of an infant's tie to attachment figures belonged to a different universe than the one inhabited by his psychoanalytic colleagues. Even an analyst of the stature of Sutherland (who was a close colleague of Bowlby during the Second World War and at the Tavistock Clinic) thought that Bowlby's contribution amounted to a 'behavioral psychoanalysis' oblivious to the dynamics of the internal world of phantasy. Phantasy was the code word used by Kleinians to describe their vision of the unconscious. Bowlby's views were a direct challenge to this vision; he should not have been surprised by the swift, negative reaction he received from his colleagues.

Luis Juri and Mario Marrone (Chapters 10 and 11) present a compelling case based on Kuhn's (1962) concept of paradigms for understanding the resistance to attachment theory within the psychoanalytic community. They believe that the revision of psychoanalytic theory proposed by Bowlby is not just a matter of offering a slightly modified view of psychoanalysis. Attachment theory proposes a completely new framework from which to understand clinical and developmental phenomena that have traditionally been interpreted with concepts of drives, libido, cathexis, fixation, regression sublimation and so forth. Attachment theory does not just tinker with different interpretations of clinical phenomena involving loss, separation or trauma, it completely re-conceptualizes how we think and see these phenomena. Any paradigm shift of this magnitude is often met by vigorous and at times vitriolic attacks by people who work within the old paradigm. Appeals to rules of evidence and to normal practices of verification and discourse are often set aside in the heat of battle. It is only after the dust has settled that the logic, reasonableness and necessity of the new paradigm becomes evident. We believe that this description of paradigm shifts is exactly what happened to attachment theory. Which takes us to our next point. What is happening that is allowing the new paradigm of attachment theory to take hold?

Part three: what has changed that has allowed a favorable reception of Bowlby's ideas?

Several factors have come into play since Bowlby first started publishing his ideas that have dramatically changed the climate of opinion in favor of Bowlby's ideas.

1. Beginning in the 1960s observations and studies carried out by sociologists, social workers, psychiatrists, clinical psychologists and family therapists highlighted the significant prevalence of child sexual, physical and emotional abuse and their consequences for later development. Maltreatment of children and family violence could no longer be ignored by clinicians and psychoanalysts. Attention to real events played right into the main strength of attachment theory: its attention to the actuality of children's experience.

2. A new model of development, strongly influenced by empirical research with infants and young children, began to take hold. Although assigning a date to this sea change is arbitrary, if forced to pick we would probably say that the publication of Lichtenberg's (1983) *Psychoanalysis and Infant Research* and Stern's (1985) *Interpersonal World of the Infant* were definite landmarks. Stern elegantly chronicled the results of this research with infants and began spelling out some of its clinical implications. The research agenda described by Stern was based on what infants *could do*, rather than focusing on their obvious immaturity. Infant researchers began to recognize the remarkable competencies that infants came equipped with, such as the capacity for cross-modal integration of stimuli coming from different sense organs, the capacity to select invariant features that characterized their interaction with caregivers and to generalize these interactions as subsymbolic schemas of self with others. This is what Stern calls RIGs – representations of interactions that become generalized. All these capacities are performed with minimal capacity to symbolize experience. Stern's RIG's are an almost identical concept to Bowlby's internal working models (IWM) concept, except that RIGs are encoded at a subsymbolic level of experience. In other words, RIGs are nonrepresentational (procedural) IWMs. This emerging model of development began to undermine the 'phantasmagoric infant' ensconced in clinical lore.

3. Simultaneously with this development, research informed by attachment theory began to be disseminated and known, and was incorporated in the thinking of some prominent empirically oriented psychoanalysts like Stern, Emde, Eagle and Lichtenberg. Research

informed by attachment theory confirmed basic tenets of Bowlby's ideas, but was compelling in its own right, enriching and expanding attachment theory in new directions. Two important strands of this research agenda are worthy of mention: the discovery of the basic patterns of attachment by Ainsworth (together with the later discovery of the disorganized pattern) and the development of the Adult Attachment Interview (AAI).

Attachment patterns and their impact on social and emotional development

Ainsworth et al.'s (1978) discovery of secure, avoidant and ambivalent patterns of attachment in infancy showed how these basic adaptive relational patterns are constructed in infancy from interactions with primary caregivers. A fourth 'pattern', the disorganized/disoriented category (this 'pattern' is probably best conceptualized as an added dimension to the basic organized patterns), was discovered within the past 20 years and has more serious pathological implications (Main and Weston, 1981; Main and Solomon, 1986; see Hesse and Main, 2000; and Cassidy and Mohr, 2002, for reviews).

The discovery of attachment patterns led to the design of several methodologically sophisticated longitudinal research studies. Key questions in these studies have been to understand how these early relational patterns affect later social and emotional development and to understand the continuities or discontinuities of these relational patterns over time. The most ambitious of these studies (now in its third decade) is being carried out at the University of Minnesota by a research team led by Byron Egeland and Alan Sroufe. This research project demonstrates how relational patterns are carried forward as (mostly) unconscious expectations and attitudes in regard to the nature, availability and responsiveness of attachment figures. In turn, unconscious expectations, together with environmental influences, begin to skew development along certain pathways. Pathways based on histories of secure attachment are more likely to promote autonomy and the development of positive relationships with peers and adults than pathways with histories of insecure or disorganized attachment (Sroufe, 1996, 1997; Cortina, 1999; Weinfield et al., 1999, for reviews).

This carefully crafted research project confirmed, for the first time, what every psychoanalytically informed clinician knows: namely, that relational patterns originating in the past continue to influence behavior and relationships in the present, and that the influences from the past are mostly unconscious. Needless to say, the relational patterns discovered by

Ainsworth and Main do not reflect the variety and complexity of patterns observed clinically. It is important to emphasize this point because there is an increasing tendency on the part of some attachment-informed clinicians to simplistically cluster their patients into these categories, without taking into account the fact that these categories have been discovered through research and do not reflect the complexity of a patient's psychic life. However, these categories do point to basic unconscious 'strategies', which emerge from infancy and childhood and continue to organize attachment relationships across the life span. This organization is largely based on representation of experience, that is, on working models of self and others (Bowlby, 1973).

Internal working models become expressed in the form of expectations and attributions of meaning in relation to attachment-relevant events and can influence the development of character-based traits and attitudes. Freud was the first to understand that 'transference' was based on early templates of experience that were carried forward toward important figures in a patient's present life. See Cortina and Marrone (Chapter 2) for further discussion of this issue.

The Adult Attachment Interview

An important strand of research developed as attention became concentrated on the study of attachment patterns at the 'level of representation' (Main et al., 1986). Here the research question is how do relational patterns, based on attachment relationships, become represented and how can this process of representation best be captured and studied?

One of the many measures used to study the process of representation is the Adult Attachment Interview (Main and Goldwyn, 1983–1998). The Adult Attachment Interview (AAI) is a clinical semi-structured interview that lasts 60 to 90 minutes. In the interview individuals are asked to describe and evaluate their experience with attachment figures beginning with their earliest memories. Questions regarding experiences of separation, loss and trauma are also part of the interview. Several 'states of mind' in regard to attachment are scored based on the degree of coherence exhibited in the interview (see the Appendix, at the end of this volume, for a description of the AAI categories and the infant attachment categories based on the Strange Situation).

These findings add to previous longitudinal research showing lawful continuities and discontinuities of attachment patterns across the first decades of life by demonstrating an *intergenerational transmission* of attachment patterns. In other words, parents with autonomous interviews in the AAI are more likely to develop a secure attachment with their infants, whereas parents with dismissive and preoccupied interviews are likely to develop, respectively, avoidant and ambivalent attachment patterns with their infants. The adult U/d category is also empirically linked to the disorganized attachment category of infancy (see Chapter 6 by Steele and Steele for a state-of-the-art description of the clinical uses of the AAI).

These results are again well known to family therapists and clinicians working with children, who see that relational patterns and conflicts running in families are often repeated from one generation to the next.

The relational turn in psychoanalysis

Perhaps a decisive factor in the growing interest in attachment theory within the psychoanalytic community is based on the shift in the center of gravity of psychoanalysis from drive theories to relational theories. No single author or school of thought is responsible for this paradigm shift. It is the result of a collective effort of reform and revision that began from the very inception of psychoanalysis with the first dissidents, Adler and Jung, and has continued unabated, in one form or another, to the present.

Greenberg and Mitchell (1983) depicted this shift in their landmark book *Object Relations in Psychoanalytic Theory*. Greenberg and Mitchell showed a distinct movement, coming from dissident groups and from within the psychoanalytic mainstream, that began mixing drive theories with object relational concepts (for instance, Melanie Klein, Bion, Kernberg), minimizing or obfuscating differences with drive theories while developing creative departures that were clearly revisionist (Winnicott, Erikson, Kohut, Mahler) or abandoning drive theories altogether in favor of 'pure' object relational, interpersonal and multi-motivational theories such as those of Fairbairn, Guntrip, Sullivan, Horney, Fromm and Bowlby.

More recently, Mitchell (1993, 1997, 2000), Atwood and Stolorow (1993) and Lichtenberg, Lachmann and Fosshage (1996), among many others, have made significant contributions to relational and multi-motivational approaches (see Chapters 12, 15 and 16 in this book for multi-motivational approaches that build on attachment theory). In Britain, the emergence of *group analysis*, pioneered by S.H. Foulkes, has also been a contributing force to the development of a relational theory. Group analysis is not only a method of group psychotherapy but a relational version of psychoanalysis, which sees individual psychological functioning as inseparable from the web of interactions that occur in the group contexts in which every person always lives (Pines, 1990).

In many ways, attachment theory finds itself more at home with these 'pure' relational and multi-motivational approaches even though there are important differences. For instance, most field theories such as Sullivan's interpersonal theory and Atwood and Stolorow's intersubjective theory shy away from explicit views on human nature. More significantly, interpersonal and intersubjective field theories lack an understanding of the biological roots of human relatedness (Cortina, 2001). Bowlby's compelling evolutionary and developmental model of the attachment relationship fills this void. There are also important 'points of contact' between Bowlby's work and key concepts formulated by authors like Kohut, Winnicott, Erikson and Mahler, who preserve some elements of drive theory while creating new departures from classic psychoanalysis (Marrone, 1998; Fonagy, 2001). Attachment theory and research, however, add a very distinctive voice to the cacophony of sounds and melodies that constitute the psychoanalytic movement.

Conclusion

Attachment theory provides a coherent and empirically supported view of normal and pathological developmental processes and clinical phenomena. Attachment theory, however, never intended to be a comprehensive view of human development, nor a theory that attempts to explain the enormous variety of clinical phenomena observed in the practice of psychoanalysis. Attachment theory is one of many psychoanalytic traditions, and needs to integrate its understanding of development with the clinical insights developed over the course of 100 years of psychoanalysis.

In line with our thoughts in regard to paradigm shifts, we are advocating that integrative attempts begin by a thoughtful and careful analysis of the similarities and differences of basic premises that underlie the understanding of clinical phenomena and clinical interventions among different psychoanalytic traditions. We think that attachment theory, built on modern biological concepts and a strong and growing empirical base, offers an indispensable platform from which to launch efforts at integration. This integration, however, should not be limited to psychoanalysis and must remain interdisciplinary. Indeed, the greatest strength of attachment theory is that it is interdisciplinary, and the cross-fertilization of attachment theory with other fields of knowledge, such as developmental psychopathology, neuroscience and anthropology, is paying huge dividends. Witness, for instance, the work of integration between attachment theory and neurobiology (Schore, 1994, 1996, 2002; Siegel, 1999), attachment and developmental psychopathology (Sroufe, 1989, 1990a, 1997; Sroufe, Egeland and Carlson, 1999), and the comparative study of attachment in different cultural settings (Gojman and Millán in this volume; Posada et al., 1995; van IJzendoorn and Sagi, 1999).

We also think there is a remarkable congruence between the theoretical and the clinical implications of attachment theory. We shall address this matter in the next chapter. We hope the book will help not only psychoanalytically informed clinicians, but psychotherapists of all stripes to appreciate, recognize and make use of the depth, richness, and enormous clinical utility of attachment theory. Nothing would have pleased Bowlby more than attachment theory returning to its clinical roots.

Notes

1. Many of the contributors are members of the International Attachment Network, an affiliation of clinicians, researchers and policy-makers interested in using and expanding attachment theory to improve the life of children and families and provide more effective clinical interventions.
2. There are now some excellent reviews of attachment theory that offer a good analysis of this shameful neglect (Eagle, 1984, 1995; Holmes, 1995; Karen, 1998; Mitchell, 2000; Slade, 2000; Fonagy, 2001).
3. Cooperative groups with altruistic members will compete for resources with other groups that may be less cooperative or altruistic (see Sober and Wilson, 1998, for a masterly rehabilitation of this group selection hypothesis).
4. These papers where published in the late 1950s and early 1960s (Bowlby, 1958, 1960a, 1960b) and became the basis of his trilogy on Attachment (1969), Separation (1973) and Loss (1980).
5. Kernberg (1993) names several factors that have contributed to this situation, such as (a) the fact that in many institutes the (so-called) didactic analyst has a say in whether a candidate will be able to graduate, (b) the lock that training analysts have over the organization and who is or is not considered legitimate, and (c) the lack of exposure to research methodologies and empirical studies.

References

Ainsworth MD, Blehar MC, Waters E and Wall S (1978) Patterns of Attachment. Hillsdale, NJ: Lawrence Erlbaum.
Arden M (2001) The development of Charles Rycroft's thought. British Journal of Psychotherapy 18(2): 245–57.

Atwood G and Stolorow R (1993) Faces in a Cloud. Intersubjectivity in Personality Theory. Northvale, NJ: Jason Aronson.

Benoit D and Parker K (1994) Stability and transmission of attachment across three generations. Child Development 65: 1444–56.

Bowlby J (1958) The nature of the child's tie to his mother. International Journal of Psycho-analysis 34: 1–23.

Bowlby J (1960a) Separation anxiety. International Journal of Psycho-analysis 41: 1–22.

Bowlby J (1960b) Grief and mourning in infancy and early childhood. The Psychoanalytic Study of the Child 15: 3–39.

Bowlby J (1969) Attachment, vol. I. New York: Basic Books.

Bowlby J (1973) Separation. Anxiety and Anger, vol. II. New York: Basic Books.

Bowlby J (1980) Attachment and Loss, vol. III. Loss. New York: Basic Books.

Bowlby J (1988) A Secure Base. New York: Basic Books.

Breger L (2000) Freud. Darkness in the Midst of Vision. New York: John Wiley and Sons.

Bretherton I (1991) The roots and growing points of attachment theory. In: CM Parkes, J Stevenson-Hinde and P Marris (eds) Attachment Across the Life Cycle. London: Routledge, pp. 9–32.

Bronfenbrenner U (1979) The Ecology of Human Development. Cambridge, Mass: Harvard University Press.

Cassidy J (2001) Truth, lies and intimacy: An attachment perspective. Attachment and Human Development 3: 121–5.

Cassidy J and Mohr JJ (2002) Unsolvable fear, trauma, and psychopathology: Theory, research and clinical considerations related to disorganized attachment across the lifespan. In press.

Cicchetti D (ed.) (1989) Rochester Symposium on Developmental Psychopathology: vol. I. The Emergence of a Discipline. Hillsdale, NJ: Erlbaum.

Cicchetti D and Nurcombe B (eds) (1998) Special Issue: Contextualism and developmental psychology. Development and Psychopathology 10 (2).

Cortina M (1996) Selection for the Rate and Timing of Development during Evolution. Read at the X World Congress of Psychiatry, August 1996, Madrid, Spain.

Cortina M (1999) Causality, adaptation and meaning: A perspective from attachment theory and research. Psychoanalytic Dialogues 9: 557–98.

Cortina M (2000) Erich Fromm's legacy: Beyond a two-person psychology. Contemporary Psychoanalysis 36: 133–42.

Cortina M (2001) Sullivan's contributions to understanding personality development in light of attachment theory and contemporary models of the mind. Contemporary Psychoanalysis 35: 193–238.

Diamond N (1996) Can we speak of internal and external reality? Group Analysis 29: 303–16.

Diamond N (1998) On Bowlby's legacy. Special contribution to: M Marrone (1998) Attachment and Interaction. London: Jessica Kingsley.

Diamond N and Marrone M (2003) Attachment and Intersubjectivity. London: Whurr.

Eagle M (1984) Recent Developments in Psychoanalysis. Cambridge, Mass: Harvard University Press.

Eagle M (1995) The developmental perspectives of attachment and psychoanalytic theory. In: S Goldberg, J Muir and J Kerr (eds) Attachment Theory. Social, Developmental and Clinical Perspectives. Hillsdale, NJ: Analytic Press, pp. 123–50.

Emde RN (1988) Development terminable and Interminable: I. Innate and motivational factors from infancy. International Journal of Psycho-analysis 69: 23–42.

Erikson EH (1950) Childhood and Society. New York: WW Norton.

Ferenczi S (1932) The Clinical Diaries of Sandor Ferenczi, ed. J Dupont (trans. EM Balint and NJ Jackson). Cambridge Mass: Harvard University Press, 1988.

Ferenczi S (1933) Confusion of tongues between adults and the child. In: Final Contributions to the Problems and Methods of Psycho-Analysis, ed. M Balint (trans. E Mosbacher). London: Karnac Books, 1980, pp. 156–67.

Fonagy P (2001) Attachment Theory and Psychoanalysis. New York: Other Press.

Freud S (1926) Inhibitions, symptoms and anxiety. Standard Edition 20: 77–175. London: Hogarth Press.

Fromm E and Maccoby M (1970) Social Character in a Mexican Village. Englewood Cliffs, NJ: Prentice Hall, 1996 edition.

Gottlieb G (1997) Synthesizing Nature–Nurture. Mahwah: NJ: Lawrence Erlbaum.

Greenberg JR and Mitchell SA (1983) Object Relations in Psychoanalytic Theory. Cambridge, Mass: Harvard University Press.

Grosskurth P (1987) Melanie Klein: Her World and Her Work. Cambridge, Mass: Harvard University Press.

Hamilton V (1985) John Bowlby: an ethological basis for psychoanalysis. In: J. Reppen: Beyond Freud: A Study of Modern Psychoanalysis. New York: Analytic Press.

Heard D and Lake B (1997) The Challenge of Attachment for Caregiving. London: Routledge.

Hesse E and Main M (2000) Disorganized infant, child, and adult attachment: collapse in behavioral and attentional strategies. Journal of the American Psychoanalytic Association 48: 1097–127.

Holmes J (1995) 'Something there is that doesn't like a wall'. John Bowlby, attachment theory and psychoanalysis. In: S Goldberg, J Muir and J Kerr (eds) Attachment Theory. Social, Developmental and Clinical Perspectives. Hillsdale, NJ: Analytic Press, pp. 19–43.

Karen R (1998) Becoming Attached: First Relationships and How They Impact our Capacity to Love. New York: International University Press.

Kernberg OF (1993) The present state of psychoanalysis. Journal of the American Psychoanalytic Association 43(1): 111–45.

Kuhn TS (1962) The Structure of Scientific Revolutions. Chicago and London: University of Chicago Press. Second Edition enlarged, 1970.

Lichtenberg J (1983) Psychoanalysis and Infant Research. Hillsdale, NJ: Analytic Press.

Lichtenberg J (1989) Psychoanalysis and Motivation. Hillsdale, NJ: Analytic Press.

Lichtenberg JD, Lachmann FM and Fosshage JI (1996) The Clinical Exchange. Hillsdale, NJ: Analytic Press.

Main M (2000a) The organized categories of infant, child and adult attachment; Flexible vs. inflexible attention under stress under attachment-related stress. Journal of the American Psychoanalytic Association 48: 1055–96.

Main M (2000b) Disorganized, infant, child and adult attachment: Collapse in behavioral and attentional strategies. Journal of the American Psychoanalytic Association 48: 1097–127.

Main M and Goldwyn R (1983–1998) Adult Attachment Scoring and Classification System. Unpublished Manuscript, University of California at Berkeley. Version 6.3.

Main M and Solomon J (1986) Discovery of a new insecure disorganized/disoriented pattern. In: TB Brazelton and M Yogman (eds) Affective Development in Infancy. Norwood, NJ: Ablex, pp. 95–124.

Main M and Weston D (1981) The quality of the toddler's relationship to mother and father: Related to conflict behavior and the readiness to establish new relationships. Child Development 52: 932–40.

Main M, Kaplan N and Cassidy J (1986) Security in infant, childhood and adulthood: A move to the level of representation. In: I Bretherton and E Waters (eds) Growing Points of Attachment Theory and Research. Monograph of the Society for Research in Child Development, 209, vol. 50, pp. 66–104.

Marrone M (1998) Attachment and Interaction. London: Jessica Kingsley Publishers.

Mitchell S (1993) Hope and Dread in Psychoanalysis. New York: Basic Books.

Mitchell S (1997) Influence and Autonomy in Psychoanalysis. Hillsdale, NJ: Analytic Press.

Mitchell S (2000) Relationality. From Attachment to Intersubjectivity. Hillsdale, NJ: Analytic Press.

Pines M (1990) Foreword to S.H. Foulkes Selected Papers. London: Karnac.

Posada G, Gao Y, Wu F, Posada R, Tascon M, Schuelmerich A, Sagi A, Kondu-Ikemura K, Halland W and Synevaag B (1995) The secure base phenomenon across cultures: children's behavior, mother's preferences, and experts' concepts. In: E Waters, BE Vaughn, G Posada and K Kondo-Ikemura (eds) Caregiving, Cultural and Cognitive Perspectives on Secure Base Behavior and Working Models. New Growing Points of Attachment Theory and Research. Monographs of the Society for Research in Child Development, Serial 244, vol. 60, pp. 27–48.

Robertson J and Robertson J (1989) Separation and the Very Young. London: Free Associations Books.

Schore AN (1994) Affect Regulation and the Origin of the Self. Hillsdale, NJ: Erlbaum.

Schore AN (1996) The experience-dependent maturation of a regulatory system in the orbital prefrontal cortex and the origin of developmental psychopathology. Development and Psychopathology 8: 59–88.

Schore AN (2002) Dysregulation of the right brain: a fundamental mechanism of traumatic attachment and the psychogenesis of posttraumatic stress. Australian and New Zealand Journal of Psychiatry 36: 122–52.

Siegel DK (1999) The Developing Mind. Toward a Neurobiology of Interpersonal Experience. New York: Guilford Press.

Slade A (2000) The development and organization of attachment: implications for psychoanalysis. Journal of the American Psychoanalytic Association 48: 1147–74.

Sober E and Wilson D (1998) Unto Others. The Evolution and Psychology of Unselfish Behavior. Cambridge, Mass: Harvard University Press.

Sroufe LA (1989) Pathways to adaptation and maladaptation. Psychopathology as developmental psychopathology. In: C Cicchetti (ed.) The Emergence of a Discipline. Rochester Symposium on Developmental Psychopathology, vol. 1. Hillsdale, NJ: Lawrence Erlbaum, pp. 13–40.

Sroufe LA (1990a) Considering normal and abnormal together: The essence of developmental psychopathology. Development and Psychopathology 2: 335–7.

Sroufe LA (1990b) An organizational perspective on the self. In: D Cicchetti and M Beegly (eds) The Self in Transition. Infancy to Childhood. Chicago: University of Chicago Press, pp. 281–307.

Sroufe LA (1996) Emotional Development. The Organization of Emotional Development in the Early Years. New York: Cambridge University Press.

Sroufe LA (1997) Psychopathology as an outcome of development. Development and Psychopathology 9: 251–68.

Sroufe LA and Waters E (1977) Attachment as an organizational construct. Child Development 48: 1184–99.

Sroufe LA, Egeland B and Carlson EA (1999) One social world. The integrated development of parent–child and peer relations. In: WA Collins and B Laursen (eds) Minnesota Symposium on Child Development, vol. 30: Relationships as Developmental Contexts. Hillsdale, NJ: Lawrence Erlbaum, pp. 241–61.

Stern DN (1985) The Interpersonal World of the Child. New York: Basic Books.

Thompson RA (1999) Early attachment and later development. In: J Cassidy and PR Shaver (eds) Handbook of Attachment. New York: Guilford Press, pp. 265–86.

Tulving E (1972) Episodic and semantic memory. In: E Tulving and W Donaldson (eds) Organization and Memory. New York: Academic Press.

van IJzendoorn MH (1995) Adult attachment representations, parental responsiveness and infant temperament: A meta-analysis on the validity of the Adult Attachment Interview. Psychological Bulletin 117: 387–403.

van IJzendoorn MH and Sagi A (1999) Cross-cultural patterns of attachment: universal and contextual dimensions. In: J Cassidy and PR Shaver (eds) Handbook of Attachment. New York: Guilford, pp. 713–35.

Waddington K (1957) The Strategy of the Genes. London: Allen and Unwin.

Waters E and Cummings EM (2000) A secure base from which to explore close relationships. Child Development 71: 164–8.

Weinfield NS, Sroufe LA, Egeland B and Carlson EA (1999) The nature of individual differences in the infant–caregiver attachment. In: J Cassidy and PR Shaver (eds) Handbook of Attachment. New York: Guilford Press, pp. 68–88.

PART 1

CLINICAL DIMENSIONS

CHAPTER 2

Attachment theory, transference and the psychoanalytic process

MAURICIO CORTINA AND MARIO MARRONE

Freud thought that the key to establishing a therapeutic relationship involved the development of an attachment between patient and therapist. According to Freud (1913):

> It remains the first aim of the treatment to attach him to it [the transference] and to the person of the doctor. To insure this, nothing needs to be done but to give it time. If one exhibits a serious interest in him, carefully clears away the resistances that crop up at the beginning and avoids making certain mistakes, he will of himself form such an attachment and link the doctor up with one of the imagos of the people by whom he was accustomed to be treated with affection. (p. 139)

In what ways does attachment theory contribute to understanding the nature of this attachment? One of the best ways to address this question is to turn to Freud's 1912 papers on technique, which continue to be an essential departure for any discussion of these matters. In the short paper on 'The dynamics of transference', Freud (1912) started out by asking the question: How is it that transference, defined as prototypes or templates or early relationships carried forward to the figure of the analyst, is both the essential vehicle for cure and the major source of resistance in treatment? For simplicity, we shall omit Freud's dated and misleading explanations based on the concept of libido as an energy source (introversion of libido, cathexis of objects, etc.) and stick to Freud's purely object relational views that are at the heart of the concept of transference. According to Freud (1912), the answer becomes clearer once we recognize that transference is not monolithic and has both positive and negative manifestations. The positive manifestation is what carries the treatment forward before the negative manifestations of transference begin to appear in the form of a resistance, e.g. falling silent and/or stopping the flow of associations. Freud strongly recommended against in-depth interpretations of any kind until a proper 'rapport' with the patient has been established. If the analyst is non-judgmental, shows interest and sympathy, the patient by his own accord will form a positive attachment 'based on the imagos of the people by whom he was accustomed to be treated with affection' (Freud, 1912, pp. 139–40). From this perspective, once a positive attachment is formed, the analyst has leverage from which to interpret the 'inevitable' resistance that will appear in the form of a negative transference.

Here, however, a complication arises. According to Freud (1912), the positive transference *also* becomes a source of resistance. To explain this form of resistance, Freud made another distinction between two types of positive transference. An 'unobjectionable positive' transference that is admissible to consciousness, and a 'positive' erotic transference, that is unconscious, and will eventually become a source of resistance to analytic work. Having confused the tender affectionate ties of a secure attachment with sexual erotic ties (see Chapter 1), Freud was *a priori* forced to view any manifestation of a positive attachment as ultimately a form of sexual or erotic instinct.

> We are thus led to the discovery that all the emotional relations of sympathy, friendship, trust and the like, which can be turned to good account in our lives, are genetically linked to sexuality and have developed from purely sexual desires through the softening of their sexual aim, however pure and non-sensual they may appear to our self-conscious perception. Originally we only know sexual objects; and psychoanalysis shows us that people who in real life are merely admired and respected may still be sexual objects for our unconscious. (Freud, 1912, p. 105)

Behind every positive manifestation of transference, Freud saw hidden sexual motives that threatened to derail the therapeutic alliance. In his later work Freud (1937) attributed the main source of resistance to the death instinct(s). In contrast, Bowlby established attachment and caregiving as independent sources of motivation, distinct from sexuality. Bowlby's theory helps us understand the nature of a positive transference without the confusion produced by Freud's conflating sexuality with attachment (see Chapter 1). A positive transference builds on the experience of attachment figures (and other significant people like teachers) that have provided a haven of safety in moments of distress and have been generally supportive, encouraging and validating. The positive experiences are represented as 'templates or imagoes' (internal working models in Bowlby's terms) that become activated in treatment and from which a therapeutic alliance is constructed. Of course, we cannot always count on positive expectations and attributions from patients. Often the predominant transference 'template' is rejecting, overstimulating or even traumatic. Only later in therapy might we discover in a patient's history alternative figures that were encouraging and gave the child positive experiences to hang on to. Hoffman (1983) calls these alternative attachment figures 'weak precursors' of more positive development. These alternative figures often do not become evident in therapy until the analyst has been tested and has gained sufficient trust from the patient (Weiss, 1993).

With patients who have been severely traumatized, we may need to build virtually from scratch 'new experiences' in therapy that create the beginnings of trust and hope. In either case, the therapeutic alliance, as Freud discovered, is built on developing a positive relationship (a 'positive transference'). Freud never abandoned the belief that developing a positive transference was the bedrock of a successful analysis. In 'Analysis terminable and interminable', written toward the end of his life (and his most sobered account of the limits of psychoanalysis as a treatment modality), Freud insisted that a friendly and affectionate attitude toward the patient 'is the strongest motive for the patient taking a share in the joint work of analysis' (Freud, 1937, p. 233).

Freud's position finds strong support from attachment theory. Bowlby (personal communication with Mario Marrone) insisted that without empathy and sensitive responsiveness the analyst could not enlist the patient's cooperation (see Chapter 3). Many negative patient reactions in the course of therapy – often attributed to resistance – may be the result of the analysts' failure to promote trust and dialogue. This approach sharply contrasts with some forms of Kleinian-oriented analysis, which confines itself from the outset to interpret the patient's 'badness' – envy, destructiveness, aggression and the like.

Bowlby thought that one of the main tasks of the analyst is to make the patient feel understood in his plight. Without this condition being met, the therapeutic alliance cannot be properly established and in some cases the analysis can become iatrogenic and re-traumatize the patient (see Marrone, 1998, pp. 155–77).

Redefining transference

We are defining transference as implicit and unconscious (occasionally explicit and conscious) expectations, attributions, beliefs and attitudes that are embodied as internal working models (IWMs) of self and others (e.g. self as unworthy of love, others untrustworthy or rejecting) carried forward in development. These experientially based templates are carried forward in development, affecting *all* relations, not just the relationship with therapists. There are several important implications of this definition of transference that we should like to explore further.

The ubiquity of transference

By defining transference as an unconscious set of expectations or attributions that affect all relations, we do not have to debate whether transference intrinsically distorts perceptions of others or whether there are also elements of a 'real relation' undistorted by transference. *All* relationships are perceived through the lenses of our expectations, attitudes and beliefs. We think the important distinction to be made is whether manifestations of transference are *more* objective or *less* objective. More objective manifestations of transference permit more balanced and coherent perceptions and evaluations of relationships. This is what most therapists mean by the 'real relationship'. Less objective manifestations of transference erode the capacity to develop more balanced and coherent perceptions and evaluations of relationships. This is what many clinicians mean by transference as a distortion.

Based on these definitions it might be possible to redefine Freud's 'unobjectionable positive transferences' as *more* objective forms of transference and Freud's negative transferences as *less* objective forms of transference. However appealing in its simplicity, we think it would be a mistake to equate positive transference with objectivity and negative transference with lack of objectivity. A person with positive expectations and attributions toward others may be very naïve or may not know enough about a particular person to be able to be objective. For instance, an analysand may start treatment with positive transference, only to find out that his analyst is unreliable and/or undermines the patient's own perceptions through interpretations that emphasize destructive impulses, and then interprets the analysand's reluctance to accept the interpretation as a 'resistance'. In this case the analysand's initial positive transference was misplaced and his growing mistrust of his analyst ('negative transference' in Freud's terms) is really a much more objective assessment of the analyst. Or a person with negative expectations, such as a strong tendency not to trust, may still be able to be objective in assessing people's motives. A suspicious and untrusting trait may even be adaptive in certain social groups or cultures. Plainly, objectivity or the lack of objectivity depends on more than the positive and negative expectations, attributions and attitudes that we carry with us (transference).

Objectivity in personal relations also depends on the capacity to reflect on our *current* experience and to be open to learning about relations. Of course, in real life no one is fully objective or unobjective.

One of the advantages of using Bowlby's IWM concept to understand transference is that working models are not based only on past relational templates. What makes IWM a 'working model' is that healthier IWMs are flexible and capable of being modified according to new experience. Using Piaget's model of adaptation, Bowlby thought that new experience was always *assimilated* to mental schemas based on past experience, but there is also a movement toward *accommodation* of the old schema (IWM) to new experience. This back and forth movement between assimilation and accommodation is what accounts for the possibility of change in IWMs. Defensive processes impede the back and forth movement between assimilation and accommodation, thus making IWMs rigid. One of the drawbacks of the concept of transference (and why the concept of the 'real relationship' emerged in the first place) is that transference is often understood as a 'transfer' of old templates (IWMs) to current relations. There is no room for change in this static view of transference since, by definition, there is no possibility of accommodating to new experience. By using the language of IWMs we can easily understand why one of the most important therapeutic tasks in psychoanalytic psychotherapy is to make IWMs more flexible and open to change with new experience (Bowlby, 1988; Marrone, 1998).

Our emphasis on the importance of trying to achieve objectivity in the analytic process might surprise readers familiar with contemporary trends in relational psychoanalysis. Many authors such as Levenson (1972), Mitchell (1993), Renik (1993) and Hirsh (1996), to name just a few, decry the use of objectivity as a standard to evaluate relationships. According to these authors, invoking objectivity is based on outmoded views of science (positivism) and philosophy (naïve realism) that hide the full participation of the analyst in co-creating with the analysand the transference–countertransference matrix. There are a host of complex issues that we believe are entangled and confused in this view. We shall address two important distinctions that often get lost in this debate.

Objectivism versus objectivity as an ideal

First, we must consider the distinction between 'objectivism' and 'objectivity as an ideal' (Cortina, 1999). *Objectivism* is based on the belief that there must be some ahistorical or transcendental foundation from which to adjudicate truth claims. This view of objectivity is based on a Platonic epistemology and on a positivistic model of science that assume that the observer should minimize participation in his observations in order not to influence them. In contrast, seeing *objectivity as an ideal* is based on a post-positivistic model of science that recognizes that we can never completely detach ourselves from what we observe (this is particularly true in the social sciences), nor can we erase our participation from the phenomena we are observing (Bernstein, 1983). The objectivity of our observations is limited and imperfect (see below). Despite these limits it is possible to aspire to increasing degrees of objectivity that allow us to make significant truth claims that can be tested. This view of objectivity is grounded on experience and is always contextualized, but nonetheless can be decentered from the immediacy of experience by reflecting on it and by testing our perceptions (Schon, 1983; Fonagy and Target, 1997).

Objectivity is not neutrality

A second issue that gets confused is the difference between objectivity and neutrality (Haskell, 1998; Cortina, 1999). What is usually meant by neutrality in psychoanalysis is that an analyst puts aside his or her values and biases (to the extent that he or she can) in order to minimize the power of suggestion, or taking sides in a conflict. This notion is akin to Anna Freud's frequently quoted definition of neutrality as remaining equidistant from the id, ego and superego. We agree with many contemporary analysts that implicit and explicit values are always present in the interaction with our patients, for better or for worse. It is dangerously disingenuous or naïve to believe that our influence in the psychoanalytic process can be eradicated or, for that matter, should be eradicated (Mitchell, 1997). We are never, and should never be, 'neutral' in this sense.

Our influence can be positive or negative. If our influence is based on our genuine concern for the patient and our desire to promote his or her growth it will have positive effects. However, our biases and values are not always helpful, or may clash with an analysand's values and biases. Moreover, influence is a two-way street between analyst and analysand. So what are we to do? To evaluate this mutual influence requires a double process: a full immersion in the relationship in order to experience it from within, and an ability to pull back from the experience in order to understand what we have learned from being immersed in it. Aspects of this process have been described in many ways: participant observation (Sullivan), a center-to-center communication (Fromm), observant participation (Erikson), projective and introjective identification (Scharff, 1992), as surrender (Ghent, 1990), or as wearing the attribution of patients (Lichtenberg, Lachmann and Fosshage, 1996).

Without being able to gain perspective and reflect on this 'immersion' with patients we run the danger of becoming absorbed in the process and 'going native' into familiar, seductive or at times coercive modes of relating that analysands bring to the interaction. To become 'attuned' to this interaction we need to be aware of values and biases that profoundly influence the way we act and perceive the world and our professional roles with patients and colleagues. Needless to say, this process of becoming aware of our own values and attitudes is incomplete and imperfect. Even a successful analysis and professional supervision and consultation will not rid us of vulnerabilities and biases, but it is the only means we have of gaining a certain degree of objectivity.

The limitations of an approach to psychoanalytic treatment based exclusively on the analysis of transference

Recognizing the universality of transference is not the same thing as assuming that all transactions in the analytic relationship are veiled or covert transferential communications. This belief is not just the mistake of novices that first learn about transference, it is a position held dogmatically by some respected practitioners in the field. Another dogmatically held belief in regard to transference is that it is only when conflicts are experienced in the 'here and now' that genuine change can take place. When transference is manifested in the analytic relation, grappling with it in the here and now can be a powerful and transformative experience. But to limit the psychoanalytic dialogue to the 'here and now' and view all communication as having covert transferential meanings is a reductionistic approach to the analytic process. This approach decontextualizes experience by failing to investigate important events in analysands' lives, which are essential for understanding current conflicts.

The 'here and now' approach also fails to explore the origin of unconscious expectations, attitudes and attributions, whether they originate from within families (attachment relationships, sibling relationships) or from cultural and social norms and values that have also been adopted as part of the process of socialization. This is what Erich Fromm (1962) called the social unconscious. In psychotherapy, transference can be fruitfully explored in relationships with lovers, spouses, friends and in the world of work. Insisting that the discussion of relational patterns and conflicts experienced outside the consulting room is a distraction from the 'real' analytic work is absurd and might also be harmful (Millán, 1996; Marrone, 1998).

A secure base model of the psychoanalytic process: tasks to be fulfilled through the analytic process

The first task of the analysis according to Bowlby (1988) is to establish a secure base. This is achieved by the regularity, frequency, continuity and confidentiality of the sessions, by the stability of the setting, by the sensitive responsiveness of the analyst, and by the gradual consolidation of the therapeutic alliance. In turn, the secure base becomes the platform for analytic exploration. We shall expand on this point in greater detail below.

The second task (Bowlby, 1988) is to assist the patient in jointly exploring his present circumstances: what situations he finds himself in, what role he plays in creating these situations, how he chooses people he forms relationships with, how they respond to him, and what the consequences of his behavior have been and are likely to be. This involves looking at the strategies the person uses to regulate access, emotional proximity and responsiveness in current attachment relationships. Simultaneously, there is an exploration of the way in which current interpersonal events may trigger or reactivate anxiety, painful affects or symptoms. At the same time, there is an exploration of how the patient talks about and reflects upon his experiences and intentions and those of the people he interacts with.

The third task (Bowlby, 1988) is to assist the patient in understanding how his experiences, patterns of relating and symptoms may be explained in terms of his attachment history, particularly from what he can remember about his childhood and adolescence. In doing so, the patient is invited to elicit and examine his internal working models and how these influence the way he feels, behaves, reacts and forecasts outcomes in the present.

Ainsworth's description of the secure base phenomenon (e.g. the use of an attachment figure as a base from which to explore the world) provides a very useful model to conceptualize some key features of the psychoanalytic process. Establishing a secure base is essential for children's development and remains a life-long need, as reactions to the terrorist attacks of September 11 so vividly demonstrated. Developing a secure base in psychotherapy is equally important and a therapeutic task in its own right (Bowlby 1988; see also Chapters 3, 4, 7 and 14 in this volume). A secure base creates a space for exploration, whether this exploration is the child's immediate environment, as in normal development, or the exploration needed in psychotherapy.

The need for a base of security in psychoanalysis is not a new idea. It is implicit in Freud's concept of an 'unobjectionable' positive transference, in Bion's concept of containment and in Winnicott's concept of the holding environment, and is explicitly stated by Sandler (1960) as the need for a 'background of safety', by Havens (1989) as the need for a 'safe place' in psychotherapy, and by Lichtenberg et al. (1996) as an 'ambience of safety'. What attachment theory adds to these concepts is an understanding and appreciation for the enormous importance of a secure attachment as a base for development (Waters and Commings, 2000). The freedom to explore the world, the ability to moderate impulses or the capacity for establishing good peer relations and intimate relations all build on the foundation of a secure base (Sroufe, 1996; Thompson, 1999; Sroufe, Egeland and Carlson, 1999).

As we noted earlier, in psychoanalysis, this exploration might lead in many directions, such as exploring defensive processes or security operations (to use Sullivan's apt term) that protect from unbearable anxiety. Or the exploration might examine grandiose fantasies originating from experiences of powerlessness and shame. Or the exploration might lead to the examination of transference and countertransference as they are manifested in and out of the consulting room. The secure base model of the psychoanalytic process does not privilege developing a 'new relation' or 'a corrective emotional experience' over insight and understanding. These two dimensions of the psychoanalytic process go hand in hand and both are indispensable. Lichtenberg et al. (1996) also voice this view, stating that the heart of the psychoanalytic process consists of developing an atmosphere of safety while maintaining a spirit of inquiry (see Chapters 4 and 18 in this volume, which also explicitly make this point).

Establishing an atmosphere of safety and trust is not always easy, and in fact may become the central task of a successful analysis. We are at times confronted and challenged by patients who bring to the clinical encounter contradictory expectations, attributions and attitudes that are chaotic and confusing. Or we may be challenged by patients who feel easily threatened, shamed or humiliated or who are in deep despair and suicidal. In these instances, patients might do in therapy what was done to them previously by attachment figures. In these circumstances our ability to remain objective, empathic or calm is tested severely, and may prove impossible to sustain. Our therapeutic mettle is forged in the crucible of these clinical encounters.

It often proves crucial that we recognize, recover, repair and apologize when it seems appropriate from these inevitable foibles, empathic failures (Kohut), enactments, and use these 'mistakes' as opportunities for growth within the analytic relationship. Much is at stake, as the outcome of any given therapy often hangs on this delicate balance of developing a secure base while pushing the limits of entrenched security operations. As important as 'getting it right' is the ability to struggle with periods of 'not getting it' and finding our way back to a new level of understanding that moves the psychoanalytic process forward. Bowlby thought that often the patient knows more than the analyst does, and that the analyst's task is to put the patient in contact with his own knowledge. Through dialogue, joint discovery, reciprocal error-correcting feedback, monitoring emotional and shared reflective thinking, patient and analyst together can aim at some commonly understood 'truth'. This goal is best achieved when the analyst does not assume he knows the truth about a patient or that his interpretations carry the weight of unquestionable authority (Bowlby, personal communication with Mario Marrone).

In this, we believe that a clinical approach informed by attachment theory is compatible with the work of many authors influenced by the self psychology and relational traditions who have pushed the boundaries of what has traditionally been considered proper 'technique' in order to meet clinical challenges. Chapter 18 in this volume is a good example of congruity in values and clinical sensibilities between attachment theory and self psychology. In Chapter 1 we mentioned fit with some relational authors such as Mitchell (1993), Hoffman (1983), Ehrenberg (1992) and Davis (2002). There is also a close compatibility of clinical approaches with some British analysts of the 'independent group', such as Abraham Brafman, Dennis Brown, Patrick Casement, Pearl King, Phil Mollon, Joan Raphael-Leff, Eric Rayner and Valerie Sinason, to name only a few.[1] To spell out these commonalities would require a chapter unto itself. In a nutshell, we think that all these traditions exhibit a clinical sensitivity to establishing a base of security with patients, and rather than shoehorning the patient to fit preconceived views, they try to draw out painful experiences and knowledge that patients have within themselves.

Peterfreund's (1983) approach is consistent with this general approach and in many ways fleshes out some of Bowlby's therapeutic tasks that we mentioned earlier. Peterfreund argued that much clinical practice is 'stereotyped' in taking the patient as 'but an example of an assumed body of clinical theory'. He contrasted this way of working with a 'heuristic' approach that encourages new awareness and understanding and uses 'search strategies' with patients to understand the psychological problems that hamper their lives. In his view, an analyst who facilitates free association in a focused way and involves the patient as a participant is likely to promote a process of joint discovery. The strategy of fostering active, independent, analytic work on the part of the patient has long been established to be a key element of the analytic process. However, it is all too often neglected.

The caregiving system and the analyst role with patients

The caregiving component of the attachment relationship offers a good model for the role of the analyst as long as we understand that there are significant differences between parent–child relationships and the analytic relationship. Parents are called to respond to normal developmental needs, whereas psychotherapists must respond to developmental histories that have gone astray. Moreover, analysands are not children, and in some areas might be more developed than their analysts (of course this applies only to work with adults) and often an important goal is to reach a greater degree of mutuality in the analytic relationship based on a deeper understanding of central conflicts and core relational themes. The importance of this goal is beautifully illustrated in the clinical case presented by Liotti and Intreccialagli in Chapter 15 in this volume. Despite these important differences, there are important commonalities.

The very nature of the analytic relationship creates conditions for analysands to seek in their analyst an attachment figure whom they can trust and to whom they can expose their vulnerabilities and conflicts. In turn, therapists and analysts are called to respond in quasi-parental fashion by listening empathetically and by understanding. Another commonality is that both parents and analysts rely on highly intuitive modes of understanding human relations. This knowledge of relationships has biological as well as developmental and psychological roots. The biological roots have developed through millions of years of hominid evolution. The psychological roots are based on the developmental history of emotional ties across the life span. We stress these points because the basic skills that make us good parents (accompanying and comforting children in moments of stress, listening, caring, encouraging, being patient, setting limits) are the same basic skills that make us good analysts. We need to build on those skills and apply them in conditions that can be very challenging and demanding. But it is important not to mystify analytic training by creating arcane procedures and esoteric jargon that is accessible only to the initiated.

Parents and analysts have specific and important roles to play and the mark of competence is that they can maintain their roles flexibly, creatively, and even playfully. Parents should not be regularly seeking comfort or solace from their children nor should analysts seek emotional needs for security through their patients. This inversion of roles portends trouble for children's development and for the course of psychotherapy.

A note on countertransference

There is a vast literature on the subject of countertransference that would have to be reviewed to address adequately the issues surrounding the use of the concept. In general, countertransference has been understood in two very different ways. The traditional definition defines countertransference as a distortion that interferes with the analyst's ability to develop a more objective view of the analysand or the analytic process. A second definition emphasizes the usefulness of the analyst's emotional responses as a vehicle to understand the analysand's unconscious communications, dissociated impulses or emotions. The traditional definition of countertransference as a distortion suffers from the same problem of viewing transference simply as a distortion. It misses the point that some of the analyst's reactions may be intuitive but fairly objective and useful responses to the analysand's expectations and attributions. Yet, as we have said earlier, in the heat of emotionally charged moments, it is sometimes very difficult to sort out who is contributing what to the analytic process. It may take a long time to find creative ways to develop an interaction that promotes growth. Occasionally we have to 'throw out the book' and find our way through the unique vicissitudes of transference and countertransference dynamics. However, we want to join others who have raised questions about 'analysing from the countertransference' (Marrone, 1998; Lachmann, 2001), which implies we can use our emotional reactions as sure-fire guides to the analytic process and as unblemished windows into the analysand's unconscious. The danger of this simplistic approach is that we have no way of separating what might be a highly idiosyncratic response to our analysands from an objective view of the interaction. As we note earlier, experiential and intersubjective approaches to the analytic process need to be complemented by the ability to pull back from the interaction in order to gain a measure of perspective and objectivity. This is a key to the psychoanalytic process.

A second point we should like to make is that we believe that the experiential and intersubjective approach to countertransference can be usefully understood by Sandler's (1976) concept of 'role responsiveness'. We think there are two dimensions to the concept of role responsiveness. First, insofar as the analytic relationship has elements of an attachment relationship, the analyst and analysand fall into different roles. As we have noted, the analyst role is quasi-parental, providing care (dare we say love), understanding and encouragement, and sets flexible limits and boundaries. The analysand comes into therapy because something important is amiss in their lives and they are looking for expert help. To the degree that analyst and analysand can develop a collaborative relationship, these roles will develop toward greater mutuality. A second dimension implicit in the concept of role responsiveness involves the reciprocity of emotional reactions and motivational systems. Seeking care should elicit the analyst's desire to provide care. A judgmental attitude (by analyst or analysand) might elicit shame or guilt, which in turn may further elicit rage or humiliation. A threat, real or perceived, may elicit an aversive fight–flight response. As analysts we are always searching for an optimal emotional response (Bacal, 1985) that matches analysands' needs.

In this chapter we have used the framework of attachment theory – as we understand it – as a base from which to understand the psychoanalytic process. We have emphasized Bowlby's (1988) thoughts of the need to establish a secure base from which the analytic exploration can proceed, by inserting the secure base model at the very heart of the psychoanalytic process. We hope that clinicians will find the secure base model of psychotherapy and our revisiting the concept of transference from an attachment perspective to be helpful. Finally, we think that the secure base model of psychotherapy can be operationalized so as to become a useful research instrument in identifying key processes that make psychoanalytic psychotherapy effective.

Note

1. Recently, some authors have endorsed general principles of attachment theory, yet they advocate and exemplify a way of working in the clinical situation that is based on very different ways of understanding clinical phenomena and the psychoanalytic process. Attachment theory today has enough internal coherence to do well without mixing it unnecessarily with radically incompatible paradigms.

References

Bacal H (1985) Optimal responsiveness and the therapeutic Process. In: A Goldberg (ed.) Progress in Self Psychology, vol. 1. New York: Guilford Press, pp. 202–27.

Bernstein JR (1983) Beyond Objectivity and Relativism. Science Hermeneutics and Praxis. Philadelphia: University of Pennsylvania Press.

Bowlby J (1988) A Secure Base. New York: Basic Books.

Cortina M (1999) Causality, adaptation and meaning. A perspective from attachment theory and research. Psychoanalytic Dialogues 9: 557–96.

Davis JM (2002) Whose bad objects are they anyway? Repetition and our elusive love affair with evil. Paper presented at the conference 'Relational Analysts at Work: Sense and Sensibility', New York.

Ehrenberg DB (1992) The Intimate Edge. Extending the Reach of Psychotherapeutic Action. New York: WW Norton.

Fonagy P and Target M (1997) Attachment and the reflective function. Their role in self-organization. Development and Psychopathology 9: 679–700.

Freud S (1912) The dynamics of transference. Standard Edition 12: 99–108. London: Hogarth Press, 1963.

Freud S (1913) On beginning the treatment (further recommendations on the technique of psychoanalysis). Standard Edition 12: 123–44. London: Hogarth Press.

Freud S (1937) Analysis terminable and interminable. Standard Edition 23: 209–254. London: Hogarth Press, 1963.

Fromm E (1962) Beyond the Chains of Illusion. My Encounter with Marx and Freud. New York: Pocket Books.

Ghent E (1990) Masochism, submission and surrender. Masochism as a perversion of surrender. Contemporary Psychoanalysis 26: 108–35.

Haskell LT (1998) Objectivity is Not Neutrality: Explanatory Schemes in History. Baltimore, Md: Johns Hopkins University Press.

Havens L (1989) A Safe Place. Laying the Groundwork of Psychotherapy. Cambridge, Mass: Harvard University Press.

Hirsh I (1996) Observing-participation, mutual enactment, and the new classical models. Contemporary Psychoanalysis 32: 364–81.

Hoffman IZ (1983) The patient as interpreter of the analyst's experience. Contemporary Psychoanalysis 19: 389–422.

Lachmann FM (2001) A farewell to countertransference. International Forum of Psychoanalysis 10: 242–6.

Levenson E (1972) The Fallacy of Understanding. New York: Basic Books.

Lichtenberg JD, Lachmann FM and Fosshage JI (1996) The Clinical Exchange. Hillsdale, NJ: Analytic Press.

Marrone M (1998) Attachment and Interaction. London: Jessica Kingsley.

Millán S (1996) The social dimensions of transference. In: M Cortina and M Maccoby. A Prophetic Analyst. Erich Fromm's Contributions to Psychoanalysis. Northvale, NJ: Jason Aronson, pp. 325–40.

Mitchell S (1993) Hope and Dread in Psychoanalysis. New York: Basic Books.

Mitchell S (1997) Influence and Autonomy in Psychoanalysis. Hillsdale, NJ: Analytic Press.

Peterfreund E (1983) The Process of Psychoanalytic Therapy. Hillsdale, NJ: Lawrence Erlbaum.

Renik O (1993) Analytic interaction. Conceptualizing technique in light of the analyst's irreducible subjectivity. Psychoanalytic Quarterly 62: 535–71.

Sandler J (1960) The background of safety. In: From Safety to Superego: Selected Papers by Joseph Sandler. London: Karnac, pp. 1–8.

Sandler J (1976) Countertransference and role responsiveness. International Review of Psychoanalysis 3: 43–7.

Scharff DE (1992) Refinding the Object and Reclaiming the Self. Northvale, NJ: Aronson.

Schon DA (1983) The Reflective Practitioner. How Professionals Think in Action. New York: Basic Books.

Sroufe LA (1996) Emotional Development The Organization of Emotional Development in the Early Years. New York: Cambridge University Press.

Sroufe LA, Egeland B and Carlson EA (1999) One social world. The integrated development of parent–child and peer relations. In: WA Collins and B Laursen (eds) Minnesota Symposium on Child Development: vol. 30, Relationships as Developmental Contexts. Hillsdale, NJ: Lawrence Erlbaum Associates, pp. 241–61.

Thompson RA (1999) Early attachment and later development. In: J Cassidy and PR Shaver (eds) Handbook of Attachment. New York: Guilford Press, pp. 265–86.

Waters E and Commings EM (2000). A secure base from which to explore close relationships. Child Development 71: 164–8.

Weiss J (1993) How Psychotherapy Works. New York: Guilford Press.

CHAPTER 3
Empathy and sensitive responsiveness

MALCOLM PINES AND MARIO MARRONE

Introduction

Managing painful affects, feelings or emotions is one of the major tasks of analytic psychotherapy, whether individual or group. Here we use the terms 'feelings', 'emotions' and 'affects' as synonymous, although the word 'affect' is most commonly used in psychoanalysis. People bring their distress, disappointment, fears of rejection, loss of love, humiliation, the range of shame affects, guilt, self-recrimination and self-hatred, low self-esteem, isolation, etc. Often these affects are the consequences of terrible traumas and violence. Thus there emerge uncontainable or unbearable feelings of existing in an experiential world where there is neither a self capable of coping with these feelings, nor a containing and responding other to help in the task.

In this context, we can ask two questions. First, where does the need to see a psychotherapist in order to get help to manage painful feelings come from? Second, how can we manage these states in psychotherapy?

Affects cannot be seen as isolated experiences. They always emerge in the context of present relationships or memories of past relationships. Affects are links between what in traditional psychoanalytic terminology we would call *self and object representations*. In the conceptual framework of attachment theory, we should say that affects are linked to *internal working models* of attachment relationships.

The task of psychotherapy involves creating a situation with capacities to hold, contain, understand and transform the emotions. Essential is a therapeutic attitude to explore these experiences sympathetically, empathically, historically, and contextually. Furthermore, it is important to understand here the developmental aspects of empathy.

As we shall explore in this chapter, the concept of *empathy* (Wilmer, 1968; Wispe, 1986) closely relates to the concept of *sensitive responsiveness* developed by attachment theorists. An important notion in attachment theory is that *sensitive responsiveness* provided by attachment figures plays a major mediating role as psychic organizer of children's development. Ainsworth et al. (1978), in the course of their observations of mother–baby interactions, concluded that the mother's capacity to respond with empathy and sensitivity is a major determinant of optimal development. Sensitive responsiveness involves being able to see things from the baby's point of view, being alert to perceive the baby's signals, interpret them accurately and respond appropriately and promptly.

One of us, Malcolm Pines, says:

I watch my wife playing with our 2½-year-old grandson, how she enters into and creates games with love and enthusiasm. I wonder at her capacity to understand his actions, to follow him as he ends one sequence of play, starts another, then another. She talks to him as they play, both responding to his initiatives and introducing her own. Inevitably there are limits to time and energy spent together, but these limits do not obtrude as I watch; the play has a quality of timelessness, where impatience, irritation, criticism, judgement have no place. For both participants the play is syntonic, cooperative, two together making one. I watch her offering new ideas for Jacob to consider: some he'll adopt, others are ignored or quickly discarded. What I am watching is love in action, love of playing together and growing together: skilful loving, bringing the experience of a lifetime of childcare into the play.

I am reminded of Hans Loewald's writings (1980), that the relationship of caregiver and child, as of analyst and patient, is that of two persons together creating a shared field of interaction in which there are two poles, the one, the more mature, the other, the more immature. Through their interaction, a gradient develops whereby they begin to approximate to each other. The more immature develops maturity; the more mature can be renewed and re-invigorated by contact with the other.

I see the grandmother of 76 becoming again the young mother of our three children, the mother who loved to play with them and to organize their games. Through play with our children she recalls, and in some ways relives, her own happy play-filled childhood. I am the watcher. I am not, cannot become, her style of player. I observe; I know that I do not have her capacities for loving play and skilful attunement to what the child desires, to what the child can accept as an intriguing, interesting novelty. I know that I am not a free player with small children in her way. I am more at home with organized games with older children where their excitement and pleasure is contained within the rules of the game. Sadly, I recognize that I am not at home in these early games with babies and toddlers in the way that mothers can be. I wonder, is this a gender issue? Probably to some extent it is, but I know that there are social and personal factors, which are significant. I cannot recall my mother spending much time in play with me and my 2-year elder brother. We were children of the 1920s when parental roles were much less flexible than nowadays. My father, an immigrant doctor, had single-handed to give most of his time and energy to building up his practice. This was at a time when he had to make his house calls on foot, as he could not yet afford a motorcar. He could be jolly and enjoyed games with older children, whereas my mother seemed to retain a somewhat rigid sense of dignity, which kept her apart in family games.

We have been exploring the theme of empathy and sensitive responsiveness in these opening passages, sharing with the reader universally accessible experiences of play that is a natural mode of relating to young children. Another grandchild of 28 months is constitutionally a happy, chubby, lively child. For him, life so far has been as secure as it can be. Though his mother has gone back to well-paid full-time work, his father, being freelance, has spent many hours a day with his son. He adores his child and very much enjoys playing with him. As a child, the father, my youngest son, has always loved fun and games and he loves the hours that he spends playing with Harry. This relationship between fathers and children was difficult for those of my generation who were, like my father, single-handed financial supporters to the family. The social context of the past two or three decades has moved the sexual stereotypes of males and females, the roles and capacities, revealing the genetic adaptability with which we are endowed. Caregiving seems to be much more equitably distributed between males and females than heretofore.

On sensitive responsiveness

The concept of *sensitive responsiveness* slightly differs from that of *empathy*. Briefly, empathy can be defined as the capacity to perceive the other's feeling states as if one were in the other's position. Sensitive responsiveness certainly involves empathy, but it also involves the responses that the mother offers in order to regulate the baby's feeling state. Needless to say, attachment theory values the importance of sensitive responsiveness from any attachment figure regardless of who the attachment figure may be, e.g. mothers, fathers or grandparents. Sensitive responsiveness plays an important role in evoking a sense of self-integration and self-worth as well as in eliciting loving, cooperative and reciprocal responses. In childhood and adolescence, one major characteristic of sensitive responsiveness is the parent's capacity to see the child as a separate human being, with his or her own needs as separate from those of others. Sensitive responsiveness does not inherently involve total identification with the other, but a sense of empathy plus the freedom and tact to choose the right strategy at any given moment to respond, sometimes in a very supportive manner, sometimes in a confrontative and boundary-setting way.

According to the description given by Ainsworth et al. (1978), sensitive responsiveness on the part of babies' mothers includes a number of characteristics, such as the capacity to perceive and appropriately respond to the baby's care-eliciting signals, the ability to respect the baby's sense of autonomy, readiness to play with the baby, etc. A sensitive mother tends to view the baby as a separate individual; she respects his or her activity-in-progress and therefore avoids interrupting. Such a mother is unlikely to get bored or self-absorbed when playing with the baby. They are accessible to close bodily contact. She can easily regain contact with the baby after returning from a period of absence. She is able to soothe the baby in distress. She is unlikely to be provoking the distress unless this happens in exceptional circumstances (e.g. holding the baby tightly when he is receiving a vaccination).

In trying to assess a mother's degree of sensitive responsiveness, several aspects of maternal behaviour have been considered:

1. *Responsiveness to crying*: this refers to the maternal readiness to try to soothe the baby when he or she is crying.
2. *Behaviour relevant to separation/reunion*: this refers to the mother's ability to initiate a pleasant interaction with the baby upon reunion, after a separation.
3. *Behaviour relevant to close bodily contact*: this refers to maternal capacity to pick up and physically hold the baby with affection, care and competence.
4. *Behaviour relevant to face-to-face interaction*: this refers to maternal capacity to establish and maintain face-to-face interaction in response to the baby's cues with appropriate aliveness.
5. *Behaviour relevant to infant obedience*: this alludes to the way the mother tries to impose discipline by means of verbal commands and physical interventions.
6. *Behaviour relevant to feeding*: this is related to the mother's capacity to synchronize her feeding interactions in accordance with the baby's rhythms and signals.

Attachment researchers accept the fact that babies differ in the kinds of signals they give, that it may take some time before a mother can learn to read the signals of her baby, and that an approximation of the optimal synchronization with the baby's signals and rhythms requires a mutual adaptation

(Ainsworth et al., 1978, p. 142). However, there is a great deal of evidence that maternal sensitivity is rooted in the mother's own attachment history (Hubbard and van IJzendoorn, 1991).

It has also been understood that maternal sensitivity is influenced by the mother's general attitude toward the baby: acceptance or rejection, and by her capacity to cooperate with the baby's intention (as opposed to interfering with them). The highly interfering mother does not respect her baby's autonomy and separateness; she tries to control him/her according to her own agenda and motivation. Miguel Hoffmann (1994), an Argentinean psychoanalyst and developmental researcher, has studied the mother's capacity to respect the young child's sense of initiative. Sensitive responsiveness is also influenced by the mother's accessibility and emotional expression. A mother may be depressed or so preoccupied with her own thoughts and activities that she would not even notice her baby, let alone acknowledge his signals.

Although we refer to *mothers* here, the same analysis could be made of *fathers'* behaviour. Early sensitive responses are crucial to set up the foundations of the person's sense of being understood, represented and reaffirmed, the degree of empathy and sensitive responsiveness that important others show in relation to the person throughout the formative years (from infancy to adolescence). Sensitive parents are able to soothe the child when he or she is upset and provide a secure base while at the same time respecting the child's sense of autonomy. During the school years, sensitivity is manifested at non-verbal as well as verbal levels. What the parent says to the son or daughter – and how they say it – is fundamentally important, particularly when the child is upset or distressed.

Sensitive responsiveness and affect regulation

In the literature on sensitive responsiveness, emphasis has been placed on the parents' capacity to contain the child's negative feelings. In turn, this capacity is related – as Fonagy et al. (1995, p. 242) suggest – to the extent to which parents are inclined to be defensive about their own negative emotional experiences. Parents may be highly defensive when in their own childhood they were not helped to deal with their own distress or painful emotions and, hence, have to resort to the consistent use of defence mechanisms. In saying this, we are placing the capacity for sensitive responsiveness in an inter-generational context. Parental defensiveness may lead to a lack of understanding or to incomplete understanding of the child's anxieties and/or painful emotional states. To a large degree, such defensiveness is the result of inadequate containment in the parent's own childhood. If the parent was not assisted to deal with certain emotions in their own childhood, they are unlikely to be entirely successful in dealing with similar affects in the child.

In the interaction between a good-enough parent (to use Winnicott's notion) and the child, there is a sequence of mutual responses. Fonagy et al. (1995, pp. 247–9) describe this sequence. Here we shall give a slightly modified version of this description. First, the child feels distress and gives an affective communication or signal. The parent perceives the signal, interprets it, forms an idea of the child's state of distress, reflects upon it and responds sensitively. In this way, the child not only experiences a reduction of their distress but also internalizes or represents a model of the parent as able to contain painful states and a model of himself as soothed. This representation fundamentally contributes to the development of the child's capacity for affect regulation.

If the parent has a deficit in his/her empathic capacity, a different sequence might take place. The child feels distress and gives an affective signal. If the parent ignores the signal (probably because he/she is taken up with his/her own internal preoccupations, which reduces attentiveness), the child will feel unresponded to. Subsequently, the child's distress will intensify. It could also happen that the child's distress reactivates unresolved emotions in the parent, who would then feel anxiety and resort to habitual defences against anxiety and painful affects. The child may then internalize the parent's defences and through them avoid an intensification of distress. Another possibility is that the parent may perceive and locate the source of the child's distress but fail to respond adequately because of a failure of competence. This failure of competence may have different sources, including tiredness due to socio-economic pressures.

If the child cannot rely on the parent to obtain a soothing response to his negative affects, he must feel either internally fragment under the impact of intense distress and anxiety or find alternative ways to reduce it. These alternative ways are most likely to be dysfunctional.

However, there has been a tendency among psychoanalysts and some developmental researchers to emphasize the importance of the containment of anxiety and negative affects for emotional regulation. Yet, recent work indicates that the development of joy is equally important. Sroufe (1996, pp. 77–100) studies the fundamental role that joy plays in optimal child development. Laughter, which is first elicited at around the age of four months, develops into a sense of joy in response to well-timed and sensitive responses in the parent–child interaction. Daniel Stern (1977, pp. 71–5) talks about the way playing and having fun in the parent–infant relationship act as affect regulators. In this context, it is possible that lack of experiences of playfulness and joy in early life could cause a developmental deficit.

As Schore (1994, p. 25) points out, critical early affective transactions with the social environment are mentally stored in the form of representations of the self emotionally interacting with significant others. This process occurs according to the child's developmental stage, as various neurophysiological and sensory systems are maturing. These mental representations involve a configuration of a representation of oneself, a representation of the significant other and a linking mediating affect. These mental representations, as Schore (1994) demonstrates throughout his work, act as regulators of affects and influence brain morphological development and neurochemical functioning.

Applications of developmental research to psychotherapy

Robert Emde (1990) outlines what he considers to be the ways in which the empathic process plays a significant role in psychotherapy:

1. The caregiving role: 'developmental empathy'.
2. The affirmative role: 'affirmative empathy'.
3. The availability of the therapist: 'empathic responsiveness'.

Through the caregiving of *developmental empathy*, the therapist creates an opportunity for the patient to discover new potentialities, as 'good-enough' parental caregivers do through constantly leading children on. Caregivers attribute intentionality to their charges, and that offer of intentionality, or the recognition of the intentionality that is latent in the child, can become purposive. Here empathy is a creative act within the therapeutic relationship. It can be playful and involve positive affects.

Affirmative empathy has to do with the way in which the therapist can enable the person to put together a sense of the continuity and coherency in their life. It also involves an affirmative sense of life-pattern and direction, whereby the person can begin to knit together past and present, to have empathy for the self of the past and for the self of the present. This comes about through the shared affective field of therapist and patient within which the patient can experience both common humanity with the therapist and their own unique experience of personality and individuality.

Therapeutic availability can foster trust, confidence and consistency of expectation. Therapeutic availability is manifested through the therapist's ability to regulate events within the shared affective field. Regulation of affect means that the therapist can handle and help the patient to learn to handle their own feeling states, to make them manageable and understandable. Making them understandable involves interpretation or, as Kohut prefers to call it, explanation. Good sensitive interpretations encourage exploration and anticipate direction; within the shared affective field of patient and therapist, the patient can use the therapist's consistency and availability to take that understanding and make it into part of the self.

Emde states that these therapeutic functions of empathy repeat some fundamental motivational aspects of development in childhood. We are endowed with inherent capacities for self-regulation, social fittedness and affective monitoring. The capacity for self-regulation enables the child to feel in control of the self; social fittedness enables the child to understand, accept and integrate with the social world; affective monitoring means that one understands one's own feelings and learns to understand those of others.

When exercised with emotionally available adults, these capacities will be developed through the following stages:

1. Consolidation of an affective core as the early stage of self-development.
2. On this basis, the self develops a sense of reciprocity, understanding of rules and empathy, understanding of others and an understanding of oneself. This initiates a world of shared meanings and early moral internalizations, a sense of right and wrong, fairness and unfairness.
3. Of particular interest to group analysts is the next stage, which Emde calls the 'executive we'.

Now the child is in a world of shared meaning structures, knowing with others and sharing in the knowledge, strength and capacities of the other, 'we two together, making One'. This 'executive we' is cognitive and affective, feeling in tune with an understanding the other.

This sense of a sharing, the use of the selfobject in Kohutian terms, is essential to the background of safety that enables separation and individuation to occur. Mahler said that at this stage the adult becomes a 'beacon of orientation' (Mahler, Pines and Bergman, 1975), both shedding light upon the world and also being a safe place to retreat to.

A relationship with this powerful other in childhood, in adult love and in psychotherapy can lead to moments of intense feelings of togetherness and shared meaning, a sense of confidence, even power in the midst of uncertainty and painful affects.

This extract from the story 'Father and I' illustrates what happens when the child looks to the parent to be such a 'beacon of orientation' but the light is out (Wilmer, 1968, p. 246).

> We went on. Father was so calm as he walked there in the darkness with even strides. Not speaking, thinking to himself. I could not understand how he could be so calm when it was so murky. I looked all around me in fear. Nothing but darkness everywhere ... Hugging close to father, I whispered, 'Father why is it so horrible when it's dark?'
> 'No, my boy, it's not horrible' he said, taking me by the hand.
> 'Yes, father, it is.'
> 'No, my child, you mustn't think that, not when we know there is a God.'
> I felt so lonely, forsaken. It was so strange that only I was afraid, not father, that we did not think the same. And strange that what he said didn't help me and stop me from being afraid. Not even what he said about God helped me.

In this fragment, the child sees his father as strong and unafraid, senses his incomprehensible fearlessness. Darkness itself is frightening, for he does not know what the unseen world is like. He reaches for his father, hugging for closeness, and asks why it is horrible when it is dark. What he is really saying is: 'why does it seem horrible to me?' However, the father in effect says, 'It is not horrible to me'. Each is speaking for himself. The father tells the child what not to think, tells him he must not think as he does. The child becomes silent, thinking inwardly, where there is no longer anything to say to father. The child now feels alone and forsaken or rejected. Moreover, he tells us why: because he and his father do not think and feel the same. This was because his father was unable to put himself in the child's place, to understand that the child had his own childish irrational or emotional reasons for being afraid, more powerfully affecting him than his father's rational ones.

Between human beings, there are profound interpenetrating and structural reciprocities without which human life could not exist. From the process of birth onwards, probably in intrauterine life, we can see synchronies between speakers and listeners, processes that have been called 'entrainment' (Condon, 1979; Condon and Sander, 1974). Infants entrain from birth, and under high speed camera and video filming can be seen to be engaged in a precisely shared 'communicative dance between mother and infant'. There is both a micro-sharing and a macro-sharing. A micro-sharing represents a form of organization that seems to flow through the body parts; what may seem to be unrelated, discrete movements have a recognized form and pattern. In macro-sharing, there is a whole body experience, which is related to that of the whole body experience of the other.

Empathy can be conceptualized as a process of mutual attunement between infant and mother, when infant and adult seem to be sharing the same affective state. This begins to give the infant a sense that he or she is in the same experiential role as the other. A very specific process occurs, when the response of the one to the other is from one unique person (an attachment figure) responding in his or her own way to what is coming from the other. The developing infant/child then experiences that 'here is one who understands me, but is different to me' and this leads to curiosity, capturing of interest, the growth of the behavioural repertoire.

Daniel Stern (1985) describes how at some time between the seventh and the ninth months the infant seems to enter into what he calls 'the experience of intersubjectivity'. This occurs when there is some shared framework of meaning which is newly arisen in a relationship in which there are some means of communications by gestures, sounds, touch and so on. Here we are using the term 'intersubjectivity' according to Stern's interpretation of it. Of course, the term can be used with different connotations (see Diamond and Marrone, 2003). Now we can see that behind the overt actions and responses of the infant are internal subjective states. This is recognized by the parents who realize now that there is a small person there in their infant. This *intersubjectivity* or *intersubjective relatedness* is built upon the foundation of previously achieved *core-relatedness*. The core-relatedness never disappears; it is always in the background, the existential bedrock of interpersonal relationships. According to Stern, the young infant had previously responded to mother's empathic gestures, her soothing, caring, but *the process itself* of empathic caring had not been registered, only the response coming from the other. Now the infant senses that there is an empathic process bridging the two minds, that a new capacity has been created. The caregiver's empathy, a process so crucial to the infant's development, now becomes a direct subject of experience. Needless to say, empathy and sensitive responsiveness are essential conditions for optimal development throughout childhood and adolescence.

The psychoanalytic concept of empathy

In a letter to her husband James, Alex Strachey, one of the translators of the Freud Standard Edition, one of the early psychoanalysts, member of the inner Bloomsbury circle, wrote: 'Empathy a vile word, elephantine, for a subtle process'. Freud had written 'empathy plays the largest part in our understanding of what is inherently foreign to our nature' and had taken the word from the aesthetician Theodore Lipps who had used it in his exploration of our responses to works of art. The literal meaning of the word is 'in-feeling, feeling into' and that 'movement in', the insertion of oneself into the psyche of another is one aspect, but not the only one of the empathic process.

In psychotherapy, a therapist can avail himself of two different facets of the empathic process, an *active* and a *passive* version. The *active* version is the entering into the other, the gathering up, discerning, grasping the other's experience; the other, the *passive* version, is giving oneself up, an openness to the experience of the other, allowing oneself to be entered into. Some of the confusion in writings about empathy has been attributed to these antithetical meanings in the concept of empathy.

Let us look at some of the uses that have been made of the concept of empathy:

1. A form of knowledge that is also an affective communication.
2. An ability to sample the affects of others, to perceive and respond in resonance.
3. A method of prolonged data gathering, for discerning complex mental states in a single act of recognition (Kohut).
4. A method of communication involving non-rational understanding.
5. An important ingredient in human development in infancy that is also an important element in the psychotherapeutic relationship (Emde, 1990).

Hans Loewald (1980, p. 360) has written about '*empathic objectivity*'. 'It is neither insight in the abstract nor any special display of a benevolent or warm attitude on the part of the analyst. What seems of essential importance is insight or self-understanding as conveyed, as mediated by the analyst, objectively stated in articulate open language. Interpretations of this kind explicate for the patient what he then discovers to have always known somehow.'

The *passive mode of empathy*: for the opening of oneself to the other, we can invoke Keats' term '*negative capability*', when man is capable of being in uncertainties, mysteries, doubts, without any irritable reaching after fact and reason. Recall Freud's description of the 'evenly hovering attention' that the analyst should allow himself when listening to his patient. This attitude involves a sort of negation of self by the therapist, a kind of self-regression to submit himself to the not-knowing, to put himself aside, for this creates the opportunity for perceptual novelty, for creativity, for an aesthetic of interpretation.

The other capability is '*positive capability*', the capacity for feeling into the other. Grasping the topography, the psychic geography, of the other person's inner world, is like seeing and appreciating the 'inscape', the felicitous word of the poet Gerard Manley Hopkins.

The active mode of empathy involves imagination, the active searching into the life of the other, while the passive mode (the openness to the other) involves resonance, vibration, and sound, different forms of listening.

The American analyst Warren Poland (1975) raised the question of why empathy has become such a feature in contemporary psychoanalysis. He places this into an historical context. In the early days of analysis, the question of the analyst to himself was 'what do I know that I can interpret'. He drew on a stock of knowledge that the observer, as possessor of secure knowledge, could impart to the less knowledgeable one, the analysand. This situation is no longer tenable. Now we understand that analyst and patient are both participants in creating a dynamic field. Within that field, each person possesses unique characteristics and the therapist brings capacities achieved through training. Nowadays the analyst has to search within himself to discover the sources of his own knowledge rather than relying upon established knowledge, to ask himself the question 'how do I know what I know to interpret' rather than 'what do I know that I can interpret'. And once we know what it is that we want to interpret, how do we convey this? For Poland, of the essence is 'tact as a psychoanalytical function'. Tact follows empathy as the way that we can use information gained via empathy for reaching a patient through interpretations. Therefore, empathy is at the sensory end of the analyst's activities, tact the motor end. 'We learn with empathy and understanding: we interpret with tact.' What is tact? Jean Cocteau wrote, 'Tact consists in knowing how far we may go too far'. Empathy involves some sort of a merger between self and other, analyst and patient; tact derives from separation. Having understood we withdraw, become separate and then re-establish contact verbally.

Therapists' tact has some of the qualities of a caregiver's soothing touch, bringing about union through touching while acknowledging the essential separateness between the parties. Empathy can sensitively guide the tact that the therapist uses in speaking with the patient. The notion of *sensitive responsiveness* involves both empathy and tact.

The concept of 'therapist's shame' has been invoked to describe the way in which a therapist, by sensitivity to the possibility of shaming the other, would himself be ashamed to do so. A sensitive awareness of shame, of over-exposure to unfeeling probing and touching, can be a good guide to a therapist's activity. Time and again, we see this exemplified in groups. One group member may be able to make contact with another with sensitivity and skill, find a shared space, enabling others to listen with patience, sensitivity and understanding; other persons who lack this capacity create space for themselves by force, manipulation, by rough handling. In analytic groups, a person can learn about his or her own styles by witnessing those of others; in this situation, new learnings can take place.

Empathy for oneself

So far, we have been writing about the empathic process as happening between separate persons. There is, as well, the concept of 'empathy for oneself' to be considered.

Self-empathy is not often referred to. Empathy for oneself implies that the observing, judging, controlling and understanding parts of the self are open to receiving and understanding, accepting and caring for the anxieties, pains, fears and conflicts which the person is experiencing. Much psychopathology arises from the rejections that a person has felt throughout his attachment history, which then are internally represented and re-enacted as lack of empathy for oneself. A pattern of role-reversal in the parent–child relationship (see Marrone, 1998, pp. 104–105) often results in the subject's tendency to be more attuned to another person's needs and emotional states than with his/her own.

Reciprocal empathy

Mr A is recognizing that he has lived in an egocentric, little boy world and has not given other people full recognition for their humanity. As he develops this from a deeper sense of himself, from a more sensitive to himself side and monitoring his feelings, which is new to him, he begins to become more empathic to his wife. He sees how she has been suffering because he lived in this self-enclosed, egocentric world, as represented by the colour of his dreams, and did not recognize the extent of her suffering. In an episode in which she was very angry, feeling unsupported by him, instead of getting angry himself, he was able to be sympathetic and the whole anger disappeared and he was able to feel empathically supportive. He looks back upon how he was before the breakdown of the marriage, when for a while he said he was living almost in a state of delusion, feeling at the top of his profession and that everything was going well in his world and completely ignoring the catastrophe that was ahead of him.

The contribution of Kohut and self-psychologists has been to emphasize the selfobject functions infants need for healthy development, to be soothed, protected, stimulated, nurtured and educated. These experiences awaken correspondence and responsiveness, develop what has been called (Brazelton and Cramer, 1990) the 'reciprocity envelope' which holds the developing infant together within the interpersonal matrix. Skin-to-skin bonding, eye-to-eye gazing, speaking and listening, all contribute to the building of this reciprocity envelope. Gaps in the envelope, distortions of homeostasis are experienced as persecutions.

Confidence in separateness develops because of a secure attachment; with the capacity for separateness begins the capacity for empathy. From birth onwards, the human condition is one of attachment and separateness, the dual track, the double helix, which forms the core of the developing self. Confidence in oneself is built up in many ways, both positive and negative, through complaints, if the infant's rage is understood and responded to appropriately. 'Complaining to the caregiver', a process with which we are all too familiar in psychotherapy, can build up confidence in the effectiveness of reasonable complaints to bring about understanding and change.

Empathy enables two to experience the pain of the one; this allows an infant to gain the experience of reciprocity and a sense of self. Failure to achieve this, failure of caregiver empathy, leads to shame, helplessness and ineffectuality, to defences that can lead to profound states of withdrawal and encapsulation.

Feeling sorry for oneself is a natural function that enables us to preserve the sense of self in the face of pain and disappointment, for then we can soothe, contain, hold ourselves, eventually recover from distress in the way that the other, the self-object had helped before.

Empathy betokens a state of faith in the relationship to an object, a sense of its protection, its nurture and its stimulation. Empathic failure leads to a sense of autistic encapsulation, withdrawal, confusion and loss of coherency. Empathy gives a memory of having been contained, of being in relationship with a mother, a father, a caregiver who was able to hear the infant's pain without shattering, thus making the pain endurable. In adult intimate relationships, reciprocal empathy and tact constitute essential elements to establish and maintain a *secure base*.

Empathy and sympathy

Empathy has begun to occupy the domain of sympathy. Sympathy was the domain of the various meanings of compassionate feeling for another person's sufferings. Sympathy is a species of humane caring, a feeling tone consonant with the plight of the other as the other experiences it. The response of sympathy is predominantly affective, nonobjective and highly personalized. In sympathy, one feels close and warm to the other, drawn to action. Sympathy is a universal human response that binds people to one another.

Empathy as experienced and used in a psychotherapeutic situation by a therapist to another, the patient, is more detached and separate, though in a situation of intimacy, in the therapeutic dyad or group. Empathy is the process of specific perception, understanding of the other knowing that the experience is that of the other and not of oneself, to communicate this understanding, to respond appropriately requiring action through thought and verbalization. Sympathy is a matter of being actively or passively influenced towards the other, an emotional contagion. These actions take a natural direction of rescue, aid and assistance. Sympathy is feeling with, a closeness.

Empathy is not a feeling with; that is sympathy; empathy is literally a 'feeling into' that represents separateness. It is less of a stimulant than sympathy to action, to rescue and assistance. Such action by a therapist is likely to arise from a sense of loss of contact with the patient, a blockage in the affective interchange, the interpersonal dialogue. When this arises, the appropriate therapeutic action is to understand what has gone awry, the derailment of the dialogue and to fill in by one's own understanding of what it is that blocks the resumption of meaningful communication.

The 'feeling into' aspect of empathy is often described through such words as discerning, grasping, gathering. This involves the use of one's imagination and understanding as a tool, as an instrument with which to grasp the experience of the other. This is *active understanding*, but there is also an *active passivity* in empathy, the act of opening oneself up to be with the person, to allow oneself to be permeated by their experience. The therapist, or the group, offers itself as environment, as container, as attentive presence. This active passivity function of the empathic process has connotations that are more feminine. There are antithetical meanings in the psychoanalytic discourse to do with empathy. It is used in different senses by persons who seem to be in dispute with each other without recognizing that they are using the concept in these antithetical ways.

There are analysts who believe that within the discourse of free association there are always unconscious wishes, conflicts and fantasies. According to this view, the task of the therapist is to bring prior knowledge – based on analytic understanding and training – to the analytic situation. In all cases, the analyst uses his or her knowledge in the service of therapy. A problem arises, however, when this knowledge is framed within a rigid paradigm. The freedom and joy of joint exploration is significantly limited by the analyst's rigid attitude, which prioritizes theoretical assumptions over empathy and dialogue (see Casement, 2002).

In contrast, there are therapists who hold a different view that what the person brings to therapy are states of being, not material for interpretation; it is more a question of an understanding acceptance and finding optimal responses. Winnicott wrote that psychotherapy in the long run is more a question of giving back to the person what they have brought with them and taking care not to take things away. Perhaps T.S. Eliot's words are appropriate here, 'And at the end of our exploring will be to arrive where we started and to know the place for the first time'.

Emanuel Peterfreund (1983), an attachment-oriented analyst from New York, who has written one of the most interesting books on the process of psychoanalytic therapy, made the distinction between a *stereotyped approach* and a *heuristic approach* to psychoanalytic psychotherapy. Even if all analysts use a basic paradigm to work clinically (Juri, 1999), what characterizes an analyst using a stereotyped approach is the way their capacity to engage the patient in joint exploratory work is impaired by adherence to a rigid model. In contrast, a heuristic analyst is able to deal with the vastness, complexity, unpredictability and multi-determined nature of the phenomena he or she confronts in psychoanalysis in ways that do not reduce all these characteristics to a limited number of theoretical assumptions. Reciprocal empathy and openness is a contributing condition for a heuristic approach.

Empathy and sensitive responsiveness in psychotherapy

Patients entering psychoanalytic psychotherapy are taking a risky step into the unknown, a journey that necessarily involves uncovering, recognizing, accepting unwelcome parts of oneself. The clinicians' responses to this journey are varied, influenced by their personalities, training, and theoretical orientations. The lines of demarcation can be traced back to the influences of Freud and Ferenczi; Freud with the surgical model, the analyst as the objective mirror in whom the patient can see their psychic life reflected; Ferenczi's experience led him to advocate empathy and sensitivity, even a mutual empathy between patient and analyst in which each could benefit the other. Freud's model largely predominates, slowly changing with growing understanding of the complexities of transference and countertransference issues. Undoubtedly the writings of Heinz Kohut and the school of self-psychology have altered the field for many, perhaps most analysts, reluctant though many may be to acknowledge this fact. The impact of self-psychology combined with advances in understanding early development processes such as attachment have been pointing to desirable and undesirable issues in analytic technique.

Relationship per se has been highlighted and a vigorous ongoing debate as to whether the therapeutic technique should be primarily interpretative in the here and now, seen as repetition of early formative experiences (whose exploration is the be-all of therapy), or whether therapy, as a new and healthier attachment, opens possibilities of 'new beginnings', or even, to use the misunderstood term, corrective emotional experience.

Consultants who, like the two authors of this chapter, have had wide experience in seeing analysands who have had previous unsatisfactory analytic experiences, and who have seen the change that can occur when such individuals experience a different analytic climate, are particularly sensitive to these issues. Therapeutic impasses (Rosenfeld, 1987) arise not from intractable and unresolvable intrapsychic dynamics (constitutionally heightened aggression, envy, greed and the like, as it is frequently proposed), but through misattunement in the analytic setting. Often the problems arise from the misapplied application of 'experience distant' theories.

Negative experiences in therapy often seem related to a therapist's insistence on interpreting what he/she sees as 'negative transference' (which refers to the patient's alleged competitiveness, envy, hatred and hidden hostility). What is seen as the patient's pathology is sometimes the product of a therapist's errors in timing and tact. Heard and Lake (1997) indicate that the therapist's inability to deal sensitively and in a timely way with the patient's communications is likely to be the result of the therapist having unresolved anxieties, which get reactivated by the material. If the therapist had an adverse attachment history, which has not been worked through properly in the therapist's own analysis, the preconditions for iatrogenic interventions are set (Marrone, 1998).

Many analyses based on the 'here-and now, you-and-me, analysing the negative transference' can be reductionistic to the point of neglecting vast areas of the patient's past and present psychological and social life. Often the analyst actively conveys to the patient the notion that he is not prepared to take seriously anything – like his memories of the past and understanding of his attachment history – which does not meet his personal interests and ideas of what meaningful material for analysis should be. Ultimately, this position involves lack of empathy and poverty of thought on the part of the analyst. The imposition of rigid theory can also be conceptualized as part of the therapist's rigid superego. Branchaft and Stolorow (1984) consider that many aspects of the borderline syndrome arise from iatrogenic causes.

If the therapist's behaviour feeds into the punitive and rigid superego aspects of the patient's personality, or repeats damaging aspects of the patient's early parental figures therapy, it is likely to re-traumatize the analysand. It is often the case that a patient who has reached impasse in dyadic therapy will flourish in group analysis applied in the Foulkesian model. The group analytic situation enables the person to share in the emotional and mental lives of others, often to begin to communicate more freely, which reduces the severity of the superego aspects of the patient that have over-intruded into therapy.

The development of the therapist's empathic abilities

What stands as an important area for further research is the way in which the therapist's own early history of receiving a certain quality of empathic responses from his caregivers – and, later on, from his own analyst – might unconsciously influence his capacity to act empathically in his current relationships, including relationships with his analysands. We know that the parental ability to act empathically cannot be intellectually learned. It can only be acquired through the emotional and cognitive experience of being at the receiving end of empathic understanding.

On the basis of our current knowledge we must assume that the four most important factors that are likely to determine a therapist's quality of empathic responsiveness are (perhaps with decreasing degree of influence):

- His/her own early attachment history.
- His/her own experiences as an analysand.
- His/her own experiences in clinical supervision.
- His/her theoretical framework or biases.

Conclusion

Advances in understanding emotional development with emphasis on the need for sensitive and empathic attunement between caregivers and infants has begun to influence the course of psychotherapy. Similarly, the understanding of the long-term consequences of a person's attachment history and intergenerational transmission of patterns of attachment should be regarded as an essential part of the therapist's training and therapeutic approach. Failure to take these developmental and attachment issues into account in shaping the therapeutic style can lead to therapeutic impasse and even to negative consequences (iatrogenia). These negative effects can be undone and remedied by further therapeutic experiences in individual or group analytic psychotherapy, where these developmental issues can be properly addressed. However, optimally, negative effects should be avoided altogether by increasing therapists' insight into the central role that empathy and sensitive responsiveness play as psychic organizers and interpersonal regulators.

References

Ainsworth MDS, Blehar M, Waters E and Wall S (1978) Patterns of Attachment. Hillsdale, NJ: Erlbaum.

Branchaft B and Stolorow RD (1984) The borderline concept as iatrogenic syndrome. In: JS Grotstein, F Solomon and J Lang (eds) The Borderline Patient, vol. 2. Hillsdale, NJ: Analytic Press.

Brazelton TB and Cramer BG (1990) The Earliest Relationship. Reading: Addison Wesley.

Casement P (2002) Learning from our Mistakes: Beyond Dogma in Psychoanalysis and Psychotherapy. London: Routledge; New York: Guilford Press.

Condon WS (1979) Neonatal entrainment and enculturation. In: M Bullova (ed.) Before Speech: The Beginning of Interpersonal Communication. Cambridge: Cambridge University Press.

Condon WS and Sander LW (1974) Neonate movement is synchronized with adult speech: interactional participation and language acquisition. Science 183: 99–101.

Diamond N and Marrone M (2003) Attachment and Intersubjectivity. London: Whurr.

Emde RE (1990) Mobilising fundamental modes of development: empathic availability and therapeutic action. Journal of the American Psychoanalytic Association 38(4): 881.

Fonagy P, Steele M, Steele H, Leigh T, Kennedy R, Mattoon G and Target M (1995) Attachment, the reflective self and borderline states. In: S Goldberg, R Muir and J Kerr (eds) Attachment Theory: Social, Developmental and Clinical Perspectives. New York: Analytic Press.

Heard D and Lake B (1997) The Challenge of Attachment for Caregiving. London: Routledge.

Hoffmann M (1994) De la iniciativa a la experiencia. Clínica Psicológica 3: 249–61.

Hubbard FOA and van IJzendoorn MH (1991) Maternal unresponsiveness and infant crying across the first 9 months. Infant Behaviour and Development 14: 299–312.

Juri L (1999) El Psicoanalista Neutral ¿Un Mito? Psicoanálisis y Paradigmas. Rosario: Homo Sapiens.

Loewald H (1980) Psychoanalysis as an art and the fantasy character of the psychoanalytic situation. In: Papers on Psychoanalysis. New Haven: Yale University Press, p. 360.

Mahler M, Pines F and Bergman A (1975) The Psychological Birth of the Human Infant. New York: Basic Books.

Marrone M (1998) Attachment and Interaction. London: Jessica Kingsley.

Peterfreund E (1983) The Process of Psychoanalytic Therapy. Hillsdale, NJ: Erlbaum.

Poland W (1975) Tact as a psychoanalytic function. International Journal of Psycho-analysis 56(1): 55.

Rosenfeld H (1987) Impasse and Interpretation. London: Tavistock.

Schore A (1994) Affect Regulation and the Origins of the Self. Hillsdale, NJ: Erlbaum.

Sroufe LA (1996) Emotional Development: The Organization of Emotional Life in the Early Years. New York: Cambridge University Press.

Stern DN (1977) The First Relationship: Infant and Mother. Cambridge, Mass: Harvard University Press.

Stern DN (1985). The Interpersonal World of the Infant. New York: Basic Books.

Wilmer HA (1968) The doctor patient relationship and the issues of pity, sympathy and empathy. British Journal of Medical Psychology 41: 243.

Wispe L (1986) The distinction between sympathy and empathy. To call forth a concept a word is needed. Journal of Personality and Social Psychology 30(2): 314.

CHAPTER 4

Implications of attachment theory for developing a therapeutic alliance and insight in psychoanalytic psychotherapy

TIRRIL HARRIS

> Having a more integrative model ... could diminish the risk of making interventions that, being pertinent for a given subtype, could become inefficient or even reinforce the pathology, when applied to a different one. Just as in medicine where even very useful medicines have clear cases in which they are contra-indicated, perhaps psychoanalytic interventions could also be thought of as indicated, or contra-indicated, and not as universally applicable. (Bleichmar, 1996, p. 957)

The substantial contribution of John Bowlby to psychoanalytic theory has been held in differing regard at different periods. Greeted with suspicion at first by professionals across the board from the hearths of psychiatry to the tabernacles of psychoanalysis, attachment theory initially won wider respect from workers in the field of ethology who had witnessed the phenomenon of imprinting (Lorenz, 1937) and then from developmental psychologists following Ainsworth's work (Ainsworth and Wittig, 1969). As respect for its message gradually spread through the ranks of child psychotherapists (Sroufe and Waters, 1977) and family therapists (Byng-Hall, 1980), its relevance for work with adult psychopathology began to be more widely acknowledged and reached those heartlands of orthodoxy, the British (Bowlby, 1977) and the American (Bowlby, 1988b) Journals of Psychiatry. During the 1990s as literally hundreds of evidence-based papers have attested to the value of Bowlby's hypotheses, this acceptance has blossomed, especially among young clinical psychologists.

However, the ramifications of this growing popularity have not been unmixed. There has been much less agreement about the theory's implications for therapeutic practice than there has about its findings in terms of developmental psychopathology; and sometimes the justified claim by its proponents that attachment theory turns Freudian theory on its head has been accompanied by parallel claims that Freudian psychoanalytic practice requires a comparable up-ending. One particular variant of this is a recent tendency to knock what has become known as 'insight therapy', and to question the importance of interpretation in the therapeutic session. Proponents challenge the role of therapist as interpreter, maintaining an almost mystical view of therapy as a 'process' rather than looking at any interchange of ideas between two people. This chapter seeks to redress the balance in this argument by following the implications of attachment theory in detail through each phase of psychotherapy. It concludes that not only is there truth on both sides, but that this 'process' can prosper only when it involves an integrated provision of challenging thoughts and emotional support. This is because on the one side (analysand's) self-reflection best arises in a context of empathic interchange, and on the other side (therapist's) true sympathy must involve reflection on the other's predicament, reflection which a truly sympathetic practitioner will want to share.

Development of internal working models of relationships

The most radical feature of attachment theory is the priority given in explaining human development to the search for proximity to a key figure imparting security. Bowlby (1969) maintained there was a separate attachment instinct over and above the drives for survival and sex. He invoked Darwinian principles to explain the origins of the strength of the attachment instinct. Children who kept physically close to key adults would have been protected from being killed by predators, and so would survive to father the next generation, whose attachment instinct would be correspondingly well developed. However, despite this added inner feature of an attachment instinct, the theory also gives special emphasis to the role of the outer world, unlike traditional psychoanalysis which stresses the importance of phantasy.

Attachment theory highlights how the ways in which each infant's attachment needs were responded to by the environment might vary, thus promoting the development of different styles of relating or defending against relating. Based on these early experiences with others, children would develop expectations about future relationships, or *internal working models*, that would shape their subsequent behaviour, often causing others to treat them in a particular way. Thus a child expecting to be bullied might in fact provoke abuse from new contacts. Some caregivers might react with 'sensitive responsiveness', recognizing the validity of the child's attachment needs and doing their best to meet them, thus helping the development of a secure attachment style. Others might be inconsistently responsive, conveying a sense that the child might need to be vigilant and press his/her demands if they were to be met, and fostering an insecure *ambivalent or preoccupied/enmeshed* attachment style in the child. Yet others might be consistently unresponsive, an external situation likely to foster disengagement by the child as a self-protective strategy against continual disappointment, that is an *insecure avoidant or dismissive* style. It seemed that each individual could be located somewhere on a map where the coordinates were anxiety and avoidance, and these could give an indication of his mode of affect regulation and of the hyperactivation or deactivation of his attachment system. Some caregivers might prove definitely abusive, but here Bowlby's insight was to see the paradox of how this might result only in pushing the child to cling more desperately to the abuser, who was one and the same as the primary caregiver.

Here Mary Main's delineation of the *disorganized* attachment style that characterized children with parents who were too frightened or too frightening was an important extension of attachment theory in the mid-1980s. As children matured, unless fate produced an alternative key caregiver of a different kind, a snowballing causal process would most likely confirm these internal working models. This process takes place as the outer world impinges upon their inner world of expectation and fantasy, with the latter in turn conditioning their style of relating to the outer world, thus reinforcing the original mode in which the outer world responded to the child.

Figure 4.1 seeks to convey this trajectory, representing the impact of the outer upon the inner world by a continuous line, and the impact of the inner upon the outer world by a dotted one, with time running from left to right. It is intended to embody the continuing influence of past events, in childhood, adolescence and early adulthood, upon the mind of the older adult. The prime purpose of the Adult Attachment Interview (AAI) (George, Kaplan and Main, 1985) is to capture this influence by paying attention not so much to the events that occurred years before between the interviewee and her parents, but also to her way of interpreting them, her style of narrating them and the way her thoughts about them are processed – in other words to her 'metacognition'. It is intuitively plausible that the narratives of preoccupied enmeshed respondents redound with long trailing sentences, often only half finished and disconnected, while the accounts of avoidant dismissive subjects tend to be monosyllabic, and laced with disclaimers about how little they can remember about that time of their life. Understanding of the different

Figure 4.1. Model of psychological development and psychotherapy

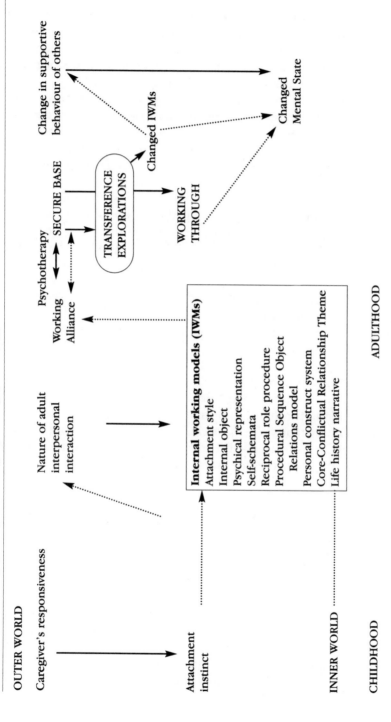

OUTER WORLD

Caregiver's responsiveness

Nature of adult interpersonal interaction

Psychotherapy

Working Alliance

SECURE BASE

TRANSFERENCE EXPLORATIONS

Change in supportive behaviour of others

Changed IWMs

WORKING THROUGH

Changed Mental State

Attachment instinct

Internal working models (IWMs)
Attachment style
Internal object
Psychical representation
Self-schemata
Reciprocal role procedure
Procedural Sequence Object Relations model
Personal construct system
Core-Conflictual Relationship Theme
Life history narrative

INNER WORLD

CHILDHOOD

ADULTHOOD

Dotted lines represent impact of inner world on outer and inner worlds
Continuous lines represent impact of outer world on inner and outer worlds

ways of remembering – semantic as opposed to episodic memory (Tulving, 1972 cited by Bowlby, 1980) – fills out this picture of how a person's style of relating has penetrated deep into their style of thinking, or their reflective function as Peter Fonagy and colleagues have named it in the manual developed to systematize its measurement across samples of different patients or research subjects (Fonagy et al., 1991).

Figure 4.1 also aims to portray the process of psychotherapy. Here the outer world, in the person of the psychotherapist, is trying to counteract the effect on the internal working models of the earlier years with a less sensitively responsive caregiver. The process of 'working through in the transference', depicted here by the oblong representing the circling dance of intersubjectivity as the sessions unfold, is seen as the source of change in the analysand's internal working models. But this is crucially dependent upon the therapy taking on the aspect of Bowlby's 'secure base' providing responsive empathy (see Marrone and Pines, Chapter 3 in this volume), without which there is a risk that a good working alliance will not be built. Once these internal working models have changed, it will be possible for the analysand to relate in a different way to others, with the result that they too may respond in a different manner, and he will feel more at home with himself.

In many ways this scheme does not depart very radically from the outlook of many object relations approaches. (The terms from other theoretical perspectives (including non-psychoanalytic ones) listed as parallels to Bowlby's notion of internal working models are intended to convey this broad similarity.) While it is particularly in focusing upon the process of working through in the transference that the contribution of attachment theory stands out most clearly – and that the role of imparting insight can be estimated – it can be a useful exercise to follow the whole process of psychotherapy according to this scheme.

Attachment theory and the stages of psychotherapy

Initial assessment

Because the attachment perspective gives due consideration to the external origin of many internal problems, it can be very helpful to use the initial assessment, before the 'fundamental rule' of free association has yet come to apply, as the source of a fully informed developmental history of the person seeking psychotherapy. By this I mean that the assessor should ask a full range of questions about current and past social circumstances, ascertaining not only the customary genogram but also information about their occupational experience. It is, of course, crucial to leave space at the beginning for the person to define how they are feeling and why they have thought of entering psychotherapy, and some standard diagnostic issues must also be covered, such as current mental state and previous psychiatric episodes; furthermore, at the end of the assessment session (or phase if more than one session seems required) it is important to give the person some idea of what will be involved in psychotherapy, including a brief explanation of the relative lack of logic of the primary process, with examples of how free association and talking about dreams can help them to find out about themselves. However, in between it can be useful to establish the key features of their development by direct questions. This does not have to feel like an interrogation: it can be explained at the beginning of the assessment that at this first meeting some questions may prove helpful to work out a plan for the therapy, but that in the subsequent sessions there will no longer be this pressure. Moreover the questions can be asked with a lightness of touch that leaves the person feeling almost as if they were spontaneously presenting their own narrative. Many people feel quite inhibited at first and are quite grateful to be guided in what they present, and the nature of the psychotherapist's questions often facilitates later talking and reflection.

While the quality of a prospective client's relationships forms an important part of most assessments, it is central to those guided by attachment theory. From what was outlined above it will be obvious that a key feature of assessment for an attachment-informed psychotherapist will be the history of key caregivers' responsiveness or insensitivity, whether there was any loss of such a key caregiver and the resulting attachment style of the person seeking therapy. Not only will it be informative in facilitating understanding of that person's particular developmental trajectory, but the specific subtype of insecure attachment will give a pointer to the particular direction a therapy may be likely to go, for example in building the working alliance or in anticipating the nature of the transference. Assessing the attachment style does not necessarily require full use of a validated instrument such as the AAI: a shortened approximation should be adequate to give an estimate of the person's location on the anxiety-avoidance map (see above). Moreover, the face-to-face situation of a clinical assessment offers many advantages over some fully validated instruments which are self-report questionnaires that do not permit use of relevant information from narrative style, gesture and tone of voice. As mentioned, the AAI has highlighted the key relevance of such cues in understanding a person's defence system when the attachment instinct has been frustrated in some manner. Thus while a full training in the AAI is not essential for an adequate attachment-informed assessment, some understanding of its approach is of considerable utility. However, there are aspects of attachment style not captured by the AAI: propensities in relating to friends, neighbours, workmates may turn out to be no less relevant for outcome than those involving family of origin. Sometimes *current* ways of relating to these latter, particularly siblings, get lost within the overall AAI protocol that focuses so much on childhood. Interactions with marital partners and older children are also omitted by the AAI but are especially key relationships. However, it is possible to supplement an approach based on a shortened AAI with one similarly based on measures of romantic relationships such as that of Hazan and Shaver (1987), or those including such partnerships along with other same-sex friendships such as Bartholomew and Horowitz (1991) or the Attachment Style Interview or ASI (Bifulco et al., 2002a, 2002b). The latter has the advantage of combining attention to the full range of adult relationships with the appreciation of coherence and other aspects of narrative style highlighted by the AAI.

While the subtypes of insecure attachment can be summarized in four or five categories (Table 4.1), it may be important to identify as early as possible very specific interactions between the prospective analysand and his key caregiver. For instance, finding out what means of discipline and reward he was subjected to in childhood may be very important. Sometimes it can be useful to explore explicitly whether the parent figure used threats of abandonment as a disciplinary measure. Bowlby has a moving account of how such parenting can prove perpetually unsettling (Bowlby, 1988a, pp. 108–9). Attachment theory suggests that knowledge of any traumatic experience, whether or not a key caregiver was involved, would be pertinent for understanding current mental state, and identifying neglect or abuse at this early stage is thus clearly useful. However, to ask explicitly about sexual abuse at this point is likely to be experienced as too intrusive, with repercussions in delaying their ability to open up in later sessions. On the other hand, for those who may be ready to disclose such information, and who may leave an assessment disappointed if they have not been given an opportunity to do so, it is possible to ask coat-trailing questions such as 'Anything else important I should know about your father? Or about anyone else in the family?' At the end of this intermediate part of the assessment it can be revealing to ask whether amid all the questions asked there is another which the psychotherapist has not asked but which they feel might have an answer of some importance about themselves. One young woman replied that in view of some of the other things I had asked her perhaps I ought to know that when she was 11 her pony had been run over by a lorry and she had witnessed this. This crucial experience, an admixture of loss and trauma, might not have emerged if I had not set the scene by my earlier focus on closeness and separation while also prompting her to see if there were other relevant experiences.

Some psychotherapies, such as cognitive behavioural therapy (CBT: Clark and Beck, 1999) or cognitive analytic therapy (CAT: Ryle, 1995), deliberately use the initial session or phase to create a jointly agreed 'sequential diagrammatic reformulation (SDR)'. CAT identifies typical 'snags' and 'dilemmas' arising in current relationships which will serve as the basis for the coming work following a 'procedural sequence object relations model' (see Figure 4.1). A similar approach identifies a 'core-conflictual relationship theme' (Luborsky et al., 1994; also see Figure 4.1). The negotiation of this joint agreement acts as a first example of the spirit of collaboration which it is hoped will prove part of the 'corrective emotional experience' of the therapy as a whole.

Building the working alliance

Implicit in the emphasis placed on assessment in psychotherapy training is the notion that the subsequent therapy will be tailored in some way to the individual characteristics that emerge at that stage. However, sometimes this does not appear to become explicit, apart from the broadest of prescriptions dictated by individuals' particular psychiatric diagnoses. Yet there is now increasing agreement that one of the best predictors of the overall success of a therapy is the quality of the working alliance (Horvath and Symonds, 1991), which requires skill to build, and that it can be premature to venture into deeper waters until such an alliance is securely developed, usually after some three months or so. Table 4.1 (over), which follows the slightly expanded categorization of attachment styles proposed by Bifulco and colleagues (2002a, 2002b), hazards an outline of the likely impact of particular attachment styles on the analysand's way of building such an alliance and suggests possible responses for a therapist facing such issues. By offering a reminder of the type of caregiving likely to have helped create such a style, the table provides a pointer to specific countervailing 'caregiving' behaviours on the therapist's part that may serve to reduce the destructive impact of the analysand's insecure attachment style on the alliance.

Whatever the attachment style of a new analysand, it is useful to give them some idea at first meeting of what they may expect upon coming to sessions, if possible giving a brief outline of the rationale for free association and mentioning something about silences during sessions. Even when this has been properly discussed before starting, one of the more difficult aspects of the early sessions is to judge their pace, and how much

Table 4.1. Using attachment classifications to build the working alliance

Attachment style and type of prior caregiver	Relevant issues for creating a supportive alliance (by disconfirming the internal working models of prior relationships)
FEARFUL (OF REJECTION): Caregiver consistently rejecting/unresponsive to needs	*Issue*: After an initial problem in talking at all, client may develop habit of speaking a lot (to be obedient and thus avoid rejection), but not about the important things or needs of which he/she may be ashamed and which he/she therefore fears will earn him/her rejection. *Focus*: Convey that therapy is non-judgemental: talking truthfully about shameful parts of the self will not call forth rejection or disapproval.
FEARFUL (OF ENGULFMENT): Caregiver imposing control/consistently unresponsive to needs	*Issue*: Client may be able to speak freely but may experience therapist's comments, especially transference interpretations, as controlling or intrusive and so be unwilling to listen/hear. May ward off therapist with a flood of talk. *Focus*: Pace interpretations gradually until client has come to feel there is room for him/her to be himself/herself.
WITHDRAWN: Caregiver consistently unresponsive/never taught the value of relating	*Issue*: Client may not have much to say, not having had as much practice in interpersonal communication as others. *Focus*: May need encouragement, even gentle 'instruction by example', before can free associate openly.
DISMISSIVE: Caregiver consistently unresponsive in any, or all, of ways outlined above	*Issue*: Client may 'dismiss' what therapy has to offer, denying the truth of valid interpretations. *Focus*: Pace interpretations until client has begun to feel the value of 'having to' confide, occasionally interpreting the behaviour of others in his/her network as a way of introducing the genuine value of attachments; remain responsive despite client's negativity.
PREOCCUPIED/ENMESHED: Caregiver inconsistently responsive	*Issue*: Client may get stuck because the boundaries of the therapeutic frame reawaken his/her ambivalence: he/she may try to manipulate some sort of change in boundaries. *Focus*: Initial flexibility may be important as it disconfirms the prior experience of inconsistent responsiveness: only then may it be possible for the client to explore why he/she had such a need for change. Too rigid adherence to the frame may make such exploration impossible as the alliance still feels too unsafe.
STANDARD/SECURE: Caregiver consistently responsive enough	*Issue*: Usually none, but sometimes the artificial nature of the therapeutic dyad may discourage a client from using the therapy. *Focus*: Show that the secure internal working model can also be applied in therapy despite constraints.

silence to allow. And of course what feels appropriate here will partly depend on whether the analysands are using couch or chair. There is much to be said for varying these arrangements according to both their attachment style and the phase of their therapy.

Following Table 4.1 from the top I shall describe building the working alliance with some analysands whose attachment styles exemplified these issues. For Fiona, whose critical mother had always preferred her brother, leaving her fearful of rejection, the classic orthodox silence in her early sessions on the couch with a previous therapist waiting for the patient to speak first had reinforced her anxiety. The sessions had felt imbued with disapproval such that when even quite mild interpretations had later been offered she felt she would never be able to measure up to what was expected. But, being fearful, she did not dare to ask what was really expected and had just stayed silent – and afraid, giving very short responses when the previous therapist later began to hazard interpretations of her silence, finally leaving the therapy after only one month. Out of obedience she had automatically gone on to the couch as indicated, but perhaps if she had been offered the chance to start in the chair this might have conveyed the sympathy of her therapist and the differences between him and her mother. For although as someone with an avoidant attachment style she tended to avoid maintaining eye contact, seated opposite him she would have had more information about his kindly interest in her than could be available from the couch. When she came to me she chose to go on the couch again, but this was partly because in the initial assessment session we had spent considerable time discussing what had felt uncomfortable in the previous therapy and how we could find a middle way to security, neither the fearful scrutiny of the chair nor the persecutory distance of the couch. We decided that together we could find a way for her to be silent with permission that made it easier for her to talk. I also moved my chair at an angle to a desk so that she would not sense me staring straight down at her on the couch. Very gradually she was able to open up.

Rejhan, also fearful of rejection, chose the chair, she later told me, because she would have felt 'at my mercy on the couch'. Keeping her eyes down she kept talking almost without drawing breath about what she was doing to meet other people's requests, but not about how that made her feel. Gradually she became able to slow down, pause for some minutes and exchange a smile.

On the other hand, Eric, a trainee technician who had been an only child with a widowed mother who longed to know and direct everything about his life, was fearful of engulfment and expressed some relief when I mentioned that we could spend parts of the sessions in silence. I explained this was because I thought he might find it easier to be truly himself and to 'listen' to how he felt about things if he did not have to report back to me immediately but spoke only when he really felt like it. Once he had come to appreciate this pace he came to enjoy telling me about thoughts he had had earlier, decided not to tell me and later changed his mind thinking it could be interesting to share them after all.

By contrast, William's silence stemmed from a withdrawn rather than a fearful style, and it was therefore less productive for his therapist (a close colleague of mine) to stay quiet. On the contrary, he came from a family culture where talking was minimal and while he got on reasonably with his workmates he did not really have friends, just acquaintances – he had never been out on a date with a girl – so had not had much practice in sharing experiences. So it was important that somewhere he should find a role model from which he could learn the enjoyment, and more basic- ally the vocabulary, of self-reflection. It is inappropriate for therapists to talk about their own self-reflections except at very rare and special junc- tures. Similarly, occasional references by therapists to how other people in therapy feel about various issues which appear to be arising for that particular analysand can help with this, but too many are apt to leave the analysand feeling second best to these other paragons of fluency who have captured the therapist's attention. My colleague specializes in com- bining group with individual work so that she saw each group member at least once weekly in individual therapy in parallel with their weekly group attendance. Her solution was therefore to include him in a group where he would have seven other role models and he became much less with- drawn. However, she runs her groups in a particular way, such that they are eminently aware of how a group can become an unsupportive envir- onment and they all try to counteract this. More traditional group therapy is not always so successful with the withdrawn.

Talking and reflecting on his own feelings was equally foreign to Derek, but so was responding to role models as he needed to defend himself against other people's feelings as well as his own. His dismissiveness was not of the angriest kind, so I was spared too much contempt, but he had little patience with what he called 'weakness' and was coming to therapy under pressure from his GP, who thought his somatic symptoms might benefit. If referred early on to a group, he would almost certainly have felt contempt for other group members without considerable initial exposure to individual sessions. As expected, his internal working models were revealed not only in the content of his sessions but also in his narrative style. He was adept at avoiding statements in the first person, thus man- aging to distance himself from his emotions: for example 'people have found it difficult to work with my boss' or 'it doesn't do to complain'. Even the phrase 'mustn't grumble' was notable for its omission of the word 'I'. However, he was occasionally able to use it, as when responding to my early explanation of the psychoanalytic method: 'Well for a start I never dream'. I was wary of compounding his disbelief by an early overemphasis on how important it was for him to talk about feelings of anxiety or anger that he denied he had. His early sessions focused on his work situation, where a supervisor was hectoring, if not harassing, him. I allowed him to talk at length about who had done what and what he had then done in return before gently interpolating that 'I found myself wondering whether he could remember what was going on in his mind while he was doing that'. By not using the word 'emotion' and by not asking directly 'what were you feeling?' I managed to get him to describe his thoughts, which often overlapped with the motivation for his deeds; and from motivation to feeling is a much easier way in to analysands who resemble closed books. But his carapace softened only marginally: his behaviour was entirely in line with Dozier and colleagues' reports about how individuals with dismissive attachment styles often try to divert the clinician's attention when sailing close to an issue which is threatening to penetrate their defences against feeling (Dozier et al., 1996). However, a month after Derek started in therapy, an unfortunate event occurred to a friend – his wife left him – that proved to be a fortunate development for the therapy; this friend, a work colleague called Stephen, did not have a dismissive attachment style. Derek had not at this point ever had any close male friends in whom he confided or who confided in him, but Stephen seemed uncomplicated in crying all over him in the office that day. It is difficult to gauge whether Derek would have allowed himself to be drafted into the role of confidant had he not had a session with me that evening. He was certainly very uncomfortable that first day. But it had given us a manner of discussing issues like the potential damage of the outdated norm that big boys don't cry, without it being too personal for Derek to let his thoughts flow. He was able to wax indignant at Stephen's wife (whom he had never met), to ask why Stephen was not more indignant himself and to begin to find value in my responses about how emotions work. The following session he came with a memory which he claimed had been triggered by our general discussions of Stephen's situation: an occasion when he had been let down by an older boy at school. Although his initial account of this was fairly brief and stiff upper lip, he was now quite willing to answer questions – which I put to him about that occasion – and was able to make quite subtle distinctions between feelings of hurt, shame and indignation which he had experienced at that time. But he still was not ready for some weeks to move on to how he had felt let down by his father, who had retired early from the forces for alcoholism. Only when his resistances had been softened by talking with me about his emotions concerning incidents less close to his core self than his parents, was he able to cease his denial of the imperfections of his childhood. (He told me originally that his father was declared invalid because of his back.)

Jeremy Holmes has neatly contrasted the different therapeutic tasks required with dismissive and preoccupied/enmeshed patients, calling them story breaking and story making. 'If the task with avoidant patients is to break open the semi-clichéd narratives they bring to therapy, with ambivalent patients it is necessary to introduce punctuation and shape into their stories – a *making* rather than a *breaking* function' (Holmes, 2000, p. 169). With Derek, I had to be involved in story breaking (removing the story that his father had been kindly and competent but physically injured) whereas with Penny, whom I discuss next, the opposite was required. She needed help to make a story out of her continual stream of remarks about how weird she felt.

Penny was preoccupied/enmeshed. The last in a series of sisters with a very intense mother and a father from abroad, she had become anorexic in her teens when the other older sisters had left home. When I first saw her (in the context of making an assessment for a clinical service) she was single and in her mid-30s, and seemed to be buffeted by currents in all directions. Drifting from course to course with temporary locum jobs she had found nowhere to live since a break-up with a boyfriend some five months previously and a residential National Health Service admission. Her woman friends, some of whom she was staying with on alternate nights, were beginning to become weary of her excuses about not finding another residence. It became clear that the assessment process with me (which required a second evaluative session because I could not report adequately on her many complicated teenage referrals in only one meeting) had given rise to a strong attachment between Penny and my therapy setting. I decided that the most ethical outcome to the assessment was for me to take her on low-fee rather than push her into a new attachment in a *trainee low-fee* setting, where her chaos might not only find no remission but also might demoralize the trainee. True to her attachment style, there were already several other alternative therapists who had carried out initial assessments waiting in the wings but I did not learn of these until after she and I had reached an agreement to start with me. These alternative therapists were finally decided against after long discussions in therapy with me.

Penny had chosen the chair, because she was familiar with this from a previous time-limited NHS-funded psychodynamic psychotherapy. However, I think it was because she so much needed to keep an eye on me. Her most characteristic feature was her need to look silently and very intently into my eyes without speaking, for minutes at a time. While I found this unsettling at first, I somehow knew I must not allow myself to be put off so I held her gaze, but gently, often giving a faint smile. Soon after such a phase, if it ended with her returning my smile, she would talk non-stop often imparting crucial extra new information. At about her seventh session she started to reach for a tissue after one of these staring matches and was later able to explain to me why she felt weepy at these points. 'I suppose it's a kind of relief,' she said, 'though I still can't believe that you do really care'. As the sessions went on she was able to catch herself increasingly often when she did not trust something emotionally and so felt she needed to impose her demands. Then she would spontaneously ask, 'Am I overreacting? Will I put them all off? Can I not trust them to get back and help me? If not why not?' But by then we both knew the answer to the latter, having explored her childhood family patterns, her older brother's dislike for her and her parent's blindness to this.

For securely attached individuals it is usually easier to build the working alliance. They are more prepared to trust and thus to open up, they are usually already more accustomed to self-reflection. However, it is important to note that within the category of 'secure' there are gradations so that the same flexibility may still be required. Sandra was in her late 40s and in therapy for training purposes; her marriage was close and confiding, as were her relationships with her late-teenage children and several women friends. However, her current security was in some sense 'earned' and there were still residues of her difficult childhood relationships. She had never been able to confide in her mother because whenever she volunteered something problematic, her mother would turn the tables to point out how something similar was even worse for her. She chose the couch and had no problem in free associating self-reflectively. Some weeks into her therapy she became very tearful in the middle of one session. After some hesitation she explained that she was becoming increasingly uncomfortable because she could not believe that from where I sat I could see all of her body and so I would not understand her emotions when she was talking. At this point I faced a critical decision: would interpretation be enough to help, or would something more behavioural be required in order to convey the message that her new therapist did really care enough for her to trust her? I judged that something more behavioural would be needed: so I told her that for sessions henceforward I would sit in the third chair which was at the extreme of the room but allowed full vision on to and from the top of the couch. But that I needed first to talk more with her about why she might be feeling like that. I was fully aware that many of my colleagues would view this decision as 'collusion'. However, I view building the working alliance as so crucial that sometimes the therapist needs to go along with the needs of the analysand (or as others would describe it 'to collude') if this alliance is to be cemented. So long as this is not done mindlessly – and by that I mean without discussing the origins of these needs with the analysand at the time of doing it – I believe it cannot really be described as 'collusion', let alone 'mindless'. I see the offer of the possibility of meeting the request as a crucial step in helping the analysand to explore the origin of the relevant needs, because when there are as yet no visions as to how they may be met the analysand will not be able to relax sufficiently to undertake this exploration. I take this up in later discussion of the frame. For Sandra, this rearrangement paid off: she felt more 'heard' and began to talk from within herself in an even more authentic way. The working alliance was consolidated.

Table 4.1 contains no mention of the AAI's U group (Unresolved as to loss or trauma). This is because in Main and colleagues' scheme this can accompany either dismissive or preoccupied styles, and does not have any special role in the formation of the working alliance. However, it is more relevant to note that the table also contains no mention of the CC or 'cannot classify' classificatory group, where there are features of several styles, thus presenting a contradictory picture. It has been suggested that those people for whom extreme dismissiveness alternates with extreme enmeshment represent a group of adults who, if they were infants, would have been called 'D babies' or Disorganized. Very often they show intensely contradictory signs of attachment style, although no systematic research has ruled out the converse – that *some* adults with such simultaneously coexisting contradictory styles might not have been disorganized as children. Techniques for building the alliance must vary depending on the relative mix of contradictory styles. Diana's childhood was not one of the most abusive or neglectful, but certainly the parents had rendered it very confusing for her and her two younger brothers. She found it difficult to speak at first but brought to all her sessions (which she religiously attended) many dramatic writings, written about a 12-year-old child in the third person, which were thrust upon me. I started to make mild interpretations about how she was trying to tell me things about a part of herself, which hindsight has proved remarkably prescient. However, at the time Diana was not verbally ready for such an approach. Her mode of communication changed as she brought with her first one stuffed toy rabbit and later a whole rucksack full of felt creatures – mice and rabbits – who, via her, were able to express feelings, which in other mouths would have been eminently disownable. When talking for the menagerie Diana was fluency itself; but asked to talk about herself she became paralysed, nowhere worse than during the occasional phone call she would make with my permission during the long summer break. She would remain tongue-tied and silent on the end of the line while I tried to assess whether there was an emergency. Later it became clear that she showed both very preoccupied and very dismissive styles, both in her relationships and in therapy. After a fair number of years in therapy Diana blossomed in a professional role, expert at finding the right vocabulary for deprived children.

I have considered this phase of therapy at length, partly because the nature of the early alliance has emerged as so crucial for outcome according to recent research (Horvath and Symonds, 1991; Piper et al., 1991). And in purely mechanical terms this must be true if failure to build an alliance leads people to leave therapy prematurely. One of the most unavailable figures in the epidemiology of psychoanalytic psychotherapy is the rate of dropout between first and fifth sessions. However, anecdotally we can estimate it to be quite high. In the absence of systematic evidence it is difficult to know to what to attribute this high rate. Low level of education or intellectual functioning is often cited as the culprit, but another way of viewing this could be as a failure to build the basic therapeutic alliance. The person in analysis has not only missed engaging with the therapist, but has come to dismiss the therapy process in general along with *all* therapists. Attachment theory offers a conceptual framework for tailoring the manner of building this alliance to the analysand's existing style of relating in a way that reduces the chance of this sort of drop-out.

Another reason for discussing this phase in such disproportionate detail is that Slade (1999) has already expounded many of the other phases with admirable clarity. But an even more powerful reason is that it typifies the aspects of psychotherapy where attachment theory has most to contribute, namely the building of a trust that permits self-disclosure without discomfort. The implication is that a similar type of 'sensitive responsiveness' is required in caregivers of infants and in psychotherapists if the child or analysand is to develop into a secure individual. Many of the points made here about flexibility in dealing with the frame as a way of responding sensitively apply equally in all phases of therapy. And many of the strategies for relating differentially to people with different types of attachment style apply across all stages of therapy. Thus Crittenden (1998, cited in Jellema, 1999) talks of those with a dismissive style being 'defended against affect' while those with a preoccupied/enmeshed style are 'defended against cognition'. Such labels fit well with what has been said about the narrative style of the two broad groupings of attachment style (avoidant and anxious–ambivalent), and in their use of the word 'defended' contain a pointer to what needs to be resolved during therapy.

It is also interesting to note a very similar bifurcation of strategies recommended in interventions designed to improve the quality of mother–infant interactions. Field and her colleagues have shown that with over-stimulating intrusive mothers, instructing the mother to imitate the infant improves this quality; with withdrawn mothers, instructing them on how attract and maintain their infant's attention has similar beneficial effects on the interaction (Malphurs et al., 1996).

The classical transference

The transference, or the relationship between analysand and therapist, is where classical psychoanalysis locates the crucial work of psychotherapy: talking together about this 'here and now' relationship is seen as the pathway to emotional change (see Chapter 2 by Cortina and Marrone for a critique of a rigid application of the 'here and now' approach to therapy). Formerly, great importance was allotted to the role of insight imparted through interpretation, but more recently there has been a greater appreciation of this relationship as offering a 'corrective emotional experience' rather than the more cognitive, almost educational, overtones of the word 'insight'. However, the notion of a 'corrective' experience struck many as uncomfortably authoritarian and this phrase has also come to be discredited, with the unfortunate consequences that the emphasis on an emotional experience, rather than a simple learning exercise involving the memorizing of interpretations, then became lost. Attachment theory implies that those coming for therapy have frequently been deprived of a secure base while growing up, with consequences for the way they 'mentalize', that is think about how both they and others behave in accord with feelings, plans and needs (Fonagy et al., 1991), with the further implication that the provision of a secure base in therapy is also essential to help reverse this process. Figure 4.1 gives a graphic presentation of the process of working through in the transference as a kind of continual repetitive circular dance amid the overwhelmingly linear portrayal of other developmental processes. This diagrammatic device aims to convey the length of time it inevitably takes to modify pathogenic internal working models by disconfirming expectations derived from earlier insensitive and unresponsive relationships, like going over the same ground several times, round and round, before the process can be complete.

Much of what has actually occurred during classical transference work has been in accord with attachment theory, even if carried out by psychoanalysts not consciously following it. This has been due to sensitive practitioners following their instincts about how to help others understand themselves. But the corollary of this is that, in the absence of systematic guidelines from attachment theory, occasionally other less helpful instincts may also have been followed. As already mentioned, many theorists have speculated that some factor common to all the different psychotherapies may play the crucial role in clinical improvement, and as early as 1986 therapeutic empathy was identified as this factor in a review of 40 studies reporting 86 findings (Orlinsky and Howard, 1986; see also Luborsky et al., 1988). A more recent study of 185 patients in cognitive behavioural therapy (CBT) for depression makes an interesting distinction between the role of empathy in increasing patients' compliance with the homework tasks required by CBT and any contribution over and above this (Burns and Nolen-Hoeksma, 1992), not dissimilar to the distinction between the contributions of empathy to, on the one hand, building the initial working alliance, and on the other to working in the transference. The CBT patients completed the 10-item ES (empathy scale) containing statements such as 'My therapist understands my words but not the way I feel inside'. The data analysis controlled for effects on improvement in depression of not only homework compliance but also initial severity of depression, income, education, sex, and age and revealed an independent contribution for therapist empathy. If such results emerge even in a highly technical form of therapy such as CBT, empathy would appear to have even more relevance for the psychodynamic therapies.

If the heart of working in the transference is the *disconfirmation* of the insecure analysand's previous internal working models, this phase of therapy may have to be more challenging, or even confrontational, than the initial alliance-building phase. The art is to maintain the empathic alliance despite these challenges. It is easier to disconfirm the consistently unresponsive behaviour of the caregivers of members of the various avoidant groups, especially if the therapy is not time-limited, than it is to disconfirm the inconsistently responsive behaviour of the caregivers of the preoccupied/enmeshed who are adept at driving most of us into inconsistency. Thus Fiona, Rejhane, Eric and Derek were all eventually able to tell me things like 'I wasn't going to tell you this but then I figured you wouldn't really think any the less of me for having felt this way and we really ought to look together at why I did'. With Penny, and even more with Diana, I was not always consistent, sometimes clumsy in picking up their feelings about how 'I' was letting them down – for example by allowing their session to be on a Monday, the national day for Bank Holidays, so that they would have to miss it or by failing to say that I agreed with them in an argument they had recently recounted. More serious were interpretations which caught them at the wrong angle (see later sections on 'Style of interpretation: emotional tone' and 'Working through'). But it was usually possible to catch up by the end of the week and rake over the coals, contrasting my intentions as seen by them and as experienced by myself. For example, I would explain to Diana that the reason I had pondered on the similarity of her feelings for a work colleague and her reactions to her brother was not because I believed she was unjust but because I wanted her to reflect on whether they came from somewhere else than purely the work situation, and that I had felt irritated when she shouted at me that I was always against her and she did not want to hear any more; now, however, I no longer felt irritated because she did seem to want me to talk again. Again, such self-disclosure, minimal though it was, might not have been acceptable in orthodox psychoanalytic practice but seemed to facilitate a greater sense of give and take by confirming her intuition. (Preoccupied/enmeshed analysands are very canny about their therapist's true feelings and it is sometimes not therapeutic to pretend one felt differently. Honesty about the therapist's feelings can be a form of validation for the person in therapy, so long as such occasions are not too frequent.) But endorsing a modicum of self-disclosure should not be taken as permission for the transference figure to depart from the role of secure base by revealing too much vulnerability.

Before moving on from thinking about the classical transference, it could be helpful to discuss some research which, though not explicitly attachment-theory based, used a measure of the Quality of Relationships (QOR) which combines elements of attachment security and of reflective function (Piper et al., 1991; Ogrodniczuk et al., 1999). These studies sought to relate both outcome and the quality of the working alliance to not merely the frequency of transference interpretations but their 'concentration', that is the relative proportion of all interventions by the therapist composed of such interpretations. The authors summarize their results as, first, underscoring the potentially negative effects of transference interpretations for patients with low QOR scores (corresponding to 'insecure' in attachment terms) and, second, suggesting that low to moderate (but not high) concentrations of such interpretations could be helpful for patients with high QOR scores (corresponding to secure). However, they are careful to point out that neither the accuracy of the interpretations nor their timing was measured and that these may have been as responsible for the findings as the concentration of transference interpretations.

The use of other aspects of the transference

One of the key aspects of attachment theory is its acknowledgement of the impact of variations in the outer world rather than allotting sole influence to phantasy. A parallel broadening of perspective is afforded by the realization that the theory of internal working models predicts that transference of an earlier childhood model can also take place on to new relationships in the adult's social network as well as on to the psychotherapist. Especially with dismissive analysands, who are even more prone to deny feelings about the therapist in the room with them than about other more distant matters, it can be useful to capitalize on this. For example, Derek was quite struck by some musings which I encouraged him to express concerning the secretary of a sports club that he attended, when the secretary (a man) behaved in a way he had not expected over his late payments of membership fees. As we worked on where such expectations had originally come from he began to be able to talk about his father more realistically and allow himself to feel the disappointment his father had caused him.

Particularly useful here are methods to examine those internal working models that would rarely be expected to arise in the classical transference for reasons such as their age- or gender-inappropriateness. Diana had occasion to change jobs several times during her long therapy and often had conflict with work colleagues who were male and slightly younger than her. This gave us an opportunity to look at the internal working models that arose in those sort of triangular situations where Diana and a young man were both accountable to one authority or parent-figure. These, of course, were not situations germane to the consulting room and I, as an older female, never really could invoke directly the feelings transferred from her younger brother. Many therapists will have found themselves involved in such explorations of external transference figures but the merit of attachment theory is that it encourages us to be on the look out to exploit such opportunities more frequently.

One aspect of the psychoanalytic process that has attracted increasing attention in the past decade is the 'helpful therapy session event'. A recent report of psychodynamic-interpersonal therapy (PI: Hardy et al., 1999) looked at how therapists had responded during those therapy events clearly concerning relationship difficulties identified as most helpful by 10 clients. The transcripts of such sessions reveal work of a kind I am extolling here when I talk of other transference work – exploring parallels between earlier and later relationship patterns to identify internal working models. It emerged that therapists responded to events evincing preoccupied attachment styles with reflection and to those manifesting dismissive styles with attempts to help clients experience feelings and upset. These responses are consonant with the implications of attachment theory.

Style of interpretation: content

As already emphasized, attachment theory implies that therapy should not impose theory through pronounced truths, but foster a joint task to develop self-reflection via a dialogue encouraging the analysand's partnership in the exploration. Even when the working alliance is successfully built there can be interpretations which are counterproductive or even 'iatrogenic', as Marrone has so strikingly described (Marrone, 1998). Two classic modes of interpreting he lists as potentially anti-therapeutic are decontextualization and double binding. The first involves insisting on the superordinate role of internal mechanisms and underestimating the effects of the external world and its social context. With its appreciation of the important role of the outer world, attachment theory is less likely to end up invalidating the analysand's sense of judgement about other people. Double binding occurs when an analysand is made to feel guilty by the therapist but the latter then interprets that the analysand's internal world is dominated by guilt. In addition, many have been undermined by the claim that the therapist is 'neutral', with the insinuation that analysands can never be properly so. Whereas it can often be especially therapeutic when therapists admit they have been in the wrong (Marrone, 1998, pp. 163–4).

These ways of offering interpretations are pretty extreme, but there are more minor ones that can also be damaging. For example, too early an insistence that analysands' unconscious feelings are 'more real' than the conscious ones runs the risk of invalidating their subjective feelings which may merely repeat a pattern that has happened all their life and confirm that they are not supposed to have the feelings they have. Moreover interpretations about breaks in therapy routine will need to be tailored to the attachment style of the analysand – those with a dismissive style can be expected to react differently to those who are more preoccupied/ enmeshed.

One of the most valuable aspects of the attachment theory perspective is that the emphasis on the role of the external world contained in its developmental perspective offers a way of extracting blame from interpretations. It is much easier for resistant analysands to own feelings of anger or anxiety if they understand that these initiated in something that came from outside during their past experience, like an abusive older sibling, than if they are made to feel such emotions indicate their own intrinsic nature, say as savage or cowardly. Penny had a sense of herself as 'pathetic' but was able to accept that her feelings of dependency, and thus she herself, were less unacceptable when constructing the narrative of her history had made them eminently understandable.

Style of interpretation: emotional tone

It follows from the above that the emotional tone of interpretations should be equally purged of blame if there is to be a chance that they will be heard and understood. Sometimes a diplomatic circumlocution comes over as less accusatory than a straightforward interpretation; for example, ' I find myself wondering if that didn't make you feel pretty angry?' rather than 'I think you feel enraged'. But even when there is no sharpness to the tone there may be other danger spots, as Marrone so clearly outlines (1998). For example, overzealous high-frequency interpreting can be experienced as invasive or disempowering, regardless of its content. Enthusiasm for 'insight provision' may be experienced as patronizing or even derogatory, especially if it concerns the analysand's anger. Attachment theory implies a mutuality of the exploratory task, a tone of give and take rather than a one-way supply of enlightenment.

Working through: emotional tone outside of interpretation

So far disconfirmation has been discussed in terms of changing internal working models of relationships since this is a particular focus of attachment theory. But although space precludes a full discussion here, mention must be made of how the attachment perspective concerns another key therapeutic task, often called 'working through'. This is perhaps a more basic form of disconfirmation, that of the relevance of previous feelings or, as Bion has put it, the 'digesting' of affective experience (Bion, 1962). The role of the secure base provided by psychotherapy is not restricted to facilitating exploration but also allows enough safety to hold someone reprocessing emotions that were too devastating to be coped with at the time. Therapies that do not feel 'safe enough' will not succeed in this task. A recent thought-provoking account of a therapeutic technique which is increasingly coming to be used with victims of trauma (accelerated information processing or eye movement desensitization and reprocessing – EMDR) draws attention to the manner in which this can be seen as parallel to this psychoanalytic practice of 'working through' (Mollon, 2001), perhaps by inducing favourable changes at a neurobiological level involving inter-hemispheric communication. In arguing for the importance of this 'inherent process of self-healing', Mollon cites a paper based on 450 case summaries submitted for certification by the American Psychoanalytic Association, which pinpointed as an almost universal phenomenon 'mental work on the painful affects associated with the re-experienced ... scenes' (Burland, 1997, pp. 469–70).

Issues of the frame

In the earlier discussion of building the working alliance, we touched on the way that flexibility in working with the frame allows attention to be paid to the specific needs of people with different attachment styles, particularly in terms of choosing couch or chair. Thus Diana, whose style of relating is best characterized as disorganized, began to talk in the first person only after she had begged me to sit on the couch with her and I had conceded on condition she would explain to me why that was so important. Once I moved over and let her put her head on my lap she was able to tell me that she needed to be 'joined on' in order to be able to talk. A better reference to attachment theory, by one who was at that time completely innocent of its nature, is difficult to conceive. This exemplifies a principle that I have found useful: namely that to first refuse a request for some amendment to usual procedures and then to try to explore why such a request has been made is often not productive since the refusal tends to set up resistances which impede self-reflection; whereas to concede the request is usually experienced by the analysand as sensitively responsive on the part of the therapist and often stimulates a greater than usual willingness to explore the reasons why the request should have been made. In other words, one should be very careful in what one dismisses as 'collusion' and therefore 'unacceptable practice'. Although it is not a clear derivative of attachment theory to reinterpret the meaning of collusion, it is certainly worth reflecting on where the boundaries between that notion and those of sensitive responsiveness begin and end. Derek once observed that he did not like having to look at one of my pictures that hung opposite the couch but was unable to get anywhere with why he disliked it. After an unusual pause I asked if he would like me to remove it during his sessions and somewhat nonplussed he agreed that I should and I immediately took it down. After another pause he said that it was remarkable how he had suddenly had a memory of his grandfather's hallway in which hung a large collection of prints. We ended up chasing a very useful association about something that had happened in grandfather's house.

However, I believe reassessment is more thoroughly needed concerning issues of the frame *surrounding* the session rather than those *within* it. The offer of telephone calls in inter-session emergencies creates a sense of greater proximity, and thus of a more secure base, than the rigid structure of no contact between sessions, especially if these are as much as one week apart. It is likely that the traditional unwillingness to allow such calls has arisen from a justified sense of self-protection by the psychotherapy profession, but what emerges consistently from other services (such as some befriending or women's counselling services) is that the offer of widespread telephone availability is not abused: people openly acknowledge how reassuring they found it to hear that they could telephone if needed, but usually add 'Of course I would only have done so in a real emergency'.

Flexibility in rearranging sessions to accord with the demands of the analysand's outer world can also heighten the therapy's secure base role. It was important to catch Fiona before she failed to request that she should be allowed to rearrange one of her sessions in order to attend a job interview and possibly jeopardized her chances of selection. Once I had shown how reasonable I thought it that some adjustment should be made for something of such importance in her life, it was easier to work on her generalized obedience to structural rules which might have prevented her doing so. With more securely attached analysands I might not make such efforts to be flexible, waiting until they themselves asked for rearrangements. A similar flexibility with regard to financial arrangements can also prove therapeutic: why curtail a promising therapy because someone has lost their job and can no longer afford their sessions?

Nowhere are the implications of attachment theory for handling the frame clearer than when considering termination. The orthodox psychoanalytic approach has often entailed seeing an analysand with sessions five days a week at one point, followed by no sessions at all as from the next week – an extremity of change that runs counter to our understanding of separation–individuation. Again, the importance allotted to proximity by attachment theory means that there should ideally be a *gradual* reduction in the frequency of sessions, perhaps passing through a phase of fortnightly or monthly meetings before they come to an end altogether.

Outer world and social context

A further implication of attachment theory's emphasis on the role of the external world is that the therapist can work in such a way that other people in the analysand's social network may somehow be utilized as adjuncts to the therapeutic process. Research on social support from partners and close friends has consistently suggested its protective (Brown and Harris, 1978; Brugha, 1995) and therapeutic (Harris et al., 1999) roles, and Figure 4.1 portrays two pathways to improved mental state from changes in internal working models, the second via changes in the supportiveness of others. After all, attachment theory reminds us that even secure adults continue to require a supportive base, and at termination of therapy the analysand will need someone to turn to who is capable of behaving supportively. It is part of the therapist's responsibility to help analysands to build such supports into their social contexts before the end of therapy.

Issues of countertransference

Finally, there have to be implications for issues of the countertransference. As Dozier and colleagues (1994) say, 'Just as a parent's secure attachment organization provides the internal resources to respond to the infant sensitively and appropriately, so it seems a clinician's secure

attachment organization may provide him or her with the resources necessary for responding sensitively and appropriately to clients'. The key
word here is, of course, 'appropriately'. These authors reported on 18
case managers whom they had assessed with Kobak's Q-set on AAI transcripts (and who were working with 27 clients): compared with secure
managers, insecure ones attended more to dependency needs and intervened in greater depth with preoccupied clients than they did with
dismissive ones. In parallel, case managers who were more preoccupied
intervened with their clients in greater depth than did case managers who
were more dismissing. The authors speculate that case managers who are
more secure seem able to attend and respond to clients' underlying
needs, whereas case managers who are insecure respond to the most
obvious presentation of needs and so miss the opportunity to provide
what Cashdon has called 'non-complementary feedback' (Cashdon,
1988). They conclude by pointing out that although they speculate about
the appropriateness of various types of interventions, outcome data are
not yet available to provide empirical support for their speculations.

In one of the few other studies of attachment theory and the countertransference, with a sample of clinical psychologists, Leiper and Casares
(2000) used Hazan and Shaver's (1987) and West and Sheldon-Keller's
(1994) measures of therapist attachment patterns to look at therapists'
work satisfaction, location of source of any difficulties experienced in the
therapeutic work and what kind of patients were found rewarding to
work with (mildly, moderately or severely disturbed). They reported that
the insecure group (a slightly lower proportion than in the general population) were more likely to locate any difficulty in themselves as therapist,
and the avoidant were more likely than the ambivalent to locate the difficulty in external circumstances, but as far as locating difficulties in the
patient was concerned there was no relation to the psychologists' attachment organization. There was no measure of patient attachment style so
it was not possible to explore notions of the fit between attachment styles
of patient and psychologist. But Leiper and Casares have set the way for
future researchers to think about a group of 'compulsive caregivers' that
are often overlooked in other classifications.

Although neither of these studies involved psychoanalysts, their presentations contain yet another implication of attachment theory by now quite
familiar to readers of this chapter: Dozier and colleagues' case managers
ranged from workers helping with housing benefit claims or food stamps to
clinicians helping people through intra-psychic issues, which would correspond more closely to the sample of Leiper and Casares, but the intervention
process hoped for by all would involve the development of a trust in a holding relationship (Winnicott, 1971) which would be the motive for change.
Indeed, Dozier and colleagues go so far as to emphasize their findings by

citing comments about 'therapeutic teachers' by Erickson, Sroufe and Egeland (1985), who respond to the underlying neediness of children who are dismissive as well as those who are preoccupied. The theme of a basic commonality of the key therapeutic ingredient across a range of caring professions suggests the area of the countertransference and empathy are the aspects of psychotherapy which need most development in the coming years. This is an area where research is only just beginning, where the self-reflectiveness of the psychotherapists is most implicated, where the implications of attachment theory are most personal for therapists, and where we as practitioners will most likely have to change. We must await their extension to a larger sample with great interest.

Diamond and colleagues' work reported in this volume (Chapter 7) represents an exciting beginning, following five patients over one year of transference–focused psychotherapy (TFP) with baseline and follow-up AAIs and pioneering a new measure of the therapist–patient relationship, the PT-AAI, where the therapist's views about the patient are seen as just as important as the patient's.

Concluding remarks: implications for the therapist's role in imparting insight

Before concluding, it is important to note that, apart from the work on the more general topic of empathy mentioned above, so far there is little research directly relating psychotherapy *outcome* to more specific attachment issues. What there is has elements of the contradictory, in that Fonagy and colleagues (1996) suggest that dismissive patients fare better than preoccupied ones, while Dozier and colleagues (2001) suggest clients with dismissive states of mind may be more resistant than others to treatment, and Horowitz and team (1996) concurred that dismissing adults do not do well in brief psychotherapy. This may partly result from the different samples studied by each group: Horowitz and colleagues were looking at *brief* therapy, Fonagy and colleagues reported on 82 patients undergoing the special therapy at the Cassel Hospital, whereas Dozier and colleagues selected clients of case management services with 'serious psychopathological disorders'. But the contradictory reports may also be due to the fact that the therapeutic services did not explicitly tailor their treatment to the attachment needs of those clients/patients in the way recommended in this chapter and therefore one group may have been less advantaged with one treatment than with the other.

It is customary to end such discussions as this with pious calls for more research, but it will be important to design any such research dealing with outcome so that it takes into account the implications of attachment theory outlined here. This will involve a closer monitoring of psychotherapy process than has been usual to chart the way in which interchanges between analysand and therapist gradually increase the capacity of the former to feel and reflect on the needs of themselves and others. The methods reported by Mergenthaler (1996) and by Hardy and colleagues (1999) have begun to point a way towards this, but attention will need to be paid not only to verbal interchanges but to tones of voice and of laughter, smiles and other gestures and the degrees to which these can be seen by both therapist and analysand. Only then will it be possible to confirm the speculations of this chapter that imparting insight in a way that helps involves an integrated cognitive-emotional interaction equivalent to the provision of attachment theory's secure base for exploration, and that old-style interpretation is not enough.

Acknowledgements

First and foremost I should like to express my gratitude to everyone who has been in therapy with me and from whom I have learnt so much. In addition, many of the ideas in this chapter derive from sharing clinical experiences with colleagues, to whom I am most grateful, in particular those in the North London supervision group of the International Attachment Network 1999–2001. I must also thank the editors of this volume for their helpful suggestions. However, any blind spots are entirely my own.

References

Ainsworth MD and Wittig BA (1969) Attachment and the exploratory behaviour of one-year olds in a strange situation. In: BM Foss (ed.) Determinants of Infant Behaviour, vol. 4. London: Methuen.

Bartholomew K and Horowitz LM (1991) Attachment styles among young adults: A test of a four-category model. Journal of Personality and Social Psychology 61: 226–44.

Bifulco AT, Moran P, Ball C and Bernazzani O (2002a) Adult Attachment Style I: Its relationship to clinical depression. Social Psychiatry and Psychiatric Epidemiology 37: 50–9.

Bifulco AT, Moran P, Ball C and Lillie A (2002b) Adult Attachment Style II: Its relationship to psychosocial depressive-vulnerability. Social Psychiatry and Psychiatric Epidemiology 37: 60–7.

Bion WR (1962) Learning from Experience. London: Heinemann.

Bleichmar HB (1996) Some subtypes of depression and their implications for psychoanalytic treatment. International Journal of Psycho-analysis 77: 935–61.

Bowlby J (1969) Attachment and Loss, vol. 1: Attachment. New York: Basic Books.

Bowlby J (1973) Attachment and Loss, vol. 2: Separation: Anxiety and Anger. New York: Basic Books.

Bowlby J (1977) The making and breaking of affectional bonds. I Aetiology and psychopathology in the light of attachment theory. II Some principles of psychotherapy. British Journal of Psychiatry 130: 201–10 and 421–31.

Bowlby J (1980) Attachment and Loss, vol. 3: Loss: Sadness and Depression. New York: Basic Books.

Bowlby J (1988a) A Secure Base: Clinical Applications of Attachment Theory. London: Routledge.

Bowlby J (1988b) Developmental psychiatry comes of age. American Journal of Psychiatry 145: 1–10.

Brown GW and Harris TO (1978) Social Origins of Depression: A Study of Psychiatric Disorder in Women. London: Tavistock Publications; New York: Free Press.

Brugha T (ed.) (1995) Social Support and Psychiatric Disorder: Research Findings and Guidelines for Clinical Practice, Cambridge: Cambridge University Press.

Burland JA (1997) The role of working through in bringing about psychic change. International Journal of Psycho-analysis 78: 469–84.

Burns D and Nolen-Hoeksma S (1992) Therapeutic empathy and recovery from depression in cognitive-behavioral therapy: a structural equation model. Journal of Consulting and Clinical Psychology 60: 441–9.

Byng-Hall J (1980) The symptom bearer as marital distance regulator: clinical implications. Family Process 19: 355–65.

Cashdon S (1988) Stage Two: Projective Identification. Object Relations Therapy. New York: Norton, pp. 96–118.

Clark DA, Beck AT with Alfred B (1999) Scientific Foundations of Cognitive Theory and Therapy of Depression. New York: John Wiley.

Crittenden P (1998) Manual of an expanded classificatory model for the Adult Attachment Interview, Unpublished Manuscript.

Dozier M, Cue KL and Barnett L (1994) Clinicians as caregivers: Role of attachment organization in treatment. Journal of Consulting and Clinical Psychology 62: 793–800.

Dozier M, Lomax L and Tyrrell C (1996) Psychotherapy's challenges for adults using deactivating attachment strategies. Unpublished manuscript, University of Delaware.

Dozier M, Lomax L, Tyrrell CL and Lee SW (2001) The challenge of treatment for clients with dismissing states of mind. Attachment and Human Development 3: 62–76.

Erickson M, Sroufe LA and Egeland B (1985) The relationship between quality of attachment and behavior problems in pre-school in a high risk sample. In: I Bretherton, and E Waters (eds) Growing points in attachment theory and research. Monographs of the Society for Research in Child Development 50 (1–2 Serial No: 209): 147–86.

Fonagy P, Moran GS, Steele M, Steele H and Higgitt AC (1991) The capacity for understanding mental states: the reflective self in parent and child and its significance for security of attachment. Infant Mental Health Journal 13: 200–16.

Fonagy P, Leigh T, Steele M, Steele H, Kennedy R, Mattoon G, Target M and Gerber A (1996) The relationship of attachment status, psychiatric classification and response to psychotherapy. Journal of Consulting and Clinical Psychology 64: 22–31.

George C, Kaplan N and Main M (1985) Adult Attachment Interview, 2nd edn. Unpublished manuscript. University of California at Berkeley.

Hardy G, Aldridge J, Davidson C, Rowe C, Reilly S and Shapiro D (1999) Therapist responsiveness to client attachment styles and issues observed in client-identified significant events in psychodynamic-interpersonal therapy. Psychotherapy Research 9: 36–53.

Harris TO, Brown GW and Robinson R (1999) Befriending as an intervention for chronic depression among women in an inner city. I: Randomized controlled trial. British Journal of Psychiatry 174: 219–25.

Hazan C and Shaver PR (1987) Romantic love conceptualized as an attachment process. Journal of Personality and Social Psychology 67: 430–45.

Holmes J (2000) Attachment theory and psychoanalysis: A rapprochement. British Journal of Psychotherapy 17: 157–72.

Horowitz LM, Rosenberg SE and Bartholomew K (1996) Interpersonal problems, attachment styles and outcome in brief psychotherapy. Journal of Consulting and Clinical Psychology 61: 549–60.

Horvath AO and Symonds BD (1991) Relation between working alliance and outcome in psychotherapy: a meta-analysis. Journal of Counseling Psychology 38: 139–49.

Jellema A (1999) Cognitive analytic therapy: developing its theory and practice via attachment theory. Clinical Psychology and Psychotherapy 6: 16–28.

Leiper R and Casares P (2000) An investigation of the attachment organization of clinical psychologists and its relationship to clinical practice. British Journal of Medical Psychology 73: 449–64.

Lorenz K (1937) Der Kumpan in der Umwelt des Vogels. Journal für Ornithologie 83: 137–213, 289–413.

Luborsky L, Crits-Christoph P, Mintz J and Auerbach A (1988) Who Will Benefit from Psychotherapy? Predicting Therapeutic Outcomes. New York: Basic Books.

Luborsky L, Popp C, Luborsky E and Mark D (1994) The core conflictual relationship theme. Psychotherapy Research 4: 172–83.

Mallinckrodt B (2000) Attachment, social competencies and therapy process. Psychotherapy Research 10: 239–66.

Malphurs J, Larrain C, Field T, Pickens J, Pelaez-Nogueras M, Yando R and Bendell D (1996) Altering withdrawn and intrusive interaction behaviors of depressed mothers. Infant Mental Health Journal 17: 152–60.

Marrone M (1998) Attachment and Interaction. London: Jessica Kingsley.

Mergenthaler E (1996) Emotion-Abstraction patterns in verbatim protocols. A new way of describing psychotherapeutic processes. Journal of Consulting and Clinical Psychology 64: 1306–15.

Mollon P (2001), Psychoanalytic perspectives on Accelerated Information Processing (EMDR). British Journal of Psychotherapy 17, 448–64.

Ogrodniczuk JS, Piper WE, Joyce AS and McCallum M (1999) Transference interpretations in short-term dynamic psychotherapy. Journal of Nervous and Mental Disease 187: 572–9.

Orlinsky DE and Howard KI (1986) Process and outcome in psychotherapy. In: SL Garfield and AE Bergin (eds) Handbook of Psychotherapy and Behavior Change, 3rd edn. New York: Wiley, pp. 344–7.

Piper WE, Azim HFA, Joyce AS and McCallum M (1991) Transference interpretations, therapeutic alliance and outcome in short-term individual psychotherapy. Archives of General Psychiatry 48: 946–53.

Ryle A (1995) Cognitive Analytic Therapy: Developments in Theory and Practice. Chichester: John Wiley & Sons.

Slade A (1999) Attachment theory and research: Implications for the theory and practice of individual psychotherapy with adults. In: J Cassidy and PR Shaver, Handbook of Attachment: Theory, Research and Clinical Applications. New York, London: Guilford.

Sroufe A and Waters E (1977) Attachment as an organizational construct. Child Development 48: 1184–9.

Tulving E (1972) Episodic and semantic memory. In: E Tulving and W Donaldson (eds) Organization of Memory. New York: Academic Press.

West M and Sheldon-Keller A (1994) Patterns of Relating: An Adult Attachment Perspective. New York: Guilford.

Winnicott DW (1971) Playing and Reality. New York: Basic Books.

CHAPTER 5

The significance of the exploration of the patient's attachment history for psychoanalytic psychotherapy

SANDRA WEINER

> Unless a therapist can enable his patient to feel some measure of security, therapy cannot even begin. (Bowlby, 1988, p. 140)

Introduction

At the time of writing, even in London, the work of John Bowlby and attachment theory has not been considered a necessary part of psychoanalytic-based psychotherapy trainings. There is a growing body of literature, e.g. Fonagy (1999), Slade (1999), Holmes (1993b, 1995) and Karen (1994), concerning itself with the varied reasons for this exclusion. The effect, until quite recently, has been to keep attachment theory within the realm of developmental psychology and research and outside the day-to-day work with patients. Bowlby himself was puzzled that a theory that was developed from his clinical work with juvenile delinquents (1944) had not been made more use of by clinicians. He noted that 'it has... been disappointing that clinicians have been slow to test the theory's uses' (1988, pp. ix–x).

This chapter attempts to show how an awareness of the attachment history of patients has significance for clinical work. Until recently, there had not been many papers that deal specifically with this topic. Some examples of this small but growing interest are the work of group analysts like Glenn (1987), who believes that the group matrix provides a 'secure base' for conducting group psychotherapy, and Marrone (1994), who teases out the relationship between attachment theory and group analysis. Holmes (1998) and Slade (1999) have considered some implications of attachment theory for individual psychotherapy using case presentations and clinical vignettes as illustrations. Arrieta Slade's chapter in

The Handbook of Attachment (Cassidy and Shaver, 1999) provides a good summary of this literature. She goes on to say that she does not believe in 'attachment therapy' (Biringen, 1994) but suggests that:

In keeping with many colleagues (Fonagy et al., 1995; Fonagy and Target, 1996; Holmes, 1993b, 1995, 1996a; Pine, 1990; Silverman, 1991; Target and Fonagy, 1996), that an understanding of the nature and dynamics of attachment *informs* rather than *defines* intervention and clinical thinking. Attachment theory offers a broad and far-reaching view of human functioning that has the potential to change the way clinicians think about and respond to their patients, and the way they understand the dynamics of the therapeutic relationship. (p. 577)

Theoretical orientation

The history of the development of Bowlby's ideas and the milestones of the Strange Situation (Ainsworth et al., 1978), the Adult Attachment Interview (George, Kaplan and Main, 1985, 1996) and the body of work on Reflective Functioning (Fonagy et al., 1991, 1995, 1997; Fonagy and Target, 1996; Target and Fonagy, 1996) have been well covered in Karen's (1994) book *Becoming Attached*.

It is largely accepted that attachment theory can be thought about as part of British object relations (Sroufe, 1986; Eagle, 1995; Holmes, 1993b) In *Thrills and Regressions* Michael Balint (1959) described two defences employed by children to manage their intense anxieties. In one strategy, which he called 'the philobatic attitude', the child rejects investment in attachments to others; this can be thought of as a dismissing attachment pattern. The other defence, which he called 'the ocnophilic attitude', occurs when the child is very clinging and dependent on the maternal object and can therefore be thought of as approximating to an enmeshed, preoccupied attachment pattern.

Karen Horney in *The Neurotic Personality of our Time* (1937) presented a theory of neurosis based on the 'basic anxiety' of childhood when parents fail to provide genuine warmth and affection. In such situations a child must search for ways to keep going and cope with a menacing world and therefore develops ad hoc strategies that become part of his/her personality. She believed that three main lines of strategy crystallize out of what is at felt at first to be chaos. The child can move towards people, against them, or away from them. In the first, the child accepts helplessness and in spite of his/her fears tries to win the affections of others and lean on them. In the second, he/she takes for granted their hostility and determines to fight. In the third, he/she wishes neither to belong nor to fight but to keep apart. I believe that the first two categories can be collapsed to form an enmeshed, preoccupied attachment pattern and the third is similar to an avoidant-dismissing pattern. The way an attachment figure meets and in the category of secure attachment modifies these strategies will set up the child's predominant response to his/her environment.

The tendency of those with preoccupied attachment patterns to lack a secure method to regulate and organize affect (Cassidy, 1994; Cassidy and Berlin, 1994; Main and Solomon, 1986) might lead to such individuals being thought of as hysterical in personality. Equally, those patients with an avoidant/dismissive attachment disposition can also be thought about as being obsessive personalities, because of their tight and highly organized structures for regulating affect (Koback and Sceery, 1998; Main, 1990).

Opposition to attachment theory has often been evident in the discussions of the role of memory in clinical work. Bowlby believed that it is 'just as necessary for analysts to study the way a child is really treated by his parents as it is to study the internal representations he has of them' (Bowlby, 1988, p. 44). This runs counter to the prevailing theoretical tradition which maintains that a patient's memories are not to be trusted and which holds that the role of phantasy is dominant. This approach, which does not accept, or at the very least views with scepticism, the patient's account of his/her history leads to interpretations of the patient's own hostile impulses and furthers the patient's sense of not being understood. Marrone (1998) describes this kind of 'persecutory therapist' in his chapter 'On iatrogenia'. In contrast, a feature of clinical work utilizing an attachment perspective is that the therapist believes in the patient's account and has the capacity to offer sensitive responsiveness and support.

Clinical illustrations

It will be clear that my clinical work has been informed by certain tendencies in current independent psychoanalytic thinking, as described by Eric Rayner (1991), which largely emphasize 'the exploration of earliest child development and the fateful effects of environmental facilitation and trauma' (p. 2). I have been fortunate to be in supervision with a psychiatrist and psychoanalyst who has written about attachment theory and who had been himself in supervision with Bowlby and I was therefore encouraged to consider attachment patterns in my patients. The clinical examples I shall use are from patients brought to this supervision.

The patients I shall discuss came from highly dysfunctional families, which inevitably led me to see their clinical cases as inextricably linked with their attachment histories. They were unable to trust significant others to provide lasting, reliable and sensitive companionship, the result being that they have shown high vulnerability to adversities in their current lives. As I shall show later in the chapter, they had childhoods in which 'parental care was at best erratic ... in which criticism and blame were frequent and bitter, and in which parents ... behaved violently towards each other' and they grew up 'to expect little or nothing in the way of love and support from any quarter' (Bowlby, 1988, p. 17).

Alan

Alan is a 30-year-old history teacher who sought therapy because he found himself becoming overwhelmed by intense feelings of rage while working in the classroom. He believed he was going mad and was so distressed that he was considering a change of profession. He is the eldest of three boys and was expected to look after his brothers and, in his words, 'keep them in line'. Although he was never physically abused himself, he witnessed scenes of great violence between his parents, describing his father as extremely violent towards his mother and recounting incidents of having to care for his brothers while his parents were fighting late at night. Such fights always ended with his father brutally beating his mother. He was aware that his involvement in the violent conflict between his parents had an ongoing influence in his life. In his childhood years his father carried on a ten-year adulterous relationship with his mother's best friend, culminating in his leaving home to live with her when the patient was in his teens. This relationship was never discussed although the woman had been like a second mother to him. He recalled no anger towards these adults at that time.

Bella

Bella is a 23-year-old single woman, living alone. She has one younger sister. Her parents had separated when she was still at university, which had greatly affected her. She had embarked on a professional training after graduating but had found it so stressful that she had walked out of the office and retreated to her childhood home in the north of England. She was prescribed antidepressants by her family GP and was subsequently able to return to work and seek therapy. She started seeing me three times a week in the hope that her depression would lift, thereby enabling her to enjoy life in London and stop being a 'miserable cow'.

Bella's mother could not afford to take time off from work when Bella was born. Her father had given up work to concentrate on being a sculptor and, as he worked from home, he looked after the baby. Bella maintained that 'it didn't matter – after all I had one parent looking after me'. She did remember that her mother had recently told her that she hated leaving work at mid-day to return home to breast-feed Bella and rushing back to work again so as not to be late. When her sister was born the family finances were better and her mother now stayed at home as the primary caregiver. Her mother had been diagnosed with breast cancer when Bella was 10 years old and she recalled feeling the loss of her mother being emotionally connected to her. She said that she felt that her mother had turned away from her to concentrate her energies on her own illness and that her mother wrote down her feelings and did not talk. Her father was scornful of her academic achievements and had always preferred a night out at the local pub to staying at home with his family.

Clinical considerations

Alan can be thought about as having an enmeshed attachment pattern. In supervision it was noted that he showed ambivalence towards therapy, which was discussed as being indicative of a possible ambivalent attachment pattern (Ainsworth et al., 1978.) However, although the idea of classification has been essential to developmental research, patients may rarely exhibit features of any one type. In referring to such an organization of character defences and attachment strategies, Bowlby (1980) talked about a 'disposition' rather than a fixed pattern. It is also important to understand that within each patient with an insecure attachment history there exist elements at an unconscious level of other insecure strategies, which may have resonances within the transference and countertransference as therapy progresses.

Bella could be thought about as having more dismissing strategies. Both patients' fear of loss exacerbated the pain of the various actual losses in their lives. Some of these adversities were partly self-induced; e.g. Alan's relationship with his previous girlfriend broke up and he consequently lost the home that she shared with him. Other adversities were not of their own making; e.g. Bella's car was broken into. Their subjective sense of vulnerability created anxieties, which in turn called for defensive manoeuvres, mainly of identifications with unreliable primary caregivers.

I became the only person in Alan and Bella's lives who proved reliable and trustworthy which, of course, made breaks even more distressing. After the first summer break, Alan's partner broke off the relationship and they gave up their flat. He had nowhere to live and camped out with various people until a friend offered him a room in his flat in a middle-class area of north-west London. When Bella's car was broken into as she was returning home for Christmas, many of her clothes and possessions were taken. She missed sessions rather than speaking about the missing objects, further exacerbating her sense of loss. When she did come to sessions she complained of various psychosomatic symptoms which kept her feeling 'different' from her friends.

Alan won promotion to a position of middle management in his school. His new responsibilities proved daunting and highly stressful. He would talk about the other teachers who were not doing their jobs properly and children who behaved badly. 'Everyone is coming to me and wanting things from me. They pester me with trivialities and I have to sort them out.' He would spend many sessions sounding off about school and I came to the understanding that what he was complaining about was the unfair demandingness of the pupils and teachers. This demandingness began to acquire a persecutory quality. He felt ineffectual and overwhelmed by their demands. This in turn magnified his sense of emptiness, deprivation and feelings of low self-esteem. One session around this time developed the theme. It was a dark early evening.

Alan: As I stood on the doorstep waiting for you to open the door I saw a dark shape, it was a large leaf blown by the wind I suppose, pass across your doorstep. I thought – that dark shape is like me – a dark piece of shit on your doorstep. That's my life right now – everything's shitty – I had to go out at lunchtime today to get some money from the bank and I was hungry. Because I'd run out of cash I hadn't eaten since yesterday and I found myself eating a pie in a horrible café round the corner from school. It was dirty and grimy and I thought that I belonged there – my clothes are shabby – I feel grubby.

He felt empty and deprived, and the horrible café was the second best he had come to expect. His clothes were shabby – he did not have enough. These feelings, it seemed to me, reactivated memories of his early history of role reversal, where he had to care for his damaged mother, and role delegation, where he had to look after his siblings for his mother. Great demands were constantly being made on him, not only in the outside world, but also by me in terms of money and time and he felt as though he got nothing back. For Alan 'everything good turns to shit'.

His lack of money became increasing apparent. He would feel empty and deprived until payday and then spend large sums in a few days only to feel impoverished again. Although it is not unusual for excessive spending to be linked with the manic phase of a bipolar disorder I began to think about what was happening in a slightly different way. I began to understand the cycle of poverty and spending as being similar to an eating disorder of starving and bingeing. For instance, McElroy et al. (1995) see comparisons between compulsive buying and binge-eating disorder. They describe these comparisons as 'the excessive amount consumed (bought) in a discrete period of time, the feeling of lack of control, the sense of urgency, the aloneness and secrecy of the activity and the subsequent feelings of shame, guilt and depression' (p. 20).

In my patient the impulse to spend was irresistible, the 'high' was craved but the crash was inevitable. I came to understand that my patient was symbolically enacting his unconscious relationship to need and desire. It was here that an understanding based on attachment history was very helpful. Alan fell into the resistant/preoccupied category, which is characterized by the relative absence of structures for regulating affect. It was at the times when Alan felt overwhelmed that he lost the ability to hold on to an organizing structure.

Of course, three times a week psychotherapy is an organizing structure in itself but Alan seemed to need more help. He admitted, with a sense of shame, that his credit card was taken away when he was at university because he overspent and exceeded its credit limit. He recalled that in his family he had a reputation as being 'bad with money'.

In the transference, he experienced my interpretations, comments and remarks as empathic and comforting. However, often he would not give me the opportunity to speak because he would be spewing forth his contempt for work colleagues, his partner and me. In such circumstances I felt as if I could no longer be his therapist. It seemed as if he was in control, reducing me to someone who had nothing to offer and who could, therefore, be discarded as useless. He would then feel empty inside and craved my help.

During the first year of Bella's therapy she was meticulous in paying me. 'I place paying you after paying the rent,' she often told me. However, she too had difficulties with money. She had squandered a small legacy from her grandmother on an electric keyboard, which she would not play. One month in the second year of therapy her cheque bounced. Her feelings of shame overwhelmed her and she missed a session. When she returned she told me that she wanted to end therapy. In subsequent sessions her psychosomatic symptoms became more prominent. She reported panic attacks, breathlessness, even an incident of vomiting on the train home after a session. She was also able to tell me about her obsessive rituals, which she knew she performed in order to ward off anxiety. In time some progress was made as she slowly felt that sense was being made of the senseless. Naming her fears and affects and containing them gradually led to understanding cause and effect. Her somatizing defences were gradually modified, but this actually left her feeling nearer to a psychological breakdown. She could no longer rely on somatization and rituals. It seemed that now she needed to defend herself against the intensity of the more primitive anxiety that she was becoming mentally fragmented and feeling that she was going mad.

If, when working with patients like Alan with an enmeshed attachment pattern it is important to provide a regularizing structure for affects, what clinical significance can be found for patients like Bella who have a more dismissing/avoidant pattern? It is my experience that such patients do all they can to protect themselves from confronting painful emotions and if they are put in touch with these feelings they become rejecting of the therapist and possibly even the therapy itself. Such was the case with Bella. It was a feature of the work with this patient that once she found that I was able to hold her in my mind and that she could give up her symptoms and begin to 'feel better', her fear of breaking down became *more* acute. Winnicott's (1974) paper 'Fear of breakdown' was extremely helpful at the time. In it he says that the word 'breakdown' is used clinically to describe 'the unthinkable state of affairs that underlies the defence organization' (p. 104). His hypothesis is that environmental failure at a time of absolute dependence gives rise to primitive agonies and nameless dreads which cannot be thought about and which have to be defended from by illness. He says, 'the clinical fear of breakdown is the fear of a breakdown that has already been experienced. It is the fear of the original agony which caused the defence organization which the patient displays as an illness syndrome' (Winnicott, 1974, p. 104).

Transference and countertransference considerations

It will be recalled that Bella had been left by her mother, who had returned to work every mid-day after feeding her baby. The risk of working with a patient like Bella is that the experience of being put in touch with such primitive agonies is too great and the patient terminates therapy. As Bella's physical symptoms lessened she began bringing material showing her terror of the changes that she felt were taking place inside her. She wanted physically to move – to make the change 'out there' instead of 'in here'. She spoke about changing jobs, moving to Amsterdam, thereby leaving her boyfriend as well as her therapy, and going to horticultural college outside London.

I was aware of her negative transference reactions. At times she felt that I was coming too close, that I was poisoning and bullying her. At the same time, she experienced me as becoming paralysed by these feelings. She communicated non-verbally her profound fear of abandonment by means of projective identification. I often felt like the helpless baby she had been when left by her mother.

Alan's former reliance on his girlfriend to comfort and sustain him gradually became transferred on to me, with the consequence that he became both super-critical of her and then, in response to those angry feelings, guilty and pathetically willing to please her. We appeared to be re-enacting in the transference his relationship with his parents as it was at those times in the past, when he believed he needed to placate them, that he also began to entertain thoughts about their trustworthiness. His ambivalence also showed in relation to me and he began to entertain thoughts about my trustworthiness. This inconsistent way of behaving with fluctuations in degrees of dependency became a feature of his therapy. Given the patient's history of childhood trauma, I was not surprised to see that in the transference I would switch suddenly from being the parent who could be turned to for comfort, to the abusive parent who treated him with contempt.

In working with both Alan and Bella, I realized that they needed something specific from me before therapy could begin in earnest. I understood that I needed to provide what Bowlby (1988) saw as the first therapeutic task, i.e.

> The conditions in which the patient can explore his representational models of himself and his attachment figures with a view to re-appraising and restructuring them in the light of the new understanding he acquires and the new experiences he has in the therapeutic relationship. (p. 138)

Most of our work together went in providing a 'secure base' from which they could tentatively explore the unhappy and painful aspects of their lives which were impossible to think about alone, without a trusted companion. As Nina Coltart (1992) said, 'patients have a great need to have their intimate personal history heard, known and used' (p. 97).

Alan spoke of his father routinely hitting his mother across the face, once even causing a deep cut near the lip, which Alan watched heal with fascination over several weeks. Together with his siblings Alan would hear the screamed verbal abuse and they would cower terrified together in Alan's bedroom waiting for the sound of the blows. His father would occasionally come into the room with blood on his hands and begin to read them a story. I kept thinking what a child would make of such scenes and eventually I began to experience it for myself.

At first I would begin to hold my breath as he spoke of the 'waiting' phase. In my mind I recalled the stories of the Blitz where when the 'buzzing' stopped one knew a bomb was overhead and about to land.

The following excerpt is an example of the violence he witnessed:

I remember once when I was about 8 looking down from the landing to the hall and seeing my mum on the floor with my dad's hands round her neck – she turned her head and saw me and told me to get some help. I ran into my room and opened the window and leant out screaming for help. A neighbour rushed in and my Dad left my mum alone. We never spoke about what had happened except that a few days later my mum wanted to know who else in the road had seen me – she made out that it was my fault some- one came in – that I'd let her down [he cries] – she told me get help!

I understood that I had been caught up in his terror and confusion as well as his unexpressed anger towards a mother who was so dismissive of his attempts to help. Later he told of his father's anger if he spoke out of turn. In the same session I talked to him in the transference of his concern about what can be spoken of with me and his fear of my anger. He stopped speaking and an angry silence developed. In the silence I ex- perienced a 'ringing' in my ears which became almost unbearable. An image came of many black birds with sharp beady eyes and pointed beaks – incredibly sinister and reminiscent of Hitchcock's *The Birds*. He left the session five minutes before the end, leaving me somewhat traumatized by the violence of his projections. I thought about how suddenly I had become the victim and he the aggressor.

Anna Freud in *The Ego and the Mechanisms of Defence* (1937) explored the basis of this defence, which she saw as a 'particular combin- ation of introjection and projection' (p. 120). Alan introjected the harsh and pitiless characteristics of his father in order to assimilate the anxiety experiences he continually suffered at his hands. By impersonating him, in the consulting room, Alan transformed those experiences from passive to active. This would be in line with Sigmund Freud's observation in *Beyond the Pleasure Principle* (1920) that

As the child passes over from the passivity of the experience to the activity of the game, he hands over the disagreeable experience to one of his play- mates and in this way revenges himself on a substitute. (p. 17)

In the context of my work with Alan, therapy was the game and I was the playmate!

Joseph Sandler in 1976 extended the definition of countertransference to include the analyst's 'free floating responsiveness', reflecting the ana- lyst's readiness to respond to the patient's attempts to manipulate or provoke him into a role that is complementary to the role the patient plays out in the transference. This role responsiveness can show itself not only in the analyst's thoughts and feelings, but also sometimes in his overt reactions. I felt reassured that my unwillingness to break the angry silences through my massive fear of retaliation could be explained by the idea of role-responsiveness. Although chronologically before the Sandler paper, I came to Heinrich Racker's book *Transference and Countertransference* (1968) later. Here the differences between concordant and complimentary identifications are made clearer. I understood that my patient's identification placed me in 'the situation of (his) dependent and incriminated ego' and that I was impelled to 'experience the situation with the context [my] patient [gave] it.' I did 'feel subjugated and accused, and [did] react to some degree with anxiety and guilt.' (p. 140).

As the therapy continued there were other occasions where he would communicate to me in the silence his profound fear of his father through his identification with him. The images left me, but now I had to endure the full horror of his experience. I was unable to speak as I had the conviction that if I did he would annihilate me. I began to call this 'walking on eggshells' and in subsequent sessions we were able to talk more freely about his experiences. It was through my extreme countertransference experience of his terror – which was unlike anything I had ever encountered in my own life – that I came to believe in a real traumatizing father.

It was a feature of his family that no one acknowledged that the children witnessed painful scenes. In his paper 'On knowing what you are not supposed to know and feeling what you are not supposed to feel' (1988), Bowlby said:

> Children not infrequently observe scenes that parents would prefer they did not observe; they form impressions that parents would prefer they did not form; and they have had experiences that parents would like to believe they have not had. Evidence shows that many of these children, aware of how their parents feel, proceed then to conform to their parents' wishes. (p. 101-2)

The disconfirmation of thoughts and feelings by Alan's parents led to cognitive disturbances in which perceptions and attributions became distorted and which could be monitored by attention to the transference and, perhaps more significantly, his capacity for reflective thought. Although a therapeutic session is not the place to be rating reflective functioning, it is possible nonetheless to be aware of any changes in the patient's ability to form a more coherent narrative.

The non-interpretive elements that support psychotherapy, i.e. the frame, the setting, the space, reliability, empathy, holding and containing, have been acknowledged by many authors and are listed by Baker (1993). These elements can facilitate a reorganization of internal working models, so that the patient feels as if he can reappraise himself and his world differently to how he had in the past. There is recognition of something different, a new beginning, and a fresh start. Balint (1968) refers to the importance of new experiences in the patient's therapy. He writes that only by 'therapeutic regression' to the area of the basic fault, which can be thought of as the area of cognitive disturbance, can there be a new beginning. I believe that Alan and Bella have been able to find in me what Ronald Baker describes as a 'new object'. He says:

> With the patient's discovery of the analyst as a new object, a new phase of growth and development may begin, especially the potential for improved external relationships. (Baker, 1993)

Both Alan and Bella have been able to form new and more appropriate relationships with partners who could give them sensitive and empathetic support, which in turn has given them much-needed self-esteem. A study by Harris, Brown and Robinson (1999) suggests that a new partner, which is classified as a 'fresh-start' experience, is 'a key-predictor of remission from depression and should become more of a routine focus in treatment' (p. 231).

Alan remains in therapy, travelling across London three times a week during the rush hour three times a week and thereby demonstrating, I believe, his devotion to therapy and the high value he places on our relationship. This relationship has enabled him to believe in his own capacity to elicit sensitive responsiveness and he has been able to modify his internal working models to ones which are far more consistent and far less persecutory. Freud in a letter to Jung stated that 'Essentially, one might say, the cure is effected by love' (1974, pp. 8–9).

I believe that non-interpretive and relationship factors, which are so significant in working with patients like Alan and Bella, are crucial in the early years of a therapy. Exploration of these patients' attachment history gives the psychoanalytic psychotherapist additional insight into the patients' internal working models and offers them hope of a happier and less fearful life in the future.

References

Ainsworth MDS, Blehar MC, Waters E. and Wall S (1978) Patterns of Attachment: A Psychological Study of the Strange Situation. Hillsdale, NJ: Lawrence Erlbaum.

Baker R (1993) The patient's discovery of the psychoanalyst as a new object. International Journal of Psycho-analysis 74: 1223–33.

Balint M (1959) Thrills and Regressions. London: Hogarth.

Balint M (1968) The Basic Fault. London: Tavistock Publications.

Biringen Z (1994) Attachment theory and research: application to clinical practice. American Journal of Orthopsychiatry 64: 404–20.

Bowlby J (1944) Forty-four juvenile thieves: their characters and home life. International Journal of Psycho-analysis 25: 19–52.

Bowlby J (1980) Attachment and Loss, vol. 3: Loss: Sadness and Depression. London: Hogarth Press.

Bowlby J (1988) A Secure Base: Clinical Applications of Attachment Theory. London: Routledge.

Cassidy J (1994) Emotion regulation: Influences of attachment relationships. In: NA Fox (ed.) The development of emotion regulation: Biological and behavioral foundations. Monographs of the Society for Research in Child Development 59(2–3, Serial No. 240): 228–50

Cassidy J and Berlin LJ (1994) The insecure/ambivalent pattern of attachment: Theory and research. Child Development 65: 971–92

Cassidy J and Shaver PR (1999) Handbook of Attachment: Theory, Research and Clinical Applications. New York: Guilford Press.

Coltart N (1992) Slouching Towards Bethlehem. London: Free Association Books.

Eagle M (1995) The developmental perspectives of attachment and psychoanalytic theory. In: S Goldberg, R Muir, and J Kerr (eds) Attachment Theory: Social, Developmental, and Clinical Perspectives. Hillsdale, NJ: Analytic Press, pp. 123–53.

Fonagy P (1999) Psychoanalytic theory from the viewpoint of attachment theory and research. In: Cassidy J and Shaver PR (eds) Handbook of Attachment. New York: Guilford Press, pp. 595–624.

Fonagy P and Target M (1996) Playing with reality: I. Theory of mind and the normal development of psychic reality. International Journal of Psycho-analysis 77: 217–33.

Fonagy P, Steele M, Moran G, Steele H and Higget AC (1991) The capacity for understanding mental states: The reflective self in parent and child and its significance for security of attachment. Infant Mental Health Journal 13: 200–16.

Fonagy P, Steele M, Steele H, Leigh T, Kennedy R, Mattoon G and Target M (1995) Attachment, the reflective self, and borderline states: The predictive specificity of the Adult Attachment Interview and pathological emotional development. In: S Goldberg, R Muir and J Kerr (eds) Attachment Theory: Social Developmental, and Clinical Perspectives. Hillsdale, NJ: Analytic Press, pp. 233–79.

Fonagy P, Steele M, Steele H and Target M (1997) Reflective functioning manual Unpublished manuscript, University College, London.

Freud A (1937) The Ego and the Mechanisms of Defence. London: Karnac Books.

Freud S (1920) Beyond the Pleasure Principle. Standard Edition, vol. 18. London: Hogarth Press.

Freud S and Jung CG (1974) The Freud/Jung Letters, ed. W McGuire, trans. R Mannheim and R Hull. Princeton, NJ: Princeton University Press.

George C, Kaplan N and Main M (1985) Adult Attachment Interview, 2nd edn. Unpublished manuscript, University of California at Berkeley.

George C, Kaplan N and Main M (1996) The Adult Attachment Interview Protocol, 3rd edn. Unpublished manuscript, University of California at Berkeley.

Glenn L (1987) Attachment theory and group analysis: the group matrix as a secure base. Group Analysis 20: 109–17.

Harris T, Brown GW and Robinson R (1999) Befriending as an intervention for chronic depression among women in an inner city 2: Role of fresh-start experiences and baseline psychosocial factors in remission from depression. British Journal of Psychiatry 174:

Holmes J (1993a) Attachment theory: A biological basis for psychotherapy. British Journal of Psychiatry 153: 752–8.

Holmes J (1993b) John Bowlby and attachment theory. London : Routledge.

Holmes J (1995) Something there is that doesn't love a wall: John Bowlby, attachment theory, and psychoanalysis. In: S Goldberg, R Muir and J Kerr (eds) Attachment Theory: Social, Developmental, and Clinical Perspectives. Hillsdale, NJ: Analytic Press, pp. 19–45.

Holmes J (1996a) Attachment, Intimacy, and Autonomy. New York: Aronson.

Holmes J (1996b) Psychotherapy and memory – an attachment perspective. British Journal of Psychotherapy 13(2): 204–18.

Holmes J (1998) Defensive and creative uses of narrative in psychotherapy: An attachment perspective. In: G Roberts and J Holmes (eds) Narrative in Psychotherapy and Psychiatry. Oxford: Oxford University Press, pp. 49–68.

Horney K. (1937) The Neurotic Personality of Our Time. New York: Norton.

Karen R (1994) Becoming Attached: First relationships and how they impact our capacity to love. New York: Oxford University Press.

Kobak RR and Sceery A (1998) Attachment in later adolescence: Working models, affect regulation, and representations of self and others. Child Development 59: 135–46.

Main M (1990) Cross-cultural studies of attachment organization: Recent studies, changing methodologies, and the concept of conditional strategies. Human Development 33: 48–61.

Main M (1994) A Move to the Level of Representation in the Study of Attachment Organization: Implications for Psychoanalysis. London: Annual Research Lecture to the British Psycho-Analytical Society.

Main M and Solomon J (1986) Discovery of a new, insecure-disorganized/disorientated attachment pattern. In: TB Brazelton and M Yongman (eds) Affective Development in Infancy. Norwood NJ: Ablex, pp. 95–124.

Marrone M (1994) Attachment theory and group analysis. In: D Brown and L Zinkin (eds) The Psyche and the Social World. London: Routledge.

Marrone M (1998) Attachment and Interaction. London: Jessica Kingsley.

McElroy SL, Keck PE and Phillips KA (1995) Kleptomania, compulsive buying, and binge-eating disorder. Journal of Clinical Psychiatry 56(4): 14–26.

Pine F (1990) Drive, Ego, Object and Self. New York: Basic Books.

Racker H (1968) Transference and Countertransference. London: Hogarth.

Rayner E (1991) The Independent Mind in British Psychoanalysis. London: Free Association Books.

Sandler J (1976) Countertransference and role responsiveness. International Review of Psychoanalysis 3: 43–7.

Silverman D (1991) Attachment patterns and Freudian theory: An integrative proposal. Psychoanalytic Psychology 8: 169–93.

Slade A (1999) Individual psychotherapy: An attachment perspective. In: J Cassidy and PR Shaver (eds) Handbook of Attachment. New York: Guilford Press, pp. 575–94.

Sroufe LA (1986) Bowlby's contribution to psychoanalytic theory and developmental psychopathology. Journal of Child Psychology and Psychiatry 27: 841–9.

Target M and Fonagy P (1996) Playing with reality: II The development of psychic reality from a theoretical perspective. International Journal of Psycho-analysis 77: 459–79.

Winnicott DW (1974) Fear of breakdown. International Review of Psychoanalysis 1: 10–17.

CHAPTER 6

Clinical uses of the Adult Attachment Interview

HOWARD STEELE AND MIRIAM STEELE

The immense clinical usefulness of an interview which thoroughly probes the family history of an adult was commented upon as early as 1949 by John Bowlby in what is widely regarded as the first paper on family therapy (Bowlby, 1949). Some 40 years later in the preface to his penultimate work, Bowlby would comment on his sense of surprise that attachment theory attracted so little attention from clinicians and, instead, remained for many years of almost exclusive interest to developmental psychology (Bowlby, 1988). This seeming paradox may be attributed in part to the deep reluctance of classical psychoanalysis to dispense with Freudian drive theory, as Bowlby proposed, in favour of an ethological account of the attachment behavioural system underpinning human development (see Steele and Steele, 1998). Bowlby's scientific perspective tended to be far wider than those that occupied his psychoanalytic colleagues in the early 1960s, and this launched him on the path of observing parent–child behaviour in the natural context, and anchoring his theorizing on reliably observed behaviours. This left him free to champion the cause of child welfare based on reliable arguments about what children *actually* experience, as opposed to speculations concerning children's fantasies.

Many colleagues helped advance this work, including James Robertson whose filmed observations of toddlers going to hospital in the early 1950s remain a moving visual testimony to the importance of young children's attachments to parents. Most notably, Bowlby had a professional partner in the attachment project who was a developmental and clinical psychologist, Mary Ainsworth (Ainsworth, 1967, 1990; Ainsworth et al., 1978). Ainsworth collected crucial observational support for, and provided inspiring conceptual extensions to, Bowlby's theory concerning the importance of the early infant–mother relationship for the child's current and subsequent mental health.

By 1988, as Bowlby himself knew and commented upon in a chapter on personality development in his book on the clinical applications of attachment theory, the tide was turning. A growing body of developmental research was documenting the influences of childhood experiences upon adult personality via administration and coding of an interview which has remarkable clinical relevance. That interview is known as the Adult Attachment Interview or AAI (George, Kaplan and Main, 1985), which – together with an accompanying specialized manual for rating and classifying adults' interview responses (Main and Goldwyn, 1998) – is attracting widespread interest from clinical psychologists, psychiatrists, social workers and related mental health professionals. This chapter provides (1) an overview of the normative findings utilizing the AAI, (2) a summary of clinical and forensic findings, and (3) a discussion of three related clinical uses of the AAI, concerning diagnosis, therapeutic action, and assessment of outcome effectiveness.

Origins and normative research findings based on the Adult Attachment Interview

Origins of the interview and evidence of inter-generational patterns

The Adult Attachment Interview was developed and first tested in the context of the Berkeley longitudinal study of attachment patterns (George et al., 1985; Main, Kaplan and Cassidy, 1985). One of the stated aims of the interview was to surprise the unconscious (George et al., 1985). The Berkeley-based group of developmental psychologists reported three classes of response to systematic questioning concerning childhood experiences and current thoughts and feelings regarding these experiences: secure (free-autonomous), insecure-dismissing and insecure-preoccupied. Furthermore, in the pioneering Berkeley study, these adult interview classifications were reported to map on to the well-known infant patterns of attachment available for their children from prior assessments made of these children's attachment relationships with mother (at 12 months) and father (at 18 months). Great excitement surrounded and followed the report of these inter-generational results. This was so because of what were already robust findings concerning the long-term social, emotional and cognitive consequences of infant patterns of attachment. Some two decades of previous work had documented both short- and long-term developmental outcomes of these infant–parent patterns of attachment. For example, secure attachments during infancy predict optimal patterns of peer relations and adjustment in the pre-school years, high levels of academic achievement in the school years, and adaptive coping in the adolescent years (see Cassidy and Shaver, 1999). Correspondingly, the insecure (avoidant, resistant and the more recently discovered disorganized) infant patterns have been shown to predict much less favourable, sometimes psychopathological, developmental outcomes.

In the original Berkeley work, mothers' interviews were uniquely related to the previously observed infant–mother relationship, and fathers' interviews were similarly predictive of the infant–father relationship. This suggested a remarkable level of cross-generational consistency, and relationship specificity, in the social and emotional meaning young children derive from their interactions with parents. These findings were confirmed in a prospective design, involving attachment interviews with expectant mothers and fathers and subsequent assessments of the infant–mother and infant–father attachment quality (Steele, Steele and Fonagy, 1996) and replicated widely across linguistic and cultural barriers (van IJzendoorn, 1995). Still many questions remain for further research and, notably, these questions have enormous clinical implications. One important line of inquiry regards the developmental trajectory from infant relationship-specific patterns of attachment (i.e. to mother or to father) to person-specific adult patterns of attachment (where the secure pattern is typified by coherence and integration stemming from the composite of earlier and current attachments). For example, does one parent, e.g. mother (Freud, 1940), have precedence in influencing the path of self-development and extent of integration achieved within the mind of the developing individual? When is such integration ordinarily achieved? These questions are the subject of much ongoing developmental research. With respect to the present chapter, it is important to note that adults from the clinical population are frequently suffering from the ongoing effects of adverse childhood experiences that not uncommonly include past trauma and/or loss. As a consequence, it seems, these interviews tend to lack an integrated state of mind concerning, and a valuing stance toward, attachment so typical of the healthy autonomous-secure adult pattern.

The capacity for arriving at, and expressing, an integrated state of mind concerning attachment

AAI research involving non-clinical samples suggests that by 17 or 18 years of age, if not sooner, individuals have developed a well-functioning capacity to report, monitor and evaluate their possibly very different types of early attachment experiences, i.e. with mother, father and others (e.g. Kobak and Sceery, 1988). Further, Main (1991) has suggested that by 10 years of age, children who have benefited from a secure early attachment to mother are more likely to demonstrate metacognitive awareness in response to probing questions exploring the nature of mind and knowledge. Relatedly, in our own longitudinal research, we have found that children as young as 6 years are advanced in their understanding of emotions if they were securely attached to their mothers at 1 year, and if their mothers' AAIs were classified autonomous-secure and *integrated* (Steele et al., 1999). This finding is relevant for two reasons. First, it offers further empirical support for the inter-generational link between parent and child. Second, it highlights the connections that need to be made with regard to the usefulness of having a working lexicon of words to describe affect experiences, affect regulation and security of attachment. Thus the concept of secure attachment seems to overlap closely with what clinicians often cite as their foremost goal in therapeutic work, i.e. to help patients 'put feelings into words' or perhaps to 'put the adult individual at ease with the child within'. Not surprisingly, the gold standard of measuring adult attachment involves close and detailed study of the words adults choose to tell their attachment stories.

We next review the systematic method of eliciting this attachment story with attention to the clinical value of the line of questioning followed. Notably, the AAI questions may be seen to comprise three distinct challenging modes of inquiry into memories for, and current evaluations of, past experiences of attachment-related distress:

1. questions that ask about negative experiences and related emotions which are part of *everyone*'s childhood experiences, including emotional upset, physical hurt, illness and separations from parents;
2. questions about negative experiences and related emotions that are part of *some people*'s childhood experiences, including loss and abuse; and
3. questions which demand that the speaker think about the possible meaning and influence upon adult personality of childhood attachment experiences, including requests that the speaker provide an account of why parents behaved as they did during childhood.

Because the adult's childhood experiences with specific caregivers (e.g. mother, father, others) are probed in detail, the interview provides a fertile ground for assessing the extent to which attachment experiences are integrated in the mind of the speaker. Ideally, an autonomous point of view arises concerning the balance an adult needs to seek between depending on important and valued others – and having such others feel that one is dependable. One expectant father, when asked about his hopes for his unborn child 20 years on, stated his awareness of this integrative balancing act as follows:

> When I think about my child's future, well I hope he or she will be strong enough to follow his or her interests and passions ... and that I will be able to make them feel that I am still there for them ... not too busy or cut off ... that they can count on me for guidance without undue interference. And, most importantly I'm sure, that they find with something like the range of feelings I share with their mother – I don't think it will be easy for them – or I – but I am looking forward to it!

Approximately 65 per cent of the normal population convey in one way or another a valuing of attachment, and a respect for exploration, which leads raters to assign their attachment interviews to the category 'autonomous-secure'.

Importantly, the trained rater first scores the narrative on a number of nine-point dimensions pertaining to probable past experience and current state of mind concerning attachment. The dimensions of probable past experience that are rated include loving, rejecting, neglecting and role-reversing experiences with each parent. The dimensions of current state of mind concerning attachment that are rated include attention to the emotional quality of parent-specific mental representations, e.g. in relation to idealization, anger or derogation. Additionally, state of mind of the interviewee is rated in terms of more global considerations including the extent to which the narrative is coherent, passive, and showing signs of metacognition (Main and Goldwyn, 1998). Of particular clinical relevance is a London-based effort to extend the scoring of metacognition (awareness of one's own thought processes) to include awareness of mental states as motivators of behaviour in oneself *and others* (Fonagy et al., 1991). This effort has led to the development of the concept of 'reflective-functioning' which we see as normatively growing out of early childhood experiences of having our inner worlds reflected upon more-or-less accurately by caregivers (e.g. Fonagy et al., 1995). Further, reflective functioning may be markedly inhibited or skewed as a result of deficient empathic responsiveness from caregivers in early childhood. In such circumstances, an elevated likelihood of psychopathological child and adult outcomes may be expected (see the discussion of criminality, and the suggestion that reflective functioning is perhaps synonymous with psychological insight, in later sections of this chapter).

For the present purposes, it is important to note that the autonomous-secure interview typically provides evidence of a balanced, non-idealizing representation of mother and father. Relatedly, the behaviours of each parent (whether favourable or adverse) during childhood are described in credible episodic detail, while the current emotional stance of the speaker is neither angry nor derogatory. These are, of course, qualities rarely observed in clinical populations, at least prior to therapeutic interventions.

Failures at integration

Beyond the 65 per cent of interviews from non-clinical samples which merit the description of organized, integrated and autonomous-secure, two insecure patterns are noted. Both of these insecure patterns reveal difficulties with integrating past negative attachment experiences into a current and balanced state of mind concerning attachment. Some of these interviews err on the side of minimizing or dismissing past difficulties with one or both parents (circa 25 per cent of the non-clinical population) while others err on the side of maximizing and becoming preoccupied with past attachment difficulties. These two alternatives to the free-autonomous group are termed insecure-dismissing and insecure-preoccupied, respectively. In the former 'dismissing' case, the speaker seems inexorably focused *consciously* on positive or normal aspects of experience, to the exclusion of what is probably (*unconsciously recognized as*) a much more mixed and negative set of actual experiences. In the latter 'preoccupied' case, the speaker seems angrily or passively gripped by past relationship difficulties that intrude upon current thoughts about relationships and are accompanied by confusing and difficult-to-control negative feelings. While this pattern is observed only about 15 per cent of the time in non-clinical samples (van IJzendoorn, 1995), the proportion of interview responses fitting this preoccupied pattern swells to over 50 per cent when clinical psychiatric populations have been assessed (van IJzendoorn and Bakermans-Kranenburg, 1996).

The disruptive influence of loss and/or trauma: resolution versus lack of resolution

A further important consideration when rating and classifying attachment interviews concerns past loss and trauma. When there is clear evidence of a significant loss or trauma (physical and/or sexual abuse) the rater or judge follows a number of specified guidelines (Main and Goldwyn, 1998) for assessing the extent to which the past trauma is resolved. In sum, this comes down to determining the extent to which the overwhelmingly negative experiences are (a) identified as such and (b) spoken about in such a way as to indicate that they have acquired the characteristics of belonging to the past without lapses in the monitoring of reason or discourse when discussing the past loss and/or trauma (after Main and Goldwyn,

1998). For example, where loss has occurred, it is important for the speaker to demonstrate full awareness of the permanence of this loss. And, where abuse has occurred in speakers' childhood experiences, it is important for speakers to at once acknowledge the abuse, and also show that they understand they are not responsible for the maltreatment they suffered. Important clues as to the extent of resolution in the speaker's mind follow from careful study of the narrative for a logical and temporally sequenced account of the trauma which is neither too brief, suggesting an attempt to minimize the significance of the trauma, nor too detailed, suggesting ongoing absorption. Interestingly, in a study of 140 college students, Hesse and van IJzendoorn (1999) report that speakers whose attachment interviews were judged unresolved with respect to past loss were statistically more likely than speakers who were judged resolved (or those who had suffered no significant losses) to score highly on an independent assessment of proneness to absorption. Thus, in a non-clinical sample, brief lapses in the monitoring of discourse or reason when discussing loss in the context of the AAI have been associated with the propensity toward absorption, measured by agreement to questionnaire items such as 'At times I feel the presence of someone who is not physically there'.

Unresolved loss and/or trauma is observed in approximately 10–15 per cent of non-clinical interviews, which are also assigned to the best fitting of three main groups, autonomous, dismissing or preoccupied. A recent finding confirms clinical intuition insofar as it has been found that a parent who is autonomous-secure throughout an AAI, save for when speaking of a past loss in an unresolved manner, does not carry the same risk in terms of their child's development. This contrasts with those parents who were both insecure and unresolved regarding a past loss in the AAI context, who were more likely to have children with disorganized infant–mother attachments (Schuengel, Bakermans-Kranenburg and van IJzendoorn, 1999).

It is a similarly positive sign when a speaker demonstrates that past trauma has been resolved. Indeed, in the non-clinical population, where childhood experiences have involved trauma, it is not uncommonly the case that the speaker conveys a sense of moving beyond the fear they felt so often as a child. Additionally, such speakers are capable of going some way toward understanding, though not necessarily forgiving, *caregiving* figure(s) who perpetrated abuse against them as children. In these circumstances, the interview often reveals a robust sense of self, interpersonal awareness and valuing of attachment so that one can say the adult who was abused is not likely to become an abuser. Such resilience invariably emerges out of the individual discovering one or more secure bases or refuges beyond the abusive relationship, such as may be provided by an extended family member, spouse or therapist. In this respect, the AAI offers a uniquely powerful clinical and legal tool insofar as it may be seen to provide a reliable indication as to whether or not abused adults are likely to repeat the pattern upon their children.

Clinical findings based on the Adult Attachment Interview

Applying the standard categorical scoring system to non-standard experiences and conditions

Research to date applying the Adult Attachment Interview in clinical contexts has revealed that loss and trauma experiences are highly common in psychiatric samples (e.g. Wallis and Steele, 2001). With respect to specific (sometimes comorbid) diagnostic groups, borderline personality disorder has been associated with high prevalence of unresolved and insecure-preoccupied interviews (Patrick et al., 1994, Fonagy et al., 1996). Eating disorders have been linked to unresolved and insecure-dismissing interviews (Cole-Detke and Kobak, 1996; Fonagy et al., 1996); and suicidality has been associated with unresolved and 'disorganized' interviews (Adam, Sheldon-Keller and West, 1996).

There have been two forensic studies reporting on the administration of AAIs to prisoners incarcerated for crimes against people and/or property. One of these studies was conducted in Holland by van IJzendoorn et al. (1997) and the other in England by Levinson and Fonagy (1998), the latter work also being the subject of discussion in Fonagy et al. (1997). While both these studies illustrate the high incidence of abuse in childhood, and the dramatically elevated prevalence of insecurity (dismissal and/or preoccupation), the English study is especially noteworthy for the contrast observed between criminals who have perpetrated violence against people as compared to violence against property. The former most violent group was observed to be almost totally lacking in any capacity for reflection upon mental states in themselves and others; in other words, when the humanity of the other is denied, severe violence becomes possible, perhaps inevitable.

For a review of DSM-IV (Diagnostic and Statistical Manual of Mental Disorders, 4th edn) Axis 1 and Axis 2 disorders, including descriptions of the disorders, relative contributions of environment and genetics to each disorder and the extent to which attachment phenomena may be implicated in each disorder, the reader may consult the recent chapter by Dozier, Chase Stovall and Albus (1999). For present purposes, it may be sufficient to relate a common thread through the Dozier et al. presentation, i.e. if a disorder is highly heritable, 'less in the way of unfavourable caregiving may be necessary for the disorder to emerge' (Dozier et al., 1999, p. 503). Thus it is not surprising that the strongest associations between insecure AAI patterns and clinical phenomena have emerged in respect of those conditions which have a low heritability rate and are correspondingly understood as relationship disturbances, i.e. borderline personality disorder, eating disorders and criminality. With respect to these adult difficulties, it may be argued that the AAI provides a detailed picture of some of the etiological or causal factors. With respect to other more heritable disorders, the AAI may be seen to provide a window upon mediating or moderating factors.

Emerging recognition of profound threats to self-integration and organization of feelings and thoughts concerning attachment

As Adam et al.'s (1996) use of the word 'disorganized' suggests, what the standard scoring system takes for granted, i.e. a primary, integrated and more-or-less organized mental and emotional stance toward attachment, may be fundamentally lacking in some speakers. This was a phenomenon noted by Hesse (1996), one of the individuals closely involved with the development of the interview coding system who has also studied a great number of interviews from clinical populations. Hesse's (1996) brief report suggested that a likely conclusion from considering some interviews, particularly those from clinical samples, is that they should be assigned to a 'cannot classify' category because they contain deeply divided states of mind concerning attachment. For example, a speaker may be insecure-dismissing with respect to a physically abusive father, e.g. speaking of him in a cold, hostile and uncaring manner, while being insecure-preoccupied with respect to an occasionally very caring mother who failed miserably at protecting the child, e.g. speaking of her in a heated, angry and involving manner. This is but one of many pathways that may lead to an attachment interview that is impossible to classify in a singular way – the common element to all these pathways appears to be severe and repeated experiences of trauma. Correspondingly, most 'cannot classify' interviews are also rated high for unresolved mourning concerning past loss and/or trauma.

In our London-based consulting work involving the AAI, we have been using the interview to help arrive at a comprehensive assessment of individuals suffering from profound dissociative difficulties. This work is confirming the clinical relevance of the 'cannot classify' category just as it is providing corollary evidence in support of the diagnostic category dissociative identity disorder (DID) or multiple personality disorder. Remarkably, the AAI when used with this population elicits multiple voices from the same individual plausibly reflecting distinct personality organizations, with unique attachment patterns. While evidence of unresolved mourning arising within the context of the AAI has been associated with evidence of dissociative symptoms outside the AAI (Hesse and van IJzendoorn, 1999), as discussed above, this is the first evidence of marked and repeated dissociation occurring within the AAI itself. In some instances, the dissociation or splitting that occurs within the interview includes the retreat of one personality and the advance of another personality, occasionally of a different gender, with a unique name and story to tell about the inevitably horrific physical, sexual and emotional abuse sustained repeatedly during childhood. The switches that occur appear to happen without the knowledge of the primary personality. The term 'cannot classify' goes only some way to capturing the attachment strategies these adults have deployed to cope with their history of life-threatening traumatic experiences (see Steele, 2002).

For example, one woman presented with a surface personality that was pleasant, polite, valuing of attachment (engaged to be married), and troubled by the distant relationship she has with her mother. This speaker was also partially able to discuss how she was rejected, abused and abandoned by this mother who also loved her (suggestive of a mildly preoccupied and resentful type of hard-earned security/autonomy). Yet as the interview progressed, a series of different attachment patterns emerged via a series of distinct voices/personalities. Notably, at no point in the interview did the interviewer ask if there was another voice/person with a different view from the one being expressed by the 'current' speaker. Staying with the present example, a marked shift was introduced by a question about who cared for her after her mother abandoned her at age 5. A different more hostile voice emerged to say that 'care means chronically abused and ruined emotionally'. This was now a male voice, not a female one, who had a tough observer 'big brother' status in the interviewee's life. He spoke with severe disapproval of any attempt by the surface personality to repair relations with her mother, saying 'I think she should tell her mother to fuck off after all she's done to her ... make her face up to reality, make her listen to what we went through'. The content of what 'we endured' included ongoing ritualized abuse over many years perpetrated and maintained within the context of being in the care of governmental social services. Interestingly, beyond the horrendously abusive experiences suffered within the context of services set up to protect children, what was perhaps the strongest source of ongoing suffering for this interviewee (in all her personas) was the abandonment by her own mother. This relates to a theme common to many of the attachment narratives provided by individuals suffering from DID. That is, while psychic pain certainly accompanies the recall of the abuse per se, this pales in comparison to the much greater pain that accompanies the recall of being betrayed by trusted caregivers and siblings.

Clinical applications of the Adult Attachment Interview

Given the depth and range of information elicited by the Adult Attachment Interview, anyone trained in the administration and (more complicated task of) coding the interview has had the repeated experience of being approached by clinicians interested in learning more about the interview. Potential clinical applications of the interview include diagnosis, treatment, and outcome evaluations in therapy, legal and social work. For example, the interview may be used to help identify relationship difficulties that may be an important focus to treatment of individuals with Axis 1 disorders. Or the interview may be used to help with court assessments of adults whose parenting capacities need to be comprehensively evaluated. Relatedly, the interview may be used to assist in assessing the suitability of adults hoping to adopt a child. And more ominously, the interview may be used to help in assessing the extent to which sex offenders have reformed themselves such that they might return to the community. In all of these and other related areas the Adult Attachment Interview is being, or will come to be, applied.

For the clinician contemplating use of the interview, what is crucial to remember is that the instrument was initially developed and tested by psychologists who have evolved an effective system for training those who use the interview. This is particularly important with respect to the system for rating and classifying interviews (Main and Goldwyn, 1998), which requires participation in an initial two-week intensive training 'institute' after which participants must complete a reliability test of some 30 interviews over a period of many months. This ensures that findings reported from different research or clinical groups may be compared, and – equally important – that ethical considerations may be thoroughly discussed and adhered to by those using the instrument. The standards of science and good clinical practice require nothing less. We have found that a useful way of incorporating the AAI into clinical work, when the clinician is not trained in the standard system of rating and classifying the interview, is for an attachment researcher with such training to offer consultation. This may include the administration of the interview, and always includes the rating and classifying of the transcription of the audio-recorded interview.

What follows is a discussion of some of the many possible clinical applications of the interview. This is the most speculative section of the current chapter as only very few studies have reached the stage of reporting results, while the vast majority are ongoing efforts of which we are aware. No doubt, many other clinical efforts involving the Adult Attachment Interview are under way, of which we have no knowledge. This discrepancy is, in part, based on the fact that there are a great many researchers and clinicians administering the interview protocol (George et al., 1985), but only a few of these are also trained to reliability in the rating and classification manual (Main and Goldwyn, 1998).

The use of the AAI in clinical diagnosis

The AAI should, of course, not be thought of as a substitute for diagnosis. However, it may be useful in identifying the particular profile of interpersonal and intrapersonal difficulties that may distinguish one depressed and/or anxious individual from another individual with similar symptoms. In other words, the interview yields a systematic and relatively deep social history. 'Deep' in this context refers to material that reflects both early memories and modes of responding to (or coping with) experience stored at diverse levels of awareness.

The finding that bipolar depressives are more likely (than unipolar depressives) to be dismissing (Fonagy et al., 1996) and unresolved (Tyrrell and Dozier, 1997) may serve as an illustration of the potential diagnostic value of the AAI and its use in therapeutic intervention. Dismissing interviews are noteworthy for the frequently unrealistically positive or highly idealized image of parent(s) that is conveyed by the speaker. Correspondingly, just as negative aspects of one's parenting experience are underplayed or denied, the self is presumed to have been unaffected by negative experiences. With respect to the speaker's representation of loss or other traumatic experiences, the interview may indicate that mourning work is ongoing. Both these observations, readily picked up by an AAI (and perhaps typical of an individual with bipolar disorder), may provide some directions along which the therapeutic intervention may proceed.

Above all else, in our experience, what the AAI is likely to provide to the diagnostician is the opportunity to discover some unsettling loss or other traumatic experience which has *not yet* been presented. 'Not yet' is put in italics so as to alert the reader to the very real possibility that unconscious defensive processes, and not only a conscious sense of

embarrassment or shame, may be preventing the individual from reporting one or more toxic traumatic events from their history. In this sense,
the AAI delivers on its promise to 'surprise the unconscious' (of the speaker) and even sometimes the therapist. A poignant example of just such a
situation occurring came within the context of parent–infant psychotherapy work that was carried out by colleagues at the Anna Freud Centre,
London. The AAI has been incorporated into selected cases as part of an
exciting initiative which will explore its use in parent–infant psychotherapy. One compelling case noted how a young mother was able to shift
dramatically in her capacity to relate to her infant after the AAI uncovered
feelings about a traumatic event that had never been explored. The young
woman, in an affect-laden moment stated 'You know, no one has ever
asked me about the event before. They all took for granted that I was just
too young to matter.'

The use of the AAI as a guide to therapeutic intervention

To our knowledge, there has not yet been any systematic attempt to
administer the AAI to a group of individuals where material from the AAI
has been used as the basis for the intervention. One might envision a
study where a comparison group who are also interviewed with the AAI
but do not receive the AAI-based intervention are included. In such a circumstance, the relative added value of the AAI-based intervention may be
assessed. Despite such a report being unavailable, there are a number of
relevant studies that have intervened using AAI-like goals with mothers
whose babies are at risk of developing insecure attachments (see
Lieberman and Zeanah, 1999, for a review and appraisal of this work).
Positive outcomes have been reported in response to these interventions
which facilitate the establishment of a secure base with the therapist, and
the exploration of current *and past* relationship difficulties. These intervention programmes often involve mothers in both individual therapy
and group therapeutic settings (e.g. Erickson, Korfmacher and Egeland,
1992), thus maximizing the potential for participants to become aware of
the toxic (transferential) influence of the past upon the present. This
opens up new ways of thinking, feeling and relating which bring immediate rewards in terms of the enhancements observed in maternal
understanding and responsiveness to infant needs, and the joyful interactions that result. Bowlby's (1988) summary of his clinical approach was
stated very much in these terms. No doubt, further work will demonstrate
the utility of the AAI to this process.
    One possible impediment to the clinician thinking the AAI useful to the
therapeutic process may be the ultimately categorical nature of the

taxonomy relied on in the research literature (as opposed to the multidimensional mode of thinking which often feels more familiar *and real* to the clinician). And, indeed, the most common element to the AAI literature is the discussion of secure versus insecure (dismissing or preoccupied) classifications on the one hand, and resolved versus unresolved classifications on the other hand. Yet, as mentioned above, there are numerous dimensions considered with respect to interviewees' probable past experiences with caregivers, and their current states of mind concerning attachment. Also, as Slade (1999) has recently reminded us, Mary Main herself has held to the view (which we heard her elaborate in 1987) that every speaker who is dismissing in the context of the AAI is unconsciously preoccupied, while the preoccupied speaker is unconsciously dismissing or restricted in feeling. In other words, there is a range of primitive to more sophisticated psychological defences or strategies available to every individual (A. Freud, 1946), with one's habitual conscious reliance on some subset of these defences being a scaffold behind which operate other, more primitive defences. Nonetheless, as Slade (1999) illustrates, the AAI classification system may help the therapist to navigate a therapeutic path that might assist the patient toward noticing the connections between conscious, verbally articulated patterns of behaviour and earlier experiences of rejection, separation, loss, and – more generally – fundamental unmet attachment needs. For patients with a dismissing attachment presentation, the therapist is alerted to the challenges of gently breaking down affectless psychological structures, born out of the need for self-protection against attachment distress. By contrast, for patients with a preoccupied attachment presentation, the therapist's time must be devoted to the 'slow creation of structures for the modulation of affect' (Slade, 1999, p. 586).

The additional consideration of treating unresolved mourning concerning past loss or trauma requires different skills, on account of the fact that the emotions surrounding the trauma have, by virtue of being unresolved, been radically dissociated and/or distorted. From an attachment perspective, this therapeutic challenge requires a gentle and monumental effort at reconstruction of the traumatic history – what, when, where, how, and why are questions that demand answers. For the individual with unresolved grief, the task is alluring but carries multiple risks of renewed terror and further dissociation. Ultimately, it is hoped that the individual may achieve a narrative that finally contains, *and relegates to the past*, the persisting loss and/or trauma.

We have explored one area of overlap between AAI research and the clinical process in London, at the Anna Freud Centre, stemming from our work on the dimensional concept of reflective functioning. Notably, ratings of this capacity in the AAIs from pregnant women we have studied in

London (Steele et al., 1996) have revealed that reflective functioning is a more powerful predictor of infant–mother attachment security than any other single AAI rating scale (see Fonagy et al., 1996). The capacity to reflect on one's own internal world and to appreciate the perspective of another individual is a crucial question in the mind of the clinician when they are assessing a patient for 'treatability'. Often there are limited resources with which to offer psychotherapy services to those that seek it and could benefit from it. The question of how to assess whether an individual might make use of treatment is a critical one for the clinician, whether in public or private practice. A familiarity with the concept of reflective functioning might have a very important role to play in this challenging area of clinical practice. An example of an adolescent boy who sought help at the Anna Freud Centre exemplifies a situation in which a capacity to reflect upon his painful situation was predictive of a good therapeutic outcome. Steven, at age 16 years, suffered from intense bullying by his schoolmates. This included being locked in a locker at school for a full hour, and having a cigarette lighter held to his cheek. He was engaging in some self-harming behaviour and was involved in a sado-masochistic relationship with his father with whom he battled on a daily basis. However, he was also able to comment at the diagnostic stage of potential treatment, 'My father will never be satisfied ... even if I was the type of boy my father thinks he'd be happy with, he still wouldn't be happy with me.' Indeed, over the course of intensive psychotherapy that followed, Steven was able to explore his own role in the difficult relationship with his father but also to see his father's contribution to the pathological situation.

The AAI and therapeutic outcome

The AAI may well be a useful guide to how well treatment has gone, particularly if it has been administered prior to treatment beginning, for later comparison with an outcome AAI. Further, the trained raters judging the interviews should be kept blind to psychiatric diagnosis and the initial classification and rating scores. All this said, if the treatment is in any way based upon material obtained from the pre-treatment interview (as we advocate above), then the AAI should not be considered as the only outcome measure, so as to maintain the possibility of achieving an independent assessment of the treatment process.

The only report of the AAI being used in a pre-treatment and post-treatment design comes from the Cassel Hospital inpatient family unit in London (Fonagy et al., 1996). This 1996 report commented on a subset (circa 35) of adults from a larger sample (circa 85) being followed over one year of treatment. No significant movement from the insecure to secure classification was observed. However, two significant outcome effects were observed. First, patients' levels of reflective functioning improved, suggesting that rating scales, rather than overall classification, may be the most useful AAI index to chart therapeutic progress. It is, after all, easier to move in a particular area, for example toward a less idealizing stance with regard to a particular parent, than to shift in several different areas, which would be necessary for a classification shift. The Fonagy et al. (1996) study also showed that those patients whose initial AAIs were insecure-dismissing were most likely to show this improvement, while those whose AAIs were insecure-preoccupied were least likely to show improvement. Slade (1999) has written at length about the particular challenges to treatment presented by patients who are primarily preoccupied. She comments on how 'progress is ... hard won. It seems to follow not from words or interpretation, but from the therapist's long-term emotional availability, and tolerance for fragmentation and chaos' (Slade, 1999, p. 588). Thus, perhaps it was the relatively short-term nature of the follow-up in the Fonagy et al. (1996) study that permitted only those patients with primarily dismissing strategies to show improvement.

A window upon the particular challenge to treatment that dismissal represents is provided by Dozier et al. (2001) based on their study of 34 patients with serious psychopathological difficulties. Patients' dismissing versus preoccupying attachment strategies were considered in relation to their behaviour in video-filmed interpersonal problem-solving sessions with significant others or case managers. Dozier et al. (2001) suggest that those patients with dismissing strategies were more likely to lack concentration in, and report more confusion following, interactions with case managers, while also showing greater rejection of significant others in interactions with them. No doubt, there are distinctive challenges presented by patients with predominantly preoccupied as opposed to dismissing profiles of attachment insecurity, and we still have much to learn about how these profiles react to treatment, and moreover, which treatments are best suited to each.

So far we have considered the AAI as reflecting characteristics of the patient which may influence diagnostic considerations of the therapist, therapeutic progress and outcome *without* commenting on characteristics of the therapist, and responses of the therapist to attachment-related characteristics of the patient. Obviously, however, every therapist has an attachment narrative of their own which will influence the therapeutic alliance formed, and the way in which the inevitable ruptures in this alliance are managed (Safran and Muran, 2000). There is one study that has systematically investigated this countertransference issue from the attachment perspective (Dozier, Cue and Barnett, 1994). These authors confirm the expectation that secure as opposed to insecure therapists are better able to negotiate successfully the challenges of treating either dismissing or preoccupied patients. This study deserves to be replicated so that its implications for the work of training and supervision of therapists may be fully explored.

Conclusion

That clinicians across the mental health field are finding in attachment theory and research much that is relevant to their work is arguably owed, in large part, to the discovery and now well-established reliability and validity of the Adult Attachment Interview (AAI). This chapter has attempted to provide an overview of this research instrument, pointing at its many possible clinical applications. A sceptic might say that it is only the research-minded clinician that will wish to become truly familiar with the interview's properties and promises. However, with the research tide turning so that even the most research-shy clinician is now being asked for audit and efficacy statistics to be produced, the AAI may offer unique and fruitful opportunities that would not have otherwise informed their work.

References

Adam KS, Sheldon-Keller AE and West M (1996) Attachment organization and history of suicidal behaviour in clinical adolescents. Journal of Clinical and Consulting Psychology 64: 264–72.

Ainsworth MDS (1967) Infancy in Uganda: Infant Care and the Growth of Love. Baltimore: Johns Hopkins University Press.

Ainsworth MDS (1990) Some considerations regarding theory and assessment relevant to attachment beyond infancy. In: MT Greenberg, D Cicchetti and EM Cummings (eds) Attachment in the Preschool Years. Chicago: University of Chicago Press, pp. 463–88.

Ainsworth MDS, Blehar MC, Waters E and Wall S (1978) Patterns of Attachment. Hillsdale, NJ: Lawrence Erlbaum.

Bowlby J (1949) The study and reduction of group tensions in the family. Human Relations 2: 123–8.

Bowlby J (1988) A Secure Base: Clinical Applications of Attachment Theory. London: Routledge; New York: Basic Books.

Cassidy J and Shaver P (eds) (1999) Handbook of Attachment: Theory, Research and Clinical Applications. London: Guilford Press.

Cole-Detke H and Kobak R (1996) Attachment processes in eating disorder and depression. Journal of Consulting and Clinical Psychology 64(2): 282–90.

Dozier M, Cue K and Barnett L (1994) Clinicians as caregivers: Role of attachment organization in treatment. Journal of Consulting and Clinical Psychology 62: 793–800.

Dozier M, Chase Stovall K and Albus KE (1999) Attachment and psychopathology in adulthood. In: J Cassidy and P Shaver (eds) Handbook of Attachment. London: Guilford Press, pp. 497–519.

Dozier M, Lomax L, Tyrrell CL and Lee SW (2001) The challenge of treatment for clients with dismissing states of mind. Attachment and Human Development 3: 62–76.

Erickson MF, Korfmacher J and Egeland BR (1992) Attachments past and present: Implications for therapeutic intervention with mother–infant dyads. Development and Psychopathology 4: 495–507.

Fonagy P, Steele M, Moran G, Steele H and Higgitt AC (1991) The capacity for understanding mental states: The reflective self in parent and child and its significance for security of attachment. Infant Mental Health Journal 13: 200–16.

Fonagy P, Steele M, Steele H, Leigh T, Kennedy R, Mattoon G and Target M (1995) Attachment, the reflective self and borderline states: The predictive specificity of the Adult Attachment Interview and pathological emotional development. In: S Goldberg, R Muir and J Kerr (eds) Attachment Theory: Social, Developmental and Clinical Perspectives. Hillsdale, NJ: Analytic Press, pp. 233–278.

Fonagy P, Leigh T, Steele M, Steele H, Kennedy R, Mattoon G, Target M and Gerber A (1996) The relation of attachment status, psychiatric classification and response to psychotherapy. Journal of Consulting and Clinical Psychology 64: 22–31.

Fonagy P, Target M, Steele M and Steele H (1997) The development of violence and crime as it relates to security of attachment. In: JD Osofsky (ed.) Children in a Violent Society. New York: Guilford Press, pp. 150–77.

Freud A (1946) The Ego and the Mechanisms of Defence. New York: International Universities Press. (Originally published 1936.)

Freud S (1940) An outline of psychoanalysis. In: J Strachey (ed. and trans.), The Standard Edition of the Complete Psychological Works of Sigmund Freud, vol. 23. London: Hogarth, pp. 137–201.

George C, Kaplan N and Main M (1985) Adult Attachment Interview, 2nd edn. Unpublished manuscript, University of California at Berkeley.

Hesse E (1996) Discourse, memory and the Adult Attachment Interview: A note with emphasis on the emerging cannot classify category. Infant Mental Health Journal 17: 4–11.

Hesse E and van IJzendoorn MH (1999) Propensities to absorption are related to lapses in the monitoring of reasoning or discourse during the Adult Attachment Interview: A preliminary investigation. Attachment and Human Development 1: 67–91.

Kobak RR and Sceery A (1988) Attachment in late adolescence: Working models, affect regulation and representations of self and others. Child Development 59: 135–46.

Levinson A and Fonagy P (1998) Criminality and attachment: The relationship between interpersonal awareness and offending in a prison population. Unpublished manuscript.

Lieberman AF and Zeanah CH (1999) Contributions of attachment theory to infant–parent psychotherapy and other interventions with infants and young children. In: J Cassidy and P Shaver (eds), Handbook of Attachment. London: Guilford Press, pp. 555–74.

Main M (1991) Metacognitive knowledge, metacognitive monitoring, and singular (coherent) vs. multiple (incoherent) models of attachment: Findings and direction for future research. In: CM Parkes, J Stevenson-Hinde and P Marris (eds) Attachment across the Life Cycle. London: Routledge, pp. 127–59.

Main M and Goldwyn R (1998) Adult attachment scoring and classification system. Unpublished manuscript, Department of Psychology, University of California, Berkeley.

Main M, Kaplan N and Cassidy J (1985) Security in infancy, childhood, and adulthood: A move to the level of representation. In: I Bretherton and E Waters (eds) Growing Points of Attachment Theory and Research. Monographs of the Society for Research in Child Development 50 (1–2, Serial No. 209): 66–104.

Patrick M, Hobson RP, Castle P, Howard R and Maughn B (1994) Personality disorder and the mental representation of early experience. Development and Psychopathology 6: 375–88.

Safran ID and Muran JC (2000) Negotiating the Therapeutic Alliance: A relational treatment guide. New York: Guilford Press.

Schuengel C, Bakermans-Kranenburg M and van IJzendoorn M (1999) Frightening, frightened and/or dissociated behavior, unresolved loss, and infant disorganization. Journal of Consulting and Clinical Psychology 67: 54–63.

Slade A (1999) Attachment theory and research: Implications for the theory and practice of individual psychotherapy with adults. In: J Cassidy and P Shaver (eds) Handbook of Attachment, pp. 575–94. London: Guilford Press.

Steele H (2002) Multiple dissociation in the context of the Adult Attachment Interview: Observations from interviewing individuals with Dissociative Identity Disorder. In: V Sinason (ed) Attachment Trauma and Multiplicity, pp. 107–121. London: Brunner-Routledge.

Steele H and Steele M (1998) Attachment and psychoanalysis: Time for reunion. Social Development 7: 92–119.

Steele H, Steele M and Fonagy P (1996) Associations among attachment classifications of mothers, fathers, and their infants: Evidence for a relationship-specific perspective. Child Development 67: 541–55.

Steele H, Steele M, Croft C and Fonagy P (1999) Infant–mother attachment at one-year predicts children's understanding of mixed emotions at six years. Social Development 8: 161–78.

Tyrrell C and Dozier M (1997) The role of attachment in therapeutic process and outcome for adults with serious psychiatric disorders. Paper presented at the biennial meeting of Society for Research in Child Development, Washington, D.C.

van IJzendoorn MH (1995) Adult attachment representations, parental responsiveness and infant attachment: A meta-analysis on the predictive validity of the
Adult Attachment Interview. Psychological Bulletin 117: 382–403.

van IJzendoorn MH and Bakermans-Kranenburg MJ (1996) Attachment representations in mothers, fathers, adolescents, and clinical groups: A meta-analytic search
for normative data. Journal of Consulting and Clinical Psychology 64: 8–21.

van IJzendoorn MH, Feldbrugge J, Derks F, de Ruiter C, Verhagen M, Phillipse M,
van der Staak C and Riksen-Walraven J (1997) Attachment representations of
personality   disordered   criminal   offenders.   American   Journal   of
Orthopsychiatry 67: 449–59.

Wallis P and Steele H (2001) Attachment representations in adolescence: Further
evidence from psychiatric residential settings. Attachment and Human
Development 3: 259–68.

CHAPTER 7

Patient–Therapist attachment: impact on the therapeutic process and outcome

DIANA DIAMOND, JOHN F. CLARKIN, K. CHASE STOVALL-MCCLOUGH, KENNETH N. LEVY, PAMELA A. FOELSCH, HILARY LEVINE AND FRANK E. YEOMANS

Introduction

Clinicians from Freud to the present have affirmed that the therapeutic relationship involves the development of attachment between patient and therapist. Indeed, Freud (1913) wrote:

> It remains the first aim of the treatment in attaching him (the patient) to the treatment and to the person of the doctor ... If one exhibits a serious interest in him, carefully clears away the resistances that crop up at the beginning and avoids making certain mistakes, he will of himself form such an attachment and link the doctor up with one of the imagos of the people by whom he was accustomed to be treated with affection. (p. 139)

Freud's definition of attachment, however, was synonymous with that of the positive transference, which he conceptualized as being twofold: first, as related to the erotic feelings towards the therapist which may function as a resistance; and second, as encompassing trusting and affectionate feelings towards the therapist, or the unobjectionable positive transference that presaged the concept of the treatment alliance (Freud, 1912). Although Freud (1912) conceptualized both aspects of positive transference as 'genetically linked with sexuality', and as having 'developed from purely sexual desires' (p. 105), he did set the stage for the further elaboration of the nature of attachment bonds between patient and therapist. Fifty years after Freud, Bowlby (1975) wrote, 'the role of the psychiatrist is seen as providing the patient with a temporary attachment figure' (p. 291).

Bowlby's definition of attachment is, of course, quite different from that of Freud. By placing the proclivity to form affectional bonds to significant others at the heart of human motivation, Bowlby (1969, 1978, 1979, 1980) expanded the spectrum of motivations beyond sexual and aggressive drives that are thought to energize human behavior and relationships, including the therapeutic one. He hypothesized that the therapeutic relationship would activate the biologically stable attachment behavioral system, which according to Bowlby is bi-directional in that infant attachment-seeking behaviors (proximity seeking) are designed to evoke and activate corresponding adult caretaking behaviors (e.g. soothing, protecting). Both types of attachment behaviors devolve from processes of mutual regulation between mother and infant, which are internalized as expectations, rule or modes of implicit relational knowledge about attachment relationships (Stern, 1985; Lyons-Ruth, 1991). Bowlby (1988) stipulated that the attachment behavioral system is active throughout the life cycle, and that 'the capacity to make intimate emotional bonds with other individuals, sometimes in the care seeking role and sometimes in the caregiving one, is ... a principal feature of effective personality functioning and mental health' (p. 121). The therapist is thought to be one of the prototypical attachment figures in adulthood (Farber, Lippert and Nevas, 1995), and the therapeutic relationship is uniquely suited to evoke and illuminate the patient's working models of attachment. Bowlby (1977) gave primacy to the consolidation of a secure attachment between patient and therapist, stipulating that the therapist's first task is to 'provide the patient with a secure base from which to explore both himself and also his relations with all those with whom he has made or might make, an affectional bond' (p. 421).

In fact, attachment concepts such as the secure base (Bowlby, 1988) have provided a new theoretical framework for aspects of the therapeutic process and relationship, including therapeutic alliance, transference, and countertransference. The term 'therapeutic alliance' is an elusive one, and there is little agreement within the psychoanalytic community about its precise definition or utility. The current controversy centers around the question about whether the treatment alliance is based in the real or nontransference relationship which provides an objective frame of reference against which transference and countertransference distortions can be examined (Greenson, 1965, 1971; Zetzel, 1956); or whether the therapeutic alliance cannot be separated from the patient's transference dispositions, and is indissolubly linked to the enactment of transference by the patient (Deserno, 1998; Schafer, 1999; see also Chapters 2 and 4 in this volume).

Despite such theoretical controversies, there is consensus that a fundamental aspect of the therapeutic or working alliance is the attachment relationship between patient and therapist, which is thought to have elements of both transference and real relationship or alliance (Bordin, 1994). Following Bowlby, for example, Henry and Strupp (1994) have stated, 'A productive alliance may be seen, in Bowlby's terms as a 'secure base' (p. 71). In similar fashion, Luborsky (1994) has written, 'The therapeutic alliance is only that part of the pattern of relationships having to do with ... positive bonds with the therapist' (p. 47). In addition, a number of clinical investigators have incorporated attachment concepts into their instruments designed to measure therapeutic alliance, such as the Working Alliance Inventory (Horvath and Greenberg, 1986), which includes subscales on the quality of the attachment bond between patient and therapist. Such alliance measures have been found to be highly predictive of therapeutic outcome regardless of the particular instrument used to measure it or the type of treatment involved (Bordin, 1994; Luborsky, 1994; Safran and Moran, 2000). Thus, there is a convergence of perspectives that anchors the therapeutic or working alliance concept in Bowlby's notions of the secure base which, while not totally immune from the vicissitudes of the transference, may buffer the treatment from the potentially pernicious aspects of negative transferences (Bordin, 1994).

However, Bowlby (1988) recognized that, particularly with severely disturbed patients, the consolidation of a secure attachment relationship with the therapist might be problematic. In the case of patients with insecure states of mind with respect to attachment, internal working models of attachment are likely to be multiple, contradictory and unintegrated, leading to complex and sometimes chaotic transferences (Farber et al., 1995; Fonagy, 1991; Main, 1995). Furthermore, particularly with more severely disturbed patients with such insecure and contradictory attachment states of mind, the therapist's feeling states, to the extent that they are nonidiosyncratic (Racker, 1968), and own attachment states of mind with respect to the patient may provide a primary source of information about the nature of such transferences and the early attachment experiences on which they are partially based (Bowlby, 1988).

An understanding of the attachment substrate of transference–countertransference dynamics has been particularly useful in psychoanalytic psychotherapy with borderline patients, for whom disorders of attachment are primary (Diamond et al., 1999a; Holmes, 1996, 1998; Slade, 1999). Clinicians, regardless of the modality in which they treat borderline patients, know that disorders of attachment lie at the heart of borderline conditions (Adler and Buie, 1979; Fonagy, 1991; Gunderson, 1996; Linehan, 1993; Liotti, 1999). The attachments formed by borderline patients, in and out of therapy, are often turbulent and chaotic with unpredictable shifts between clinging and repudiation, intense idealization and scathing devaluation, terrors of abandonment often leading to gross intrusions into the therapist's life, or sudden unilateral rejection of others, including the therapist. All of these features are particularly evident in the transference. Hence close attention to the management, containment, and working through of the transference is essential with borderline patients. Borderline patients vacillate between a collaborative and rageful stance towards the therapist and between reflectiveness and self-destructive acting out from one session to the next. Recently these characteristics of borderline pathology have been reinterpreted as the behavioral correlates of insecure attachment representations that have been demonstrated to characterize borderline patients (Dazzi, 1998; Fonagy, 1991; Fonagy et al., 1995; Gunderson, 1996). While there is now a substantial body of research linking insecure attachment patterns to borderline disorders, there have been few investigations on the ways in which such patterns may configure aspects of the therapeutic process and relationship.

As part of an NIMH-funded longitudinal study (John F. Clarkin, PI; NIMH MH-5370502) at the Personality Disorders Institute (PDI) at New York Presbyterian Hospital on the effectiveness of a form of psychoanalytically oriented psychotherapy for borderline patients called transference focused psychotherapy (TFP), we have been examining the possible relationship between borderline patients' attachment organization, that is the working models they hold of attachment relationships, and treatment process and outcome. Transference-Focused Psychotherapy (TFP) is based on object relations theory (Kernberg, 1975, 1976), and is designed to achieve change in the patient's representational world through the interpretation of the transference relationship with particular emphasis on the here and now (Clarkin, Yeomans and Kernberg, 1999). In TFP, the transference is the vehicle for mobilizing and transforming maladaptive behaviors and the insecure attachment patterns which may fuel them. Clinical researchers at the PDI have described the tactics and techniques of TFP in two volumes of a treatment manual (Kernberg et al., 1989; Clarkin et al., 1999). and have delineated how complex treatment issues may be addressed in TFP as well as how it may be tailored to the needs of the individual patient (Koenigsberg et al., 2000). Outcome studies from this project with 23 patients have indicated that after one year of TFP, borderline patients showed a significant diminution of suicide attempts and behaviors, a decrease in medical risk and severity of medical condition following self-injurious behaviors, and a decrease of hospitalizations (Clarkin et al., 2001). In addition to changing self-destructive and maladaptive behaviors, TFP is designed to change the pathogenic object relations that are thought to underlie the chronic self-destructiveness, affective instability and distorted cognitions of borderline patients. Hence, as part of our investigations of the efficacy of TFP, we have been investigating changes in representations of self and attachment figures as well as behavior.

In this study we have been using the Adult Attachment Interview, a semi-structured clinical interview designed by Mary Main and colleagues (AAI; George, Kaplan and Main, 1985, 1996), to assess change in attachment organization and the representational states that underlie them in borderline patients over the course of one year of TFP. Preliminary data analysis on changes in attachment organization of 20 patients after one year of TFP showed that there was a significant improvement in the coherence of narrative on the AAI), although a minority of the sample showed a shift to overall security of attachment at one year (Levy, 2002). We have also been investigating the way in which patients' states of mind with respect to attachment in childhood, as assessed on the AAI, are related to states of mind with respect to attachment in the therapeutic relationship on the part of both patient and therapist. The latter is being assessed through an interview adapted from the AAI, called the Patient–Therapist Adult Attachment Interview or PT-AAI (George et al., 1996; Diamond et al., 1999b). Like the AAI, the PT-AAI is designed to assess states of mind with regard to attachment, or the conscious and unconscious rules that the individual has developed for organizing attachment-related experiences, feelings and thoughts, but within the context of the therapeutic rather than the parent–child relationship. In developing the PT-AAI, we have been attempting to advance our understanding of how attachment status might affect both transference–countertransference dynamics (Dozier and Tyrrell, 1998; Fonagy, 1991; Holmes, 1995, 1996; Szajnberg and Crittenden, 1997) and the quality and nature of the therapeutic alliance (Mackie, 1981; Slade, 1999). In this chapter, we shall present partial findings on five patients, two of whom shifted to secure states of mind after one year of TFP on the AAI and three of whom did not. We shall also present findings on our use of the PT-AAI to assess the impact of attachment organization on therapeutic process and the therapeutic relationship. Finally, we shall present findings on changes in patients' symptomatology and personality organization over the course of one year of TFP.

Attachment and the therapeutic relationship

The limited empirical studies on the implications of attachment state of mind for the psychotherapeutic process and relationship suggest that patients' internal working models of attachment affect a number of aspects of the therapeutic endeavor, including (1) the nature of the patient's symptom reporting, (2) the capacity to make use of treatment, (3) the quality of the therapeutic alliance, and (4) treatment outcome (Dozier, 1990; Dozier, Cue and Barnett, 1993; Korfmacher et al., 1997, Fonagy et al., 1996, Tyrrell et al., 1999). For example, patients classified with preoccupied states of mind with respect to attachment on the AAI tend to report higher levels of symptomatology on self- report measures such as the Hopkins Symptom Checklist-90 (Derogatis, 1977) and the Minnesota Multiphasic Personality Inventory-2 (MMPI-2) as compared with those who are classified with secure and dismissing states of mind (Butcher et al., 1989; Kobak and Sceery, 1988; Pianta, Egeland and Adam, 1996). These findings are consistent with a preoccupied attachment state of mind in which the self is presented as victimized, needy and over-whelmed by attachment experiences. Pianta et al. (1996) also showed that dismissing women reported fewer symptoms of hysteria on the MMPI. Again, this is consistent with a dismissing state of mind in which the self is presented as strong, independent and uninterested in, or unaf-fected by, attachment relationships. Interestingly, although a dismissing state of mind is not associated with higher levels of self-reported symp-tomatology, Dozier and Lee (1995) found that clinicians and research interviewers rated these patients as *more* symptomatic than preoccupied patients.

The extent to which patients engage in or make use of treatment has also been found to vary as a function of attachment state of mind. In a study that examined the effects of a long-term intervention for high-risk pregnant women, Korfmacher et al. (1997) found mothers rated as autonomous/secure were easier to work with and more involved in treat-ment than mothers rated as unresolved and dismissing. Autonomous mothers were also more likely to engage in problem-solving and sup-portive therapy compared to dismissing mothers, who engaged in more superficial interactions, and unresolved mothers, who required signifi-cantly more crisis intervention. Similar findings were obtained in a study of patients with serious psychiatric disorders involved in case manage-ment (Dozier, 1990). Clinicians rated patients with more secure states of mind as being more cooperative with treatment compared to those with less secure states of mind. Deactivation of attachment, or dismissing states of mind, were associated with less help seeking, less self-disclosure, and poorer treatment use compared to those with hyperactivating, or preoc-cupied, states of mind.[1]

These studies are consistent with the idea that attachment states of mind reflect unconscious rules that guide how one approaches, interprets, reacts to, and organizes relationship experiences. Bowlby suggested that the main task of the therapist is to challenge or disconfirm patients' usual style of relating to attachment figures, which involves bringing the patient's characteristic internal working models of attachment to awareness and challenging the perceptions and expectations of self and other inherent in them, while maintaining a working alliance. Thus, it is not surprising that the therapist's own attachment state of mind has also been found to affect the treatment process. For example, Dozier and colleagues (Dozier, Cue and Barnett, 1993) found that clinicians with more secure states of mind with respect to attachment were more likely to challenge patients' own strategies for relating (i.e., intervene in greater depth with deactivating patients and in less depth with hyperactivating patients) whereas more insecure clinicians tended to mirror the patient's interpersonal style (i.e., intervene in greater depth with hyperactivating patients and in less depth with deactivating patients). Dozier et al. (1993) suggest that secure clinicians were more flexible in their approach to each client and were better equipped to understand and tolerate patients' negative reactions to their efforts. Other studies also by Dozier and her colleagues (Tyrrell et al., 1999) indicate that the best treatment outcomes and overall ratings of treatment alliance occur when patients' and therapists' attachment state of mind are complementary rather than concordant. In such treatments, the therapist is able to challenge the patient's characteristic ways of regulating affect and distress in interpersonal contexts, leading to better therapeutic outcomes.

While the foregoing studies indicate that attachment state of mind affects a number of aspects of treatment process and outcome with severely disturbed patients, a major limitation of the research described above is that it has been conducted with patients with Axis 1 disorders (including schizophrenia, schizoaffective, bipolar disorder and major depression), who were being treated with supportive psychotherapy and/or case management. Hence there is a necessity for further research that examines the impact of patients' and therapists' states of mind with respect to attachment on the treatment process and effectiveness with patients with Axis 2 disorders and neurotic disorders who are being treated with psychoanalytically oriented psychotherapy or psychoanalysis. The following research findings on changes in attachment status with borderline patients in psychodynamic treatment, although preliminary, hopefully will contribute to filling in this gap, and will show how attachment measures, particularly the AAI and the PT-AAI, may provide a window into crucial aspects of the therapeutic process and relationship.

Methods

This section presents a brief description of the measures and procedures relevant to our findings on the five patients and their therapists, selected from the complete NIMH sample of 23 patients. A comprehensive description of the overall study and assessment procedures is beyond the scope of this chapter and can be found elsewhere (see Diamond et al., 1999a; Clarkin et al., 2001; Clarkin and Levy, in press). For the subset of patients in this chapter, the average age of the patients was 30.4, range 23–38. Four patients were Caucasian, one mixed race. All patients were diagnosed with borderline personality organization (Kernberg, 1975) and borderline personality disorder (American Psychiatric Association, DSM-IV, 1994). All had made at least one para-suicidal gesture (severe self-injurious gesture) within eight weeks of admission to our research project. The four therapists in the study are all clinicians with postdoctoral and/or psychoanalytic training, who had substantial experience as therapists and researchers in the Borderline Psychotherapy Project. All therapists participated in a weekly peer supervision meeting led by senior clinicians in the project. All therapists were monitored for their adherence and competence in TFP, which is described in more detail below.

Transference-focused psychotherapy

The primary goal of TFP is to help borderline patients develop images of self and others that are integrated, multidimensional and cohesive, to modify primitive defensive operations, and to resolve identity diffusion. Briefly, TFP stipulates a specific sequence of treatment phases and guidelines for phase-appropriate interventions with the emphasis on the transference at each stage as the vehicle for the transformation of primitive (e.g. fragmented, split) to advanced (e.g. complex, integrated) object relations. TFP is designed to contain and work with the intense, chaotic transferences that borderline patients develop as a result of their split, polarized internal world. TFP involves several major treatment phases including: (1) an initial contract-setting phase designed to identify and contain the major areas of self-destructive acting-out; (2) an early treatment phase which involves the identification of dominant object-relational patterns as they are lived out in transference; (3) a mid-phase of treatment which focuses on the integration of split, polarized and part-object identifications via here-and-now transference interpretations; (4) an advanced stage of treatment where genetic interpretations link current relational and transference patterns with early experiences.

During the first year of treatment (the time period depicted in the following clinical case material), the primary focus is on the predominant affect-laden themes that emerge in the relationship between borderline patients and their therapists in the here-and-now of the transference.

TFP has roots in several branches of psychoanalytic theory, the full exposition of which is beyond the scope of this chapter and can be found elsewhere (Clarkin, Yeomans and Kernberg, 1999; Koenigsberg et al., 2000). In brief, TFP is consistent with certain aspects of Kleinian theory and technique in that it stipulates that individuals experience external reality through the structure of their internal object worlds, and emphasizes the early interpretation of the transference in the here and now as a route to that internal world of object relations dyads. TFP differs from Kleinian approaches, however, in its emphasis on the frame, its frequency of sessions (two times per week, as opposed to four or five times), and its focus on both oedipal and pre-oedipal issues even in the early stages of treatment. TFP uses the concept of the therapist as the third party, who is in part a subject in the transference–countertransference relationship and in part an objective observer of that relationship. The boundaries and structure of TFP introduce or encourage an identification with the observing, limiting function of the therapist, and catalyze early triangulation; this can lift the patient out of the symbiosis of a purely dyadic transference and introduce archaic oedipal material, which is interpreted along with the pre-oedipal from the early stages of treatment on.

Second, TFP is consistent with some of the theorists of the British Independent school in its emphasis on the importance of the therapist's countertransference, or the monitoring of his or her own feelings states and fantasies relating to the patient as an important source of information about the patient's self and object world (Kohon, 1986; Koenigsberg et al., 2000). TFP also is consistent with aspects of Bowlby's approaches to treatment, based on attachment theory. While it does not emphasize as much as did Bowlby the necessity of linking transference interpretations to the patient's attachment history, TFP does consistently link the transference to current relationships. TFP is also consistent with Bowlby's theory that patients may experience the therapist in polarized and contradictory ways that reflect the dichotomous nature of internal working models of attachment. 'Not infrequently, the patient shifts during therapy from treating his therapist as though he was one or the other of his parents behaving towards him in the way one of his parents had treated him' (Bowlby, 1988, p. 144). Hence, Bowlby's observations about the dramatic role reversals that may occur in the transference relationship as the patient recreates all aspects of the internal working model of attachment with the therapist are consistent with the monitoring and interpretation of such role reversals in TFP. Although TFP stipulates a specific sequence of treatment phases and specific guidelines for phase appropriate interventions, the progression through these phases varies according to individual patient characteristics and the nature of the unique patient–therapist dyad. The patient's attachment status or current state of mind regarding early attachment relationships is a major patient characteristic that we have found to affect the course of TFP for borderline patients (Diamond et al., 1999a; Koenigsberg et al., 2000).

Measures (see Table 7.1)

Adult Attachment Interview

At four months and one year after the beginning of treatment, patients were given the Adult Attachment Interview (AAI), a semi-structured clinical interview designed to elicit thoughts, feelings and memories about early attachment experiences (George et al., 1985, 1996). The AAIs were rated for attachment classification by raters who were blind to all identifying information about the patients or the study, as well as to the time of administration of the interview, and who were trained to reliability by Main and Hesse in the Five Way Adult Attachment Classification System. Based on specific subscale ratings, the AAIs were assigned to one of five primary classifications: Secure/Autonomous, Preoccupied, Dismissing, Unresolved, or Cannot Classify (Main and Goldwyn, 1998; see Hesse, 1999 and the Appendix to this volume, for a more complete description of the AAI and its scoring system).

Table 7.1. Attachment and symptomatology measures

Adult Attachment Interview (AAI):
Semi-structured clinical interview
Scored for state of mind with respect to attachment and reflective function (see Appendix)

Patient–Therapist Adult Attachment Interview (PT-AAI):
Semi-structured clinical interview adapted from AAI
Scored for state of mind with respect to attachment and reflective function

Parasuicide History Interview (PHI):
Measures the topography, intent, medical severity, precipitating events and outcomes of parasuicidal behavior during the target time period

Inventory of Personality Organization (IPO):
Classifies patients according to level of personality organization; Subscales assess Identity Diffusion, Primitive Defenses, Reality Testing, Quality of Object Relations (normal scale), Aggression, and Moral Values

Patient–Therapist Adult Attachment Interview

Patients' and therapists' state of mind with respect to attachment in the therapeutic relationship was assessed at one year through the PT-AAI. The PT-AAI follows the same format and order of questions as the AAI, with minor changes in the wording of questions to fit the context of the patient–therapist as opposed to parent–child relationship. The PT-AAI consists of 28 questions asked in a set order. Speakers are asked to describe their relationship with their patient/therapist generally and then to choose five words to describe the relationship with the patient/therapist, supporting these descriptors with specific examples or incidents. Speakers are also asked what they did when upset, or hurt, in the course of therapy. The interview also includes questions about the individual's response to separations from the patient/therapist, about times when the individual felt rejected by the patient/therapist, and about whether the individual has ever felt threatened by the patient/therapist in the course of the treatment. In addition, speakers are asked why they think the patient/therapist acted the way he or she did in the course of treatment, and are asked to describe and evaluate the effects of psychotherapy. As is the case with the AAI, the technique has been described as having the effect of 'surprising the unconscious' (George et al., 1985, 1996) in that it allows numerous opportunities for the interviewee to elaborate on, contradict, support or fail to support previous statements or generalizations. There are additional questions designed to evaluate the extent to which therapists and patients can formulate a coherent understanding of the therapeutic interaction. The interview evaluates the quality of the therapist's understanding of the patient as well as the extent to which the patient has internalized the therapist's understanding of him or her, and has been helped by such understanding in other interpersonal contexts.

The technique of administering and scoring the PT-AAI is parallel to that of administering and scoring the AAI. An adult attachment classification of the patient and/or therapist may be derived from the first 16 questions of the PT-AAI using an adaptation of the five-way Adult Attachment Scoring and Classification System (Main and Goldwyn, 1998). The interviews are assigned to one of five primary classifications: Secure/Autonomous, Preoccupied, Dismissing, Unresolved, or Cannot Classify. These classifications are derived from three classes of subscale ratings, which have been adapted to fit the context of the patient–therapist relationship by Diamond et al. (2001). While revision of the majority of the subscales has necessitated only minor changes in wording, revision of the subscales designed to assess the speaker's experience of the relationship has involved minor changes in wording and conceptualization to fit the context of the patient–therapist relationship. For example, the subscale for loving versus unloving behaviors between parent and child has been changed to liking versus not-liking between patient and therapist; that is the extent to which the patient and therapist maintain positive feelings despite the vicissitudes of the transference. Similarly, the AAI subscale for involving, or the extent to which the parent attempts to involve the child or to seek parenting from the child, has been revised to assess the extent to which patient and therapist seek attention or caretaking from each other in ways that go beyond the frame of the therapeutic relationship.

Measures of symptomatology and personality organization

Assessments of the patients' clinical status and symptomatology occurred at four-month intervals throughout the year-long treatment. Here we shall report only the data on self-destructive symptomatology, as measured by the Parasuicide History Interview (PHI). The Parasuicide History Interview (PHI; Linehan, Wagner and Cox, 1989) measures the topography, intent, medical severity, social context, precipitating and concurrent events, and outcomes of suicidal and parasuicidal behaviors during a target period. Each episode of parasuicidal behaviors is coded separately as to medical risk, suicide intent, impulsivity – all of which are associated with lethality of parasuicidal behavior.

The level of personality organization was also assessed at admission to the study and at one year through an instrument called the Inventory of Personality Organization (IPO) (Kernberg and Clarkin, 1995; Lenzenweger et al., 2001), which classifies patients according to level of personality organization (e.g. neurotic, borderline and psychotic) based on assessments of Identity Diffusion, Primitive Defenses, and Reality Testing.

Results

The findings for the five patients and therapists at one year indicate that all patients showed shifts in attachment organization on the AAI after one year of TFP. All patients were initially rated as insecure, with the majority having a primary AAI classification of unresolved for trauma and/or loss (U) (Table 7.2).[2] This finding is consistent with previous research by Fonagy and colleagues (1996), who found in their investigations of AAI classifications among a number of Axis 1 and Axis 2 disorders that 98 per cent of patients with BPD diagnoses were classified with lack of resolution with respect to loss and trauma on the AAI and 75 per cent as preoccupied. In addition, all patients showed a change in their state of mind with respect to attachment after one year of TFP, with two patients showing a shift from unresolved and insecure states of mind to secure states of mind, and three from unresolved and insecure states of mind to Cannot Classify or mixed states of mind with respect to attachment.

Table 7.2. Adult Attachment Interview (AAI) classification for five patients

Patients	AAI Time 1 (four months)	AAI Time 2 (one year)
Patient A	U/E3b/E2 Unresolved Angry/conflicted Fearfully preoccupied with traumatic events	F5/U Secure/Autonomous Somewhat resentful/Conflicted Unresolved
Patient B	Ds2 Devaluing of Attachment	F1a Setting aside of attachment
Patient C	U/E1/E2 Unresolved Passively preoccupied Angry/Conflicted	CC/U/E3/E2/Ds3 Cannot Classify Unresolved Fearfully preoccupied with traumatic events Angry/conflicted Restricted in feeling
Patient D	U/Ds2/Ds3 Unresolved Dismissing of attachment Restricting in feeling	CC/U/Ds2/E3 Cannot Classify Unresolved Devaluing of attachment Fearfully preoccupied with traumatic events
Patient E	E3b Fearfully preoccupied with traumatic events Loss of memory	CC/Ds1/E2 Cannot Classify Dismissing of attachment Fearfully preoccupied with traumatic events

This change in attachment status is surprising since it suggests a shift in what has been repeatedly found in a number of studies to be a stable attribute of adult personality functioning. The AAI has been shown to have a high level of test–retest stability over a two- to three-month period (Bakermans-Kranenburg and van IJzendoorn, 1993; Sagi et al., 1994), as well as stability over an 18-month to four-year period (Crowell et al., 1996; Ammaniti et al., 1996) including one study which indicates stability between prebirth AAI interviews and interviews conducted 11 months after the birth of the first child (Benoit and Parker, 1994; see Hesse, 1999, for review). Thus, our findings suggest that the therapeutic work in TFP catalyzes a shift in the individual's characteristic mode of organizing attachment-related information and experiences. We shall amplify these findings further in the next section where we focus on specific cases in depth.

Table 7.3. Patient–Therapist Adult Attachment Interview (PT-AAI) classification for five patients and their therapists after one-year of TFP

Patient	Patient PT-AAI	Therapist PT-AAI
Patient A	F5 Secure/Autonomous Somewhat resentful/conflicted	F5 Secure/Autonomous Somewhat resentful/conflicted
Patient B	Ds3 Restricted in feeling Incomplete dismissal	F3 Secure/Autonomous
Patient C	E3 Fearfully preoccupied by traumatic events	F5 Secure/Autonomous Somewhat resentful/conflicted
Patient D	E2 Angry/Conflicted	F2 Secure/Autonomous Somewhat restricting of attachment
Patient E	Ds2 Devaluing of attachment	F3 Secure/Autonomous

With regards to the PT-AAI findings (Table 7.3), all five therapists were rated with secure states of mind with respect to the patient, although there was variability in the secure subclassifications of the therapists from those who were judged secure, but remained somewhat constricted and inhibited in discussing their feelings about the therapeutic experience (F1) to those who were judged secure, but expressed moderate, albeit contained and coherent, feelings of anger and conflict about their experience with the patient (F5). These findings are consistent with those of Dozier and colleagues (Dozier et al., 1996; Dozier and Tyrrell, 1998; Tyrrell et al., 1999) who found little variability in clinicians' AAI ratings, with the majority of clinicians tending to be classified with secure states of mind with regard to their own childhood attachment experiences. In contrast, the five patients' states of mind with respect to the therapist at one year on the PT-AAI showed considerable variability. Two patients were classified with secure states of mind with respect to the therapist at one year, two with preoccupied states of mind, and one with a dismissing state of mind. Given that all the patients were rated with insecure states of mind with respect to attachment vis-à-vis their parents at four months, there is some continuity between the state of mind with respect to childhood attachment and the PT-AAI ratings for the majority of the patients.

Specifically, the PT-AAI classification seems to capture aspects of the patients' own childhood attachment experiences as reflected in their AAI classifications at four months and/or one year. In each case, the patient's own state of mind regarding the therapeutic relationship was consistent with major aspects of how the patient organized her own childhood attachment relationships at one year into treatment. For patient A, the states of mind regarding childhood attachment figures and the state of mind with respect to attachment to the therapist were identical. Although patient B showed improvement in her organization of childhood attachment experiences (moving from dismissing to secure/autonomous), she was still judged as dismissing with regard to her therapist at one year. Patients C and D were assessed as preoccupied/enmeshed with their therapeutic relationship one year into treatment, which is consistent with a major aspect of how they also represented their own childhood attachment experiences. Similarly for patient E; the dismissing approach to the therapist at year one echoes the dismissing themes evident in her AAI classification at year one (CC/Ds1/E2). These findings suggest that the PT-AAI in combination with the AAI given over the course of therapy may be useful in tracking the transference as it unfolds over time, reflecting aspects of the early relationship with the parents as well as shifts in defensive and representational structures.

Table 7.4. Suicide and parasuicide behavior change in five patients following one year of TFP (prior year and treatment year comparison on Parasuicide History Interview (PHI))

PHI	Patient	Prior year	Treatment year
Total	A	4	3
	B	6	1
	C	25	12
	D	6	1
	E	65	230
Parasuicide	A	2	0
	B	0	1
	C	24	11
	D	4	1
	E	64	230
Suicide	A	2	1
	B	2	0
	C	2	1
	D	1	0
	E	1	0

The ratings of changes in symptomatology and personality organization are presented in Tables 7.4 and 7.5. These data on the five patients ought to be considered in the context of the research findings on the total sample of 23 patients, since it is difficult to do any meaningful statistical analyses on such a small sample, and since there are some interesting patterns in this subsample of five patients which diverge from the overall group findings. The most significant change for all five patients, which was consistent with the findings for the group of 23 patients from which they were drawn, was the diminution of suicidal acts over the course of one year of treatment as assessed on the Parasuicide History Inventory (PHI) (see Clarkin et al., in press). We took a total of the suicidal events for the year prior to treatment as reported on the PHI for each of the five patients and compared it to the events during the treatment year.

Table 7.5. Structural change in five patients following one-year of TFP – Inventory of Personality Organization (IPO)

IPO Scales	Patient	Pre	Post	Adult norms
Primitive Defenses	A	69	43	30 ± 7
	B	56	48	
	C	83	83	
	D	72	34	
	E	53	60	
Identity Diffusion	A	72	45	38 ± 9
	B	63	62	
	C	83	90	
	D	67	29	
	E	61	56	
Reality Testing	A	61	31	22 ± 6
	B	51	46	
	C	53	47	
	D	49	23	
	E	38	56	
Normal	A	53	55	
	B	33	57	
	C	49	80	
	D	50	75	
	E	70	83	

However, if we examine the data for individual patients, we see that while patients A, C and D showed a diminution of these behaviors, patients B and E did not. Upon closer look, we see that although patient

E showed an increase in self-reported parasuicidal behaviors, she was actually demonstrating low levels of parasuicidal behaviors (holding her finger under hot water) throughout treatment. She began to report these behaviors as parasuicidal only when she became more aware in treatment that these behaviors represented an expression of self-destructive tendencies. Patient B reported no parasuicidal behaviors at the beginning of treatment and admitted to one such behavior at the end of treatment. Patient B was also the only patient rated as dismissing (Ds2) with regard to childhood attachment on the AAI at admission to the study and rated as secure (F1) at one year. The increase in her report of parasuicidal behaviors may in fact accompany a diminution of the dismissing dynamics that have been associated with under-reporting of symptoms in patients who are observed by clinicians to be highly symptomatic.

Table 7.5 shows changes in personality organization for the five patients as measured by the IPO after one year of therapy. On the measure of personality organization, there was minimal change on the subscales for all five patients after one year of treatment, which is consistent with the idea that borderline patients will not show changes in level of personality organization from borderline to neurotic in such a time span. However, there are significant improvements over the year of treatment for the group of five patients on the Normal scale that assesses the quality of object relations. The greatest degree of change was observed in patients A and D. In fact patient A's scores went from above the inpatient norms at admission to slightly above the non-clinical sample norm scores at one year. Since a major goal of TFP is to ameliorate the pathogenic object relations and defenses that lead to chronic affective, behavioral and cognitive disturbances in borderline patients, it is not surprising that the greatest area of change is in the arena of object relations.

Finally, as was the case with the larger sample of 23 patients from which our subsample of five was drawn, the patients tended to show a significant reduction in service utilization including number of hospitalizations (Clarkin et al., 2001).

Clinical examples

Unresolved/Preoccupied patients: patients A and C

We shall present four cases in greater depth, including excerpts from the AAI and PT-AAI interviews, in order to illustrate the application of attachment theory and research to the therapy dyad. The four patients include two who were initially rated with preoccupied states of mind and two who were initially rated with dismissing states of mind with respect to attachment on the AAI.

Brief history: patient A

Patient A was the only child in a family that was chaotic and enmeshed, partly as a result of a major traumatic accident that occurred before her birth. She had a brother who was killed as a result of injuries sustained when he was hit by a car, two years before the patient's birth. Her brother had suffered a serious head injury as a result of the accident, and he died during surgery following the accident. Subsequently, patient A's mother developed a chronic illness and depended on patient A for emotional and physical caretaking. Patient A described her relationship with her mother as 'joined at the hip.' Patient A thought her parents believed her to be the reincarnation of the child; at one point they shaved her head so that she would resemble her brother who had had his head shaved after the accident. Her father, a research scientist, was an alcoholic who she described as alternately cruel, seductive and pathetic. The parents frequently separated and reunited during patient A's childhood, and both eroticized their relationship with her by engaging in a number of overt and covert sexualized interactions. In addition, she recollected various bizarre and traumatic incidents from her childhood, including witnessing her father drowning her pets.

The clinical course for patient A during the first year of therapy was extremely tempestuous, and punctuated by ongoing urges towards self-mutilation. It was necessary to hospitalize her briefly on three occasions in the first six months of treatment. At one point she engaged in an affair that escalated into a murder-suicide pact that threatened her safety and that of her therapist. After this stormy beginning, however, she settled into the therapy, ceased self-destructive acting out and became increasingly involved in and committed to her treatment, in which she chose to continue when the research year ended.

AAI: patient A

On the AAI, patient A received a primary attachment classification of unresolved (U) and a secondary classification of preoccupied (E), with specific subtypes of fearfully preoccupied with traumatic events for which she showed loss of memory (E3b), and a second subtype of angry/conflicted (E2). As is the case for those with a primary classification of unresolved, patient A's attachment interview showed evidence of a breakdown in discourse strategies and a loss of memory related to past traumatic experiences, as the following passage, in which she describes the violent behavior on the part of her father, indicates.

> We kept getting ... we kept getting replacement pets. And then when they would get full-grown and they were boring, my father didn't like them anymore and he'd get rid of them. But I – all I knew though when I was a kid

is that they disappeared ... And it wasn't until I was older, and I think I was like in fifth or sixth grade and I saw my dad killing my pet ... that was pretty horrible ...he um he strangled it ... I forgot for like a couple of years before I remembered it ... it was so upsetting ... And then I wasn't like sure if I had seen it or not, and I thought you know I must've like made this up...

A preoccupation with such early traumatic experiences was not limited to her discussion of loss and trauma, but generally pervaded patient A's AAI discourse. As is the case with many preoccupied speakers, she also included rapid oscillations between positive and negative valuations of attachment figures as indicated by the five adjectives she used to describe her mother: 'intimate, neurotic, desperate, scared and confusing'. Although she was relatively open and forthcoming, her interview showed many long, confusing, grammatically entangled passages listing the faults of her parents and their malignant influences.

At one year, patient A received a primary classification of secure on the AAI, and a secondary classification of unresolved. She remained on the preoccupied end of the secure category (F5), indicating that she continued to show some moderate anger and resentment towards attachment figures, but was coherent, contained and even humorous about it. She expressed greater acceptance and understanding of her own and her parents' imperfections, and although she was not totally forgiving, she was able to gain some perspective on her early experiences, as the following response to the question, 'Why do you think your parents parented you the way they did during your childhood?' indicates:

I think because they were – scared and – messed up themselves and had had horrible childhoods themselves ... and as much as I – I'm furious at them for things, I really do think that they just couldn't do any differently ... My Mom at least just wasn't – she wasn't physically well enough to care for me – she was paralyzed and ill and that made her unable to see like the gray areas ... And that's what prevented her from learning how to be a better parent when – even after she read the books.

Whereas at the beginning of treatment, patient A's AAI suggested a notable lack of personal identity apart from overwhelming traumatic experiences and her involving anger about them, at one year, she was contained and coherent in her discourse, suggesting a strong sense of self, although she remained somewhat resentful.

PT-AAI: patient A

On the PT-AAI, patient A was rated with a secure state of mind with respect to the therapist although, as was the case with her AAI at one year, she continued to be somewhat resentful and conflicted about her therapy, leading to a rating of F5. She reported that initially she thought the therapist would forget about her between sessions, but that 'there was a gradual change of trusting him more'. Asked to give five words that reflected her relationship with her therapist, patient A chose, 'reliable, dignified, important, mildly frustrating, and confusing'. She was able to support her descriptions with semantic memories. In general, patient A was coherent in her description of her therapist, describing him and the relationship in ways that were balanced and believable to the reader. For instance, she admitted having felt rejected and frustrated by her therapist but took ownership of these feelings and did not inappropriately blame the therapist. She was able to discuss negative aspects of the relationship openly in a contained and objective manner. For example, in speaking about the relationship and how it had changed over the course of therapy, she stated:

> Well in the beginning I, I guess I was a little bit skeptical – about – the whole idea of things being so sort of strict ... I felt that he was pretty cold, I guess ... and then of course because I felt, you know, I was paranoid of those type of things I ... tried to be tricky in a really lame, sad, borderline way ... but uh it was worth it to me at that point ... and now I feel like ... I don't feel like it's necessary to outsmart him or anything and there's probably very little point to trying anyway ... I think things have like settled and all the sort of bullshit parts of me seem to have, you know gone home to rest.

Reflecting on what separations from her therapist were like for her, she said that they were 'stressful' and at times, 'seemingly endless', but they became progressively easier for her to manage. In fact, as illustrated below in her response to the question 'What are separations from him like for you?' she shows the development of 'secure base' behaviors, including valuing of attachment and missing the therapist during separations (Bowlby, 1973; Main, 1999):

> Well, the last one was in June – and I handled it pretty well. In fact, I even quit smoking for a week to show that I wasn't bothered by it at all. But, ... at the same time as that I started to think I needed a new therapist. So, gee, I – I guess there's probably a connection. Um, I didn't think anything was wrong at the time, but I guess I must've been a little bit angry. And this time he's leaving for the first week of January and I'm actually dreading it ...

In the above passage we also see the capacity to monitor and reflect on her own thinking, which is also a characteristic of secure speakers.

In addition, patient A talked about changes in her self-destructive behaviors during the course of treatment. For example, when asked what she does when she's upset, she replied, 'Well I used to try to kill myself.

And you know I got it out of my system.' She acknowledged that now she tends to 'talk about it a lot' or to get dizzy when upset. In her response to questions about how her experiences with the therapist have affected her personality, Patient A again showed indications of being able to use her therapist as a secure base.

> I guess I feel a little more secure in general just because he has been so reli- able as a steadying influence ... I kind of feel like I survive the unreliable things in day-to-day life better because there's something that's sort of steady. And just having one thing ... that is kind of safe helps with all the things that aren't safe. The way a home would ideally feel when you're a kid ...

This characterization of the therapeutic relationship as a home or haven of safety is reminiscent of Bowlby's (1988) conception of the therapeutic relationship as a secure base. Her experience of her therapist as a secure base allowed her to explore and endure the painful and problematic aspects of her relationships and experience, including those related to the therapeutic situation. For example, negative transferential feelings were evident in her feelings of being rejected by the therapist when he would not read her short stories, and also in her sense of being pressured by him to go further in her career even though she acknowledged that 'I can't blame him for it since he's never said these things.' Her growing security in the relationship allowed her to react with some perspective on such intense feelings as those expressed above.

PT-AAI: therapist, patient A

The therapist was classified as secure/autonomous with respect to the patient on the PT-AAI, although his rating of F5 indicated some mild anger and resentment about aspects of the therapeutic relationship. He report- ed initially being intimidated and at times threatened by patient A, whose dramatic episodes of self-destructive acting out (e.g., cutting her wrists in the emergency room and engaging in dangerous sado-masochistic liaisons) threatened his safety as well as that of his patient. Despite the tempestuous initial phases of the treatment, certain aspects of her pre- sentation captivated the therapist. For example, he described her as 'the most creative patient I've ever had', and stated, 'I've had to be on guard because it would be easy to be sidetracked by that.' His engagement with this patient was evident in the five words he used to describe her at one year, 'committed, stable, creative, interesting and enjoyable'. At the same time he remained vigilant about his engagement, since he was aware that her 'MO ... is to engage treaters rather than get treatment from them.'

The therapist reported not being overly anxious about patient A's safe- ty during separations. 'She's the kind of patient who apparently would always make the therapist miserable just before vacation – she doesn't torture me in that way ... so ... I haven't had any reason to think she was a particular risk and I haven't worried about her.' He said that when he thought of her outside of sessions it was less with trepidation than with pleasure and curiosity about her communications, as the following statement indicates:

> She came in a few weeks ago and said she was writing a book. And she'd written a couple of chapters. And that book was about a well-intentioned therapist whose very own interventions that were meant to try and help the patient led to her suicide ... not every patient is as clever as that in finding ways to you know, communicate their combination of attachment and devaluation ... so I never know what to expect, but it's often clever.

Interestingly enough, the PT-AAIs for patient A and her therapist were both rated as secure/autonomous (F5) at one year, indicating that although there were pockets of resentment or conflict about the therapeutic relationship, both had a rational, accepting and even humorous overview of the difficulties in the relationship, and about their respective contributions to them.

Brief history: patient C

Fragmented family relationships and dislocations from infancy characterized patient C's early life. The patient's mother, an actress, met her father while working on a film in Los Angeles. They married and had one child, patient C, but never lived together; patient C alternated between her mother and father's homes on opposite coasts for most of her childhood. Her mother worked in the theater industry in New York and did not want to leave her aging parents whom she supported. Patient C reported that she and her mother were extremely close and that her mother, 'did everything for me.' She also recollected times when her mother left her alone or became violent after going on drinking binges. When her parents were together, they argued constantly and patient C reports that she did everything to keep them together, including on several occasions standing between them when they physically attacked each other. When patient C was 10 years old her mother had major surgery that left her debilitated and unable to work. Subsequently she became addicted to painkillers, and patient C would often return home from school to find her 'zoned out' or in a stuporous state. Patient C's father and mother divorced when she was 12, and after the divorce patient C rarely saw her father, and described their relationship as 'distant' and 'empty'. Despite these negative experiences, patient C talked about her family in a somewhat hallowed way, and remained preoccupied with pleasing her parents. Although she married at a young age she remained extremely involved with her mother, whom she saw on a daily basis and with whom she engaged in various impulsive and destructive activities such as shoplifting and drinking. Her self-destructive behaviors, including chronic but superficial cutting and bingeing, and suicide attempts led to repeated hospitalizations and ultimately to her referral to the psychotherapy project.

The clinical course for patient C during the first year of therapy was characterized by numerous attempts to engage the therapist through self-destructive threats and actions. Patient C reported that throughout the treatment year she vacillated between 'sabotaging her treatment' by 'giving in to her impulses of wanting to really cut myself' and wanting 'this relationship with her (the therapist) to continue to work out'. She acknowledged that there was a part of her that could not give up the 'role of the near dangerous near fatal suicide patient'. She attended therapy regularly and eagerly and was quite forthcoming in sessions, but her chronic, intractable self-injurious behaviors led to repeated interruptions and crises in the treatment. By the end of the treatment year, the therapy had been partially successful in bringing the patient's self-injurious behaviors under control, but she continued to be preoccupied with fantasies and maneuvers designed to cast her therapist into the role of rescuer. When the therapist offered patient C the possibility of continuing at a reduced fee at the end of the research year, she readily accepted.

AAI: patient C

On the AAI at the beginning of therapy, patient C strove to give a hallowed view of her childhood and presented as preoccupied with pleasing her parents, particularly mother; but the overall impression was one of inchoate, diffuse negativity with respect to early attachment figures. In addition, her discourse showed considerable disorganization and disorientation around discussions of loss and trauma, leading to a primary classification of unresolved, and a secondary classification of passively preoccupied with early attachment figures (U/E1/E2). There was much evidence of extreme oscillation and ambivalence in her descriptions of her early experience. For example, in response to the question 'Did your parents hold you?' she replied:

> Yeah, I mean I have to say even if my dad – even though he wasn't really close – like you couldn't get through to him emotionally I mean, I don't feel like I was ever starved – love starved for, you know, my parents hugging me and – um, and that goes for both of them. I don't have a memory of them hugging me ... I mean, I do, I just, you know, it's just um – I mean, I guess it happened through my whole childhood ...

On the one hand, she recollected her mother as providing a haven of safety. 'My mother always sort of protected me and it was just sort of ... I mean even to this day I feel like if I could just, you know ... when things are really bad, if I could just ... become like this child again and just, you know be in her arms or something it would be safe'. On the other hand, she described her mother as chaotic and unpredictable, at times leaving her alone in the house during her childhood, or spoiling holidays and good times with rage attacks or drugged stupors. For example, in support of her description of the relationship as chaotic, she related a memory of her mother hurling a globe that she had given her husband as a Christmas present across the room. She recalled, 'what started off like a peaceful holiday just turned, you know, totally upside down'.

Despite such negative experiences, patient C remained preoccupied with her sense of having failed to please her parents and especially her mother in childhood and still to this day. For example, when asked about the current sources of satisfaction and dissatisfaction in her relationship with her mother, she replied, 'Um satisfaction with my mother, is that I ... I feel like no matter what I do it's never gonna be right and, it's never gonna be enough, and never gonna please her ...' One is left with the sense of a young woman who is struggling to move beyond her entanglement with early attachment relationships, but whose sense of personal identity remains weak and confused.

When asked about experiences of loss on the AAI, patient C showed strong evidence of lapses in reasoning, orientation and monitoring of her discourse. For example, she confounded her description of four deaths that occurred in close proximity, those of her grandmother, grandfather, aunt and cousin, in ways that showed temporal disorientation and lapses into confusional states combined with avoidance of any coherent discussion of the experience of the losses or their impact on her.

At one year, patient C's primary attachment classification shifted to Cannot Classify, with secondary classifications of unresolved (U), angrily and fearfully preoccupied (E2/E3) and restricting in feeling (Ds3) (i.e. CC/U/E2/E3/Ds3). Thus, there was evidence of a shift in her state of mind with respect to attachment experiences and objects from one of pervasive inchoate negativity (E1) to more focused anger (E2) and pervasive preoccupation with early traumatic experiences (E3) combined with defensive attempts to dismiss the emotional impact of these experiences on her current functioning (Ds3). For example, the following passage provides an example of focused anger:

> I always felt close to my Mom, but we were never honest with each other about anger. It was like was never – it was like taboo for us to be angry at each other. And now ... now I'm scared of our relationship because now there's my husband involved in it and – she tends to attack. She's uh – in

the last couple of years I've realized and I don't know if she was always so critical, and I just couldn't see it or if she's becoming critical right now. 'Cause I always used to think she was my strong supporter but ... my mother is like so critical of me, you know ....

At one year, while patient C was more forthcoming about her anger and resentment about attachment experiences, she also attempted to discount their emotional impact and downplayed their effect on her current functioning. This defensive tendency to 'normalize' her experiences with her parents is typical of dismissing speakers and is evident in the following statement in response to the question about why her parents behaved the way they did: 'I really feel like they probably did the best they could ... with what they had ... I guess you know that they, you know that that's, you know, you couldn't do anything better than what you were taught to do, you know .... what someone teaches – how can you do something other than what you were told to do ....'

PT-AAI: patient C

Patient C showed the same mental entanglement, passive dependency, and oscillatory tendencies with respect to her therapist on the PT-AAI as she showed in regard to her parents, and particularly to her mother, on the AAI at time 1. As was the case with the mother on the AAI, the five adjectives that she used to describe her therapist, 'comforting, conflicting, dependent, productive and scary' were quite polarized, reflecting the sense of the therapist as both a secure base and as potentially harmful. She reported that she sometimes found the therapy to be comforting and that often when she reached the therapist's office, 'it just felt like going home after being through some sort of storm'. Patient C described separations from the therapist as extremely 'anxiety provoking', and took little comfort in the therapist's reported assurances that she thought of the patient while she was away. Significantly, she likened herself to an infant who is unable to evoke any representation of her mother in her absence, and is unable to be soothed by her presence, as the following passage indicates:

> She (the therapist) said she'd think about me, you know? But it's like I said yesterday, it would be very hard to understand, you know, it – it, it feels like, you know, you go through the door and that's it, you know. And, um, – and I always liken that to, like I guess a baby and an in, crying and sees its mother, and then cry when the, the moment the mother walks away it's like, Oh, she's not there and ... started crying again.

The above description of her responses to separation from the therapist is strikingly similar to the Strange Situation (Ainsworth et al., 1978) behaviors of infants rated with anxious-ambivalent attachment. Anxious ambivalent infants (type C) have been observed to display high levels of negative affect and/or to display mixed negative affects (anger, fear, and desire for comfort). Such infants have been observed to cry inconsolably when the mother leaves and to alternate between clinging and angry repudiation of mother upon her return (Ainsworth et al., 1978).

Interestingly, the most striking aspect of patient C's PT-AAI was her pre-occupation with fantasies of life-saving rescue by her therapist. She reported, 'and I, I wanted her to, I wanted her to rescue me, you know, and I wanted to feel that she would rescue me and take care of me instead of me trying to take care of myself.' Her overwhelming preoccupation was not only with being rescued by her therapist, but also with her own self-destructive impulses that seemed out of her control, as well as with graphic fantasies involving the therapist being present as she lay dying. Such fantasies came up repeatedly during the interview not only where relevant, but also in regard to other topics, leading to her PT-AAI rating of fearfully preoccupied by traumatic events or E3. Despite indications throughout the PT-AAI that she experienced her therapist as a soothing containing object, she stated that when she was upset during the course of the treatment, her first thought was to hurt herself. She also reported that the primary function of this preoccupation with self-injury devolved from her fantasy that it was the most effective way to engage her treaters. On the PT-AAI she repeatedly elaborated a fantasy of cutting herself, bleeding to the point of death, being taken unconscious to the hospital and awakening to find the concerned faces of her therapist and psychopharmacologist hovering over her. For example, in response to the question about how her therapist responded when she was upset, she became absorbed in such a fantasy:

> I guess my fantasy about it would be, um, I'd just want her to take care of me, you know ... so I have told her that I've, you know, that, like, if, you know, one day someone could, oh, you could have this fantasy about the way you wanted it and that would be that someone would, and this came from having a dream similar to this um, that I would be, I don't know, found in a – hot bathtub, you know, bleeding and that she (the therapist) and Person 2 (her psychopharmacologist) would, you know, whether I lived, it depended on them that, I don't want, there are times where I don't want – myself to be surviving because of me, I want it to be because they rescued me. You know, or took care of me, and stuff like that.

In the above passage we see the immersion in terrifying dreams and fantasies characteristic of those rated as fearfully preoccupied with traumatic events. Patient C concluded by saying that she knew that if she acted on these impulses, it could 'definitely end my treatment, you know. I mean, it's definitely not saying that I want to be in treatment'. Thus, her attachment to her therapist conflicted with her attachment to self-destructive behaviors, which for this patient functioned as an attachment object in its own right (Holmes, 1996).

Over the course of the treatment year, patient C came to see her self-destructive behaviors and cravings for rescue from the therapist as attempts to reverse her early relationship with her mother, who numbed herself with drugs and who looked to the patient for caretaking. 'I had to be there for her and take care of her,' she stated, and 'now I guess I want to do the same thing and I feel it's my turn'. That such insights were only partially successful in limiting patient C's self-destructive behaviors may be attributed in part to her lack of any consistent identity apart from such object relational scenarios of rescued/rescuer, and to her fearful preoccupation with these scenarios, past and present, in fantasy and reality, which invade the discourse of her PT-AAI.

PT-AAI: therapist, patient C

Perhaps as a result of patient C's preoccupation with such scenarios, and with casting all current relationships into their procrustean bed, the therapist had a difficult time describing her relationship with patient C apart from them. The five words that she offered to describe the patient, 'suspicious, tentative, uneasy, false, doomed', conveyed the combination of incisive candor balanced by reflectiveness, and moderate anger contained by rueful humor that characterized the therapist's PT-AAI. The therapist gave compelling and vivid examples to illustrate these adjectives. For example, in response to the word 'doomed' she expressed her concern about the ways in which patient C's attachment to self-destructive fantasies and actions consistently undermined her treatment.

> I think, that this is a hopeless case. I think that her pleasure in, uh, creating melodramas is so great that nothing can compete with it. She is an addictive kind of person. I think she's addicted to her fantasy, and ah, nothing could ever be better than, than that.

The therapist stated candidly that patient C's overwhelming and fearful preoccupation with traumatic fantasies and events posed formidable obstacles to a successful treatment. Although in fact suicide attempts and parasuicidal gestures diminished for this patient over the course of the treatment year (by over 50 per cent compared to the year prior to treatment), the focus on suicidal behaviors, fantasies and ideation reflected the patient's fearful preoccupation with the trauma of self-injury. As is characteristic of speakers with secure states of mind with respect to attachment, the therapist readily acknowledged her own contributions to the difficulties in this treatment, and showed a sense of ease with the imperfection in herself as a therapist. For example, the therapist ruefully acknowledged that her work with patient C was rendered more difficult by the ways in which she saw the disliked as well as the valued aspects of herself reflected in the patient. For example, she stated, 'there are certain aspiring sublimatory, sublimating aspects of my character that I see in her in miniature', adding that she appreciated the fact that the patient was going to school, read a lot and wrote a lot and wanted to learn. Further, she showed some appreciation of the rudimentary gains made in the treatment, describing such gains as the 'very gradual, incremental creep ... toward, um, I wouldn't say toward genuineness, but toward pre-genuineness'. For the most part, however, the therapist took a humorous and rueful stance about her work with this patient, despite the glimmers of angry preoccupation or derogating dismissal in her PT-AAI interview noted above. She showed a great deal of insight and compassion about the transference distortions that fueled patient C's chronic self-injurious behaviors, even while she expressed some sadness about her inability to help the patient to totally eliminate these behaviors. For example, when asked why the patient acted the way she did, she replied that patient C's repeated self-injurious behaviors devolved from her experience 'of the other person as ... as zoned out' and unavailable, like her mother who abandoned her emotionally. The therapist concluded by stating that patient C's behavior throughout the treatment year could be understood as an 'alternation between being and having, this zoned out mother'.

Summary

It is significant that in the two cases described above, the patients had virtually identical AAI ratings at the beginning of treatment, while the therapists had identical ratings on the PT-AAI at one year. Further, both patients showed improvements in suicidal and parasuicidal gestures on the PHI. Yet the course of treatment and treatment outcome for the two patients differed significantly. Both patients were initially classified with unresolved/preoccupied states of mind on the AAI at four months. However, patient A shifted to a secure, autonomous classification on the AAI at one year, and showed improvements in personality organization as measured by the IPO. Patient C, on the other hand, continued to be rated with an insecure attachment classification at one year, although she showed a shift to Cannot Classify attachment status, and minimal change in personality organization on the IPO. In addition, although the therapists of both patients were classified as secure/autonomous (F5) on the

PT-AAI at one year, patient A was reclassified with a secure state of mind with respect to her therapist, while patient C was classified with a preoccupied state of mind.

We can surmise that the differences in the therapeutic process and outcome for the two patients is reflected in and devolves from the differences in the nature of the transference relationship, which is captured by the PT-AAI ratings. Patient A was able to find a secure base in the therapeutic relationship that helped to contain and detoxify the heinous projections and near violent enactments that characterized the early phases of the treatment. Further, the therapist was able to tolerate the welter of pleasurable and frightening feelings she evoked in him, and to use them to therapeutic advantage. In contrast, patient C's fearful experiences related to attachment pervaded the therapeutic relationship, leading to her PT-AAI classification of E3. Patient C could not control or shift her attention away from her preoccupation with traumatic frightening events, but was driven to reenact them in relation to the therapist, despite the indications of the therapist's capacity to coherently express her own sometimes conflictual and angry feelings towards the patient.

Dismissing patients: patients B and D

Brief history: patient B

Patient B was from a family that she depicted as cold, conflictual and combative, with embattled parents who were minimally attentive and affectionate. She reported having few memories of her parents, who for their part sometimes forgot her birthday. Her father, who was severely depressed, was often absent for weeks at a time and, when present, was sporadically violent, on one occasion driving a car into the house. She described her mother as alternately affectionate and rejecting. The family environment, according to the patient, was: 'Just cold ... It was empty ... not much furniture ... Everything was slate and stone, and she (mother) just never did anything to make it warm. It was like, really cold ... there was nothing warm ... It was just cold ...' The patient states that as a child she felt that she was not really important and that no one would care if she were not there.

Patient B's clinical course was relatively smooth and uneventful, despite the fact that she had been referred to our project by another therapist who terminated with her after she made a near lethal suicide attempt that seemed to come out of the blue. Although patient B dutifully participated in one year of treatment, her engagement with her therapist remained somewhat limited and self-protective. In her retrospective account of the therapy at one year, she characterized her therapist as 'concerned' about her and 'interested' in what she had to say, but she described their relationship as 'not that personal'. Patient B reported that the therapy definitely helped her, and made her 'realize more about myself ... why I do things and why I feel the way I feel sometimes, and you know where it comes from.' Indeed, she made significant gains during the treatment year, including committing herself to one of the several relationships she had been juggling, returning to school to earn an advanced degree, and ceasing all self-destructive acting out. Partly as a result of these gains and his sense that she could go further, the therapist reported that he was surprised and disappointed when she ended treatment at the end of the one year required by the research project. He felt that she was retreating from exploring what could help her to enrich her life. He described their relationship as 'formal and distant ... she would kind of close off to what I was saying and dismiss it in a devaluing way'.

AAI: patient B

Patient B had a barren and constricted manner of expressing herself on the AAI, and initially received a primary classification of dismissing of attachment (D), with the specific subtype of devaluing of attachment (Ds2). She could recall few memories of her childhood and depicted her parents in a uniformly detached and/or derogating manner. She also minimized the significance of attachment relationships and associated feelings, focusing instead on her personal strengths and autonomy in childhood and currently. The words that came to mind in describing her relationship with her mother were 'cold, sometimes warm, not very motherly, calm and sparse', but she could provide only the barest specific memories to back up her generalizations. 'It's just a feeling ... I don't even really remember that much of it. It's strange but I don't really remember my interactions with her really well ... there's very little I really remember.' Instead she kept reiterating that the family environment was 'Just cold ... our whole house was kind of that way ... nothing warm or inviting about it ... We never had a family room ... It was empty ... not much furniture ... Everything was slate and stone.' The patient stated that as a child she felt upset a lot, and used to retreat to an attic hideaway where she comforted herself in isolation. The five words she chose to describe her childhood relationship with her father, 'tumultuous, scaring, loud, violent and [I] felt guilty' were more vivid and specific. But generally, like most dismissing speakers, she tended to distance herself from attachment experiences and affects and to discount their impact on her current functioning, as indicated in the following response to the question of how having lived with her father's episodic threats and acts of violence might influence her now as an adult: 'I'm sure it must but I don't know how really. I mean, I'm sure if, you know, if you have a great, you know perfectly adjusted childhood it probably helps you as a result. But I don't know specifically how it affects me.' Or, she tended to put a positive cast on negative experiences. For example, in response to the question 'Why do you think your parents behaved the way they did during your childhood?', patient B replied:

> I think, they just, that's them. I think it was the best that they could do and that's their personalities and, you know ... I just think that was ... it wasn't intentional. I mean, I don't think that ... that's just the way they are. And they were trying to do better than their parents had done ... that was just their personalities.

At one year, patient B was reclassified with a secure state of mind with respect to attachment, although she remained on the dismissing end of secure. Her classification of (F1) indicates that she had re-evaluated and consciously 'set aside' early disappointing attachment relationships and redirected her attention to new experiences and relationships. In contrast to her initial AAI responses, which were detached and poorly substantiated, at one year, she was clear, simple, concise and coherent in expressing her feelings about attachment relationships and experiences, and often got to the heart of the matter. For example, she was able to portray her parents' inadequacies more forthrightly, while still being somewhat forgiving towards her parents, as the following response to the question, 'why do you think your parents behaved the way they did during your childhood?' indicates:

> I think they did the best they knew how ... my mother was one of ten children and to her we had a good life compared to what she had. She had a bad life or she thought – you know – her father used to run away ... and she didn't have enough to eat or even a room when she was growing up. So for us to even have a bedroom ... even though she never had any idea of how to make it warm ... or some place a child would want to be in, to her it was just nice that ... we had it.

Compared with her response to the same question at four months, her response at one year showed increased openness and capacity to take her parents' point of view, without the defensive distance that was evident in her earlier response. Although, at one year, she still remained somewhat constricted in her discussion of attachment experiences and relationships she did not block, avoid questions, or derogate attachment relationships, as was the case in her earlier interview.

PT-AAI: patient B

Patient B's evaluation of her therapist and the treatment on the PT-AAI suggests that she struggled to deactivate or dismiss her emotions and thoughts in the relationship. On the PT-AAI, she described her therapist as 'professional', 'controlled' 'understanding' and 'concerned' about her, but said that their relationship was 'not that personal'. The few episodic memories that she offered to illustrate these five words were rather vague and unconvincing. About the therapist being concerned about her, she stated, 'I think he was always concerned, like he always seemed interested ... you know in what I was talking about.' She also minimized the significance of separations from the therapist and reported not feeling anything when informed about an upcoming vacation, but stated 'maybe there was once or twice when I got depressed when he was away and I said to myself that I couldn't wait till he came back ... but I didn't really miss him greatly when he left.' In general, patient B was able to access both positive and negative aspects of the relationship, but she tended to minimize negative qualities with 'upbeat' statements and to emphasize her personal strengths. For example, when asked how the therapist responded when she was upset, she added, 'He'd ... give me an idea of why I was feeling the way I was feeling ... Um I didn't get that upset this year.' In general she minimized the impact of the relationship on her functioning, and showed little insight into why her therapist did therapy the way he did. For example, in speaking about the relationship and its effects, patient B stated:

> Um ... I don't know ... when we started, you know, actually setting up sessions it was more, you know regimented and more, um, structured and um ... you know, I don't think our relationship changed ... I didn't really know him in the beginning anyway so it didn't really, you know, change. It was just that he was a little different the first two times I met with him, than – he was afterwards. I – I don't know – I mean ... I don't know. I can't really say what my relationship was with him exactly ... I don't know.

At other times, patient B reported that the therapy definitely helped her and made her 'realize more about myself ... why I do things and why I feel the way I feel, and you know, where it comes from.' However, other statements indicated that the therapeutic explorations challenged her tendency to distance herself from the affective experience of relationships – which undoubtedly contributed to her decision to terminate after one year when the research year ended. For example, she stated:

> I didn't want him or anybody to know I was angry ... consciously, I didn't know I didn't want anybody to know, if you know what I mean. But he'd say

or start digging into things and find out why I was angry and then I'd realize something really made me mad, but I didn't want to be mad. With my parents, for example, I didn't want to be angry with them.

In the above statement there is also a sense of heightened anxiety and insecurity that has been associated with a shift from dismissing to secure attachment organization (Hazan and Shaver, 1994). Although she remained defensively distanced from the relationship with her therapist, the experience clearly allowed her a safe base to begin to explore and understand herself and the nature of her relationship with her parents.

PT-AAI: therapist, patient B

On the PT-AAI, the therapist was somewhat unilateral in describing his relationship with patient B as evidenced in the five words he chose to describe it: 'distant, rigid, formal, cold and superficial'. He reported feelings of rejection and exclusion from her life, and freely acknowledged his frustration with her tendency to 'close off to what I was saying and dismiss it in a devaluing way'. He stated:

> I don't think she ever wanted me to see everything going on inside of her, so she would be well behaved and withholding at the same time ... it was hard to figure out how to get to the deeper levels ... we did make some progress with that ... But on the whole I'd say that the relationship was formal, distant.

The therapist reported that he rarely thought about patient B outside of the treatment situation, and that he had no fantasies about her. Acknowledging that he felt rejected and disappointed by patient B's decision to leave treatment after one year, he understood it as patient B's way of turning the tables on others by whom she felt 'chronically dismissed'. The therapist stated:

> She seemed to have identification with narcissistic cold rejecting parents who left her feeling very tenuous about her claim on just being alive. She always seemed to feel like an afterthought and resented not being more of a priority in the lives of people ... She seemed to be extremely wary of any connection to anybody because it didn't register to her that it could be real, and so she walled herself off in an isolated, protected state, and simultaneously, without much awareness, treated people with the very narcissistic indifference that she felt she was the object of.

Interestingly, on the PT-AAI whereas the therapist was classified with a secure state of mind with respect to patient B (F3), she was classified with a dismissing state of mind with respect to the therapist (Ds3), which close-ly approximated her original state of mind with respect to her early attachment relationships (Ds2). There are slight differences between these two classifications that denote some change. Whereas in Ds2 tran-scripts, speakers often express a unilateral derogation of attachment relationships and experiences that are not well recollected, in Ds3 tran-scripts, speakers show some capacity to recall and recount negative experiences, but the expression of feelings about these experiences remains somewhat restricted and the individual claims to have been ultimately strengthened by them. The slight difference may have afforded patient B just enough of a platform from which to begin to tentatively understand her early experiences and their impact on her development, resulting in her eventual autonomous stance regarding her early experi-ences after one year of therapy.

Brief history: patient D

Patient D's family was fragmented by her mother's sudden death from a brain aneurysm when patient D was 5. After her mother's death, she and her younger sister and brother were 'constantly pushed from person to person'. They lived briefly with their father, but he was unable to cope with the demands of raising three children. At times he was violent, and she recalled threatening and abusive behaviors on her father's part towards herself and her siblings. Eventually she and her siblings were sent to live with foster parents, who later adopted them. Although her foster parents provided a home for them, patient D stated, 'They never became my parents.' From the time of their adoption when patient D was 8, she had only intermittent contact with her father, who would visit irregularly, at one point going for over a year without seeing her and her siblings.

Patient D's foster mother developed breast cancer while the patient was in her last year of college and she dropped out to care for her. She found this caretaking role to be taxing and resented the interruption in her education, since she was a serious and successful student and planned on a career in law. After six months, she returned to college, where she began to act out self-destructively by bingeing, cutting herself and abusing alcohol. Her foster mother died several weeks before her graduation. Patient D moved to a different part of the country, and enrolled in law school. However, her self-injurious behavior and alcohol abuse, which had started in early adolescence, intensified. After a suicide attempt and brief hospitalization, she was referred to the therapy project.

The clinical course for patient D during the first year was relatively uneventful in that she attended sessions fairly regularly, and was forthcoming with her therapist about issues relating to self-destructiveness and safety. However, throughout her treatment, she devalued the therapy and its efficacy. Her psychosocial functioning improved markedly, and by the end of the treatment year she was planning to return to law school. Her self-injurious behaviors also decreased markedly by the end of the first year of treatment.

AAI: patient D

On the AAI at four months, patient D was rated with a primary classification of unresolved for trauma and loss, and a secondary classification of dismissing with a specific subtype of Ds2, devaluing of attachment. Her classification as unresolved devolved from her decompensation and hospitalization after her foster mother's death, for which she still felt personally responsible, together with her lack of memory for her mother's death during her childhood. For example, she stated that she believed she had caused her foster mother's death because she had left her in the final stages of her illness to complete her last semester of college. In addition, she minimized the significance of mother's death at age 5, and its impact on her early development, stating, 'I don't think about it.'

A sense of devaluation and deactivation of attachment pervaded patient D's AAI. Although she provided an unflinching portrait of the hardships and losses of her childhood, she avoided exploring the emotional experience of the events she described, and focused instead on her independence and on the personal strengths, which enabled her to survive. Throughout the interview, she expressed contempt for attachment figures and for attachment-related experiences. In general, the adjectives that she gave to describe her relationship with her parents were strikingly lacking in emotional or relational content, and were either not well substantiated or were illustrated with overly concrete examples. For example, the words that came to mind with regard to her mother were 'blue, Coca-Cola, mulberries, aloneness and something religious' while the words she gave to describe her father were 'absence, English leather, old socks, and sick a lot'. In elaborating on 'blue' with respect to mother, she replied somewhat concretely, 'her eyes were blue ... and the um, the uh, dress she used to wear all the time was blue', while she elaborates on 'absence' with regard to father somewhat vaguely, as follows: 'He was never there. And even when he – I guess even when he was – he was physically there I don't remember him being there.' The adjectives she gave to describe her foster mother, 'hot soup, French lessons, yelling, threatening, and snot', do have some emotional resonance, but were somewhat negatively toned. She also derogated this tie as in her elaboration of the word 'hot soup', in which she denigrated her foster mother's attempts to empathize with the losses patient D had endured. 'She used to spoil us rotten when we first got there because we had such a hard tragic life ... we heard how many times ... that we had such a hard, tragic life that it became irrelevant ... but she used to make hot soup and she had rheumatoid arthritis so it was a big deal for her.' Patient D candidly acknowledged that she 'felt constantly upset as a child' but that she never did anything about it because she and her siblings were 'not allowed to get upset'. She also reported feeling constantly rejected as a child, but states that 'it's something that I don't think about ... it's easier not to think about it ... because it could destroy me.'

This latter statement shows striking insight into the defensive aspects of her derogating stance with respect to attachment relationships. In a similar vein, patient D made perceptive observations about how her childhood experiences have affected her adult functioning, stating that she shies away from emotional involvements with others and is uncomfortable with physical contact or affection. She emphasized autonomy, personal strengths, and resiliency both as a child (e.g. 'I used to seem completely independent of them when I was younger though. I never felt attached to them') and currently ('people are easier to deal with if they're not important to you'). She summed up the impact of her early experiences on her adult functioning by stating 'I don't have any sense of security with anybody ... it doesn't matter what they promise ... I still feel threatened.'

At one year, patient D showed a mixed state of mind with respect to attachment and was rated as Cannot Classify. She continued to show pockets of linguistic disorientation and disorganization around early experiences of loss and trauma (U), to devalue attachment relationships and experiences and to discount their impact on her current functioning (Ds2). At the same time references to early traumatic experiences and losses pervaded her discourse, indicating some mental preoccupation with these experiences. Hence we might surmise that the therapeutic work posed a challenge to her stance of cool active derogation towards attachment figures and attachment-related experiences. As a result, at one year into the treatment, she displayed elements of a dismissing approach mixed with mental preoccupation, which resulted in a Cannot Classify attachment classification. It seems that her usual defense strategies were breaking down to reveal the true overwhelming impact of her history.

PT-AAI: patient D

Patient D's combination of derogation and preoccupation with respect to attachment relationships was also reflected in her narrative account of her therapeutic experience on the PT-AAI. The five words she gave to describe her therapist: 'Wizard of Oz, seating arrangements, rigidity, chess and disconnection' reflected the impersonality, derogation and detachment that characterize the words she gave to describe her parents and foster mother and father. Elaborating on the word disconnection, she volunteered that she was never able to establish any sense of safety or security with her therapist, and in fact was hospitalized in the course of her treatment so that she could have a safe place to 'deal with things I needed to work on, including her self-destructiveness'.

> There wasn't an internal sense of safety … Um, only when I got stressed out about things then I felt like I was completely alone. Um, I didn't feel any sense like I could; I didn't feel open enough to discuss everything with him when I was there. I didn't feel a sense of security that could kind of pull me through whatever I was going through whenever I wasn't there.

She did acknowledge that there must have been 'some kind of connection' with the therapist, but stated, 'It wasn't a very deep one.' She described her experience as 'like going to see um, a calculus professor'. Indeed, her interview was replete with such impersonal metaphors for the therapist and her treatment, which she referred to as a 'scientific experiment' or 'chess game'.

Although the patient insisted that there was little emotional engagement with the therapist, there were several indications in the interview of preoccupied anger at the therapist, involving long passages listing his faults and shortcomings. The patient consistently blamed the therapist for the difficulties and dissatisfactions with the therapeutic relationship, at times using exaggerative language designed to gain the agreement and empathy of the interviewer. For example, in the specific examples she provided to illustrate the word 'rigidity', she railed against the therapist's proclivity to connect her account of her reactions and feelings to significant others outside the therapy to issues in the therapeutic relationship.

> Things were brought back into that room that had no reason to be brought back into that room. Um, and if they did, they didn't at that particular moment.

The patient vilified the therapist for attempting to address issues about the transference and the therapeutic relationship. She stated, 'It was a big deal that I would even say that aloud in the first place. Um, and the idea of somebody saying, – 'And how does that relate to us?' – is very … anticlimactic.' The above passage indicates that she was often caught up in angry recounting of his faults and inadequacies, indicating that her relationship with the therapist was characterized by a degree of mental entanglement. Her involving anger towards the therapist ultimately led to the rating of preoccupied attachment with the angry/conflicted subtype

(E2) despite her conscious attempts to dismiss him from consideration. In keeping with her angrily preoccupied stance, she worried continually that he would end their treatment: 'Like I could do something wrong and I wouldn't be completely aware of how it was wrong and I could be dismissed because of that; or I could be dismissed because I didn't fit anymore.' In elaborating on her concerns about the therapist ending the treatment, she reported that the psychiatrist at the hospital who referred her to the project did not seem to know what to do with her, and that they had her evaluated by a number of specialists before they ultimately referred her. She stated 'And it always seemed like I was being handed on to someone else cause I never fit anywhere ... so it seemed like that could very possibly happen ... because it happened before.' Not surprisingly, given the fears of being 'dismissed' expressed above, patient D reported that throughout the treatment year she was fearful of forming a 'strong attachment' to the therapist that would involve an 'unhealthy merging'. When the treatment year ended, she chose to leave therapy, which she denigrated by saying to the interviewer at the end of the PT-AAI, 'You've given our relationship a whole lot more thought than I did.'

PT-AAI: therapist, patient D

On the PT-AAI, the therapist was somewhat held back in talking about his feelings about patient D and her treatment. Although his general approach was collaborative and his interview was generally coherent, his comments about the therapy were sometimes superficial and intellectualized, and he seemed at times to sidestep his emotional reactions to the patient. He described the relationship between himself and patient D as 'strained' and 'lacking in trust' from the outset, and showed some mild incoherence when talking about her devaluation of him and the therapy, as indicated in the following passage:

> She felt in a strained relationship with me from the outset. And in fact that strain and the, ah, the, – ah, ... her feeling of l-lack of trust, – ah continued through the whole treatment. It was, it was a center of what went on between us. Ah, and, the interesting thing is I ah, I would say I like the patient ... Ah, ah, the, ah, from the beginning. So I, I think that ah, even though that she scathing, contemptuous, devaluing of me ...

When asked to give five words to describe patient D, the therapist chose 'adversarial, contradictory, fearful, mistrustful, respectful'. He also added 'hardworking', These words had a somewhat negative valence, but were well substantiated and the anger contained. For example, about fearful, he said, 'her fear of being dumped was continual'. He described one incident in particular when the patient came to the session drunk and feared that he would throw her out. About mistrustful, he said that she was someone who 'had deeply distrustful feelings in the presence of a strong attachment' but stated 'this was understandable to me on the basis of the patient's life history'. At times his statements about her were somewhat contradictory. For example, he said 'she was always honest with me ... so despite the strong evidence of contempt of me, ... I felt treated decently by her.'

Taking some responsibility for his own contribution to the difficulties in the therapeutic relationship, the therapist acknowledged that when he was upset with the patient he would 'clam up ... I wouldn't say much'. He recognized that the patient might have experienced his reserve as withholding at times. At the same time, he expressed liking for the patient, whom he described as 'a young woman with real substance'. His empathy and understanding for her comes through in his response to the question, 'Why do you think the patient acted the way she did?' He provided a visceral image of patient D as 'a horrendously traumatized individual' who seemed to be 'a person in a train wreck bleeding'. He understood her leaving therapy as a recapitulation of 'the shaping experiences of her life that are constantly being enacted and constantly provoking abandonments', and described her as still in the grip of 'heartbreaking' family events, including the mother's death, her abandonment by the father, and her premature responsibility for her younger siblings for whom she assumed a maternal role.

The therapist observed that the treatment foundered on the shoals of a fixed negative transference towards the therapist as an unfeeling, neglecting paternal object who failed to provide protection for the patient. For example, he described a dream of the patient, which illuminated her negative representation of the therapist:

And ah, in the dream, um, she's in um crawling through in the living room of her parents' home in front of these plastic tunnels for kids. Someone dangerous behind her is chasing her. And ah, as she's coming out of the tunnel, her father is sitting in his chair and ah, in the dream is totally unresponsive.

He reported that the patient referred to the dream extensively in her treatment, and that 'at one point 'she said to me speaking of me as that father that I don't provide her a feeling of safety and that ah, therefore she saw me as dangerous.'

This statement indicating that he was somewhat held back and restricting of affect in his relationship with the patient, in combination with statements indicating he cared about her and valued his relationship with her, led to a rating of secure/autonomous on the PT-AAI for the therapist, but with the subtype of F2 (somewhat restricting while still valuing of attachment). As is the case with speakers with secure states of mind, the therapist talked openly about his imperfections as a therapist and about the limited success of the treatment. Although he saw the patient as more functional at the end of the research year, he reported that he was only partially successful in addressing and working with this 'horrendously traumatized' patient's 'defensive omnipotence and control'. He also acknowledged that he 'felt saddened' by her decision to end the treatment after the research year, and that he was left with 'certain ... self-critical feelings about myself' as a result of what he considered a 'premature termination', although she completed the research required by the project and showed major symptomatic improvement.

Summary

Both patients B and D showed evidence of dismissing states of mind with respect to attachment on the AAI at four months. At one year, patient B showed a shift to a secure state of mind with respect to attachment, some increase in measures of self-destructive symptomatology (as well minor decreases on other symptomatology measures), and minimal change on the IPO. Patient D showed a shift to Cannot Classify status on the AAI at one year, substantial decrease on measures of symptomatology, and substantial change on the IPO. While the therapists for both patients were rated with secure states of mind with respect to attachment on the PT-AAI, the patients both retained insecure states with respect to the therapist, with patient B being rated as dismissing and patient D an angrily preoccupied. It appears that for dismissing patients, the emergence of preoccupied anger and/or increased report of symptomatology may in fact involve a way station on the way to intrapsychic and behavioral change.

Discussion

The findings presented above on the patterns of change in attachment organization and symptomatology for four patients lend support to the idea that an understanding of attachment states of mind as assessed on the AAI and the PT-AAI provided a lens which reveals a heretofore neglected and sometime hidden aspect of the therapeutic process and relationship. Our findings suggest that knowledge of the patient's attachment state of mind may help to comprehend the patient's characteristic modes of affect regulation and defense, transference and countertransference dynamics, and responses to separations and endings in the therapeutic situation. In addition, an understanding of the patient's dominant attachment state of mind may help the clinician to understand differential responses to treatment interventions with individual patients, particularly in a structured dynamic therapy such as TFP.

The above cases also indicate that the patient's state of mind with respect to attachment, and the therapist's response to it may constitute a 'third term', or 'analytic third' (Ogden, 1994), which reflects the 'unique dialectic generated by (between) the separate subjectivities' (p. 4) of patient and therapist. Insecure attachment classifications tend to involve contradictory, incompatible working models of attachment (Main, 1999), so that while there is usually one dominant attachment state of mind (except in the case of those rated as Cannot Classify), there are other states of mind that emerge in the course of therapy. As Ammaniti (1999) has pointed out, it is likely that even patients with insecure states of mind have had some experience of attachment security with secondary attachment figures, which may emerge in the therapeutic situation. Hence the clinician in practice must remain attuned to the often fleeting emergence of multiple states of mind, including secure states that may emerge from an exploration of the patient's history and from the here-and-now therapeutic interactions with the therapist. The somewhat different treatment outcomes with patients and therapists with similar attachment ratings described above speaks to these points.

The findings on the patterns of change for five patients in attachment organization and self-report symptomatology lend support to the idea that the AAI is a valid and reliable measure of intrapsychic and symptomatic change in borderline patients, although the findings also suggest different trajectories of change. We shall first address the shift to security in two of our patients, because we were surprised that these patients were judged by independent blind raters to have shifted their primary attachment classification from insecure to secure after only one year of therapy, given the severity of their pathology and our experience that it generally takes years of treatment before such patients make substantial long-term changes. We want to emphasize that a secure state of mind with respect to attachment is not necessarily synonymous with secure attachment overall. We may surmise that the shift to secure status for these two patients indicates a change in the organization and coherence of their verbal discourse, and in the capacity to use such discourse to cope with and coherently verbalize impulses and affects that heretofore were expressed through self-destructive acting out. If one assumes that acting out involves the inability to symbolize or reflect on the internal states of self and other, and that it represents 'discharge to ward off psychic reality' (Green, 1993, p. 77), then the capacity to demonstrate a secure state of mind on the AAI shows some increased capacity to tolerate and represent psychic reality coherently. The findings on the ways in which changes in attachment classification were paralleled for the majority of patients by a decrease in levels of self-reported symptomatology and particularly in self-injurious impulses and actions provide support for this formulation.

The shift to Cannot Classify status in three of our patients who show a mixture of dismissing and preoccupied states of mind after one year of therapy indicates that a reorganization of attachment may be in process. Cannot Classify indicates that there is no overriding state of mind with respect to attachment discernible in the interview, and/or may connote inconsistencies in the individual's characteristic mode of organizing attachment-related information and experiences. We may surmise that through the focus on the here-and-now interactions between patient and therapist in the early and mid-phases of transference focused psychotherapy, therapists are challenging the patient's characteristic mode of approaching relationships and regulating emotions. The emphasis in the first year of TFP on the integration of the individual's split polarized and part object identifications through interpretation of object relational patterns as they emerge in the here and now of transference relationship may also precipitate a shift in patients' characteristic ways of regulating affect and hence in patients' defensive strategies. In object relations as well as attachment theory, each self-object-affect unit or internal working model of attachment is thought to involve linking affects. Hence integration in the world of object relations fostered through TFP involves concomitant modulation and integration of affect, and shifts from more primitive to higher-level defenses.

Previous research does indeed suggest that adults with different states of mind with respect to attachment rely on different defense mechanisms, with dismissing adults more likely to use repression and other ideational defenses and preoccupied/unresolved adults more likely to rely on more primitive defenses of splitting, projection and dissociation (Slade, 1993; Levine, 2001). It is probable that the shift to Cannot Classify status in three of our patients after one year of TFP denotes a shift in defensive strategies. Further, the admixtures of dismissing, preoccupied and unresolved states of mind that are characteristic of Cannot Classify interviews may suggest shifts between primitive and higher-level defenses, which would be expected after one year of intensive psychodynamic therapy in borderline patients.

Our preliminary research findings with the PT-AAI indicate that it is a fruitful instrument for assessing patients' and therapists' states of mind with respect to attachment in the therapeutic relationship. Our findings suggest that the PT-AAI provides an instrument to track one aspect of the transference, the attachment state of mind with respect to the therapist, and to investigate the ways in which it recapitulates aspects of the attachment state of mind with respect to parents on the AAI. The PT-AAI is also designed to assess how the attachment behavioral system of the patient and the corresponding caregiving system of the therapist may be activated in the therapeutic situation, and may affect therapeutic process and outcome. When we began this study, we had expected that at one year the PT-AAI might reflect the attachment state of mind towards the parents at the initial assessment point, and might provide a way of tracking the transference, but in fact we see this continuity with only one patient (patient B, dismissing with respect to parents and therapist). Even with this case, however, there are some changes in that the patient was initially classified as Ds2 or devaluing of attachment relationships and experiences on the AAI, but was classified on the PT-AAI at one year as Ds3, that is with incomplete dismissal of attachment relationships, although still somewhat restricted in feeling.

Thus, our findings suggest that the PT-AAI indeed captures aspects of the transference, but that those aspects do not necessarily directly reflect the attachment status to the parents at the beginning of treatment. Instead they may reflect aspects of the relationship with the parents that begin to emerge after one year of treatment. Furthermore, the fact that the AAI classification changes, while the PT-AAI classification shows echoes of the initial state of mind with respect to early attachment figures, suggests that conflicts from the past are now being reenacted with the therapist, while the extra-therapeutic relationships may be more secure and healthy (at least in two cases).

Our findings also suggest that the PT-AAI may be useful for differentiating between transference as the recapitulation of insecure states of mind that may potentially disrupt the treatment or lead to premature termination, and the treatment alliance, which involves finding a secure state of mind or secure base in the therapeutic relationship. While the development of a secure state of mind with respect to the therapist was associated with the most optimal treatment outcome, the development of an insecure state of mind in the transference is not necessarily inconsistent with a positive therapeutic outcome at one year, as indicated by the fact that decreased symptomatology, particularly in self-injurious behaviors, and/or shifts in personality organization were seen in two cases (patient D and to a lesser extent patient C) who showed preoccupied state of mind with respect to the therapist at one year.

In sum, our findings with the PT-AAI thus far indicate that patients' and therapists' states of mind with respect to attachment in the therapeutic relationship configure aspects of both transference and countertransference, and the therapeutic or working alliance between patient and therapist. The PT-AAI findings suggest that there are various proportions of transference and working alliance in the attachment aspects of the therapeutic relationship. The PT-AAI, like other measures of working alliance, may be 'heavily loaded with transference' (Bordin, 1994, pp. 16–17). As Bordin (1994), Luborsky (1994) and others have pointed out, we need measures and instruments that will get at transference, alliance, and the ways in which they might be discriminable and/or overlapping. The PT-AAI is sensitive to both dimensions of the therapeutic relationship. In its capacity to assess the extent to which the patient has established a secure base in the treatment, it functions as a measure of therapeutic alliance; in its capacity to assess, in conjunction with the AAI, the extent to which the patient has recapitulated states of mind with respect to early attachment figures in the relationship with the therapist, it functions as a measure of transference. Further research with this instrument will hopefully lead to further clarification of these issues.

Clearly, future research should also focus more closely on the therapeutic process that may contribute to divergent therapeutic outcomes, even in therapeutic dyads where the attachment status of patients and therapists is similar. For example, in cases A and C, the patients and therapists had virtually identical AAI ratings (unresolved with regard to loss and trauma and preoccupied (E2/E3 for patient A and E1/E2 for patient C) at the beginning of treatment; with both therapists classified as F5 on the PT-AAI. Researchers in early mother–infant interaction, particularly the work of Stern, Tronick, Lyons-Ruth and the Boston group on the study of change in psychoanalysis, have micro-analyzed the myriad socio-emotional exchanges between mothers and infants that lead to the formation of different types of attachment relationships, and their findings suggest directions for future research (see Stern et al., 1998). For example, Tronick (2000) has suggested that each mother–infant dyad establishes its own unique interactional rhythms characterized by different vocalizations, gestures and facial expressions, and further that the chronic repetition of such micro-patterns between infant and caretaker generates implicit relational procedures that dynamically organize what happens in the transactions and structure knowledge about how they are together. So through such micro-transactions or patterns, the infant learns both general schemes and highly singular ways of being with another that are unique to each relationship the infant experiences. Tronick and his colleagues pay as much attention to the power of such singular interaction processes to reshape the internal world as to the power of the internal world to shape such transactions. Part of the uniqueness of each dyad is the level of thickness or specific fittedness in the dyad. Specific fittedness emerges out of the myriad micro-exchanges between infant and caretakers, so that the implicit procedures and knowing are specific to that dyad. 'Thickness' refers to the range of contexts and activities that are experienced and mutually regulated by infant and caretaker; and to the density of the transactions that may be either positively or negatively valenced. So specific fittedness is generated between mother and infant along with levels of thickness or thinness of the interaction. The concept of specific fittedness in conjunction with attachment concepts amplifies our understanding of the process of change in psychotherapy and psychoanalysis. Because the internal world is made up of such co-constructed implicit relational scenarios, new relational scenarios can modify it, according to Tronick and others. Every time we interact, we co-create something new, with each partner potentially modifying the transactional rhythms and constraints of the other. But in some cases the singularity and thickness of relationships raises a formidable barrier to change, or to the extent to which new procedures and knowledge can be created through transactions with another. Tronick (2000) believes that we come to present interactions with different levels of constraint based on the thickness or thinness and degree of singularity of past socio-emotional exchanges and implicit relational scenarios that they generate. Where such socio-emotional exchanges were very 'thick' in a negative direction, there may be multiple constraints on the extent to which new transactions can lead to change. Such was the case in part with patient C, whose thickness and singularity of the relationship with the mother, past and present, posed formidable constraints on the extent to which new relational scenarios could be co-constructed with the therapist.

In sum, the cases presented above suggest that the patient's state of mind with respect to attachment may in fact function as an important factor in the co-construction of transference and countertransference dynamics in the clinical situation. Just as in the course of development the causal relationships discovered by attachment research are not simple and linear, but rather the result of goodness of fit between the individual's inner organization and the multifaceted contexts in which it evolves, so also the patient's attachment status does not necessarily lead to one particular transference–countertransference dynamic or pattern, but rather a multiplicity of transference and countertransference possibilities, dependent on the goodness of fit in the therapeutic dyad.

Acknowledgments

We thank our colleagues at the Personality Disorders Institute who contributed to the research and clinical work that shaped this chapter, including Drs Ann Appelbaum, Steve Bauer, Otto Kernberg, Paulina Kernberg, Harold Koenigsberg, Michael Stone, and Kay Haran, and the many postdoctoral fellows, residents and scholars who have visited and trained in our institute. We have benefited from their wisdom and expertise.

Notes

1. In the studies of Dozier and colleagues, hyperactivating strategies are linked to preoccupied attachment status. However, the research of Main and colleagues has indicated that that hyperactivation is linked with the U/D (disorganized) status in adults and children. Although individuals with preoccupied or anxious ambivalent attachment tend to maximize attachment, they are not necessarily hyperactivating. Hyperactivation is a concept linked conceptually and neurophysiologically to fear (George, personal communication, 2001).
2. It should be noted that these findings are based on five patients and that we do not yet know the percentage of unresolved subjects in the complete sample.

References

Adler G and Buie D (1979) Aloneness and borderline pathology: The possible relevance of child development issues. International Journal of Psycho-analysis 60: 83–96.

Ainsworth MDS (1985) Patterns of mother infant attachments: antecedents and effects on development. Bulletin of the New York Academy of Medicine 61: 792–812.

Ainsworth M, Blehar MC, Waters E and Wall S (1978) Patterns of Attachment: A Psychological Study of the Strange Situation. Hillsdale, NJ: Erlbaum.

American Psychiatric Association (1994) Diagnostic and Statistical Manual of Mental Disorders, 4th edn. Washington, DC: American Psychiatric Association.

Ammaniti M (1999) How attachment theory can contribute to the understanding of affective functioning in psychoanalysis. Psychoanalytic Inquiry 19: 757–84.

Ammaniti M, Speranza AM and Candelori C (1996) Stability of attachment in children and intergenerational transmission of attachment. Psychiatria dell'Infanzia e dell' Adolscenza 63: 313–32.

Bakermans-Kranenburg MJ and van IJzendoorn MH (1993) A psychometric study of the Adult Attachment Interview: Reliability and discriminant validity. Developmental Psychology 29: 870–9.

Benoit D and Parker K (1994) Stability and transmission of attachment across three generations. Child Development 64: 1444–56.

Bordin ES (1994) Theory and research on the therapeutic working alliance: New directions. In: AO Horvath and LS Greenberg (eds) The Working Alliance: Theory, Research and Practice. New York: John Wiley, pp. 13–37.

Bowlby J (1969) Attachment and Loss, vol. 1: Attachment. New York: Basic Books, 1982.

Bowlby J (1973) Attachment and Loss, vol. 2: Separation. New York: Basic Books.

Bowlby J (1975) Attachment theory, separation anxiety and mourning. In: American Handbook of Psychiatry, 2nd edn, vol. 6. New York: Basic Books, pp. 290–308.

Bowlby J (1977) The making and breaking of affectional bonds. I. Aetiology and psychopathology in the light of attachment theory. British Journal of Psychiatry 130: 201–210.

Bowlby J (1978) Attachment Theory and its Therapeutic Implications. Chicago: University of Chicago Press.

Bowlby J (1979) The Making and Breaking of Affectional Bonds. London: Tavistock Publications.

Bowlby J (1980) Attachment and Loss, vol. 3: Loss, Sadness and Depression. New York: Basic Books.

Bowlby J (1988) A Secure Base: Parent–child Attachment and Healthy Human Development. New York: Basic Books.

Butcher JN, Dahlsrom WG, Graham JR, Tellegen A and Kaemmer B (1989) Minnesota Multiphasic Personality Inventory-2 (MMPI-2). Manual for Administration and Scoring. Minneapolis: University of Minnesota Press.

Clarkin JF and Levy KN (in press) Empirical status of transference-focused psychotherapy. Psychoanalytic Inquiry.

Clarkin JF, Yeomans F and Kernberg OS (1999) Transference-focused Psychodynamic Therapy for Borderline Personality Disorder Patients. New York: John Wiley.

Clarkin J, Foelsch P, Levy K, Hull J, Delaney J and Kernberg OF (2001) The development of a psychodynamic treatment for patients with borderline personality disorder: A preliminary study of behavioral change. Journal of Personality Disorders 15: 487–95.

Crowell JA, Waters E, Treboux D, O'Connor E., Colon-Downs C, Feider O, Golby B and Posada G (1996) Discriminant validity of the Adult Attachment Interview. Child Development 67: 2584–99.

Dazzi S (1998) Some thoughts concerning borderline pathology and fear of aloneness. Journal of the American Academy of Psychoanalysis 26: 69–84.

Derogatis LR (1977) SCL-90 Administration, Scoring, and Procedures Manual. I. Baltimore, Md: Johns Hopkins University Press.

Deserno H (1998) The analyst and the working alliance: The reemergence of convention in psychoanalysis. Madison: Conn: International Universities Press.

Diamond D, Clarkin J, Levine H, Levy K, Foelsch P and Yeomans F (1999a) Borderline Conditions and Attachment: A Preliminary Report. Psychoanalytic Inquiry 19(5): 831–84.

Diamond D, Bartocetti L, Levy K, Clarkin J and Foelsch P (1999b) Attachment and Personality Organization: Measures of Structure and Change in TFP Treatment. Presented at the 30th Annual Meeting of the Society for Psychotherapy Research, Braga, Portugal, June.

Diamond D, Clarkin JF, Stovall KC and Levy KN (2001) Scoring System for the Patient–Therapist Adult Attachment Interview. New York, NY: The City University of New York, Unpublished research manual, in preparation.

Dozier M (1990) Attachment organization and treatment use for adults with serious psychopathological disorders. Development and Psychopathology 2: 47–60.

Dozier M and Lee SW (1995) Discrepancies between self and other report of psychiatric symptomatology: Effects of dismissing attachment strategies. Development and Psychopathology 7: 217–26.

Dozier M and Tyrrell C (1998) The role of attachment in the therapeutic relationship. In: JA Simpson and WS Rholes (eds) Attachment Theory and Close
  Relationships. New York: Guilford Press.
Dozier M, Cue K and Barnett L (1993) Clinicians as caregivers: Role of attachment
  organization in treatment. Journal of Consulting and Clinical Psychology 62:
  793–800.
Dozier M, Lomax L and Tyrrell C (1996) Psychotherapy's challenge for adults
  using deactivating attachment strategies. Unpublished manuscript, University
  of Delaware.
Farber BA, Lippert RA and Nevas DB (1995) The therapist as attachment figure.
  Psychotherapy 32: 204–12.
Fonagy P (1991) Thinking about thinking. International Journal of Psycho-analysis 72: 639–56.
Fonagy P (1998a) Moments of change in psychoanalytic theory: Discussion of a
  new theory of psychic change. Infant Mental Health Journal 19: 346–53.
Fonagy P (1998b) An attachment theory approach to the treatment of the difficult
  patient. Bulletin of the Menninger Clinic 62: 147–68.
Fonagy P, Steele M, Steele H, Leigh T, Kennedy R, Mattoon G and Target M (1995)
  Attachment, the reflective self and borderline states: The predictive specificity
  of the Adult Attachment Interview and pathological emotional development. In:
  S Goldberg, R Muir and J Kerr (eds) Attachment Theory: Social, Developmental
  and Clinical Perspectives. Hillsdale, NJ: Analytic Press, pp. 233–79.
Fonagy P, Leigh T, Steele M, Steele H, Kennedy R, Mattoon G, Target M and Gerber
  A (1996) The relation of attachment status, psychiatric classification and
  response to psychotherapy. Journal of Consulting and Clinical Psychology 64,
  22–31.
Fonagy P, Steele, M, Steele H and Target M (1997) Reflective-Functioning Manual:
  Version 4.1. For Application to the Adult Attachment Interviews. Unpublished
  manuscript, University College London.
Freud S (1912) The dynamics of transference. Standard Edition 12. London:
  Hogarth Press.
Freud S (1913) On beginning the treatment. Standard Edition 13. London:
  Hogarth Press.
Freud S (1915) Observations on transference love. Standard Edition 14, 12.
  London: Hogarth Press.
Frieswyk SH, Gabbard GO, Horwitz L, Allen JG, Colson DB, Newsom GE and
  Coyne L (1994) In: AO Horvath and LS Greenberg (eds) The Working Alliance:
  Theory, Research and Practice. New York: John Wiley, pp. 199–224.
George C, Kaplan N and Main M (1985) The Berkeley Adult Attachment Interview.
  Unpublished manuscript, Department of Psychology, University of California,
  Berkeley.
George C, Kaplan N and Main M (1996) Adult Attachment Interview, 3rd edn.
  Unpublished manuscript, Department of Psychology, University of California,
  Berkeley.
Green A (1993) The analyst, symbolization and absence in the analytic setting. In:
  On Private Madness. Madison, Conn: International Universities Press.

Greenson R (1965) The working alliance and the transference neurosis: In: Explorations in Psychoanalysis. New York: International Universities Press, 1978, pp. 199–224.

Greenson RR (1971) The nontransference relationship in the psychoanalytic situation. In: Explorations in Psychoanalysis, New York: International Universities Press, 1978, pp. 425–41.

Gunderson J (1996) The borderline patient's intolerance of aloneness: Insecure attachments and therapist's availability. American Journal of Psychiatry 153: 752–8.

Hazan C and Shaver PR (1994) Attachment as an organizational framework for research on close relationships. Psychological Inquiry 5: 1–22.

Henry WP and Strupp H (1994) The therapeutic alliance as interpersonal process. In: AO Horvath and LS Greenberg (eds) The Working Alliance: Theory, Research and Practice. New York: John Wiley & Sons, pp. 51–85.

Hesse E (1999) The adult attachment interview. In: J Cassidy and PR Shaver (eds) Handbook of Attachment: Theory, Research and Clinical Applications. New York: Guilford Press.

Hesse E and Main M (1999) Second-generation effects of unresolved trauma in nonmaltreating parents: dissociated, frightened, and threatening parental behavior. Psychoanalytic Inquiry 19(5): 481–541.

Holmes J (1995) Something there is that doesn't love a wall: John Bowlby, attachment theory and psychoanalysis. In: S Goldberg, R Muir and J Kerr (eds) Attachment Theory: Social, Developmental and Clinical Perspectives. Hillsdale, NJ: Analytic Press, pp. 19–43.

Holmes J (1996) Attachment, Intimacy and Autonomy: Using Attachment Theory in Adult Psychotherapy. Northvale, NJ, London: Jason Aronson.

Holmes J (1998) The changing aims of psychoanalytic psychotherapy. International Journal of Psycho-analysis 79: 227–40.

Horvath O and Greenberg LS (1986) Relation between Working Alliance Inventory. In: LS Greenberg and WS Pinsof (eds) The Psychotherapeutic Process: A Research Handbook. New York: Guilford Press, pp. 529–56.

Kernberg O (1975) Borderline Conditions and Pathological Narcissism. New York: Jason Aronson.

Kernberg O (1976) Object Relations Theory and Clinical Psychoanalysis. New York: Jason Aronson.

Kernberg OF and Clarkin JF (1995) The Inventory of Personality Organization. White Plains, NY: The New York Presbyterian Hospital/Weill Medical Center of Cornell University.

Kernberg OF, Selzer MA, Koenigsberg HW, Carr AC and Appelbaum AH (1989) Psychodynamic Psychotherapy of Borderline Patients. New York: Basic Books.

Kobak R and Sceery A (1988) Attachment in late adolescence: Working models, affect regulation, and representations of self and others. Child Development 59: 135–46.

Kobak R and Shaver PR (1987, June) Strategies for maintaining felt security: Implications for adaptation and psychopathology. Paper prepared for the conference on Attachment and Loss in honor of John Bowlby's 80th birthday, London.

Koenigsberg H, Kernberg O, Stone M, Appelbaum A, Yeomans F and Diamond D (2000) Borderline Patients: Extending the Limits of Treatability. New York: Basic Books.

Kohon G (ed.) (1986) The British School of Psychoanalysis: The Independent Tradition. New Haven: Yale University Press.

Korfmacher J, Adam E, Ogawa J and Egeland B (1997) Adult attachment: Implications for the therapeutic process in a home visitation intervention. Applied Developmental Science 1: 43–52.

Lenzenweger MF, Clarkin JF, Kernberg OF and Foelsch PA (2001) The Inventory of Personality Organization: Psychometric properties, factorial composition and criterion relations with affect, aggressive dyscontrol, psychosis-proneness, and self domains in a nonclinical sample. Psychological Assessment 13: 577–91.

Levine HA (2001) Intrapsychic and symptomatic change in patients with borderline psychopathology. Unpublished doctoral dissertation. City University of New York.

Levy KN (2002, May) Change in attachment organization during the long-term treatment of patients with borderline personality disorder. Invited panelist, Integrative treatments for borderline personality disorder. XVIII Annual Conference of the Society for the Exploration of Psychotherapy Integration, San Francisco, Calif.

Linehan MM (1993) Cognitive-Behavioral Treatment of Borderline Personality Disorder. New York: Guilford Press.

Linehan MM, Wagner AW and Cox G (1989) Parasuicide History Interview: Comprehensive Assessment of Parasuicide Behavior. Seattle: University of Washington.

Liotti G (1999) Understanding the dissociative processes: The contributions of attachment theory. Psychoanalytic Inquiry, 19(5).

Luborsky L (1994) In: AO Horvath and LS Greenberg (eds) The Working Alliance: Theory, Research and Practice. New York: John Wiley, pp. 38–51.

Lyons-Ruth K (1999) The two person unconscious: Intersubjective dialogue, enactive relational representation, and the emergence of new forms of relational organization. Psychoanalytic Inquiry 19(4): 576–616.

Mackie AJ (1981) Attachment theory: Its relevance to the therapeutic alliance. British Journal of Medical Psychology 54: 201–12.

Main M (1991) Metacognitive knowledge, metacognitive monitoring, and singular (coherent) vs. multiple (incoherent) models of attachment: Findings and directions for future research. In: CM Parkes, J Stevenson-Hinde and P Marris (eds) Attachment Across the Life Cycle. London: Routledge, pp. 127–59.

Main M (1995) Attachment: Overview, with implications for clinical work. In: S Goldberg, R Muir, and J Kerr (eds) Attachment Theory: Social, Developmental and Clinical Perspectives. Hillsdale, NJ: Analytic Press, pp. 233–79.

Main M (1999) Epilogue. Attachment Theory: Eighteen points with suggestions for future studies. In: J Cassidy and PR Shaver (eds) Handbook of Attachment: Theory, Research and Clinical Applications. New York: Guilford Press.

Main M and Goldwyn R (1998) Adult attachment scoring and classifications system. Unpublished scoring manual. Department of Psychology. University of California, Berkeley.

Main M, Kaplan N and Cassidy J (1985) Security in infancy, childhood, and adulthood: A move to the level of representation. In: I Bretherton and E Waters (eds) Growing Points in Attachment Theory and Research (Monograph for the Society for Research in Child Development). Chicago: University of Chicago Press 209: 66–104.

Ogden TH (1994) The analytic third – working with intersubjective facts. International Journal of Psycho-analysis 75: 3–20.

Pianta R, Egeland B and Adam E (1996) Adult attachment classification and self-reported psychiatric symptomatology as assessed by the MMPI-2. Journal of Consulting and Clinical Psychology 64: 273–81.

Racker H (1968) Transference and Countertransference. London: Maresfield Library.

Sable P (1992) Attachment theory: Application to clinical practice with adults. Clinical Social Work Journal 20: 271–83.

Safran JD and Moran JC (2000) Negotiating the Therapeutic Alliance: A Relational Treatment Guide. New York: Guilford Press.

Sagi A, van IJzendoorn MGH, Scharf MY, Joels T, Loren-Karie N, Mayselless O and Aviezer O (1994) Stability and discriminant validity of the Adult Attachment Interview: A psychometric study in young Israeli adults. Developmental Psychology 30: 771–7.

Schafer R (1983) The analyst's empathic activity. In: The Analytic Attitude. New York: Basic Books, pp. 34–57.

Schafer R (1999) The Contemporary Kleinians of London. Madison, Conn: International Universities Press.

Slade A (1993) Affect regulation and defense: Clinical and theoretical considerations. Paper presented at the biennial meetings of the Society for Research in Child Development, New Orleans, La.

Slade A (1999) Attachment theory and research: Implications for theory and practice of individual psychotherapy. In: J Cassidy and P Shaver (eds) Handbook of Attachment Theory and Research. New York: Guilford Press.

Stern D (1985) The Interpersonal World of the Infant. New York: Basic Books.

Stern DN, Sander LW, Nahum JP, Harrison AM, Lyons-Ruth K, Morgan A, Bruschweiler-Stern N and Tronick EZ (1998) Non-interpretive mechanisms in psychoanalytic therapy: The 'something more' than interpretation. International. Journal of Psychoanalysis 79: 902–21.

Szajnberg NM and Crittenden PM (1997) The transference refracted through the lens of attachment. Journal of the American Academy of Psychoanalysis 25(3): 409–38.

Tronick E (2000) The Implicit Organization, Thickness and Specificity of Infant-Adult Relationships. Presented at: Attachment: Current Developments in Research, Theory, and Application. Sponsored by The Center for Attachment Studies of the Derner Institute of Advanced Psychological Studies at Adelphi University, December 1, 2000.

Tyrrell C, Dozier M, Teague GB and Fallot RD (1999) Effective treatment relationships for persons with serious psychiatric disorders: The importance of attachment states of mind. Journal of Consulting and Clinical Psychology 67: 725–33.

Yeomans F, Selzer M and Clarkin JF (1992) Treating the Borderline Patient: A Contract Based Approach. New York: Basic Books.

Zetzel E (1956) The analytic situation: In: RE Litman (ed.) Psychoanalysis in the Americas. New York: International Universities Press.

CHAPTER 8

Integrating attachment and social character approaches to clinical training: case studies from a Mexican Nahuatl village

SONIA GOJMAN DE MILLÁN AND SALVADOR MILLÁN

> Psychoanalysts are doctors not of the body, but of culture and the mind, of words and symbols. Midwives of meaning. (Gargiulo, 1997, *Soul on the Couch*)

This chapter illustrates four different methodological perspectives that can be integrated into the training process for clinical therapists. We shall argue that becoming acquainted with attachment research tools and with socio-psychoanalytic assessment can enhance the development of the clinicians' observational skills, their insight and their scientific research practices.

To illustrate the methodological perspectives, we shall present two cases[1] from a study conducted in a Mexican Nahuatl village,[2] pointing to the socio-cultural-ethnic basis that serves as an underlying structure for the development of meaning (Fromm, 1941; Gojman, 1997; Millán, 1996; Gojman and Millán, 2000). A clinical vignette from a woman living in Mexico City, who shares the same social origins, will also be presented.

Introduction

The field of attachment research originated in the central idea of John Bowlby (1958, 1960a, 1960b) that 'the mechanisms underlying the infant's tie to the mother originally emerged as a result of evolutionary pressures' and not as a secondary outcome from an associational learning process. This 'strikingly strong tie, evident particularly when disrupted' (Cassidy and Shaver, 1999) has been systematically observed by attachment researchers through the development of a series of instruments that gauge interpersonal communication. These interpersonal communications have, on the other hand, been found to 'contain traces of developmental history' (Sroufe et al., 1999).

The *Strange Situation Procedure* (Ainsworth et al., 1978) is a 20-minute structured laboratory procedure that focuses upon the infant's response to two separations from, and reunions with, the parent across eight (three-minute) videotaped episodes. 'The infants' responses yield three traditional categories of attachment with respect to their particular parent: Secure, Avoidant and Resistant/Ambivalent; a fourth category, Disorganized-Disoriented was subsequently added' (Hesse, 1999a). Each of them has been shown to be related to the way in which the caregiver treats the infant during home observations. 'It has consistently been found that a parent's "sensitive responsiveness" across the first year of life is the best predictor of infant security of attachment at one year of age (Bretherton, 1985; Isabella, 1993; Smith and Pederson, 1988). Parental rejection of infant attachment behavior and particularly of physical contact with the infant predicts avoidance (Ainsworth et al., 1978; Main and Stadtman, 1981), while inconsistent responsiveness coupled with a tendency to discourage autonomy and independence predicts the insecure-ambivalent/preoccupied infant response pattern' (Main, 1994).

The *Adult Attachment Interview* (George, Kaplan and Main, 1984, 1985, 1996) is a 'semi-structured protocol focusing upon an individual's descriptions and evaluation of salient early attachment experiences and the effects of these experiences on current personality and functioning'. The interview is analyzed via an accompanying scoring and classification system (Main and Goldwin, 1985–1996, 1998) that includes a set of general categories for 'identifying five differing overall states of mind with respect to attachment (secure, dismissing, preoccupied, unresolved and cannot classify), as well as continuous scales for scoring the text with respect to both the speaker's current state of mind and his or her inferred childhood experiences' (Hesse, 1999a). In analyzing these narratives, the researcher does not focus on the content of what is said, but rather on the way in which it is said, on the way in which the discourse or communication with the interviewer is structured, on 'the extent to which it is collaborative/consistent, giving a unified, yet free-flowing picture of the subject's experiences, feelings and viewpoints within the interview' (Main and Stadtman, 1981; Main, Kaplan and Cassidy, 1985; Main and Solomon, 1986; Main and Hesse, 1990; Main, 1993; Hesse, 1999a; Lyons-Ruth and Jacobvitz, 1999) or, on the contrary, is inconsistent and/or non-collaborative.

The *Social Character Questionnaire* was developed originally by Erich Fromm (1932, 1984) as a practical resource for studying the interrelations between a person's emotional attitudes, rooted in his/her character, and the overall socioeconomic conditions under which she or he lives (Fromm, 1968, 1970). The aim of the social character concept is to apply psychoanalytic categories to social investigation. The questionnaire comprises a series of open-ended questions that lead to psychoanalytic interpretation. The answers are taken not as raw material or coded according to behavioral categories and are not analyzed in terms of the frequency of each single answer or by factor analysis. The main effort is not directed toward statistical elaboration – as in a conventional questionnaire – but rather to following and focusing all of these steps to interpret the answers in terms of their unconscious or unintended meaning (Fromm and Maccoby, 1970, 1996). The interpretation of the questionnaire may be at odds with what a person consciously believes or thinks about him- or herself. No single answer expresses a particular social character orientation. The answers are scored in the context of the whole questionnaire as a total system (Millán, 1993). It comprises not only the external conditions but the internalized unconscious motivations, attitudes, values, etc., that become integrated through the subject's early relations to significant others.

An invitation to the reader

We now describe two infant–mother dyads from a traditionally preserved Indian peasant village in Mexico[3] in two distinct situations: videotaped home observations (HO) and the Strange Situation Procedure (SSP). We invite the reader to try to match up the descriptions of home observations with the strange situation procedures and immediately assess the accuracy of these conjectures. We shall then shift our focus to these two mothers' Social Character Questionnaires (SCQ) and to their Adult Attachment Interviews (AAI). Our aim is to illustrate the degree to which the four different methodological perspectives (HO, SSP, AAI and SCQ) can complement each other and to explore how clinically coherent they can be.[4]

Videotaped home observations

Case 1: Maria and her baby

(a) As she feeds her 12-month-old baby, Maria is concentrating on non-verbal interchange with her infant. She responds to the baby's signals, giving it the time it needs to swallow, smiling and putting words to the baby's 'obvious' gestures. The baby seems to anticipate its mother's response. It signals what it wants, and provokes the reactions from its responsive mother.

(b) Four months later: Maria is preparing the water to bathe her 16-month-old baby, gathering some in a plastic bucket, so that she can combine it with some more water that she had previously warmed to obtain the desired temperature. Her mother-in-law brings a towel and the baby's clothes. The baby likes to be bathed. It smiles and gurgles, to which signals Maria responds most of the time in her native Nahuatl language, though also sometimes in Spanish. It seems as if they are talking to each other. Maria explains to the baby what she is about to do. She is careful with the soap so that it does not get into the baby's eyes. From time to time, the seated baby looks back at her mother, who is bathing her from behind. The mother notices, and responds by looking at her baby, both looking and smiling at each other. The baby is interested in the persons who are filming (almost as if inviting them into the bath with her). When by the end Maria cannot easily convince the baby to let herself be removed from the bath, she tells the baby something in Nahuatl. The baby immediately cooperates, getting ready to be taken out of the washtub, dried and dressed (Maria explains that she offered to take her baby to the street to see the horse, which her baby loves to do).

Case 2: Celonia and her baby

(a) Celonia breastfeeds her 14-month-old baby in a natural, experienced and familiar manner. She touches the baby's hair, combing it with her hand several times, and touches its chest in a soothing gesture, as if it were about to cry. Oddly, the mother's face seems to be without any emotional expression, almost as if she were in some way absent. The baby barely moves or interacts with its mother, except for the feeding. It falls asleep while eating and continues to move its mouth in a reflexive movement with the breast in it, but without eating any more. The breast slips out of the baby's mouth as it falls into a deeper sleep. Celonia then begins to change the baby's diapers while it is lying asleep on her lap, without waking it up.

(b) Three months later: Celonia is turning on the water hose from the ground to bathe her 17-month-old baby. The baby obviously does not like it at all. It resists being bathed, protests and cries throughout the bath. Celonia does not pay attention to these protest signals nor does she respond to them. She continues to bathe her baby in a mechanical kind of way just as if the baby were not objecting. She forces the baby to stand up. She does not notice that the soap is getting into its eyes, and does not register or acknowledge that the soap hurts. When she is finished, she breastfeeds her baby, who calms down while eating and looks attentively at us as we are filming the scene.

Strange Situation Procedure

Perhaps it is not too difficult to guess which of the following Strange Situation scenes are from Maria and her baby – the first dyad's home observation we just described – and which from Celonia and her baby, the second one.

Strange Situation X

Mother and baby enter the room. The mother puts the baby on the floor and shows it the toys. The baby looks at mother, then at the toys and again at mother. It begins exploring, establishing occasional eye contact with mother from time to time. The baby gives one of the toys to its mother, who accepts it and then gives it back to the baby. The baby looks at the stranger when she enters the room. It slows down her exploration of toys. The baby remains still seated, with her hands down for a moment, while the mother and the stranger start talking between them. The baby begins to explore again and notices when the mother leaves the room. The baby points at the chair, as if signaling that it is aware of her absence. Then it gestures twice toward the door through which mother exited. The baby does not cry, but seems to be upset. When the mother comes back, the baby looks at her and shows her the mirror through which we are taping. The baby then shows the mother the toys. One of them plays a tune. The baby bobs its head in delight while giving it to mother. The mother laughs and asks her baby if she is dancing. The baby bobs its head again as if responding that she is. The mother goes to her chair and sits down. The baby stops playing and looks at the mother, then approaches her a few times, bringing her toys and playing with them with her. The baby cries when the mother leaves the room for the second time. She nevertheless settles down a bit and explores the toys intermittently, combining her interest in the toys with bouts and expressions of distress over mother's absence. When the stranger (rather than the mother) comes in, the baby continues to cry but calms down as the stranger insistently tries to engage her with different toys, naming them and changing them whenever the baby says no with her head. When the stranger picks her up, the baby begins to cry again, resisting the stranger by kicking her feet. The baby shows the stranger the door through which her mother left. The stranger sits down on the floor and the baby stops crying when the stranger puts the baby on her lap. The baby continues to show attention to toys and to the stranger with some crying, staying still for a few seconds until her mother comes back. The baby looks at her mother, smiles, and extends her arms to her while orienting all of her body towards her mother. As the baby is picked up, she looks at the stranger as she leaves the room. The baby is evidently relieved when the mother sits down on the floor with the baby on her lap. The baby is completely and immediately settled, and resumes playing and exploring toys with the mother.

This strange situation shows a baby that is securely attached to her mother.

Strange Situation Y

As she enters the room, the mother places her baby on the floor, carefully fixing the baby's bonnet and placing him as if afraid that the baby will not be able to stay seated. The baby explores the toys a little, crawling while holding them in his hand, and looks to establish eye contact with his mother several times. One of the toys produces music; the baby shakes it and shows it to his mother with vocal sounds. When the stranger enters the room, the baby looks at his mother and at the stranger and continues to play with the toy that produces music, pushing it from one side of the room to the other. The baby notices when the mother goes away, and remains seated as the stranger interacts with the baby and picks him up. He begins to cry aloud. The baby looks at the door, through which his mother left, crying and only looking at the toys or touching them for seconds. The baby continues crying. When his mother comes back he does not appear to hear her call, perhaps because of his own loud crying. When the baby notices her, he seems to be going toward her, but she passes the baby by, and goes around it without sitting down, then picks the baby up who simultaneously avoids being picked up and resists being put down. She feeds it, insistently massaging the baby's cheek, then combing his hair and gently patting his arm. The baby gags and coughs. He sits down. Mother puts the baby down to the floor. The baby cries aloud. The mother feeds the baby while checking its diapers and pants. The mother tries to put down the baby to leave for the second separation but the baby cries and she tries to calm him down with pats on his arm while carrying him for a while. The mother is advised to put the baby down and leave the room. She does so and the baby cries aloud, crawling to the door where he continues to cry until the stranger comes in. The stranger tries to calm the baby, who cries even louder every time she picks him up or interacts with him. The baby cries incessantly till the cry reaches a wail. The baby cries, coughing and eventually gagging and continuing to cry as loud as he can. When the mother calls the baby's name, the baby looks at the mother, crying. The baby stops for a moment and coughs. Mother goes to her chair; the baby reinitiates his exploration of toys but pouts. He looks at the mother while exploring the toys as she speaks to him. The mother extends her arms as if calling the baby to her, and the baby continues to explore the toys, pouting. The mother picks the baby up and tries to calm him down. The baby resumes his crying when mother tries to put him down. The baby explores the toys, emitting at the same time occasional wails.

This baby qualifies as CC/disorganized/resistantly[5] attached to his mother.

Corresponding cases

Maria's baby corresponds to the first strange situation, X, while Celonia's baby corresponds to the second strange situation, Y.

The strange situation procedure with Maria and her baby shows an example of a baby securely attached to its mother, while Celonia's with her baby is one of a cannot classify/disorganized/resistant attachment. As we see with Maria and her baby in the two reunion episodes, her baby's confident expectation in her mother is shown by how she greets her return and by how quickly and promptly she settles and is able to return to play. Throughout the strange situation procedure, it is obvious that there is also significant affection shared between Maria and her baby. The baby shows her mother the toys and engages her in play. With Celonia and her baby the situation is quite different. The baby is enormously distressed and is not able to settle, despite the efforts Celonia makes to calm him down. The quality of the baby's play is poor and the baby continues to wail as he explores the toys.

These reactions in the strange situations were predictable, based on the home observations. Maria was consistently attentive to her baby's signals in both observations. She knew her baby well and was able to get her to cooperate when she was resisting leaving the bath water by offering her one of her favorite activities. In contrast, Celonia nursed her baby competently but seemed absent. She was less skilled in getting her baby to cooperate with the bath and seemed oblivious to the baby's protests, and at times intrusive. The baby's attachment patterns seem to consistently reflect the responsiveness of Maria and Celonia to their babies' needs. This consistent relation between sensitive responsiveness and security of attachment has been documented repeatedly through a number of empirical studies (Main et al., 1985; Hesse, 1999a; and Sroufe and Fleeson, 1986; Sroufe, 1989).

As we shall show shortly in describing Maria's and Celonia's AAI, their 'states of mind' in regard to their own attachment histories with their parents are also related to their babies' patterns of attachment. This relationship between AAI's coherence of mind of the parents and their infants' attachment strategies has been observed in numerous empirical studies. These studies prove indirectly, but systematically, that a caregiver's responsiveness to the babies' needs is related to subtle unconscious but clearly distinguishable mental structures, which are called 'states of mind' by Main (Main, Kaplan and Cassidy, 1985), a manifestation of what Bowlby used to call 'internal working models' (Bowlby, 1973).

We now turn to another instrument, the Social Character Interview, in order to provide a social and cultural context from which to understand Maria's and Celonia's responses to the AAI, as the background structure of meaning.

The Social Character Interviews of Maria and Celonia

Both of these mothers live in an extremely poor indigenous peasant community and speak Nahuatl, their original language. Maria has become fluent in Spanish, while Celonia is barely capable of expressing herself in it. Celonia responded to the SCQ with the help of a Nahuatl translator.

Maria lives in the patriarchal extended family household of her husband. Her husband's grandfather is well known in the village because of his knowledge of its oral traditions; he contributed to a compilation of oral tradition that was published in a bilingual (Nahuatl–Spanish) book about the village. One of his sons (Maria's father-in-law) is an important member of the local Human Rights Committee. Maria's husband has had special opportunities for educating himself. He has just finished his studies, having gone for several years to the state capital to get a degree. Maria's family of origin is quite different. Her father was a peasant who complemented his living with a very small business that for the past few years has also been selling prepared food (tacos) in the village.

The social character interview of Maria indicates that she is in the process of transforming herself, from the traditional receptive character based on submissiveness to one centered on taking care of herself by having an active, independent attitude, critical of authority and intent upon furthering her education, which she pursued against her father's wishes.

Maria ran away from home during adolescence when she felt her father was mistreating her and in spite of having basically been able to rely on his support and understanding during her childhood. His attitudes contrasted with her mother's jealous and aggressive controlling attitude, which became more pronounced during her adolescent years.

Maria believes that children should not be afraid of parents and that one 'should give them the opportunity to express what they feel, to become self-reliant'. Her dreams are an expression of her wishes for her family: in one, she sees herself being married in the church, and having a house of her own with her husband and two children. In a second dream, she sees her baby very happily walking by herself. Then she dreamt that the baby was sick and vomiting. She interpreted this as a sign that she should be more careful with her baby and not let herself be distracted by her dreams of good fortune.

Celonia's husband is a 'jornalero', as was her father, both peasants who are employed to cultivate the plots of land of others. She also lives on a plot of land that has been loaned to her family, where they have built their home out of bamboo.

Celonia's Social Character Questionnaire shows her as a submissive, dependent, traditionally receptive woman. She defines herself by listing socially proscribed attributes she states she does not exhibit, implying that she does not misbehave. Her role in society is, she believes, clear. She fulfills this role by being obedient and attentive to her husband, without acknowledging or valuing her own activities, her work, or even her maternal tasks. She considers physical punishment as an acceptable way to teach children to conform to parental authority. She readily resorts to punishment when her children do not obey her, although perhaps not with the same severity as the punishment her parents used on her when she was a child.

Celonia believes children should be obedient and be afraid of their parents because otherwise they do things they are not allowed to do. Her favorite activity is embroidery, because it allows her to 'earn some money while being near or taking care of the children'. A recent hardship in her life is having to stay all morning at the kindergarten which her 3-year-old son attends because he cries incessantly and cannot adapt to it, so much so that the teacher has advised her to stay, and has even refused to receive him if she does not stay with him.

Her dreams reflect the type of life she lives and the fears and damage that can come from such a harsh environment, but also her own despair and completely repressed violence. In one of them she witnesses an extremely bloody and violent scene in which a man is murdered. In another one she loses her 6-year-old boy in the market of the nearest village and never finds him again.

Although both women come from extremely poor backgrounds, the different opportunities they have had to develop themselves and to use these opportunities to their benefit have had an enormous impact on their lives. As a child Celonia was forced to actively contribute to the survival of her family. The hard life she lived did not leave time to develop her interests or to engage in recreational activities. Maria's everyday living conditions were not easy either, but she had her father's support as a child, and was able to attend school in the village. She also benefited in many ways from the community efforts of Prade, a group aimed at facilitating the development of the people in the village. This outstanding and sustained community effort spanning three decades has contributed to creating for many people in the village completely new perspectives from which to change their lives (Sanchez and Almeida, 1992).

Adult Attachment Interviews of Celonia and Maria

Celonia's Adult Attachment Interview reflects the extreme experiences she underwent as a child. Her parents are scored at the extreme end of the scales of role reversal and pressure to achieve. As early as from 3 to 5 years old, Celonia was forced to perform fieldwork, harvesting coffee, carrying water and firewood, feeding the chickens and the pigs. She says she had to be especially solicitous to respond to her father's thirst and hunger. She would invariably receive a severe beating when she tried to resist him. Her beatings by her father distinctly constitute traumatic experiences as identified in the scoring manual for the AAI (Main and Goldwyn, 1998) and, if lapses in the monitoring of reasoning or discourse occur when these experiences are described by the parent, these traumatic experiences can affect the next generation, as revealed in the Strange Situation Procedure (Main and Hesse, 1990). Unfortunately, we cannot be certain whether or not Celonia manifests unresolved trauma (i.e. lapses or slips in her reasoning or discourse) because her Spanish is too limited. Her malapropisms in the AAI as they are recorded might be a sign of this disorganization, or they could also be the result of limited language abilities. As coders, the language difficulties in translation from Celonia's native tongue leave us uncertain of her dominant classification. It is clear, however, that Celonia's AAI will be placed in an insecure category.

The Adult Attachment Interview of Maria seems to be autonomous,[6] her language is coherent and fluid, despite her not particularly favorable childhood development. Her experiences of her father during her childhood – as inferred from her AAI responses – seem to have been primarily loving (a rating of 4 to 5 in the 9-point 'loving experiences' scales, which was the average in the non-risk sample in Baltimore). We have yet to see how common or uncommon this pattern may be in this group of women. In contrast, Maria's experiences of her mother, as inferred from her AAI, were much less supportive, providing her with very little attention. In the scale of experience that code for inferred loving experience behavior she scored quite low, 2.5. This low rating is in the AAI system considered as an instrumental, non-affectionate but elemental caring. Her mother's inferred behavior in fact appears aggressive and, like Celonia's mother, Maria's mother scores quite high on the involving role-reversing scale. This scale uses the speaker's description of childhood experiences as a base to infer the degree of parental intrusiveness and/or the degree to which a parent uses the child to meet his/her own needs (Main and Goldwyn, 1998). The degree of her mother's intrusiveness was greatly increased when Maria started having male friends and began to date in adolescence (though not to be counted in her AAI scores because of being out of the age span). At that time, even her father ended up losing the understanding and emotionally supporting contact he had maintained with Maria and on which she had relied during childhood.

There are some outstanding signs of what Mary Main calls 'metacognitive' processes in her transcript (see Main, 1991): 'a monitoring of her process of thought and recall which takes place while the interview is in progress'. These are expected to be mainly in autonomous transcripts, and 'seem to manifest themselves in a free-flowing, flexible, and continuous awareness of possible logical contradictions and erroneous personal biases, of the fallibility of personal memory' (Main and Goldwyn, 1985), suggesting also that she 'may be aware of aspects of the appearance–reality distinction, that things might not be as they appear, and indeed appearances are never certain' (Main and Goldwyn, 1998, p. 101). As an example, we can quote Maria's words by the end of her telling why she decided, as an adolescent to go away from her home. Maria's mother used to scold her for coming home late after school even when she had explained that she went to do schoolwork with her classmates – which her mother did not approve of, like most of the other parents in the village, because the reunions involved gender interactions without 'adequate complete adult supervision'. Maria's mother frequently pushed her around and pulled her hair. She says 'People in the village are "very communicative" and especially one woman who used to go to my house and tell my mother that we used to misbehave when coming back from school ... I remember I got tired of being pressured by that ... she believed other people more than ourselves, and yes ... with the fact that everyday it was the same and she used to get angry at me ... *I don't know if we were wrong or they were, or if they are wrong* ... but she believed in what they were telling her and did not try to understand us ... and, as I said, I tired of that ... I decided to go away.'

Some disorientation seems to be present in Maria's transcript with respect to two losses, but both seem to be contained and refer to a repeated confusion or contradiction of the time when the deaths of her paternal grandfather and of her great-aunt (whom she calls 'grandmother'') took place. These seeming time confusions may perhaps be attributed to the possible existence of various other uncles, who are repeatedly mentioned as grandfathers and thus easily confused in her answers. Her score on the 9-point scale for 'lapses in the monitoring of reasoning or discourse' therefore remains below 6, and does not predict disorganization in her baby.

Early human experience and the assessment of interpersonal relations

The theoretical contributions of John Bowlby (1958, 1960a and b, 1969, 1979, 1980, 1988) and the prospective studies derived from it (Sroufe, 1989, 1990, 1997; Sroufe and Waters, 1977; Sroufe and Wards, 1980; Sroufe and Rutter, 1984; Sroufe and Fleeson, 1986; Sroufe et al., 1999; Aguilar et al., 2000) have been tremendously enriching for analysts' and therapists' clinical understanding of early human experience.

The instruments developed in the field of attachment research can be used as practical resources to gauge interpersonal communication, which is transcendental to the clinical practice. The methodological advances in the past 30 years led to the development of instruments like the Strange Situation (Ainsworth et al., 1978; Ainsworth, 1985) and the Adult Attachment Interview (Main and Stadtman, 1981; Main, Kaplan and Cassidy, 1985; Main and Solomon, 1986; Main and Hesse, 1990; Main, 1993; Hesse, 1999a; Lyons-Ruth and Jacobvitz, 1999) both centered in the interacting processes (between infant/caregiver or interviewer/interviewed). Clinicians may use these instruments as a way to enhance their observational skills regarding these processes and to test clinical hypotheses with precision and consistency. These instruments assess 'interpersonal communications' that have been found to contain 'traces of developmental history' (Sroufe et al., 1999). The systematization of some of these instruments has offered an experimental opportunity to refine, calibrate and specify relevant and consistent axes of interpersonal communication.

As anyone who has worked in the clinical psychoanalytic field would expect, 'unconscious processes' embedded in early experiences are transformed into subtle signs or forms of communication (Sroufe et al., 1999).

Individual previous experiences are adopted as behavioral strategies to deal with others. We can learn to carefully decode these pre-verbal messages and understand their 'repetitious' (transference-like) nature (see Freud, 1914).

Just as infants' responses to their caregivers' return after the brief separations – during the strange situation (SSP) – contain clues to their previous experiences with these caregivers, the narratives of adults produced in the interaction with the interviewer – during the AAI – reflect their ways of interacting with their infants. The analysis of these narratives as mentioned above is not focused on the content of what is said, but on the way it is said and the collaborative/coherent way of communicating with the interviewer.

The AAI system for analyzing the transcripts is at once similar to, yet very different from, the way in which we as clinicians work in psychoanalysis: we focus not only on the content or manifest meaning of communication. We focus as well on the traces of individual personal meaning. We then carefully follow how their previous background and personal history get interwoven in the transference to us, dynamically manifested in the patient's interactions with us as therapists. These individual experiences are nevertheless not forged in isolation but through adaptation to and participation in a particular social community and a cultural environment. These factors constitute the individual's context (see also Devereux, 1967).

The social communitarian context and the development of meaning

Erich Fromm (1932, 1935, 1941, 1947, 1962) formulated a socially informed psychoanalytic perspective, one that recognizes context as a main source of unconscious processes and in the development of meaning. His concept of social character (with its Interpretative Questionnaire (the SCQ)) created a frame of reference and a practical resource for developing psychoanalytically informed field research (Fromm and Maccoby, 1970, 1996).

A socially rooted understanding of dynamic unconscious processes recognizes that personal individual experiences are affected by the social institutions (the family, the school, religion) in which they are forged. Developmental history and early experiences are influenced by the socioeconomic conditions which are, according to Fromm, crucial for the functioning of the social system as a whole, and the adaptive responses they pose to its members.[8] This social psychoanalytic approach requires a careful and critical examination of social institutions. It can be developed through the study of 'normalcy', that is to say, through the assessment of character traits prevalent in diverse non-clinical populations (Gojman, 1996a). The study of non-clinical populations creates, for analysts, an experiential opportunity to gain a unique socio-analytic perspective and lends crucial insights on human development (Funk, 1982, 1992; Gojman, 1996b).

The concept of social character was originally postulated by Fromm (1930) as the 'character matrix common to all members of the group' (Fromm, 1932); 'the drive structure, the libidinous and largely unconscious attitude of a group', the 'character of a society'. Fromm took the dynamic concept of character – for him one of Freud's greatest contributions to the science of man – as the basis for his application of psychoanalytic categories to the study of social groups. Thus character was conceived not only as the individual strivings and needs, structured in terms of Freud's dynamic character concept (Freud, 1908), but as the character traits that are common to most members of each group or class within a given society (Millán and Gojman, 2000). These traits 'do not refer to the complete, highly individualized, in fact unique character structure as it exists in the individual, but to a character matrix, which has developed as an adaptation to the economic, social and cultural conditions common to that group' (Fromm and Maccoby, 1996, 1970).

The concept of social character explains how psychic strivings and needs in general are transformed into the specific form of psychic strivings and needs that every society requires for its own function. There is no 'society' in general, says Fromm, in emphasizing specificity and diversity, 'only specific social structures; each society and class demands different kinds of functioning from its members' (Fromm and Maccoby, 1970, 1996). Differing social contexts demand that its members relate differently to each other, i.e. as equals, or as superiors, or inferiors.

The crucial importance of childhood experiences (very much mediated by the child's constitution) by no means excludes later changes in character, according to Fromm. His understanding of social character formation, which recognizes the need for human relatedness as a fundamental key for human growth (Millán, 1996), is impressively coherent with attachment theory and has been supported by the outcomes of its most sophisticated current methodological research findings.

Both Fromm's and Bowlby's understanding of emotional development focus centrally on the enormous importance of early and pre-oedipal phases of development. Preverbal early experiences may have special significance, as posited by Sroufe et al. (1999), because they are not accessible to verbal recall; 'unconscious processes' are set in the initial phases, which are immensely important, but not absolutely determinant, to how experiences become interpreted later on. 'Prior history is part of the current context, playing a role in selection, engagement, and interpretation of subsequent experience and the use of available environmental support' (Sroufe et al., 1999, p. 1). Meaning does determine in a large part what is lived through the ways in which experiences become interpreted, and through these interpretations the subjects become involved in different experiences that can either close or open alternative modes of relation.

Clinical vignette

We briefly present a clinical vignette of a 40-year-old woman, whom we will call Socorro, in order to illustrate how some aspects of the contributing perspectives that we have mentioned have informed our clinical practice. Thus we look at the patient within the large, social, economic and cultural context and within the social context of family life, attachment relationships, losses and trauma.

Socorro is a severe-looking, dominant, very successful business woman, who comes from very humble origins. She had participated (without fully realizing it) in the male–female gender confrontations of a broken traditional peasant family that had to migrate to a very large city. Her father was a worker who had established two simultaneous families to compensate for his lost pride as a 'macho', and his weak dependent submission to a matriarchal social environment.

Socorro entered her treatment with a female analyst after struggling to recover from the loss of her mother nearly two years earlier. The analyst had met her once before that event, but Socorro had not been able to make up her mind whether to start treatment with a male analyst, as advised in order for her 'to work on her difficulties in developing stable relationships with men'. Soon after the consultation came the sudden and completely unexpected death of her mother due to an infectious disease, which her father, who was previously infected, had survived.

Socorro was depressed, full of guilt for 'not having been more aware of her mother's critical health condition' and for 'not having taken her to the hospital when she was pleading to be taken'. When speaking of these events later, she repeatedly tempered her guilt by saying that she was merely following the doctor's instructions and that she thought that her mother would get better just as her father had. The initial work dealt with her unbearable hatred towards her father, her tremendously ambivalent relationship with her mother and the continuous acrimony woven into her parents' marriage. She also talked about her role as a kind of spousal substitute with her mother whenever her father was absent. She realized how she had adopted her mother's role since she had passed away, replacing her not only in all of the housekeeping responsibilities, but also in identifying with her mother and engaging in tremendously resentful and jealous scenes toward her father. She also realized that she was repeating or reviving her mother's eternal recriminations against her father and was experiencing her mother's anxiety over her father's long-standing extramarital relationship, in which he had fathered a number of children. Through the therapeutic process, Socorro's identification with her mother and hatred towards her father began to gradually ameliorate.

Relieved of her conflicted feelings towards her father and towards her mother's death, Socorro became involved, some time later, in a relationship with a man who was kind to her. She precipitously agreed to marry him, even though she was thoroughly aware that she was taking a risk in not having known him long enough or having had sufficient time to develop the relationship. Soon after the couple married, and despite Socorro's advanced age, they had a baby girl. Socorro began to experience anxiety crises, with overwhelming and disproportionate fears centering around 'fatal events that can happen to the baby'. Although the AAI was not administered to Socorro, we should note that such fears of loss of a child if observed during the AAI would have placed Socorro in a rare insecure subcategory, 'Fear of loss from an unknown source'.

In a session, after the analyst had started integrating her knowledge and work with Adult Attachment Interviews, she begin to listen differently to Socorro's references to an event in her childhood that prompted us to include this vignette. She had undoubtedly made previous mention of the death of her 9-month-old baby brother when she was about 7 years old, and how her mother's mourning never seemed to end, aggravating her eternal unhappiness.

As the therapist listened to her speak of the experience, this time she noticed that Socorro seemed to tell it in a disorganized-disoriented way, a spatial disorientation surrounding a loss, as would be coded on the AAI system if she had made this statements during the interview.

While Socorro was describing the circumstances of the death, she alluded to images of the baby as if she had been in two places at the same time: in the first image she is in the room where the corpse of the baby was lying. Her mother had forbidden her to enter this room and thus it would have been unlikely that Socorro would have been in it. A second image was of seeing from the adjoining room, which, as she had stated before, was the room she and her older brothers were strictly confined to.

This time the therapist asked her to go beyond her early statement of fact that 'the baby got sick, from a stomach disease that worsened and worsened each day and did not respond to the medical treatment'. Socorro then remembered clearly, for the first time, that her mother blamed her for the death of this baby.

Socorro and her two older brothers had stayed home by themselves with the baby a few days before, on an afternoon when their mother went out, something she rarely did. Socorro, being the girl, was expected to look after the baby, which she remembers she did. Nothing seemed to have gone wrong until after the death of the baby, when the 'cause of the fatal event' seemed to have been that the infant had very probably ingested a piece of a balloon from the floor, while he was crawling.

In sum, Socorro suffered an initial unexplained fear of loss of her infant child. In listening to her speak about the death of an infant sibling when she was 7 years of age, we observed *spatial disorientation* of a kind that would have been termed unresolved/disorganized in the AAI. Finally, tracing this back to experiences she found herself remembering for the first time in the analytic hour, we see her mother had blamed her for the death of her infant sibling. This external and potentially real-life experience (of course we cannot know the 'real' event) may have occasioned Socorro's extraordinary anxiety, although she did not recall it until the analyst worked together with her on her memories regarding the event that was under her 'lapse of reasoning'.

We think that paying attention to these events, even while they refer to outside external and real world experiences, is essential to the clinician's reconstruction of the patient's developmental history. Those experiences in the outside world become established and interwoven with the internal representations of the mind. Previous history becomes part of and confirms the meaning attributed to the current context.

Scrutinizing individual experiences as well as appreciating their social significance contributed meaningfully to understand crucial events in Socorro's early experiences. These experiences had remained unconscious and played a central role in dynamic aspects of her psyche.

The social and cultural conditions of her upbringing are common in Mexico as a basically feudal social system that is beginning to be transformed into a modern capitalistic system.[9] The dynamic transition of women's roles from a society based on ancient matriarchal and on feudal patriarchal structures to modern gender roles poses critical choices and contradictions. These affect all aspects of their daily lives: the socialization of their offspring, the type of family organization that is being forged, and the type of work available to women outside of their families. Whether this modernization encourages the development of women and brings an improvement in their lives, or whether it has the opposite effect, depends on how flexible a women's character is (Fromm, 1947), or in terms of attachment theory, how autonomous and coherent their states of mind are. It is these emotionally ridden strategies that determine if they can adapt and respond to the process of change, and what use they can make of the resources they have at their disposal. Women's previous experiences and current opportunities available to them have a crucial effect on the development of their character structure and the way they cope with the many dilemmas that they face.

This case shows how the training in the AAI system can encourage clinicians to listen to specific ways of recounting traumatic events. With its postulates on loss and the relevance of the mourning processes, attachment theory is finding its place in clinical practice. Attachment theory has its origins in the earliest biologically biased establishment of a regulatory system of survival: when the individual is physically at risk, the tendency to seek an attachment figure takes precedence over all others (Main, 1999). The emotional link to caregivers and the urge to find relief by being in contact with them can transform memories, the meaning of events and the possibilities or limitations of consciousness (Bowlby, 1979). Attachment also affects the adopted value system, beliefs and social character traits throughout their formation (Fromm, 1947).

Witnessing and repeatedly viewing the subtle non-verbal and transcendental impacts of mother–infant interchange through the assessment of the strange situation and the videotaped home observations as a part of the process of being trained as clinicians,[10] as well as the diverse ways in which adults describe early experiences with their caregivers in the AAI transcripts, and being able to see and compare these diverse perspectives later on, can sharpen our understanding of interactive processes and the ways of communicating. It also gives clinicians an opportunity to be exposed to vivid early processes and to experience and confront the strong emotional reactions that are frequently elicited in themselves as observers.

The relationship between the different attachment assessments and the social character interpretative questionnaire of the mothers, with its more clinical psychoanalytically oriented view, shows that the complementary perspectives can sensitize both kinds of approach to human development. From the methodologically sophisticated attachment instruments we must look towards the clinically oriented view of social character dynamics, and vice versa. From the clinical perspective we must work for a broader understanding of, and focus on, the subtle assessments of attachment instruments, which vividly illustrate the primary non-conscious interpersonal exchanges of the dyads. This confirms once more that the meaning we assign to events is a result of our relationships with others. The processes of socialization revolve around the central axis of the primary relationships with caregivers. The repression of consciousness is rooted in the need to relate (Fromm, 1993).

Acknowledgments

We thank Mary Main, Catherine Silver and Teresa Villarreal for their comments on a previous draft. The research has been developed in the Seminario de Sociopsicoanálisis AC (Semsoac) – a group of professionals (psychologists, psychiatrist, psychoanalysts, anthropologists, sociologists and others) that has conducted multiple participative action studies with the purpose of widening consciousness as a tool for fostering social change (see Gojman 1977, 1992, 1993, 1997; Millán, 1992, 1993, 1996; Millán and Gojman, 1997).

Notes

1. Each of the dyads was assessed by means of: (a) two videotaped home observations; (b) Ainsworth's Strange Situation Procedure (Ainsworth et al., 1978; Sroufe and Fleeson, 1986); (c) the Social Character Interview (Fromm and Maccoby, 1970; Gojman, 1991, 1992; Millán, 1993), and (d) the Adult Attachment Interview, AAI (George, Kaplan and Main, 1984, 1985, 1996; Hesse, 1999a, 1999b; Main, Kaplan and Cassidy 1985; Main, 1993).
2. These two cases are part of a 12-case pilot study of social character traits and attachment in Indian Mexican women (Gojman and Millán, 2000). The village is one of 3500 inhabitants living in the mountains of the Sierra Norte de Puebla, Mexico. They are traditional peasants who maintain their ancestral traditions, and cultivate corn, coffee, pepper and beans. Their culture, Indian language (Nahuatl), traditional medicine, costume, beliefs and legends have persisted in spite of the pervasive pressures of Western modernization.
3. We gratefully acknowledge the collaboration of Francisco Sanchez and Beatriz Acevedo throughout the fieldwork in the community. They both are members of Prade AC, a group that has been working to enhance the quality of life in the village for almost 30 years. They call it a 'synergic process' (Almeida and Sanchez, 1989; Sanchez and Almeida, 1991, 1992), and we have witnessed its outstanding vitality. We carried out the fieldwork with the collaboration of the following members of the Seminario de Sociopsicoanálisis: A. Barroso, J.

Bustamante, M. Cortina, G. Sanchez and C. Sierra. The middle-class Mexico City dyads with whom they will be compared have included the participation of: E. Arriaga, A. Cortes, M. Gonzalez, P. Gonzalez, C. Juarez, A. Rodarte and G. Rosete.

4. The two Social Character Questionnaires were scored blind by Salvador Millán. The mother's responsiveness to these babies during the home observations was scored by Ana Maria Barroso and Guadalupe Sanchez.

5. 'Cannot classify (CC)' as seen in this case (Main and Hesse, personal communication) refers to the infant's characteristic simultaneous opposing attachment strategies. This classification has recently been described in the scoring system as the fifth kind of attachment pattern. The various patterns involved in each case get listed one after the other in the order of best fitting categories (Main and Goldwyn, 1998, p. 179). Both CC and Disorganized categories, found in Celonia's baby, have been found to be not infrequently associated with latter pathological development (Hesse and Main, 2001; Hesse, 1999b).

6. 'Autonomy', as understood and observed by Main and Goldwyn in the AAI system, involves a strong open valuing of attachment relationships, regarding attachment-related experiences as influential and not denying their importance while simultaneously appearing objective regarding any particular relationship or experience. 'Security' in the strange situation also involves on the part of the infant the open manifestation of missing the caregiver and proximity seeking as well as greeting him/her at return after brief separations.

7. A title that is commonly used in these extended families (ME Sanchez, personal communication, 2001).

8. An interesting outline of the evolution of analytic Marxism can be found in Gargarella's book *Las Teorías de la Justicia Después de Rawls* (Gargarella, 1999, Chapter 4).

9. See: Millán and Gojman (1997), Gojman (1997), Sanchez (2001), Barroso (2001), Sierra (2001) and Bustamante (2001).

10. In the training program for analytic therapists the socio-analytic group Seminario de Sociopsicoanálisis has added to the candidate's clinical practice, one year of the weekly Esther Bick's Baby Observations (Bick, 1964). Towards the end of the year the dyads are studied by means of the Attachment and Social Character instruments. The assessments are then scored blindly with respect to each other and to the baby observations. The resultant comparison giving a combined multifaceted view.

References

Aguilar B, Sroufe A, Egeland B and Carlson E (2000) Distinguishing the early-onset and persistent adolescence-onset antisocial behavior types: From birth to 16 years. Development and Psychopathology 12: 109–32.

Ainsworth M (1985) Patterns of mother–infant attachment: Antecedents of development. Bulletin of the New York Academy of Medicine 61: 771–90.

Ainsworth MD, Blehar MC, Waters E and Wall S (1978) Patterns of Attachment. Hillsdale, NJ: Lawrence Erlbaum.

Almeida E and Sanchez ME (1989) Theory and Practice at Tzinacapan, Mexico. Psychology and Developing Societies 1: 237–50.

Barroso AM (2001) In the theater of confusion: Mourning and its consequences for a four year old child. International Forum of Psychoanalysis 10: 35–55.

Bick E (1964) Notes on infant observation in psychoanalytical training. International Journal of Psycho-analysis 45: 23–56.

Bustamante JJ (2001) Understanding hope. Persons in the process of dying. International Forum of Psychoanalysis 10: 1–15.

Bowlby J (1958) The nature of the child's tie to his mother. International Journal of Psycho-analysis 39: 350–73.

Bowlby J (1960a) Separation anxiety. International Journal of Psycho-analysis 41: 1–25.

Bowlby J (1960b) Grief and mourning in infancy. Psychoanalytic Study of the Child 15: 3–39.

Bowlby J (1969) Attachment, vol. 1, New York: Basic Books.

Bowlby J (1973) Separation, vol. 2. New York: Basic Books.

Bowlby J (1979) On knowing what you are not supposed to know and feeling what you are not supposed to feel. Canadian Journal of Psychiatry 24: 120–35.

Bowlby J (1980) Loss, vol. 3. New York: Basic Books.

Bowlby J (1988) A Secure Base. Clinical Applications of Attachment Theory. London: Routledge.

Bretherton I (1985) Attachment Theory: Retrospect and Prospect. In: I Bretherton and E Waters (eds) Monographs of the Society for Research in Child Development, vol 50, pp. 66–104.

Cassidy J and Shaver PR (1999) Handbook of Attachment. Theory, Research, and Clinical Applications. New York: Guilford Press.

Devereux G (1967) From Anxiety to Method in the Behavioral Sciences. Mouton and Co. and Ecole Practique de Hautes Etudes.

Freud S (1908) Character and Anal Eroticism. Standard Edition, vol. 9. London: Hogarth Press 1958, pp. 9–157.

Freud S (1914) Remembering, repeating and working through. Standard Edition, vol. 12. London: Hogarth Press 1958, pp. 109–20.

Fromm E (1930) Die Entwicklung des Christusdogmas. In: Imago 16 English translation: The Dogma of Christ. New York: Holt, Rinehart & Winston, 1963.

Fromm E (1932) Ueber Methode und Aufgabe Einer Analytischen Sozialpsychology' Zeitschrift für Sozialforschung, Hirschfeld-Leipzig. Published in English as: The Method and Function of an Analytic Social

Psychology. In: E. Fromm. The Crisis of Psychoanalysis, Essays on Freud, Marx and Social Psychology. New York: Holt, Rinehart & Winston 1970, pp. 110–34.

Fromm E (1935) Die Gesseschaftliche Bedingtheit der Psychoanalytischen Therapie. In: R Funk (ed.) Gesamtausgabe, vol. I: Analytische Sozialpsychologie (1989). Stuttgart: Deutscher Taschenbuch Verlag, pp. 115–38.

Fromm E (1941) Escape from Freedom. New York: Holt, Rinehart & Winston.

Fromm E (1947) Man for Himself. New York: Rinehart.

Fromm E (1962) Beyond The Chains of Illusion, My Encounter with Freud and Marx. New York: Simon and Schuster.

Fromm E (1968) The Revolution of Hope. New York: Harper & Row.

Fromm E (1970) The Crisis of Psychoanalysis, Essays on Freud, Marx and Social psychology. New York: Holt, Rinehart & Winston.

Fromm E (1984) The Working Class in Weimar Germany. Cambridge, Mass: Harvard University Press.

Fromm E (1993) El Arte de Escuchar Obra póstuma IV a cargo de Rainer Funk. Piados.

Fromm E and Maccoby M (1970) Social Character in a Mexican Village. Englewood Cliffs, NJ: Prentice Hall. Also published in Spanish: Sociopsicoanálisis del Campesino Mexicano (1970) by Fondo de Cultura Económica Mexico.

Fromm E and Maccoby M (1996) Social Character in a Mexican Village. New Brunswick and London: Transactions Publishers. (Originally published in 1970 by Prentice-Hall.)

Funk R (1982) Erich Fromm: The Courage to be Human. New York: Continuum Publishing.

Funk R (1992) Fromm's approach to psychoanalytic theory and its relevance to therapeutic work. Cuadernos IV: Social Character, its Study an experiential Interchange 1992. Ed. Seminario de Sociopsicoanálisis Mexico: I MPAC, pp. 17–42.

Gargarella R (1999) Marxismo analítico y teoria de la justicia. Capítulo 4. Las Teorías de la Justicia después de Rawls. Piados. Barcelona, pp. 99–122.

Gargiulo G (1997) Inner mind/outer mind and the quest for the 'I'. In: C Spezzano and G Gargiulo (eds) Soul on the Couch. Spirituality, Religion, and Morality in Contemporary Psychoanalysis. Hillsdale NJ, London: Analytic Press, pp. 1–9.

George C, Kaplan N and Main M (1984, 1985, 1996) Adult Attachment Interview Protocol. Unpublished Manuscript, University of California at Berkeley.

Gojman S (1977) In: P Reining et al., Village Women, Their Changing Lives and Fertility. Washington DC: American Association for the Advancement of Sciences.

Gojman S (1991) Revaloración del Cuestionario Interpretativo en una Comunidad Minera después de Tres Años de Trabajo Comunitario (Diseño Experimental Pre y Post Aplicación a la Experiencia de Trabajo de Grupo). The Final Report to the National Council of Sciences and Technology (CONACYT), Mexico.

Gojman S (1992) A Socio-psychoanalytic Intervention Process in a Mexican Mining Village. Science of Man. Yearbook of the International Erich Fromm Society; Wissenschaft Vom Menschen,, Jahrbuch der Internationalen Erich Fromm Gessellschaft, vol. 3, Science of Man, vol. 3. Munster: Lit-Verl, pp. 47–56.

Gojman S (1993) An Overview of the Mexican Project of Sociopsychoanalytic Participative Research in a Mining Community. In: Cuadernos IV: Social Character, its study: An experiential Interchange. Ed. Seminario de Sociopsicoanálisis. Mexico: IMPAC, pp. 59–84.

Gojman S (1996a) The Voice of Sentiopil, Son of the Corn. Ancient Nahuatl Prophet for Our Times. Presented at the IFPS Conference, Athens.

Gojman S (1996b) The analyst as a person: Fromm's approach to psychoanalytic training and practice. In: M Cortina and M Maccoby (eds) A Prophetic Analyst, Erich Fromm's Contribution to Psychoanalysis. Northvale, NJ, London: J. Aronson, pp. 235–8.

Gojman S (1997) A socioeconomic dimension of the therapeutic relationship. International Forum of Psychoanalysis 6: 241–52.

Gojman S and Millán S (2000) Attachment patterns and social character in a Nahuatl village. Socialization processes through social character interviews and videotaped attachment current methodology. Fromm Forum. International Erich Fromm Society, Germany.

Hesse E (1999a) The Adult Attachment Interview: Historical and current perspectives. In: J Cassidy and P Shaver (eds) Handbook of Attachment Theory, Research, and Clinical Applications. London: Guilford Press, pp. 395–433.

Hesse E (1999b) Unclassifiable and Disorganized Responses in the Adult Attachment Interview and in the Infant Strange Situation Procedure: Theoretical proposal and Empirical Findings. Doctoral Dissertation, Leiden University.

Hesse E and Main M (2001) Disorganized infant, child, and adult attachment: Collapse in behavioral and attentional strategies. Journal of the American Psychoanalytic Association 48: 1097–127.

Isabella RA (1993) Origins of attachment: Maternal interactive behavior across the first year. Child Development, 64: 605–21.

Lyons-Ruth K and Jacobvitz D (1999) Attachment disorganization: Unresolved loss, relational violence and lapses in behavior and attentional strategies. In: J Cassidy and P Shaver (eds) Handbook of Attachment. Theory, Research, and Clinical Application. London: Guilford Press, pp. 520–54.

Main M (1991) Metacognitive knowledge, metacognitive monitoring and singular (coherent) vs. multiple (incoherent) models of attachment: Findings and directions for future research. In: CM Parkes, J Stevenson-Hinde and P Marris (eds) Attachment Across the Life Cycle. London: Routledge, pp. 127–59.

Main M (1993) Discourse prediction and recent studies in attachment: Implications for psychoanalysis. Journal of the American Psychoanalytic Association 41: 209–44.

Main M (1994) A move to the level of representations in the study of attachment organization: Implications for psychoanalysis. Annual Research Lecture of the British Psychoanalytic Society, London. 6 July.

Main M (1999) Mary D. Salter Ainsworth: tribute and portrait. Psychoanalytic Inquiry 19: 682–736.

Main M and Goldwyn R (1985–1996, 1998) Adult Attachment Scoring and Classification System. Unpublished manuscript, University of California at Berkeley, Version 6.3.

Main M and Hesse E (1990) Parents unresolved traumatic experiences are related to infant disorganized attachment status: Is frightened and/or frightening parental behavior the linking mechanism? In: MT Greenberg, D Cicchetti and MG Commings (eds) Attachment in the Preschool Years: Theory, Research and Intervention. Chicago: University of Chicago Press, pp. 161–82.

Main M and Solomon J (1986) Discovery of a new insecure, Disorganized/Disoriented attachment pattern. In: TB Brazelton and M Yugman (eds) Affective Development in Infancy. Norwood, NJ: Ablex, pp. 95–124.

Main M and Stadtman J (1981) Infants response to physical rejection by the mother: Aggression avoidance and conflict. Journal of the American Academy of Child Psychiatry 20: 292–307.

Main M, Kaplan N and Cassidy J (1985) Security in infancy, childhood and adulthood. A move to the level of representations. In: I Bretherton and E Waters (eds) Growing Points in Attachment Theory and Research. Monographs in the Society for Research in Child Development 50: 66–104.

Millán S (1992) The Third World and Social Character. Science of Man, Yearbook of the International Erich Fromm Society; Wissenschaft Vom Menschen, Jahrbuch der Internationalen Erich Fromm Gesellschaft, vol. 3. Munster: Lit-Verl, pp. 57–68.

Millán S (1993) Methodology for the evaluation of the interpretative questionnaire used during the sessions of the Mexican seminar of Sociopsychoanalysis. In: Cuadernos IV: Social Character, its Study an experiential Interchange. Ed. Seminario de Sociopsicoanálisis Mexico: I MPAC, pp. 107–124.

Millán S (1996) The social dimension of transference. In: M Cortina and M Maccoby, A Prophetic Analyst, Erich Fromm's Contribution to Psychoanalysis. Northvale, NJ and London: J Aronson, pp. 325–40.

Millán S and Gojman S (1997) The Weekly Clinical Group Supervision Chaired by Erich Fromm presented in 'Erich Fromm – Psychoanalyst and Supervisor'. International Conference April 4–5 in Ascona Switzerland.

Millán S and Gojman S (2000) The legacy of Fromm in Mexico. International Forum of Psychoanalysis 9(3–4): 207–16.

Sanchez G (2001) Mother as messenger of love and death. International Forum of Psychoanalysis 10(1): 57–63

Sanchez ME and Almeida E (1991) La Relación Humana Simétrica: Fuente de Acción y de Conocimiento. In: Cuadernos II. Ed. Seminario de Sociopsicoanálisis. Mexico: IMPAC, pp. 30–43.

Sanchez ME and Almeida E (1992) Synergistic development and participatory action research in a Nahuatl community. American Sociologist 23(4): 83–99.

Sierra C (2001) A story of losses and the creation of an alternate world. International Forum of Psychoanalysis 10(1): 64–71.

Smith PB and Pederson D (1988) Maternal sensitivity and patterns of infant–mother attachment. Child Development 50: 1097–101.

Sroufe A (1989) Pathways to adaptation and maladaptation: Psychopathology as developmental deviation. In: D Cicchetti (ed.) Rochester Symposium on Developmental Psychopathology. Hillsdale, NJ: Lawrence Erlbaum, pp. 13–41.

Sroufe A (1990) An organizational perspective on the self. In: D Cicchetti and M Beeghly (eds) The Self in Transition: Infancy to Childhood. Chicago: University of Chicago Press, pp. 281–307.

Sroufe A (1997) Psychopathology as an outcome of development. Development and Psychopathology, Vol. 9. New York: Cambridge University Press, pp. 251–68.

Sroufe A and Fleeson J (1986) Attachment and the construction of relationships. In: W Hartup and Z Rubin (eds) Relationships and Development. Hillsdale, NJ: Erlbaum, pp. 51–72.

Sroufe A and Rutter M (1984) The domain of developmental psychopathology. Child Development 54: 173–81.

Sroufe A and Wards J (1980) Seductive behavior of mothers of toddlers: Occurrence, correlation and family origins. Child Development 51: 1223–7.

Sroufe A and Waters E (1977) Attachment as an organizational construct. Child Development 48: 1184–99.

Sroufe A, Carlson E, Levy AK and Egeland B (1999) Implications of attachment theory for developmental psychopathology. Development and Psychopathology, Vol. 11. New York: Cambridge University Press, pp 1–14.

Taller de Tradición Oral de la Sociedad Agropecuaria del CEPEC (1994) Les Oimos Contar a Nuestros Abuelos. Etnohistoria. Instituto Nacional de Antropología e Historia, Mexico.

CHAPTER 9

Applications of attachment theory to the treatment of latency age children

JUNE W. SROUFE

There has been an increasing body of work that addresses the application of attachment research and assessment procedures to clinical work with infants, young children and their parents (Cassidy and Shaver, 1999). Several studies have focused on the relationship between attachment status and risk factors for psychopathology. Other projects have evaluated the outcome of intervention with caregivers and their infants. Still other programs have been designed to intervene with parents and young children after difficulties have emerged, such as feeding or sleeping problems. In each of these approaches, given the age of the child, attachment status can be considered to be an important determinant of functioning. As children grow, however, attachment history becomes integrated within a complex organization that is further determined by later developmental tasks as well as unique factors that define individual experience. Understanding the role of attachment history in later functioning becomes more challenging and, perhaps as a result, the application of attachment research and assessment instruments to clinical work with latency age children has been slower to develop.

With regard to attachment considerations, latency age children form a unique group. Unlike infants, for whom attachment is the overriding organizational structure, for the older child attachment history is embedded within a developmental outcome that has been shaped by additional influences. In the toddler period, the child asserts its independence and gains a sense of personal agency and predictability. In this stage, regularity as well as consistent and lovingly set limits from the parents support the child's growth. A sense of agency, instrumental competence and self-management are further elaborated in the pre-school years; and gender identity is consolidated while children begin to learn the complex set of rules that govern social behavior.

By the age of 6, most children are well on their way towards mastery of these developmental tasks and have evolved a personal adaptation that started with attachment but is now a much more complicated organization with attachment at its core. New developmental challenges emerge that uniquely define the school age period. The basic rules of social life that the pre-schooler is exposed to are transformed into a complicated social system, involving the beginnings of true friendship and establishing a position in a social group (Hartup, 1992). Moreover, the school age child is confronted with the demands of the school setting and is expected to exhibit mastery of particular tasks. Mastery and competence in the physical world outside the home become of central importance and, along with competence in the social world, define the developmental status of the child in this era. Nonetheless, attachment continues to be a primary force in the lives of school-age children.

The place of attachment in development

The attachment relationship is at the heart of development, the first and most global relationship experience of life. John Bowlby (1969/1982) saw attachment as having the important evolutionary function of protection from predation, as well as serving as a secure base from which the child can explore its world. The optimal situation for the child is one in which the balance between attachment and exploration stimulates healthy development.

Felt security is experienced by the child when there is an optimal balance between attachment and exploration. The child feels secure in the expectation that the caregiver will be available if needed. Over time and countless social interactions, children internalize their experiences as more general and fine-tuned expectations for themselves and others in relationships. These internalized representations form the core of personality, as well as influence the direction of further development. That core of personality may be denoted as basic trust of others and as self-esteem – basic trust of self.

The foundation of emotional regulation is also established within the context of the attachment relationship (Sroufe, 1996). The young infant has little capacity to regulate its own state of arousal effectively. If aroused by hunger, pain or other discomfort, it will cry with increasing intensity until its needs are met. The caregiver serves the vital role of responding promptly and appropriately to the expressions of need from the child, helping the child through meeting of needs or other soothing behaviors. In this way the child begins to count upon the caregiver to be available as an important resource.

The caregiver also may stimulate arousal through games and play. Tickling, laughing together, playing peek-a-boo, all are activities that increase arousal in a social and pleasurable way. These activities are not only fun for mother and child but also provide another opportunity for the child to experience the regulation of arousal with pleasure. To the extent that the mother is sensitive to the capacities of the child to contain the arousal, the child will gain an important and positive experience. These multiple experiences of arousal modulation within the context of both positive and negative emotion provide the foundation for confident expectations regarding the regulation of arousal. At the same time they provide a format for practicing self-regulation long before the child has the capacity to manage arousal independently. Research suggests also that these experiences are integral for literally tuning excitatory and inhibitory systems in the central nervous system (Schore, 1994). In all these ways, such dyadic experiences form the foundation of later more independent self-regulation of emotion.

From the very beginning, the child develops within a relationship context. For most infants, the world is a fascinating and provocative environment, and at the same time, a safe and well-defended haven. Over time, the primary caregiver has attended to and learned the unique and subtle cues for care expressed by the infant. Over time, a smoothly functioning relationship develops in which the child can explore the world.

However, not all infant–caregiver relationships develop this pattern of functioning in which there is an optimal attachment/exploration balance. In some cases, the caregiver is not sensitive to the cues of the child and responds in a rejecting or inconsistent way. The rejection may be subtle but, if chronic, engenders in the child a complementary response that will compensate for that rejection by cutting off direct expression of attachment needs in times of stress. In the same way, the child who experiences inconsistent care will develop a complementary role, ultimately creating a relationship pattern characterized by chronic intensification of attachment signals and undue vigilance concerning possible threat (Main and Hesse, 1990). These are the patterns of avoidant and resistant attachment described by Ainsworth (Ainsworth et al., 1978; see also Appendix to this volume).

These variations in attachment have documented developmental consequences. In a longitudinal study of child development done at Minnesota, children were studied whose attachment history was assessed in infancy. In the pre-school years, the anxious/resistant pattern was associated with immaturity, low frustration tolerance, victimization and observed dependency on teachers (Sroufe, 1983). In latency, it was revealed in low social status, an inability to balance the complexities of the social world, and lack of effectance (Elicker, Englund and Sroufe, 1992). Ultimately, these children were found to be at risk for anxiety disorders (Warren et al., 1997).

Quite distinctive outcomes were associated with the avoidant pattern. In the pre-school years, this pattern was associated with lack of empathy for and emotional distance from others (Sroufe, 1983). In latency, the avoidant pattern was associated with social isolation, difficulty forming close friendships, and aggression (Shulman, Elicker and Sroufe, 1994). Paradoxically, the children in this group were similar to the children in the resistant group in that they also displayed high levels of dependency (Sroufe, Fox and Pancake, 1983). As Bowlby (1973) predicted, early movement away from dependency actually compromises later self-reliance. These children were at risk for later conduct disorders (Renken et al., 1989).

It is also noteworthy that in the pre-school, the children in the two insecure groups evoked very different responses from the teachers when they expressed their dependency needs or misbehaved (Sroufe and Fleeson, 1988). The most common response of the teachers to the children with anxious/resistant histories was to treat them as though they were younger than they in fact were. Teachers spent more time with them and gave them more reassurance than they did the children in the secure group. Expectations for behavior were modified such that these children were not expected to perform at the same level as the other children, perhaps missing an opportunity to challenge the child and stimulate growth. The children with avoidant histories were treated very differently, in spite of expressing similar high levels of dependency. These children were less well liked by the teachers and more likely to be isolated if they misbehaved. The very rejection that the child experienced in its attachment relationship was reproduced in the teacher–student relationship. Moreover, the children with secure attachment histories were more well-liked and treated in an age-normative way by the teachers.

In each of the three groupings based on attachment history, teachers varied in their response to their students in predictable ways. These are important findings for clinicians. The responses invoked within us may well reflect the attachment history of the child. If, as clinicians, we fail to appreciate this aspect of countertransference we may unwittingly serve to reinforce the child's distorted and ultimately maladaptive experience of the world.

To fully understand the place of attachment in the development of the latency age child, it also must be remembered that the relationship between the child and the primary caregivers does not fade in importance as the child grows and other developmental tasks become central.

Instead, the role of the parent in shaping the development of the child changes to fit the needs of the period. Parents differ in the strengths they bring to each developmental stage. One parent may do very well with an infant but, for complex reasons, be much less able to respond to the autonomy strivings of the toddler. As a consequence, the child's adaptation may be compromised. By the time the child reaches the school-age period, one is presented with an individual for whom attachment experiences have been a formative influence, but also for whom many other vital and transforming experiences also are of critical importance. Some of these experiences are universal and forged within the context of normal development; still others are unique to the individual child, yet also are of importance in determining the course of individual development.

The role of experience in individual development

In his writings on attachment, Bowlby diverged from classical analytic theory by placing emphasis on real experiences instead of internal conflict as the important determinant of personality development. Bowlby argued that early experience with the caregiver leads to an internal set of 'working models', which one then uses in further interaction with the world. With development, inner working models can be modified through profound and/or persistent experience. Such is the foundation of long-term therapy.

Certain experiences can be overwhelming to a child's adaptation. When this occurs, the normal pattern of coping may break down. Mary Main noted that some of the children in Ainsworth's Strange Situation Procedure exhibited contradictory behavior or an otherwise incoherent strategy for coping with the separation experience (Main and Hesse, 1990). In the presence of the caregiver, these children exhibited anomalous behaviors suggestive of contradictory urges (approaching a parent with head averted) or behaviors that involved apprehension either directly (fearful facial expressions) or indirectly (disoriented behaviors, including dazed and trance-like expressions). She hypothesized that the child was in conflict, even afraid, and unable to maintain a coherent strategy. One situation that could lead to this problem is when the caregiver becomes a source of fear due to child abuse. In this case, when aroused, the child would experience contradictory impulses, since human evolutionary history disposes the child to both run *to* the attachment figure when frightened, and to run *from* the source of the fright. When the parent is both, the child is placed in an unresolvable paradox. Being unable to hold these simultaneous contradictory impulses, the child experiences a breakdown in the usual way of coping and shows signs of disorganization. Indeed, it has been found that the Disorganized/ Disoriented (D) pattern, as it is called, is associated with risk factors such as parental child maltreatment (George and Main 1979; Carlson et al., 1989; Lyons-Ruth et al., 1991).

However, other disruptive experiences can also lead to signs of disorganization. Any frightening experience from which there is no escape may serve as the catalyst for a breakdown in coherent functioning. Some additional risk factors found to be associated with disorganized attachment include parental bipolar disorder (DeMulder and Radke-Yarrow, 1991), and parental alcohol intake (O'Connor, Sigman and Brill, 1987). Recent research has focused on the prevalence of unresolved losses in the history of the caregiver and its effect on the infant. Unresolved losses in the history of the parent, assessed prenatally, were found to be predictive of frightened or frightening behavior with the infant (Jacobvitz, Hazen and Riggs, 1997). Frightening or frightened behavior, while in the presence of the infant, has also been shown to be associated with disorganized attachment status (Schuengel et al., 1997).

The critical underlying affect of disorganization is fear. Over time, without intervention, fear without resolution leads to maladaptation. To date, disorganization in infancy is linked to externalizing behavior, including aggression, in latency (Lyons-Ruth, Alpern and Repacholi, 1993), and to dissociative symptoms throughout childhood and adolescence (Carlson, 1998). It is not a new observation that many aggressive school-age children are coping with high levels of internal fear. Incorporation of attachment theory, as well as theory regarding the effects of fearful experiences on children, advances our work.

Attachment and clinical practice with latency age children

Even though attachment experiences are at the core, it is difficult as well as hazardous to draw a direct connection between early attachment and a particular pattern of symptoms in a latency age child, due to the embedded nature of development. Nonetheless, attachment considerations can be important guides in considering the origins of a problem as well as the subsequent recommendations. As previously mentioned, there are patterns of behavior in latency that are associated with early attachment; in some cases a presenting problem is clearly linked to enduring attitudes about the social world that stem from the infant period. For example, a child may be seen in the clinical setting whose presenting problem is chronic bullying by peers. The parents and school professionals have intervened at length but to no avail. The child is unable to make use of the help that is offered and persistently behaves in ways that draw negative attention and ridicule from others. In addition, the child presents as immature and highly dependent and perhaps also fussy and passively non-compliant. From an attachment perspective, one might search for long-standing attitudes about how social relations are to be conducted. Underlying the child's inability to extricate himself from the bullying may be a belief that relationships are unfair, unpredictable and filled with conflict. In this case, it is possible that current social difficulties stem from these attitudes established in very early childhood.

Attachment experience may also be considered as a factor in cases where the presenting problem apparently is not relational in origin. For example, evaluation of a depressed child may reveal that the child is friendless and in a fundamental way does not really see the social world as a source of support. In some cases, it may be concluded that friendlessness is an outcome of depression. In another view, one may question the origins and longevity of those beliefs. A child who has never experienced the rewards of a mutually satisfying relationship will not seek support from others when sad and lonely, contributing to the intensity of those feelings. If experience dictates that needs for care will be rejected, turning from others at moments of need is understandable. Recommendations for intervention in these cases and others will be influenced by consideration of attachment history. A child who has a history of positive care and connection with others will more likely respond to efforts to reinstate a richer social life. A child with little expectation of reward within a relationship will not be able to respond to brief interventions based on trust within a relationship. In this case, a long-term therapy is likely indicated (ideally including parental and family work), and expectations for change would be modified in acknowledgment of the unique challenges.

Assessment

At this time direct and reliable evaluation of attachment security can be done only at very young ages. As described in the Appendix to this volume, the Strange Situation Laboratory Procedure dependably assesses the quality of attachment security in infants aged 12 to 18 months. Validity studies for its use at older ages have yielded mixed results (Cassidy, 2001). A Q-sort technique also has been developed to assess quality of attachment in somewhat older children up to the age of 4½ (Waters and Deane, 1985). With this method, the parent is given a list of items that describe children in relationships and asked to distribute them into categories to best describe their own child. This instrument has been shown to relate to earlier Strange Situation assessments of attachment and is based on direct observation of the attachment–exploration balance in the home. This Q-sort technique has not yet been used in clinical settings. However, it is relatively easy to administer and score and probably could be adapted for clinical use and possibly use with older children.

Just as attachment history is embedded in the development of the older child, assessment of attachment history will be embedded in a broader evaluation. For example, several projective techniques have been modified for research purposes to reveal themes of attachment and could readily be included in a personality assessment (see Bretherton and Munholland, 1999, for a review). An evaluation of self and kinetic family drawings developed in Berkeley and elaborated at Minnesota was used in research with children aged 6 to 8. It includes particular signs that signify each of the three categories of security and also signs that point to disorganization. When these signs are considered collectively, or integrated into broader scales, they are related both to infant attachment history and to current aspects of functioning, such as peer competence and behavior problems (Fury, Carlson and Sroufe, 1997).

Others have used either fantasy play or stories completed by young children in response to stems (Bretherton, 1990; George and Solomon, 1996; Rosenberg, 1984; Warren et al., 2000). Typically, stories used involve separation themes (e.g. while cared for by a babysitter you become lost in the woods). Those with secure histories much more commonly bring such threatening circumstances to a successful ending (the parents come to find them). In general, in the play of young children with secure histories, conflict routinely is successfully resolved.

With older children, TAT-type stories and sentence completions have been used (McCrone et al., 1994). For example, stories told showing apparent conflict among peers are more commonly followed by resolution in the accounts of those with secure attachment histories. Likewise, sentence stems such as, 'my mother will always...' and 'My mother likes when...' are followed by themes of time together, sharing, and being available.

Another instrument that was originally developed to assess the state of mind with regard to attachment in adults is the Adult Attachment Interview (George, Kaplan and Main, 1984). This instrument (see Appendix) has been modified and used to assess attachment status in 10-year-olds with promising results, but at this point no outside validating confirmation (Target, 2000). However, the Adult Attachment Interview can be used with parents to gain an understanding of some of the attitudes they bring to the clinical setting.

Many important connections between adult attachment status and childhood attachment have been made. For example, an expectant mother's state of mind with regard to attachment as assessed by the Adult Attachment Interview is later predictive of her 1-year-old infant's attachment classification as assessed in the Strange Situation Procedure (van IJzendoorn, 1995). Several studies have also shown a link between parental unresolved status and child disorganization (Main and Hesse, 1990; Lyons-Ruth et al., 1991; van IJzendoorn, 1995). What these linkages confirm is the connection between how the parent views the world and the child's unique pattern of adaptation. Research with the Adult Attachment Interview (AAI) that enlightens clinical work with latency age children currently is limited, but does promise to be fruitful.

Apart from formal diagnostic procedures, critical information of a more inferential nature regarding attachment history can be obtained from the developmental history. For example, caregiver descriptions of the child's nature in infancy are often quite revealing of early relationship dynamics. A parent's description of a child in infancy as being motivated to cause trouble for the parent, being constitutionally unable to behave responsively, or generally 'very good' without further information about how the child was unique are examples of descriptions that might lead the interviewer to consider the possibility of an insecure attachment history. Questions may be added to a developmental history interview that point specifically to the quality of the relationship between the caregiver and child.

Also of importance is the timing and nature of early disruptions in the family relationship system and subsequently the child's ability to organize his experience coherently. Questions of this sort are often asked, although in regard to attachment history they take on a specific meaning. If events occurred that would compromise the quality of caregiver responsivity, a more in-depth probe of the nature, extent and response to that disruption would be indicated, and one would look for signs of disorganization in other phases of the evaluation.

Another indirect source of information is the social history of the child and the child's attitudes about peer relationships. Evidence of empathy for others suggests a positive attitude about relationships in general and an expectation that people are responsive to one another. Current functioning with peers is also relevant, and a careful assessment of those relations is revealing. Some children can be superficially social and yet have no real friends. Others may state that they have friends but with closer questioning reveal that they feel left out and alone. Good social functioning in latency is complex. In the Minnesota study, mentioned before, it was discovered that children with secure histories are much more likely at age 10 to be involved in stable, loyal friendships, to be effective in the same-gen-der peer group, to be able to coordinate the competing demands of friendship and group participation and to maintain age-normative gender boundaries (Sroufe, Egeland and Carlson, 1999).

Finally, how the child relates to the therapist is an important source of information about the child's capacity for trust in his or her self and the outside social world. It could be said that children most often resist com-ing to see a therapist, and children with secure attachment histories are typical in this way. Even an angry resistance to a clinical visit may simply mean that the child is confident in his or her permission to express out-rage at the prospect of being labeled deficient in some way. One also would expect to see hesitancy and resistance to joining the initial process, especially if it entails a discussion of the child's problems. Aspects of social behavior that may reflect attachment qualities include (1) how the child uses the caregiver as a resource, especially in separating from that person, (2) the quality of cooperation and the regard for honesty in pre-sentation with the therapist, and (3) the quality of emotional regulation that is exhibited.

Recommendations and treatment

Attachment history can be taken into account when making recommen-dations for a course of treatment. After an assessment of the seriousness and severity of the problems, the type and length of treatment may be affected by awareness of the child's attachment history and subsequent social functioning. The child who has a secure attachment history and lit-tle experience that would disrupt his trusting expectations of the social world is a good candidate for a relationship-based therapy. This is not to say that the child will immediately engage the therapist. On the contrary, the child with the secure history and good current social functioning may take some time to relax and get to know the therapist. Indeed, this cau-tious approach characterized those with secure histories in the Minnesota pre-school project (Sroufe, 1983). On the first day of school they were attentive and interested in both teachers and peers, but they did not immediately interact with a wide range of social partners. Preferences for play partners developed over time. In contrast, those with avoidant his-tories were immediately friendly and engaging of numerous partners; only in time did they become isolated. As previously mentioned, the anx-ious/resistant children, from the first day, seemed immature when compared to the others and required greater assistance from the teachers to adjust to the new setting.

A child with an avoidant attachment history may seem superficially able to respond to the therapy situation but in fact is likely to take longer to truly develop trust. These children are likely to evoke feelings of pity in the therapist in place of genuine empathy, and will ultimately search for rejection in the therapist, however subtle or unintended. The child with an anxious/resistant attachment history might also become readily engaged in the therapy-based activities, but over time will likely exhibit the same ambivalent and unstable behavior that has been the norm for the child. To the therapist, these children can be experienced as very needy, dependent and immature. Regular and on-time attendance in sessions might become a problem. Feelings invoked might include frustration and helplessness.

Attachment history may be included in determination of the length of treatment. For some children, a long-term corrective relationship experience is clearly indicated precisely because of uneven or otherwise inadequate early care. As is already well known, children who appear to have experienced early trauma and who exhibit signs of disorganization usually need a lengthy therapy to fully address the effects of trauma. The parents of the child with the avoidant style may be confused about the value of a relationship-based treatment and resist the commitment to the long-term intervention.

The attachment status of the parent can be an important consideration in determining prognosis and treatment. A parent who is insensitive to and/or rejecting of his/her child can be the fundamental stumbling block to real change for the child. Likewise, the inconsistent caregiver who is unable to provide calm reliable care and limit-setting can undermine the recovery of the child. Sensitivity to the needs of the parent and assisting them in improving parenting behaviors is often the centerpiece of child therapy.

Case illustration

The following is a summary of a case in which incorporation of attachment considerations was a part of the diagnosis, recommendations and treatment. It illustrates the complexity of the task of assessing attachment status in latency, how it is embedded in a complicated organization and, at the same time, how it may enrich the process beyond conventional symptom-based formulations.

Amanda was my client in therapy for two separate periods of time. The first was from ages 6½ to 7 and the second was from 7½ to almost 9. She is the second of three children, with an older brother and a younger sister. The family is intact and Amanda's father is a very busy professional. Her mother does not work outside the home.

Amanda's parents chose to consult a psychologist because of their concern about her behavior at home. Their concern was that she had been increasingly exhibiting unusual, repetitive tic-like behaviors, was irritable when anyone interfered with her routines and was often quite angry, especially with her younger sister.

The developmental history revealed that Amanda had been a planned child whose mother had a relatively pleasant pregnancy and delivery. In the first 18 months of her life Amanda was described as being a happy, loving, very expressive and clever child. She had not experienced serious illnesses or injuries. Amanda's parents stated that at 18 months she changed, developing sleep problems, and becoming a 'bundle of energy'. At the same time, she also began to develop an unusual ability to focus on one activity for long periods of time, a habit that continued to the present. The first time she came to see me her focus was on music. She was considered by her music teachers to be gifted.

Most of Amanda's tics were transient and included behaviors such as clicking her tongue, rubbing her tongue and then her ear, or hitting her head with the palm of her hand. She also stated that she had obsessive thoughts, usually a tune or a phrase that she could not get out of her head, especially when she was trying to go to sleep. One tic was more chronic and seemed to serve the function of a compulsion; that is, Amanda felt compelled to rub her forearm on an object for an extended period of time prior to most transitions. She sometimes would be late for school because she had not finished her rubbing ritual.

Socially, Amanda was, by mother's report, well liked. She had several friends, both in the neighborhood and in school, and was sought out as a play partner. Most days after school, she played with her friends and also enjoyed a wide range of physical activities, such as tennis and skiing. Her school performance was at a high level, and she was very well liked by her teachers. She did not noticeably exhibit tics in school.

Considering this particular symptom picture, Amanda met the criteria for two diagnoses, transient tic disorder (possibly chronic tic disorder) and obsessive compulsive disorder. In addition, given her sleep problems, the high level of irritability she was experiencing, and the inferred worry, other diagnoses of depression or anxiety could be considered.

At this point I shall present my subjective appraisal of Amanda's early attachment experience and my reasons for coming to these conclusions. Often with symptoms as serious as these in a first-grader, one finds evidence for fairly negative early relationship experiences. However, in Amanda's case, it was my view that she had had a good early attachment experience and would have been considered secure. There were three sources of information that led me to this conclusion. First, her mother reported that it had been a pleasant time for both of them: 'Even though I was busier with two children, I really enjoyed that period of time. Amanda was a great baby.' Moreover, in describing her current difficulties, Amanda's mother balanced the detailing of her problems with assertions about the strength of Amanda's character, her empathy for others and her underlying cooperative spirit. She wanted me to know that in spite of Amanda's frustrating behavior and her own concern about that, Amanda was a special child and that she was very proud of her. She neither exaggerated her description of the symptoms nor minimized her concern about them. This is in contrast to the parental report that highlights the failures of the child, or the defensive denial of very real problems that a child may be struggling with.

Second, when I did interact with her, I found Amanda to be appropriately shy and reticent at first, but when I asked her questions about her life, she was able to answer honestly and in a straightforward manner. She showed what I should call a trusting vulnerability in responding to me. She had actually been quite outraged that her mother had decided to bring her to see me. Most children at first resist coming to see a therapist. To them, it means that people think something may be wrong with them. It often happens that the more secure children express this resistance in the form of simple outrage, perhaps because they have an essential core of confidence that they are fundamentally sound. 'I'm good!' declared Amanda.

Third, the report of her current social adaptation supported my impression that Amanda had had a secure early start. As noted above, she had friends, was well liked by her peers and teachers, and demonstrated an empathy for others. An example of her capacity for empathy is shown in her response to a child that visited her house very often. The child was in her older brother's class at school and would come home to Amanda's house with her brother, saying that his mother had agreed to let him eat there. The child lived in a very poor neighborhood and was ultimately discovered to be living only with his 18-year-old sister who was seldom home. Amanda's mother reported taking him home more than once to a completely dark house at eight in the evening. This boy's particular adaptation was to be charming, a good game player and always 'on the go'. Amanda thought that he was funny and sometimes liked to play games with this child but primarily found him to be a source of unneeded stimulation in her home every night for dinner. This put her in a quandary. She admitted that she did not like him at her house so much, but, after discovering the state of his living situation, was quite worried about rejecting him and sending him home to an empty house and no food. Her resolution was that her mother must find some help for the child and demanded that she go to the principal to get that help.

Given these strengths, it seemed plausible that Amanda had an early secure foundation. Clues to her difficulties lay elsewhere. Consider what Amanda experienced between her infancy and her first meeting with me. It may be remembered that her disposition had changed at 18 months when she became a 'bundle of energy'. It turns out that when Amanda was 18 months old, her mother was in a very serious car accident and nearly died. Moreover, as a result of the initial accident, there were two subsequent hospitalizations that also carried the risk of death. In addition, in at least the first circumstance, the babysitters were incompetent and frightening to the children. Before the age of 5, Amanda had experienced the near loss of her mother three times. Prior to one of her later visits to see me, she asked her mother who would take care of her if she went to the hospital again. When Amanda's mother repeated that question to me later in her presence, I asked Amanda if she thought her mother would go back to the hospital again. She replied that she could not be sure her mother would stay well.

Based on Bowlby's contention that one's (primarily relational) experience forms the foundation of one's development, my working hypothesis was that Amanda's early attachment had been secure but that, beginning at 18 months, she had experienced overwhelming trauma that had finally resulted in her presenting symptoms. Note, however, that these symptoms are embedded (in a complex constellation of strengths) in a personality that has at its core an important foundation of trust and self-worth.

When Amanda first visited me, I asked her to do a kinetic family drawing which was evaluated by Dr Elizabeth Carlson using the system developed by Main and elaborated at Minnesota (Figure 9.1). As would be obvious to almost anyone, there is a lot of distress in this picture. Dr Carlson gave it a rating of 5 on the 5-point scale pertaining to D (Disorganized) status. D signs include: (1) a chaotic scene, (2) frightening people (faces), (3) an incomplete self, (4) disjointed limb, and an appearance of incoherence. I had the benefit of hearing the story behind this picture, so I would say that there is more coherence than is first apparent. Nonetheless, one can readily see that this child is coping with a high level of distress.

The story Amanda told with this picture is that the children have unexpectedly gained an ability to fly. Dad is running to keep people safe, mother is worried that they will fall and hurt their heads. Little sister has

Figure 9.1.

her eyes popping out and big brother is running to catch the baby. Amanda is flying off but will land in the pool if she falls.

In this somewhat unusual picture, there are signs from all of the attachment categories. Incomplete figures are signs of general insecurity. The mask-like appearance on father's face is considered a sign of avoidance and the unusually small figure is considered a sign of ambivalence. Most of the signs are of security, however, including detailed individual drawings of all family members, excepting herself. There is a sense of personal individuation and a sensitive understanding of emotion and dynamics. Moreover, she is able to tell this rather alarming story with some completeness, of course with the exception of her own diminished and incomplete figure. I also like the fact that there are members of her family who are attempting to help the others.

How I then came to understand this case, the meaning of the symptoms, the likely causes, and thoughts about prognosis – all questions that parents will ask – was shaped by my developmental perspective with early attachment as the core. The meaning of the symptoms is complex, as always. I saw the trauma at 18 months as the beginning of Amanda's chronic distress. At 18 months children are consolidating their attachment foundation and just beginning to explore the world in a more autonomous manner. Over the next couple of years, they are gaining an important hold on predictability in their lives. Because Amanda experienced this trauma that was anything but predictable or manageable and also because the adults in her life were unable to fully respond to her due to their own trauma, she did what she could to control her life by focusing on distracting activities and some self-soothing behaviors. Later, when two more alarming hospitalizations had occurred, she continued with the same defensive style but developed more complicated tics and obsessions. The rather primitive nature of the basic symptoms can be attributed to the age at which she experienced the trauma, before having much language and more sophisticated defenses. It may be noted that her older brother was also worried about possible disasters, but having been older when the original crisis occurred, evolved a more verbal coping style. He talked a lot about his worries.

The second factor that needs mentioning is the fairly high level of anger that Amanda was experiencing and that was also alarming to her. It is a clinical observation that otherwise well-functioning children will contain their distress while the family is in crisis or transition, but then when the crisis passes and the family reestablishes some stability, they become more symptomatic, acting out their frustrations. This family had been doing quite well for about one year and in general was beginning to relax more. This is the time when Amanda began to exhibit her anger. Naturally this would be a source of conflict for her, because she would not really understand the source of her anger and it would seem powerful to her. In addition, she probably had some worry that she might have the power to cause another health problem for her mother. From other drawings and clinical material, it was clear that she was angry with her mother for going away and not taking care of her. In fact, the whole family was upset with mother for scaring them so much. This became the focus of Amanda's first phase of treatment.

To address the current high level of worry, I recommended to the parents that Amanda attend weekly individual therapy, and that mother and father when necessary attend parent guidance sessions to discuss various aspects of the case. With them I emphasized that her good early beginning was an important factor in how speedily she could respond to treatment.

Predictably, after six months, Amanda was much less angry and only exhibiting one tic. Her parents were not yet ready to join in a family session and decided to take a break from therapy. Six months later they came back because Amanda's behavior was slipping into the old patterns. I then suggested that they commit to a year of therapy. They agreed to do so, and Amanda spent that year in what I call rebuilding. This was done with dollhouse play. Her mother also attended frequent parent sessions in which she discussed her own response to threatening situations.

In a case like this, with a generally well-functioning family, I usually recommend family sessions to talk about the traumas. In this case we never met as a group to talk about the hospitalizations. The parents were not ready for that step. Understanding the link between the accident and the change in Amanda's behavior was very difficult for them, in my view, because they experienced the same trauma and associated disorientation. It was quite late during the second phase of therapy when they began to connect the changes in Amanda's behavior with the accident. It frequently occurs that traumatic experiences interfere with verbal processing of the events. This is especially striking in individuals like these, who are otherwise straightforward and cooperative in discussion. One family meeting was held in which another important family transition was discussed. This session provided an opportunity to discuss in general how each family member copes with change and threat. The parents reported a very positive response to that session.

In sum, the case of Amanda is an example of a child with a secure early start who suffered an overwhelming trauma. For understandable reasons, she lacked adequate support and as a result became symptomatic. In therapy, in spite of rather serious symptoms, she was able to make good use our relationship to improve her situation. If her beginning had been different, she would have been armed with a different set of tools to cope with the trauma. For purposes of illustration, it is useful to consider how she would have responded if her early attachment had been anxious.

The outcome for Amanda probably would have been very different had she begun life with an insecure attachment. If her attachment status had been avoidant, she would have emerged from infancy with the perspective that she could not always rely on her mother to be available to her. She would have learned to hide her needs and be less likely to express them in an understandable way. She would have been less prepared to even know what her feelings were. Then, at 18 months the trauma of her mother's accident would have been experienced within this context of suppression and avoidance. It is possible that on the surface she would have responded in the same way as the secure Amanda did. She might have developed sleep problems and self-soothing behaviors. But underneath the surface, it can be assumed that she would have struggled to maintain her basic avoidant strategy; that is, to turn away from arousing aspects of the situation, including her own feelings. Later, when the family was assured that the danger had passed, the avoidant Amanda would be much less likely to admit to feelings of anger toward her mother. If, in spite of herself, she expressed her resentments, it would have been in very indirect and confusing ways, and would not have led to obtaining the care that she needed. Without intervention the fearful aspects of the trauma would have remained powerful and might have led to life-long changes in her functioning. In the therapeutic context, she would have been superficially social but unable to count on the relational context to be a source of support. Accessing the feelings associated with the trauma would have been quite difficult and would have occurred only after a secure base was fully established with the therapist.

If Amanda had a history of anxious/resistant attachment, she probably would have developed a different set of expectations about the world before the accident occurred. In general, she would have expected that her needs would be met at some times but not at others, and that there was no regularity to the pattern of availability. She would have been immature in her behavior and emotional regulation. At 18 months, when the accident occurred, the anxious/resistant Amanda's vulnerable hold on emotional regulation might well have slipped, leading to symptoms of emotional dysregulation which might have appeared in the sleep problems or eating problems, tantrums, motor restlessness, aggression, and so on. For the anxious/resistant infant–caregiver pair, the unpredictability of the hospitalizations would have added pressure to a system that was already weakened by inconsistency. One can expect that in this case Amanda's mother would have responded to her daughter's increasing demands with greater inconsistency, at times providing responsive care but more often, due to her own compromised resources, becoming very frustrated with the demanding child. The anxious/resistant Amanda probably would have been viewed as a behavior problem from early childhood, manifested perhaps in frustration and tantrums or perhaps in social anxiety and school avoidance. In therapy she might have presented as an immature, anxious child who exhibited symptoms associated with anxiety, hyperactivity and learning problems.

If Amanda's early attachment classification had been disorganized prior to her mother's accident, the effect of the trauma would have been quite serious. An underlying tendency to disorganize under stressful conditions would have been exaggerated in the phase of coping with the separations and the unsatisfactory childcare. Instead of, or in addition to, the compulsive behaviors, she might have been inclined to more dissociative behaviors and emotional volatility.

In the Minnesota longitudinal study, it was demonstrated empirically that traumatic experience occurring following a foundation of disorganized attachment in infancy was much more strongly associated with dissociative symptoms in late adolescence than was the case for trauma in the context of a secure attachment (Ogawa et al., 1997). It is thought that early disorganization is the foundation not only of dissociative symptoms, but also of multiple personality disorder. In Amanda's case much more serious symptoms would have been expected than were seen.

Conclusion

When parents bring their children to a psychologist, they also bring a set of questions. These questions commonly cover a range from what exactly is the problem, to what caused it, and how can it be made better. Indeed, as practitioners, these are the questions we ask ourselves, and the answers to them are critical in determining whether our interventions are appropriate and effective. What we consider to be of importance in the development of clinical formulations will dictate what answers are arrived at. When attempting to understand the difficulties a child is experiencing, we are rarely able to understand the situation fully without contextual considerations. Children's behavior and emotional problems seldom arise independently of the context of the child's past history or of the surrounding cultural context. In our efforts to answer important clinical questions, we gather data from a variety of sources and create a formulation aimed at answering these questions.

One source of information is the parents and other professionals who are involved in the child's life. Not only can they elaborate on the early history of the child; they also can describe more broadly the larger framework within which the child lives. This is not inconsequential. Our effectiveness is compromised if we fail to address cultural contextual aspects, including family, school and so on, of a child's life (Cortina, 2000). A child attending a private school exists in a different educational environment than one who attends a large metropolitan school; a child raised in a deeply religious home is different from one who is not. All children are embedded within their culture and will reflect those roles in their behavior. An appreciation of cultural factors illuminates the task of understanding a troubled child.

Like the child who is nested within the cultural context, problematic outcomes are nested within a complex personality organization. Full delineation of a child's difficulties can best be done by taking into account all-important aspects of development, starting with the attachment relationship. The attachment relationship is the context within which the core of personality develops. Then, at subsequent stages of development, the child is influenced by new experiences so that adjustments and readjustments to the core of personality are made. Some children's difficulties are long standing and deeply entwined in the child's personality; others are more transient and superficial, yet all impact and are impacted by the child's early attachment strategies. Considerations of attachment history are always relevant in a personality assessment that seeks to answer questions of etiology because attachment is the first and most global of relationships, and therefore affects a child's responses to later life events.

Attachment considerations are also important in determining recommendations for a course of treatment. What a child expects from the social world will influence the effectiveness of a relationship-based intervention. If a child has carefully learned to function in the world without revealing emotional vulnerability, or has developed an orientation toward rendering useless any aid that is offered, a therapy can be severely hindered. How the child began life in its social world will strongly affect the treatment process. Efforts to incorporate an appreciation of early attachment experiences in clinical work have great potential to enrich our understanding and increase our effectiveness.

References

Ainsworth M, Blehar M, Waters E and Wall S (1978) Patterns of Attachment. Hillsdale, NJ: Erlbaum.

Bowlby J (1969/1982) Attachment and Loss, 2nd edn. New York: Basic Books.

Bowlby J (1973) Separation. New York: Basic Books.

Bretherton I (1990) Pouring new wine into old bottles: The social self as internal working model. In: M Gunnar and LA Sroufe (eds) Minnesota Symposia on Child Psychology. Hillsdale, NJ: Erlbaum, pp. 1–41.

Bretherton I and Munholland K (1999) Internal working models of attachment relationships: A construct revisited. In: J Cassidy and P Shaver (eds) Handbook of Attachment. New York: Guilford, pp. 89–114.

Carlson EA (1998) A prospective longitudinal study of disorganized/disoriented attachment. Child Development 69: 1970–9.

Carlson V, Cicchetti D, Barnett D and Braunwald K (1989) Disorganized/disoriented attachment relationships in maltreated infants. Developmental Psychology 25: 525–31.

Cassidy J (2001) Unsolvable fear, trauma, and psychopathology: theory, research, and clinical considerations related to disorganized attachment across the life span. Clinical Psychology: Science and Practice 8: 275–98.

Cassidy J and Shaver P (1999) Handbook of Attachment. New York: Guilford.

Cortina M (2000), Erich Fromm's Legacy: Beyond a two-person psychology. Contemporary Psychoanalysis 36: 133–42.

DeMulder EK and Radke-Yarrow M (1991) Attachment with affectively ill and well mothers: Concurrent behavioral correlates. Development and Psychopathology 3: 227–42.

Elicker J, Englund M and Sroufe LA (1992) Predicting peer competence and peer relationships in childhood from early parent–child relationships. In: R Parke and G Ladd (eds) Family–peer Relationships: Modes of Linkage. Hillsdale, NJ: Erlbaum, pp. 77–106.

Fury G, Carlson E and Sroufe LA (1997) Children's representations of attachment relationships in family drawings. Child Development 68: 1154–64.

George C and Main M (1979) Social interaction of young abused children: Approach, avoidance, and aggression. Child Development 50: 306–18.

George C and Solomon J (1996) Representational models of relationships: Links between caregiving and attachment. Infant Mental Health Journal 17: 198–216.

George C, Kaplan N and Main M (1984) Adult Attachment Interview, 1st edn. Unpublished manuscript. University of California at Berkeley.

Hartup W (1992) Peer relations in early and middle childhood. In: VB Van Hasselt and M Hersen (eds) Handbook of Social Development: A Life Span Perspective. New York: Plenum Press, pp. 257–81.

Jacobvitz D, Hazen N and Riggs S (1997, April). Disorganized mental processes in mothers, frightening/frightened caregiving, and disoriented/disorganized behavior in infancy. In: D Jacobvitz (Chair), Caregiving Correlates and Longitudinal Outcomes of Disorganized Attachments in Infants. Symposium conducted at the biennial meeting of the Society for Research in Child Development, Washington, DC.

Lyons-Ruth K, Repacholi B, McLeod S and Silva E (1991) Disorganized attachment behavior in infancy: Short-term stability, maternal and infant correlates, and risk-related subtypes. Development and Psychopathology 3: 377–96.

Lyons-Ruth K, Alpern L and Repacholi B (1993) Disorganized infant attachment classification and maternal psychosocial problems as predictors of hostile-aggressive behavior in the preschool classroom. Child Development 64: 572–85.

Main M and Hesse E (1990) Parents' unresolved traumatic experiences are related to infant disorganized attachment status: Is frightened and/or frightening parental behavior the linking mechanism? In: MT Greenberg, D Cicchetti and EM Cummings (eds) Attachment in the Preschool Years: Theory, Research, and Intervention. Chicago: University of Chicago Press, pp. 161–82.

McCrone E, Egeland B, Kalkoske M and Carlson E (1994) Relations between early maltreatment and mental representations of relationships assessed with projective story telling in middle childhood. Development and Psychopathology 6: 99–120.

O'Connor MJ, Sigman M and Brill N (1987) Disorganization of attachment in relation to maternal alcohol consumption. Journal of Consulting and Clinical Psychology 55: 831–6.

Ogawa J, Sroufe LA, Weinfield NS, Carlson E and Egeland B (1997) Development and the fragmented self: A longitudinal study of dissociative symptomatology in a non-clinical sample. Development and Psychopathology 9: 855–1164.

Renken B, Egeland B, Marvinney D, Sroufe LA and Mangelsdorf S (1989) Early childhood antecedents of aggression and passive-withdrawal in early elementary school. Journal of Personality 57(2): 257–81.

Rosenberg DM (1984) The quality and content of preschool fantasy play: Correlates in concurrent social-personality function and early mother–child attachment relationships. Unpublished doctoral dissertation, University of Minnesota.

Schore AN (1994) Affect Regulation and the Origin of the Self: The Neurobiology of Emotional Development. Hillsdale, NJ: Erlbaum.

Schuengel C, van IJzendoorn M, Bakermans-Kranenburg M and Blom M (1997, April) Frightening, frightened and/or dissociated behavior, unresolved loss, and infant disorganization. In D. Jacobvitz (Chair), Caregiving Correlates and Longitudinal Outcomes of Disorganized Attachments in Infants. Symposium conducted at the biennial meeting of the Society for Research in Child Development, Washington, DC.

Shulman S, Elicker J and Sroufe LA (1994) Stages of friendship growth in preadolescence as related to attachment history. Journal of Social and Personal Relationships 11: 341–61.

Sroufe LA (1983) Infant–caregiver attachment and patterns of adaptation in preschool: The roots of maladaptation and competence. In: M Perlmutter (ed.) Minnesota Symposium in Child Psychology, vol. 16. Hillsdale, NJ: Erlbaum, pp. 41–83.

Sroufe LA (1996) Emotional Development: The Organization of Emotional Life in the Early Years. New York: Cambridge University Press.

Sroufe LA and Fleeson J (1988) The coherence of family relationships. In: RA Hinde and J Stevenson-Hinde (Eds.), Relationships Within Families: Mutual Influences. Oxford: Oxford University Press, pp. 27–47.

Sroufe LA, Fox N and Pancake V (1983) Attachment and dependency in developmental perspective. Child Development 54(6): 1615–27.

Sroufe LA, Egeland B and Carlson E (1999) One social world: The integrated development of parent–child and peer relationships. In: WA Collins and B Laursen (eds) Relationships as Developmental Context: The 30th Minnesota Symposium on Child Psychology. Hillsdale, NJ: Erlbaum, pp. 241–62.

Target M (2000) Paper presented at attachment conference, New York University.

van IJzendoorn MH (1995) Adult attachment representations, parental responsiveness, and infant attachment: A meta-analysis on the predictive validity of the Adult Attachment Interview. Psychological Bulletin 117: 387–403.

Warren S, Huston L, Egeland B and Sroufe LA (1997) Child and adolescent anxiety disorders and early attachment. Journal of the American Academy of Child and Adolescent Psychiatry 36: 637–44.

Warren S, Emde R and Sroufe LA (2000) Internal representations: Predicting anxiety from children's play narratives. Journal of the American Academy of Child and Adolescent Psychiatry 39(1): 100–7.

Waters E and Deane K (1985) Defining and assessing individual differences in attachment relationships: Q-methodology and the organization of behavior in infancy and early childhood. In: I Bretherton and E Waters (eds) Growing points of attachment theory and research. Monographs of the Society for Research in Child Development 50 (1–2, Ser. No. 209): 41–65.

CHAPTER 10

Revisiting Freud in the light of attachment theory: Little Hans' father – oedipal rival or attachment figure?

Luis J. Juri

> Daddy, don't trot away from me!
> Little Hans (Freud, 1909, p. 45)

Little Hans

In 1908 Freud treated – through the father – a 5-year-old child named Herbert Graf for a period of four months. The case is known in psycho-analytic literature as 'Little Hans'. The child was afraid that a horse would bite him in the street, a fear that was considered by Freud as zoophobia. In the case history, published in 1909, Freud considered Little Hans a 'small Oedipus', who wanted to displace his father so he could be alone with his 'beautiful mother' (Freud, 1909). The child's phobia was inter-preted as a fear of paternal punishment (the dangerous horse of the story) because of the incestuous wishes toward the mother. Due to his ambiva-lent feelings toward his father – tenderness and hostility – Little Hans displaced the conflict from the representation of the 'father' to the repre-sentation of the 'horse', a displacement through which emerged the fear of animals, which became a symptom.

Little Hans died in 1973, at the age of 70; the same year John Bowlby published *Separation: Anger and Anxiety* (Bowlby, 1973), the second volume of three works where he re-examined the Little Hans history. Bowlby's significant contribution lies in the formulation of attachment as a new motivational system. For him 'attachment' signifies a disposition to maintain proximity and contact (affection bonds) with a figure that has the character of protector, termed the 'attachment figure'.

In his re-examination of the case history of Little Hans, Bowlby uses a paradigm based on attachment theory, arriving at different conclusions. In Bowlby's analysis of the case history, his central point is that:

... distinct from and preceding any fear of horses, Hans was afraid that his mother might go away and leave him. (Bowlby, 1973, p. 327)

Bowlby attributes that fear to the threats of abandonment of the child made explicitly and implicitly by the mother. Carefully reviewing the text, he finds repeatedly proof that Little Hans' states of anxiety are linked with the fears of separation. Little Hans' symptoms coincide with the formation of an anxious attachment that manifests itself as a fear of loss of the attachment figure (separation anxiety) and as clinging behaviours.

Freud had noticed the repeated maternal threats in the case history, but he centred the weight of his interpretation on the sexual wishes of the child (Oedipus). According to Bowlby (1973) Little Hans feared that his mother would make the threats of abandonment come true, leaving him alone, fears that would be the product of the representational model of his mother as 'potentially abandoning' (Marrone, 1993), constructed from the verbal maternal threats (via the semantic route) and with other experiences such as separation from the mother due to the birth of the little sister Hanna (via the episodic route). Fear and not a sexual wish are seen as driving Little Hans to have contact with his mother. The fear of being abandoned has stimulated a wish for attachment.

The father of Little Hans

Those of us who have become familiar with the concept of paradigm (Kuhn, 1962, 1977) cannot forget that all clinical material is selected and endowed with significance in accordance with the theoretical beliefs of the analyst. Freud listened to the account given by Hans' father on the child's phobia using his theory of infantile sexuality that he had formulated four years previously. Freud was interested in ascertaining whether Hans' phobia, in Freud's own words:

... supports the assertions which I put forward in my 'Three Essays on the Theory of Sexuality'. (Freud, 1909, p. 101)

In 'Three Essays on the Theory of Sexuality' (1905) Freud had presented his vision of the sexual life of a child and developed his ideas on the libido, erogenous pleasure and autoeroticism. Freud analysed Hans' symptoms based on these tenets, seeking the confirmation of his thesis in the case history. Freud's beliefs where transmitted to Hans' father, who admired his ideas. The child's father oriented the conversations with his son in the direction of Freud's theories, which clearly biased his questions and contributions. Freud's paradigm is evident throughout the pages of the case history, and his analysis of Hans – performed via the father– was carried out under these tenets.

As a logical result, the interpretations of the horse of the child's phobia received the 'theoretical load' of the paradigm. The celebrated horse of the case history is a psychoanalytical illustration of the epistemologist Thomas Kuhn's assertion that data are never neutral (Kuhn, 1962). Kuhn questioned the traditional division between the language of observation (that is neutral) and theoretical language (that is explanatory). Data and observations are supposedly contaminated by the observer's paradigm (Kuhn, 1962, 1977). The horse of the phobia has therefore received the theoretical load of the different analysts who have dealt with it, the present work being no exception.

The phobia first appeared after Hans saw a large, heavy horse fall. The interpretation given by his father suggested that the child's wish was that he (the father) would fall in the same way, and even suffer death as a result. This interpretation satisfied Freud as it fitted his recent discoveries, i.e. the Oedipus complex and his theories on child sexuality. Guided by these assumptions, Hans' father inevitably had to interpret the horse as a symbolic rival of the child. Hans' conflict with his father – over his erotic inclinations towards his mother – was displaced from the representation of the father to that of the horses, by which he was afraid of being bitten (castration) and whom he wished to see fall and die (death of the oedipal rival). These interpretations were constructed under the 'sway of wish'. Thus behind Hans' anxiety towards falling horses could be conjectured the hostile wish towards his father (Juri, 1999).

Nevertheless, Freud had also wondered on one occasion whether the horse could also be seen as representing Little Hans' mother. Freud wrote:

> ... Hans had always observed horses with interest on account of their large widdlers, that he had supposed that his mother must have a widdler like a horse, and so on. We might thus be led to think that a horse was merely a substitute for his mother. (Freud, 1909, p. 27)

In a conversation between Little Hans and his mother, the child clearly demonstrates the association pointed out by Freud:

> *Hans:* 'I was looking to see if you 'got a widdler too.'
> *Mother:* 'Of course, Didn't you know that?'
> *Hans:* 'No. I thought you were so big you'd have a widdler like a horse.'
> (Freud, 1909, p. 10)

Hans compares his mother to a horse. It is worth noting that the child's mother once claimed she has a 'widdler', which reinforced Hans' association of his mother with horses. During the dialogue the mother makes no distinction between men and women, which suggests that the representation of the mother with the big 'widdler' could have been maintained.

In spite of this evidence, which is present in the case history, Freud opted for associating the animal with the father. In a joint interview between Freud, Hans and his father, Freud comments that a fragment of the issue of the horses had been clarified. He was referring to what the horses had on their eyes, and the black around the mouth. Freud jokingly asked Little Hans if his horses wore goggles, which Little Hans denied. Freud then asked if his father wore glasses, which Hans also denied and which was against all evidence. The black around the horse's mouth appeared to be the father's moustache, reinforcing the connection between the horse and the father. Freud explained to Hans that it was inevitable that he should believe that his father was angry with him because of his (the child's) excessive love of his mother, but that this was not the case. The connection established by Freud between the dangerous horse and Hans' father fitted the logic of the paradigm. According to the Oedipus theory it was due to his own sexual wishes toward his mother that Hans should inevitably fear his father and therefore believe that his father was angry with him. Thus the horse of the story, by necessity, had to represent a castrating father. This was the 'theoretical load' which the horse of Hans' phobia received. However, the text contains abundant proof for thinking that Hans might have feared his mother more than his father, and associated her with horses. Together with evidence of affectionate behaviour towards Hans, it can be seen that the mother

(a) carried out repeated threats (Freud, 1909, pp. 8,16, 35, 44);
(b) assigned herself a 'widdler' (Freud, 1909, pp. 9, 10);
(c) relished challenges (Freud, 1909, p. 18);
(d) had a rejecting attitude (Freud, 1909, pp. 19, 22, 28).

Hans' father, despite certain conflicts with the child, showed himself to be

(a) a calming influence (Freud, 1909, p. 44);
(b) empathetic (Freud, 1909, p. 19).

I believe that it is reasonable to think that Hans' father did not represent a dreaded rival for the child, but rather a protective attachment figure (Juri, 2001). I am aware that I approach this case history with other theoretical beliefs and that my observations possess the 'theoretical load' of attachment theory and the view of child development influenced by John Bowlby's work.

Let us follow how Hans manifests his attachment to his father. At one stage of the conversations which took place between the second and third of April, Hans had moved close to his father, who said to him:

> *I:* 'So you come to me because you're frightened?'
> *Hans:* 'When I'm not with you I'm frightened; when I'm not in bed with you, then I'm frightened.'
>
> (Freud, 1909, p. 44)

Hans' expression 'When I'm not with you I'm frightened' suggests that the father exerts a calming influence on the child, dispelling his fears, rather than being a problematic rival. In the same conversation, Little Hans reproaches his father for not taking into account his affection for him.

> *Hans:* 'Yes. Why did you tell me I'm fond of Mummy and that's why I'm frightened, when I'm fond of you?'
>
> (Freud, 1909, p. 44)

The child rightly protests because the father cannot recognize the child's affection towards him. Nor is he able to perceive Hans' anxiety regarding his repeated trips away from home. In the same dialogue Hans says to his father:

> *Hans:* 'When you're away, I'm afraid you're not coming home.'
> *I:* 'And have I ever threatened you that I shan't come home?'
> *Hans:* 'Not you, but Mummy. Mummy's told me she won't come back.'
>
> (Freud, 1909, p. 44)

The child is afraid that his father will not return, a fear undoubtedly increased by the fear of abandonment by his mother. Hans' fear is not only about his mother leaving but also about his losing his father. His words 'When you are away' referring to his father, could be linked to the latter's repeated trips from Gmunden to Vienna and to the anxiety these separations appeared to arouse in the child. The father, however, failed to recognize the influence of these trips as he was convinced that Hans wished him to leave, thus enabling the child to be alone with his mother.

Unlike the father's reading of the situation, I suppose Hans harboured a feeling of attachment to his father, looking for safety in the bond. This supposition coincides with his father's accepting and comforting attitude. He assures the child that he does not have a threatening attitude (unlike the mother, who has an inclination towards threats of all kinds). But the father was 'blind' towards Hans' affectionate and anxious approach to him because his beliefs and expectations led him to suppose an oedipal unconscious rivalry. Hans, however, I believe, becomes uneasy because he fears that his loving and non-threatening father may go away and leave him. On one occasion, when his father is about to leave the breakfast table, Hans makes the following request:

> *Hans:* 'Daddy, don't trot away from me!'
>
> (Freud, 1909, p. 45)

The father was struck by the child's use of the word 'trot away' ('davon-rennen') rather than 'leave' ('davonlaufen') and he replies:

> *I:* 'Oho! So you are afraid of the horse trotting away from you.'
>
> (Freud, 1909, p. 45)

The child identifies the father with a horse, but not one that bites but with a horse's trotting away. Freud did not ignore Hans' tenderness towards his father, but he considered it to be exacerbated reactively, and existing with-in a conflict of ambivalence (tenderness–hostility). The father is unable to perceive his son's wish for a secure figure (one who does not 'trot away') because he is guided by the idea that 'my son wishes to get rid of me and take my place as father' (Freud, 1909, p. 39). The child's affection cannot be perceived by the father as a loving gesture (bond of attachment) as long as he is theoretically bound to consider Hans to be an incestuous rival.

I suspect that the child was attempting to find in the father the 'secure base' (Bowlby, 1988) which the mother was only partly providing. Hans' mother was inconsistent and did not provide security. On the one hand, she was an affectionate mother who received the child into her bed and consoled him but on the other hand, as has previously been mentioned, she also used threats, rejected the child and was provocative. Consequently, she constituted an 'insecure base' for the child, threaten-ing not to return. This behaviour would account for Hans' turning to his father in his search for security.

Following this line of thought, we are faced with the question of Hans' hostility towards his father. On several occasions, Hans demonstrated aggression towards his father. Once he hit him on the hand, and then kissed him on the same hand (Freud, 1909, p. 43). Again, surprisingly, there was an instance in which the child unexpectedly head-butted the father in the stomach (Freud, 1909, p. 43). This aggression would coin-cide with the oedipal rivalry present, marking hostility with the sexual competitor, only to be converted subsequently into anxiety. However, we can ask the question: Could the child's hostility have any other plausible explanation? An event that had an influence on Hans' aggressive attitude towards both his father and mother was the birth of his younger sister Hanna. According to Freud, Hanna's birth was the 'big event' in Hans' life. The brief sequence of events that follows shows the moment of the appearance of the horse phobia and an anxiety dream in relation to the birth of Hanna.

Hans' age at:

Birth of Hanna	3 years 6 months
Changing bedrooms	4 years or 4 years 6 months
Dream of anxiety	4 years 9 months (2 or 3 January?)
Fear of horses	4 years 9 months (8 January)

Hans' mother went into labour at 5 a.m., at which time his bed was moved into another room. The child would never forget the moment, and in future conversations with his father he would make ironic references to the event with a patently hostile attitude.

> *I:* 'Did you see how the stork brought Hanna?'
> *Hans:* 'Why, I was asleep, you know. A stork can't bring a little girl or a little boy in the morning.'
> *I:* 'Why?'
> *Hans:* 'He can't. A stork can't do it. Do you know why? So the people shan't see. And then, all at once, in the morning, there's a little girl there.'
>
> (Freud, 1909, p.74)

Hans' words were 'all at once, in the morning, there's a little girl there', showing that Hanna's birth was unexpected and probably not without a certain degree of trauma. Hans caught a sore throat shortly after the birth of his sister. In the throes of fever, he was heard saying:

> 'But I don't want a baby sister!'
>
> (Freud, 1909, p. 11)

The arrival of Hanna, together with the subsequent deprivations and distancing to which the child was subjected, contributed to increasing his anxiety over the separation with his mother together with producing hostility associated with this anxiety. Bowlby's theory assigns an attachment-related function to the aggressive reaction. Hostility may arise due to whatever has caused separation from the attachment figure (e.g. the birth of Hanna) or as an attempt to be reunited with the threatened figure. The functional aggression can become dysfunctional when the hostility is aimed at targets such as vengeance or the suffering of the other (Bowlby, 1979, 1988).

Bowlby agrees with Freud over the role of Hanna's birth in the appearance of Hans' symptoms. Freud attributes the child's anxiety – at least in part – to his separation from his parents, caused by the birth of his little sister, and he even went so far as to attribute to the event a share of Hans' hostility towards his father. According to Bowlby, Freud did not deepen his perception of the state of anxiety suffered by Little Hans as a result of the separation he suffered (Bowlby, 1973). In fact, it was hardly to be expected that Freud would pursue this direction. Freud related a certain degree of hostility of the child towards his father with the latter's lies about the stork. But, for Freud, the child's aggression over the story of the stork served to reinforce his hostility resulting from the oedipal rivalry. A central tenet was the competition with the sexual rival. The hostility arising from another source 'reinforces' the oedipal hostility, which signifies that it is of a secondary importance. Freud observed that Hans suffered deprivation due to the birth of Hanna and pointed out the separation from his mother suffered by the child. Likewise, Freud stated that the child experienced a revival of the pleasure-giving moments of his infancy, aroused by his perception of his mother's care of Hanna. Freud wrote that 'the erotic need was incremented' as a result of 'both influxes' (Freud, 1909, p. 107). Sexual motivation ('erotic need') prevailed over other possible motives such as the wish for attachment produced by separation anxiety. It must be remembered that Freud recognized only sex and nutrition as motivation for bonding. The notion of attachment is a distinct motivation from sexuality and nutrition and does not appear in psychoanalysis until Bowlby makes his contribution. Although attachment and sexuality are different motivational systems, they are not contradictory, but rather, interrelated. According to Nicola Diamond:

> What can be said is that sexuality emerges in the developing infant in the context of attachment tie. Attachment and sexuality become fundamentally interrelated and overlie each other. (Diamond, 1998)

In parallel fashion, Bowlby gives priority to separation anxiety. This phenomenon, undoubtedly observed in the 1909 case history, played the role of a secondary tenet, whereas the central tenets for Freud were the pleasure principle, the wish fulfilment, the oedipal sexual motivation. These tenets are seen at work in the assessment of the report on Hans' fears sent to Freud by the father, in which we read:

... in fact nothing throws him into greater alarm than when a cart drives off ... (Freud, 1909, p. 45)

Hans' 'greater alarm' was not related to the child's fear of losing his parents, which was aroused by the departure of the carriage. The separation anxiety was disregarded in favour of the idea that the child wished his father to go away so as to be alone with his mother (Oedipus).

Little Hans' father wrote:

The repressed wish that I should drive to the station, for then he would be alone with his mother (the wish that 'the horse should drive off') is turned into fear of the horse's driving off. (Freud, 1909, p. 45)

The father suspects that behind Hans' anxiety lies a repressed wish for him to leave. The logic of the paradigm leads him to infer that the child wishes to eliminate his sexual rival. This supposition is related not only to the oedipal sexual motivation, but also to the thesis that the psychical apparatus is mobilized exclusively by wish (Freud, 1900, p. 598). These tenets lead to the conclusion that there was a wish (sexual wish) operating behind the anxiety, when the child heard a carriage departing. In 'Inhibition, Symptoms and Anxiety' (1926) Freud modified his theory on anxiety. In this text Freud held that the anxiety of the child came from fear of the loss of the object. This represented a re-elaborating of the anxiety theory. In the new theory, anxiety is considered a signal of danger, whereas in his first theory, anxiety arose from uncontrolled libidinal tension. In the new theory, anxiety is linked to the helplessness of the psychical and biological state of the infant ('hilflosigkeit') and is given a relational function. The anxiety signal would be at the service of the maintenance of the link, to give a warning alarm when threatened with danger of loss. John Bowlby finds affinities with the Freud of 'Inhibition, Symptoms and Anxiety', for the value assigned in that text to separation anxiety, which coincides with the importance that it has in his theories regarding attachment.

Bowlby's revision of Freud's case history focuses primarily on Hans' relationship with his mother. The weight assigned aetiologically to the mother's threats of leaving the home are responsible for this bias on the part of the author. Nevertheless it could be argued that the excessive emphasis placed on the maternal role in attachment theory in its beginnings might have underestimated the role of the father.

Marrone has drawn attention to the fact that Bowlby and Ainsworth's early work emphasizes the role of the mother and is therefore consistent with my analysis of the case history. More recently, attachment theory has focused more on the role of the father (Marrone, 1998). In my opinion, a theoretical framework centring on the mother–infant relationship should include an analysis of the paternal function. In the present chapter, I have pointed out numerous indications that show a wish on the part of Hans to get close to his father in his search for a 'secure base'. I believe that the mother's shortcomings in providing a secure base prompted the child to turn to his father for the satisfaction of his need for security. Whilst revisiting the case of 'Little Hans' from the point of view of attachment theory, I therefore feel that it is necessary to incorporate the wish for attachment the child sought from his father, his need for security within this relationship, and his anxiety at his imaginary departure.

The reader will note that in my analysis the child's father plays a similar role to that of the mother. I should like to point out that I do not consider my analysis of the relationship between Hans and his father as a generalized formulation regarding the role of the father. Quite the contrary, I have no intention whatsoever of 'maternalizing' the latter. My observations in this work are strictly limited to my re-reading of the case history. John Bowlby has shown how a father can carry out roles that are distinct from the mother's, such as taking part in physical activities with boys, or becoming a companion in their games (Bowlby, 1988). I wish to present the issue of the role of the father as a starting point for reflection within attachment theory.

An intersubjective reading of the 'Little Hans' case history

Continuing my analysis of the case history, I should like to point out that Hans' symptoms could be observed within the conceptual framework of an isolated psyche or using a paradigm that includes an intersubjective context. In the work of 1909 the accent was placed on endogenous determinants. The libido, as an internal energy source, would be seen to be the motivation drawing Hans towards his mother, as described by Freud in the following text:

> ... it becomes quite clear why he was so fearful in the evening, if we suppose that at bedtime he was overwhelmed by an intensification of his libido for its object was his mother, and its aim may perhaps have been to sleep with her. (Freud, 1909, p. 25)

The figure of the libido that 'overwhelmed' Little Hans provides a fitting metaphor of the model of endogenous energy source with which the child in the case history is analysed. The idea that a wish, in this case sexual, originates autonomously inside the subject derives from a model that sees the mental apparatus as a closed, or quasi-closed unit, with a tendency to discharge excitement. Although Freud in no way ignored the influence of external factors, the emphasis he places on the endogenous pole in the functioning of the psyche and in the aetiology of the symptoms left partially in the shadows the influence of the bonding context-kinship at the root of Little Hans' wishes and fears. It is particularly true for Freud's economic model. By assigning a structuring role to identification, Freud was to give a place to 'others' in the organization of the psyche (Freud, 1923).

Although Bowlby never employed the term 'intersubjectivity', its use does not contradict his ideas, since affective bonds play a central role in his thinking (see Diamond, in Marrone, 1998). Bowlby focuses on the interplay between individual psyches and the influence of internal models (representational models) in the arousal of wishes, fears and the perception of others (Bowlby, 1988).

In Hans' intersubjective context, we find the representational model of his mother as a 'potentially abandoning figure'. The 'representational models' or 'working models', are cognitive structures (unconscious system of beliefs) which drive the appearance of fears, wishes, expectations, etc. The representational models are constructed in two ways: (a) via the episodic route (the 'seen' and the 'heard' by the child), and (b) the semantic route (what is 'said to him' by the parents through the language). Representational models of attachment figure – the basis for the representation of others – and representational models of the self – the basis of the self and of self-esteem – are incorporated through these routes (Bowlby, 1980; Marrone, 1993; Steele and Cassidy, 1999). The construction of the representational models does not depend solely on lived experiences with attachment figures. Intrapsychic operations may also have a role to play. For example, we can see the imaginary efforts made by a subject in order to be reunited with an absent figure (Marrone, 2001). The representational models govern the appearance of fears, desires, expectations, hopes, etc., and may intervene in the construction of dreams or symptoms.

The representational model of Little Hans' mother as a 'potentially abandoning figure' (Marrone, 1993) dominated the appearance of Hans' fear of abandonment and the subsequent defensive displacements. Hans' representational model was constructed both semantically, from the maternal threats of abandonment, and episodically, from events such as the birth of his younger sister Hanna, causing the child to feel deprivation and distancing from his mother. In my opinion, the child's fear of being abandoned by his mother (a 'potentially abandoning' figure) was displaced towards his father, generating in Hans the fear that he might also abandon him ('Daddy, don't trot away from me!). However, the figure of the father appears to be only 'moderately abandoning', representing a lesser risk for the child, in comparison with the figure of the mother, whilst he also appears as a calming influence. Hans observed to his father that when he was with him he felt soothed and that he also assuaged his fears of being abandoned (Freud, 1909, p. 44).

I believe that Hans' fear of abandonment was displaced from the representation of his mother and father towards the representation of the horses and carriages. Consequently, the anxiety he felt on the departure of the carriages can be seen to represent his anxiety over the potential departure of his parents, and his fear of a definitive separation from them ('Mummy's told me she's not coming back'). The displacement from the representation of the potentially abandoning parents towards the dangerous horses and departing carriages implies a defensive operation-taking place in the child's psyche. The idea causing his anxiety (abandonment by his parents and loneliness) is relegated to his unconscious – albeit partially – by means of a process of 'defensive exclusion' (Bowlby, 1980) whilst a substitute fear appears in the conscious self. No matter how anxiety-provoking the fear of horses or carriages may be, it is undoubtedly less disturbing than the intolerable idea of being separated from his parents.

In a very brief clinical history, I should like to show certain similarities between the respective events occurring in Hans' and Sylvia's cases. In the latter case, a 6-year-old girl was terrified at the idea that chairs and furniture would fly and hit her. She called the furniture 'Daleks' and it took two years of therapy and interviews with her mother to reveal their true identity. Sylvia's father had been a violent man who during his fits of anger would throw and break the furniture. On one occasion, he had even thrown his daughter around the room. But however terrifying these 'Daleks' undoubtedly were, they were less terrifying than the idea, which had been relegated to her unconscious, that her own father hated her so much that he was capable of physical aggression towards her. By means of this displacement Sylvia, in her imagination, was seeking to save her figure of attachment (Bowlby, 1985).

Hans both saw and heard evidence that was to serve to construct the representation of his mother as 'potentially abandoning.' His wish for attachment to his mother is therefore not due to an internal accumulation of stimuli seeking a channel of discharge (sexual libido), but rather the activation of the model of his mother as 'a potentially abandoning figure'. The activation of this representation (for either internal or external motives) arouses Hans' separation anxiety and his craving for security, whereas contact with his mother produces a calming effect on the child, dispelling his fears. Parts of the case history provide examples of the activation and deactivation of attachment as a function of the child's contact with his mother. A few days before the appearance of the child's phobia with horses, and on a number of separate occasions, Hans suffered fits of anxiety, which resulted in fits of weeping. He was subsequently soothed by contact with his mother (Freud, 1909, p. 24). It is difficult to explain these mood swings where states of anxiety alternate with calm – the latter produced by contact with a particular figure – as a function of the theory of accumulation and discharge of endogenous stimuli driving the individual (libido). It would appear more feasible to conceive these sequences as the activation and defusing of representational models in a given context.

On one occasion (during the course of a walk to Schönbrun), Freud rightly observes that despite the presence of the mother, Hans experienced a fit of anxiety, ascribed by Freud to an unsatiated craving of the child's libido. According to Freud, the accent was put on economic and endogenous factors. The intersubjective stance on the issue I adopt in this chapter leads us to inquire into the emotional state of the mother and the mother–child exchanges which took place during the walk under discussion. These latter questions cannot be adequately understood in Freud's internal energy source model.

The reader may notice the existence of a counterpoint between two paradigms: (a) that of an isolated or quasi-isolated psyche, whose processes predominantly originate within the individual and (b) that of the subjective interacting, of interrelated psyches (Bowlby, 1969; Stolorow, Atwood and Brandchatt, 1994). In this chapter I hold a model of a psyche which is constructed and which operates within an intersubjective context. This model is analogous to an open system, one of whose defining features is the maintenance of an exchange with the environment (Bowlby, 1969). Throughout this chapter, Hans' symptoms were analysed in relation to the affective context of the case, which implies taking into account the interactions and subjective experiences of the child with reference to his attachment figures.

Table 10.1 shows Hans' relationship with his parents using Freud's oedipal theoretical framework contrasted with Bowlby's attachment theory, which is my espoused paradigm.

Table 10.1. Little Hans' case history

Freud	Bowlby
Oedipus	Attachment
Mother: libido object	Mother: attachment figure
Father: oedipal rival	Father: attachment figure
Little Hans' wish to get rid of the father (rivalry)	Little Hans' wishes for his father not to 'trot away' (wish for a secure attachment)
Sexual wishes	Attachment wishes
Castration anxiety	Separation anxiety
Economic–instinctive paradigm	Attachment–survival paradigm

It is worthwhile noting that the theoretical framework of attachment theory does not ignore the issue of father–son rivalry, or the triangular relationships which characterize the Oedipus conflict. However, it attributes the rivalry and triangular relations to the vicissitudes of attachment relationships. As Bowlby put it in a personal conversation with Mario Marrone, 'In life there are many triangular situations in which the subject is afraid of being the excluded third party, and wishes to ally himself with one of the other parties. Such situations are more common in people who feel rejected or insecure. But why ascribe a universal, sexual character to this triangularity?'

In this light, I believe that Hanna's birth created a triangular situation in Hans' life. The child is known to have felt insecure, due to his fear of being abandoned by his parents. The birth of his little sister increased the child's fear of separation from his attachment figures, giving rise to the jealousy and rivalry he felt towards Hanna, together with his hostile reactions towards his mother and his father, which are usually attributed to the existence of an oedipal conflict.

References

Bowlby J (1969) Attachment and Loss, vol. 1: Attachment. London: Hogarth Press.

Bowlby J (1973) Attachment and Loss, vol. 2: Separation: Anxiety and Anger. London: Hogarth Press.

Bowlby J (1979) The Making and Breaking of Affectional Bonds. London: Tavistock Publications.

Bowlby J (1980) Attachment and Loss, vol. 3: Loss: Sadness and Depression. London: Hogarth Press.

Bowlby J (1985) El papel de la experiencia de la infancia en el trastorno cognitivo. In: A Freeman and M Mahoney (eds) Cognicion y psicoterapia. Buenos Aires: Paidos.

Bowlby J (1988) A Secure Base. New York: Basic Books.

Diamond N (1998) On Bowlby's legacy. In: M Marrone, Attachment and Interaction. London: Jessica Kingsley.

Freud S (1905) Three Essays on the Theory of Sexuality. Standard Edition 7: 123–243.

Freud S (1909) Analysis of a Phobia in a Five-year-old Boy. Standard Edition 10:1–147.

Freud S (1923) The Ego and the Id. Standard Edition 19: 1–59.

Freud S (1926) Inhibitions, Symptoms and Anxiety. Standard Edition 20: 75–176.

Juri L (1999) El psicoanalista neutral. ¿Un mito? Homo Sapiens Ediciones. Rosario.

Juri L (2001) Juanito ¿Edipo o Apego? In: M Marrone, La Teoria del Apego. Un enfoque actual. Madrid: Editorial Psimatica.

Kuhn T (1962) The Structure of Scientific Revolutions. University of Chicago Press.

Kuhn T (1977) The Essential Tension. University of Chicago Press.

Marrone M (1993) Los Modelos Representacionales. Teoría del Apego y Relaciones Afectivas. Bilbao: Servicio Editorial del País Vasco.

Marrone M (1998) Attachment and Interaction. London: Jessica Kingsley.

Marrone M (2001) La Teoria del Apego. Un enfoque actual. Madrid: Editorial Psimatica.

Steele H and Cassidy J (eds) (1999) Internal Working Models Revisited. Attachment and Human Development, vol. 1, No. 3 (Special Issue). London: Routledge.

Stolorow R, Atwood G and Brandchatt B (1994) The Intersubjective Perspective. New York: Aronson.

CHAPTER 11

Attachment and bereavement

LUIS J. JURI AND MARIO MARRONE

Introduction

We should like to begin this chapter by highlighting two important points:
Many people believe that attachment theory is basically – if not exclusively – concerned with early development. Bowlby never formulated
attachment theory in such a restricted framework. Attachment theory is
fundamentally interested in the study of attachment relationships and
their influence on psychic, psychosomatic and psychosocial life across the
life cycle. Studies on loss and bereavement in adult life clearly demonstrate this assertion.

The second point is that the study of bereavement – carried out in the
framework of attachment theory – underlines some areas of coincidence
and divergence between Freudian thinking and attachment theory. This is
important not only to clarify conceptual matters but to keep attachment
theory linked to its source: psychoanalysis.

Mourning according to Freud

The basic text, which set the ground in psychoanalysis for the study of
bereavement, was 'Mourning and Melancholia'. Freud (1917 [1915] p.
243) defined mourning as reaction to the loss of a loved person, or to the
loss of some abstraction which has taken the place of one, such as one's
country, liberty, an ideal, and so on. Freud (1917 [1915]) made the distinction between mourning – or normal bereavement – and melancholia
– or pathological bereavement. According to Freud, the distinguishing
mental features of melancholia are a profoundly painful dejection, cessa-
tion of interest in the outside world, loss of the capacity to love, inhibition
of all activity, and a lowering of the self-esteem.

Moreover, Freud (p. 245) suggested that melancholia is in some way related to an object-loss, which is withdrawn from consciousness, in the sense that the person may know *whom* he has lost but not *what he has lost in him*. Instead, in mourning, 'there is nothing about the loss that is unconscious'. This may seem a controversial statement. It sounds strange that the creator of psychoanalysis would refer to certain mental processes as devoid of unconscious components. However, what Freud probably meant was that mourning was more straightforward than pathological bereavement.

Of course, Freud used the well-established concept of *object*, which attachment theorists replace by 'person', 'attachment figure' or 'representation of the other' or 'internal working model' of an attachment figure (Marrone, 1998, p. 110). Here, in referring to Freud's work, we shall keep the term 'object'. In 'Mourning and Melancholia', Freud introduced the term *'work of mourning'*. He said (p. 244), 'In what, now, does the work which mourning performs consist? I do not think there is anything far-fetched in presenting it in the following way. Reality testing has shown that the loved object no longer exists, and it proceeds to demand that all libido shall be withdrawn from its attachments to that object. This demand arouses understandable opposition. It is a matter of general observation that people never willingly abandon a libidinal position, not even, indeed, when a substitute is already beckoning to them.'

Here, of course, Freud was using the concept of 'libido' according to his own metapsychology. In this context, the libido is the dynamic manifestation in psychic life of the sexual drive. Freud regarded attachment as subservient to sexuality and not – as Bowlby eventually proposed – as a discrete motivational force, separate from the sexual drive. Freud conceptualized attachment as a libidinal investment or cathexis. Therefore, mourning involves a withdrawal of such cathexis.

According to Freud (pp. 244–5), mourning involves a process of detachment of the libido. This process is carried out bit by bit, a great expense of time and energy. Each single one of the memories and expectations in which the libido is bound to the object is brought up for this process to occur. When the work of mourning is completed, in Freud's words, the *ego* becomes free and uninhibited again. This task is fulfilled by the ego.

Freud used the word 'ego' with two different meanings. On the one hand, *ego* was the person or *self* as distinct from other individuals. On the other hand, the *ego* was the part of the mind that involves particular attributes and functions. Various ego functions, such as reality testing, judgement, thinking, impulse control and defence, were proposed and defined throughout Freud's writings, beginning with his 'Project for a Scientific Psychology' (1895). Reality testing plays an important role in providing an accurate perception and acknowledgement on what is going on internally and externally.

In the process of mourning, withdrawal of the libido from the object is accomplished through reality testing. In 'Inhibitions, Symptoms and Anxiety' (1926 [1925], p. 172), Freud said that mourning occurs under the influence of reality testing; for the latter function demands categorically from the bereaved person that he should separate himself from the object, since it no longer exists. It has often been said that the process of mourning is equivalent to 'killing the dead'. The phrase clearly expresses a view that the process of mourning consists of separating self from the object. Such a definition of the process of mourning has become classic and influenced the thinking of several generations of analysts.

According to Freud, the successful outcome of the work of mourning consists of the withdrawal of libido from the lost object, so that it can be displaced to a new one. This process is understood in terms of energy that needs to locate a new target. Freud (1894, 1895, 1915, 1920) used metaphors based on analogies with hydraulic and electric systems to explain his views in this respect. It is well known that Freud's metapsychology was the result of an attempt to place psychoanalysis in the nineteenth century natural sciences, heavily influenced by physics. In this context, the sexual drive was regarded as the source of the libido and the libido as energy that is invested in mental representations of the object. The economic model (see Marrone, 1998, pp. 33–4) is not a secondary hypothesis in Freudian theory. Freud (1915) considered it as one of the most fundamental premises to understand psychological processes, including the development of psychopathology.

The dominant paradigm in Freud's thinking was characterized by a view of the mind as a closed or almost closed system. He conceptualized the mind as an entity that was relatively isolated from the environment and world of interactions with others. In this context, in the process of mourning, a normal or pathological outcome was seen as fundamentally determined from within by internal forces. Largely, the fate of mourning was to depend on the intrapsychic itinerary of the libido. Freud also thought that identification with the lost person plays an important role in the process of mourning and that identification is almost exclusively oral in character. In attachment theory, identification is a mechanism that is independent from orality.

Bowlby (1980, pp. 26–7) adopted and elaborated the view advanced by Freud in the final pages of 'Inhibition, Symptoms and Anxiety'

(1926). In this context, when the subject fears the loss of the attachment figure, he is likely to experience anxiety. When the subject has reasons to believe that the attachment figure has been permanently lost, he is bound to experience pain. In attachment theory, the basic source of anxiety is insecurity in relation to the constant and sensitive availability of the attachment figure. Of course, this view greatly differs from Melanie Klein's view, which attributed the origin of anxiety to fear of annihilation and persecution, in a way that seemed largely independent of interpersonal events.

The work of mourning according to attachment theory

Although Bowlby is known for his concern with understanding child–caregiver attachments, he viewed close and intimate relationships between adults within the same theoretical framework he used to look at the child–parent relationship. In this sense, Bowlby remained clearly anchored in the psychoanalytic tradition, but modified some of its metapsychological assumptions.

Bowlby did not accept Freud's *economic point of view*, which involved propositions concerning the role of a hypothetical psychological energy, and he postulated a new concept of instinctual behaviour within which the need to form and sustain attachment relationships was considered to be primary and distinct from the sexual motivation. Furthermore, he clearly reformulated some fundamental points of psychoanalytic theory according to an interpersonal model. Finally, he borrowed from modern biology a control theory or cybernetic model to understand psychic organization and functioning.

Bowlby examined the work of mourning according to the theoretical framework of attachment theory. In Bowlby's view, attachment ensures protection and survival. Having durable and intimate relationships with specific others is a basic condition of existence. The nature and quality of early parent–child relationships is a determinant of future development. Yet, attachment plays an important role throughout the life cycle, including attachment between adults. Therefore, the disruption or loss of an attachment relationship is likely to have a severe impact on the bereaved person. Bowlby (1980, p. 7) highlighted the point that loss of a loved person is one of the most intensely painful experiences any human being can suffer. It is painful to experience and painful to witness. To the bereaved, nothing but the return of the lost person can bring true comfort. Freud (1926, p. 172), in the last paragraph of

'Inhibition, Symptoms and Anxiety', also acknowledged the pain of loss.

In Bowlby's terms, the process of mourning takes place in the context of an attachment relationship – which is then broken – and not, strictly speaking, as Freud suggested, as the sudden frustration of libidinal cathexis, which requires withdrawal. Furthermore, traditionally, in psychoanalytic writings, emphasis has been placed on identification with the lost object as the main process involved in mourning. Such identification has often been considered compensatory for the loss. However, attachment studies show that identification is not the main process intervening in mourning.

A pioneering figure in studying and understanding bereavement from the attachment perspective is the distinguished psychiatrist Colin Murray Parkes. He joined Bowlby's team at the Tavistock Clinic (London) in 1962. From then up till Bowlby's death in 1992, they maintained a close professional relationship. Parkes studied important aspects of the bereavement process. His studies showing that the work of mourning goes through several distinct phases have been one of his major contributions. He also described different forms of bereavement in accordance with the bereaved person's attachment organization.

Furthermore, Bowlby and Parkes established the distinction between child and adult bereavement. In the past, some psychoanalysts believed that children who were facing a significant loss do not go through a mourning process. This notion proved to be false. At the age of 5, the majority of children can understand the difference between a temporary separation and a permanent separation. Gradually, they learn that death is inevitable and universal. Children who permanently lose their main attachment figure develop a state of vulnerability, which can eventually lead to serious emotional problems and psychiatric pathology. Their immediate response can be despair, behavioural problems or marked withdrawal. Enuresis, constipation and sleep disturbance can accompany the clinical picture. A child who lost one parent may fear that he can lose the other one. In the same way, children react negatively to the death of a sibling. Rutter (1966) observed that the propensity to develop psychiatric disturbance increases by 500 per cent as the result of a loss of a parent.

When these children reach adulthood, many of them show their emotional scars. Their vulnerability can be fertile soil for depression, chronic anxiety, suicidal tendencies, etc. There is clear evidence that loss of a parent is a major factor that creates vulnerability to psychiatric disturbance in childhood (Brown, Bifulco and Harris, 1987). This situation has a greater impact when substitutive care is inadequate.

Phases of bereavement in adult life

According to Bowlby and Parkes (Bowlby, 1979, 1980, p. 85; Parkes, 1972), there are four phases in the bereavement process. These phases should not be regarded as fixed and universal stages. In each individual they manifest in particular ways, both in terms of duration and sequence.

These phases are:

1. Phase of numbing.
2. Phase of yearning and searching for the lost figure, lasting some months and sometimes for years.
3. Phase of disorganization and despair.
4. Phase of greater or lesser degree of reorganization.

The *phase of numbing* usually lasts from a few hours to a week and may be interrupted by outbursts of extremely intense distress and/or anger. Frequent comments like 'I can't believe it!' or 'it can't be real' reflect the refusal to accept the distressing news. Numbing is an attempt at using denial as a defence mechanism at a point where the person cannot cope with the sudden realization of the loss. The emotional and cognitive recognition of the loss involves a process of mental reorganization that requires time. Sometimes there appear moments of elation, based on an illusory fantasy of reunion with the lost person.

One form of pathological reaction is to prolong this phase over a period of weeks, months or even for the rest of the subject's life. The emotional anaesthesia may continue as if nothing has really happened in the life of the person. This could be the result of an emotional blockage, which is only broken at times by anxiety-ridden dreams or psychosomatic disturbance. In other cases, the lack of response simply indicates that the subject has never felt a deep attachment with the lost person, perhaps as the result of having an avoidant personality structure.

The *phase of searching* starts when the person begins to consciously acknowledge the reality of the loss. During this phase, the person may experience outbursts of weepiness and anguish accompanied by psychosomatic manifestations. There is restlessness, insomnia and preoccupation with thoughts of the lost person, combined with a sense of his actual presence. There is an intense conscious or unconscious wish to be reunited with the lost person, which can also manifest itself in dreams. The bereaved person may misperceive a number of signals from the environment as an indication that the other is about to turn up. At times, such misperceptions can become illusions with disturbing quality.

Another common feature of the second phase of mourning is anger. Anger is directed at the lost person, for having left and at people held responsible for the death. There can be profound hostility towards the dead person for all sort of reasons, but anger arising out of the loss itself is to be expected in most cases. None of these features should be considered as pathological. Bereaved people oscillate between grieving and meeting the other demands of life – eating, sleeping, working, caring for surviving children, and so on.

When there is pathology, it manifests as an absence of grief or, at the opposite pole, as a long and chronic process of mourning and longing to regain the lost other, which never leads to resolution. This interminable process may manifest in the way the subject talks about the loss. It can also show in 'family museums', where objects that belonged to the dead person are kept intact, as if it were in preparation for the eventual return.

The *phase of disorganization and despair* begins when the person gives up hope of being reunited with the lost person. Grief, at this stage, can be very intense. There may be a process of endless examination of how and why the loss occurred. As Bowlby (1980, p. 93) said, for mourning to have a favourable outcome it appears to be necessary for a bereaved person to endure this buffeting of emotion.

The *phase of reorganization* begins when the person has accepted the reality of the loss. In conjunction with this process and because of it, there is a reorganization of the person's representation of the lost person. This also involves a restructuring of the system of meaning and style of life, which had been formerly related to the existence of the other that is no longer there. Things have changed and life cannot go on as it was. This acceptance is not a purely cognitive act. There is a painful modification of personal identity. The subject is no longer a husband or wife but a widower or a widow. The subject is no longer part of a family with five members, now he is part of a family with four members. The resolution of this phase makes it possible for the person to make plans for the future, perhaps substitute the lost person with a new attachment and make adjustments to his notion of himself in relation to his world.

Vulnerability, resilience and the course of bereavement

Unlike Freud, Bowlby did not think that the bereavement process (in its normal or pathological variants) depends on intrapsychic factors. Bowlby and attachment theory conceptualize the course of bereavement as a complex set of factors, including the subject's personality, his own attachment history, the quality and length of the relationship with the lost person, the circumstances under which the loss occurred and so on. Furthermore, the quality and extent of the subject's immediate social network (family and friends) facilitate or obstruct the normal course of bereavement. The course of bereavement is not entirely played on an inner stage.

Whom the subject has lost (a spouse, a parent, a sibling, a child, a friend) is important as well as the age of the subject and the age of the lost person. The circumstances under which the loss has occurred (sudden accident, murder, political event, long or short illness, etc.) are also important. Some losses, such as those that occurred as the result of war, criminal act or accident, may also be an integral part of traumatic events. In these cases, the loss leads not only to mourning but to traumatic responses. Immigration and exile involve simultaneous and prolonged or final separation from many friends and relatives. However, they also entail the loss of a cultural milieu and a physical space with all the inherent symbolic elements.

Colin Murray Parkes (1975) has studied other forms of loss, such as loss of a limb or part of the body. Brown et al. (1987) have also studied a particular form of bereavement, which they call 'the loss of a cherished idea'. This mainly refers to a situation whereby a person has to give up a cherished idea about who an attachment figure may be (a spouse, an adolescent son, a parent, a sibling) in the light of new evidence. This may happen, for example, when a father discovers that his adolescent son is a drug addict, the wife discovers that her husband is bisexual and is having a homosexual affair, the sister discovers that her brother is a criminal and has been convicted, and so on and so forth. In all these cases, the loss of the cherished idea involves a reorganization of the mental representation of the other.

To summarize and complete this account, we can say that studies on bereavement inspired by attachment theory show that the course of bereavement depends on a number of factors:

1. The nature, depth, duration and quality of the relationship that the subject has had with the lost person.
2. The subject's attachment history.
3. The defence mechanism that the subject normally uses in situations of loss and deprivation.
4. The extent and quality of the support that the bereaved person receives from his social network.

Vulnerability factors preceding the loss normally determine the degree to which psychiatric or psychotherapeutic intervention may be necessary.

People with a history of secure attachment to parental figures are less likely to need clinical interventions than those who did not follow an optimal pathway (Parkes, 2001).

Factors likely to contribute to vulnerability or resilience in the face of bereavement can be classified as follows:

Preceding factors

- Childhood attachment experiences.
- Attachment experiences in later life.
- Previous psychiatric history, particularly depression.
- Previous history of life crisis (including previous losses) and degree of subsequent resolution.
- Quality of the relationship that the subject had with the lost person.
- Kinship with the lost person (spouse, offspring, sibling, parent, aunt, uncle, grandparent, cousin, friend or other).
- Degree of emotional and practical dependency that the subject had with the lost person.
- Degree of ambivalence that the subject had with the lost person.
- Form and timing of the death (sudden, expected, traumatic, single or multiple loss, etc.)
- Whether there has been a period of separation before the death occurred.

Concurrent factors

- Age and gender of the bereaved subject and the dead person.
- Personality of the bereaved subject, particularly in relation to his tendency to inhibit expression of feelings, fall in state of sadness, etc.
- Status and socioeconomic resources of the bereaved person.
- Nationality and sociocultural and ethnic origin of the subject.
- Subject's religion, including the possibility of participating in religious ceremonies and religious community.

Subsequent factors

- Social support or isolation of the subject.
- Stress or calmness in the life of the subject.
- New opportunities (such as forming a new relationship).
- Success or failure in other aspects of the subject's life.

We should mention here that if the subject has lost someone with whom he/she had a couple relationship, the process of mourning can continue after forming a new couple relationship. Mourning for the lost person and starting a new relationship may not necessarily be mutually incompatible. Where pathology shows is when seeking a new relationship is part of a manic attempt to deal with underlying feelings of loss and depression.

Among the subsequent factors, we should include certain disturbances that originate in the process of bereavement, which – in turn – make it more difficult. We should include here *medical complications* (such as immunological failure and psychosomatic diseases) as well as *psychiatric complications* (such as dissociative fugues; see Marrone, 1998, pp. 186–7; depression, etc). We shall deal with these aspects later in this chapter.

The urge to recover the lost person and restore the relationship

Bowlby and Parkes have observed that in the majority of cases the bereaved person experiences a strong conscious or unconscious urge to recover the lost person and restore the broken relationship. This is a key point in the understanding of bereavement and fits well with attachment theory (Parkes, 1972; Bowlby, 1980). The subject, instead of trying to internally 'kill the dead', is searching for the dead, trying to recover him/her.

The urge to recover the other may manifest in persistent thinking about the other, sometimes to the point of ruminating in an obsessional way. This can be seen as an attempt on the part of the analyst to keep the bond in the realm of thinking. Some subjects express the fear of blurring the mental image and memories of the lost person. Often the subject has dreams in which the lost person is alive. Waking up to the reality of the loss is profoundly disappointing and painful. Many of these dreams have a wish-fulfilment aim. In them the dead person is not only alive but also younger, with a healthy aspect, as if there was no risk of becoming ill and dying. If the work of mourning had the aim of taking distance from memories of the dead person, bereaved people do not seem to be able to meet this demand. Of course, the bereavement process is complex and variable. The bereaved subject oscillates between believing in the irrevocable reality of death and a sense of disbelief (with an inherent search for the other and hope of recovering the other). Bowlby held the view that, in the course of evolution, irretrievable losses are statistically insignificant. Human beings experience reversible separations from their attachment figures. Because of this, we are biologically equipped to react as if all losses could lead to reunion. In this context, anger is directed at trying to induce reunion.

The main purpose of anger is to make the other feel obliged to come back to honour the mutual commitment. In this context, aggression can be viewed not as an emotion *per se*, but as a piece of behaviour that expresses either anger or hate. Anger is retentive. The function of anger is to promote a favourable, just and sensitive response from the attachment figure. When the attachment figure does not adequately respond, or else responds in an inconsistent way, anger can become chronic. Hatred, instead, is expulsive. The person who hates feels so invalidated in his/her sense of self by the other, that getting rid of the other becomes the primary aim. In this context, we can understand why anger is an emotion that arises in the bereavement process.

Illusory ideas of reunion, searching, weepiness and anger are aimed at reunion. They also constitute a re-edition of a child's strategies to evoke a positive response on the part of the caregiver. Early attachment patterns may be reactivated.

From this perspective, we can see why it is very misleading to see the normal work of mourning as an attempt to eliminate the feeling of being attached to the lost person. A normal mourning process is better understood as a way of *preserving* the memory of the lost person with an altered sense of meaning.

Mourning and identification

What is the place of identification in trying to recover the lost person? In 'Mourning and Melancholia' Freud (1917) indicates that the love for the object finds refuge in identification. In other words, renunciation of the object derives from identification with that object. The investment in the object is replaced by identification with the object. According to this reference framework, the investment in the object is transformed into a narcissistic investment, from a representation of the object into a representation of the ego (or self). This self-investment is more resistant to the frustration of not having the external object anymore.

Bowlby (1980, p. 13) endorsed Freud's idea that enacting the role of the missing person is often a manifestation of identification. In this context, identification with the lost person is a way of trying to retain it inside oneself. However, Bowlby (1980, p. 26) thought that identification is neither the only, not even the main, process involved in mourning. Here, Bowlby objected to some notion, which has been prominent in psychoanalysis since Freud (1921) formulated it in 'Group Psychology and the Analysis of the Ego', that 'identification is the original form of emotional tie with an object [and that] in a regressive way it becomes a substitute for a libidinal tie' (Freud, 1921, pp. 107–8). In terms of attachment theory, identification is not the original form of emotional tie. It is a defence mechanism that the subject uses under specific conditions. Emotional ties are formed as the result of a specific motivational system, quite different in nature from sexuality and defensive processes. Moreover, what psychoanalysts often ascribe to identification is a large array of processes, which – strictly speaking – do not always fall into the realm of identification. This does not mean that Bowlby disregarded the concept of identification. He was particularly interested in the way a person may consciously and – more often – unconsciously identify with values, character traits and behavioural patterns of parental figures. He observed that where there has been an abusive or dysfunctional parent–child relationship, the child (and later the adult) might treat others as he has been treated (see Marrone, 1998, pp. 138–9). Therefore, a person may identify with aspects of a lost parent, but such identification may be largely independent from the mourning process.

Permanence of the absent other

As we have indicated, for Freud, normal mourning involves a withdrawal of libidinal cathexis from the lost object and its investment in a new object. In this way, the ego breaks its links with the annihilated other. The ego obtains normal narcissistic satisfaction out of continuing to live, instead of following the fate of the dead object. In this theoretical context, the work of mourning is a gradual detachment (Laplanche and Pontalis, 1983).

Bowlby saw this process differently. According to him, the favourable outcome of normal bereavement does not necessarily consist of an emotional detachment from the lost object. Remaining emotionally attached to the lost person is compatible with the acceptance of the death and the psychological and socio-psychological reorganization that mourning involves. The continuous representation of and bond with the lost person can manifest as a sense of constant inner company by the other, by pursuing the same projects and values that the dead person had or by being localized in a specific and adequate place (a photograph, the grave, etc.). This mental state is reached once the acute pain that follows the lost recedes. While there is pain and sadness, in optimal circumstances there is also preservation of the attachment with the lost person. The resolution of the intense initial state of pain and sadness seem to be the gradual result of a complex process, whereby there is greater acceptance of the reality of the loss but also a reorganization on the representation and meaning of the relationship.

Studies with widows have shown that the continuous, albeit modified, presence of the other in the subject's representational world is part of normal bereavement. It is not uncommon that the widow has internal conversations with her deceased husband. This persistent attachment is compatible with the development of the widow's capacity to reorganize her life with an ever-increasing sense of autonomy and independence from the lost husband. The persistence of this sense of attachment often allows the widow to reorganize her life in a meaningful way. This sense of enduring attachment rests on values and projects that were profoundly shared in the marriage.

Our thesis that an adequate outcome of bereavement involves the persistence of a sense of internal accompaniment by the dead person is not a minor point. It contradicts one of the basic premises of the traditional psychoanalytic theorizing, which holds the view that the work of mourning has a precise task, which is a withdrawal of cathexis from the lost object. The latter is based on the economic point of view in metapsychology. As far as the work of mourning is conceptualized in terms of energy, the loss of the object leads to a displacement of energy to a new representation. In this context, the ego acts as a regulator of energy.

Bowlby's thinking departs from such an assumption. In terms of attachment theory, psychic life is fundamentally organized by attachment needs. Affect regulation is a process highly intertwined with mental states in relation to attachment, rather than a derivative of energy control. Given the fact that, in Bowlby's reference framework, attachments are the source of security and trust, in optimal circumstances the persistence of the affectional tie with the lost person fulfils an important function. The presence of the lost person as an internal companion helps the subject to use it as a secure base from which to explore new directions in life and, consequently, reorganize his position in the world and his aims in life.

Of course, we are not referring here to pathological bereavement, as is the case with chronic mourning and mislocation. In these examples, there is no true internal companion but a frozen object in an unresolved mourning.

On mislocation

Bowlby (1980, pp. 161–9) talks about 'mislocation', which occurs in unresolved or chronic mourning. A mislocation is a way of trying to locate the lost person somewhere inappropriately. One common form of mislocation is that of regarding a new or different person as a substitute for someone lost. In some cases, such a mislocation can take bizarre and extremely damaging forms. One of us had a psychotherapist in supervision who treated a man with a serious identity disturbance. This man was the second child of a couple who lost their first child when he was 8. He was six years younger than the older brother. Following the death of his brother, his parents constantly tried to impose on him characteristics of the dead brother. In another example, the parents tried to impose a female identity on their young son, following the death of his older sister, which resulted in a severe form of gender identity confusion. In fact, to attribute to another person the complete personal identity of someone lost is easier when the recipient is a child, because a child is more malleable than the adult is. Bowlby also thought that the process of identification with the lost other might also be conceptualized as a *mislocation into the self.*

How can we understand this process of mislocation? We would advance the following hypothesis. The process of normal bereavement relates to the process of symbolization. Essentially, symbolization is the process of instituting a representation of the other in its absence. In Freud's description (see 'Beyond the Pleasure Principle', Freud, 1920), an 18-month-old child – in the temporary absence of his mother – plays with a wooden reel with a piece of string tied round it. He holds the reel by the string and very skilfully throws it away saying, 'gone'. Then he pulls the reel back by the string, to make it reappear, saying 'there'. In this way, the child is symbolically mastering the anxiety that arises as the result of mother's temporary absence. We would suggest that when the child's representational world is marked by a high level of insecurity, his capacity to symbolize and built a representation of mother in her absence is impaired. Anxiety is too high for him to play with a notion of separation. Therefore, in the absence of a symbolized representation of her, he needs to have her concrete presence to mitigate his anxieties. Later on in life, following loss, grief becomes unmanageable and can be assuaged only by the real presence of the other. This will give rise to the process of mislocation.

Lack of grief

In our clinical experience, there can be two main sets of reasons to explain such a reaction. In some cases, it seems that the person feels bereaved but cannot openly express his/her emotions. In other cases, the sense of attachment to the dead person was weak or poor.

Martin is a 47-year-old Englishman, who works as an accountant. He has never been married and has had short-lived heterosexual relationships. His pattern of behaviour in these relationships has been to keep an emotional distance from his partner and to feel little grief following the break-up. He has two sisters, both divorced, who emigrated to a remote country. Martin has a circle of friends but does not feel close to anyone. He seeks therapy because of an ill-defined inner sense of emptiness.

In his therapy, Martin keeps saying that he feels nothing for his therapist. He says, 'I do not feel involved with you. I continue coming to my sessions because I think I need therapy, but I do not feel I have a relationship with you.' In the course of his therapy, both parents died. In addition, a friend died in a motor accident. Martin felt nothing. He reported these deaths as facts, with an emotionless tone of voice. What happened in Martin's early life? How can we explain his style of relating and his emotionless response to loss?

It became clear, through a difficult and long analysis, that Martin has developed strong avoidant defences against closeness and intimacy, in order to ward off painful feelings from childhood. He was a neglected child. His parents were hospital nurses who worked opposite shifts. At home, they were consistently cold and distant. The family rarely met as a group. In the evening the norm was not to sit at the table and eat a cooked meal. The children normally made themselves beans on toast or a sandwich and ate in front of the television.

Mourning and divorce

The process of mourning in relation to the loss of a partner or spouse through separation or divorce has been studied by Robert S. Weiss (1975), a researcher from Boston, who had close contact with Colin Murray Parkes and John Bowlby.

From the point of view of attachment theory, we could say that a couple, when it is formed, has already vulnerability or resilience to interpersonal conflicts, given by each other's attachment history. Couples formed by people who have been securely attached to both parents are more likely to manage, survive and learn from interpersonal conflict and adversity than those formed by insecure partners.

The fact that, in separation and divorce, the loss is the result of a break down of communication, of loss of affection and trust in each other or intolerance to tension and conflict, makes the process of bereavement complex and idiosyncratic. Furthermore, the lost person is still alive but not accessible. Separation occurs not because someone has died but because of the couple's state of mind.

If the relationship had enough depth, length and meaning, for months after the end of the marriage, the events leading to its breakdown are likely to occupy the thoughts of the separated husband and wife. At the same time, as in the case of bereavement following death, the process goes through several stages. The first stage is that of *separation distress*, associated with an intense discomfort because of the other's inaccessibility. Separation distress is an analogue to the child's response to the threat of abandonment. The presence of a friend or a new partner may relieve but not cure separation distress. All attachment relationships are highly specific to each member of the relationship. One cannot be easily substituted by the other.

The person who made the decision to separate may go though a similar process to the one who is left. The person may feel tense, vulnerable, preoccupied with the image of the other and with memories of past moments in the relationship. He or she may find it difficult to concentrate, may lack motivation to continue with normal pursuits (hobbies, study, work, etc.) and experience profound sadness and unhappiness. However, in some cases, the separation, instead of producing grief, gives rise to a permanent or intermittent state of euphoria. Such a state of euphoria could be a manic reaction, to deny loss. It could also be the final outcome of a gradual process of emotional detachment that went on before the actual separation occurred. In the latter case, the person may feel liberated after years of feeling oppressed. The person is then free to pursue new interests and gain a new sense of personal identity. However, even though a state of euphoria may help the person to handle the emotions of separation, an underlying state of fragility may persist.

Feelings of loneliness and sadness may be exacerbated by anniversaries of important dates in the history of the relationship, or by visiting places where important events took place. A new relationship can be formed during this period, so that the processes of establishing a new relationship and emotionally distancing oneself from the previous partner or spouse can occur simultaneously. However, some people cannot tolerate having to go through one process and the other simultaneously. One possible explanation is that changing partners often involves a profound process of identity reorganization.

In some cases, the couple breaks up because one partner has been having an extramarital affair. People have affairs for all sort of reasons. Here we cannot discuss the complexity of the problem. Deceit and betrayal constitute the key issue. However, not in all cases does an affair lead to dissolution of the relationship. What really matters is that the affair might yet be another symptom of a dysfunctional relationship and is likely to become a new problem in itself. When the affair leads to dissolution of the couple relationship, the issues posed by who is left excluded and who has a new companion do not directly correlate with the degree of suffering that one or the other may experience. In this context, emotional responses are more complex than in the loss of a partner because of death.

In many cases, the bereavement process following a marital break-up is very similar to the work of mourning following a death. Eventually, the individual reaches a state of reorganization. This involves greater emotional stability, regaining hope of having a better life in the future, an increase of self-esteem and a readjustment of the sense of personal identity.

Preceding, concurrent and subsequent factors play a part in determining the course of bereavement following a marital break-up. As in mourning following death, grief following marital break-up may produce minimal responses, or lead to chronic or pathological bereavement. In some cases, the separated person may experience total denigration or idealization of the former partner or spouse. Intense emotions or defences against these emotions (jealousy, humiliation, anger, shame, guilt, etc.) can be experienced. For instance, a female patient blamed herself for the break-up of the marriage, even when, objectively, she knew that her husband was a very difficult man to live with. The analysis revealed that – as a child – her parents always blamed her for all sorts of adversity. She ended up believing that anything that went wrong was her fault. Another patient with a history of role reversal in her childhood continued to look after her emotionally ill husband, even after separation, to the detriment of her own legitimate interests.

The analysis of patients who are separating often reveals how the attachment history of each individual has significantly contributed to the emergence and lack of resolution of marital problems as well as to the way each partner deal with the loss. As a general principle, we can say that the function of a good marriage is to create a system of emotional regulation through mutual empathy and reflective capacity. A marriage in crisis reflects fundamental failures in these capacities and the way each partner deals with the separation – particularly if a psychotherapist or good friends do not assist them.

Often, psychotherapists have to work with a patient in a difficult partnership or marriage. Not infrequently, when they see that a relationship becomes chronically destructive or dysfunctional they try to promote a separation. However, an important principle in analytic practice is not to tell the patient how he should conduct his life. But a lesson they must learn is that the break-up is likely to trigger difficult emotional responses and that the patient should be warned what lies ahead of a separation.

If there are children of the marriage, the situation is even more complex. Accessibility to, and authority over, the children may decrease considerably. The marital conflicts – as well as the intergenerational disturbance underlying them – may also be reflected in the way children's development is affected. The analyst should be attentive to this issue. Often, the separated partner loses friends who remain loyal to the former spouse, adding more losses to the main loss.

Divergent psychoanalytic interpretations

We should like to offer a critical analysis of a vignette taken from a book by Nasio (1996). Nasio is an Argentinean psychoanalyst who lives in Paris and works within a Freudian and Lacanian theoretical framework. Nasio refers to one of his patients, a 38-year-old woman called Clemence. Clemence, after trying hard and long to resolve her problem of infertility, finally managed to get pregnant. Unfortunately, her baby, Laurent, died shortly after his birth. Clemence's bereavement is intense. She is inconsolable. Over a long period, following the baby's death, Nasio simply accompanied Clemence with her pain.

Eight months later, in the course of a session, Nasio said to Clemence, '... if you have a second child, I mean a brother or sister of Laurent ...' Clemence, feeling taken by surprise, responds, 'It is the first time someone mentions a sister or brother of Laurent!'

For Nasio, this was a crucial moment in the analysis of the bereavement. Clemence understood that a future child would not take the place of Laurent. Therefore, having another child would not take away her love for her dead baby. In this way, Laurent could still be loved and also be the first child of the couple. Having another child would not imply having to withdraw the affection she had for her first baby. To put it differently, the baby would remain alive in her inner world, with all her memories of his short life and the deep affection for him still present in their mind. According to the theoretical understanding implicit in this clinical vignette, Clemence does not 'kill the dead', does not withdraw her libido, she *reorganizes* her mental representation of the lost baby.

To recapture what we have said so far, for Freud the work of mourning takes place under the ruling of the reality principle, which demands a withdrawal of libido from the lost object. This was Freud's thesis, even if he did not overlook the subject's wish to recover the lost object. Freud thought that the bereaved person over-invests the lost object before withdrawing the libido. Bowlby, instead, did not believe that the reality principle was the determinant factor that prompted the work of mourning but the need to preserve the attachment, albeit in a reorganized form.

In this context, we could say that it is the attachment motivational system that directs the bereavement process. If, as attachment theory holds, the attachment bond serves a protective function, it follows that relying on the mental representation of the lost person can act in optimal circumstances as a 'secure base' to explore a new world without the concrete presence of the other. The attempt to recover the lost person does not lead to failure but to new encounters. There is profound pain and sadness but there is growth and a reorganization of meaning.

Freud and Bowlby coincided in recognizing that the work of mourning implied the recognition of the reality of the loss. Where they differ is in the description of the pathways that lead to such recognition. For Freud, reality testing promotes the abandonment of the other. For Bowlby, the second phase of the bereavement process involves an intense wish to recover the accessibility of the lost other. The failure of this wish – in the third and fourth phases of the process – leads to an acceptance of the reality of the loss and a reorganization of the internal representation of the relationship and the sense of self with reference to the other.

In Freud's terms, the normal outcome of the bereavement process is to separate from the object, because it no longer exists. For Bowlby (1980) acceptance of the loss is compatible with the persistence of the attachment. Table 11.1 sets out their two positions.

Table 11.1. Freud's and Bowlby's views on mourning

Freud	Bowlby
Mourning: Reaction to loss	Mourning: Reaction to loss
Aim: detachment	Aim: reorganization of attachment representation
Process: withdrawal and reinvestment of libidinal cathexis. Reality testing	Process: preservation of the other's protective function
Normal mourning: withdrawal of libido	Normal mourning: making the absence of the other compatible with the persistence of the internal attachment
Psychic function: stimulus control	Psychic function: affect regulation
Notion of psyche: closed system	Notion of psyche: intersubjective system
Underlying paradigm: economic and energetic models	Underlying paradigm: attachment system

In order to avoid reductionistic formulations, we must remember that Freud accepted the possibility of maintaining the attachment to the lost object. Moreover, Bowlby did not consider the persistence of the attachment to be always a positive outcome, since some forms of persistent attachment reveal a pathological process. Here we are trying to describe and compare two different paradigms rather than falling into a reductionistic stance.

Childhood bereavement

There was a time when psychoanalysts believed that children do not mourn. Bowlby said that children do mourn, although their bereavement process may not be noticed. Furthermore, they are profoundly affected by loss of significant others. 'Grief and mourning in infancy and early childhood' (Bowlby, 1960) was one of Bowlby's early seminal papers. Bowlby (1980, p. 320) noted that if childhood mourning is to follow a favourable course, certain conditions are required. The child should have enjoyed a reasonably secure relationship with his parents prior to the loss. He should be allowed to discuss the loss, receive accurate information about the circumstances surrounding it and participate in family grieving. Finally, he should have the comforting presence of the surviving caregivers. Children have less knowledge and understanding of issues of life and death than adults have. In the great majority of cases in which children are described as having failed to respond noticeably to a parent's death, it seems more likely that both the information given and the opportunity to discuss its significance were so inadequate that the child has failed to grasp the nature of what happened (Bowlby, 1980, p. 291). This is another important element of attachment theory, based on the notion that clear communications in the family and the ability to share and articulate thoughts, feelings and ideas are essential for the development of the child's capacity for reflective thinking and affect regulation.

Bowlby (1980, p. 345) refers to cases where the individual who experienced a significant early loss appears to be composed and self-assured while, at a deeper level, there is pain and grief. He called these coexistent mental states 'segregated systems'. Obviously, the first system is built upon defences against pain. Here, we do not intend to review the literature on childhood bereavement. It is, however, important to mention Bowlby's contribution to the study of such an important process.

Bowlby (1980, pp. 356–8) discusses clinical material related to a boy called James, aged 6, whose father died in hospital after a short illness. A child analyst on the staff of the Tavistock Clinic treated James. Following the loss of his father, James had become disturbed, particularly aggressive and quarrelsome. Under these circumstances, his mother decided to seek professional help.

In the course of his therapy, on one occasion James came readily to the therapist's room and dived immediately into an open drawer of toys made ready for him. Following his reactions, the therapist asked if he was looking for daddy. 'Yes', he replied immediately. In the course of his initial sessions, James showed a marked interest and doubts as to where his daddy might be and the wish to be reunited with him. He sadly added,

'Sometimes I forget what he looks like ... I try to think of him and he's not there.' James had an urgent desire to see his father again, even if it meant his dying too. He expressed the idea that he wanted to commit suicide with all his family so they could all be with daddy again.

Here, we should take the opportunity to explore a related issue, that of a child's reaction to parental suicide. A parent's suicide in childhood involves three main aspects. The first is that if a parent has committed suicide, he/she is likely to have experienced mental problems prior to the suicide act, which may have affected the way he/she treated the child. The second aspect is the loss itself. The third component is the traumatic element of knowing that a parent has killed himself/herself.

Traditionally, suicide was considered a sadistic attack on an internal object, lodged in the ego (or *self*) through identification. In 'Mourning and Melancholia', Freud says that ambivalence towards the object is turned to the self, which now identifies with the abandoned object. The complaints of the melancholic subject (*klagen*) must be regarded as grievances against the object (*anklagen*). Given the fact that by means of identification the object's shadow falls on the ego (or *self*), sadism is directed towards oneself. This gives rise to a dangerous disposition to commit suicide.

We cannot entirely discard Freud's hypothesis, which seems right in many cases. However, we should also consider the possibility of suicidal wishes being an expression of the subject's desire to be reunited with the lost person. In this context the suicidal person's death would not aim at killing the hated object but at a reunion with the lost other.

Additional concepts

Beyond the mere description and explanation of normal reactions to loss, Freud also proposed a theoretical reference framework to study and understand pathological bereavement. The pathology of bereavement includes manifestations such as absence of grief, delayed grief, prolonged and intense grief, actings-out, psychosomatic reactions, inordinate sense of guilt, manic responses, etc. It is interesting to note that attachment researchers have extensively studied the two major variants of pathological bereavement, absence of grief or intense and prolonged grief. In different moments of the life cycle, reactions to loss seem to reproduce the basic patterns of response to brief separation, studied in children aged 12 to 18 months with the Strange Situation Procedure. Insecurely attached children may react to brief episodes of separation from mother in different ways. One group of children under-react to the separation.

Another group over-reacts in a dramatic way, showing intense stress, anxiety and anger. A third group of children reacts with a disorganization of attachment strategies.

One fundamental idea in Bowlby's thinking is that whenever an individual of whatever age reacts to separation from an attachment figure, the pattern of response reflects (a) the organization of predominant internal working models of attachment relationships – or representational system – that the individual has, together with (b) his usual defence mechanisms and strategies in dealing with separation anxiety. Such a process is determined to an important degree by the experiences that the person may have had with his significant others throughout his attachment history, particularly his early attachment history.

Patterns of relating and interactions in couples are largely built upon the interconnection of each partner's representational system. Similarly, reactions to the rupture of the relationship, because of death of one partner or divorce, are also determined by these systems.

In adult life, individuals who have an avoidant organization of attachment strategies may have the tendency to behave in relation to couple relationships in one of two ways: either they may avoid forming relationships (as happens with some people who remain single for many years if not for ever) or they may form close relationships but not feel deeply involved at an emotional level. One interesting point of study is whether the person feels deeply but does not allow himself to consciously recognize his depth of involvement, or whether the person has never been able to establish a profound affectional tie with the other. If the latter was the case, the fact that the person does not seem to experience grief is not the result of repressing it. Simply, the person has not been able to forge a meaningful and pervasive tie with the other. However, whatever the case may be, what is clear is that underneath it all there is a defensive character structure against pain and hurt stemming out of abandonment, rejection or neglect. Bowlby, in his clinical work, observed that individuals with the tendency to repress feelings or inhibit their expression grew up in families where – as a child – showing feelings was not approved of or facilitated.

On the other hand, individuals who tend to go through a long and dramatic bereavement process may have an attachment history of inconsistent parenting. If the attachment figures alternated between moments of empathic availability and moments of withdrawal or rejection, the child may not have had the possibility of structuring a stable defensive pattern. In this context, a sense of inner vulnerability remains near the surface. Moreover, the child may have learned that crying and/or expressing anger louder and longer were effective strategies to elicit a caring response. In adult relationships, these individuals tend to seek care in an emotionally intense yet ambivalent way. In the face of loss, the sense of vulnerability and need for reassurances increases dramatically and cannot lead to satisfactory resolution.

The therapy of bereavement

The technical approach to the problem of bereavement depends to a large degree on the therapist's paradigms. The previously internalized paradigms govern the selection and interpretation of clinical data and shape technical procedures.

In using attachment theory to understand bereavement and, at the same time, discussing clinical cases where mourning is a dominant issue, it is important to establish if the loss occurred prior to starting therapy or during the therapeutic process. In some cases, a recent loss or an unresolved mourning in relation to a much earlier loss may be one of the main determining factors in seeking a consultation with a psychotherapist. In these cases, it is important that the initial assessment takes into account not only the loss itself but the total interpersonal situation of the patient, past and present, particularly his attachment history. In certain cases, the patient needs only a relatively brief and focalized approach. In other cases, reaction to a loss may be the tip of the iceberg and a long, intensive and extensive analytic undertaking may be indicated.

According to attachment theory, the main tasks in the therapy of bereaved subjects are:

1. To allow the subject to express his feelings, pain, hidden wishes, etc., including anger or hatred towards the deceased person and those whom the subject makes responsible for the loss.
2. To find words to name these feelings.
3. To examine the subject's attachment history, including the quality of the relationship with the lost person as well as other significant people in the person's earlier life.

To fulfil these tasks, it is essential to respect the subject's feelings and to show empathy. Under such conditions, the patient may be able to express his rational or irrational fears, anger, hatred, and sense of loneliness and illusory projects to recover the lost person. It is not at all helpful to become a *representative of reality* and demand a renunciation of the attachment with the lost person.

Often, friends and patients remind the bereaved subject that the loss is irretrievable. The subject knows this at some level but needs the time that his internal processing may require. Even if the bereavement is prolonged, it is not appropriate for the therapist to show irritation because the process is taking longer than expected. A London-based analyst said to his bereaved patient, with a disapproving tone of voice, 'You can't mourn!' What the patient may need most is to be allowed to be internally in touch with the lost person. For this reason, some patients react unfavourably if the therapist tries to offer consolation.

Worden (1991) has proposed that the first task of bereavement therapy is to help the patient accept the reality of the loss. In order to achieve this aim, the therapist should use clear and definite remarks, such as 'Your son is dead'. One may wonder if such a technique may not inhibit the patient's free expression of feelings and his search for empathy and sensitive responsiveness. Even worse, such an approach may block the subject's quest for reunion with the lost person, which – in our view – is the core point of departure in the work of mourning.

The patient needs to be understood if he denies reality, if he has mad ideas about finding the lost person again and/or experiences anger against people he justly or unjustly blames for the death (doctors, nurses, etc.) or even against himself. Only if the therapist captures the full meaning of these reactions, and offers his understanding to the patient with empathy, will he be able to provide a secure base.

Without establishing an *empathic secure base*, the therapist may find it difficult to elicit the patient's full cooperation to take a step further and examine the *internal working models* of the self in relation to the lost figure. These internal working models influence the course and length of the bereavement process.

The bereavement process is likely to be more difficult and painful if the bereaved subject sees the other as irreplaceable and himself as unable to tolerate the loss and find new meaning for his life. This representation is normally based on the whole constellation of internal working models of early relationships. When there is a favourable outcome, the pain diminishes, the absence of the other is tolerated and the inner presence finds a satisfactory space in the subject's representational world. At this stage, the subject can get in contact with memories of past experiences with the lost person without pain.

But what happens when the lost relationship was so troubled by conflict and ambivalence that the subject has little to treasure internally? We know that some subjects have the tendency to minimize the negative aspects of the lost person and maximize the positive aspects. Other individuals, although they experience grief, also have intense negative feelings towards the lost other. Bowlby (personal communication) insisted that early attachments are formed on the basis of familiarity rather than on the basis of their quality. Children get attached to their caregivers even when they are unsatisfactory or abusive. For this reason, paradoxically as it may seem, some individuals experience deep grief and quest for reunion as a response to the loss of an unsatisfactory companion. In these cases, the work of analysis will have to be more extensive and the detailed exploration of the patient's early history an indispensable condition.

References

Birtchnell J (1970) Early parent death and mental illness. British Journal of Psychiatry 116: 281–8.

Bowlby J (1960) Grief and mourning in infancy and early childhood. The Psychoanalytic Study of the Child 15: 3–39.

Bowlby J (1979) The Making and Breaking of Affectional Bonds. London: Routledge.

Bowlby J (1980) Attachment and Loss, vol. 3. London: Hogarth Press.

Brown GW, Bifulco A and Harris TO (1987) Life events, vulnerability and onset of depression: some refinements. British Journal of Psychiatry 150: 30–42.

Freud S (1894) The Neuro-Psychoses of Defence. Standard Edition 23: 41–61. London: The Hogarth Press.

Freud S (1895) Project for a Scientific Psychology. Standard Edition 1: 281–381. London: The Hogarth Press.

Freud S (1915) Instincts and their Vicissitudes. Standard Edition 14: 109–40. London: The Hogarth Press.

Freud S (1917) Mourning and Melancholia. Standard Edition 14: 237–58. London: The Hogarth Press.

Freud S (1920) Beyond the Pleasure Principle. Standard Edition 18: 1–63. London: The Hogarth Press.

Freud S (1921) Group Psychology and the Analysis of the Ego. Standard Edition 18: 107–108. London: The Hogarth Press.

Freud S (1926) Inhibitions, Symptoms and Anxiety. Standard Edition 20: 75–174. London: The Hogarth Press.

Juri L (1999) El psicoanalista neutral ¿Un mito? Psicoanálisis y paradigmas. Rosario: Homo Sapiens Ediciones.

Laplanche JB and Pontalis JB (1983) The Language of Psycho-Analysis. London: The Hogarth Press.

Marrone M (1998) Attachment and Interaction. London: Jessica Kingsley.

Nasio JD (1996) El libro del dolor y del amor. Barcelona: Gedisa Editorial.

Parkes CM (1972) Bereavement. London: Tavistock Publications; 3rd edn: London: Routledge, 1986.

Parkes CM (1973) Factors determining the persistence of phantom pain in the amputee. Journal of Psychosomatic Medicine 17: 97–108.

Parkes CM (1975) Psycho-social transitions: comparison between reactions to loss of a limb and loss of spouse. British Journal of Psychiatry 127: 204–21.

Parkes CM (2001) Lecture given at the First International Conference of the International Attachment Network. Birmingham, September 2001.

Rutter M (1966) Children of Sick Parents. Oxford: Oxford University Press.

Weiss RS (1975) Marital Separation. New York: Basic Books.

Worden W (1991) Grief Counselling and Grief Therapy. New York: Springer.

PART 2

THEORETICAL CONSIDERATIONS

CHAPTER 12

Defensive processes, emotions and internal working models: a perspective from attachment theory and contemporary models of the mind[1]

MAURICIO CORTINA

Introduction

Bowlby's trilogy (1969, 1972, 1980) on attachment, separation and loss not only introduced a new theory of attachment ties across the life span, it also sketched a new information processing approach toward under-standing defensive processes, emotions and internal representations. This chapter reviews Bowlby's information processing approach and builds on it using contemporary models of the mind that are consistent with Bowlby's general approach. The chapter is organized in five parts:

- Part I shows how Bowlby's information processing approach to the mind and Edelman's theory of neuronal selection address problems inherent in Freud's theory of repression.
- Part II shows the relationship between an information processing approach and a 'holistic' theory of emotion. It also considers the links between emotion and motivation.
- Part III looks at defensive processes in light of the previous outline on information processing models of emotions and motivation.
- Part IV reviews Bowlby's concept of internal working models in light of contemporary developments in attachment theory, developmental psychology and cognitive science.
- Part V compares Bowlby's model of internal working models with related concepts of projective identification and phantasy from the object relations tradition.

Part I. Where Freud got stumped: conceptualizing repression

As Freud grappled with the mechanism of repression he came upon a major stumbling block. In the topographical model of the mind consisting of three subsystems, the conscious, preconscious and unconscious, Freud vacillated in attributing to the conscious or preconscious subsystems the role of censorship and of initiating repression. In this model, the unconscious is identified with what is dynamically repressed, and the preconscious with what is only functionally or descriptively unconscious and hence, accessible to consciousness. The topographical model ran into problems once Freud made the central clinical discovery that people are often unaware of repressing their experience ('resistance'). If the repressed and repressing forces are both dynamically unconscious, repression could no longer be seen as originating from the conscious or preconscious subsystems.

In order to get around this problem, in his structural theory (id, ego, superego) Freud (1923) located the repressing forces in the unconscious part of the ego, whereas the content – the drives that are repressed – were located in the id. As Gill (1963) and more recently Lachmann (1999) observe, although the repressing function and the repressed experience are now located in different mental structures (the ego and the id respectively), many problems remained unsolved. The distinction between the unconscious part of the ego that does the repressing and the repressed id seems arbitrary. If the unconscious ego and the id are both dynamically repressed, on what basis can one say they are different structures? Or is this just an ad hoc solution that was pointing toward a more intractable problem? To complicate matters even more, if the source of libidinal energy resides in the id how does the ego mobilize anti-cathectic energy to oppose the cathectic energy emanating from the id? Freud vacillated on this point, sometimes attributing the source of libido to the ego. This solution posed more questions than it answered. How do drives gain their cathectic energy from the ego?

The tendency to reify mental structures (id, ego, superego) and to imbue them with agent-like qualities was lampooned by Ryle (1949) and more recently by Dennett (1991) with his concept of the 'Cartesian Theater'. According to Ryle and Dennett, the tendency of postulating ghost-like agents ('the ghost in the machine') that orchestrate mental processes can be traced to Descartes. Descartes' philosophical dualism separates the spirit from body and mind. The brain belonged to the same mechanistic universe that Galileo and Newton had discovered, while the spirit belonged to an immaterial world. Ryle argues that mental processes are not things, not pieces of clockwork located in space as envisioned by Descartes. Nor is the mind driven by quasi-physical energies as assumed by Freud.

The mind is an enormously complex organ processing vast amounts of information. Until recently, attempts to conceptualize the nature of the mind have fallen into two types of reductionism: (1) mechanistic approaches, such as Freud's, that reduced the complexity of the mental processes – drives, emotions, defensive processes – using the scientific paradigm of the day based on a tension-reduction energy model; and (2) epiphenomenalist approaches that consider 'only the physical world as real and thoughts and feelings as no more than shadows playing no real part in life's drama' (Bowlby, 1969/1982, p. 106).

Exorcising the ghost in the machine (or how to solve the problem of conceptualizing repression)

Even if we discard Freud's psychic energy concepts, his theory of repression encountered two major obstacles:

1. How to solve the 'little person within the mind' problem; a master censor or interpreter (the ghost in the machine) that acts as gatekeeper allowing some experience to reaching consciousness while excluding others. The censor problem leads to an infinite regress: how did he get there and who in turn controls the censor?
2. How to solve the problem of repressed emotion without resorting to a 'master censor' that keeps felt emotion from being experienced.

Bowlby attacked these problems from two complementary perspectives. Leaning heavily on Langer's (1967) subtle and profound analysis, he argued that feelings are part of a physiologic process and not things separate from the process. Noting that to feel is a verb, Langer thought that to say 'I have a feeling' is very deceptive. The phenomenon usually ascribed to having a feeling is really that an organism feels something. According to Langer what is felt is a phase of a process. Just as iron heated to a critical degree becomes red, and redness is not a thing separate from the heating process, a felt state is part of a physiological process, instead of a product separate from the process. A felt state is a state of being, not a thing we have or possess. This analysis transforms the question from how a physical process can be transformed into something non-physical to a more manageable (but still very difficult) question of how the phase of feeling is attained physiologically and how the process may pass into unfelt phases again. Our understanding of this question has been brilliantly addressed by LeDoux (1996) by showing how fear is processed at unconscious and conscious levels.

Bowlby sketched a second perspective from which to approach the problem in his third volume on Attachment and Loss in the chapter entitled 'An information processing approach to defence'. Bowlby observed that whether information is derived from the environment or from the organism:

> Sensory inflow goes through many stages of selection, interpretation and appraisal before it can have any influence on behavior, either immediately or later. This processing occurs in a succession of stages, all but the preliminary of which require that the inflow be related to matching information already stored in long-term memory ... for most purposes the inflow of interest to psychologist and the common man alike is that which having been selected, interpreted and appraised goes forward to influence mood or behavior and/or stored in long-term memory. The fact that in the course of having been processed the vast proportion of initial information is routinely excluded, for one of several reasons, is ignored. For the understanding of pathological conditions, by contrast, the interest lies in the opposite direction, namely what is being excluded, and perhaps above all, why it should be excluded. (Bowlby, 1980, pp. 44–5)

When the information is evaluated as potentially dangerous, the process of defensive activity, defensive belief or defensive exclusion will be mobilized. When the information is already stored in long-term memory, defensive exclusion results in different degrees of amnesia, whereas new information arriving from sense organs will be subject to different degrees of compartmentalization, filtering or perceptual blocking.

Viewing the processing of information in general, and defensive processes in particular, as operating in multiple stages that are coordinated with memory systems opens up new vistas to problems that Freud was struggling with and which seemed to be intractable. Appraising, selecting and interpreting experience is not a function of a single structure of the mind such as the ego or superego; *it is what the brain does*. How does the mind go about filtering and sorting information while creating meaning out of this complex information processing organ?

Edelman's model of the brain

Perhaps no one has contributed more to transforming the 'little person in the mind' conundrum from a puzzle into a problem that can be operationalized and researched than Edelman (1987, 1992; Edelman and Tononi, 2000). According to Edelman the brain is perpetually in the process of recreating itself through twin processes: neuronal group selection and reentrant signaling. We constantly confront new information and new situations. How does the brain cope with this bewildering source of new information? Taking his cue from Darwinian selection, Edelman believes that the basic unit in the brain consists of groups or units of neuronal networks consisting of 50 to 10,000 neurons. There are perhaps a hundred million of such groups. Experience that proves to be of value for the organism is 'mapped' into these neuronal networks. A 'map' is not a representation in the ordinary sense, but an interconnected series of neuronal networks that respond collectively to certain elemental categories or tendencies, such as colors in the visual world or a particular situation that triggers a feeling in the emotional world. Edelman calls these elementary categories 'values' because they orient the developing organism toward selecting a limited amount of stimuli from an enormous array of possibilities. From a psychoanalytic perspective, the most fundamental values that organize the mind are based on motivational systems (Bowlby, 1969, 1972; Lichtenberg, 1989; Liotti and Intreccialagli, 1998).

Neuronal selection: prenatal and postnatal

Two selective processes operate in the brain. During embryonic phases of development neurons extend myriad branches to adjoining sections of the brain, creating an immense repertoire of neuronal circuits. Circuits that become functionally connected fire together, strengthening these connections ('neurons that fire together wire together') As a result, neurons in some neuronal groups become more closely connected than other groups.

A second process of neuronal selection filters and sorts postnatal experience. We now know that throughout postnatal development, the brain goes through cycles of synaptic proliferation and pruning. Neuronal networks that are not strengthened through use are pruned. The surviving neuronal networks are selected and become part of the architecture of the brain (Edelman, 1987; Schore, 1994). Experience that is salient and meaningful is literally mapped in the brain by this 'Darwinian' process of experiential selection. Initially, the selection of experience that is salient is based on organismic 'values'. Edelman's organismic values become transformed through social and cultural experience into complex systems of value and meaning.

Reentrant signaling

A second process is necessary. The neuronal networks that survive the developmental and experiential selection processes need to be coordinated, otherwise we should not be able to develop a coherent view of the environment or ourselves. The goal is achieved through reentrant signaling, which describes a process whereby neuronal networks that 'map' experience and internal states are in continuous and active communication with each other. The brain makes maps of its own maps and categories of its own categorizations by a process that can ascend indefinitely to ever more generalized pictures of the world. This is more than just a process of feedback that corrects its own errors, such as the feedback system envisioned by Bowlby in his goal-correcting attachment system. As we develop, a premium is put on the capacity to develop greater adaptive flexibility. New functional units that can 'learn' from experience are needed for this end. The concept of reentrant signaling accounts for this growth and differentiation by means of networks of neuronal units that are in a continuous process of communication and coordination, creating and recreating ever more complex maps of the world and of ourselves in relationship to the world. Reentry consists of this ongoing recursive signaling between reciprocally connected neuronal networks that map experience of the world and internal states. Neuronal networks that map experience are widely distributed throughout the brain, particularly throughout the complex thalamo-cortical brain system (Edelman and Tononi, 2000).

The twin concepts of neuronal selection and reentry signaling do away with the need to postulate a master interpreter or master censor functioning as a gatekeeper that sorts and filters information. These functions are collectively created. Edelman's picture of the brain is of a vast orchestral ensemble of players in continuous communication with each other. Even though there are several sections in this vast ensemble, like a wind section or the string section ('neuronal networks'), there is no master conductor that coordinates these sections. Like a giant jazz ensemble, each section is constantly feeding and inspiring each other as they improvise and create new music. The musical experience created by the improvising orchestral ensemble is similar to the coherence of experience that results from reentry processes. Edelman's model of integrative brain processes is intimately tied to a model of increasing complexity and differentiation (Edelman and Tononi, 2000). New properties emerge with increased complexity.

Edelman's explanation of how brain processes create a coherent view of the world out of a massive information flow is consistent with a long developmental tradition emphasizing the unity of development. As Loevinger (1976) put it, 'striving to master, to integrate, to make sense of experience, is the essence of the ego itself' (p. 59). Paraphrasing Loevinger, Ogawa et al. (1997) express the same thought in the language of the self, 'integration is not a function of the self, integration is what the self is' (p. 871). Edelman adds that integration is what the brain does. This formulation of the self is also at the heart of Kohut's view of the self as a coherent center of initiative and purpose.

The theme of unity of development which facilitates differentiation and individuation has been a key feature in the classical developmental tradition in the work of authors such as Werner (1948), Erikson (1950), Piaget (1952, 1971) and Vygotsky (1978). This unbroken tradition continues to influence contemporary developmentalists and psychoanalysts such as Stern (1985), Loevinger (1976), Sameroff (1989), Gottlieb (1997), Sroufe (1996), Emde et al. (1991), Emde (1994), Schore (1994), Lichtenberg (1989) and Lachmann (2001). An organismic model of the mind that looks at normality and pathology together in order to understand development is central to the new field of developmental psychopathology (Cicchetti, 1989; Cicchetti and Richters, 1997).

Even a superficial scanning of the developmental, cognitive, psychoanalytic and neuroscience literatures shows we are in the midst of a paradigm shift that can be characterized as follows:

1. A shift from reified psychic structures to brain processes that select, coordinate and evaluate staggering amounts of information.
2. A shift from primitive drives to adaptive emotional, behavioral and motivational systems, honed in by millions of years of biological evolution.
3. A shift from a mechanistic tension-reduction model that leads to a discussion of psychic energy and its vicissitudes, to an organismic model that leads to a discussion of adaptation, salience and meaning.

Before looking at defensive processes within this framework, it is important to understand where emotion and motivation fit into this model of the mind.

Part II. Towards a holistic theory of emotions

Feelings and emotions have a special role to play in this informational approach to the mind. As Tomkins (1962, 1963), Langer (1967), Lazarus (1991) and Lichtenberg, Lachmann and Fosshage (1992) have noted, feelings amplify and guide the selection of experience, particularly experience that has proved to have adaptive evolutionary and developmental significance. Feelings and emotions are psycho-physiological markers (Damasio 1994, 1999) that alert the organism to important information coming from within the organism or the environment.

Together with the organismic purposes and goals that they serve (read motivational systems), emotions function as important organizers of experience and are the intuitive source for the capacity for empathic communication (see below). With cognitive development, proto-emotions, such as distress/frustration, wariness and pleasure/contentment, are transformed into 'primary' emotions such as anger, fear and joy that embody core relational themes while serving organismic goals and purposes.

Emotions confer an incipient sense of meaning to interactions with the surround (Lazarus, 1991; Sroufe, 1996). Emotions are further shaped by
attitudes, beliefs and meanings rooted in family life and culture. As Fromm
(1947) observed, families act as 'psychic agents of society', socializing children into conscious and unconscious attitudes and beliefs embedded in the
cultural and socioeconomic conditions in which they live.

This formulation of the role of feelings as psycho-biological markers follows Darwin's (1955) view of emotions and bears close resemblance to
Freud's (1925) theory of signal anxiety. Indeed, if one rids Freud's theory
of signal anxiety of its tension-reduction energy assumptions and its reify-
ing tendencies, the basic premisses of the theory are sound. Any
experience that is perceived unconsciously as dangerous because it resembles conditions that in the past created a sense of helplessness will trigger
automatically a signal of anxiety and mobilize defensive operations.

We can go a long way toward solving Freud's problem of repression if
we extend his signal theory of anxiety to a general theory of emotions that
recognizes that all emotions act as organismic signals that highlight significant interactions with the surround. Since all emotions have a signaling
function, they are inevitably linked with conscious and unconscious evaluations that promote adaptation. In our species, the repertoire of emotions
and their meaning is dramatically enhanced due to the acquisition of language and the expanded symbolizing capacities associated with possessing
a big brain.

Following Lazarus (1991) and Sroufe (1996) and others, I adopt a
'holistic' view of information processing and emotions that includes several phases linking cognition, emotion and motivation with the creation
of coherence and meaning:

1. An unconscious or conscious cognitive appraisal phase that may or may
   not become linked to feeling states.
2. An autonomic nervous system (ANS) phase (a physiological and vege-
   tative state of arousal and tension build-up).
3. An experiential phase (the 'felt phase' of emotional processing). The felt
   phase may be integrated with more complex systems of meaning. We
   usually refer to these complex feeling states as 'emotions' (see below for
   further discussion of the difference between feelings and emotions).
4. A motor communicative phase characterized by facial expressions and
   postures related to different emotions.
5. A conative or motivational phase – a tendency to mobilize or to
   inhibit goal-directed behaviors.

All phases of processing information may be encoded in short- and/or
long-term memory and at subsymbolic and symbolic levels (see

below).This list of phases does not imply an invariant sequence of information processing and activation from cognitive appraisals–ANS phase–experiential or felt phase–motor communicative phase–action tendency. This is an issue that needs to be researched. It is likely that different sequences are possible depending on different circumstances (see the discussion of this matter in Ekman and Davidson, 1994, and Sroufe, 1996). Furthermore, phases of information processing are linked by feedback and feedforward loops or perhaps by reentry loops. For instance, the activation of the felt phase might lead to a reappraisal of an environmental stimulus, which in turn might lead to a self-correcting behavioral response.

There are several merits in this holistic approach. First, all phases of information processing are regarded as important, without privileging any single phase (cognitive, experiential or motivational) as the defining organizing principle of development. A holistic perspective avoids needless debates among competing theories that emphasize the primacy of emotion, cognition or motivation for development. Emotion and cognition become integrated through development, creating ever-wider circles of meaning. In turn, evolving structures of meaning redefine human goals and purposes. Second, it provides conceptual links between cognitive, emotional and motivational processes without conflating them (see below). Third, it builds on Bowlby's information processing model, elaborating some aspects of the theory with new developments in attachment theory and contemporary models of the mind.

Different phases of information processing are not all linked together with the same affinity or associative strength. The links between cognition, emotion, motivation and meaning change with development and with shifting contexts. Furthermore, the vast majority of appraisal processes are nonconscious and do not reach the felt or experiential phase. If, however, information has adaptive significance and is meaningful, information will likely be 'amplified' by being further processed to a felt phase; otherwise non-salient information will remain encoded at nonconscious levels. Of course, appraisal processes may also be dynamically repressed (see Part III of this chapter).

From this holistic perspective, human development is a process of integration of all phases of processing information, from unconscious and conscious cognitive appraisals, memory systems, ANS arousal, felt experiential and motivational phases to the creation of meaning. The flow of information, coming from within the organism or from the environment, becomes progressively integrated in ever increasing circles of meaning that facilitate exploration, while promoting competency, adaptive flexibility and freedom (freedom *to*, Fromm, 1941). I hasten to add that this definition is meaningless unless grounded in history, culture and in the actuality of people's lives.

The role of the attachment relationship in promoting and regulating emotional development

Early in development, the integrating process depends heavily on the regulating role of attachment figures. Through empathic interactions and soothing responses, caregivers help to integrate infants' growing capacity to tolerate the build-up of arousal and stimulation with emerging cognitive capacities while creating a sense of security (Sroufe, 1996). As the child develops, the roles parents have to play will change. By the time a child is 2 to 3 years old, parents need to set limits, occasionally reigning in their toddler's impulsiveness and exuberance when there is danger of losing control or the child's poor judgement puts him in jeopardy. As young children begin to internalize the external-regulating role of parents, new competencies and new challenges emerge that shift the balance between emotional regulation, emotional expression and exploration. It is worth emphasizing that the build-up of arousal is associated not only with unpleasant affects such as distress, wariness, fear and shame, but also with positive affects such as pleasure, interest and joy. Parents who develop secure attachments with their infants intuitively know how to stay within the 'zone of proximal development' of their children, encouraging their development beyond where they are, yet not exceeding their capacity to tolerate stimulation and novelty (Vygotsky, 1978; Sroufe, 1996).

From birth, infants are bathed in language and parents attribute meaning to infants' communications, needs and physiological states, a point that Hans Loewald stressed repeatedly (Mitchell, 2000). Most of the time, positive attributions are validating, promoting cognitive and emotional development. Occasionally, attributions can be invalidating and malignant, projecting dreaded or unwanted aspects of parents' selves on to their young children. I shall return to this subject at the end of the chapter when I discuss the concept of projective identification.

A note on the use of terms

Following Sroufe (1996), I occasionally substitute the word 'evaluation' for the word 'appraisal' to call attention to the fact that 'emotional' evaluations, whether unconscious or conscious, are always made from the perspective of what is considered to be of value for an individual at any given moment. Otherwise, I have adopted Bowlby's terms. Feeling is used as a general-purpose term to describe the felt or experiential phase of information processing. Feeling (as opposed to affect or emotion) is the preferred usage for the felt phase of the process, since feeling is the only one of the three words (affect, feeling and emotion) derived from the verb (to feel) having the exact meaning as itself. Emotion is used as an inclusive term to denote the unconscious as well as the conscious phases of the 'emotional' processing of information. I sometimes use the word *affect* as a general-purpose term to avoid the awkward 'feeling states'.

Are emotion and motivation synonymous?

There is a considerable overlap in functions attributed to emotions and to motivational systems. Motivational systems such as the careseeking attachment system, the parental caregiving system, the sexual mating system, the exploratory system or the aversive fight/flight system often spring into action following some felt emotional state such as anxiety, fear, anger, love or lust. As I have emphasized, emotion and motivation are accompanied by cognitive evaluations that may be unconscious or conscious. Perhaps because of some of these overlapping processes and functions and trenchant critiques that have made drive theories rightfully obsolete, some authors including Atwood and Stolorow (1999) and Demos (1993) have taken the position that a theory of affects based on Tomkins' (1962, 1963) groundbreaking work is a substitute for drive theories. In effect, their proposal collapses affect and motivation into the same construct. I believe this is a mistake, for the following reasons:

1. Although the unconscious and the felt phase of emotion may serve as an interpersonal communication and organismic signal that triggers a motivational system, there is more to a motivational system than its trigger. Motivational systems are directed toward goals reached through behavior. Behavior is monitored in terms of whether the goal is reached or not. Bowlby (1969) conceived of this goal-correcting mechanism as operating as a control system. Purpose is built into behavior from the moment of birth and so are control systems that monitor the attainment of goals. Aside from goal-correcting control systems, there is also a need for an internal map that will guide the organism toward its objectives. Bowlby (1969) called these maps internal working models (IWMs), traditionally referred to as internal representations. In short, motivational systems have several components: goals, the signaling function of emotions, goal correcting control systems and IWMs.

2. By conflating emotion and motivation we can lose sight of the purposes and goals that are implicit in emotional signals. For instance, the meaning of an infant's anger following an unexpected separation from an attachment figure is to try to regain contact. To regain contact

is the goal of the attachment system. The meaning of jealousy is to keep a loved one from leaving. This is the goal of the sexual system (sexuality is frequently mixed with attachment needs). The purpose of fear in a life-threatening situation is to flee from danger. This is the goal of the fight/flight aversive system (Lichtenberg, 1989). The meaning of shame associated with appeasement gestures (or pride in winning competitive challenges) is to avoid conflict from escalating into violence within hierarchical social systems. This is the goal of the ranking system (De Waal, 1989; Heard and Lake, 1997; Liotti and Intrecciagli, 1998; Chapter 15, this volume).

3. Lazarus (1991) notes that although emotions are idiosyncratic to each individual, emotions also express core relational themes that cut across different cultural contexts. The idea of core relational themes comes close to Bowlby's ideas on instinctively rooted motivational systems, Lichtenberg's (1989) multimotivational system and Liotti and Intrecciagli's (1998; Chapter 15, this volume) interpersonal motivational system (see also Heard and Lake, 1997, for very similar views on multimotivational systems). For example, the core relational meaning of fear is an immediate assessment of danger; anger is an assessment of a demeaning offense to me or mine; envy an assessment of wanting a coveted attribute belonging to someone else. Motivational systems and core relational themes associated with particular emotions have been selected through the course of primate and human evolution because of their adaptive value, even though on occasion they prove not to be adaptive. But whether adaptive or not, from an evolutionary perspective, motivational systems associated with emotions, on average, have promoted survival and reproductive success.

4. Humans are intrinsically motivated to construct higher-order systems of meaning (Fromm, 1973; Maccoby, 1988; Bruner, 1990). The roots of the need to create meaning can be traced to the self-organizing properties of the mind. Through neuronal selection and reentry signaling processes and new learning, 'rough drafts' or internal working models of the world are continually being created and re-created. These integrative processes are the basis from which we develop a coherent experience of the world. Integrative processes operating throughout development have been radically transformed by symbolic capacities and language during the course of human evolution. The need to make sense of the world is expressed in many ways, such as the need for a 'frame of orientation and devotion' (Fromm, 1973), a desire to give artistic expression to our perceptions and dreams, the creation of myths, an appreciation of beauty and harmony. These higher-order needs constitute a new motivational system that is quintessentially

human – from here on this motivational system will be referred to as the 'meaning system'. One of Fromm's (1973) most profound insights was to have linked human destructiveness with the need to create meaning, a radical departure from Freud, who linked destructiveness with atavistic impulses. Emotions and moods associated with the meaning system range from the contemplative to the intensely passionate: 'epistemic' emotions such as surprise, a passionate interest in understanding the world or a sense of wonder, awe in contemplating nature, or genocidal hatreds based on fanatical ideologies.

5. The communicative role of emotions builds on the function of emotions as psycho-physiological markers that signal salient interactions with the environment. During the course of evolution emotions associated with characteristic facial expressions and body postures were selected due to their adaptive value (Darwin, 1955). In humans, the communicative role of emotions becomes radically enhanced and transformed by language.

In sum, emotions serve many masters. Emotions can be in the service of interpersonal motivational systems such as the attachment, caregiving or ranking systems that we share with other species. Emotions are also associated with uniquely human systems of meaning and purpose. Last but not least, emotions are intuitive forms of knowledge that serve as vehicles for highly effective, non-verbal modes of communication. Some authors, such as Aitken and Trevarthen (1997), consider this intuitive form of communication as a 'primary motive' that is present from birth to promote social interaction between caregivers and infants.

Part III. Some examples of the defensive uncoupling of cognitive, emotional and motivational processes

The concept of 'unconscious emotion' is confusing because in common use 'feeling' and 'emotion' are used interchangeably, so the felt phase of an emotion and 'unconscious emotions' are conflated.

The approach taken by Langer, Bowlby and LeDoux, among others, begins to resolve this confusion. Conceptualizing the activation of feelings as a phase in the multistage evaluative, selective and interpretive processes, by necessity implies different degrees of information processing of emotion. Many of these selective and evaluative processes take place at non-conscious levels before inducing the felt stage of the process.

To illustrate the hypothesis of the delinking of the unconscious cognitive and the felt phase of information processing I shall begin by using two neurological cases as 'experiments in nature'. These 'experiments' help us understand something about the neurobiology of cognitive-emotional processes that normally operate in seamless fashion, but become delinked when particular brain centers are damaged. I then proceed with the example of psychological trauma and avoidant patterns of attachment to illustrate how the evaluative and the felt phases of emotional processing can become functionally and temporarily delinked by means of defensive processes.

A startling example of cognitive/emotional delinking was cleverly demonstrated by Claparede over a century ago (described by Westen, 1997). Claparede shook hands with an amnesic patient suffering from Korsakoff's syndrome. Claparede concealed a pin between his fingers, and pricked the patient's hands as their hands clasped. Patients with Korsakoff's syndrome have bilateral damage to the hippocampus, which is now known to be essential for the consolidation of new information encoded at symbolic levels – sometimes referred to as explicit or declarative memory. Because this deficit leads to amnesia for recent events, upon meeting again, the patient was unable to recognize Claparede. Nonetheless he was unwilling to shake his hand. When asked about his 'impolite' behavior, the patient was unable to give an explanation.

Damasio (1999) describes a similar case. The patient, known as David, had suffered a rare bilateral damage to temporal lobes that included damage to the hippocampus and the amygdala. Both of these anatomical structures are often thought of as the emotional processing centers of the brain that have multiple connections to the prefrontal, parietal and visual cortices and the autonomic nervous system. David had severe defects in learning and memory. He was unable to recognize people he knew and was unable to recall events that transpired between them. Nonetheless, he showed some clear preferences among people in the nursing staff. This observation led Damasio and his team to carry out an experiment that they dubbed the 'good guy/bad guy experiment'. For a week, David interacted for equal amounts of time with a 'good guy' who was always welcoming and rewarded David, a 'neutral guy' who was neither friendly nor unfriendly and a bad guy (in this case an attractive woman) whose manner was brusque and engaged David in very tedious tasks. David was then given photographs of the three persons and asked whether he knew any of them and to select the picture of the person he liked the most. Although David had no recollection of ever meeting the people in the photograph, he performed spectacularly, picking the picture of the good guy as most liked, showing a strong dislike for the bad guy (despite the fact that she was very attractive) and an indifferent response to the neutral guy.

Clearly, both of these patients had been able to evaluate and develop preferences that influenced their behavior at non-conscious levels. Claparede's patient refused the handshake and David was able to pass with flying colors the good guy/bad guy test. What they were not able to do, due to the bilateral neurological damage to the hippocampus and the temporal lobes, was to consciously connect their feelings with the person that had induced their feeling states. These cases show dramatically the devastating effects of damage to the hippocampus and temporal lobes, which uncouple the cognitive and felt phase of emotional processes. What appear to be unconscious feelings are actually the result of a rupture between cognitive and the felt stage of an appraisal process.

Delinking the cognitive and the felt phase of emotional processes in cases of trauma

As 'experiments in nature', neurological conditions that rupture different phases of emotional processes provide a blueprint that allows us to think about defensive processes that are psychological in origin and that functionally delink these processes. In this section I shall address the delinking effects of trauma in attachment relationships. Bowlby thought that the degree of dysfunction observed in the development of attachment relationships would depend on the degree to which the behavioral, emotional and cognitive components of the attachment system become 'inactivated'. In cases of severe loss, prolonged or repeated separations or maltreatment by attachment figures, the attachment system in the child can become more or less permanently disconnected. According to Bowlby, a continual activation of the attachment system produces a degree of distress in young children that is unbearable and can produce a 'segregation' of painful experience into different self systems or internal working models (Bowlby, 1980). When the term 'dissociation' is used in a broad sense as reflecting a failure of 'integrative process of identity, memory, or consciousness' (American Psychiatric Association, 1994), the concept of segregated systems might be seen as an example of a dissociative process (Liotti, 1992; Solomon and George, 1999).

Children's attachment behavior may be permanently disconnected, rather than being temporarily inactivated, when they experience repeated separations and losses from attachment figures. In these often-chaotic circumstances, there have not been adult caregivers that can offset the losses and comfort the children. Children learn that they cannot risk expressing their basic need for security and comfort. Their basic trust in the world is broken. They manage their distress by withdrawing from close relationships that make them feel vulnerable or through other means such as establishing relationships based on control, domination, submission or exploitation.

Of course, there are other experiences that are not necessarily attachment related that can be traumatic, such as being exposed to violence within the family or community or being the victim of violence. What all these experiences have in common is they engender an overwhelming sense of fear/terror and helplessness. In these circumstances, emotions become segregated from the rest of the child's developing personality. This almost always implies different degrees of uncoupling between the cognitive, the motivational and the felt phases of information processing.

A note on the disregulation of emotion in traumatic conditions

Several lines of research seem to indicate that trauma causes a hypofunction of the inhibitory role of the prefrontal cortex and its connections with the hippocampus and hyperfunction of amygdala-mediated emotion (Le Doux, 1996; Chefetz, 2000). These impairments lead to states of chronic stress and disregulation of emotion. Disregulated emotion is accompanied by hyperarousal of the autonomic nervous system. Traumatized patients come to identify strong emotion and the disregulation and hyperarousal of the autonomic nervous system as a sign of great danger (Chefetz, 2000). In effect, they become 'phobic' toward strong emotion and often resort to dissociative strategies, obsessional thinking, avoidant behaviors and the dampening of all emotion in an attempt to control the state of hyperarousal.

There is growing evidence that overwhelming emotion experienced under traumatic conditions can lead to a functional impairment of the hippocampus (Bremmer, 1998, quoted by Chefetz, 2000). Neuro-imaging techniques using positron emission tomography (PET) scans also show that patients who were asked to read aloud first person accounts of documented traumatic experience had an increased perfusion of the amygdala and decreased perfusion of Broca's area, an area that is known to be a critical language center (Rauch et al., 1996). There are now five studies that have replicated these findings (Chefetz, 2000). The decreased perfusion to language centers was a surprising finding, indicating that there is a mild functional expressive aphasia in traumatized patients that compromises their ability to describe their experience coherently. As Chefetz notes, narrative capacities rely on intact hippocampal function and its connections with the prefrontal cortex and language centers that provide the neurological connections to the denotative processes of language.

Delinking cognition, emotion and motivation in children with avoidant patterns of attachment

Can cognitive/emotional/motivational processes become delinked in psychological conditions that do not involve severe trauma? Bowlby believed this would indeed be the case in situations where the challenge to children's coping capacities were less severe. In these cases the different components of the attachment system would be only temporarily deactivated rather than disconnected. Children who develop an avoidant attachment toward their caregivers are a good example of this milder form of assault to the attachment system. This group of caregivers often rebuff their children's wish to be comforted when the child is distressed. The rejection of the child's needs may take many forms and be more or less harsh, but in every case it leads to a temporary deactivation of the attachment system.

This defensive strategy can be seen clearly as early as 12 months of age in the Strange Situation. During the two reunion episodes, these young children behave as if they were indifferent to their parents' return and turn their attention to the toys in the room. Although it would seem from their behavior that these children are not distressed, studies measuring heart rates (Sroufe and Waters, 1977) or saliva cortisol levels (Spangler and Grossman, 1993) show a significant degree of autonomic arousal. Two components of the attachment system are temporarily delinked (deactivated) in this example. The action tendency (the children seeking the comfort they need) and the experiential or felt phase (muting their distress by focusing on the toys rather than on the attachment figure). However, these unconscious phases leading to the felt phase are fully active: namely, the assessment of danger (the parent leaving the room) and the phase of autonomic activation that accompanies the assessment of danger.

How do we know that the deactivation of the behavioral and felt components of the attachment system are temporary rather than permanent? Longitudinal and naturalistic observations show that these children can become very clingy in the home environment or when the perceived threat is extremely frightening, in which case they override the avoidant strategy and seek attachment figures. As they grow older, children who are avoidant in their attachment show their need for comfort and protection in roundabout and hidden ways, but nonetheless are judged by their teachers or camp counselors as more emotionally dependent than children secure in their attachment (Sroufe and Fleeson, 1986; Sroufe, Egeland and Carlson, 1999).

Taken together, these examples of neurological and psychological dysfunction show that 'repressed emotion', so called, can be better understood as a temporary or permanent delinking of different phases of complex cognitive and emotional processes that normally would become integrated during unconscious and conscious (felt) phases of the emotional processing of information.

Part IV. The internalization of experience: Bowlby's concept of internal working models (IWMs)

I have found Sroufe and Fleeson's (1986) relational propositions a very useful framework from which to approach the internalization of experience:

1. Relationships are wholes, i.e. they are more than simple combinations of the individual characteristics of people.
2. There is continuity and coherence of close relationships over time.
3. The whole relationship 'resides' in each individual.
4. Previous relationships are carried forward to later close relationships (the effect of relationships upon relationships, transference in psychoanalytic terms).

Clinicians and researchers belonging to different schools of thought can probably attest to the face validity of these propositions. Research on the effects of attachment relationships on development have empirically confirmed these relational propositions (for summaries see Cortina, 1999; Sroufe and Fleeson, 1986; Sroufe, 1996, 1997; Weinfield et al., 1999).

For purposes of our discussion, the crux of the matter hinges on what we mean by relationships 'residing' in individuals and how this process of 'residence' takes place. In the psychoanalytic and cognitive science literature there are many terms that have been used to describe and name the process of internalization: introjection, identification, good and bad objects, personifications, internal representations, emotional schemas and Bowlby's internal working models. This is a field strewn with boulders. There are advantages and disadvantages of each one of these terms tied to the phenomena they are trying to capture, as well as to the theoretical commitments that each one of these terms carries with it. Exploring these issues would require a book in itself. Here I shall stick to exploring Bowlby's concept of IWM and current concepts from cognitive and developmental research consistent with Bowlby's general approach.

Bowlby (1969) notes that goal-corrected behaviors, such as attachment behaviors directed at maintaining a state of security, require a plan to reach their goal. Maps can be thought of as schematic representations that help an organism navigate its way through the environment to reach its goals. However, Bowlby thought that a map, with is topographic image, is inadequate because it is too static a concept. Bowlby came up with the concept of a 'working model' to convey the idea that internal representations are dynamic processes that are updated and revised according to the vicissitudes of internal states and changing environmental landscapes. The concept of working model also suggests that internal representations are not passive copies of reality. Representations are actively selected and schematized models of the world.

Bowlby realized that for an organism to reach its goals, at least two complementary representational models were necessary. An 'organismic' model representing internal states and an 'environmental' model representing changing external realities. When the goals have to do with relationships, the two complementary representational models are of self and of others. These models are constructed at conscious and unconscious levels. Furthermore, language brings in a whole new dimension to these internal models. By means of language we can create much more sophisticated models and narratives that communicate our experience with greater precision and richer meaning.

According to Bowlby, when a young child is fortunate to have parents that are emotionally responsive to his or her needs, the child develops internal working models that are complementary: others as reliable and trustworthy, and self as lovable and competent. These internal models begin to exert a positive influence on future development by carrying forward expectations (and later in life, attributions, see below) based on these mostly non-conscious and sometimes dynamically unconscious assumptions of self and others. If environmental conditions that produced these models do not change substantially, models of self and others remain unchanged. These IWMs are carried forward as a set of expectations and attributions that skew development toward maladaptive paths.

With the discovery of Ainsworth's anxious patterns of attachment and the discovery of disorganized attachments, more specific hypotheses of internal working models of self and others have been developed.

Children with a history of resistant attachments have caregivers that are inconsistent or overstimulating in their care. Hence, these children will develop models of others as inconsistent or unreliable and models of self as ineffective or weak in eliciting care.

Children with histories of avoidant attachment have caregivers who have rebuffed their need for comfort when distressed. Hence, they will develop models of others as rejecting of their emotional needs and of self as unlovable.

There is substantial evidence to support the view that unless the care-givers' capacity for emotional responsiveness changes, the child's internal working models of self and others will persist and exert their negative toll as development proceeds (Cortina, 1999; Weinfield et al., 1999).

Episodic and semantic memory systems

Bowlby made use of Tulving's dual memory model (1972) in an attempt to understand how a person might come to develop multiple and contradic-tory IWMs of self and others, a phenomenon observed frequently in patients with histories of trauma and severe personality disorders. According to Tulving, information can be stored according to personal auto-biographical experiences (episodic memory) or according to its meaning (semantic memory). In the first case, information is stored as temporally dated episodes or events. In contrast, in the semantic type of storage, infor-mation exists as general facts, propositions about the world and about others. As Bowlby (1980) notes, one reason for the discrepancies between the information in one type of storage and another may be due to:

> A difference in the source from which each derives the dominant portion of its information. Whereas for information going into episodic storage the dominant part seems likely to derive from what the person himself perceives and a subordinate part only from what he may be told of the episode. For what goes into semantic storage the emphasis might well be reversed, with what he is told being dominant over what he himself might think. (p. 63)

Clinically we often see people who carry with them negative self-attribu-tions such as being lazy, selfish, difficult, the 'black sheep' of the family. In trying to disentangle negative attributions made by family members and significant figures in their life from the reality of those attributions, it is often useful to examine episodic memories to see what can be learned from these episodes. Lichtenberg, Lachmann and Fosshage's (1992) clin-ical use of 'model scenes' is a good example of the usefulness of examining prototypical episodic memories. The close examination of model scenes can serve as vehicles to enter the emotional architecture of family life. Often a close examination of model scenes allows patients to see their behavior, attitudes and emotions in a more positive light. This exercise may also reveal that patients carry incompatible IWMs. For example, a powerful IWM based on negative attributions made by a parent (encoded as a semantic memory) may be at odds with a weaker IWM (encoded as episodic memories) based on positive experiences with other people.

The distinction between episodic and semantic memory has also been used creatively by George, Kaplan and Main (1996) in designing the Adult Attachment Interview. As part of the interview, individuals are asked to provide five adjectives that describe their relationship with each parent, starting with their earliest memories. In the follow-up questions, individuals are asked to give specific memories that exemplify each adjective. For instance, if a person says their mother was loving (a semantic IWM), the interviewer probes for specific memories that support the adjective (an episodic IWM). The discrepancy between the episodic and semantic memories becomes an important criterion for scoring the AAI as coherent or not.

When Bowlby applied Tulving's (1972) dual memory system to clinical work, the distinction between experience encoded at subsymbolic and symbolic levels was yet to be fully appreciated. Bowlby's use of Tulving's dual memory system is even more relevant in light of the contemporary procedural/implicit and declarative/explicit distinction. The concept of implicit or procedural memory can be seen as an extension of episodic memory encoded at subsymbolic and non-representational levels (see Chapters 15 by Liotti and Intreccialagli and 17 by Nicola Diamond for some clinical implications of these ideas).

Implicit (procedural) and explicit (declarative) memory systems

Within the past two decades of research in cognitive psychology, near consensus has been reached that memory is encoded or mapped at two levels:

1. An implicit or procedural memory system that is subsymbolic, non-verbal and non-representational.
2. An explicit or declarative memory system that is symbolic, verbal and representational.

As Bauer at al. (2000) note, the distinctions between implicit versus procedural and the explicit versus declarative classifications are not identical, but they overlap considerably. Regardless of differences, there is agreement that memory is not a unitary system and different systems serve different functions and rules of operations. Declarative memory is what we generally mean by remembering and involves the recall of names, places, events, etc. Implicit or procedural memory involves a variety of activities that are primarily learned and encoded at non-conscious levels such as routines, habits, skills, some types of classical conditioning, and most important for our purposes, interpersonal patterns and configurations.

The following is a summary from Bauer et al. (2000):
Declarative memory:

- Fast (e.g. can be learned by one trial).
- Fallible (e.g. memory traces degrade, retrieval failures are common).
- Flexible (not tied to a specific modality or context).

Procedural memory:

- Slow (with the exception of priming, it builds up from gradual and incremental learning and repeated practice).
- Reliable (once a skill, habit or interpersonal configuration is learned, it is not easily forgotten).
- Inflexible (procedural memory is activated only as specific skills, habits or interpersonal patterns, priming being the exception).

Interpersonal patterns constructed by infants with their caregivers are clearly procedural. What is being mapped in the brain are most likely rules of action, or more precisely, rules of interaction or coaction (Gottlieb, 1997). These interactive rules involve routines (who does what to whom), mutually induced gestures, patterns of escalating and de-escalating arousal, of safety regulation and comfort seeking that develop a rhythm and intensity that are unique to each interactive pair.

It is important to emphasize that experience encoded at procedural levels is sub-symbolic and therefore non-representational. We are used to thinking of the internalization of experience as being representational, so this statement may come as a surprise. But a moment's reflection should dispel this misconception. When experience is not encoded symbolically it just *is*. Early experience is carried forward as sets of expectations that cannot be remembered at a semantic, declarative level, they can be 'remembered' only behaviorally or somatically in the context of situations that trigger implicit memories. The Strange Situation is a striking example of how memories encoded at subsymbolic levels (and expectations based on these memories) influence infants' behavior during parental departures and reunions. These expectations have powerful effects on development; to a large extent, their power resides in memory systems that are non-representational. It is only with the emergence of symbolic capacities that young children can begin to map experience in representational memory systems.[2]

The Boston Process of Change Study Group has extended the concept of procedural knowledge to include interpersonal and intersubjective procedures (such as how to relate, how to get attention and how to 'joke around') as a special category of procedural knowledge that they have called 'implicit relational knowing'. According to the Boston Group, traditional interpretations can change only the 'explicit or declarative landscape', but the process of change often requires 'something more'. This 'something more' can be conceptualized as therapeutic changes made at the level of implicit relational, which often elude interpretative approaches (Stern et al., 1998).

Normally, there should be a fluid interaction between these two forms of encoding relationships, particularly for information that has developmental and adaptive significance. Much of the information mapped in the implicit or procedural format is not (and should not be) transposed to the explicit or declarative format, otherwise conscious processes would be overwhelmed with unnecessary information. Because of its adaptive significance, implicit relational knowledge that we use spontaneously when we parent, develop friendships or become lovers, may be transformed through language into words and narratives (explicit relational knowing). Language, however, can never completely capture the global quality of subsymbolic experience, except in the hands of gifted writers and artists and ordinary people with the extraordinary capacity to express basic experiences with simple eloquence, grace and wisdom.

How is implicit relational knowing transformed into explicit relational knowing? Bucci (1997) uses the concept of the referential cycle to refer to the bidirectional process whereby experience encoded sub-symbolically (implicit knowledge) is transformed into symbols and narratives (explicit knowledge) and vice versa. To explain this process, Bucci proposes a third way of encoding experience that shares some features of symbolic and sub-symbolic modes of encoding experience: a non-verbal symbolic code or processor. This third transitional format can be expressed in the form of visual images, often packed with symbolic meaning, as is evident in dreams and art. We can discover the multifaceted nature of these images when we are awake and begin to 'free associate' about these images and express them in words. Bucci believes that before sub-symbolic procedural knowledge can be transformed into symbols and language, the referential process cycles through this intermediate code. Karmiloff-Smith (1992) uses the term 'representational re-description' to describe a similar process of transformation from pre-verbal to verbal experience.

Liotti's hypothesis of the origin of multiple and contradictory internal working models

Liotti (1995, 1999) has put forth a very interesting proposal linking attachment research on disorganized/disoriented patterns (from here on referred to as the disorganized attachment patterns) with Karpman's

(1968) descriptions of the 'drama triangle'. The disorganized attachment patterns were discovered by Main and Weston (1981) by reviewing a series of Strange Situation (SS) cases that did not fit well into Ainsworth's secure, ambivalent and avoidant attachment patterns. When some of these atypical cases were forced into the typical secure, avoidant and resistant categories the results were counter-intuitive. For instance, some infants known to be maltreated appeared secure in the SS. Main and Solomon (1986) found something in common with all these infants. Some appeared dazed or disoriented and exhibited atypical behaviors such as freezing, approaching the parent with head averted, rocking on hands and knees, moving away from the parent to the wall, rising to greet the parent, then falling prone on the face, mixing avoidant with resistant behaviors. All these behaviors can occasionally be observed in the absence of the parent during the SS, but with this group of infants these behaviors were intensified in the presence of the parent.

In a now classic paper, Main and Hesse (1990) interpreted the children's behavior as a breakdown of attachment behavior induced by an irresolvable conflict. Young children are highly motivated to seek comfort when distressed. However, if the parent shows signs of being frightened or shows frightening behaviors, as many of these parents do, the infant faces a classic approach/avoidance dilemma. The distress is telling the young child to seek comfort from their caregivers, but the caregivers' fright is signaling danger, a signal that normally leads the child to flee. This dilemma leads to a breakdown of coping capabilities and hence the disorganized-disoriented behaviors observed in the SS. Caregivers' unintegrated frightened or frightening responses to their infants' distress are the driving factor leading to disorganization in their infants.

According to Liotti, when patients with a history of disorganized attachment encounter further unfavorable events in life, their organization of IWMs can become very unstable and contradictory. Contradictory IWMs may be reenacted in the form of the victim, the persecutor and the rescuer roles (VPR roles), particularly in moments of crisis. As Karpman observed, these roles show up regularly in fairy tales, plays and myths but also appear clinically – Karpman's 'drama triangle'. Liotti notes that the drama triangle appears frequently in patients with dissociative symptoms and severe personality disorder (Liotti, 1999, Liotti et al., 2000).

How are the patterns of the rescuer, victim and persecutor constructed? Liotti (1999) suggests that young children faced with a caregiver who is frightening, and perhaps has been denigrating too, will construct the image of self as being a 'helpless victim'. Another, equally plausible and complementary construction of meaning, however, is possible: since the child may observe the fright of an attachment figure while he or she is approaching her, the child may construct the self as the cause of the caregiver's expressed fear. This might lead to an image of the self as being intrinsically evil and frightening, and the attachment figure as the helpless victim of the child. This self-image might become 'actualized' if the child develops a controlling-punitive way of relating to his parent. If, however, in the sequence of parent–child interactions the parent is somehow comforted and distracted from painful intrusive memories of traumas and seeks comfort from her child, the child might construct the image of the omnipotent rescuer of a fragile parent. This event sets in motion the premature activation of the caregiving motivational system in the child, and the inversion of roles in the attachment relationship. At the same time, the child, in the arms of a now warmly affectionate parent, will experience comfort from his own distress, and will have grounds for constructing the caregiver as a loving rescuer.

A good example of how children 'internalize' and enact these roles in the arena of peer relations comes from the longitudinal attachment research project carried out by Troy and Sroufe (1987). Children with histories of secure, resistant and avoidant attachment patterns were evenly distributed. Extensive videotaped observations of the children interacting among themselves and with counselors were analyzed and coded. The findings are striking. Only children with avoidant attachment histories became victimizers (the persecutor in Karpman's terms) and only children with histories of resistant attachment became victims. Securely attached children usually chose other secure children to play with, and did not allow the bullies to tease them, nor did they tease other children. Children with avoidant attachment have mothers who are rejecting of their needs when distressed, whereas children with resistant attachment have mothers who are inconsistent and feel insecure in their mothering roles. These experiences of rejection and helplessness are then played out in the arena of peer relations. This research strongly supports Sroufe and Fleeson's (1986) relational propositions, namely, that relationships are wholes that 'reside' in each individual and precious relationships are carried forward to later relationships.

The popularity of the concept of enactment in contemporary psychoanalysis might be based on the growing realization that it is only after finding ourselves embroiled in confusing and at times chaotic implicit relational patterns that we can begin to work ourselves out of them by finding words to describe these uncanny interpersonal exchanges. Very often, the clinical challenge is how to contain these disturbing enactments so they can be articulated and understood. I think, however, it is an exaggeration to say that therapists invariably join the enactment before they can understand it. The degree to which therapists can pull back from being drawn into confusing and chaotic exchanges varies from patient to patient, and with the personality of the therapist.

Part V. Comparison with some object relational concepts

Bion's model of unconscious mother–infant communication

The concept of projective identification overlaps with the phenomena that are being described as VPR role enactments, patterns and negative attributions (see below), particularly when played out within a therapeutic setting. In addition, Bion (1967) elaborated Klein's original concept of projective identification to understand how, under normal conditions, the mothering figure contains primitive anxieties and impulses and communicates emotionally with her infant. There are similarities as well as basic differences between how Bion and attacment theorists understand how parents regulate emotion and communicate with their infants.

Attachment theory as well as Bion's concept of container/contained assumes that the attachment figure has an important regulating role in modulating arousal levels and heightened emotional states. They differ on how these interpersonal processes take 'residence' in the interacting pair. According to Bion (1967), the infant projects primitive anxieties and impulses into the mother so she can help him modulate unbearable states of arousal and inchoate experience. The mother 'takes in' these projected impulses through a process of introjective identification and 'reverie' (Bion, 1967; Scharff, 1992). By 'metabolizing' their infants' distress, parents allow their infant to 'reintroject' unbearable impulses and inchoate experience into a more manageable form. This is the process of containment, in which the mother is the container. According to this neo-Kleinian paradigm, the back and forth between projective identification, reverie and introjective identification are the basic processes involved in unconscious communication between parents and young children. Pathology in this schema emerges when infants persist in the excessive use of projective 'evacuations' without any containment from the mothering figure.

Attachment theorists and infant researchers explain the 'containing' function using a completely different paradigm. Parents' intuitive knowledge on how to respond to infants developed over the course of millions of years of hominid evolution. However, the quality of their parenting is strongly influenced by their own history and social norms. An 'ordinary devoted mother'(Winnicott, 1949) is capable of responding to an infant's needs sensitively. In turn, infants bring to this interchange with their care-givers an ability to respond to rhythm and timing of these proto-conversations, as well as to basic facial expressions and affective tone of their caregivers. This capacity is described by Emde et al. (1991) as social fittedness.

It is worth restating that parents transpose their intuitive empathic capacity into language, a running commentary that adds meaning to inter-actions with their infants. Although infants can respond only to the timing, tonality and rhythm of the language of caregivers, with time, lan-guage begins to be incorporated into the referential cycle of young children, providing a new sense of meaning and purpose to their interac-tions with caregivers. For further discussion on the regulatory role of attachment figures see Emde et al. (1991), Schore (1994, 1997), Sroufe (1996) and Silverman (1998).

Clearly, infants' experience is not as inchoate as the object relations tradition would lead us to believe. Infants' capacities to engage in early interactions with caregivers and parents' intuitive regulatory role in modulating this interaction are the basis of parent–infant communication. This intuitive form of communication does not require the convoluted projective and introjective mechanisms that are the basis of Bion's inter-personal construct of projective identification.

The construct of projective identification used to understand the *normal* communication between parent and infant should be discarded. The question remains, is there a useful *clinical* role left for phenomena described under the rubric of projective identification that cannot be bet-ter understood from the perspective of contemporary developmental research, attachment theory and some self-psychological perspectives (Lichtenberg, 1989; Lachmann, 2001)?

Lieberman (1992) and Silverman and Lieberman (1999) believe that the concept of projective identification as developed by Ogden (1982) is complementary to Bowlby's IWM concepts if 'projection' is conceived as a form of negative and coercive maternal misattribution (see also Seligman, 1999). Moreover, Lieberman and Silverman think that the con-struct of projective identifications, as developed by Ogden (1982), allows us to understand the psychological mechanisms involved in the transmis-sion of violence from one generation to the next. According to Ogden (1982) the first phase in the cycle of projective identification involves the projector ridding himself of intolerable internal experience and locating that experience in the other. The second phase consists in the projector putting pressure on the recipient to accept the projection, and the third phase consists of the recipient beginning to act and feel in accordance with the disowned projection generated by the projector.

I do not object to this use of projective identification as long as it is clear that the coercive misattribution(s) flow from the parent to the infant and *not* vice versa. On this point, I regrettably part company with Silverman and Lieberman (1999) who, taking the neo-Kleinian view, believe these misattributions are bidirectional. Infants and young children are a captive audience for parental misattributions and cannot escape their coercive, and at times violent nature, but they do not have the capacity to attribute intentions and needs to others. Whatever 'attributions' infants may have toward their parents take the form of expectations that are implicit in the attachment relationship. In order to attribute intentions, motives or needs to parents, it is necessary for infants to have developed the idea that parents have agendas and needs of their own, a capacity usually known as 'theory of mind' (Fonagy and Target, 1997). There is almost complete scientific consensus that a theory of mind does not develop until children are 3 or 4 years old (see Wellman, Cross and Watson, 2001, and the ensuing commentary on their meta-analysis). Even if infants had that capacity to attribute needs and intentions to others, it seems odd to believe that babies would be able to coerce or induce attributions, let alone misattributions, on to their parents.

That parents can subtly or harshly force their misattributions on their children does not necessarily imply any malevolence on their part. In fact, most of the damage inflicted by these projections is based on parents' sincere belief that their perceptions are accurate; they are not aware that they are forcing their misperceptions and misattributions on the child. As Ogden's last phase in the projective identification cycle proposes, the fact that *some* children assume the role assigned to them by their parents only confirms the parent's belief in the validity of the misattributions. I emphasize the 'some' because, like Demos (1999), I have witnessed a few instances where children were able to resist a persistent onslaught of parental misattribution and maintain a sense of psychic integrity. I have also found in these cases an important adult figure that gave the child an alternative view of itself, which I believe explains their resilience in the face of extreme adversity.

Fantasy understood as the capacity for imagination

The misrepresentation of early experience, whether conscious or not, is often referred to as 'phantasy' in the psychoanalytic literature. However, fantasy, understood as the capacity for imagination, is based on symbolizing capacities. Symbolic functions and imaginative capabilities do not emerge – in rudimentary form – until the second year of life, a developmental insight that was well established by Piaget (1962/1951). Fantasy is not part of the mental repertoire of infants and hence cannot distort the subsymbolic experience of infants (see Chapter 13 by Jean Knox for a similar point of view). Any distortion of experience during infancy is introduced by attachment figures because of lack of emotional responsiveness, coercive misattributions, abusive and frightening behavior and/or frightened affect. The only 'defenses' available to infants to cope with these parental impingements are behavioral (withdrawing, shutting down) and/or shifting attention away from distressing events while focusing on other activities – Sullivan's selective inattention and Bowlby's defensive activity. As I have noted earlier, processes that integrate memory systems with emotion, cognition and motivation may be unhinged, leading to different degrees of segregation and fragmentation among these systems.

This does not exclude the possibility that infants may contribute to problems in the attachment relationship. For instance, within poverty samples there is some evidence to suggest that infants that are temperamentally inhibited or 'fussy' might contribute to the insecurity of the attachment with primary caregivers (Weinfield et al., 1999). However, in non-poverty samples the same temperamental vulnerability is transformed by a responsive caregiving relationship; in these samples, a difficult temperament does not predict anxious attachment (Sroufe, personal communication). Attachment figures who are able to provide a secure base for young children can cope with a range of temperamental variation by becoming sensitively responsive to each temperamental type. A recent twin study (O'Conner and Craft, 2001) and adoption study (Dozier et al., 2001) fully support the view that parental responsiveness and 'state of mind' in regard to attachment are the main factors that contribute to the security or insecurity of infant attachment.

This view of young children's limited mentalizing and coping capabilities, but remarkable abilities to extract common features in their interactions with caregivers, is consistent with 50 years of developmental research. This view represents a significant departure from most psychoanalytic theories derived from object relations traditions, whether 'phantasy' is linked with drive concepts (the traditional view) or with imagination, as some contemporary authors have begun using the term (Mitchell, 2000).

Young children have no choice but to take in at sub-symbolic levels the impact of parents' emotional attitudes and beliefs, for better or for worse. They cannot generate fantasies in regard to these relationships until the capacity for imagination is well established by the third year of life. Once the capacity for imagination emerges, it becomes a tool that can potentially liberate the human mind from the actuality of the moment by recreating the past and imagining the future. Imagination can also be used in the service of defensive processes. Fantasies are a symbolic elaboration of experience, initially mapped at sub-symbolic levels. The symbolic elaboration of experience introduces, for the first time in evolutionary history, a species with the capacity to create infinitely complex shades of meaning and purpose, ranging from the demonic to the divine.

In criticizing the view of the infant as possessing a 'weak ego', Erikson (1964) wrote:

> It is here that our traditional concept of reality fails to account for the fundamental fact that the infant, while not able to test what we call our reality, is competent in his actuality. True, all beginnings are characterized by vulnerability, but as long as vulnerability is accompanied by active adaptation to protective conditions, it is not a state of weakness. (p. 176).

In summary, I believe we should turn the traditional psychoanalytic view of development on its head. In the traditional view, phantasy (in the form of primitive drives and inchoate experience) comes first and the impact of reality comes later. In contemporary views of development the actuality of infant's sub-symbolic experience (implicit relational knowing) comes first, and fantasy, understood as the capacity for imagination, comes later.

Conclusion

To understand how defensive processes disrupt emotional regulation, memory systems and motivation, we need a model of the mind that takes into account the unity of development and the coherence of experience amidst an enormous diversity of mental states. By unity of development I mean the progressive integration of unconscious and conscious cognitive appraisals, emotions, memory systems and motivational systems into wider circles of meaning and purpose. Under normal conditions these integrative processes lead to greater competency, adaptive flexibility and freedom. This chapter builds on Bowlby's information processing approach to the mind and Edelman's theory of neuronal selection to explain how the brain might accomplish the staggering feat of integrating enormous amounts of information while creating a sense of unity and coherence. This feat has to be explained without postulating a homunculus ('little person in the mind') that integrates and censors information – as Freud did in his theory of repression. I show how information may be processed in phases that integrate unconscious and conscious cognitive appraisals with the activation of autonomic nervous system, emotions and motivational systems. Some defensive processes come into play by delinking cognitive, experiential and motivational phases of information processing. Other defensive processes operate by interfering in the integration of memory systems, which encode experience at several levels, along semantic versus episodic and procedural versus declarative lines. Still other defensive processes operate by skewing internal working models of self and others (that carry with them maladaptive, contradictory and distorted expectations and attributions) into conflict-ridden developmental pathways. In the final section of this chapter I compare this model of development and defensive processes with traditional concepts of projective identification and phantasy.

Acknowledgments

I thank Barbara Lenkerd, Jon Frederickson, Giovanni Liotti, Jean Knox and Alan Sroufe for their helpful comments.

Notes

1. An earlier version of this paper was presented on 5 April 2001 at the conference 'Frontiers of Practice. The New Dialogue between Attachment Theory and British Object Relations', University of Virginia.
2. Edelman and Tononi (2000) take the position that all memory systems are nonrepresentational. In contrast, Bucci (1997), following a long developmental tradition, believes that non-representational memory systems are not the only systems available to the human mind. According to Bucci, representational memory based on symbols and language are an emergent property in evolution. Symbolic representational systems are modeled on classic 'serial' processors. The non-representational memory systems that Edelman and Tononi have in mind have a different brain architecture modeled on parallel distributive processors (PDP). The debate hinges on whether the human brain is composed of one or two main 'architectures': a non-representational architecture modeled as a PDP system (Edelman's belief) or a second architecture modeled on serial processors.

References

Aitken JK and Trevarthen C (1997) Self/Other organization in human development. Development and Psychopathology 9: 653–77.
American Psychiatric Association (1994) Diagnostic and Statistical Manual of Mental Disorders, IV. Washington, DC: American Psychiatric Association.
Atwood GE and Stolorow G (1999) Faces in a Cloud, Northvale, NJ: Jason Aronson.

Bauer PJ, Werner JA, Droop PL and Wewerka SS (2000) Parameters of remembering and forgetting in the transition from infancy to early childhood. Monographs of the Society for Research in Child Development, Serial No. 263, Vol. 65, No. 4.

Bion WR (1967) Second Thoughts. London. Heinemann.

Bowlby J (1969) Attachment, vol. I. New York: Basic Books.

Bowlby J (1972) Separation. Anxiety and Anger, vol. II. New York: Basic Books.

Bowlby J (1980) Attachment and Loss, vol. III. Loss. New York: Basic Books.

Bremner JD (1998) Neuroimaging of Posttraumatic Stress Disorder. Psychiatric Annals 28: 445–52.

Bruner I (1990) Acts of Meaning. Cambridge: Cambridge University Press.

Bucci W (1997) Psychoanalysis and Cognitive Science. A Multiple Code Theory. New York: Guilford Press.

Chefetz RA (2000) Affect dysregulation as a way of life. Journal of the American Academy of Psychoanalysis 28: 289–303.

Cicchetti D (ed.) (1989) The Emergence of a Discipline. Rochester Symposium of Developmental Psychopathology. Hillsdale, NJ: Lawrence Erlbaum.

Cicchetti D and Richters JE (eds) (1997) Special Issue. Conceptual and Scientific Underpinnings of Research in Developmental Psychopathology, vol. 9. Hillsdale, NJ: Lawrence Erlbaum.

Cortina M (1999) Causality, adaptation and meaning. A perspective from attachment theory and research. Psychoanalytic Dialogues 9: 557–96.

Damasio AR (1994) Descartes' Error. New York: Grosset/Putnam.

Damasio AR (1999) The Feeling of What Happens. Body and Emotion in the Making of Consciousness. New York: Harcourt Brace and Company.

Darwin C (1955) The Expression of the Emotions in Man and Animals. New York: The Philosophical Library.

Demos EV (1993) Developmental foundations for the capacity for self-analysis: parallels in the roles of caregivers and analysts. In: JW Barron (ed.) Self-analysis. Critical Inquiries, Personal Visions. Hillsdale, NJ: Analytic Press, pp. 1–27.

Demos EV (1999) The Search for Psychological Models: Commentary on Papers by Stephen Seligman and Robin C. Silverman and Alicia Lieberman. Psychoanalytic Dialogues 9: 204–19.

Dennett DC (1991) Consciousness Explained. Boston: Little, Brown and Company.

De Waal F (1989). Peacemaking among Primates. Cambridge, Mass: Harvard University Press.

Dozier M, Stovall CK, Albus EK and Bates B (2001) Attachment for infants in foster care. The role of caregiver state of mind. Child Development 72: 1467–77.

Edelman GM (1987) Neuronal Darwinism. The Theory of Neuronal Selection. New York: Basic Books.

Edelman GM (1992) Bright Air, Brilliant Fire. On Matters of the Mind. New York: Basic Books.

Edelman GM and Tononi G (2000) A Universe of Consciousness. How Matter Becomes Imagination. New York: Basic Books.

Ekman P and Davidson RC (eds) (1994) The Nature of Emotion. Oxford University Press.

Emde RN (1994) Individuality, context and the search for meaning. Child Development 65: 719-37.

Emde RN, Biringen Z, Clyman RB and Oppenheim D (1991) The moral self in infancy. Affective core and procedural knowledge. Developmental Review 11: 251–70.

Erikson EH (1950/1963) Childhood and Society, 2nd edn. New York: WW Norton.

Erikson EH (1964) Insight and Responsibility. New York: WW Norton.

Fonagy P and Target M (1997) Attachment and reflective function. Their role in self-organization. Development and Psychopathology 9: 679–700.

Freud S (1923) The Ego and the Id. Standard Edition 19: 3–66. London: Hogarth Press, 1957.

Freud S (1925) Inhibitions, Symptoms, and Anxiety. Standard Edition 20: 87–172. London: Hogarth Press, 1957.

Fromm E (1941) Escape from Freedom. New York: Farrar & Rinehart.

Fromm E (1947) Man for Himself. Greenwich, Conn: Fawcett Publications.

Fromm E (1973) The Anatomy of Human Destructiveness. New York: Holt, Rinehart & Winston.

George C, Kaplan N and Main M (1996) Adult Attachment Interview. Unpublished manuscript, Department of Psychology, University of California, Berkeley (3rd edn).

Gill M (1963) Topography and Systems in Psychoanalytic Theory. New York: International University Press.

Gottlieb G (1997) Synthesizing Nature-Nurture. Mahwah, NJ: Lawrence Erlbaum.

Heard D and Lake B (1997) The Challenge of Attachment for Caregiving. New York: Routledge.

Karmiloff-Smith A (1992) Beyond Modularity. Cambridge, Mass: MIT Press.

Karpman J (1968) Fairy tales and script drama analysis. Transactional Analysis Bulletin 27: 157–61.

Lachmann FM (1999) Unconscious and Model Scenes. Presented at the 1999 annual conference of the Institute of Contemporary Psychotherapy and Psychoanalysis, Bethesda, Md.

Lachmann FM (2001) Some contributions of empirical infant research to adult psychoanalysis. Psychoanalytic Dialogues 11: 167–85.

Langer SK (1967) Mind: An Essay on Human Feeling, vol. I. Baltimore: Johns Hopkins University Press.

Lazarus RS (1991) Emotion and Adaptation. New York: Oxford University Press.

LeDoux J (1996) The Emotional Brain. New York: Simon & Schuster.

Lichtenberg JD (1989) Psychoanalysis and Motivation. Hillsdale, NJ: Analytic Press.

Lichtenberg J, Lachmann MF and Fosshage LJ (1992) Self and Motivational Systems. Hillsdale, NJ: Analytic Press.

Lieberman AF (1992) Infant-parent psychotherapy with toddlers. Development and Psychopathology 4: 559–74.

Liotti G (1992) Disorganized/disoriented attachment in the etiology of dissociative disorders. Dissociation 5: 196–204.

Liotti G (1995) Disorganized/disoriented attachment in the psychotherapy of the dissociative disorders. In: S Goldberg, R Muir and J Kerr (eds) Attachment Theory. Social, Developmental and Clinical Perspective, Hillsdale, NJ: Analytic Press, pp. 343–63.

Liotti G (1999) Understanding the dissociative process: The contribution of attachment theory. Psychoanalytic Inquiry 19: 757–83.

Liotti G and Intreccialagli B (1998). In: C Perris and P McGorry (eds) Cognitive Psychotherapy of the Psychotic and Personality Disorders. Chichester: Wiley, pp. 333–49.

Liotti G, Pasquine P and The Italian Group for the Study of Dissociation (2000) Predictive factors for the development of borderline personality disorder. Acta Psychiatrica Scandinavica 102: 240–89.

Loevinger J (1976) Ego Development. San Francisco: Jossey-Bass.

Maccoby M (1988) Why Work. New York: Simon & Schuster.

Main M and Hesse E (1990) Parents' unresolved traumatic experiences are related to infant disorganization status. In: MT Greenberg, D Cicchetti, and EM Cummings (eds) Attachment in the Preschool Years. Theory, Research and Intervention. Chicago: Chicago University Press, pp. 161–82.

Main M and Solomon J (1986) Discovery of a new insecure disorganized/disoriented pattern. In: TB Brazelton and M Yogman (eds) Affective Development in Infancy. Norwood, NJ: Ablex, pp. 95–124.

Main M and Weston D (1981) The quality of the toddler's relationship to mother and father: Related to conflict behavior and the readiness to establish new relationships. Child Development 52: 932–40.

Mitchell S (2000) Relationality. From Attachment to Intersubjectivity. Hillsdale, NJ: Analytic Press.

O'Conner GT and Craft MC (2001) A twin study of attachment in preschool children. Child Development 72: 1287–300.

Ogawa JR, Sroufe LA, Weinfield EA, Carlson EA and Egeland B (1997) Development and the fragmented self: Longitudinal study of dissociative symptomatology in a nonclinical population. Development and Psychopathology 9: 855–79.

Ogden T (1982) Projective Identification and Psychotherapeutic Technique. New York: Jason Aronson.

Piaget J (1952) The origins of intelligence in children. New York: International University Press.

Piaget J (1962) Play, Dreams and Imitation in Childhood. New York: WW Norton.

Piaget J (1971) Biology and Knowledge. Chicago: University of Chicago Press.

Rauch SL, van der Kolk BA, Fisher RE, Albert NM, Orr SP, Savage CR, Fishman AJ, Jenike MA and Pitman RK (1996) A symptom provocation study of posttraumatic stress disorder using positron emission tomography and script driven imagery. Archives of General Psychiatry 53: 380–7.

Ryle G (1949) The Concept of Mind. New York: Barnes and Noble, 1965.

Sameroff AJ (1989) Models of developmental regulation: The environtype. In: D Cicchetti (ed.) The Emergence of a Discipline. Rochester Symposium on Developmental Psychopathology. Hillsdale, NJ: Lawrence Erlbaum, pp. 41–68.

Scharff DE (1992) Redefining the Object and Reclaiming the Self. Northvale, NJ: Jason Aronson.

Schore AN (1994) Affect Regulation and the Origin of the Self. The Neurobiology of Emotional Development. Hillsdale, NJ: Lawrence Erlbaum.

Schore AN (1997) Early organization of the nonlinear right brain and the development of a predisposition for psychiatric disorders. Development and Psychopathology 9: 595–631.

Seligman S (1999) Integrating Kleinian theory and intersubjective infant research. Observing projective identification. Psychoanalytic Dialogues 9: 129–59.

Silverman DK (1998) The tie that binds. Affect regulation, attachment and psychoanalysis. Psychoanalytic Psychology 15: 187–212.

Silverman RC and Lieberman AF (1999) Negative maternal attributions, projective identification, and the intergenerational transmission of violent relational patterns. Psychoanalytic Dialogues 9: 161–86.

Solomon J and George C (1999) The place of disorganization in attachment theory. Linking classic observations with contemporary findings. In: J Solomon and C George (eds) Attachment Disorganization. New York: Guilford Press, pp. 3–39.

Spangler G and Grossman G (1993) Behavior organization in securely and insecurely attached infants. Child Development 63: 1439–50.

Sroufe LA (1996) Emotional Development The Organization of Emotional Development in the Early Years. New York: Cambridge University Press.

Sroufe LA (1997) Psychopathology as an outcome of development. Development and Psychopathology 9: 251–67.

Sroufe LA and Fleeson J (1986) Attachment and the construction of relationships. In: WW Hartup and Z Rubin (eds) Relationships and Development. Hillsdale, NJ: Lawrence Erlbaum, pp. 51–7.

Sroufe LA and Waters E (1977) Heart rate as a convergent measure in clinical and developmental research. Merrill-Palmer Quarterly 23: 3–27.

Sroufe LA, Egeland B and Carlson EA (1999) One social world. The integrated development of parent-child and peer relations. In: Minnesota Symposium on Child Development, vol. 30: WA Collins and B Laursen (eds) Relationships as Developmental Contexts. Hillsdale, NJ: Lawrence Erlbaum, pp. 241–61.

Stern D (1985) The Interpersonal World of the Infant. New York: Basic Books.

Stern D, Sandler L, Nahum J, Harrison A, Lyons-Ruth K, Moran A, Brushweiler-Stern N and Tronick E (1998) Noninterpretive mechanisms in psychoanalytic therapies. The 'something more' than interpretation. International Journal of Psycho-analysis 79: 903–21.

Tomkins SS (1962) Affect, Imagery and Consciousness, vol. I: The Positive Affects. New York: Springer.

Tomkins SS (1963) Affect, Imagery and Consciousness, vol. II: The Negative Affects. New York: Springer.

Troy M and Sroufe LA (1987) Victimization among preschoolers. Role of attachment relationship history. Journal of the American Academy of Child and Adolescent Psychiatry 20: 166–72.

Tulving E (1972) Episodic and semantic memory. In: E Tulving and W Donaldson (eds) Organization of Memory. New York: Academic Press, pp. 162–79.

Vygotsky SL (1978) Mind in Society. The Development of Higher Psychological Processes. Cambridge, Mass: Harvard University Press.

Weinfield NS, Sroufe LA, Egeland B and Carlson E (1999) The nature of individual differences in infant–caregiver attachment. In: J Cassidy and PR Shaver (eds) Handbook of Attachment. Theory Research and Clinical Implications. New York: Guilford Press, pp. 68–88.

Wellman HA, Cross D and Watson J (2001) Meta-analysis of theory-of-mind devel-
    opment: The truth about false belief. Child Development 72: 655–84.
Werner H (1948) Comparative Psychology of Mental Development. New York:
    International University Press.
Westen D (1997) The Scientific Status of Unconscious Processes. Is Freud Really
    Dead? Paper presented at the Rapaport-Klein Study Group, Stockbridge, Mass.
Winnicott DW (1949) An Ordinary Devoted Mother and her Baby. New York: Basic
    Books.

CHAPTER 13

Attachment theory as a bridge between cognitive science and psychodynamic theory

JEAN KNOX

Introduction

In the first half of the twentieth century, the classical theory of behaviourism dominated academic psychology; it was a theory that represents the low point of any attempt to understand the human psyche, because it simply did away with mind altogether. One of the most famous behaviourists, B.F. Skinner, actually said, 'The question is not whether machines think but whether men do' (Pinker, 1997, p. 62). Behaviourism treated humans as mindless automatons whose essential spirit, our hopes, fears, desires and beliefs were all treated as an irritating irrelevance. It was a psychology of stimulus-response, reflex arcs and salivating dogs which alienated generations of potential psychologists through its absolute denial of the vital role that subjective experience and emotions play in the way we all function as human beings.

Then, in the 1950s and 1960s, a revolution began to take place in academic psychology, a revolution essentially linked to the development of the computer. A computer-based model for the human mind may initially seem to be just as reductive as behaviourism because it also might seem to imply a predetermined set of rules governing the way the mind works, like a form of 'Windows' software installed in our heads, but this is very far from the truth about the computational theory of mind, or cognitive science.

Cognitive science is revolutionary in relation to behaviourism and crucially important to analysts and psychotherapists (of all theoretical orientations) because it explores the way the mind deals with information, and information can include anything that goes on in the human mind; perceptions, emotions, hopes, beliefs, desires, dreams, fantasies, the experience of bodily sensations; all these are information, all of equal value in the computational theory of mind even though some of them may be more difficult to investigate than others.

Cognitive science and its relevance to psychotherapy

Since cognitive science is a description of all the ways in which scientists try to understand the way the mind computes or processes information, it is therefore apparent that cognitive science covers many of the areas that psychotherapists are exploring clinically. We do aim to be therapeutic with our patients but we also draw on our clinical work to attempt to gain an ever more accurate understanding of how the human mind works, an understanding based on the remarkable pioneering work of Freud, Jung, Klein and those who followed them. In our attempts to gain a better understanding of human mental functioning, psychotherapists are cognitive scientists as well, investigating the way our patients process the information of their dreams, fantasies and memories.

However, the early pioneers of psychoanalysis and analytical psychology were still struggling with nineteenth-century models of the mind, based on the regulation of instinct and the hydraulic model of limited quantities of energy which were channelled towards an instinct-satisfying object and discharged (Sandler, 1997, p. 72). What was missing was the information-processing view of mind, which cognitive science now offers us. Cognitive science is based on a representational–computational view of mind in which knowledge is constituted by mental representations and cognitive activity consists in the manipulation of these representations, i.e. the application of computational operations to them (Shanon, 1993, p. 2). Most information processing takes place without conscious attention being paid to the representations being computed, although some are available to be made conscious and can become so under certain conditions. Mandler highlights the fact that attention and consciousness should be distinguished from each other and wishes to 'define attention as being independent of consciousness and to restrict it to the potential intake of information' (Mandler, 1984, p. 62). The significance of this cannot be overestimated; the implication is that unconscious information processing is a normal state of affairs in the human mind and does not by any means always result from the activation of psychodynamic mechanisms such as repression or dissociation. In Chapter 12 in this volume Cortina explores this in detail, pointing out that: 'Appraising, selecting and interpreting experience is not a function of an agency of the mind such as the id or the ego or superego. *It is what the brain does.*'

On the other hand, I should not want to give the impression that I am suggesting that we can ultimately reduce the mystery of the human spirit to a series of computations, the processing of packets of information. We cannot and should not try to explain away the numinous or demonic aspects of our experience, painting, poetry, religion, our dreams or intuitions, the overwhelming experience of passionate love or hate, the tenderness of intimacy and the symbols that express these emotions. As therapists, much of our skill lies in being attuned to the transforming symbols that our patients unconsciously communicate to us in the session; as therapists we cannot be merely scientific objective observers of our patients' mental processes but must also allow ourselves to be drawn in and sometimes taken over emotionally; we must be able to feel love and hate, sometimes towards and sometimes with or on behalf of our patients.

It is this intuitive response to symbolic communication that plays as important a part in therapy as objective understanding. Although much of the focus in this chapter is on the scientific contributions that attachment theory brings to psychotherapy, it is also a framework that has emotions and relationship at its core. Bowlby never undervalued the central role of intuitive responsiveness in therapy, writing that: 'Clearly the best therapy is done by a therapist who is naturally intuitive and also guided by the appropriate theory' (Bowlby, 1991, p. 16). Mario Marrone points out that 'sensitive responsiveness' is recognized to be a major psychic organizer. Mary Ainsworth showed, by means of the 'Strange Situation' experiments, that what matters most in determining a developmental pathway is the caregiver's sensitive responsiveness (Marrone, 1998, p. 42). Allan Schore has offered a neurophysiological explanation for the key role that emotions play in psychological development, suggesting that early emotional experiences directly affect the growth and maturation of interconnections in the prefrontal cortex and the limbic system of the infant's brain and that the adult brain retains the plasticity necessary for similar effects to be produced by the patient's relationship with the therapist:

> Prefrontal areas are known to continue maturing well into adulthood, perhaps throughout the lifespan. Affect regulatory dialogs mediated by a psychotherapist may induce literal structural change in the form of new patterns of growth of cortico-limbic circuitries, especially in the right hemisphere which contains representations of self-and-object relationships. (Schore, 1994, p. 468)

However, Bowlby's comment about the value of intuition also refers to 'the appropriate theory' and psychotherapists do need to be clearer about the value of the scientific approach in relation to the theoretical models that underpin our clinical practice. This value lies in the discipline of the scientific method, which is always trying to narrow down its field of investigation to make each problem it tries to solve into as small and precise as possible in order to exclude all the variables that might confuse the answer; if successful, scientists can produce the evidence with some confidence that the experimental results are relevant to the question being asked.

In contrast, all psychodynamic theories fall, at times, into the trap of trying to offer an explanation for all mental phenomena. We run the risk of working with increasingly outdated and inaccurate models of the human mind if we avoid subjecting them to the rigour of scientific scepticism, for fear that the numinous or spiritual will be destroyed by the scientific advances in understanding the way the mind actually works, the ways in which it processes information. Richard Dawkins argues in his book *Unweaving the Rainbow* that scientific understanding of the physics of the rainbow can produce just as much wonder as the belief that it is a symbol of God's covenant with Noah after the flood. Dawkins says:

> The feeling of awed wonder that science can give us is one of the highest experiences of which the human psyche is capable. It is a deep aesthetic passion to rank with the finest that music and poetry can deliver. It is truly one of the things that makes life worth living and it does so, if anything, more effectively if it convinces us that the time we have for living it is finite. (Dawkins, 1998, p. x)

I think that the more scientifically accurate our models of the human mind are, the better therapists we become because we can be much more relaxed about the fact that there is so much we do not know. The requirement to support theories with empirical evidence means that a scientist does learn to live with uncertainty, with the possibility that new evidence may at any moment cast doubt on a model that he or she has spent a lifetime developing. In contrast, rigid analytic dogmas, like rigid religious dogmas, can at times seem to demand absolute conviction and certainty from their supporters, so that new evidence which might require revision of the model is seen as a threat. This authoritarian strand can be traced back to Freud's inability to tolerate dissent from his view of the psyche and his need for 'disciples who would accept his doctrine without reservation' (Ellenberger, 1970, p. 669); it re-emerged with full force in the rejection of Bowlby's revolutionary ideas by the majority of the psychoanalytic community in his day (Holmes, 1993, p. 6).

The danger for a therapist whose mind is closed to new discoveries and developments in theory or practice is that he or she will miss valuable opportunities to increase his or her therapeutic effectiveness. Daniel Stern has vividly described how crucial this open-mindedness is clinically; he has identified unpredicted 'moments of truth' which suddenly arise in a session, moments which are laden with emotional significance and with potential importance for the immediate or long-term future, a 'kairos' moment which must be seized or be lost. Stern says that in one of these 'now' moments, the patient and therapist are surprised and taken off guard by its unpredictability. Both may defend against the anxiety this creates by resorting to established technique. Stern says, 'if the therapist "knows" what to do, he has probably missed the "now" moment' (Stern, 1998; Stern et al., 1998).

Unfortunately, this view is not shared by all therapists. The rapidly evolving research in cognitive science and developmental psychology may be seen as a threat to some therapists because the findings from this research begin to break down the rather outdated divisions between therapeutic schools and to undermine the absolute authority of the analytic pioneers such as Freud, Jung and Klein, who could not be right about all aspects of their theory however inspired they were. André Green, for example, is openly critical of the contribution that empirical research, such as that undertaken by Daniel Stern, can make to analytic theory and practice and has recently written that: 'the procedures of research (even if those involved were adults who had experienced a psychoanalysis) were inadequate because they were not applicable to the type of mental functioning of the patient in the analytic session, and with the corresponding state of mind of the analyst listening to the free association of the patient with his free-floating attention' (Green, 2001, p. 67).

In contrast, there are many contemporary psychoanalysts who do integrate findings from developmental psychology and cognitive science into their theoretical models (Shapiro and Emde, 1995). Attachment theory has played an increasingly important role in such studies and makes an essential contribution to our understanding of the distortions of mental representations of key people in a child's early life; attachment theory arose largely out of Bowlby's recognition that psychological and psychoanalytic theories must be compatible with contemporary evolutionary and ethological science (Bowlby, 1988, p. 5; Bretherton, 1995, p. 62). In other words, different levels of explanation of psychological processing must be compatible with each other:

1. Psychodynamic. The clinical level of explanation.
2. Information processing–attachment theory (cognitive science; developmental studies).

Both principally involve observation under experimental conditions.

3. Ethology (evolutionary mechanisms). Theoretical explanation concerning the biological mechanisms that underpin the clinical and
experimental phenomena of levels 1 and 2.

Attachment theory as a bridge between science and psychotherapy

Grossman emphasizes the urgency of the task of building bridges
between psychodynamic theories and academic models of the mind, saying 'two psychologies have existed side by side for more than a hundred
years, and the shakiness of the bridges between them has every so often
been deplored'. He goes on to state that 'Attachment is not one relationship among others; it is the very foundation of healthy individual
development. More, it is the precondition for developing a coherent
mind, even if it is, finally, insufficient by itself for understanding the whole
mind. Scientifically, attachment theory has done nothing less than bridge
the gap between individual experience and objective research'
(Grossman, 1995, p. 116).

The points of convergence between attachment theory and contemporary psychoanalytic models of the psyche have been fairly extensively
mapped, particularly by Morris Eagle (1995, p. 123). The focus in this
chapter will be more on the points of contact between attachment theory
and analytical psychology, the Jungian model of the psyche. Many of the
areas in which Jung's ideas sharply diverged from those of Freud can be
seen to be points of convergence with attachment theory and I shall highlight some of these key areas throughout this chapter. These similarities
in the theoretical models offered by analytical psychology and attachment
theory have so far not been examined in the literature in any depth.

The use of the term 'instinct'

There is a vital point of clarification about the nature of the concept of
instinct which needs to be made here as a key part of identifying the role
of attachment theory as a bridge between cognitive science and psychodynamic models of the mind. One of the most clear-cut distinctions
between Freud and Jung, which precipitated the final break between
them, was their sharp divergence over the nature and role of instinct and
the place of instinctual drive in shaping psychological processes. Jung criticized Freud on this account, saying that 'Unlike Freud, who after a proper
psychological start reverted to the ancient assumption of the sovereignty

of the physical constitution, trying to turn everything back in theory into instinctual processes conditioned by the body, I start with the sovereignty of the psyche' (Jung, 1921, para. 968). Jung rejected the sexual definition of libido, instead identifying it as a neutral psychic energy which is not attached to a specific instinct. He wrote: 'I cannot see the real aetiology of neurosis in the various manifestations of infantile sexual development and the fantasies to which they give rise' (Jung, 1916, para. 574).

Jung's view gains support from the work of developmental psychologists such as Daniel Stern and Lichtenberg who have shown fairly conclusively that instinctual drive theory should be discarded as an explanation for human psychological development. On the basis of his and others' empirical research, Stern said:

> [I]nfants from the beginning mainly experience reality. Their subjective experiences suffer no distortion by virtue of wishes or defences but only those made inevitable by perceptual or cognitive immaturity... the capacity for defensive, that is psychodynamic distortions of reality is a later developing capacity requiring more cognitive processes than are initially available. Reality experience precedes fantasy distortions in development. (Stern, 1985, p. 255)

The problem with Freud's instinctual drive theory, also adopted wholeheartedly by Klein, is that it is a nineteenth-century hydraulic model, based on outdated concepts, such as those of quantities of energy and the need to reduce instinctual arousal and tension to a minimum. Eagle points out that in this model: 'the infant's attachment to mother is secondary to the latter's role in gratification of the infant's hunger drive; that the vicissitudes of the sexual drive are primary determinants of personality development; and that the reduction in excitation is a superordinate motive underlying a wide range of behaviors' (Eagle, 1995, p. 123). In this chapter it is this Freudian model that I mean when I refer to instinctual drive theory.

In contrast, in attachment theory, instinct is conceptualized much more in terms of dynamic, interactive patterns of relationship and behaviour, in a way that is much more in keeping with recent ethological research. Attachment is seen as a primary motivational system, not dependent on hunger or libido (Marrone, 1998, p. 36). Once again we can see how important it is that theoretical explanations at the psychodynamic or information processing level are compatible with, and keep up to date with, research findings from biology and ethology. This is a process that requires constant reassessment of models as new research findings emerge in relevant fields. Even though Bowlby's concept of instinct is much more contemporary than Freud's, new findings in developmental psychology may require some further revision of the notion of instinct and I shall explore this in the section on innate structures below.

Turning to other aspects of attachment theory as a bridge between science and psychotherapy, Bowlby himself recognized that attachment theory was an information-processing model involving special categories of mental representations, those concerning relationships with key attachment figures; an information-processing approach provides a vehicle for us to examine and clarify the nature of these mental representations (Bowlby, 1980, p. 55). Most psychodynamic theories describe such mental representations of attachment figures as 'internal objects', which are thought to be, at least partly, schematized representations of a child's parents and other key figures of early life, although there is wide variation between psychodynamic explanations for the ways in which such representations or 'internal objects' are formed (Perlow, 1995).

Attachment theory provides a model in which interpersonal experiences with key attachment figures are encoded and stored as mental representations and cumulative experiences of this kind are gradually built up in the mind into schematic representations of generalized patterns of such interactions, called 'internal working models' (Bowlby, 1988, p. 129). These 'internal working models' influence a person's perceptions of, and attitudes and behaviour towards, all subsequent emotionally important relationships but are not themselves accessible to conscious awareness.

The concept of 'internal working models' therefore plays a crucial part in forming a bridge between psychodynamic theory and cognitive science; it gives an information-processing account of the way in which mental representations of relationships with key attachment figures are formed and stored in implicit memory, an account that is much more compatible with evidence from developmental psychology and research on the nature of memory than the psychodynamic concept of 'internal objects', as Bowlby himself suggested (Bowlby, 1988, p. 120). As a further bridge to cognitive science, the retrieval of 'internal working models' can be linked to the phenomena of state-dependent retrieval, in which any information learnt in one situation is preferentially recalled when a person is again in that situation, and mood-congruent retrieval, in which an emotional state leads to preferential recall of information with the same emotional content. Relationships that retrieve a particular 'internal working model' will also retrieve information learnt on previous occasions when that working model was retrieved and the emotions that accompany the retrieved 'internal working model' will lead to preferential recall of similar emotional experiences. The concept of the 'internal working model' can be used to shed new light on three pivotal issues in psychotherapeutic theory and practice: the nature of memory, the ways in which unconscious fantasy arises, and the question as to what, precisely, constitute the innate, inherited aspects of the human psyche.

Memory

Let me, therefore, begin to illustrate some of these general themes by focusing on the question of memory, a topic of central importance to the psychotherapeutic endeavour and one that has shown therapists how vulnerable we are to public censure when our theoretical models for understanding memory processes are shown by scientific investigation to be faulty or inadequate.

Two statements illustrate our difficulty:

- A memory may be true but may be repressed for long periods of time and then recovered.
- A memory may be held with great clarity and conviction but is actually false.

'True' means that the memory reflects real events which took place, whilst 'false' means that the events which seem to be remembered did not in reality occur. Both these statements are accurate and as therapists we must have a theoretical model of memory which allows for both these possibilities. John Morton, who chaired the British Psychological Society Working Party on recovered memories, summarized this in the statement:

> Sometimes we remember events pretty much as they happened, sometimes we remember fabrications as if they were reality and sometimes we do a bit of both. Even when we do recount things as they happened, we are, simultaneously, likely to be remembering details incorrectly. All memories are a mixture of reproduction and reconstruction. (Morton et al., 1995)

There has been considerable scientific research conducted on the whole area of true and false memory which provides evidence that false memories can be constructed quite easily and then held with great conviction, particularly when strengthened by frequent rehearsal. A beautiful example is given by Piaget himself from his own childhood:

> One of my first memories would date if it were true, from my second year. I can still see, most clearly, the following scene, in which I believed, until I

was about fifteen. I was sitting in my pram, which my nurse was pushing in the Champs Elysées, when a man tried to kidnap me. I was held in by the strap fastened round me whilst my nurse bravely tried to stand between the thief and me. She received various scratches and I can still see vaguely those on her face ...

When I was about fifteen, my parent received a letter from my former nurse ... she wanted to confess her past faults, and in particular to return the watch she had been given as a reward. She had made up the whole story ... I must therefore have heard as a child, the account of this story, which my parents believed, and projected into the past in the form of a visual memory. (Piaget, 1962)

Subsequently there has been considerable experimental evidence for such false remembering. One such study showed that the test subjects could be made to 'remember' that they had been lost in a shopping mall when young; as part of this study, one 42-year-old subject was falsely convinced by his sister that he had been lost as a small child. She gave a vivid invented account of the event to him and a day later the test subject was sure that he could remember some of the events she described. Loftus describes five other subjects who were led quite easily to 'remember' events that had never taken place (Loftus and Coan, 1994).

However, Loftus, who has conducted a whole range of experiments on the memory process, has also said that she too believes that it is possible to lose contact with memories for a long time, a statement from one of the most authoritative scientists who study memory and which contrasts with the conclusion of the Royal College of Psychiatrists' Working Party that recovery of long-forgotten memories of abuse was most unlikely. However, this report was criticized for failing to take into account research which demonstrates that while it is possible for false memories to be firmly implanted by suggestion, it is also possible for memories to be unavailable to recall for long periods of time and then recovered.

There are both experimental studies and clinical studies that are relevant to this issue. Carefully conducted experimental studies have demonstrated a phenomenon called state-dependent retrieval, which essentially means that we are more likely to remember an event that occurred under certain specific conditions if those conditions are reproduced at the time we try to recall the event. One particularly striking experiment showed that deep sea divers showed better recall of material they had learnt underwater when they were again underwater as opposed to recall when they were on land (Bower, 1981). Other studies have shown that, although alcohol has a generally adverse effect on memory, experiences that occurred when a person was drunk are more likely to be recalled when that person is drunk again than when they are sober (Eich, 1980). Changes in mood can contribute to state-dependent retrieval, so that events that occurred in one particular mood or frame of mind are more likely to be recalled when in the same state of mind again.

This phenomenon of state-dependent retrieval is clearly highly relevant to the issue of lost, then recovered memories. A child who is being sexually abused by a parent experiences intense and distressing emotions. The experience is often kept totally secret, usually at the bidding of the abuser, who calls it 'our secret', and may remain unintegrated into the rest of that child's life as she grows up; she may form satisfactory emotional and sexual relationships as an adult and the abuse remains either unavailable to recall, or if it is remembered it may be recalled without any re-experiencing of the intense emotional pain felt at the time of the abuse. However, at any time that person may suddenly find herself vividly reliving the abuse in the most painful and terrifying way if something happens to trigger state-dependent retrieval. Some patients have described this experience as a result of watching the programmes or advertisements that warn about child abuse; the advertisements have actually been experienced as abusive themselves because the words and images, the picture of bedclothes moving, the words 'come and sit over here' have actually triggered an acutely painful reliving of their particular experience of abuse with all the distress they felt at the time.

Clinical studies have also demonstrated that memories may be lost and then recovered, although strenuous efforts have been made by a number of scientists to discount such findings as evidence of repression (Pope and Hudson, 1995). One frequently quoted study is by Williams, who followed up children with documented evidence of childhood sexual abuse into adult life; she found that adults who had documented experience of childhood abuse sometimes do not report these experiences at interview even when asked about such events; sometimes they would report the general experience of maltreatment but would seem not to remember specific episodes, of which there was documentary evidence from childhood notes (Williams, 1994). Most strikingly of all, 12 per cent of these adults with documented evidence of childhood sexual abuse completely denied that they had ever been abused by anyone at any time. Simple forgetting does not seem an adequate explanation for this kind of failure to recall highly significant traumatic experiences.

So far, I have described remembering specific events from the past, the kind of memory we are all familiar with and which is usually called declarative or explicit memory by cognitive scientists. However, in an editorial in the *International Journal of Psycho-analysis*, Peter Fonagy questions the role of this kind of memory in relation to therapeutic effectiveness; he says:

The aims of psychoanalysis have been greatly elaborated over the hundred years since Freud's original model of undoing repression and recovering memory into consciousness. But these advances have not brought with them an updating of the role of memory in the therapeutic process, nor a clear and consistent theory of therapeutic effect. Some still appear to believe that the recovery of memory is part of the therapeutic action of the treatment. There is no evidence for this and in my view to cling to this idea is damaging to the field. (Fonagy, 1999)

So, if psychotherapy does not bring about change solely by means of the recovery of autobiographical memories, what is the role of memory in therapy? There has been an explosion of scientific research on the nature of memory, research that has demonstrated that there are several different types of memory and that some forms of memory can operate complete-ly outside conscious awareness without any psychodynamic process such as repression or splitting being involved. A most striking illustration of this is the phenomenon of blind-sight, where damage to the occipital cor-tex results in the loss of the conscious sense of vision; in other words the patient apparently cannot see. However, Weiskrantz found that when a light was flashed in the part of the patient's visual field affected by the brain damage, the patient said he could not see anything, but when asked to guess the location of the flash he could do so quite accurately as though he were capable of some sort of unconscious perception (Weiskrantz, 1986). The word 'unconscious' can simply mean outside awareness rather than dynamically repressed, and as therapists we do need to have some understanding of this kind of research; otherwise we shall be looking for psychodynamic explanations for such phenomena where none exist.

There is another way in which memories can exert an active influence, but without that person being aware of any conscious memory. Implicit memory is a form of memory in which past events influence our thoughts, actions and perceptions but outside consciousness. This can be quite a simple perceptual priming effect such as the fact that subliminal messages or advertisements, flashed on to a screen so briefly that we are not aware we have seen them, can be shown to influence our judgements and choices. However, implicit memory may also involve complex conceptual knowledge, an unconscious memory, not for specific events but rather a kind of generalized knowledge about how to do things, procedural knowledge, and what things mean, semantic knowledge. Implicit memory is a kind of abstract generalized set of unconscious rules, guidelines and expectations about how the world works and how one functions in it (Schacter, 1996, Chapter 6). Christopher Bollas' formulation of the 'unthought known' suggests that he is describing aspects of implicit memory, although his concept also implies that there is innate instinctual knowledge which is activated by facilitating parenting, which is not a feature of implicit memory (Bollas, 1987, 1989).

Implicit memory as the basis for the transference

Clarifying the relevance of the concept of implicit memory to the theoretical framework which informs our clinical work shows that the concept of implicit memory also has direct implications for our clinical practice, particularly in the way we conceptualize the transference, and I should like to explore these applications further here.

Implicit memory forms the basis for most of the unconscious patterns of attitude, behaviour and expectations that our patients bring to their sessions; out of the experiences of a lifetime, some of which the patient consciously remembers, but most of which he or she does not, a whole set of models of the world are constructed in implicit memory and these models structure or pattern the way that person relates to any new experience. Thus, implicit memory is the basis for the transference. The transference does not arise as an expression of instinctual drives that somehow spontaneously produce complex mental imagery and fantasy, which is then projected out on to real people. Transference arises out of the internalization of actual people and real events in the world and gradually produces an unconscious pattern of generalized expectations about relationships.

The person who most clearly understood this was John Bowlby, whose views were unacceptable to many of his psychoanalytic colleagues at the time. The concept of implicit memory helps us to understand how internal working models develop, without our needing the psychoanalytic model of instinctual drive theory to explain why internal reality can differ so much from external reality. Implicit memory helps us to see how multiple real-life events become aggregated, mixed up together and that the fears or hopes that a person has at the time can also become incorporated into the memory of events.

The end result of this process of internalization of multiple experiences was described by Bowlby as an 'internal working model'; internal working models can be thought of as internal maps organizing our perception of the world (Bowlby, 1988, p. 129). A securely attached child will have internal working models of other people as reliable and predictable and will bring this generalized expectation into the transference, whereas an anxiously attached child will have working models of other people as rejecting, dangerous or otherwise unreliable. Internal working models are the most obvious clinical examples of implicit memory; they are really forms of unconscious memory of an abstract kind and demonstrate that it is possible for memories to be unconscious without being dynamically repressed. Working model 'memories' can never become a conscious memory of an event. The memories of events have been turned into an abstract pattern which can be consciously discovered only when it is relived, for example in the transference, and can then be analysed and modified.

Clinical illustrations

1. A patient has given me many descriptions of her parents, both doctors, as people who are unable to live with anxiety, uncertainty or helplessness and always look for someone to blame. She has many clear memories of occasions when her parents have blamed her or anyone other than themselves when things went wrong, but remembering these examples has not produced any change in the constant non-specific anxiety that she lives with every day and which was one of the reasons she came into therapy.

   However, during the course of the therapy she has gradually realized how much her anxiety arises because she waits to be blamed, including by me; she is constantly unconsciously expecting someone to say 'it's your fault'; much of the work in the therapy has involved a gradual recognition that quite often we are all helpless to prevent or solve problems, which may be just the way life is at times and it is not her task to put things right for her internal parents. The working model in this case seemed to be of a pattern of relationship in which she, the child, was made responsible for allaying parental anxiety and would be blamed if she failed to do so. This pattern gradually emerged in her relationship with me, and making this conscious in our interactions is what has brought about change rather than the memories of actual childhood events.

2. Another patient has described the fact that her mother had numerous illnesses and sudden unexpected hospital admissions when my patient was a small child, which she remembers as experiences of abandonment. Her father was emotionally unable and unwilling to provide the secure parenting she needed at these times, but an uncle who lived with them did offer her care and security; however, after a year or so, this uncle started to abuse her sexually when he was looking after her.

   As an adult she married a man whose work made it necessary for him to be away from home for periods of days or weeks without any prior warning and once again she felt profoundly abandoned, so much so that she was unable to function independently and would spend days in the house without going out, often curled up on her bed in a depressed state. She then met a man who was caring and protective towards her, helping her to manage practical aspects of her life whilst her husband was away; a sexual relationship developed between them, but this soon became abusive.

It seemed to me that unconscious 'working model' memories of abandonment were activated in adult life by her husband's absences, and this led to the recreation of a pattern of relationship with an initially caring man who then became sexually abusive, like her uncle. The 'internal working model' acted as an unconscious script, which possibly even influenced her initial attraction to a man with a similar personality to her uncle. In the analysis, she has become aware that she may have also unconsciously evoked the abusive attitude which her lover developed towards her, through her own attitude of neediness, seductiveness and passive compliance towards him. She realizes that she was relating to him on the basis of an unconscious belief that the only people who wanted to care for her would also abuse her and that she had to accept this because the alternative was to be abandoned. An unconscious 'working model' such as this might have led her to evoke abuse as a necessary, though painful, proof that she would not be abandoned.

In psychotherapy, the unconscious patterns that are laid down in internal working models may, from time to time, be illustrated by specific memories from childhood, but the remembering of these particular events is not sufficient in itself to bring about change in therapy. This also depends upon the slow modification of the patient's internal working models of self–other relationships through the relationship with the analyst; this creates its own working models, which are hopefully more positive and which can be gradually integrated with existing working models or exist alongside them as alternatives. The formation of new 'internal working models' would probably be accompanied by, and indeed rooted in, the restructuring of neuronal pathways in the prefrontal cortex and limbic systems described in the quote from Allan Schore, above.

The concepts of implicit memory and the internal working model have profound implications for our understanding of psychopathology and for the theoretical models which inform our clinical practice. The overcoming of repression and dissociation still have a central part to play in analytic practice but there is an increasing recognition amongst analysts that our task is also one of constructing new internal working models of relationships with our patients. This approach has been explored by psychoanalysts such as Owen Renik, Robert Emde and the psychoanalytic 'Process of Change' study group, who suggest that analysis creates new implicit patterns of interpersonal relationship (Renik, 2000; Emde, 1999; Stern et al., 1998). For Jungians, this 'synthetic' or constructive function of analysis is very familiar because Jung himself proposed that: 'The aim of the constructive method, therefore, is to elicit from the unconscious product a meaning that relates to the subject's future attitude' (Jung, 1921, para. 702). Jung always sharply disagreed with Freud's view that analysis should concern itself only with the reductive exploration of infantile memory and fantasy and recognized the importance of allowing new attitudes to emerge in the patient's psyche.

Fantasy

Some aspects of the scientific investigation of memory can also help us when we turn to the question of the nature of fantasy. Instinctual drive theory, which proposes that unconscious fantasy is a direct expression of instinctual drives, is a theory that many psychoanalysts believe in with great passion partly, I think, because it provides an explanation for the distortions of external reality which are so evident in our clinical work. We do need to be able to account for the way in which internal objects are formed and why they can differ so much from the actual people, usually parents, who have played such a central part in the formation of our internal world. The psychoanalytic model of instinctual drives, originally propounded by Freud and emphasized by Klein, gives us an easy answer by proposing that the external reality is relatively unimportant and that the magical or terrifying 'good' or 'bad' internal object arises as a direct expression of the 'life' and 'death' instincts. External reality is not considered to play any part in the formation of unconscious fantasy in its purest form, at least in the earliest stages of development. Thus Melanie Klein said that 'the child anticipates, by reason of his own cannibalistic and sadistic impulses, such punishment as castration, being cut into pieces, eaten up, etc. and lives in perpetual dread of them' (Klein, 1927); one of her closest supporters, Joan Riviere, said, 'psychoanalysis is Freud's discovery of what goes on in the imagination ... it has no concern with anything else, it is not concerned with the real world' (Holmes, 1993, p. 130).

This Kleinian position is one that has had considerable influence not only in psychoanalytic theory but also on the models of developmentally orientated Jungians. This does create certain theoretical incompatibilities

which Jungians have not really addressed because Jung himself emphatic-
ally rejected Freud's instinctual drive theory, arguing that the innate
structures of the human mind do not come with prepackaged mental contents, but instead are predispositions which organize information coming
from the environment. The fact that there are certain similarities between
his concept of archetypal polarization and the good and bad polarization
of the Kleinian model is not enough to overcome the fundamental differences between the two theoretical frameworks. In Klein's model of
fantasy, the contents of the fantasy arise from within as though certain
images pre-exist fully formed in the brain and are waiting to be released
by a good feed or an experience of frustration. Although Klein acknow-
ledges the role of external reality in contributing to unconscious fantasy,
it seems only to play the part of a trigger which releases innate unconscious fantasies. Jung, on the contrary, understood that mental imagery
always has its origin in external experience which is then internalized and
modified by innate or archetypal expectation.

In contrast to the Kleinian position that I have just outlined, we can see
that cognitive science research really draws us towards the conclusion
that memory can become fantasy and fantasy can become memory. In a
symposium on the subject of recovered memory, Peter Fonagy, professor
of psychoanalysis at University College London, made a similar point:

> We are setting up truth against falsehood, history against phantasy, fact
> against desire. ... (but) these pairs of opposites do not exist independently
> ... the dialectic of fact and desire is that fact makes desire and then desire
> makes fact, in an interminable sequence of events and thoughts that are
> repeated throughout life. (Fonagy, 1997, p. 126)

If, as I am suggesting, we should reject the idea that unconscious fantasy
arises directly from instinctual drives, then we need to investigate what
alternative explanations for the development of unconscious fantasy are
offered by research based on attachment theory and cognitive science. The
related concepts of implicit memory and the internal working model can
also give us new ways of thinking about the nature of fantasy as well as
adding to our understanding of memory itself. Wishes and desires, fears
and defences not only influence and distort the way we experience events
but also form part of that experience and so themselves become incorporated into the memories of events. Internal working models, the
unconscious patterns of beliefs and expectations about relationships that
are built up through the process of internalization, are not only a form of
memory, but they are also a new way of conceptualizing unconscious fantasy. The child's own emotions and the imaginative narratives he or she

constructs to make sense of the world or to maintain a positive sense of identity become included in unconscious 'working models' as they develop. Working models of relationships are internal objects, which include all the child's conscious and unconscious imaginative material and his or her sense of identity as well as being generalized memories of real experience.

For example, a child who is subject to random and unpredictable violence from a parent will feel not only pain and terror but also a sense of complete helplessness, with no power to influence the parent's behaviour or to have any control over the situation. In addition, without any apparent cause for the parent's cruelty, the child has to face the intolerable fact that the parent is at that moment hostile, malevolent and sadistic towards the child. I think that for any child to feel this is unbearable and that it may be preferable in that situation for the child to construct a belief or fantasy that she has done something to cause the parent to behave in this sadistic way; such an imaginative belief would allow the child to retain some sense of cause and effect, some belief that she actually does have some control over the situation because she did something wrong which provoked this violent response. The belief that she caused the parent's violence by some bad behaviour also allows the child to retain the belief that the parent will love her again, that it is the bad behaviour that is being punished and not that the parent really hates the child.

This kind of defensive belief becomes part of the unconscious 'working model' of relationships with key attachment figures and may emerge in relationships in adult life in the form of an unconscious fantasy that she is responsible for others' bad behaviour and should be punished for it; it might be quite easy for this person to become a battered spouse as a kind of enactment of the unconscious fantasy and/or memory. The internal working model produces a pattern of implicit beliefs and expectations that determine, for example, the choice of a partner and the nature of the relationship that subsequently develops. A person's unconscious fantasy that she is to blame if her partner is abusive could evoke the same belief in him and easily lead to the re-creation of the childhood experience.

Attachment theory also offers us another way to understand the development of fantasy in the growing child's mind, namely that of intergenerational transmission of attachment patterns. The research done by Ainsworth, Main, Fonagy and others has demonstrated clearly that the internal working models of the parents powerfully influence the growing child's internal working models, reflected in the patterns of attachment that the child shows; a mother who has a dismissive rating on the Adult Attachment Interview, a pattern which demonstrates an avoidance of emotionally painful memories about her own life, is most likely to have a child who shows an avoidant pattern of attachment (Steele et al., 1996).

It seems that the parent's internal working models are communicated to and internalized by their children, becoming part of that child's internal world; in other words, part of that child's fantasy. There is considerable research evidence that demonstrates this kind of intergenerational transmission of attachment patterns and, by implication, the internal working models which underpin that behaviour. An experiment by Broussard (1970) explored mothers' fantasies about their babies soon after birth by asking them to rate their firstborn babies as better than average or not better than average at the end of the babies' first month. Babies whose mothers had rated them as 'not better than average' were three times more likely to show clinical psychological problems at the age of 4 than the babies whose mothers had rated them better than average at one month. The predictive power of the mother's initial fantasy of the worth of their infants continued to the age of 10, when the negatively viewed infants still had markedly greater diagnosable mental disorder than the more positively viewed babies.

In this discussion of fantasy, I should emphasize that we do not need to lose the richness of the internal world of object relationships and unconscious fantasy if we reject the explanation that they derive from instinctual drives. For most psychotherapists, the core of our work, which differentiates our profession from other forms of psychological treatment, is the fact that we explore unconscious fantasy and the internal object world of, and with, our patients. Attachment theory and cognitive science do not in the least take that away from us; on the contrary, they offer us exciting new ways of demonstrating the existence of that internal world through the interpersonal research tools that are being developed. The key difference is that in attachment theory, the internal world is formed by a process of internalization of real experiences and real relationships, which are then imaginatively reconstructed and endlessly reworked internally, into generalized patterns of belief and expectation about relationships between oneself and key attachment figures, about oneself in the world, patterns which then powerfully influence all subsequent relationships.

Of all the psychodynamic models that preceded attachment theory, the one that seems to have most closely anticipated the 'internal working model' was Jung's concept of the 'complex' and Jung does seem to have recognized the concept of unconscious patterns that influence us without our being aware of them, long before the name of 'implicit memory' had been used to describe this. Jung suggested that a complex consisted of 'the *image* of a certain psychic situation which is strongly accentuated emotionally and is, moreover incompatible with the habitual attitude of consciousness. This image has a powerful inner coherence, it has its own wholeness and, in addition, a relatively high degree of autonomy, so that it is subject to the control of the conscious mind only to a limited extent and therefore behaves like an animated foreign body in the sphere of consciousness ... Every constellation of a complex postulates a disturbed state of consciousness. The unity of consciousness is disrupted and the intentions of the will are impeded or made impossible. Even memory is often noticeably affected, as we have seen' (Jung. 1934, para. 200–3).

Many of these ideas are strikingly compatible with the findings of contemporary research-based cognitive science in a way in which many original Freudian and Kleinian theoretical formulations, such as 'drives', the 'death instinct' and 'unconscious phantasy' are not (Knox, 1999). Jung regards psychic contents as mental representations, images formed in large part from sensory perception rather than generated by unconscious fantasy. Jung's description of the complex as evidence of the dissociated nature of consciousness has many features in common with the contemporary view of cognitive scientists, who have demonstrated the dissociation between explicit and implicit memory experimentally (Marcel, 1988). Jung also recognized that emotion is not merely a visceral or physiological experience but is inextricably bound up with cognition, a view that has been independently elaborated within an information-processing framework by George Mandler (1984, p. 47). Jung constantly emphasized the emotional basis of the complex: 'The entire mass of memories has a definite feeling-tone, a lively feeling [of irritation, anger, etc.]. Every molecule [of the complex] participates in this feeling tone, so that, whether it appears by itself or in conjunction with others, it always carries this feeling-tone with it'. Jung compared this to Wagnerian music, saying:

> The leitmotif, as a sort of feeling-tone, denotes a complex of ideas which is essential to the dramatic structure. Each time one or the other complex is stimulated by something someone says or does, the relevant leitmotif is sounded in one of its variants. It is exactly the same in psychic life: the leitmotifs are the feeling tones of our complexes, our actions and moods are modulations of the leitmotifs. ... The individual representations are combined according to the different laws of association (similarity, co-existence etc.) but are selected and grouped into larger combinations by an affect.
>
> (Jung, 1907, p. 34)

In this discussion of the nature of fantasy, I have attempted to apply the concept of implicit memory directly to the clinical situation and the experience of the transference. As a clinical manifestation of internal working models in action, the transference can be described as both a form of memory and as a form of fantasy; the internal working model is the vehicle through which the concept of fantasy can be integrated with

contemporary scientific accounts of the ways in which the mind processes information; instinctual drive theory becomes superfluous as an
explanation for the distortions that our patients bring to the consulting
room.

The question of innate mental contents

I shall finally turn to the subject of innate mental contents to see whether
cognitive science can also help us to define and describe them better. I
have investigated the psychoanalytic concept of instinctual drive in the
previous section on the nature of fantasy and I now want to turn to the
alternative model for innate mental structures, the Jungian concept of
archetypes. I did not discuss archetypes in any depth when exploring fantasy and many Jungians would say that they do not use Klein's model of
fantasy at all and that, like Jung, they do not regard instinctual drives as
the source of fantasy. Instead, many Jungians consider archetypes to be
the source of the distortions of external reality and of our memories that
fantasy creates.

There has been considerable debate in the *Journal of Analytical
Psychology* on the nature of archetypes and some authors would like to
discard the biological basis of archetypes altogether and regard them as
cultural symbolic forms (Pietikainen, 1998). I think the problem with
this view is that archetypes then would cease to have any explanatory
value in relation to individual human psychology and become interesting anthropological abstractions, which cannot have any claim to being
part of the universal human psyche. We are biological animals and we
think, fantasize and produce mental imagery with our brains. Any theory of universal human mental processes has to be compatible with the
working of the human brain; if archetypes are part of the universal
human psyche, their imagery must arise out of the neurological
processes of the brain.

The problem this creates for Jungians is, I think, the same as the problem that instinctual drive theory creates for Freudians and Kleinians. It
seems as though, in both theoretical frameworks, the innate aspects of the
psyche are often thought of as pre-formed packets of imagery and fantasy,
waiting to pop out fully formed given the right environmental trigger; on
the contrary, the growing body of research from cognitive science is that
the human brain just does not work in this way and young infants are simply not capable of the complexity of imagery and conceptual thought
which both instinctual drive theory and this form of archetypal theory
seem to require. Cognitive science does offer us a way of thinking about

the innate aspects of the psyche. There is increasing scientific evidence that innate structures of the mind certainly do exist but that, like the internal working models of implicit memory, they exist in a form that is itself inaccessible to consciousness; there are no collective thoughts or images waiting to emerge into consciousness like butterflies from a chrysalis when activated by the right environmental cue. Innate structures of the mind may be no more than sets of instructions which orient attention towards and select external events and experiences. The crucial difference between innate structures and internal working models is that innate structures are a direct expression of genetic codes, a set of hard-wired information-processing instructions about how to attend to and prioritize stimuli; on the other hand, internal working models contain much more information-rich generalized patterns which are created from accumulations of experiences and so represent the meaningful patterns that have been learnt about the real world. Innate structures are pre-experiential potentialities and internal working models are post-experiential constructions.

In a previous paper, I discussed the similarities between Jung's concept of archetypes and the primitive structures described as image schemas by cognitive scientists such as Johnson and Mandler (Knox, 1997). I discussed the function of image schemas in providing a set of conceptual and spatial meanings and illustrated this with a description of a series of experiments that have shown that infants' capacity to recognize faces depends on an innate mechanism which contains primal structural information about the pattern and nature of a human face. These experiments showed that it is the activation of this primal mechanism that makes human faces so much more interesting to infants than many other stimuli. In itself the mechanism does not distinguish between faces, but by focusing the infant's attention on any face it provides maximum opportunity for the infant to form a schematic representation of the human face (Johnson and Morton, 1991). The image schema is not itself innate, but one of the very earliest cognitive developments and its formation depends upon innate mechanisms. The similarity between image schemas and the concept of archetypes has also been noticed by Kotsch, who regards archetypes not as concrete images but as unconscious structures which antedate conscious experience and as irrepresentable sources of images and ideas; archetypes 'order experience without appearing in it' (Kotsch, 2000).

The concept of image schemas has mainly been experimentally investigated in relation to infancy because they offer a way of understanding the infant's preverbal and preconceptual structures for organizing and making sense of experience. However, Johnson does suggest that image schemas 'exist at a level of generality and abstraction that allows them to serve repeatedly as identifying patterns in an indefinitely large number of experiences, perceptions and image formations for objects that are similarly structured in the relevant ways' (Johnson, 1987, p. 28). One illustration he gives is that of an 'in–out' schema which organizes a whole range of experiences, from physical movements, such as reaching *into* a cupboard to metaphorical uses of the schema, such as entering *into* a conversation. The problem remains that it is extremely difficult to provide experimental evidence to demonstrate this extension of the image schema into the realm of language and metaphor.

Johnson also begins to explore the crucial question of the biological nature of image schemas. He says that although image schemas are definite structures, they are dynamic patterns rather than fixed and static images. By dynamic, Johnson means that image schemas are the means by which we construct order and are not passive receptacles into which experience is poured. They are thus relatively fluid patterns that become altered in different contexts.

The newly evolving field of evolutionary psychology has introduced new complexities into the field. Cosmides and Tooby describe the artificial intelligence research which has dramatically demonstrated the vital part that pre-programmed knowledge plays in problem-solving in the simplest tasks set for computers or robots. This is called a 'frame' in artificial intelligence and Cosmides and Tooby draw on this research to suggest that there are also frames in the human mind:

> A frame provides a 'world view'; it carves the world into defined categories of entities and properties, defines how these categories are related to each other, suggests operations that might be performed, defines what goal is to be achieved, provides methods for interpreting observations in terms of the problem space and other knowledge, provides criteria to discriminate success from failure, suggests what information is lacking and how to get it and so on. (Cosmides and Tooby, 1992, p. 106)

How could such complex innate structures have developed in evolutionary terms? A debate rages currently among the giants in this field, such as Gould and Lewontin, who argue that many complex biological features such as language are the emergent products of complex interactions between genetic predispositions and the environment, and Dennett, Pinker, Dawkins and Cosmides and Tooby, who are more reductionist, convinced that these are the direct products of natural selection 'which creates reliably developing architectures that come equipped with the right frames and frame-builders necessary to solve the adaptive problems the species faced during its history' (Cosmides and Tooby, 1992, p. 107; Dennett, 1999, p. 51). Antonio Damasio, a neurologist who has conducted extensive research on the nature of consciousness, has also suggested that complex knowledge can be stored genetically, in his concept of 'dispositions'. He points out that humans, as complex organisms, have to respond to a large variety of complex and varied tasks, saying:

> The machinery needed to perform these demanding tasks is complicated and requires a nervous system. It requires a vast stock of dispositions, a substantial part of which must be provided by the genome and be innate, although some dispositions can be modified by learning and additional stocks of dispositions can be acquired through experience. (Damasio, 1999, p. 139)

However, some of the most recent research in developmental psychology begins to cast doubt on this kind of view, that complex propositional knowledge can be encoded in the human genome. In the discussion earlier in this chapter on the nature of instinct, I suggested that even Bowlby's ideas about instinct, advanced as they were for his time, need to be updated. For example, the recent discoveries about the human genome suggest that humans have only about 30,000 genes, not nearly enough to encode all the complex mental instructions that the more determinist evolutionary psychologists would require.

The alternative view is offered by developmental psychologists such as Annette Karmiloff-Smith, who suggests that many of the early patterns of behaviour in infants that we have considered to be innate are really early developmental products of gene–environment interaction. This is a model of the human mind in which the gene plays the role of a catalyst, 'kick-starting' developmental processes which then self-organize to produce increasingly complex cognitive content, rather than a model in which the gene itself contains complex cognitive content (Karmiloff-Smith, 1999). This developmental view would require a modification of the concept of instinct, in so far as the word is assumed to refer to complex cognitive content as well as to automatic patterns of behaviour.

Although, like Freud, Jung contradicted himself at times, there is a lot of evidence that he viewed archetypes as innate predispositions with an organizing function but no complex cognitive content. We need to gain a clearer understanding of the extent to which mental content can be 'hard-wired' because genetically inherited or, on the other hand, consists of self-organizing patterns that emerge as a central part of the development of meaning by the human brain, as Saunders and Skar (2001) have recently proposed.

Conclusion

In summary, scientific evidence suggests the following to us about the human mind:

1. Innate mechanisms focus the infant's attention on to features in the environment that are crucial to the infant's survival; these mechanisms are biologically based and have arisen by the process of natural selection because they improve chances of survival. Innate mechanisms are activated by environmental cues, interacting with them and organizing them, leading to the formation of primitive spatial and conceptual representations (image schemas). These form the foundation on which later, more complex representations can be built.
2. The environment provides information, which is then taken in and stored in different forms in memory, some as conscious memories of specific events and some as unconscious patterns in implicit memory. In particular, patterns of relationship between self and other people are stored in implicit memory in the form of internal working models, which can be considered to be both a form of memory and a form of fantasy because the wishes, fears, dreams that we bring to an experience become incorporated into the memory of that experience. These internal working models offer us a new way of understanding object relationships and they pattern our expectations and perception of the present. They therefore form the basis of the transference in therapy. Although conscious memories of specific past events are often very useful illustrations that can trigger the activation of internal working models, it is not the recovery of repressed memories in itself that brings about change in psychotherapy, but the gradual modification of the unconscious working models as they are enacted and worked through in the transference.

References

Bollas C (1987) The Shadow of the Object: Psychoanalysis of the Unthought Known. London: Free Association Books.
Bollas C (1989) Forces of Destiny: Psychoanalysis and Human Idiom. London: Free Association Books.
Bower GH (1981) Mood and Memory. American Psychologist 36: 129–48.
Bowlby J (1988) A Secure Base. Clinical Applications of Attachment Theory. London: Hogarth.
Bowlby J (1980) Attachment and Loss, vol. 3: Loss: Sadness and Depression. London: Hogarth Press and Institute of Psychoanalysis.

Bowlby J (1991) The role of the psychotherapist's personal resources in the therapeutic situation. Tavistock Gazette (autumn).

Bretherton I (1995) The Origins of Attachment Theory. In: S Goldberg, R Muir and J Kerr (eds) Attachment Theory. Social, Developmental and Clinical Perspectives. Hillsdale, NJ and London: Analytic Press.

Broussard E (1970) Maternal perception of the neonate as related to development. Child Psychiatry and Human Development 1: 16–25.

Cosmides L and Tooby J (1992) The Psychological Foundations of Culture. In: The Adapted Mind: Evolutionary Psychology and the Generation of Culture. New York and Oxford: Oxford University Press.

Damasio A (1999) The Feeling of What Happens. Body, Emotion and the Making of Consciousness. London: Heinemann.

Dawkins R (1998) Unweaving the Rainbow. London: Allen Lane/The Penguin Press.

Dennett DC (1999) Darwin's Dangerous Idea. Evolution and the Meanings of Life. London: Allen Lane/The Penguin Press.

Eagle M (1995) The developmental perspectives of attachment and psychoanalytic theory. In: S Goldberg, R Muir, and J Kerr (eds) Attachment Theory. Social, Developmental and Clinical Perspectives. Hillsdale NJ, London: Analytic Press.

Eich JE (1980) The cue-dependent nature of state-dependent retrieval. Memory and Cognition 8: 157–73.

Ellenberger HE (1970) The Discovery of the Unconscious: The History and Evolution of Dynamic Psychiatry. London: Allen Lane.

Emde R (1999) Moving ahead; integrating influences of affective processes for development and for psychoanalysis. International Journal of Psycho-analysis 80(2): 317–40.

Fonagy P (1997) Panel discussion. In: J Sandler and P Fonagy (eds) Recovered Memories of Abuse. True or False? London: Karnac Books.

Fonagy P (1999) Memory and therapeutic action. International Journal of Psychoanalysis 80: 215.

Green A (2001) Science and science fiction. In: J Sandler, AM Sandler and YM Davies (eds) Clinical and Observational Psychoanalytic Research: Roots of a Controversy. London: Karnac Books.

Grossman K (1995) The evolution and history of attachment research. In: S Goldberg, R Muir, and J Kerr (eds) Attachment Theory. Social, Developmental and Clinical Perspectives. Hillsdale, NJ and London: Analytic Press.

Holmes J (1993) John Bowlby and Attachment Theory. London and New York: Routledge.

Johnson M (1987) The Body in the Mind: The Bodily Basis of Meaning, Imagination and Reason. Chicago and London: University of Chicago Press.

Johnson MH and Morton J (1991) Biology and Cognitive Development. The Case of Face Recognition. Oxford: Blackwell.

Jung CG (1907) The psychology of Dementia Praecox. Complete Works, vol. 3. London: Routledge and Kegan Paul.

Jung CG (1916) Psychoanalysis and neurosis. Complete Works, vol. 4. London: Routledge and Kegan Paul.

Jung CG (1921) Definitions. Complete Works, vol. 6. London: Routledge and Kegan Paul.

Jung CG (1934) A review of the complex theory. Complete Works, vol. 8. London: Routledge and Kegan Paul.

Karmiloff-Smith A (1999) Beyond Modularity. A Developmental Perspective on Cognitive Science. Cambridge, Mass and London: MIT Press.

Klein M (1927) Symposium on child-analysis. In: Love, Guilt and Reparation and Other Works. New York: Delacorte, 1975.

Knox J (1997) Internal objects – a theoretical analysis of Jungian and Kleinian models. Journal of Analytical Psychology 42: 653–66.

Knox J (1999) The relevance of attachment theory to a contemporary Jungian view of the internal world: internal working models, implicit memory and internal objects. Journal of Analytical Psychology 44(4): 511–30.

Kotsch W (2000) Jung's mediatory science as a psychology beyond objectivism. Journal of Analytical Psychology 45(2): 217–44.

Loftus EF and Coan JA (1994) The construction of childhood memories. In: J Peters (ed.) The Child Witness in Context: Cognitive, Social and Legal Perspectives. New York: Kluwer.

Mandler G (1984) Mind and Body. Psychology of Emotion and Stress. New York and London: WW Norton.

Marcel AJ (1988) In: Marcel and Bisiach (eds) Consciousness in Contemporary Science. Oxford: Clarendon Press.

Marrone M (1998) Attachment and Interaction. London: Jessica Kingsley.

Morton J, Andrews B, Brewin B, Davies G and Mollon P (1995) Recovered Memories – The Report of the Working Party of The British Psychological Society. Leicester: The British Psychological Society.

Perlow M (1995) Understanding Mental Objects. London and New York: Routledge.

Piaget J (1962) Play, Dreams and Imitation in Childhood. New York: WW Norton.

Pietikainen P (1998) Archetypes as symbolic forms. Journal of Analytical Psychology 43(3): 325–44.

Pinker S (1997) How the Mind Works. London: Allen Lane/The Penguin Press.

Pope HG and Hudson JI (1995) Can memories of childhood sexual abuse be repressed? Psychological Medicine 25: 121–6.

Renik O (2000) Subjectivity and unconsciousness. Journal of Analytical Psychology 45(1): 3–20.

Sandler J (1997) Freud's Models of the Mind. An Introduction. London: Karnac Books.

Saunders P and Skar P (2001) Archetypes, complexes and self-organization. Journal of Analytical Psychology 46: 305–23.

Schacter D (1996) Searching for Memory: the Brain, the Mind and the Past. New York: Basic Books.

Schore A (1994) Affect Regulation and the Origin of the Self: The Neurobiology of Emotional Development. Hillsdale, NJ: Lawrence Erlbaum.

Shanon B (1993). The Representational and the Presentational. An Essay on Cognition and the Study of Mind. New York and London: Harvester Wheatsheaf.

Shapiro T and Emde RN (1995) Research in Psychoanalysis. Process, Development, Outcome. Madison, CT: International Universities Press.

Steele H, Steele M and Fonagy P (1996) Associations among attachment classifications of mothers, fathers and their infants: Evidence for a relationship-specific perspective. Child Development 67: 541–55.

Stern D (1985) The Interpersonal World of the Infant. New York: Basic Books.

Stern D (1998) The process of therapeutic change involving implicit knowledge: some implications of developmental observations for adult psychotherapy. Infant Mental Health Journal 19: 300–8.

Stern D, Sander LW, Nahum J, Harrison AM, Lyons-Ruth K, Morgan A and Bruschweiler-Stern N and Tronick E (1998) Non-interpretative mechanism in psychoanalytic therapy: the 'something more' than interpretation. International Journal of Psycho-analysis 79(5): 903–36.

Weiskrantz L (1986) Blindsight: a Case Study and Implications. Oxford: Oxford University Press, Oxford Psychology Series 12.

Williams L (1994) Recall of childhood trauma. A prospective study of women's memories of childhood sexual abuse. Journal of Consulting and Clinical Psychology 62: 1167–76.

CHAPTER 14

The psychoanalytic process in the light of attachment theory

RAFAEL CRISTÓBAL

Introduction

Freud, like Marx and other children of the Enlightenment, dreamed of a scientific depth psychology. Freud aspired to create a science of the soul that would take the place occupied by divinities and demons. All his life he lived in the hope of finding the grammar for the unconscious. His work 'The Interpretation of Dreams' constitutes both a bold attempt to reach this dream and a failure of the dream. The doctrine of the grammar of the unconscious implies that there exists a stable code that permits the translation between symbolic meanings and the contents of the psyche. Psychoanalytic science would be based on the knowledge of this grammar. The psychoanalyst initiated into the nature of the unconscious would be able to interpret the meaning of symbols, symptoms, dreams and free associations based on an understanding of the laws that had transformed the contents of the psyche by censorship and repression. Unfortunately, Freud's dream of a grammar for the unconscious has not been confirmed by experimental and empirical methods nor has it been possible to achieve a consensus among psychoanalysts who shared Freud's dream on what constitutes the basic elements of this grammar.

So what is left of Freud's dream if a grammar of the unconscious is unattainable? Psychoanalysis has been forced to retreat from this lofty dream. Yet within the past two decades new developments, from within psychoanalysis and in the neighbouring fields of developmental psychology, infant research, cognitive science and the neurosciences, have combined to produced new hope that a less grandiose but still ambitious in-depth psychology might emerge from Freud's tattered vision. In many ways attachment theory is an inheritor of this dream. Bowlby took some of the most valuable elements of Freud's vision and recast many of them within a modern evolutionary framework.

The model of the psychic apparatus in Bowlby's work

Bowlby's model of the psychic apparatus is a huge step beyond Freud's metapsychology. Bowlby's revision of Freud's metapsychology accomplishes Freud's dream of creating a scientific psychology (Freud, 1895) in ways he could not have imagined. Bowlby has been able to build a paradigm of the psychic apparatus in accordance with behavioural biology and the empirical sciences of the mind. In so doing, the advantages are obvious and manifold. On the one hand, Bowlby's model is a less cumbersome and more comprehensive model of psychic phenomena. This model also has the advantage of dispensing with outdated scientific concepts such as psychic energy, tension-reducing drives, the nirvana principle (the pleasure/unpleasure principle) and so on. Bowlby's revision makes it easier to understand causal connections between theory and clinical data. Bowlby's revision facilitates an interdisciplinary dialogue with other fields such as cognitive psychology, ethology, neurobiology, sociology and systems theory. This cross-fertilization of ideas is mutually enriching, infusing psychoanalysis with new ideas and new findings and providing these other fields with a wealth of psychoanalytical knowledge. As Ainsworth (1967) put it, 'In effect, what Bowlby has attempted is to update psychoanalytic theory in the light of recent advances in biology.' This advance requires that all explanatory theories of the phenomena obtained from clinical observations from the couch should meet the criteria of the empirical method. Otherwise, psychoanalytic theories will inevitably retain the epistemological status of heuristic hypotheses. Bowlby started this task in the field of attachment. What remains is the huge task of sifting the postulates and valuable clinical observation amassed over a century by psychoanalysis through the filter of empirical methodologies. Until this task has been accomplished, we are compelled to move between a few verified concepts and concepts that have the status of heuristic hypothesis. In other words, we have to use both a nomothetic and an analogical language (Piaget, 1970; Fonagy et al., 1995). Concepts such as Bowlby's internal working models will coexist with others like ego and superego. This mixed framework is the one I shall be using in this chapter.

The evolutionary framework of attachment theory

In opposition to Freudian individualistic psychology and the central role played in Kleinian theory of innate aggression, attachment theory regards human beings as social animals born with the capacity to relate to other human beings and to live in their presence (Bowlby, 1974; Suomi and Harlow, 1971, 1972). However, the immature condition in which the human being comes into the world does not allow him to express attachment behaviours as early as other primates do (Suomi, 1976). Despite this immaturity, the study of infants' neurobiological dispositions reveals the extent to which infants are oriented towards the encounter with others (Schore, 1996). The evolutionary development of the human child corresponds with that of the primates, but in general is more delayed (Harlow, 1958; Harlow and Harlow, 1965; Harlow et al., 1972). Exploration starting at the age of 6 months is followed by the maturing of fear behaviour some months later. Curiosity and exploration are controlled, by servo-mechanisms, in which felt security, fear and avoidance behaviour play important roles. Fear behaviour has matured in most children by the eighth month of life. Exploration is at the base of animal and human cognitive development and play. Fear and avoidance play similar roles in relation to withdrawal and behavioural inhibition. Anaclitic depression described by Spitz (1946) has been found by ethologists in primates reared in the absence of the mother or surrogates once the fear behaviour has matured (Harlow, 1970).

Between the fourth and sixth months of life, the cognitive development of the child allows him to discriminate between caregivers. Once infants develop an exclusive relationship with an attachment figure, they signal their preference with smiles, stammers and babbles (Bowlby, 1974; Brazelton, 1995). Bowlby calls this phase of attachment a phase of 'falling in love' (Bowlby, 1980). This bond will last throughout life.

Attachment behaviour develops through bodily contacts and caresses, visual expressions of smiles and auditory signals, tender sounds and sweet nothings. On an internal level, at a cognitive and emotional level, attachment behaviours are accompanied by intense emotions (Bowlby, 1974). The qualities of these emotions are expressed through words of tenderness, through affection and fondness. On exercising attachment behaviours one feels intimate joy, and its imaginary scenarios are suffused with light. Some family celebrations such as Christmas with its colours, light and gestures manifest these inner scenarios of attachment.

Bowlby must be credited with having placed the roots of human anxiety in the interplay between fear behaviour and the presence or absence of primary caregivers. Anxiety and the susceptibility to intense fear is found to be dependent on the availability and responsiveness of the attachment figure. Once the fear behaviour emerges, the child withdraws from the source of fear and seeks proximity to an attachment figure. The contact with the attachment figure terminates the fear and the child returns to exploration and play. In the absence or unavailability of this figure, play and exploration decrease and the child remains frightened. The very absence of the attachment figure is an important stress factor that generates anxiety and anger. This behavioural outline constitutes the paradigm of animal and human fear and anxiety. Bowlby has devoted all of his second volume of *Attachment and Loss* to the study of human fear, anxiety and anger connected with separation from attachment figures.

The emotional and physical availability and attunement of the attachment figure protects the child against fear generated by novelty or by perceived threats. Confidence in her presence and attunement of her responses builds in the child a sense of trust in the attachment figure (Bowlby, 1974; Ainsworth and Wittig, 1969). Conversely, the growth of exploration and play creates a sense of self-confidence. Within the framework of this harmonious relationship – a secure attachment – the child is able to store experiences (Crandell, 1994) during the early sensorimotor phase of development (Piaget and Inhelder, 1966). In other words, young children are able to create a biographical narrative and to construct a sense of self-history (Holmes, 1993). The dialogue between the child and his caregivers about the relationship develops a meta-knowledge which becomes the basis for self-reflection (Fonagy et al., 1995).

By 12 months, the basic patterns of secure or insecure relationships has already been established and they can be assessed by experimental procedures such as the Strange Situation (Ainsworth et al., 1978. See Appendix to this volume for a description of the procedure). The Strange Situation test activates the attachment behaviour and shows that there are qualitative differences of attachment relationships among different mother–infant dyads (see Appendix). The relational experience is encoded in memory as internal working models. During the sensorimotor phase of development, internal working models are first encoded at subsymbolic levels. With the development of semiotic functions and language, internal working models are encoded at symbolic levels and as narratives (see Chapters 12 and 13 in this volume).

These working models tend to endure throughout life although they can change if new experiences provide new internal models. Internal working models can also change through the ability of humans to reflect on their experience (Fonagy, 1999; Grossmann, 1999). In adulthood, romantic relationships and couple relationships will reproduce the patterns of attachment encoded as internal working models that developed through childhood.

Pathways to psychopathology

So far, research informed by attachment theory has focused primarily on the observed aspects of attachment relationships and their vicissitudes as they unfold developmentally in their healthy and pathological dimensions (Ainsworth et al., 1978; Sroufe, 1996, 1997; Sroufe et al., 1999). Only fleeting references have been made to the inner world of fantasies and feelings, which have been the traditional emphasis of psychoanalysis (for an exception see the work of Main, 2000, and Hesse and Main, 2000). What remains to be done is the huge task of sifting the hypotheses made in the psychoanalytical literature (the discourse of the couch) through the filter of empirical methods. Only then will psychoanalysis reach the status of scientific knowledge. Until this task is completed, traditional interpretative and hermeneutic theories of psychoanalysis can have the status only of conjectural hypotheses.

Efforts to establish a correspondence between the 'discourse from the couch' and empirical research are only beginning to appear. For now, we have no choice but to remain in the sphere of establishing hermeneutic correspondences between the paradigms derived from attachment theory and psychoanalytic traditions based on different models of the mind. We can provisionally attribute heuristic value to the interpretations based on free associations, dreams, myths, and to emotional phenomena arising from the transference. We can also attempt to reinterpret clinical phenomena derived from different psychoanalytic models in the light of attachment theory and research (see Chapter 10 in this volume as an example of this effort). Traditional psychoanalytic models consider the discourse derived from the couch and from transference as a privileged entry into the inner world of the patient. Attachment theory will be valuable in looking at this inner world from a new perspective based on what we have learned in regard to developmental pathways and their vicissitudes.

The pathology of attachment

In accordance with the central role attributed by our paradigm to the attachment relationship in human psychology and psychopathology, analytic attention should be focused on a person's ability to observe current relationships in light of experiences with parental figures – stored as working models of self and others. This corresponds roughly to the relationships in Freud's model between ego and superego.

Bowlby and other psychoanalytic observers, freed from the bias of a theory based exclusively on sexuality and aggression, see this relationship as moving in a continuum between opposite poles. One pole is the consistency of the parental presence and the attunement of parental responses to their children, thus creating a harmonic, secure relationship. The other pole corresponds to the breakdown of the attachment relationship and disharmony. Bowlby emphasized the enormous importance of parents instilling a sense of confidence in their children and strengthening their sense of agency. These are the parental attributes that create a secure attachment. The importance of consistent parental responses was already envisioned by some of the first psychoanalytic writers. In regard to self-esteem Fenichel (1945) said: 'An Ego who feels loved feels strong and an Ego who feels lost is weak and exposed to dangers' (Fenichel, 1945, p. 35).

There is a plethora of clinical phenomena observed in psychoanalytic practice that are part of the human condition that attachment theory has addressed only tangentially, or is just beginning to address. To name just a few: the analyses of recollections and memories of self object experiences made by Kohut (1971), the phenomenology of religion, the mystical experience (Otto, 1963; Mircea Eliade, 1949/1970), and states of falling in love (Freud, 1914; Fenichel, 1945). More recently, however, a few articles have begun to appear in regard to attachment and romantic love (Mohr, 1999) and attachment and religion (Kirkpatrick, 1999). These phenomena are accompanied by feelings of joy or admiration and by imaginary scenarios made up of grandiosity, omnipotence, glory, absolute beauty, goodness and wisdom at a representational level.

There are some important points of contact between self psychology and attachment theory. Kohut (1971) noted that the quality of omnipotence is a feature of phenomena pertaining to an early or 'archaic' period of development. Children's pride in their performance – called in the psychoanalytic jargon 'exhibition' – and the delightful mirroring response from parents are the two poles of a harmonious attachment relationship. Kohut emphasizes the enormous importance of parental attitudes in facilitating the development of a cohesive construction of the self. In the mirror of the parental gaze, the young child, like Narcissus in the waters of the lake, discovers his own image. In the absence of this gaze of delight and admiration by parents, emerging exhibitionist behaviours cannot be integrated in the self. The child not only identifies his image in the gaze of the other, but also finds a meaning in it. The delight of the parental figure confers on the child's 'narcissistic' behaviours a sense of wholeness and beauty, while an indifferent and censuring attitude deprives it of its value and confers on him the attribute of badness. This psychological phenomenon is recalled in the vampire myth. The vampire thirsty for the blood of living beings does not find his image reflected in a mirror.

From an attachment perspective the self–object function is understood in terms of the importance given to attachment figures in regulation affects and levels of arousal of young children (Sroufe, 1996) and validating the child's uniqueness, as Mary Ainsworth (1967) often emphasized. This requires that parents be able to go beyond their own needs and wishes and be able to perceive children in all their uniqueness.

Returning to the theme of attachment and pathology, on the side of conflict and breakdown, there is the anger, despair, depression and detachment following separation from an attachment figure or trauma in the attachment relationship. This corresponds roughly to the narcissistic rage, grandiosity and cold isolation in Kohut's theorizing. All these emotional reactions – derived from aggression and fear activated in the child by the unavailability, insensitivity or absence of attunement of parental figures – might also correspond to Melanie Klein's aggressiveness observed in schizo-paranoid and depressive positions. The pathology of obsessive-compulsive neurosis is often a reaction to parental aggression, lack of attunement or withdrawal. In turn, the child responds with a convoluted labyrinth and symbolic displacement of aggressive behaviour. Mistrust, suspicion and resentment toward others will inevitably be the result of deformities based on adverse experience registered in the form of internal working models.

The repression of instincts: demonic possessions and satanic beliefs

Rejection or neglect of children's needs (based on instinctive motivational systems) by parents will lead sooner or later to the inhibition or repression of these needs (drives, in the Freudian model) and more or less anger towards attachment figures. The fact that attachment theory has relegated sexuality and aggression to secondary drives in early development does not mean that sexuality and aggression, as well as other of motivational systems, are unimportant. Bowlby specifically focused on the study of attachment behaviour, but at the same time has opened the way to integrate other instinctive and behavioural systems into their rightful place within the developmental tree that leads to the formation of the human personality. There is an enormous amount of work to be done in exploring the developmental significance of different instinctive systems that form part of the human personality and the human condition. In any case, human beings, like other species within the animal kingdom, need to develop and expand the full spectrum of innate behaviours for their own welfare and for correct functioning. The elimination or inhibition of one of the motivational behavioural systems is no less an injury than having an organ damaged or a limb torn off.

Bowlby has shown that some of the most painful and the most powerful ways of truncating development is the loss, or the threat of loss, of an attachment figure. The violence inflicted on the child can be seen in the common street scene of a child enraged with a parent feigning to walk away and leaving the child in distress.

The main consequences of repression are:

1. The subject will be mutilated by the deprivation in his personality of the full expression of motivational systems and more or less injured depending on the intensity of the repression.
2. As a consequence of aggression caused by repression, imagoes of self and the object will be damaged by guilt and resentment and will acquire a quality of 'badness'. Resentment and suspicion toward the other, and guilt and insecurity toward oneself, will be the consequences of the defeat of the child in the conflict between the healthy development of motivational behaviour and their repression.
3. Since repressed behavioural systems do not disappear through repression, a state of active tension will remain with a strong tendency for the repressed behaviour to become activated in roundabout ways. Any occasion will be exploited by the repressed motivation to break through the repression. Consequently the subject will feel tempted and in danger of falling into temptation.
4. Similarly to what happens to attachment figures by virtue of repression and conflict, the repressed drives – through the effect of hate and fear – will lose their original beauty and charm and become obscure, contemptible and bad. The charming and pleasant behaviours associated with innate dispositions can become 'demonized' by becoming transformed into negative feelings like fear, guilt, disgust or shame.

Satanization is a notion belonging to the mythical paradigm which metaphorically expresses in symbolic language the destiny of motivational systems, and needs associated with these motivational systems, when these needs are repressed by parental condemnation and humiliation. The Babylonian myth, which first appeared in the Book of Daniel and then in the Apocalypse, was subsequently elaborated in the Middle Ages. The myth tells the story of the rebellion of angels against God. The most brilliant and beautiful angel of them all headed this revolt: Luzbel or Lucifer, which means beautiful light and bearer of the light. After a great battle in the heavens, Lucifer and his angels were defeated by the archangel Michael (Mi-ka-el in Hebrew means 'He who is like God') who expelled Lucifer and his troops to hell. Lucifer became Satan and his angels became purveyors of evil. As in the Babylonian myth, innate dispositions, by means of repression, lose all their original beauty and light and become evil and monstrous. Rancorous and thirsty for revenge, as in the Babylonian mythology, repressed behaviours and impulses stalk the human being and turn him against God (parental figures) and against himself. Henceforward, the return of the repressed will not be in its original form. The repressed has been demonized.

The persistence of the belief in diabolic possession and satanism challenge the paradigms of our scientific culture. Despite the rationalistic impact of the Enlightenment, the very survival of this ancient myth shows its power and the huge appeal it has for human beings. Part of the power of this mythic paradigm is due to the fact that it captures important aspects of psychological phenomena: the inner world of conflicts, tormenting obsessions, repressed impulses and destructive passions.

Taken in its right context, satanism and experiences of being possessed by demonic forces provide heuristic hypotheses of great value for understanding and testing hypotheses in regard to the fate of repressed or dissociated behaviour. The psychological impact of feeling possessed by demons, the urgency of repressed impulse to break through consciousness, the internal organization of the repression experienced as an alien force, its effects on self-identity and on loss of a sense of agency all attest to the value of understanding this myth as a metaphoric expression of repressed and/or dissociated experience.

Studies on the subject of dissociation and hypnotic trance such as the work of Hilgard (1974) suggest that although there is a principal system upon which the idea of self is based, other subsystems that coexist with it are not always communicating with each other. Chapter 8 of the Gospel of St Luke narrates the answer of a possessed man to Jesus's question: 'Jesus asked: "What is your name?" He said: "Legion" ' (Luke 8.30). In each of us, many subsystems can coexist in dissociated form and can be experienced as being possessed by a drive or behaviours that are not integrated in the principal system that forms what we consider to be our main identity. The multiple personality produced by severe trauma and abuse is the extreme pole of a continuum.

In satanic mythology, demons lie patiently, waiting for the right time to draw humans to forbidden acts by luring them through pleasure. This strength of repressed impulse can be compared to a roaring lion seeking someone to devour (I Peter 5.8). The experience of forbidden impulses as waiting for the appropriate moment in which to spring into action follows the laws of instinctive behaviour (Lorenz, 1937, 1954) and threatens to reopen the conflict in which the subject was wounded and defeated. This tendency of forbidden impulses to spring into action is the main source of anxiety (Freud, 1926). Bowlby perhaps has not focused sufficiently on this source of anxiety.

As legends, myths and fairy tales show us, repressed instinctive behaviours take multifarious routes in order to break through consciousness and tempt humans. Clinical reports are very important sources of psychological knowledge that helps us understand the transformations undergone by the repressed drives. Nocturnal dreams, daydreams, free associations, slips of tongue and other symptoms are the pathways taken by repressed unconscious impulses. Defence mechanisms are constructed to protect against the pain of traumatic experience and from the anxiety and guilt generated by the return of the repressed. Bowlby in the second and third volume of his trilogy has made a remarkable conceptualization of the psychoanalytic theory of defences in the light of cognitive science.

In the next section of this chapter I discuss specific ways in which attachment theory approaches transference and clinical material, the discourse from the couch.

The goals of the psychoanalytic process: understanding and reconciliation

As a consequence of his individualistic psychology, in his study of neurosis, Freud focused his attention almost exclusively on the distorted pathways of repressed drives. The superego was considered only as an agent that produced fears of castration and that punished desire. Freud was unable to perceive the need for emotionally responsive attachment figures that construct children's positive self-representations and enhance their development. For this reason, he conceived analysis as a cognitive process and not as an encounter in which analyst and analysand meet to relive the old and forgotten wounds produced by the encounter with parental figures that produced psychic conflict. Through the analytic relationship, an attempt is made to develop understanding and acceptance, to make peace and repair shattered self-images full of hate, resentment and despair.

Psychoanalytic goals are reached through a process that gradually leads to reconciliation. A reconciliation among all the components of conflict recorded in internal working models: reconciliation between the agents of repression and internal demons, between the adult figures that created the need for repression and the repressed strata full of fear, anger and contempt. The psychoanalytic process thus reopens conflicts that had led to condemnation and satanization. It helps analysands confront omnipotent parental imagoes and helps to consign the power of these imagoes to oblivion. Psychoanalysis can be conceived as a process that accomplishes this reconciliation: a process that starts by opening the locks and breaking the bars that imprison the self. The process conjures images of Pinel opening the cells of the mentally ill at La Salpêtrière.

Plainly, the psychoanalytic process is much more than just a cognitive process. The process of 'working through' is sometimes a dramatic dialogue that fosters understanding and forgiveness and minimizes blame. Nothing will be achieved if there are winners and losers. Forgiveness allows for the healing and restoration of damaged images of self and others (Holmes, 1999). Only a process of reconciliation can lead the self to become self-confident and autonomous.

The psychoanalytic process begins as a confrontation and ends in reconciliation. Step by step the original harmony between the subject with his inner world and the parental figures is being restored: joy, confirmation and praise replace criticism, rejection and blame. If the satanic myth reveals the dynamics of the repressed drives, the myth of paradise, present in all cosmogonies (Mircea Eliade, 1949/1970), reveals this original harmony.

For the healing process to be set in motion some general conditions are required.

Feigned neutrality versus an authentic neutrality

The first act of this dramatic process is the meeting between two human beings. On the one hand, we have an individual with all his characteristic ways of being, searching for another to relieve his sufferings. On the other, we have an analyst with greater or lesser feelings of empathy towards this person. Despite the formalities of a professional meeting, from the first moment, idiosyncrasies determined by the individual's internal working models will be revealed.

The traditional concept of neutrality, inspired by a cognitive conception of the psychoanalytic process, has been used as a way to capture the patient's characteristic relational patterns. But there are other important reasons for maintaining a neutral stance that is not just based on a cognitive conception of the psychoanalytic process, as we shall see later.

In the traditional view of neutrality, the analyst is supposed to minimize disclosures or signals to the patient. To maintain a neutral stance, it has often been suggested that analysis should be conducted within an atmosphere of abstinence, thus minimizing gratification that will get in the way of the patient's task of remembering rather than repeating conflicts.

Another image that has been used to convey an ideal attitude of neutrality is that of presenting a blank screen to the patient so he can project all his conflicts without any interference from the analyst. Attachment theory suggests a very different conception of neutrality (see Chapter 2 for a distinction between the concept of neutrality and objectivity).

As Marrone (1998) has pointed out, the 'opaque analyst' is no more than a myth, an incoherent myth at that. An effort to limit or minimize any kind of signals conveys a message that will be interpreted by the patient according to his own psychology. An opaque attitude risks being interpreted by the patient as a repetition of the type of rejection he suffered in his past from parental figures. Or another patient might interpret the silence as criticism or indifference. Marrone (1998) considers this opaque behaviour a 'false neutrality', since more often than not it does not correspond to the real feelings that the analyst has toward the patient. The traditional view of neutrality is dysfunctional because it has negative consequences for the process itself (Marrone, 1998). Feigned neutrality is more likely to entrench the patient in his position of fear and submission, thus preventing him from developing self-confidence to explore his inner world and to break out in his movement toward autonomy.

In contrast a 'true or authentic' neutrality resembles good parenting. It consists of 'holding' the fears, anxieties, rejections and suspicions of the patient (Winnicott, 1948). The acceptance conferred by authentic neutrality is generous and does not take advantage of the patient's weaknesses. It mirrors back to the patient what he is doing and therefore heightens his awareness. If naturalness is the first rule for true neutrality, neutrality needs something more to be of help to the analytic process: a sympathetic gaze.

The need for a empathetic regard for the patient

Another condition for setting the psychoanalytic process in motion is based on the positive regard the therapist has for the patient (see Chapters 3 and 4 of this book). When drives have become distorted because of guilt and pain, the sense of oppression and hate that follow will be exposed only if the analysand perceives in the eyes of the analyst a positive regard toward him. A positive regard counters the view projected from the superego. It helps to heal disastrous events of childhood and aspires to restore the original state of harmony, as is expressed poetically in the biblical myth of paradise. Just as a condemned man can dare to confess his acts only to his defence counsel, so patients can reveal their hurt, shame, anger and hate only if the analyst is perceived as being on their side.

The capacity of the analysts to maintain a caring and empathetic attitude toward analysands is not a voluntary act but the consequence of his having first seen within himself legitimate needs that have been deformed by defences. This is the reason why a didactic psychoanalysis is needed. Only if the analyst has been able to look at his own deformities with empathy and understanding, will he be able to see beyond the disfigured inner world of the patient.

The analytic process is opened precisely at the point when the analyst has become an ally to the patient, who can see beyond his deformities, beyond his guilt and shame, and contemplate the patient's legitimate needs in all their beauty. The analyst establishes himself as the defence counsel for the patient in a reopened proceeding that had been previously foreclosed by guilt, self-condemnation and shame. The position as defence counsel, the capacity to maintain a positive regard for the patient, must be maintained even when the analyst himself becomes the object of resentment and aggression. It is exactly at this moment when neutrality is particularly needed. The containment of the patient's aggression by the analyst and mirroring of it back to him in an understanding way allows the process to move forward.

So, 'working through' is a process in which the analysand rebels against and confronts parental figures, where he acts against agents of disavowal and repression. The process comes to a resolution when the capacity for comprehension, forgiveness and reconciliation has been restored. In this way the superego will be transformed from a persecutory agent to a more benign conscience that is well-wishing and compassionate, from Koeforas to Eumenides, as in the Aeschylus tragedy. This restorative process is possible only if the analyst is present at times as a defence counsel, at times as a helper of the patient's investigative work of unmasking the disguises in which his legitimate needs have been camouflaged, and at other times as the depository of parental imagoes.

The analytic process has, therefore, both cognitive and experiential aspects. Cognitive, because what is repressed does not emerge simply in its original form, but in the deformations and disguises generated by defence mechanisms. Experiential, because the restoration of the self is possible only after an emotional encounter with the analyst that restores the capacity to have faith in oneself and others.

The cognitive aspects of the psychoanalytical process can be compared to an archaeological research or anatomical dissection, in which the interpretation represents a tool or scalpel. Interpretation has been a major issue in psychoanalytical thinking. As we understand it, interpretation is oriented towards unmasking the disguised needs and drives and, in so doing, elucidating the truth about events that had been hidden.

Interpretation can be a source of anxiety because it opens wounds. It is a delicate act to be handled with mastery because it confronts the hidden wound behind the defence as well as the critical and blaming superego. Handling resistances is one of the most difficult tasks of the psychoanalytical art. A caring, patient and sympathetic attitude restores faith in the capacities of the patient and therefore is a key for accomplishing interpretative tasks. The patient will accept interpretations when his increased sense of security allows him to look at a painful part of his experience by giving it a new meaning and thus alleviating guilt and shame associated with the experience.

The rhythm of the analyst should be in tune with the possibilities of the analysand to advance through the analytic process. Wild interpretations risk wounding the patient, making him more subdued. Sympathy and patience are a positive form of neutrality in the same way that parental attunement validates the child. Sympathy and caring are founded on the faith of the analyst in the possibilities of the patient. Faith and confidence in the patient enables the analyst to wait for the right moment to make the interpretation.

An egalitarian versus a dogmatic praxis in psychoanalysis

Many psychoanalytic schools position themselves as doctrines. The search for truth is not based on a spirit of free inquiry and respect for empirical methods, but on the authority of the master. Because of this, psychoanalysis has become a closed system in which any dissidence with respect to the authority of the analyst and the psychoanalytic doctrine will inevitably be interpreted as resistance and will be condemned. Consequently, the patient's perceptions are systematically invalidated. A dogmatic interpretation is nothing less than an exercise of violence that reproduces the interaction in which the subject was invalidated, injured and repressed. It perpetuates authoritarian and repressive dynamics and so hinders the emergence of a liberating revolt. Dogmatic approaches in analysis are a major obstacle to the accomplishment of the analytical process and lead to an identification with the aggressor. If the subject is in a training analysis, he risks adopting a scholastic manner with an uncritical submission to the doctrines of his master.

Feelings of personal incompetence are often rooted in submission to the omnipotent parental figures as developmental psychology and human ethology show, and this submission may be a crucial factor predisposing to neurotic disorders. Dogmatic interpretations, even if accurate, will maintain the patient in a state of fearful retraction. Free associations are an exercise of free movement. Dogmatic interpretations deprive the subject of the possibility of exploring autonomously the meaning of his perceptions and free associations.

When the analytic process is conducted in an egalitarian atmosphere, analysands are encouraged to gradually take up the role of interpreting aim-inhibited or disguised impulses. The place of the analyst is to be present in the patient's exploratory activity – a step behind, yet a step ahead – assisting him when frightened or disorientated by giving meaning to the fright. At this stage, the offer of a meaning is a light in the patient's darkness and a sign of the analyst's presence. The sense of alarm decreases, fear behaviour is terminated by the presence of the new attachment figure, and exploration is renewed.

The truth about oneself – as with all human truth – is realized only in the context of relationships. Interpretation is always – and can only be – an offer of meaning from the analyst to the patient. This offer is the true initiator of the egalitarian dialogue in which the patient always has the last word about the meaning of the content of his discourse or a feeling in the transference.

An analysis conducted in the framework of an egalitarian praxis affirms the belief that no one is in full possession of the truth. It stimulates into action an individual inhibited because of his feelings of incompetence and the underdevelopment of his capacities. It facilitates exploration and play and restores the capacity to make decisions with greater confidence and integrity. In sum, an egalitarian praxis increases the individual's capacity to think and act autonomously.

The need for a revolt

Revolt is a necessary act in the analytic process. It is the only possible way for anger and resentment to be transformed from submission to productive, liberating action.

Through revolt, the repressed conflict is opened for examination. Once this act of freedom is initiated, the 'working through' is a process in which the analysand can examine working models of self and others, begins to question working models that are oppressive and condemning, begins to fight against these 'bad objects' and to understand and forgive parental figures that had failed him. Throughout this dramatic process, as anger is liberated, the satanized forces start to retrieve their original beauty and begin to be seen in another light. The analyst divides into two figures: he can become the target of anger and thus the depository of bad images and he must become the ally of the irate child and his defence counsel against the aggressive attacks from his superego. It is through this interplay that the analysis progresses.

The Oedipus myth versus the story of reconciliation between Jacob and Esau

In Freudian thinking, the Oedipus complex is the last battle the human being fights against his parental figures. The myth of Oedipus is taken by Freud as the central paradigm for understanding neurosis. The intergenerational conflict in Oedipus ends in strife, condemnation and guilt, with Oedipus killing the father and marrying the mother.

Much has been said in regard to the role of the Oedipus complex in structuring conflict. In Lacan's theorizing, the possession of the paternal phallus is what is at stake in the myth. According to Lacan (1966) castration means the renunciation of narcissistic omnipotence and the acceptance of limitations imposed by social laws. Through the resolution of the Oedipus conflict, the subject migrates from the subjectivity of desire to acceptance of social reality and its rules.

Attachment theory sharply diverges from this line of theorizing. While it was a stroke of genius that Freud was able to appreciate the Oedipus story as a metaphor for human psychological development, Freudian theory concerns itself only with the masculine half of humanity, namely the competitive relationship between fathers and sons within a patriarchal society. In the attachment paradigm the origin of reality and social rules begins much earlier within the context of an attachment relationship, often a mother–child relationship. Through cognitive development, affect regulation and by imitation, attachment figures instil at unconscious levels social rules and expectations. Other social rules will be learned later in development through interaction and play with peers (Piaget and Inhelder, 1966).

The Oedipus conflict can be considered a modern version of original sin in the Jewish-Christian tradition. Morality, according to Freud, develops as a consequence of having transgressed the most important of all commands: the prohibition against incest and patricide. In *Totem and Taboo* Freud speculated that civilization is founded on this guilt-ridden complex that compels the brothers to renounce the paternal phallus and so organize as an egalitarian fraternity. But the longing for the denied paternal phallus will threaten the guilty society of brothers. The temptation of absolute power will emerge at any time, making way for dictatorship.

Genesis narrates another intergenerational story of a clash between parents and children and between brothers, but with a very different outcome. This story has been painted by artists of the highest calibre, including Delacroix, and is rendered poetically in Chapter 32 of Genesis. Jacob asks his wives, children and servants to leave him alone on the eve before the meeting of reconciliation with his brother Esau. Esau, you might remember, had stolen Jacob's primogeniture, aided by their mother's cunning.

> The same night he got up and, taking his two wives, his two slave girls and his eleven children, crossed the ford of Jabbok. After he had taken them across the stream, he sent all his possessions over too. And Jacob was left alone. Then someone wrestled with Jacob through the night and until day-break. But seeing that he could not master him, the stranger struck him on the hip socket, and Jacob's hip was dislocated. As Jacob wrestled with the stranger the stranger said: 'Let me go, for day is breaking'. Jacob replied, 'I will not let you go unless you bless me'. The stranger says, 'What is your name?' 'Jacob' he replies. Then the stranger says 'No longer are you to be called Jacob, but Israel since you have shown your strength against God and Men and have prevailed. Then Jacob asked, 'Please tell me your name'. He replied: 'Why do you ask my name?' With that, he blessed Jacob. Jacob named the place Peniel, 'Because I have seen God face to face' he said, 'and have survived'. The sun rose as he passed Peniel, limping from his hip. (Genesis 32, 23–32)

Unlike in the Oedipus myth, in this story God is not killed, neither does he try to kill Jacob, but limits himself to containing Jacob's fury. The story ends with God blessing Jacob and giving him another name: 'No longer are you to be called Jacob, but Israel since you have shown your strength against God and men and have prevailed'.

A follower of Lacan's theory will interpret the story of Jacob as rivalry between brothers competing for the paternal phallus and the hostility of the mother against her husband, by displacing the female penis envy by favouring the weak son. But what we want to draw attention to in this story is the behaviour of God who represents the paternal figure. He is not destroyed by *the son's aggression*, he does not counterattack but contains the fury of the son and in the end he blesses him because he has demonstrated his strength against him and has prevailed.

The contrast between the two stories is striking: in Freud's vision the only outcome for the conflict between generations is hate: hate calls for the death of the hated one. Oedipus is overcome by the guilt and finds himself immersed in loneliness inhabited by his desire and insatiable needs. At the other extreme, Jacob emerges from the encounter with God (the father figure) confirmed in his strength and blessed by him. Henceforward, he will be able to prevail among men. Instead of maintaining a rivalry for the primogeniture, he will renounce it and reconcile himself with his brother; a totally different outcome to that of the Oedipus myth. The presence of the Father now resides in Jacob. Power has no importance for him now.

Underlying this story we find the loving regard of God towards Jacob. God does not feel threatened by the strength of Jacob because he is able to see beyond his fury and hate: he is able to understand the resentment of Jacob and see beyond his resentment to his original innocence. The father is attached to the son. His regard is a loving regard. This is the difference between a psychology based on loneliness and hate and one based upon attachment and love.

Conclusion

To liberate the subject from hate, suspiciousness and resentment it is often essential for these impulses to be acted out in the transference. Throughout the analytic process this repressed revolt and fury will be expressed in many guises. This expression of hate is necessary to rid oneself of the fear of one's destructiveness. In the analytic process it is crucial that the analyst be capable of containing the patient's fury and, like the Angel of YHWH, appreciate the strength of the patient's feelings and mirror them back to him. The patient will no longer fear his destructiveness but see it the way that the analyst sees it: as a protest against the threat of loss or separation from attachment, or as an expression of an injured and angry child who has been rejected, humiliated or neglected. Only in this way can the analysand appreciate his original worth and discover the reasons for his 'demonized' hate. Thus, the door to love is opened. In the confrontation with our demons, the imagoes of self and of parental figures spring back to life restored in a more loving fashion, and reconciliation is made possible.

As Holmes (1999) pointed out, an analysis is successful only if it ends in reconciliation with the parental figures of the working models (or the superego). This outcome is not envisaged in Freud's perspective because his theoretical framework and individualistic psychology prevented him from imagining such a possibility. In Freudian thinking, the goal of the analysis is to make the subject aware of his desires and phantasmata, so that 'where before was the id now the ego shall be'.

In the light of attachment theory, the goal of analysis is certainly to retrieve the demonized drives and phantasies camouflaged by the defence mechanisms. But for this to happen this task must be accomplished in a loving dialogue with an analyst. This dialogue reopens the biographical conflict with parental figures and may help restore broken relationships. Only then can the power of guilt, hate and shame be overcome.

Reconciliation and forgiveness of the hurts inflicted by parental figures is the fundamental step in the analytical process because from our theoretical framework the attachment figures are fundamental for the sense of security and integrity throughout life and for the development of the self. The retrieval of parts of the self buried in the unconscious through an egalitarian dialogue between patient and analyst leads to a new narrative of the analysand's life and a new perspective from which to understand parental figures. This understanding enhances the reflective function, an essential ingredient of the analytic process (Fonagy et al., 1995; Diamond, 2000). Biographical coherence is restored and, with it, the patent's identity as a loving human being.

References

Ainsworth MD (1967) Infancy in Uganda: Infant Care and the Growth of Love. Baltimore, Md: Johns Hopkins University Press.

Ainsworth MD and Wittig BA (1969) Attachment and the exploratory behavior of one-years olds in a strange situation. In: BM Foss (ed.) Determinants of Infant Behaviour, vol. 4. London: Methuen.

Ainsworth MD, Blehar MC, Waters E and Wall S (1978) Patterns of Attachment: A Psychological Study of the Strange Situation. Hillsdale, NJ: Erlbaum.

Bowlby J (1974) Attachment and Loss, vol. I: Attachment. London: Hogarth Press and Institute of Psycho-Analysis.

Bowlby J (1980) Attachment and Loss, vol. III: Loss. Sadness and Depression. London: Hogarth Press and Institute of Psycho-Analysis.

Brazelton TB (1995) Your Child's Emotional and Behavioural Development. Harmondsworth: Penguin Books.

Comte A (1825) Considerations Philosophiques sur les sciences et les savants. Le producteur 1825, 7, 8, 10. Paris.

Crandell LE (1994) Representational models of attachment: Replication and reorganizational processes. Unpublished doctoral dissertation, Michigan State University, E. Lansing.

Diamond N (2000) Intersubjectivity and reflective function. Psychotherapy Section Newsletter. The British Psychological Society 28: 30–43.

Eliade M (1949/1970) Traité d'histoire des religions. Paris: Payot.

Fenichel O (1945) The Psychoanalytic Theory of Neurosis. New York: WW Norton. Traducción española: Teoría Psicoanalítica de las Neurosis. Buenos Aires: Paidos, 1966.

Fonagy P (1999) The transgenerational transmission of holocaust trauma: lessons learned from the analysis of an adolescent with obsessive-compulsive disorder. Attachment and Human Development 1: 92–114.

Fonagy P, Steele H, Leig T, Kennedy R, Mattoon G and Target M (1995) Attachment, the reflective self and borderline states: The predictive specificity of the adult attachment interview and pathological emotional development. In: S Goldberg, R Muir and J Kerr (eds) Attachment Theory. Social, Developmental, and Clinical Perspectives. Hillsdale, NJ: Analytic Press, pp. 233–78.

Freud S (1894) Anxiety and neurosis. Standard Edition 3: 90–115. London: Hogarth Press.

Freud S (1895) Project for a Scientific Psychology. Standard Edition 1: London: Hogarth Press.

Freud S (1905) Three Essays on the Theory of Sexuality. Standard Edition 3: 135–245. London: Hogarth Press, 1953.

Freud S (1914) On Narcissism. Standard Edition 14: 69–102. London: Hogarth Press, 1957.

Freud S (1920) Beyond the Pleasure Principle. Standard Edition 18: 7–64. London: Hogarth Press.

Freud S (1926) Inhibitions, Symptoms and Anxiety. Standard Edition 20: 87–172. London: Hogarth Press.

Freud S (1940) An Outline of Psycho-analysis. Standard Edition 23: 139–195. London: Hogarth Press.

Grossmann KE (1999) Old and new internal working models of attachment: the organization of feelings and language. Attachment and Human Development 1: 253–69.

Harlow HF (1958) The nature of love. American Psychologist 13: 673–85.

Harlow HF (1970) Love Created – Love Destroyed – Love Regained. Colloques internationaux du CNRS No 198. Modèles animaux du comportement humain: 14–60.

Harlow HF and Harlow MK (1965) The affectional systems. In: AM Schirier, HF Harlow and F Stollnitz (eds) Behavior of Nonhuman Primates, vol. 2. New York: Academic Press, pp. 287–334.

Harlow HF, Gluck JP and Suomi SJ (1972) Generalization of behavioral data between nonhuman and human animals. American Psychologist 27: 709–16.

Hesse E and Main M (2000) Disorganized, infant, child and adult attachment: Collapse in behavioral and attentional strategies. Journal of the American Psychoanalytic Association 48: 1097–127.

Hilgard ER (1974) Toward a neo-dissociation theory: multiple cognitive controls in human functioning. Perspectives in Biology and Medicine 17: 301–16.

Holmes J (1993) Attachment theory: a biological basis for psychotherapy? British Journal of Psychiatry 163: 430–8.

Holmes J (1999) Ghost in the consulting room: an attachment perspective on intergenerational transmission. Attachment and Human Development 1(1): 115–31.

Kirkpatrick LA (1999) Attachment and religious representation and behavior. In: J Cassidy and PR Shaver (eds) Handbook of Attachment. New York: Guilford, pp. 803–22.

Kohut H (1966) Forms and transformations of narcissism. Journal of the American Psychoanalytic Association 14: 243–72.

Kohut H (1971) The Analysis of the Self. New York. International Universities Press.

Lacan J (1966) écrits II. L'aggresivité dans la Psychanalyse. Paris: Editions du Seuil.

Lorenz K (1937) Uber die Bildung des Instinktbegriffes. Natrurwissenschaften 25. Eng. trans. The Establishment of the Instinct Concept. In: K Lorenz, Studies in Animal and Human Behaviour, vol. I. London: Methuen, 1970.

Lorenz K (1954) Psychologie et Philogenèse. In: Evolution der Organismen. Herberer G (ed.) Eng. trans. The Establishment of the Instinct Concept. In: K Lorenz, Studies in Animal and Human Behaviour, vol. I. London: Methuen, 1970.

Main M (2000) The organized categories of infant, child and adult attachment; Flexible vs. inflexible attention under stress under attachment-related stress. Journal of the American Psychoanalytic Association 48: 1055–96.

Malinowsky B (1932) The Sexual Life of Savages. London: Routledge & Kegan Paul.

Malinowsky B (1963) Mutterrechtliche Familie und Oedipus Komplex. In: Internalionaler Psychoanalytischer Verlag. Vienna. Reprinted in Estudios de Psicología primitiva. Buenos Aires: Paidos.

Marrone M (1998) Attachment and Interaction. London: Jessica Kingsley.

Mead M (1968) Coming of Age in Samoa. New York: William Morrow & Company.

Mohr JJ (1999). Same sex romantic attachments In: J Cassidy and PR Shaver (eds) Handbook of Attachment. New York: Guilford, pp. 378–93.

Otto R (1963) Das Heilige. Beck'sche Verlagsbuchhandlung. Munich 1963. Trad. Esp. Lo Santo. Alianza Editorial, 1980.

Piaget J (1970) La situation des sciences de l'Homme dans le système de sciences. In: Tendences Principales de la recherche dans les sciences sociales et humaines. Partie I: Sciences sociales. Unesco, pp. 44–120.

Piaget J and Inhelder B (1966). La psychologie de l'enfant. Paris: Presses Universitaires de France.

Schore AN (1996) The experience-dependent maturation of a regulatory system on the orbital frontal cortex and the origin of developmental psychopathology. Development and Psychology 8: 59–87.

Spitz RA (1946) Anaclitic depression. Psychoanalytic Study of the Child 2: 313–42.

Sroufe LA (1996) Emotional Development. The Organization of Emotional Development in the Early Years. New York: Cambridge University Press.

Sroufe LA (1997) Psychopathology as an outcome of development. Development and Psychopathology 9: 251–68.

Sroufe LA, Egeland B and Carlson EA (1999) One social world. The integrated development of parent–child and peer relations. In: WA Collins and B Laursen (eds) Minnesota Symposium on Child Development, vol. 30: Relationships as Developmental Contexts. Hillsdale, NJ: Lawrence Erlbaum, pp. 241–61.

Suomi SJ (1976) Experience Précoce et Développement social du Singe Rhesus. Psychiatrie de l'Enfant XIX(1): 279–302.

Suomi SJ and Harlow HF (1971) Monkeys at play. Natural History 80: 72–6.

Suomi SJ and Harlow HF (1972) The role and reason of peer friendship in rhesus monkeys. In: M Lewis and A Rosenblum (eds) Peer Relations and Friendship: ETS Symposium on the origins of behaviour. New York: John Wiley & Sons.

Winnicott DW (1948) Paediatrics and psychology. British Journal of Medical Psychology 34: 1–9. Reprinted in Collected Papers by DW Winnicott. London: Tavistock Publications, 1958.

Chapter 15

Disorganized attachment, motivational systems and metacognitive monitoring in the treatment of a patient with borderline syndrome[1]

Giovanni Liotti and Bruno Intreccialagli

Introduction

Deficits in metacognitive monitoring and the related deficit in the development of 'Theory of Mind' are particularly difficult obstacles to overcome in the treatment of patients within the 'borderline continuum' – borderline personality disorder, other personality disorders of the dramatic cluster, and dissociative identity disorder. Metacognitive monitoring is the capacity to monitor and reflect on one's own thoughts and feelings (Flavell, 1979; Metcalfe and Shinamura, 1994), whereas the related concept of Theory of Mind (ToM: Leslie, 1987; Whiten, 1991) refers to the capacity to conceive the content of other people's mind as different from one's own. Fonagy and his collaborators have discussed the importance of taking into account metacognitive deficits when treating borderline patients (Fonagy, 1991, 1995; Fonagy and Target, 1996; Fonagy et al., 1995). They also believe that defective metacognitive development (reflective-self capacity) is linked to insecure attachment, a hypothesis that has been successfully tested and confirmed by other researchers (Meins, 1997).

In general, insecure attachments are a moderate risk factor in the development of many psychopathological disorders (for a review of contemporary research on this theme, see Dozier, Stovall and Albus, 1999). In particular, disorganized attachment seems to be a major risk factor for the development of borderline disorders and other disorders implying dissociative experiences (Carlson, 1998; Fonagy, 1999; Hesse and van IJzendoorn, 1998; Hesse and Main, 1999; Liotti, 1993, 1995, 1999a, 1999b, 2000; Liotti, Pasquini and The Italian Group for the Study of Dissociation, 2000; Ogawa et al., 1997; for a review, see Lyons-Ruth and Jacobvitz, 1999).

Research in developmental psychopathology and reflections on the process of psychotherapy with the borderline syndrome thus converge in pointing toward an important theme for the treatment of patients within the borderline continuum, a theme in which disorganized attachment and hindered metacognitive development are intertwined. One of the consequences of linking an interpersonal experience (insecure and disorganized attachment) with a metacognitive deficit is that it suggests that developing a new and positive interpersonal experience in psychotherapy with borderline patients may be a necessary condition for fostering a better metacognitive capacity. A new interpersonal experience often precedes any cognitive change that can be obtained through interpretation or restructuring of pathogenic beliefs.

In this chapter we use the treatment of a patient with borderline psychopathology to illustrate a way of using the therapeutic relationship in order to foster metacognitive capacity, an approach based on attachment theory and research. The process of change involved restoring the patient's metacognitive capacities and correcting the emotional, motivational and cognitive dynamics by gradually transforming a former insecure-disorganized attachment into a more secure attachment relationship with the therapist.

In order to take full advantage of knowledge of attachment dynamics it is necessary to recognize that the behavioural control system regulating attachment interactions is only one among a number of motivational systems with an evolutionary and developmental basis. Each of these motivational systems regulates a particular aspect of human relationships. Before illustrating how the psychotherapist can manage attachment dynamics during the treatment of a serious personality disorder, it is therefore necessary to define the different, evolved control systems that regulate human interpersonal motivation.

Inborn and developmental bases of interpersonal motivational systems

Evolutionary and ethological considerations strongly support the hypothesis that humans are born with multiple, evolved algorithms for the processing of socio-emotional information (Cosmides, 1989). Another way to express the same idea is to say that human beings are endowed with a set of innate dispositions to engage in a few basic forms of interpersonal interaction. This alternative formulation does not commit us to computer metaphors (algorithms) that can be misleading (Gilbert, 1989; Edelman, 1992; Gilbert et al., 2000). These innate dispositions, being the result of evolutionary processes, are also present in other primates and, with the exception of the tendency to cooperate on equal grounds, also in other mammals and in birds.

As a function of learning in interpersonal contexts, the evolved inborn dispositions to different forms of social behaviour in humans give way to complex control systems, each of which regulates a particular domain of interpersonal behaviour. The development of simple innate relational dispositions into complex, goal-corrected behavioural control systems has been masterfully illustrated by Bowlby (1982, 1988) in the case of the attachment system.

The innately based control systems are goal-corrected through cybernetic principles of feedback and feed-forward by orienting behaviour toward particular interpersonal goals. Some of these goals might include seeking protective proximity of a potential caregiver, finding sexual mates, establishing a high social rank, and cooperating with others in the prospect of obtaining shared advantages. Since the interpersonal behavioural systems are defined by their goals, it is useful to conceive them as interpersonal motivational systems. Ethological observation, evolutionary considerations and across-species comparison concur in identifying at least five distinct interpersonal motivational systems (Gilbert, 1989; Gilbert et al., 2000):

1. The attachment system (activated by global feelings of vulnerability, and aiming at the achievement and maintenance of proximity to a caregiver).
2. The caregiving system (activated by emotional signals of distress emitted by a well-known member of one's social group or family, and aiming at reducing such distress).
3. The agonistic or competitive system (activated by competition for limited resources, and aimed at defining social ranks of reciprocal dominance and submission; it implies various subroutines: ritualized aggression, yielding, withdrawal, dominance).
4. The sexual mating system (activated by rising levels of sexual hormones, and aiming at sexual intercourse).
5. The cooperative system (activated by the perception of a shared goal, implies the ability to cooperate, on equal grounds, toward the achievement of the goal).

The attachment system becomes fully active by the last trimester of the first year of life, even though it continues to develop through the life cycle. Other motivational systems also require the development and maturation of the organism before they become fully operative. For instance, the competitive, agonistic system requires the ability to stand strongly on one's feet before it can operate, and this is the reason why it seems to come on to the stage only between the second and the fourth year of life (the so-called 'terrible twos'). The caregiving system usually begins to be active in child-hood with instances of doll-play, care of pets, and social play. The cooperative system becomes active with the development of peer relations during pre-school and the so-called latency period of childhood. The sex-ual system, in the ethological, evolutionary view of motivation, cannot become fully operant before adolescence, even though there are early expressions of the sexual system taking the form of auto-erotic stimulation and sexual exploration with peers (the normal expression of sexual exploration, however, never crosses generational boundaries unless sexu-al activity is initiated by adults who seduce or coerce sexuality on vulnerable children). A mature expression of sexuality during adolescence and adulthood requires the integration of sexuality with the attachment system, the caregiving system, the agonistic system (e.g. dealing maturely with issues of power in the relationship) and the cooperative systems.

Interpersonal life may be conceived as governed by the sequential operation of the five motivational systems. When the appropriate inter-personal context arises, there is a shift from one system to another in controlling thoughts, feelings and behaviour. The shift from one motiva-tional system to another is regulated by:

1. Inner needs (e.g. rising levels of sexual hormones facilitate the shift from other interpersonal motivational systems to the sexual system).
2. Environmental contingencies (e.g. the evaluation that a given environ-mental resource is available in limited amounts is likely to activate the agonistic system; the perception of environmental dangers activates the attachment system).
3. Emotions expressed by other people (e.g. a child's tears activate the parent's caregiving system, a cooperative smile activates the coopera-tive system, an expression of aggressive challenge activates the agonistic system).

Each interpersonal motivational system comprises an inborn component (a set of innate rules attributing meaning to socio-emotional signals, and value to particular interpersonal goals) and a learned component (cogni-tive schemas summarizing past experiences in the exercise of each system). Cognitive schemas also shape expectations as to the likelihood of success in reaching the goals of interpersonal systems. Bowlby (1982, 1988), in his study of the attachment system, uses the construct of 'inter-nal working model' (IWM) to designate the learned component of an interpersonal motivational system. Safran and Segal (1990) call this learned component 'interpersonal schema' in order to emphasize its being a cognitive structure concerned with the representation of self and other people. Interpersonal schemas variously articulate and develop the basic way of constructing self and other people that are coordinated by the different interpersonal motivational systems. For instance, the schemas developed on the basis of a secure attachment convey a view of the self as both normally vulnerable and trusting when the attachment system is active. The vulnerability of the self, in other words, is regarded as transient. Above all, a sense of vulnerability does not undermine a basic trust in self and other people. This sense of trust is constructed on the basis of positive attachment relationships. The schemas of an insecure attachment, on the contrary, may induce a representation of the self as unworthy of help or abnormally vulnerable and of the potential caregiver as intrusive, threatening or rejecting (see, for example, Bowlby, 1988).

For a psychotherapist, it is particularly important to foster the development of the cooperative system, since the cooperative system implies a way of constructing the self and other people on equal grounds, whilst the caregiving, the attachment and the agonistic systems imply asymmetrical interpersonal schemas. When the caregiving system is operative, a potential caregiver is construed as stronger or wiser than the person seeking care, while the self in relationship to the caregiver is perceived as vulnerable. When the attachment system is active the self is conceived as weak or endangered. The agonistic system, in its yielding subroutine, facilitates a cognitive construction of the self as subjugated, defective or even menial, whilst in its dominant subroutine induces a view of the self as basically powerful and proud.

Lichtenberg and his collaborators (Lichtenberg, 1989; Lichtenberg, Lachmann and Fosshage, 1992) have developed an approach to the study of human motivation, based on infant observation and the empathic analysis of patients' experiences in psychotherapy that has many similarities to the approach that we are proposing. Both approaches are based on the premiss that any attempt to reduce motivational theory to a single view of human motivation, or to one or two basic drives, is simplistic and misleading. Lichtenberg (1989) derives his multimotivational approach from infant observation and developmental theories. The ethological-evolutionary theory of human interpersonal motivation, like attachment theory, is derived from ethological observations as well as from developmental considerations. It is rewarding to note that (the different emphasis on infant observation versus ethological across-species observations notwithstanding) there is an overlap between Lichtenberg's multimotivational theory and ours. Lichtenberg identifies at least three basic and distinct motivational systems mediating, respectively, sexual encounters, attachment–caregiving interactions, and competitive–aggressive interchanges. Two other motivational systems identified by Lichtenberg, one mediating homeostatic needs and the other exploration, are also acknowledged by an evolutionary approach to motivational processes. The difference in this regard is that an evolutionary approach distinguishes between the social or interpersonal motivational systems in the strict meaning of the term, and the evolutionarily older systems concerning the regulation of the homeostatic needs of the organism. Behavioural goals related to the homeostatic needs of the organism can be pursued without any exchange of social signals, while the social motivational systems by definition imply non-verbal communication. For the same reason, the evolutionary approach distinguishes between the social motivational systems and the exploratory system, on the grounds that exploration of the environment does not necessarily imply social interchanges, and can be performed by the individual in isolation. Clearly, however, the interpersonal motivational systems (IMS), as defined by the evolutionary approach, are dynamically interconnected with, although functionally distinct from, the homeostatic and the exploratory systems. The relation between secure attachment and confident exploration of the environment (Bowlby, 1988) is a good example of this dynamic interconnection.

Emotional processes and interpersonal motivational systems

The innate IMS (interpersonal motivational systems), at the beginning of human life, process only procedural (implicit, non-verbal) knowledge, mainly related to the exchange of emotional signals. The processing of this type of procedural knowledge takes place mainly at the unconscious or preconscious level of mental operations. Emotions – as Bowlby (1982) has convincingly argued – are often the first phase of the processing of procedural interpersonal information, governed by an inborn unconscious 'algorithm' or rule, which becomes conscious.

Looking in this way at the relationship between emotion and interpersonal motivation, we can conclude that emotions are intuitive forms of knowledge encoded procedurally, rather than motivational forces. Emotions are information on the disposition to act toward a given interpersonal goal (Frijda, 1986). This disposition has inborn roots, and is unconscious in the first stages of the mental-brain operations it governs. Therefore emotions, in themselves, are not organizing principles of mental processes: rather, they are the subjectively felt result of the organizing activities of motivational systems.

Damasio (1999) has recently formulated a solid, coherent and empirically supported neuropsychological theory of emotions, feelings and consciousness. According to Damasio, emotions and feelings are the result of unconscious brain processes and these processes are part of the very origin of consciousness. We think that the unconscious brain processes described by Damasio, when they operate on implicit socioemotional information (from which the subjectively conscious experience of interpersonal emotions emerge), are the neurological counterpart of the inborn algorithms postulated by Cosmides (1989) as constituting the evolved foundation of the IMS. From another neuropsychological perspective, the inborn foundation of the IMS may be considered akin to the brain processes, selected by evolution and ethologically defined, that Edelman (1989) calls 'values of the biological Self' (Migone and Liotti, 1998). The operation of Edelman's 'values' implies brain processes, located in the brain stem and the limbic system, that lie at the foundation of emotional experience and are unconscious: in order for their results to become conscious, they must be linked to the 'categories' of perception and cognition (value-category memories) through re-entrant signalling with the neural groups of the thalamo-cortical system (Edelman, 1989).

In summary, according to this model, IMS have their origin in distinct, evolved and therefore basically inborn neuronal groups or brain modules. Each IMS develops ontogenetically to form the basic building blocks of human personality and each IMS has a distinct set of basic emotions that become integrated in this development.

A clinically important corollary of this view of the relationship between IMS and emotions is that each IMS has a characteristic group of emotions and affects linked to changes in the environment. The activation of these emotions is linked to conscious or unconscious appraisals that monitor the changing environmental landscape (Gilbert, 1989). The attachment system, during its operations, may yield the experience of separation anxiety, attachment-related anger, sadness consequent to losses, joy at reunion after a separation, emotional coldness and detachment after a prolonged or traumatic separation, felt security and trust as a response to the predictable offer of help and comfort when one is distressed. The caregiving system is characterized by emotions of protective tenderness, anxious solicitude, and guilt (e.g. for having deserted a significant other who was needing help). The competitive, agonistic system also has its typical emotions and affects: competitive anger, fear of being judged inferior and of being defeated, humiliation and shame at the prospect of defeat and deserved criticism, sadness for having been clearly defeated, pride for the victory, scorn toward the loser, envy toward the winner. Sexual desire, sensual pleasure, chaste modesty and jealousy are emotions that are typically implied by the operations of the sexual system. Feelings of loyalty and friendship, shared enthusiasm, guilt and disappointment for a failure in an expected cooperation are the mark of the operations of the cooperative system.

Cognition, metacognition and the interpersonal motivational systems

Young children perceive in self and in others specific emotions organized by the operations of a given IMS. These perceptions are first organized in structures of implicit memory that are the foundation of IWMs (Amini et al., 1996). Starting with the second year of life and with the emergence of symbolizing capacities, IWMs can process information at declarative or explicit levels (propositional knowledge). Children also begin to name emotions and attribute cause and meaning to emotions (explicit, semantic knowledge). Later in development, children are able to rehearse specific episodes in which a given emotion has been experienced (autobiographical, episodic knowledge), and thereupon begin to reflect on possible alternative meanings of those emotions and interpersonal events (metacognitive capacity).

A smooth, cohesive development of declarative knowledge, congruent with the corresponding implicit or procedural knowledge, is likely to be the condition for an optimal growth of metacognitive capacities. Such a smooth development can be seriously hindered by unhappy or traumatic interpersonal interactions. Most psychotherapists would agree that as a result of adverse interpersonal experience (particularly early interpersonal experience), the types and contents of declarative knowledge implied in the operations of an IMS may be at strong variance with the original structure and meaning of the system's procedural knowledge (Bowlby, 1985; Gilbert, 1989, 1992; Liotti, 1991, 1994). Cortina (Chapter 12, this volume) cogently argues that, as a result of unhappy attachment relationships, a temporal delinking of the cognitive and emotional components of attachment can take place.

The interpersonal experiences that produce such a dissociation between the declarative and the procedural aspects of the emotional-cognitive processes regulated by an IMS will also, by definition, hinder the metacognitive monitoring of the mental operations governed by that system. A deficit of metacognitive monitoring in the meaning domain of a given motivational system means that any experience regulated by that system (one's own interpersonal attitudes, emotions and motives, as well as those of people one is interacting with) becomes a topic on which it is difficult or impossible to reflect.

Empirical findings (Fonagy, 1995; Fonagy et al., 1995; Meins, 1997), clinical observations and theoretical reflections (Liotti, 1994) converge in indicating that secure attachment and cooperative relationships in childhood are ideal interpersonal antecedents for developing high metacognitive capacities. Both insecure attachment relationships and other non-cooperative types of human interactions (e.g. interactions governed primarily by the competitive or the premature activation of the sexual IMS) are less likely to foster the development of metacognitive capacity (Liotti, 1994). Since optimal metacognitive development is related to the experience of secure attachment and of cooperative interchanges, it is in principle possible to foster a patient's metacognitive capacities by developing a proper therapeutic relationship in which a secure attachment and cooperation on equal grounds become aims of the therapeutic dialogues. An atmosphere of real and enduring cooperation, however, becomes possible only in later phases of the therapeutic dialogue in patients within the borderline continuum, once a more secure attachment has been established. The following clinical case illustrates how the therapist, in achieving this goal, can make use of attachment theory in the context of the ethological-evolutionary theory of multiple IMS.

Case description

Ms Silvia Q, a 30-year-old single woman, was referred to Dr Intreccialagli for individual psychotherapy by her former psychiatrist. The referring psychiatrist reported the following:

Ms Q is the youngest of three sisters. Their father died 15 years ago. Ms Q had scarcely met him since she was 4 years old. At that time, Ms Q's parents went through a conflictual conjugal separation, motivated by the father's emotional difficulties (a psychotic breakdown could be inferred). Ms Q's mother, having to earn a living, was forced to leave her daughters in the care of their maternal grandparents. To grow up in such a home environment seemed to foster the three girls' wishes for autonomy. When about 20, each of the three sisters got a job and was able to live on her own.

Ms Q was offered employment by an international business firm on the basis that her excellent knowledge of a foreign language allowed her to work abroad for a while. This she did successfully. At the age of 27, Ms Q reached such a level of expertise in her work as to be called back to Italy by the main branch of her firm. Her mother, at about the same time, retired. Silvia and her mother decided to live together. Shortly thereafter, Silvia fell in love with Giulio, a 35-year-old bachelor still living with his widowed mother.

In this interpersonal context – living with her mother, which was quite new, and beginning a relationship with Giulio – Ms Q fell emotionally ill. She became dysphoric, was verbally aggressive toward her mother, and grew morbidly jealous of Giulio. Then at times she became incoherent in her speech and thought, and occasionally uttered the ungrounded suspicion that people at work were secretly hostile to her. She also felt that the numbers and numerals she met with in her daily life (phone numbers, street numbers, licence plates, totals in bills, numerals printed in clothes and shoes) could have concealed meanings. She yielded to the compulsion of ruminating for hours on the fancied cabalistic connections of these numbers. At times, Ms Q looked deeply absorbed in her thoughts, as if she was in a trance: she was then unable, even for as long as one hour, to respond to her mother's, her sisters' or Giulio's invitations to pay attention to outside reality. Abrupt changes of mood and attitudes were also noticed by Silvia's relatives.

Not surprisingly, her work performance, which had been so good for over seven years, began to deteriorate, and Ms Q received negative evaluations from her boss. As a consequence, she ventilated the idea of quitting her job. This prospect alarmed her mother, who insisted that Silvia consult a psychiatrist. Ms Q reacted with fear and expressed distrust of the possibility that psychiatry could help her. She eventually agreed, however, to meet a psychiatrist for a joint interview together with her mother. In this way an attempt at helping Ms Q through conjoint family therapy could begin. Two years of conjoint sessions, however, did not yield significant benefits. The only positive result of the family sessions was Ms Q's new acceptance of individual psychotherapy.

In the two years of treatment the referring psychiatrist and family therapist prescribed various psychotropic drugs. Although Ms Q's compliance with the drugs had been far from satisfactory, it had been possible to assess that neither antidepressant nor neuroleptic drugs, either alone or in combination, could significantly reduce her ailments. After a few sessions of family therapy and the first prescriptions of neuroleptic drugs, Ms Q began to report troublesome experiences of depersonalization.

As far as the diagnosis is concerned, the referring psychiatrist hypothesized first a schizophrenic disorder, then a borderline syndrome with severe dissociative experiences, sporadic paranoid ideation, and obsessive-compulsive symptoms in comorbidity. However, since Ms Q sometimes expressed the vague feeling that a concealed will or personality, somehow related to her inner world but separated from her self, was competing with her own will in determining her choices and the direction of her own thoughts, the diagnosis of a dissociative identity disorder could not be ruled out.

The first phase of the treatment

When Ms Q sat for the first time in front of her new psychotherapist, it soon became evident that her cooperative motivational system was difficult to access. Ms Q moved her chair about one metre away from the therapist's desk, and started to talk hesitantly, with her gaze at times fixed in the middle distance, at times instead inexpressively fixed on the therapist's face. She soon stated her sceptical attitude toward psychotherapy. However, when the therapist suggested that he and Ms Q could try jointly to identify an area of her experience that both of them could regard as worthy of exploration, Ms Q did not refuse the suggestion. After a brief pause of reflection, she replied: 'I would like to know why I am so jealous of my boyfriend'.

At the end of the first session, the therapist had reason to believe that Ms Q could, at least for a moment, conceive herself and the therapist as people sharing a common goal and engaged in a common enterprise (exploring the meaning of her jealousy). This observation, whilst it suggested that the prospect of establishing a therapeutic alliance was not a desperate one, did not imply that the cooperative system could, for a long time, motivate their interpersonal behaviour and guide Ms Q's interpersonal cognition. Rather, Ms Q's psychopathological problems, and her behaviour during most of the first session, clearly suggested that a motivational system implying asymmetrical interpersonal schemas (i.e. either the attachment or the agonistic system) would soon come to govern Ms Q's attitude toward the therapist.

In the following sessions, Ms Q continued to move her chair away from the desk. The therapist had the impression that she was frankly afraid of meeting him and talking to him. Her gaze expressed fear, her voice was trembling, her words few, fragmented, incoherent. She seemed unable to concentrate her attention on the topic of her attitudes toward her boyfriend Giulio, or on any other topic, for more than a few minutes. Her ability to report on emotions and thoughts, not to mention her capacity to reflect on them (metacognition), was almost nil. Confusedly, she turned time and again to the idea that a sort of hidden, malevolent will – she was not sure whether she regarded it as extraneous or as somehow connected to her inner world – was threatening her work and her love relationship. Maybe – sometimes she whispered with a trance-like expression on her face – the concealed meaning of numbers and numerals could reveal the intentions of this malignant will.

Paying close attention both to his own emotions, evoked by Ms Q's behaviour in the session, and to Ms Q's interpersonal attitudes in the therapeutic relationship (in a way much like the one suggested by Safran and Segal, 1990), the therapist was able to hypothesize that the attachment system was guiding his patient's behaviour in the therapeutic relationship. Ms Q's interpersonal (non-verbal) behaviour was such as to make her therapist feel protective (rather than cooperative, annoyed, dominant, or seductive) toward her. Since emotions expressed as a function of a person's attachment system tend to activate the caregiving motivational system in his or her partner, the therapist's protective feelings were a hint that the attachment system was regulating Ms Q's behavior in the therapeutic relationship. Moreover, the quality of Ms Q's fear in the therapeutic relationship was more suggestive of the type of fear characterizing disorganized attachment (Main and Hesse, 1990; Liotti, 1992, 1995, 1999a, 1999b, 2000; Lyons-Ruth and Jacobvitz, 1999) than of the type of fear that might be expressed in competitive interactions (i.e. aggressive interactions motivated by the agonistic system, and aimed at defining ranks of dominance or power in the relationship: Gilbert, 1989, 1992).

A metaphor summarizes the therapist's impressions and hypotheses concerning the motivational systems governing Ms Q's behaviour in the therapeutic relationship: Ms Q acted like a frightened child who hopes to find comfort in a parent's arms, but is also afraid of some obscure threat if she yields to this hope and approaches the attachment figure. This form of fearful attachment in a child has been found by developmentalists to be related to a parent's frightened and/or frightening attitudes, which in turn are often due to an unresolved mourning process, or to a post-traumatic stress reaction plaguing the parent's emotional life while she or he is taking care of the child (Main and Hesse, 1990; Lyons-Ruth and Jacobvitz, 1999). As a consequence of being frightened by the same person who is providing comfort and protection from fear, the child's attachment behaviour becomes disorganized and disoriented. Very likely, the internal working models related to disorganized attachments are multiple, fragmented and dissociated. A predisposition to dissociative reactions may be set in motion by early disorganized attachment (Carlson, 1998; Liotti, 1992, 1993, 1995, 1999a, 1999b; Ogawa et al., 1997). Also, the development of the basis for a future borderline disorder may be set in motion (Fonagy, 1999; Liotti, 2000; Liotti et al., 2000).

Ms Q's therapist was aware that an unexamined internal working model of fearful, disorganized attachment might become the basis for a patient's unconsciously construing either the self or the attachment figure as threatening, frightening or evil (Liotti, 1995, 1999a, 1999b, 2000). If the therapist takes such an attitude in the therapeutic relationship as to foster the activation of the patient's attachment system (for instance trying explicitly to offer comfort and reassurance), the result could be, paradoxically, an increase in the patient's fear. On the other hand, if the therapist takes a straightforwardly directive role in the relationship with a frightened patient, he or she could induce the activation of the yielding subroutine (Gilbert, 1992) of the agonistic system in the patient. This, too, could be counterproductive if the therapist's aim is (a) to reduce the likelihood of the patient's experiencing fear and discomfort in the therapeutic relationship, and (b) to increase the likelihood of a proper exercise of metacognitive capacity.

On the basis of these assumptions, Ms Q's therapist decided to limit himself to listening to his patient's confused discourse with an inner empathic attitude. He did not try to dispute Ms Q's beliefs in the concealed operations of a malevolent 'will', nor did he explicitly try to reassure and convince her that she had nothing to fear in the therapeutic relationship. He also abstained from explanations, critical comments, or interpretations of any sort. He hoped that Ms Q could gradually and spontaneously acknowledge that he was available to listen and, whenever possible, to understand and help her. If Ms Q and her therapist could begin to construct the therapeutic relationship based on a secure (instead of fearful and disorganized) attachment, or on a cooperative basis, then it could be hoped that the therapeutic relationship could foster the exercise and the development of Ms Q's metacognitive capacities.

The second phase of the treatment

After two months, and nine sessions, Ms Q gave up the habit of moving her seat from the therapist's desk before starting to speak. During the tenth session, looking more relaxed, for the first time she asked if she could smoke a cigarette. Her therapist did not smoke, and there was no ashtray in the therapy room.

The therapist thought that Ms Q's request could mean that she was (consciously or not) testing his way of experiencing the therapeutic relationship. The therapist imagined that something like the following question could be tacitly taking shape in Ms Q's thoughts: 'Are you so rigidly dominant as to forbid any request of mine that could even slightly annoy you? Are you going to judge me negatively if I show a bit of slightly improper behaviour?' Perhaps, at the deeper (mainly unconscious) level of the inborn algorithms governing the construing of interpersonal events, the attachment system (in Ms Q until then functioning according to an IWM of fearful, disorganized attachment) was giving way to the agonistic system. It was important not to allow Ms Q the possibility of construing the therapeutic relationship according to the mentality governed by the agonistic system (i.e. of construing the therapist as overwhelming and the self as either rebellious or subjugated).

The therapist took out an ashtray from his desk drawer and answered: 'Yes, you can. I do not smoke, however. If the smoke begins to annoy me, I'll let you know'. Ms Q lit her cigarette, and started to speak – and then answer the therapist's comments and questions – in a way that was decidedly more syntonic and coherent than had ever been the case before. After that session, she seemed more able to concentrate on the theme that had been selected in the first session as the goal of joint exploration, namely her jealousy. The therapist thought (and, monitoring his own emotions, also felt) that he was witnessing a major change in the motivational attunement within the therapeutic relationship. Gradually, a transformation of her fearful attitudes (based on a disorganized attachment) and dominant and submissive attitudes (based on the agonistic system) gave way to an atmosphere where moments of cooperation and a sense of safety began to emerge creating a secure attachment. Correspondingly – and in keeping with hypotheses relating the optimal development of metacognitive capacity to secure attachments and to cooperative interactions (Fonagy, 1995, 1999; Liotti, 1994) – Ms Q's thought processes became more oriented and wider in scope.

Noticing this progress, the therapist thought that his patient could now be ready for an investigation of her own memories. Ms Q was still unable to observe her present automatic thoughts, or to relate emotional experiences to her way of construing interpersonal events. Perhaps, however, in the more relaxed atmosphere of the therapeutic relationship, she could apply her limited metacognitive capacity to the mere report of memories of childhood experiences that could be helpful for the therapist's understanding of past traumas. The therapist, then, invited Ms Q to dwell on her past family interactions: 'I would understand your present experiences better if you could tell me something of your past family history'. She seemed willing to comply with this invitation. However, whenever Ms Q tried to offer information concerning family events, her thought processes became again confused, incoherent, full of logical lapses and time lapses. Ms Q, for instance, could narrate a given interaction with her mother in such a way as to give the impression that she was reporting a quite recent episode. Then, cues emerged in her narrative which suggested that the episode could actually have happened when Ms Q was a child. She seemed either unconcerned with the need to make the time scale of her reported memories clear to the listener, or unable to orient herself in such a time scale. As a consequence, the therapist sometimes felt dazed or confused while trying to make sense of Ms Q's narratives. He had to make an intense effort of attention in order to avoid disorientation. He had to ask for dates, periods of the year, names of the persons involved, in order to make sense of Ms Q's flow of confused memories. His patient did not seem troubled or annoyed by these questions. Rather, she looked grateful for his requests for clarification. Thanks to the fact that another person was striving to orient himself in the reconstruction of her past, Ms Q seemed to begin to make sense, for the first time, of her own personal memories.

It is important to emphasize that Ms Q's therapist, although aware of alternative theoretical approaches that could explain what was happening in the therapeutic process, was committed to the cognitive, developmental and interpersonal model outlined above. He knew that Kohut's self-psychology (see, for example, Wolf, 1988) could explain Ms Q's difficulties and her uncertain progress in psychotherapy in terms of empathy, empathic failures, and consequent cohesion or loss of cohesion of the self. He, however, was committed to interpreting the same observations in terms of the IMS active at a given moment, interpersonal cognitive schemas connected to the operations of those motivational systems, and hindrances to or facilitation of the exercise and development of metacognitive capacities. His goal, as a consequence of this theoretical orientation, was to maintain the motivational set-up on the register of secure attachment and/or cooperation, and thereupon to facilitate the exercise of his patient's metacognitive capacity.

The third phase of the treatment

In order to maintain the motivational set-up of the therapeutic relationship on the register of secure attachment and cooperation, considerable therapeutic skills had to be exerted. Ms Q often betrayed, in the therapeutic relationship, the tendency to motivational shifts from cooperation to dominance–submission and to sexual seductiveness, or from secure attachment to insecure, disorganized attachment. For instance, on one occasion (during the 22nd session) she asked her therapist not to address her any more as 'Miss Q', but to call her 'Silvia'. To this, the therapist replied, rather warmly but firmly, that this could be accepted provided that she: (1) was prepared to remember that their relationship was a cooperative and professional one, aimed at the joint goal of clarifying the roots of her jealousy, and (2) was prepared to reciprocate by calling him by first name (Bruno) rather than 'Doctor I'. To this, Ms Q replied that she felt unable to call him by first name. Then, the therapist said, it seemed more sensible to refuse her request, and to go on with 'Miss Q' and 'Doctor I': Addressing each other more formally did not in any way diminish the positive feelings and mutual appreciation they had for each other and would keep them on their main task, which was to understand the nature of her emotional problems (extreme jealousy).

In instances such as the one described above, the therapist was aware that his response to Ms Q's request could have been explained using other theoretical models. Weiss's theory of psychotherapy (Weiss, 1993) would have suggested that Ms Q was unconsciously testing the therapist's capacity to disconfirm one of her irrational, tacitly held, pathogenic beliefs. For instance, Ms Q could tacitly (unconsciously) harbour a pathogenic belief of the type: 'If I get close to another person and expect his or her acceptance, help and comfort, then he or she will either reject or deservedly downgrade me, and I should accept this in order not to be rejected'. If Ms Q's request to be addressed by her first name, and to continue addressing her therapist as 'Doctor I', had been accepted, such an irrational belief would have been confirmed, and the unconscious test would not have been passed. To 'pass the test' would, according to Weiss, both reduce Ms Q's level of anxiety in the therapeutic relationship and facilitate her conscious access to the previously unconscious irrational belief that had guided her request.

While the therapist was sympathetic to Weiss's theory, he based his decision not to accept Ms Q's proposal on the simpler idea that to resist the motivational shift toward dominance–submission (a patronizing 'Doctor I' and an inept 'Ms Q'), and to foster the operations of the co-operative motivational system, could facilitate his patient's resort to metacognition. Metacognition entails, among other capacities, the ability to monitor the relationships that one's thinking processes may establish between a given piece of autobiographic memory (episodic knowledge: see Schacter, 1996) and the inner world of generalized meaning structures (semantic structures). In order to foster Ms Q's metacognitive capacities, and taking into account her difficulty in reporting childhood memories in a meaningful way, the therapist suggested basing the reconstruction of Ms Q's memories on a series of old family photographs. (Ms Q – perhaps in accordance with Weiss's hypothesis that an insightful search for previously unconscious episodes and meanings may follow the therapist's passing a test – had spontaneously brought and shown the therapist, during the 24th session, one of these old photographs, portraying Ms Q, when 5 years old, with her mother). Each photograph could evoke episodes of Ms Q's childhood. They could be defined – as to time, place and persons involved – more clearly than Ms Q had previously been able to do. Meaning could be attributed or reattributed to these episodes. Such a simultaneous exercise of episodic memory and semantic knowledge, taking place in an interpersonal atmosphere of cooperation or of a newly emerging secure attachment, could foster the development of Ms Q's metacognitive capacities. A similar cognitive approach to the psychotherapeutic problem of how to help a patient develop the higher integrative functions of memory and consciousness may stem from Bucci's (1985, 1993) work on the relationships between non-verbal and verbal coding.

Ms Q and the therapist spent part of each of the following 50 sessions observing and commenting on two or three of her family photographs, both old and recent. The rest of the session was usually devoted to commenting on Ms Q's present relationships with her mother and her boyfriend, Giulio. In the process of examining the photos, Ms Q became progressively more clear, concise and coherent in her speech, and better oriented as to time, place and attribution of meaning. Interestingly, during this process she suggested a change in the joint goal of therapy: rather than be concerned mainly with the meaning and causes of her abnormal jealousy, she now wished to know why other people find it so difficult to understand her, why she felt 'mixed up' so often, and why such a confusion had come to plague her subjective experience of herself and other people just in that period of her life. This request for a change of the set goal for the therapeutic dialogues was a clear sign of a major growth of Ms Q's metacognitive capacities. To be aware of one's own confusion, and to wish to regain a more lucid state of mind, is possible, of course, only when the disorder of the higher integrative functions of consciousness and memory is remitting. Not surprisingly, Ms Q's complaints relating to feelings of depersonalization diminished drastically.

Ms Q's family history

Ordering the family photographs (there were hundreds of them, portraying uncles, aunts, grandparents, cousins, family friends, besides Ms Q's parents and sisters) in a clear time sequence, and reflecting on each of the persons portrayed in them on the basis of her therapist's questions and comments, restored the continuity and coherence of Ms Q's memory of herself and of meaningful people of her past.

Particular care and time was spent by the therapist in trying to explore Ms Q's memories of her father. He had left home, after a dramatic conjugal quarrel of which Ms Q had only a vague but still frightening memory, when she was 4. Thereafter she met him only rarely – allegedly because he was often emotionally or physically very ill – until he died when Ms Q was 14. Notwithstanding the care and time the therapist employed in trying to reconstruct Ms Q's memories of her father, her comments on the pictures in which he was present remained laconic and emotionally cold, in striking contrast with the flow of emotion-ridden memories often evoked by the pictures of other people. 'Here he was still at home'; 'Here he was already ill'; 'Here we were visiting him ... I was probably 6 or 7 years old ... I remember having spent almost all day on his shoulders ... He used to bring me around like that, since I was the little one'; 'Here Giulio, my mother's younger brother, had accompanied the three of us [namely, Ms Q and her two sisters] to visit him'.

There was, then, another Giulio in Ms Q's life, besides her boyfriend. Giulio, the brother of Ms Q's mother, was about the same age as Ms Q's older sister. He was, for most of the sessions spent examining the photos, the only other person besides Ms Q's father who did not evoke emotion-ridden memories, but only rather laconic comments. When about one year had elapsed from the beginning of therapy, Ms Q casually examined a photo portraying her father when still at home immediately after having dwelled on a recent picture of 'uncle Giulio' (now a young man). Only then did she notice the striking resemblance between the two men. The therapist had already observed the likeness, which was quite surprising for two supposedly unrelated persons as a man and his brother-in-law, but abstained from making a remark about it until Ms Q, too, explicitly came to notice it.

For Ms Q, to acknowledge the striking resemblance between her father and 'uncle Giulio' came as a shock. Not only did 'uncle Giulio' resemble her father, he also resembled Ms Q and her sisters, while he did not show any likeness of features with other relatives of Ms Q's mother. Reflecting on this resemblance, Ms Q expressed a sequence of strong emotions – surprise, shame, fear, anger and sadness – while an hypothesis for the reasons for such a likeness of features emerged: Giulio was born from the secret sexual relationship between Ms Q's father and her maternal grandmother.

This hypothesis, which later found confirmation from the dialogues between Ms Q and her mother, became the new organizing principle for the reconstruction of the patient's early developmental history. The sexual affair between Ms Q's father and his mother-in-law had been kept secret. The secret was unveiled shortly after Ms Q was born, when the resemblance between Giulio (then about 5 years old) and Ms Q's father became all too evident. Ms Q's mother was obviously deeply distressed by the discovery of the twofold betrayal, by her mother and her husband. The emotional turmoil that followed affected all Ms Q's caregivers, who were all frightened by the consequences of the misdeed. Since all her caregivers were frightened (and therefore frightening to an infant), Ms Q's early patterns of attachment – to her mother, her father, and her grandparents – all became disorganized and disoriented (Main and Hesse, 1990; Lyons-Ruth and Jacobvitz, 1999). Disorganized attachment is related to the construction of a multiple IWM of self and other people (Main, 1991). In this multiple, dissociated or fragmented IWM, the construction of representations both of the self and of the attachment figures may shift dramatically between the non-integrated stereotypes of the Rescuer, the Persecutor and the Victim (Liotti, 1995, 1999a, 1999b, 2000). This shift between dissociated, incompatible and dramatic representations of the self and the attachment figures may become the antecedent of dissociative processes deeply affecting the integrative functions of consciousness and memory (Fonagy, 1999; Lichtenberg, Lachmann and Fosshage, 1992, pp. 164–8; Liotti, 1992, 1993, 1994, 1995, 199a, 199b, 2000).

Other negative factors then added to the predisposition to dissociate that had been set in motion by the early experience of a disorganized attachment. The prolonged, conflictive process of separation between Ms Q's parents offered plenty of occasions for traumatic experiences, to which the young child reacted with the dissociative processes already facilitated by her multiple, incoherent internal working models. The family secret (Giulio being the son of Ms Q's father and maternal grandmother) was maintained in the communication between the older family members and the four children (Giulio, Ms Q and her sisters). The deeply distorted family communication, very likely, further hindered Ms Q's already threatened integrative functions of consciousness and memory. Ms Q's metacognitive capacity, as a consequence, could not develop properly. It is likely that Giulio and the two older sisters, not having experienced disorganization of early attachment (the frightening secret was discovered by Ms Q's mother and her maternal grandfather when the other children were already aged 3 or older, while Ms Q was just an infant), were relatively less affected with regard to the coherence of internal working models and the development of metacognitive capacities.

The meaning of Ms Q's symptoms

During the reconstruction of the 'family secret', Ms Q and her therapist shared the feeling of a cooperative striving toward a common goal: to understand the meaning of the strange and distressing experiences that had started to plague the patient's life shortly after her going to live with her mother. As a result of these reflections, Ms Q came to believe that, as soon as she had the opportunity of living with her mother after having spent so many years far apart from her, she felt that there was a secret that her mother was keeping concealed from her. However, Ms Q was then unable to reflect consciously on this feeling, or intuition. She had, very likely, the semi-conscious intuition that the secret had to do with being unfaithful in a love relationship. The fact that in that very period of her life she was for the first time involved in a romantic relationship – moreover, with a man who bore the same name, Giulio, as the man she believed to be her uncle and whose birth was part of the secret – created the basis for her abnormal, irrational, ego-dystonic jealousy. Her cabalistic obsession with the meaning of numbers could have been the result of the semi-conscious intuition that the secret had to do with dates: the strange closeness of the dates of birth of her older sister and of 'uncle

Giulio', for instance. How come that, more than 20 years after her mother's birth, her grandparents had decided to have another child? Was it not strange that her maternal grandmother and her mother were pregnant almost at the same time? And what about the unacknowledged resemblance between 'uncle Giulio' and Ms Q's father?

All this emotion-ridden and doubt-inducing information, we can now hypothesize, was processed outside Ms Q's consciousness. This information was also shut off from the communication with her mother and other relatives (see Bowlby, 1985, for a discussion of the cognitive-emotional consequences of such distortions in family communication). Therefore, they tended to emerge in Ms Q's consciousness and communication only as chaotic, irrational fragments of ideation and affects. Ms Q's reduced metacognitive capacities did not allow for a sufficiently critical evaluation of her now very unusual and distressing subjective experience of herself and of significant others. Both her relational and her subjective life began to deteriorate. So, the stage was set for the development of her serious psychiatric disorder.

This process of self-reflection, which took place within the context of a therapeutic relationship that was now both supportive and cooperative, clearly fostered the development of Ms Q's metacognitive capacity. The newly developed metacognitive resource allowed for the solution of her relational problems.

The final phase of the treatment

Ms Q became able to monitor carefully her thoughts and feelings during and after the often disappointing interactions with her boyfriend Giulio. Thanks to such a metacognitive monitoring, the state of mind that was once globally experienced as 'jealousy' revealed itself to be quite a complex one.

Ms Q had many quite justified negative thoughts and feelings related to her boyfriend's attitudes. Giulio, who was 35 years old, had never been able to complete his university studies, to find a job, and to live on his own (he was still living with his widowed mother, totally depending on her for financial support). He was egocentric, prone to daydreaming, socially rather withdrawn. When Ms Q reflected on these aspects of Giulio's style of life, she often came close to concluding that she would have to end such an unpromising relationship. She came close to, but did not clearly formulate, such a conclusion in her mind, because as soon as the mental representation of herself leaving Giulio forever began to take form, she felt intense emotions of fear and sadness. After this painful emotional experience, Ms Q had fantasies of

Giulio being unfaithful to her, deserting her for another woman, or otherwise betraying their love. These fantasies, which actually were just the last link of a complex chain of thoughts and feelings, were the only mental contents that she had been able to recover from her memory when required to provide reasons for her jealous, aggressive behaviour toward Giulio. When, however, Ms Q became capable of proper metacognitive monitoring, the whole chain of thoughts and feelings became easily retrievable. It then became possible to reflect on why such intense feelings of anguish accompanied the prospect of leaving Giulio.

The final phase of Ms Q's treatment mainly consisted in the application of classic cognitive therapy techniques to her catastrophizing way of construing the prospect of separation from a lover. She was now able to detect automatic thoughts and to reflect critically on the related pathogenic beliefs (e.g. 'If I abandon a man who loves me, I'll prove my unworthiness, and nobody will love me in the future').

As a result of this process of revision of irrational beliefs related to the themes of loneliness, Ms Q decided to put an end to her unhappy relationship with Giulio. Shortly thereafter, she also decided to live on her own. She had forgiven her mother for having kept the events that led to the divorce, and the real identity of 'uncle Giulio', a secret for so long. However, Ms Q now felt that it was impossible to create a trusting relationship with her mother, and that she would appreciate the freedom of living apart from her mother more than she feared the consequent loneliness. She also felt that she had now regained her capacity to go on in life without depending on other people's support, and that it was therefore possible to end the therapy. The whole therapeutic process had lasted about two and a half years.

At a follow-up interview, about one year after the end of the treatment, Ms Q reported on her satisfactory adaptation to work, and a new and much happier romantic relationship. None of her former symptoms had recurred.

Concluding remarks

This case presentation shows the importance of detecting moments in the therapeutic dialogue in which the attachment system becomes active in the patient, carefully discriminating them from moments in which other IMS organize the patient's mental operations. It also illustrates the need to balance the therapist's compassionate responses to the patient's attachment needs with a constant attempt at restoring, as promptly as possible, a cooperative motivational register in the therapeutic relationship. This is particularly important when the patient's attachment system is functioning according to an IWM of disorganized attachment, as is very likely to be the case in borderline syndromes.

Whenever a therapist responds with an excessive caregiving attitude to the patient's attachment needs, there is the obvious risk of 'infantilizing' the patient. In the face of a disorganized IWM of attachment, however, there is the further risk of evoking frightened and dissociated reactions in the patient. The patient may unconsciously strive to avoid the painful experiences linked to the activation of the IWM of disorganized attachment within the therapeutic relationship, through interpersonal manoeuvres linked to the competitive (agonistic) or the sexual motivational system (in this way, the patient keeps the attachment system with its dissociated, dramatic IWM at a stake, through the activation of another motivational system within the ongoing interpersonal exchange). In the face of such manoeuvres, the therapist should keep in mind that only cooperation and secure attachment within the therapeutic relationship are compatible with a proper exercise of metacognitive capacities. Even careful interpretations of the patient's agonistic or sexual manoeuvres, given the patient's limited metacognitive capacity, are not likely in themselves to bring the motivational register in the therapeutic relationship back to the cooperation and secure attachment. Therefore, it is important that the therapist use, in such circumstances, any intervention (including silence or expressed disagreement) that seems better able to convey to the patient his or her intention (a) to offer help, empathic comfort and acceptance whenever the patient is seriously distressed, and (b) to proceed to the cooperative pursuing of a shared goal (e.g. exploration of the patient's present inner experience or past autobiographical memory) immediately thereafter. The therapist's intervention should also make clear to the patient his or her intention to avoid any other type of human interaction within the therapeutic relationship.

However difficult this constant striving of the therapist toward the ideal goals of developing a secure attachment and a cooperative relationship may be in the face of the patient's IWM of disorganized attachment, pursuing these goals may be very rewarding in terms of increasingly efficient metacognitive capacity displayed by the patient. The clinical case illustrates, in a particularly clear way, how such a progressive recovering of metacognitive capacities may take place even when the therapist abstains from any interpretation of unconscious mental processes, or from any technique of cognitive restructuring and modification. It may seem to an external observer that in a psychotherapeutic process, like the one in which Ms Q was engaged, the therapist merely listens to the patient's story and comments on it according to common sense. The therapist's work, however, requires great expertise in carefully monitoring the sequence of motivational systems intervening in the therapeutic relationship, with particular attention paid to the dynamics of the attachment system.

Acknowledgments

The authors gratefully acknowledge Mauricio Cortina's critical comments, which have contributed to shape many ideas expressed in this chapter, and his help in rendering it accessible to an English audience.

Note

1. This chapter is a modified, expanded and updated version of a previous paper, originally published as a chapter in the book edited by C. Perris and P. McGorry, *Cognitive Psychotherapy of Psychotic and Personality Disorders*, with the title 'Metacognition and motivational systems in psychotherapy' (Wiley, Chichester, UK, 1998, pp. 333–49).

References

Amini F, Lewis T, Lannon R, Louie A, Baumbacher G, McGuinness T and Zirker E (1996) Affect, attachment, memory: Contributions toward psychobiological integration. Psychiatry 59: 213–39.

Bowlby J (1982) Attachment and Loss, vol. 1, 2nd edn. London: Hogarth Press.

Bowlby J (1985) The role of childhood experience in cognitive disturbance. In: MJ Mahoney and A Freeman (eds) Cognition and Psychotherapy. New York: Plenum, pp. 181–200.

Bowlby J (1988) A Secure Base. London: Routledge.

Bucci W (1985) Dual coding: A cognitive model for psychoanalytic research. Journal of the American Psychoanalytic Association 33: 571–607.

Bucci W (1993) The development of emotional meaning in free association: a multiple code theory. In: A Wilson and JE Gedo (eds) Hierarchical Concepts in Psychoanalysis. New York: Guilford Press, pp. 3–47.

Carlson EA (1998) A prospective longitudinal study of disorganized/disoriented attachment. Child Development 69: 1970–9.

Cosmides L (1989) The logic of social exchange: Has natural selection shaped how humans reason? Cognition 31: 187–276.

Damasio A (1999) The Feeling of what Happens: Body and Emotion in the Making of Consciousness. New York: Harcourt Brace.

Dozier M, Stovall KC and Albus KE (1999) Attachment and psychopathology in adulthood. In J Cassidy and PR Shaver (eds) Handbook of Attachment. New York: Guilford Press, pp. 497–519.

Edelman GM (1989) The Remembered Present: A Biological Theory of Consciousness. New York: Basic Books.

Edelman GM (1992) Bright Air, Brilliant Fire: On the Matter of the Mind. New York: Basic Books.

Flavell JH (1979) Metacognition and cognitive monitoring: A new area of cognitive-developmental inquiry. American Psychologist 34: 906–11.

Fonagy P (1991) Thinking about thinking: Some clinical and theoretical considerations concerning the treatment of borderline patients. International Journal of Psychoanalysis 72: 639–56.

Fonagy P (1995) The influence of attachment on the representational world in the pre-school years. Paper presented at the Conference 'Attaccamento: Teoria, ricerca e implicazioni cliniche' [Attachment: Theory, research and clinical applications]. Rome, 23 June 1995.

Fonagy P (1999) The transgenerational transmission of holocaust trauma: Lessons learned from the analysis of an adolescent with obsessive-compulsive disorder. Attachment and Human Development 1: 92–114.

Fonagy P and Target M (1996) Playing with reality: 1. Theory of mind and the normal development of psychic reality. International Journal of Psychoanalysis 77: 217–33.

Fonagy P, Steele M, Steele H, Leigh T, Kennedy A and Target M (1995) The predictive specificity of the Adult Attachment Interview: Implications for psychodynamic theories of normal and pathological development. In: S Goldberg and J Kerr (eds) John Bowlby's Attachment Theory: History, Research and Clinical Applications. Hillsdale, NJ: Analytic Press, pp. 233–78.

Frijda N (1986) The Emotions. Cambridge, UK: Cambridge University Press.

Gilbert P (1989) Human Nature and Suffering. London: Lawrence Erlbaum Associates.

Gilbert P (1992) Depression: the Evolution of Powerlessness. New York: Guilford Press.

Gilbert P, Bailey KG and McGuire MT (2000) Evolutionary psychotherapy: principles and outline. In: P Gilbert and KG Bailey (eds) Genes on the Couch: Explorations in Evolutionary Psychotherapy. Hove, UK: Brunner-Routledge, pp. 3–27.

Hesse E and Main M (1999) Second-generation effects of unresolved trauma: Dissociated, frightened and threatening parental behavior. Psychoanalytic Inquiry 19: 30–61.

Hesse E and van IJzendoorn M (1998) Parental loss of close family member and propensities toward absorption in the offspring. Developmental Science 1: 299–305.

Leslie A (1987) Pretence and representation: the origins of 'theory of mind'. Psychological Review 94: 412–26.

Lichtenberg JD (1989) Psychoanalysis and Motivation. Hillsdale, NJ: Analytic Press.

Lichtenberg JD, Lachmann F and Fosshage J (1992) Self and Motivational Systems: Toward a Theory of Technique. Hillsdale, NJ: Analytic Press.

Liotti G (1991) Insecure attachment and agoraphobia. In: CM Parkes, J Stevenson-Hinde and P Marris (eds) Attachment across the Life Cycle. London: Routledge, pp. 216–33.

Liotti G (1992) Disorganized/disoriented attachment in the etiology of the dissociative disorders. Dissociation 5: 196–204.

Liotti G (1993) Disorganized attachment and dissociative experiences: An illustration of the ethological-developmental approach to cognitive therapy. In: KT Kuehlvein and H Rosen (eds) Cognitive Therapies in Action. San Francisco: Jossey-Bass, pp. 213–39.

Liotti G (1994) La dimensione interpersonale della coscienza [The interpersonal dimension of consciousness]. Rome: NIS.

Liotti G (1995) Disorganized attachment in the psychotherapy of the dissociative disorders. In: S Goldberg and J Kerr (eds) John Bowlby's Attachment Theory: History, Research and Clinical Applications. Hillsdale, NJ: Analytic Press, pp. 343–63.

Liotti G (1999a) Understanding the dissociative processes: The contribution of attachment theory. Psychoanalytic Inquiry 19: 757–83.

Liotti G (1999b) Disorganized attachment as a model for the understanding of dissociative psychopathology. In: J Solomon and C George (eds) Attachment Disorganization. New York: Guilford Press, pp. 291–317.

Liotti G (2000) Disorganized attachment, models of borderline pathology, and evolutionary psychotherapy. In: P Gilbert and K Bailey (eds) Genes on the Couch: Explorations in Evolutionary Psychotherapy. Hove, UK: Brunner-Routledge, pp. 232–56.

Liotti G, Pasquini P and The Italian Group for the Study of Dissociation (2000) Predictive factors for borderline personality disorder: Patients' early traumatic experiences and losses suffered by the attachment figure. Acta Psychiatrica Scandinavica 102: 282–9.

Lyons-Ruth K and Jacobvitz D (1999) Attachment disorganization: Unresolved loss, relational violence and lapses in behavioral and attentional strategies. In: J Cassidy and PR Shaver (eds) Handbook of Attachment. New York: Guilford Press, pp. 520–54.

Main M (1991) Metacognitive knowledge, metacognitive monitoring and singular (coherent) vs. multiple (incoherent) model of attachment. In: CM Parkes, J Stevenson-Hinde and P Marris (eds) Attachment across the Life Cycle. London: Routledge, pp. 127–59.

Main M and Hesse E (1990) Parents' unresolved traumatic experiences are related to infant disorganized attachment status: Is frightened and/or frightening parental behavior the linking mechanism? In: MT Greenberg, D Cicchetti and EM Cummings (eds) Attachment in the Preschool Years. Chicago: University of Chicago Press, pp. 161–82.

Meins E (1997) Security of Attachment and the Social Development of Cognition. Hove, UK: Psychology Press.

Metcalfe J and Shinamura AP (1994) Metacognition. Cambridge, Mass: The MIT Press.

Migone P and Liotti G (1998) Psychoanalysis and cognitive-evolutionary psychology. An attempt at integration. International Journal of Psychoanalysis 79: 1071–95.

Ogawa JR, Sroufe, LA, Weinfield NS, Carlson EA and Egeland B (1997) Development and the fragmented self: Longitudinal study of dissociative symptomatology in a nonclinical sample. Development and Psychopathology 9: 855–79.
Safran J and Segal Z (1990) Interpersonal Process in Cognitive Therapy. New York: Basic Books.
Schacter DL (1996) Searching for Memory: The Brain, the Mind and the Past. New York: Basic Books.
Whiten A (ed.) (1991) Natural Theories of Mind. Oxford: Blackwell.
Weiss J (1993) How Psychotherapy Works. New York: Guilford.
Wolf ES (1988) Treating the Self. New York: Guilford.

CHAPTER 16

Attachment and intimacy in adult relationships

HUGO BLEICHMAR

Introduction

In earlier papers I elaborated on the idea that the psyche functions as a set of motivational systems that respond to different needs and wishes: namely, the need and wish for self-preservation and heteropreservation (preserving the other, being responsible for the well-being of the other), needs and wishes for attachment, sexual needs and wishes, needs and wishes for psychobiological regulation, and narcissistic wishes. The motivational systems are in turn monitored by means of an alarm (anxiety) system when the needs and wishes are not fulfilled, with several defence systems (which include aggressiveness), and with executive capabilities to perform their functions associated with each system (Bleichmar, 1997, 1999, 2001). Each of the motivational systems has its own organizational laws, and subsystems or dimensions can be established and give motivational systems their particular configurations. This is what I have worked on especially for the narcissistic system (Bleichmar, 1981, and, particularly, 2000. See also Chapter 15 by Liotti and Intreccialagli in this volume for another multimotivational systems model).

The motivational systems may acquire a different primacy or hierarchy in each individual. There are people whose needs for attachment enable them to forgo sexuality and narcissistic satisfaction, accepting all sorts of humiliations. Others, because of their narcissistic wishes, forgo needs for attachment so as to show that they are independent, even ignoring their own self-preservation and preferring to die rather than having to face what they feel to be shame and dishonour. On the other hand, there are people whose need for self-preservation causes them to forgo any sexual or narcissistic wish.

The more or less stable hierarchical predominance of one or several motivational systems determines the possibility of defining certain personality structures based on the importance of each system, although there may be an alternation in the relative predominance of motivational systems at different times in life and in different intersubjective contexts. Moreover, the interplay among motivational systems and the linking of processes among them give rise to certain psychopathological configurations, as I proposed in my work on subtypes of depressive disorders in which I showed that there is no single cause for these disorders (Bleichmar, 1996).

Although there is a modular organization of the psyche, the modularity is not absolute. Motivational systems have interactive effects among each other. For example, the narcissistic system can trigger sexuality, which is activated so as to enable the subject to obtain a grandiose image of himself (machismo, for instance), with sexuality losing its nature of purely urge-driven pleasure and becoming oversignified as an expression of the subject's potency. Sexuality is therefore activated or deactivated on the basis of the narcissistic gratification or anxiety that it produces.

The origin of my ideas are based in the studies of Chomsky and Fodor on the modularity of the mind. Chomsky postulated that for language to work, three components – a syntactic one, a semantic one and a phonological one – have to be articulated; they are independent, and each has its own laws of organization. Indeed, they are now known to reside in different parts of the brain (Gazzaniga et al., 1998). Apart from the studies of Chomsky and Fodor, the notion of modularity is currently receiving wide support from neuroscience research (Bechara et al., 1995; LeDoux, 1996; McGaugh and Cahill, 1997; Lane et al., 1997; Pally, 1997; Morris et al., 1998; for a more ample bibliography, see *Journal of Neuro-Psychoanalysis*, Nos 1 and 2; also, on Internet: 'Aperturas Psicoanalíticas' (http://www.aperturas.org), section on Neuroscience, Nos. 1, 2, 3 and 4).

In psychoanalysis, Lichtenberg (1989) and Stern (1985) deserve recognition for having been the first authors to clearly pose the need to go beyond the description of the psyche merely in terms of a few forces – Eros and Thanatos, libido and aggressiveness, etc. – and to describe specific motivational systems.

The concept of the object of motivational systems

With respect to the object, two questions that could help us clarify it are: how does the other enter into the subject's psyche and upon what inner need does it install itself? Taking this into account, we can characterize the object, in a broad sense, as that which meets certain specific functions of the motivational systems and satisfies their wishes and needs.

When this formulation of the object is applied to any couple – be it parent/child, an adult couple, or analyst/analysand – this leads to the following sets of questions: what does each member of a couple represent for the other in terms of motivational systems? Is the encounter, and the relationship between two subjects, based on the fact that each subject satisfies a wish of the same motivational system, for instance the sexual/sensual one, or the narcissistic one – i.e. couples of reciprocal idealization. Or is the encounter made possible because, for example, one subject is the object of narcissistic activity for the other while the second subject soothes attachment anxieties, or self-preservation needs of the first?

As can be seen by these questions, it is possible to develop a typology of couples based on the different configurations of the roles – real or imaginary – that each subject plays in the motivational systems of the other.

The mother, father or analyst, as actual people in the outer world, are multiple objects, simultaneously present, coexisting in relation to the functions they can each fulfil: attachment object, object of sexual drive, of the psychic regulation of biological functions, object of self-preservation, narcissistic object – mirroring, etc.

The object can fulfil some of these functions successfully and others unsuccessfully. For instance, it can adequately stimulate eroticism at the expense of annihilating individuation and the emergence of any desire beyond eroticism. It may adequately sustain the subject's narcissism at the cost of inhibiting the development of sensuality or of ego resources. It can also be pathological for the subject's alarm system: for example, a phobic parent, out of his/her own needs, may require constant contact with the subject, thus satisfying certain dimensions of attachment, specifically constancy of presence, but filling the subject with anxiety, making it difficult for him to sleep, and deregulating him biologically.

An analyst may be an object for the subject that fulfils his/her attachment needs. He is stable, and the regularity of the analytic setting also provides stability, thus proving reliable for attachment. But at the same time, the analyst, with his interpretations, can make the subject feel that he is continually defending himself, that he is hiding and/or distorting the truth, and that he requires the other to tell him what is happening inside of him. In these cases, the analyst is a disturbing object for the subject's narcissism, for the development of ego resources, for the attainment of a feeling of potency.

Attachment and intimacy

I should like now to explore the relationships between wishes for attachment – and their variants – and an area of intersubjectivity that unleashes intense desires and tensions, namely the feeling of intimacy. That is to say, the experience of self and other being or not being in the same emotional space. The space is shared; the subject can feel that he is joyfully merged with the other without losing his own sense of being. Or conversely the subject can experience the painful sensation of loneliness in the presence of the other, of emptiness, of the other being outside that space, of being unreachable, even if there is close physical contact. This experience is not easy to describe in words, because conventional language is hardly adequate to convey the profound experience of what the encounter between the subject and the other is like. This experience is constructed gradually and begins with the earliest emotional exchanges between caregivers and young children from precursors such as a smile in the first months of life that provokes a smile from the other – an encounter of smiles. This intersubjective experience can reach sophisticated expression such as the pleasure of sharing a common belief.

Pain-loaded expressions like 'I feel you are distant', 'we don't understand each other', 'it's as though we lived in two different worlds', are trying to convey in words something that belongs to another order: the feeling of loneliness precisely when one is physically accompanied.

A distinction must therefore be made between the feeling of not being in the same mental space and feelings of loneliness caused by the physical absence of the other, by the loss of the object of attachment. In this case, the other may be missed but there is not the Tantalus-like suffering caused by the other being present but in another psychological locus, by the subject not occupying the desired place in the mind of the other, not being able to reach the other with his feelings and thoughts so as to trigger in the other the resonance needed to permit the experience of being together, the experience of intimacy. In these circumstances it may be preferable to break with the other, not to see him again, so as to avoid experiencing the pain of the emotional non-encounter precisely when the other is physically present. Hatred may even be strengthened in an attempt to destroy the longing for intimacy that is the basis of suffering.

Attachment and intimacy are, therefore, two conditions whose relationship deserves to be precisely defined. The ideas of Bowlby (1969, 1973, 1980) about attachment met with much opposition among psychoanalysts while also giving rise to many important studies (Ainsworth et al., 1978; Atkinson and Zucker, 1997; Bailly, 1997; Bernardi, 1998; Lebovici, 1991; Marrone, 1998; Murray Parkes et al., 1991; Ortiz Barón and Yárnoz Yaben, 1993; Sperling and Berman, 1994; Vollin and Notaro, 1998,

Cassidy and Shaver, 1999). A contributing factor in this respect was the fact that his ideas questioned Freud's theses about the determinant role of sexuality in fixation on the object, whereas Bowlby considered attachment to be independent from sexuality and not triggered by sexual desire, but by an independent source of motivation that, from a neo-Darwinian standpoint, would serve the function of self-preservation at an evolutionary scale (Slavin and Kriegman, 1992).

I also believe that another cause for the rejection of Bowlby's ideas by the psychoanalytic community was the fact that many of the studies about attachment were predominantly of a behavioural nature and did not go into the subject's phantasy but tried to describe patterns of behaviour in the face of the presence, absence and return of the object of the attachment. Bowlby made it clear that attachment depends on internal schemes that mould the forms that they adopt – internal schemes that he called 'working models'. However, subsequent research on attachment did not focus on subjectivity, the intrapsychic aspect, nor on the complexity of the motivational structure within the subject which determines his search for a relationship with the external object. It is this dimension that I propose to explore from the perspective of the 'modular-transformational' model.

I point out in previous papers (Bleichmar 1997, 1999) that, in order to understand what drives attachment, attention must be placed on the various motivational systems or modules that mobilize the psyche, rather than on any single motivation. The attachment system, which is a system in itself – Bowlby's merit is in having revealed this – is activated by multiple needs and wishes. It is available to ensure the encounter with that significant other that fulfils various needs and wishes of the subject. It is a module, a component, of the mental organization that is articulated with other modules – needs and wishes for self-preservation, sexual needs and wishes, narcissistic wishes, needs and wishes for psychobiological regulation, etc. It is a system independent from sexuality or self-preservation, but not autonomous with respect to these forces. It is reinforced by them and enables them to be fulfilled. We should therefore study the different types of objects that attachment becomes linked to, based upon the motivation that activates and sustains the attachment system.

The object of attachment is occasionally that which makes it possible to obtain a feeling of basic security – the self-preservation system – as is evidenced, for example, in the attachment relationship of the phobic individual with his counterphobic companion.

In other instances, it is sexual pleasure that selects the object as the object of attachment from among all other objects available to the subject. This view is consistent with Freud's thesis that what fulfils the sex drive determines the choice of the object, which has received confirmation from rigorous studies in neuroscience (Insel, 1997).

But the object of attachment may also be what contributes to the subject's psychic regulation, to reducing his anxiety, to organizing his mind, to counteracting fragmentation anxiety, to providing a feeling of vitality and enthusiasm. The feeling of revitalization, of emptiness, of boredom because of the absence of the object of attachment makes the subject seek the object compulsively.

The object of attachment may be predominantly an other who sustains the subject's self-esteem, an other to be merged with so as to acquire a feeling of worth. This is a narcissizing object with two functions that Kohut called mirroring and parental idealized imago, to which I have added the function of the 'object of narcissistic activity', and the object that acts as 'narcissistic possession of the self' (Bleichmar, 1981).

On the other hand, a distinction must be made between attachment driven by the pleasure (sexual or narcissizing need, for example) that arises in the relationship with the other and attachment driven by defensive manoeuvres that counter anxieties of separation, of loneliness, of psychobiological deregulation, and of intense feelings of inferiority. In these cases, attachment is secondary to anxiety, as in the defensive symbiosis, that functions as a defence against the terror of disintegration.

In short, attachment takes place with an object that can be defined by what it fulfils – an object of self-preservation, of narcissism, of sexuality, or of regulation of psychobiological needs. In all these cases, there is a phantasy element in the attachment behaviour (search for pleasure or flight from displeasure), which drives that behaviour, and a procedural memory, which organizes it (Stern, 1985; Pally, 1997). The advantage of thinking in terms of motivational systems is that it makes it possible to specify the kinds of objects sought in each case.

Pleasure in intimacy

The pleasure in the feeling of intimacy brought about by the encounter with the other is an additional motivation for attachment that cannot be reduced to sexuality, nor to the feeling of protection for self-preservation, nor to valuation in the area of self-esteem and narcissism, nor to psychobiological regulation. For some subjects, a self-preservation attachment need is enough, e.g. a phobic patient with a panic crisis or a hypochondriac may have a solid and compulsive attachment to the analyst – never missing a session, feeling intense separation anxieties – but in his mind the other is merely an instrument or thing that protects him, rather than a person with feelings and needs of their own that he would want to share.

The same is true of attachment triggered by sexuality, where the satisfaction provided by the object is sufficient for an attachment on that object to arise. This was Freud's conception: the object as that which permits satisfaction of the drive, whereby the drive achieves its aim.

Conversely, other subjects do not seek protection or sexual gratification from the object, do not call on the object to regulate them psychobiologically or to balance their self-esteem. What these other subjects need is to feel that they are in the same emotional space as the other, to feel that there is a meeting of minds. So just as we propose to describe objects of sexuality, of self-preservation, of narcissism, of psychobiological regulation (Lichtenberg, 1989), it is also necessary to recognize the existence of an 'object of intimacy'.

The subject may have all these objects separately located in different people – the friend in intimacy is clearly different from a sexual or self-preservation object – or may reside in a single individual who performs several functions simultaneously. The complex articulation among the different objects, with dissociations and condensations, alerts us to the fact that expressions like 'separation anxiety' are too all-encompassing and need to be specified as to what the object in play is, what its functions are with respect to one or several motivational systems.

Types of intimacy

The feeling of intimacy is achieved in different ways. There are subjects who experience the sensation of being in the same psychological space as the other if both parties feel each other's bodies. Or, to put it more precisely, *if each one's body is pleasurably represented in the mind of the other*. The kind of contact that becomes an index of being together is very varied: whereas for some people direct sexuality is essential, for others it is enough to pass close by the other and fleetingly brush some part of the other's body, provided that this slight touch is also an index for the other of sharing a presence. This 'object of corporal intimacy' is different from the 'object of corporal attachment' in that the subject seeks the contact only so as to feel on his body the body of the other, in that he wants to sleep with the other in his arms so that the other's presence provides heat/sensuality to his own body. When, on the contrary, it is the body of intimacy that is wanted, it is also necessary for the mind of the other to feel the body of the subject. This is an encounter between two minds in which the body of the other is lived as the desiring party, not as the object of a desire that exists only in the subject.

Other subjects live intimacy as something based on sharing the same affective state, be it of happiness, of sadness, of surprise, of interest, of horror and disgust, etc. When it is the longing to cohabit this emotional space that dominates the subject, he/she does everything that is necessary to activate the desired affective state in the other: communication is an action on the other meant to produce affective resonance, to make the other vibrate on the same wavelength. Indeed, the feeling itself is hyper-trophied, the emotion is 'hysterized', so as to drag the other along. Or, inversely, the subject mimics the other's state of mind so as to feel that he is with the other. In both cases, affect is not something in itself; its worth does not lie in its quality of expressing internal states but in its use as a means of achieving encounter with the other. So, in the analysis scenario, the question that will guide how the analyst grasps the patient is not only 'what is he feeling?' but also 'is he feeling this so as to feel something else?' Through this intersubjective dialectic of feeling, an attempt is being made to achieve the feeling of intimacy with the other. Feeling is an instrument for reaching that intimacy.

So pleasure is obtained by suffering with the other, which leads to one form of masochism: suffering arises from the fact that it permits achieve-ment of the feeling of intimacy with the other who is also suffering. Often, this form of intimacy is first experienced in the relationships with parents or siblings. We often hear descriptions from analysands of one parent hav-ing to suffer in his or her relationship with the other parent, or of parents' sufferings on behalf of their children. This is often the air that was breathed in the families of masochistic patients. These intersubjective ways of being are then recreated in relationships with others. The uncon-scious pact to suffer with the other, by talking about or recalling painful facts and experiences – whether friend, partner or analyst – is of a bitter-sweet nature because it recreates the feeling of an intimate encounter.

The addiction to shared suffering, which constitutes a character struc-ture type, leads us right into the role of intersubjectivity in the genesis of the psychopathology of masochism. This was originally studied as a pure-ly individual phenomenon: a force within the subject that produced pleasure – sexual masochism – or mitigated guilt – moral masochism (Freud, 1924), or achieved a feeling of cohesion of the self (Kohut, 1971). But the roots of pleasure in suffering, and of its re-actualization at pres-ent may be linked to suffering as a privileged way of feeling oneself in communion with the other. Hence the risk of a sort of masochistic trans-ference–countertransference in which patient and analyst obtain a feeling of intimacy by focusing on painful experiences. The analyst thinks he is being empathic with his type of patient, whereas what is really happening in some cases is that he is enacting the complementary role for a patient who needs to suffer in order to acquire a feeling of intimacy.

Incidentally, just as inclusion of the intersubjective dimension for understanding masochism is a step forward, so is going more deeply into the motivations that generate and maintain a narcissistic personality. Together with the purely intrapsychic motivations, with the defensive movements in which narcissistic exaltation and the grandiose self serve to counteract feelings of envy or aggressiveness – 'if I am grandiose, there is nothing for me to envy, I feel no anger' (the Kleinian position, e.g. of Kernberg, 1975) or because they help to compensate for failures of narcissization by the objects of the self (Kohut, 1971) – there is another cause that lies in the fact that the grandiose self is an offering that the child makes to the parents who require this sort of exaltation from him/her. There are parents who unconsciously demand that their child should display a narcissistic exaltation as a condition not only for granting the child their presence and their recognition, but also for allowing the child to share their intimacy. Parents and child dream together phantasies of grandiosity. This experience will later mould the predominant way in which the narcissistic personality will demand from the other a state of grandiose exaltation that must be shared.

Notions such as those of 'false self' or of an 'as if' personality may cover up, in their different ways, the structured character based on the use of mimicry to achieve intimacy: feelings, thoughts and attitudes are shaped until they match those of the other so as to achieve that most basic of feelings, the feeling of intimacy.

Threefold dimension of affects: expression, communication-induction and accommodation

Much of the subject's emotional development, his acquisition of the other's emotional vocabulary, his emotional identification with parents, partner or analyst, takes place to enable him to feel that he is with the other, to unite himself with the other. This makes it imperative to revise the widespread notion that affects are exclusively the expression of an inner state, the subject's reaction to certain representations. In other words, that a subject dominated by representations signifying danger will feel fear; or a person who loses the object will be overcome by sadness; or a person who manages to fulfil a wish will become happy, and so on. In all these cases, the affect is a result, part of a mental state, an automatic correlation of certain ideas. This is a purely intrapsychic dimension, because affects can be experienced in absolute loneliness.

In addition to this intrapsychic dimension of emotion – it does not require the presence of the other and is not directed towards the other – I should like to highlight two other dimensions. One of them is better known, emotion as communication, in which the subject activates or intensifies an emotion so as to reach the other and make him feel what the subject is feeling (projective identification as communication). If the other (parents or analyst) is 'deaf', the subject has to intensify his emotional state in an effort to make himself heard. This is why some patients develop anxiety or sadness that increases if the analyst does not 'listen' or when the feeling of not being listened to arises from the transfer to him of an inner object – that was real in the past or is a purely imaginary construction – of insensitive non-empathic parents who did not realize the subject's emotional state. This is a 'communication-induction' emotion, which produces in the other an emotional response and a position (a role in the relationship) from which the other will respond to the subject's demand expressed in the form of that particular emotion. The affective state is an instrument in the exchanges with the other so as to make him feel and behave in the desired way.

In addition, when the longing is to share a psychic space, the emotion performs a function that might be called 'fusional', a means of producing the encounter. The emotion stops being a component of cognitive-affective inner states and becomes exclusively a way of generating the encounter. If the parents pay attention and respond positively only when the subject shows happiness, this affective state is not one of the inner states (emotion as expression) but is the subject's self-imposed way of trying to be with the other (for another discussion of the multiple functions of emotions, see Chapter 12 by Cortina in this volume).

From this viewpoint, the genesis of the hypomanic character is not always due to a defence against something that the subject is trying to deny – a pure intrapsychic manoeuvre – but may be the result of the other's call for the subject to be someone who makes him/her happy. If this is the subject's inner relationship with another who 'obliged' him to be happy, to be excited, to show narcissistic exaltation, when the subject is in analysis he may, in projecting that other on to the analyst, need to deny or to be happy for the other. This is done not just to defend against negative self-representations, but so as to feel that he is pleasing the other.

This demonstrates yet again that the subject may mobilize defences if he or she perceives that there is a real or imaginary demand from the other to conform to his emotional or defensive structure. This is an intersubjective cause of defence that has been little studied, in which the subject becomes alienated from himself by virtue of emotional and defensive ways of being of the other. The impact of the other on the subject compels the subject to forge a bond that he or she wishes to have with the other (see Fairbairn, 1943, for the study of the moral defence as a way of keeping a much-needed relationship with a significant other).

Different ways of achieving the feeling of intimacy

Although sharing an emotional state – whether by imposing on the other or by accommodating to the other – is one of the privileged ways of achieving the feeling of intimacy, it should not be universalized. Some people get this feeling of a shared mental space when they do something practical in which the other intervenes – cooking, arranging an object, painting a room, choosing a purchase. This activity acts as a semiotic indicator for the subject of 'being with'. The other participant in the event may not express emotions, but the fact of picking up the screwdriver asked for, or which he foresees that the subject will need to finish the job, is what furnishes the feeling of union. 'Help me to lay the table or to make the bed' may be the way in daily life of trying to give shape to the longing for encounter. There are families that get together to talk, to tell each other about affective states and to make the rest of the family live them; there are also other families that reach the common space of intimacy in the practical chores that they share.

As the foregoing exposition indicates, it is not the body, nor emotions, nor activities, that are decisive for some people; rather, there is a certain very specific quality of intersubjective experience which is what they want, the feeling of intimacy. Yet, there are other people who seek only to experience enjoyment with their bodies, without interesting themselves in any other type of relationship with the object; that is, their goal is primarily one of drive satisfaction. This is why the dispute between Fairbairn (1952) – the libido seeks the relationship with the object – and the Freudian position – the object is a means of obtaining satisfaction of the drive – dichotomizes what are, in fact, multiple possible forms of the relationship between subject and object: the body can be used to reach a feeling of union with the object, or on the contrary, the encounter itself can be used as a way of fulfilling a sexual wish. And this will depend not on an innate quality of the subject but on the experiences with which the subject's psyche has been structured, on what the parents were looking for in their contact with the subject or amongst themselves.

It will also depend, and not to a lesser degree, on the transformations imprinted on the experiences by unconscious phantasy, on the complex interaction of the inner and the external. If experiencing emotions, for example, is perceived as something dangerous and the subject defensively blocks any emergence of emotions, the achievement of the feeling of intimacy will follow other paths, which may depend, in turn, on the narcissization of certain functions – that of thinking, for example – and their products – thoughts.

There is a non-linear relationship in the exchanges with parental figures which alerts us against any mechanical conception of generational transmission: if the parents' way of feeling was to flood the subject with anguishing emotionality, the subject's rejection of that emotionality may determine that he seeks intimacy by sharing silence: he/she feels that the two people in the new relationship 'are being with' the other because both of them experience the same pleasure of silence and the concomitant emotional calm.

Identification is undoubtedly important for reproducing in children the kinds of bonds they had with their parents, but the subject's anxieties and wishes impose transformations when new dimensions are brought in. There is internalization in some cases, but what always predominates is an internalization-transformation process.

Intimacy in the analytic scenario

Wishes guided by the search for intimacy may imprint their course on the analytic scenario. For instance, if the analyst wants the patient only to use insight or to behave in a particular way inspired by certain ideals of health/sickness, he will be helping to structure his patient's psyche using a goal-oriented motivation. Metaphorically, the situation will be three-pronged: patient, analyst and the therapeutic goal. For the analyst, the patient will be an object to be transformed; for the patient, the analyst will be an object/instrument for achieving certain ends. Analyst and patient will focus on the goal, and if as a result the wish 'to be with' the other is ignored, in some patients this will strengthen a psychic structure in which this wish was insufficiently developed. This is what happens with certain personalities oriented towards actions in the outside world for whom encounter with the other is a contingency that is added, and has to be borne, on the path towards their goals.

In order to achieve a sense of 'being with' their analysts, some patients will mould all their activities accordingly: They will associate, they will recount their dreams, and they will even change because this is what the analyst wants. Talking will be a way of 'being with' the analyst, of attaining a feeling of intimacy. Even insight will be at the service of the basic need to share a psychological space. From this perspective, an alarm must be sounded in regard to the paradox of analysands that have a pseudo insight of always having functioned as an 'as if' personality, but are driven by the unconscious motivation of feeling united with the other by any means. In their analysis, they use this pseudo insight in order to feel united with their analysts. The outcome is a strengthening of the 'as if' character.

Symmetrically, if the analyst's prevailing wish is 'to be with' the analysand, this tendency that already dominated the psyche of some patients will be strengthened, while in others it will give rise to what was never developed. As a result, the analyst should not have any *a priori* valuation of either attitude. The analyst must be careful of not privileging an intersubjective encounter, the 'being with' the other, or seeking insight, because of the iatrogenic risk of treating each patient the same regardless of the type of problem that each patient will present in the analysis.

Another way in which certain people reach the feeling of intimacy is by sharing beliefs or thinking alike. Examples include certain ideological communities – political, religious, scientific or professional movements – in which thinking alike is what furnishes the feeling of communion and of intimacy. Leaders or followers may feel that they must form a unit. Their way of 'being with' the other is by sharing a creed. Anyone who deviates from this shared creed runs the risk of being excluded from the community and the sense of intimacy that comes from belonging to the community.

In the cognitive domain, there is something that goes beyond the ability of ideas to produce, or not to produce, the feeling of intimacy. Problems will arise if a person whose psyche is organized by certain ways of reasoning, which conform to the way conventional discourse links thoughts and arguments, comes into contact with somebody who thinks more in primary process terms; for instance, by associating thoughts and feelings intuitively, by jumping from one topic to another, or returning to the previous topic, leaving undetermined who is being talked about (e.g. saying 'then he came' without explaining who it is that came). Encounters between people who have different cognitive styles may produce a form of cognitive dissonance, a feeling of unease, and ultimately, a lack of encounter. The surfeit of details given by some obsessional people may overwhelm others who are more intuitive in their cognitive approach. The flows of ideas that organize their respective thinking follow different paths. They may organize their idea differently, have a different sense of what is important and the order in which things should be talked about. Their notions of what to expect in the next moment in the dialogue might be totally different. Needless to say, this will lead to another form of rupture in the search for intimacy.

Alternatively, the other's speed of thinking, either too fast or too slow for the interlocutor, makes the subject feel that he cannot keep pace; these asynchronies are perceived as a non-encounter. In the feeling of being in the same psychological space, this leads to consideration of the importance of the phenomenon of attunement, of the rhythms of two participants in an interaction, an issue that was strongly highlighted by Stern (1985).

Attunement or rhythm extends to encounters of all kinds: corporal, affective, instrumental or cognitive. Attunement is of interest as something that goes beyond the possibility of a given action being performed successfully – sexuality in the couple, or breastfeeding, or therapy, for example – because it intervenes decisively for achieving the supraordinate dimension we are discussing, the feeling of intimacy. The dimension is supraordinated in the sense that the rhythm which makes the sexual encounter possible in turn makes possible something that the subject may be seeking above everything else, namely the feeling of psychological communion.

So there are four dimensions of 'being with' the other: affective, cognitive, instrumental and corporal. In the analytic situation they are reduced to three because of the exclusion of the corporal dimension, not only for doctrinal reasons, but because of the disastrous consequences when the corporal dimension is transgressed. These four dimensions will be the vectors by which the vicissitudes of the feeling of intimacy will travel for both participants. The content and rhythm of affect, of shared work – the instrumental, the famous 'working alliance' – of the consonance/dissonance of the cognitive styles will shape the possibility of the feeling of intimacy, with its pleasures and anxieties.

The questions that can be asked in this respect will be: what is the patient doing emotionally, instrumentally or cognitively to get the analyst to share in his own psychic space, or to avoid his doing so if it causes anxiety? What is the analyst doing emotionally, instrumentally or cognitively to achieve matching objectives of approximation or distancing, of sharing or separating psychological spaces? What are both of them doing, regardless of what they want, out of mere compulsion to repeat, that goes against what they want and propose?

And even more importantly: what if analyst and subject have different methods for feeling that the other is in their psychological space, or for keeping the spaces apart? For example, for the analyst an optimum characterological way of 'being with' the other may be cognitive – thinking alike, sharing insights, constructions, theories about the functioning of the psyche – whereas for the patient the optimum way of 'being with' the other may be an emotional encounter, sharing the same emotional state. Conflict between the two is inherent to the structure of that encounter, and what for the analyst might be considered to be resistance by the patient against the cognitive encounter, to insight, could just as legitimately be experienced by the patient as the analyst's resistance against the affective encounter. With a dash of irony one might ask whether it was Irma who resisted Freud's interpretations or Freud who resisted Irma's affect. In other words, does the patient resist the analyst's interpretations because their content arouses anxiety – the classical view – or because of narcissistic negative transference – there is no doubt that this does happen – or because analyst and patient sometimes have different unconscious definitions and needs of the meaning of 'being with' the other, of the way of seeking to reach the feeling of intimacy?

Self/non-self differentiation in the 'intimacy space' and its relationship with the concept of 'transitional space'

What relation exists between the concept of 'intimacy space' and that of 'transitional space' developed by several authors following Winnicott's 'potential space' (1971)? The expression 'transitional space' tries to describe a sort of illusory experience in which the differences between inner/outer, subjective/objective, 'self/non-self' become irrelevant, making it possible for the subject not to be overwhelmed by a reality with which he will have to struggle throughout his life and which is always traumatizing. It is a space of creativity in which the attitude of the other – the mother, the analyst, etc. – is what enables the illusion to be maintained, accepting that illusory reality of the person who lives it in this way, gradually introducing reality in small doses. In *Playing and Reality* Winnicott stressed that the illusion is the result of an attitude of the other, 'of a breeding technique', in which the subject is not asked whether it was he who created the object or found it in reality; in other words, he is allowed to leave undetermined the difference between the inner, his phantasy and reality.

In contrast, the feeling of intimacy arises in relation to an other who is indeed recognized as separate from the subject – existing in reality. The subject, while maintaining that feeling of separateness, simultaneously experiences the sharing of feelings, thoughts and ideas with the other. *Intimacy is the feeling of union in the midst of a differentiation between self and other: we are separate beings but we feel and think alike.* It is the tension between separation and union that makes the pleasure of intimacy possible. So it is not total fusion or loss of individuation. Intimacy requires a 'theory of the mind', in the sense currently given to it: the attribution of mental states to the other (Fonagy and Target, 1996).

Since the feeling of intimacy with the other is always a subjective construction, it can vary, depending on the moment and the people involved: on the one hand, the subject may wish for and believe that there is intimacy but this does not match what the other is actually feeling. This is related to what Kohut (1971) described as 'twin transference', in which the patient sees the analyst as having the same wishes and thoughts as he (the patient) has. On the other hand, the feeling of intimacy may relate to the perception, more consistent with what is happening to the other, that this concordance between the subject and the other does indeed exist. The whole range of possible experiences are to be found between these two poles of the most arbitrary subjectivity and the closest approximation to reality, which is never attainable, never completely objective, always constructed.

Accordingly, the feeling of intimacy is a subjective construction for each of the participants, regulated by their wishes, by their anxieties and defences, but at the same time created by the two participants. In the analytic situation we should be alert to the possibility that feelings of intimacy may be, for both patient and analyst, a pure illusion – one of the poles mentioned earlier – or something approaching the reality of what both are feeling.

Anxieties in the face of intimacy

However, before going more deeply into the possible combinations that arise from two interacting subjectivities, consideration must be given to the anxieties in the face of intimacy, because the discussion so far has assumed that the feeling of intimacy is always something desired. For some people the encounter with the other is loaded with fear. This may have originated in interpersonal experiences with significant others, or by identification with others who transmitted to the subject how they should experience intimacy, or through phantasy, or through a combination of all the above. The net result is a fear of being invaded, overrun, blamed, pursued and punished, saddened, overexcited and infected with anxiety, forced to do what they do not want to do. Or it may result in being disturbed in their rhythms, or cognitively disorganized. The shared space is experienced as being trapped in a lions' cage.

In some relationships between adolescents and their parents, the adolescents reject the parents because intimacy involves the feeling of invasion at any of the levels described earlier. The same is true of certain couples, with the additional fact that the other may be rejected in one of the types of intimacy. For example, in sexual intimacy, not as a narcissistic retaliation against offences of the other, not to fulfil the wish to frustrate the wish of the other, not for lack of sexual desire, not because sexuality is experienced with anxiety about corporal penetration, but for another reason on top of all these: that sexuality is signified as intimacy, which is what causes anxiety because of what it has represented in the subject's history. Over the sexual encounter looms the signification that 'being with' threatens the integrity of the self in any of the dimensions mentioned above.

One of the types of intimacy that may trigger most rejection and mobilize defences is the traumatizing impact of the other's affect on the subject. If the affect is excessive, changing or chaotic – e.g. borderline parents – the subject defends himself, going so far as to eliminate any wish for contact. In the analytic situation, if the analyst is anxious, if how he speaks or his tone of voice conveys alarm, if he is a worrier like parents who want their children to feel the seriousness of what is at issue, then the patient may tend to isolate himself, to 'resist'. This is not due to a narcissistic rivalry, but to an emotional state in which he feels emotionally flooded and is disorganizing for his psyche.

It is this level of interaction, which does not depend on the thematic content of what is said, that has been most disregarded in psychoanalysis. The disregard has got to such a point that, not infrequently, when an analyst attempts to describe to colleagues his participation in the analytical dialogue, the form of words used is 'I told him (the patient) that ...', omitting the reflection on the so-called 'paralinguistic' series that would require the addition to that bald statement 'I told him in a tone of ... (alarm, harshness, gravity, affective distance, emotional over-involvement, etc.) and with a ... (hurried, tumultuous, slow, etc.) rhythm'. On very few occasions do we analysts include these characteristics when describing our work.

Expectations for intimacy

Like any other type of wish, the wish for intimacy is experienced as a set of expectations that the subject wishes will be fulfilled. There may be a foreboding that intimacy will never be attained that there will be no way of reaching the other. Despair occurs occasionally when there is a feeling that the other – the partner in a couple, for example – does not share a view that is self-evident for the subject. These views are based on socially learned rules of reciprocal obligations, how each one should regulate his relationship with the other. This condition is illustrated by the case of a female patient who, after chiding her partner for inappropriate behaviour, received a reply from her partner that seemed to her totally unreasonable based on arguments 'taken from nowhere and totally devoid of logic'. After these arguments, the patient would feel desperate and become angry.

Anyone who has had the experience in childhood of living with irrational parents may reach a point when they give up making any effort to achieve intimacy and will therefore not communicate their thoughts, feelings or movements. A schizoid state and silence become a method of protection against the anxieties of non-encounter, against the feeling that it is not possible to establish a common basis for dialogue and understanding.

On other occasions, without reaching desperation, the expectation is that the other will come to understand the subject only if the subject forces the feelings he wants to communicate on to the other. When one of my patients wanted to convey an idea, an anxiety or a worry to me, he started to shout, taking it for granted that I would not understand him. The common expression 'you don't understand me' does not always arise from the lack of understanding, but from the subject's repeated experiences of not being able to reach a feeling of intimacy with the other and to share the same mental space.

The loss of the object of intimacy – the object in which the wish for intimacy is fulfilled – may provoke emotional reactions equivalent to those described by Spitz for hospitalism and by Bowlby for the loss of the object. Namely, a phase of protest to force the re-encounter with the other. If despite the protest, the object of intimacy does not seem disposed to do what is asked of him, the phase of desperation and detachment sets in.

Defences against intimacy

The ways available to the subject for keeping the other at a distance, or directly out of the shared space – i.e. the defences against the anxieties of intimacy – can range from physical distancing or schizoid withdrawal in the presence of the other (so well studied by British analysts), to dissociated states in which the subject keeps part of himself outside the organization of the personality involved in the exchanges with the other – multiple selves (Bromberg, 1996), to aggressiveness, to keeping the other at a distance (Mahler, 1981; Bleichmar, 1997).

Moreover, intimacy may be sought in one of its multiple forms – corporal, affective, instrumental or cognitive – while rejecting the other forms, not because they involve intimacy but because they affect the feeling of security in the motivational systems of narcissism, self-preservation and regulation of the psychobiological equilibrium. Thus, one member of a couple may seek intimacy on the sexual plane but this means coming into contact with an other who deregulates him/her psychobiologically and fills him with anxiety, or who transmits his sadness, or who wants to impose his ideas and so creates tension in the narcissistic system. Conversely, intimacy may be oversignified by the narcissistic system: 'he/she shares with me, so he/she values me', thereby reinforcing the subject's search.

This reaction of the other based on the different motivational systems – acceptance or rejection – allows for a more accurate description of what is called ambivalence. Ambivalence is a pervasive phenomenon in all relationships precisely because the subject is bound by a multiplicity of motivational systems as well as by the types of search and rejection strategies that are activated in relationships – and the counter-reactions to these interactive strategies. Rather than ambivalence between two categories (love–hate), what we find are multiple sources of ambivalence based on complementary motivational systems that are activated between participants in any given interaction.

Non-encounters among types of search for intimacy

Non-encounters arise from the multiple combinations that can be generated by the interplay of the wish for intimacy, the ways of achieving it, and the needs felt by a subject from his motivational systems. Ferenczi (1933) spoke of confusion of languages to refer to the situation in which someone addresses an other in search of care and protection and the other responds with a sexual wish. It makes no difference if the first person is a child and the other is an adult: the decisive part of Ferenczi's contribution is that it illustrates one of the variants of the non-encounter between two subjectivities.

Just as sexuality may be something in itself, because of drive-derived pleasure, or may be an instrument for achieving intimacy, so the wishes and needs of the other motivational systems can be achieved without intimacy being involved. Narcissistic pleasure is obtainable in some cases precisely because the subject feels that what the other feels or thinks or does is of no interest to him; he represents himself as absolutely autonomous. Psychobiological regulation or self-preservation is better achieved by some people in solitude, without the physical, emotional, instrumental or cognitive presence of the other. However, the feeling of intimacy is based on feeling safe and protected; when intimacy is not achieved the subject may experience himself as being in danger.

Since the psyche does not function on a rational calculation that maximizes benefits and minimizes damages, but is driven more or less blindly by differing motivational forces, each pushing in its own direction, a person may have an intense desire for intimacy and seek it on the emotional or corporal plane but comes up against an other who deregulates him via the narcissistic, sensual/sexual or self-preservation system, with the result that the subject will end up fleeing from contact. Or, inversely, a person may be pushed by strong needs of his narcissistic system towards confrontation with the other, towards demarcation and difference so as to feel himself superior, thereby frustrating simultaneous and equally intense wishes for intimacy.

Consequently, in each encounter with the other, the subject is exposed not only to the intrapsychic contradictions between his own motivational systems, but also to the contradictions arising from the interplay with the motivational systems of the other. And the same can also be said for the encounter in analysis, in which wishes for and anxieties about intimacy are activated in analyst and patient, specifically in their respective domains, together with encounters/non-encounters between the wishes and needs of their respective motivational systems.

Questions arise in the search for and rejection of intimacy between analyst and analysand. What will be the consequences when both of them seek intimacy, when both of them reject it, when one seeks it and the other rejects it? In addition to the analyst's character structure, how does the analyst's theoretical and technical orientation contribute to strengthening the search for or flight from intimacy? Analysts who are followers of Freud or Klein or Kohut or Lacan or analysts who have an intersubjective or interpersonal orientation will obviously generate different interactive fields in regard to intimacy.

The different combinations or ways in which a person seeks intimacy, the relationship between intimacy and attachment and between attachment and the other motivational systems are different for each subject. This shows us once again that the psyche functions as a component-articulating system in which different modules, when they are articulated, undergo and imprint transformations on the others. The same thing happens, but in an even more complex way, when two subjectivities come into contact with each other.

Why is intimacy sought?

If, as stated earlier, the wish for intimacy is not reduced to the customary motivations leading to self-preservative or sexual or narcissistic attachment, if the wish for intimacy is a condition with a specificity of its own, why then is intimacy sought? Failure to answer this question exposes us to the risk of turning intimacy into an entelechy. What happens when we feel we are sharing a state of mind with the other? Our state of mind is validated. That is to say, we are confirmed in the feeling that we exist, in the validity of our perceptions and thoughts, insofar as what we are and what we feel exists for the other.

The feeling of being a subject is a reflection of the fact that we are formed by the encounter with the other: most often the child wants, almost dictatorially, the adult to look at what she is looking at. The child's validation requires re-creating the constituent moments of the psyche, when the other provides the meaning of an experience. Even something that is a biological given, namely smiling, is reciprocated in the smile of the adult who joyfully smiles back at the same moment. The pleasure of a certain kind of food is created by the pleasure observed in the significant other in the presence of that food; or the functional pleasure of the first steps toward motor controls requires the jubilant response of the other who helps to bring it into being.

The subject never ceases to require that a real or imaginary other bear witness to its existence and to the emotional validity to his or her experience. The pleasure encountered in intimacy is precisely that of re-validation. That is why intimacy is of a vivifying nature, which is prior to the ability to establish a sense of one's own worth. This is a later development, which requires a system of valuations, a scale of preferences, an ego ideal, an ability to compare the representation of the self with that of the ego ideal (Bleichmar, 1978). The vivifying experience is a much more general and all-encompassing one in which the other's libido, the other's joy, impels the subject's pleasure in being, thinking, feeling and acting.

But when a subject makes the painful discovery that the other's emotional state, interests and wishes may differ greatly from his own, the wish for mental re-encounter will become an engine of the psyche. The pleasure of intimacy is the affirmation of being human in the encounter with the other, who confirms the subject's life experiences.

Inner obstacles to intimacy

This need of the subject to validate the other within himself in order for intimacy to arise puts us on track for ascertaining the possible conditions that can conspire against the emergence of intimacy. It is not only the external object that contributes to the confirmation of self – a factor that Kohut should be recognized for having stressed – but also the subject's own aggressiveness can deteriorate and corrode the representation of the object that may confirm him. A tendentious criticism of the external object deprives the subject of the capacity for intimate pleasure. In devaluating the object from which something is expected it also creates an obstacle for the internalization of positive experience. This was the contribution of M. Klein (1940), who highlighted the inner conditions of the subject that conspire against the ability to make use of the external object for his own development.

An important implication for analytical therapy is that the reaffirmation of the subject, and the derived vitalization of the self, requires confirmation by the analyst. This reaffirmation is based not only on the confirmation of the other, as is clearly shown in studies on attachment and the importance of the external figures. Validation also depends on inner conditions of the subject, such as the level of aggressiveness that might be present (with its sundry causes), which prevents the external object – the analyst, in this case – from providing a vitalizing and confirming experience for the analysand. This combination of conditions makes plain to us, once again, the risks of extreme polarization among schools, a polarization that we should strive to overcome in psychoanalysis.

Conclusion

This chapter examines the motivational systems that activate and sustain attachment behaviour from the standpoint of the 'modular-transformational' approach (Bleichmar, 1997, 1999) and tries to define psychoanalytically the different types of objects of attachment. It describes the specificity of the wish for intimacy, the ways in which the subject tries to fulfil that wish, the types of suffering caused when the wish is not fulfilled – which are clearly differentiable from attachment rupture anxieties – and certain kinds of personality structures that act as defences against the anxieties provoked by intimacy. Also addressed is one form of pathology of intimacy, namely the shared pain of masochism, that serves the function of re-creating a feeling of intersubjective communion. The chapter reconceptualizes affect within a model that takes into account the intrapsychic and the intersubjective, identifying three dimensions: the expressive, the communicational-inductive and a third one in which the subject imposes on himself the affect of the other so as to feel himself merging with the other.

The foregoing concepts are applied to the analytic situation in order to establish variants, in the analyst/analysed relation, of the different combinations of encounters/non-encounters among the respective types of wishes for attachment or intimacy, of anxieties in the face of such wishes, and of types of defences that may be triggered in the two participants.

References

Ainsworth MDS, Blehar MC, Waters E and Wall S (1978) Patterns of Attachment. A Psychological Study of the Strange Situation. Hillsdale, NJ: Erlbaum.

Atkinson L and Zucker K (eds) (1997) Attachment and Psychopathology. New York: Guilford Press.

Bailly D (1997) Angustia de separación. Barcelona: Masson, SA.

Bechara A, Tranel D, Damasio H, Adolphs A, Rockland C and Damasio AR (1995) Double dissociation of conditioning and declarative knowledge relative to the amygdala and hippocampus in humans. Science 269 (5227): 1115.

Bernardi R (1998) Informe del panel: Attachment representations in adult years: Implications for psychoanalysis. International Journal of Psycho-Analysis 79: 798–801.

Bleichmar H (1978) Le discours totalisant: le moi idéal et l'idéal du moi: les effets de deux types de discours. Topique 29: 85–112.

Bleichmar H (1981) El narcisismo. Estudio sobre la enunciación y la gramática inconsciente. Buenos Aires: Nueva Visión.

Bleichmar H (1996) Some subtypes of depression and their implications for psychoanalytic therapy. International Journal of Psycho-Analysis 77: 935–61.

Bleichmar H (1997) Avances en Psicoterapia Psicoanalítica. Hacia una técnica de intervenciones específicas. Barcelona: Paidós.

Bleichmar H (1999) Fundamentos y aplicaciones del enfoque modular-transformacional. Aperturas psicoanalíticas, No. 1. Journal on the Internet http://www.aperturas.org

Bleichmar H (2000) Aplicación del enfoque Modular-Transformacional al diagnóstico y tratamiento de los trastornos narcisistas. Aperturas psicoanalíticas, No. 5. Journal on the Internet http://www.aperturas.org

Bleichmar H (2001) El cambio terapéutico a la luz de los conocimientos actuales sobre la memoria y los m´ltiples procesamientos inconscientes Aperturas psicoanalíticas, No. 9. Journal on the Internet http://www.aperturas.org

Bowlby J (1969) Attachment and Loss, vol. 1: Attachment. New York: Basic Books. (El vínculo afectivo. Barcelona: Paidós).

Bowlby J (1973) Attachment and Loss, vol. 2: Separation, Anxiety and Anger. New York: Basic Books.

Bowlby J (1980) Attachment and Loss, vol. 3: Loss, Sadness and Depression. New York: Basic Books.

Bromberg PM (1996) Standing in spaces: The multiplicity of self and the psychoanalytic relationship. Contemporary Psychoanalysis 32: 509–36.

Cassidy J and Shaver R (1999) Handbook of Attachment. Theory, Research, and Clinical Applications. New York: Guilford Press.

Fairbairn WRD (1943) The repression and the return of bad objects (with special reference to the 'war neuroses'). Psychoanalytic Studies of the Personality. London: Tavistock (1952).

Fairbairn R (1952) Psychoanalytic Studies of the Personality. London: Tavistock.

Ferenczi S (1933) Confusión de lenguas entre los adultos y el niño. In: Psicoanálisis, vol. IV, p. 139. Barcelona: Espasa Calpe, 1984.

Fonagy P and Target M (1996) Playing with reality: I. Theory of mind and the normal development of psychic reality. International Journal of Psycho-analysis 77: 217–33.

Freud S (1924) The economic problems of masochism. Standard Edition 19: 155-74. London: Hogarth Press.

Gazzaniga MS, Ivry RB and Mangun GR (1998) Cognitive Neuroscience. The Biology of the Mind. New York: WW Norton.

Insel TR (1997). A neurobiological basis of social attachment. American Journal of Psychiatry 154: 726-34.

Kernberg O (1975) Borderline Conditions and Pathological Narcissism. New York: Jason Aronson.

Klein M (1940) El duelo y su relación con los estados maníaco-depresivos. In: Obras completas de Melanie Klein, vol. 1. Barcelona: Paidós, pp. 346-71.

Kohut H (1971) El análisis del sí mismo. Buenos Aires: Amorrortu.

Lane RD, Reiman EM, Ahern GL, Schwartz GE and Davidson RJ (1997) Neuroanatomical correlates of happiness, sadness, and disgust. American Journal of Psychiatry 154: 926-33.

Lebovici S (1991) La théorie de l'attachement et la psychanalyse contemporaine. Psychiatrie de l'enfant 34: 309-39.

LeDoux J (1996) The Emotional Brain. The Mysterious Underpinning of Emotional Life. New York: Simon & Schuster.

Lichtenberg JD (1989) Psychoanalysis and Motivation. Hillsdale, NJ: Analytic Press.

Mahler M (1981) Agression in the service of separation-individuation. Case study of a mother–daughter relationship. Psychoanalytic Quarterly 50: 625-38.

Marrone M (1998) Attachment and Interaction. London: Jessica Kingsley.

McGaugh JL and Cahill L (1997) Interaction of neuromodulatory systems in modulating memory storage. Behavioural Brain Research 83: 31-8.

Morris JS, Öhman A and Dolan RJ (1998) Conscious and unconscious emotional learning in the human amygdala. Nature 393: 467-70.

Murray Parkes C, Stevenson-Hinde J and Marris P (1991) Attachment Across the Life Cycle. London: Routledge.

Ortiz Barón MJ and Yárnoz Yaben S (1993) Teoría del apego y relaciones afectivas. Bilbao: Servicio Editorial de la Universidad del País Vasco.

Pally R (1997) Memory: brain systems that link past, present and future. International Journal of Psycho-analysis 78: 1223-34.

Slavin MO and Kriegman D (1992) The Adaptive Design of the Human Psyche. Psychoanalysis, Evolutionary Biology, and the Therapeutic Process. New York: Guilford Press.

Sperling M and Berman W (1994) Attachment in Adults. Clinical and Developmental Perspectives. New York: Guilford Press.

Stern D (1985) The Interpersonal World of the Infant. A View from Psychoanalysis and Developmental Psychology. New York: Basic Books.

Volling BL and Notaro PC (1998) Adult attachment styles: relations with emotional well-being, marriage, and parenting. Family Relations 47: 355-67.

Winnicott DW (1971) Playing and Reality. London: Tavistock.

PART 3

ATTACHMENT, SEXUALITY AND THE BODY

CHAPTER 17

Attachment, trauma and the body

NICOLA DIAMOND

Introduction

In this chapter I intend to explore how trauma lives on as a bodily experience, well after the event. In doing so, I find in Freud and in further work developed out of attachment thinking a way of conceptualizing the significance of the body for understanding trauma. Inevitably, the body is located in an interpersonal field and is directly affected by relationships. Attachment theory has developed our understanding of both the nature of trauma and its aftermath. Trauma can be experienced as the result of a variety of factors, such as medical (a serious illness), atmospheric (a hurricane), mechanical (a motor accident), and so on. Here, I am referring to a more specific form of trauma that originates in attachment relationships. Trauma, in this context, can be conceptualized as an interpersonal phenomenon. It involves a fundamental disruption and disturbance in affiliative bonds.

It is now established that social stressors are more detrimental than non-social aversive stimuli (Sgoifo et al., 1999; Schore, 2001, p. 206). It has been recognized that when trauma – such as in the case of sexual abuse – is inflicted by another person, the individual is far more likely to experience profound emotional disturbance, even more so when the abuser is a member of the family or attachment figure (Main and Hesse, 1990).

Proposal of the chapter

In the realm of interpersonal disturbance and trauma, neglect as well as intrusive relating can be traumatizing in the context of development. In this chapter we shall briefly consider both types of trauma, but our main focus will be on sexual abuse and its impact on the developing person from a psychoanalytic attachment perspective.

One of the questions that will be asked in respect of the kind of trauma under investigation is: what is traumatic about trauma? The answer will be found in the fact that experience is traumatic when it is found to be overwhelming for the individual. The experience is traumatic when it continues well after the interpersonal event (or series of interpersonal encounters as in accumulative trauma) and cannot be assimilated and made into sense. We shall consider trauma as unprocessed affect derived from the other that lives on in unintegrated somatic states. Trauma brings about an affective alteration of psychobiological being, which then continues by being autostimulated, affecting thoughts, bodily-motor perception, memory, neurological and hormonal function, as well as other somatic states.

We shall explore the way that trauma brings about a fundamental disturbance in the bodily self and a sense of agency; the way the trauma lives on in a body and how the intrusion by the other leaves its mark in reoccurring bodily states. Bodily memories are experienced as unprocessed sensory fragments that repeatedly return to disrupt any sense of bodily and subjective cohesion.

We shall look to the way attachment theory reformulates psychoanalytic thinking and returns our emphasis back to the body. There will be two coterminous descriptions in the analysis: an exploration of the basis of psychobiological disturbance and a phenomenological description of experience. For although there are neurobiological processes simultaneous with every perceptual experience (they are one and the same process), the neurobiological descriptions are nevertheless unsatisfactory in themselves for they do not capture the quality of the experiential phenomena. That is why it is necessary to offer a phenomonological description of the experience of trauma as well.

Background: attachment and psychoanalysis

Early on in psychoanalysis, the conception of trauma had drawn on analogies from medical surgery and in this way had linked trauma to the body. In fact, the word 'trauma' derives from the Greek, meaning 'wound' or 'to pierce'. In the context of medicine and surgery, trauma refers either to an injury where the skin is broken due to an external violence or to an internal contusion, as in the case of closed head-brain trauma. In either case, trauma concerns the effects of such violation and malformation on the organism as a whole.

Freud (1920), in 'Beyond the pleasure principle', drew on the idea of a breach in the skin's protective barrier, as the organism becomes inundated by too many stimuli aggressing it from without, breaking through the surface of the body. Freud noted that the organism lacks a shield that would help filter the stimuli and reduce their intensity. In other words, the organism has not developed a tough emotional skin and is thus left exposed, open to attack. Moreover, in Freud's metapsychology, the ability to process and manage affective stimuli is linked with the ego. Trauma implies a fundamental disturbance in ego function. The ego is the agency that unifies and coheres psychological experience.

The idea of an organism encountering an over-stimulating environment, forming a breach in the protective barrier, became interpreted in Kleinian thought as a metaphor for the mind's processes. Needless to say, Kleinian readings of Freud have become dominant in the British context. In this setting, there is a certain reading of Bion's notion of the mind as a container applied to an understanding of trauma. Here, there is the idea that a person's ability to think implies that affects are contained in mental thoughts. In this context, trauma is understood as the loss of that capacity, as the failure of the mind to act as a protective shield, as the inability to process affective stimuli into meaningful thoughts. From a Kleinian perspective, such an understanding of trauma offers an explanation of trauma both in terms of the psychic effects of trauma, and the psychological vulnerability that leads certain individuals to be more easily traumatized than others. In other words, from this perspective, there are particular individuals who lack a capacity to process and thus symbolize affective states. Of course, as we shall see, this begs certain questions from an attachment perspective, such as how to explain differences in vulnerability and resilience.

There are a number of difficulties with the Kleinian model; psychic vulnerability is not sufficiently contextualized. The fact that certain individuals have a greater propensity to become traumatized should not be left inadequately examined. Second, there is an insufficient analysis of the precise nature of interpersonal trauma and its impact on development. Third, this model at its worst can leave us with the false idea that trauma exists inside a metapsychology of the mind. This would leave out of the account the impact trauma has on brain/body processes and the style of attachment disturbance that induced the trauma. In contrast, an attachment approach would provide a detailed exploration of the relationships that created the trauma and would not divorce the traumatized individual from this context.

In reference to the first difficulty, the case of a psychic vulnerability, John Bowlby (1969) would point out that the attachment relationship directly influences the child's capacity to cope with stress. Attachment theory explains why certain individuals have greater susceptibility to trauma than others. Insecure attachment in childhood (particularly when there have been cumulative traumatic events in the family) increase vulnerability to trauma in later life. More recently, some attachment researchers have argued that resiliency can be better explained as being the product of relational histories that have provided protection in the face of trauma, rather than being the result of some children having 'the right stuff' that makes them invulnerable to trauma. As Sroufe (1996) points out, resilience does not emerge out of nowhere. It always has to be viewed as the outcome of a developmental process relating to the quality of an attachment relationship that enables the child to make sense of what has happened to him/her. If a secure attachment figure is not available in the parents, there may be a relative, a teacher or a friend who is emotionally resourceful and enables the child to make a secure attachment and help him/her think, or maybe a person is met in later life. Sroufe places emphasis on the importance of self-esteem, a sense of self-worth that the child develops. What is recognized as important is the sensitive responsiveness and emotional understanding that the other provides which enables the child to develop a reflective capacity (Fonagy et al., 1995) and to perceive and understand its own feeling states and others. What Main (1991) describes as metacognitive functioning makes it possible to reflect on a difficult traumatic attachment history and make emotional sense out of it.

For Bowlby, psychological life could never be reified or in any way decontextualized. The focus for Bowlby, as I have suggested (Diamond, 1998, pp. 200–2), has been to consolidate the move away from a 'one person psychology' towards a 'multiperson psychology'. In Bowlby's view, the object of study for psychoanalysis was not the internal world as such but the link between the individual and the world of others. Although Bowlby did not talk about philosophy, his work involved a philosophical shift at the root of psychoanalysis. Attachment theory challenges a reified metapsychology of mind rooted in Descartes' dualistic split between mind/body and world. For Bowlby (1988, p. 142) the contrast between the internal and external, or as a biologist, the distinction between organism and environment, never made any sense.

From the biological point of view, it is increasingly recognized that there is a direct relationship between organism and environment. Contemporary attachment theory considers biology as part of an open system, as experience dependent. In other words, the development of biological regulatory functions and neural networks is fundamentally reliant on interaction with others. Therefore, I emphasize the way attachment theory brings back the body to psychoanalysis. There is no false abstraction of mind because trauma lives on as a brain–body experience. Furthermore, it shows the direct interdependent relation between the body and the interpersonal environment.

An attachment approach shows that Freud's idea in 'Beyond the pleasure principle' (1920) of the vesicle confronting a hostile environment is no longer to be read as a metaphor, but should be better understood as a description of an interpersonal encounter in which the aggressor is the other. Freud's (1923) famous phrase, 'the ego is first and foremost a bodily ego' is an important one and we need to retain its most general sense. Trauma occurs at the overlapping interface of body and the world of others. Freud (1920) referred to an encounter between the skin surface of the vesicle and overwhelming stimuli. He described what takes place, as the skin surface is directly exposed to contact with the world of others. We meet the world as embodied beings, precisely as a projection of a body surface into that world. The overwhelming stimulus is better understood as a perturbing affective exchange that brings about a breach in the child's stimulus barrier. The outcome is a breach in the child and adult's capacity to develop psychobiological modes of regulating and understanding feeling and body states. And as we shall explore later, the breach also refers to a fundamental disruption in the experience of bodily self and agency.

Trauma, abuse and the family

So far we have allowed for the fact that interpersonal trauma is a varied phenomenon. However, each form of abuse has its specificity. In the family there can be emotional abuse that may not take physical form, or there can be physical violence rather than sexual abuse, or there can be abuse that has all these aspects. In this chapter, we shall be focusing on the impact of sexual abuse in the context of exploring sibling relations within the family.

Juliet Mitchell (2000) argues for the importance of the sibling relationship, and reinstates its centrality. She argues that priority has always been given to the oedipal complex in psychoanalysis. Such an emphasis has focused attention away from other key relations, such as sibling relationships. For Mitchell the key theme in regard to sibling conflict is rivalry over exclusive love from the mother that comes with the inevitable displacement that occurs with the birth of another sibling. This feeling of rivalry gives rise to murderous destructive feelings directed at the favoured sibling. Attachment theory has potentially always been more open to a broader view of relationships in the family and the question of the relationship of siblings in the context of attachment has been recognized (see Brunori, 1996). But with few exceptions (Sroufe, Egeland and Carlson, 1999), to date little has been written on the subject. Of course when exploring the familial relationships, this can include relatives and friends or people known by the family who have played a role as an attachment figure and the intergenerational family history.

Attachment needs to be explored in the broader family context and dynamic. In disturbed families there is a complex system whereby abuse between siblings may be the expression of disturbance of attachment in the whole family. The clinical illustration that follows later will explore sexual abuse that takes place between two brothers.

Attachment, trauma and the neurosciences

The brain that processes emotional and interactive experiences is directly linked to bodily processes. The right hemisphere is associated with the development of emotional somatic and non-verbal interpersonal understanding and these are stored in procedural memory of the right brain. The right brain is directly linked to the brain stem and autonomic nervous system. Allan Schore (2001), explicitly inspired by attachment theory, has explored the negative impact of traumatic attachments on brain development. Trauma causes impairment in right brain functions (orbitofrontal dysfunction) and a predisposition to post-traumatic stress disorder. He highlights the fact that the 'disorganized/disorientated' early attachment pattern (normally associated with abuse and severe neglect) leads to serious deficit in the capacity to regulate feelings and bodily states. Alterations in brain–body processes are brought about in the context of the quality of the individual's attachment relationships, past and present.

Optimal attachment experiences stimulate the proliferation of neural networks. In contrast, negative affective states can inhibit the production of neural networks, or result in the case of early development in radical pruning that destroys neural cells and their connections. There is some evidence (Van der Kolk et al., 1989) that opioids are released with repeated negative experiences, which then encourages a form of addiction to heightened negative states. Rather than an avoidance of the distress, we see in traumatized persons the 'seeking out' of further traumatic situations (Mollon, 1996, p. 72)

Schore (2001) points out that in neuroscience there should no longer be an intra-brain focus. In his view, it is now possible to investigate inter-brain transactions. There is a direct emotional transmission between brains, particularly the right hemispheres. In optimal circumstances, this results in the co-regulation of psychobiological states. This, he points out, is the neurobiological basis for the phenomenon of intersubjectivity. However, in the case of gross misattunement there are disturbances in the development of the right brain and regulatory capacities. The importance of this description is that it accounts for the way interactions with another can profoundly affect psychobiological experience, directly influencing brain–body processes.

Children who have experienced abuse show EEG abnormalities in frontal temporal lobe and anterior brain region. Perry et al. (1995) identify a dual state of disassociation and hyperarousal in the abused child, affecting the sympathetic nervous system as well as the parasympathetic system. All these changes are accompanied by hormonal and neurochemical correlates, leading to what Schore (2001) calls 'hypermetabolic state of the brain'.

In summary, trauma, both at critical periods of growth and throughout development, can lead to detrimental effects on brain functioning. The emotional regulating limbic system as well as the hypothalamic-pituitary-adrenal and sympathetic nervous system can be permanently affected. As a result, in later life, high states of anxiety with accompanying disassociation can be triggered in everyday situations, and are no longer reserved for trauma-inducing environments. Van der Kolk et al. (1996) note the fundamental loss of the ability to regulate feelings and bodily states.

Bodily memory and trauma

Research shows that memory of trauma is stored in a way that significantly differs from storage of non-traumatic memories. Memories of traumatic events are experienced bodily. Perry (1994; Perry et al., 1995) and Van der Kolk et al. (1996) have looked at the relation between the laying down of neural networks and bodily memory in traumatized persons. Van der Kolk notes that when we are in stress-inducing situations, the secretion of endogenous stress hormones affects how the memories are laid down. They play a role in long-term activation and intensification of traumatic memories.

Sensitization is a particular state whereby the person who has been traumatized tends to experience a reactivation of feelings and memories linked with the original trauma in everyday situations, which in themselves may not be traumatic or warrant such a response. Traumatic memories live on as disassociated sensory and perceptual fragments and somatic effects. The experience remains unassimilated and unprocessed; sensory fragments are somatized with no linguistic components. Van der

Kolk et al. (1996) call such states 'speechless terror'. Experiments have shown that the linguistic left brain functions are literally knocked out of action, leaving the emotional right brain split off from language expression.

Perry (1994) and Bessel and Van der Kolk (1996) give an account of how the repetition reactivates the neural network, intensifying and solidifying it. Perry describes the way neurons are experience dependent: 'they are designed to change in response to external signals'. He explains that in the traumatized child in an abusive relationship there is a repetitive pattern of neural activation. The more frequently this pattern is activated, the more indelible the memory will be. This is because the activation of stress hormones increases the force of the memory trace (Bessel and Van der Kolk, 1996).

Yovell (2000) further describes the neurobiology of traumatic memories. He states that for traumatic memory there is a dual and paradoxical process. There is the intense 'flashbulb' memory and there is the partial memory or the experience of amnesia.

There are two forms of memory system: *declarative memory* (the conscious recollection of factual details mediated to a large extent by the hippocampus) and *procedural memory*, which is mediated in part by the amygdala (see Chapters 12 and 13 in this volume). The amygdala is mainly responsible for mediating emotional experience, particularly of fear and anxiety

In the flashbulb memory there is the vivid reliving of the event in the present, which can take the form of a somatic experience. This type of memory is of the same order as that which Van der Kolk is referring to. Yovell describes the physiological process underlying this kind of memory. As a reaction to the traumatic situation, stress hormones such as adrenaline and noradrenaline are produced and simultaneously activate both the hippocampus and amygdala, producing enhanced and intense remembering.

Traumatic induced amnesia is very common in cases of sexual abuse and other situations that induce disassociation. Le Doux (1998) describes the way very high levels of cortisol are produced, which increase the activity of the amygdala whilst the hippocampus is bypassed. Very high levels of cortisol decrease the activity of the hippocampus, to the point of bringing about a partial or total shutdown of hippocampal activity. In such cases there is thus either a hazy, patchy conscious recall or no conscious declarative memory at all.

Although the emotional memory will remain, the associated fear and anxiety wait to re-emerge at a later date. Repeated or ongoing psychogenic trauma injures the hippocampus, ultimately killing neurons. In cases of severe abuse, the altered states of memory function may well relate to damage of the hippocampus.

There is also evidence that the right emotional brain and the nature of procedural memory (storage of non-verbal interpersonal understanding of the self in relation with others) can be developmentally affected by adverse experiences. The extreme case of the Romanian orphans demonstrates a case of privation and impaired development of the emotional right brain. These orphans as babies were deprived of interaction with another human being. On a PET scan of a Romanian orphan aged about 8, there were areas of the frontal-occipital lobes that had negligible activity.

Traumatic experiences in the form of disturbed interactions with others produce negative affect and can impair the development of procedural memory and right brain functioning, and the capacity to develop emotional thinking, memory, a sense of self and an interpersonal understanding of relationships (Schore, 2001). Traumatic interactions within the first two years of life (particularly in critical periods) can have profound long-lasting effects on emotional brain development; however, adverse effects on development continue throughout childhood.

The bodily self/memory and the experience of agency

The affect that is communicated in an abusive interaction is likely to disturb fundamentally the child's experience of self and agency (see also Mollon, 1996). The sexual abuser is unable to perceive the child as separate from his own needs and imposes his desires on to the child. The child may experience an annihilation of his subjective bodily space. Abuse is much more than mere insensitivity and intrusion. It can be an entire negation of the child as a subject.

Trevarthen (1980, 1993), Hoffman (1994), Stern (1977, 1985) and others highlight the importance of parental respect for the child's sense of agency. This involves treating the child as a being with feelings and intentions. When there is a denial of the child's intentional space in the interaction there can be disturbances in subjective being.

Fonagy et al. (1995) identify how a child with an abusive parent can learn to cut off from the mental state of the abuser as a way of escaping the annihilating murderous and frightening state of mind of the other. They also (Fonagy and Target, 1997) quote research undertaken with abusive families that explore the way the interaction systematically undermines the child's right to be. The child in this context fails to be treated as a subject with intentionality, or as having a right to needs and feeling states. Children from these families have shown impoverished vocabulary for subjective experiences and they lack comprehension of feeling states.

Bowlby (1988) writes of the experience of 'knowing what you are not supposed to know and feeling what you are not supposed to feel'. He refers to disturbed forms of communications whereby parents weave a narrative that disguises the true course of events. This leads to cognitive disturbance in the child. While the child may adopt the parental view at the level of semantic memory, he may recall episodic events that contradict the narrative internalized from the parents. For Bowlby the child has recourse to his true feelings and knowledge of events, although they may be buried and not clearly articulated.

I should like further to suggest that when parents produce a dominant narrative that provides a language and mode of articulating an experience, it might be very difficult if not impossible for a child to find means of reflecting on what the truth is. The child's truth becomes confounded with the parent's truth, without any simple recourse to an autonomous experience. If there has been no dialogue with the parent or surrogate other, no co-thinking that enables the child to reflect on experience, the narrative of the parents articulates the experience of the child and the child is left bereft without the means to represent his own experience.

Again, if the child's rights to feelings and subjective states are not recognized and nurtured by a sensitive and responsive other, then the self will not be brought into representation. This is, of course, only more so when the abusive relation actively annihilates the subjective space of the child. The internal working model of self in relation to other will be altered, whereby the other dominates the self. There is a fundamental disturbance in agency whereby autobiographical memory that permits self-representation is impaired. Although autobiographical memory continues to develop, it becomes more incoherent with gaps and inconsistencies.

It was thought that autobiographical memory was rooted in declarative recall. It is now known that autobiographical memory is also a form of procedural knowledge (Schore, 2001). Given that procedural knowledge is linked to somatic, non-verbal understanding and that trauma can affect development of the right brain, it follows that disturbances in the sense of agency can be rooted developmentally with the experience of the somatic self.

Freud (1920) observed the compulsion to repeat painful experiences. He hypothesized this was done in order to master such experiences, to become an agent again who is in control. In the case of a traumatized person, the painful experiences are relived again and again as a situation that renders the subject helpless, with no control and no mastery. There is a painful repetition of being taken over, rather than being agent of the experience. The narrative of the traumatic memory dictates the subject, there is no active role in telling the sequences of events. Again we can see that there is a disturbance in the sense of agency. This compulsive reliving of the trauma is often experienced as a bodily manifestation. One of the striking features of these bodily symptoms is that they occur as a repeated sensory experience that takes the subject by surprise. The sensation feels like it is 'happening to me', that 'it (the sensation) is doing it to me', 'it takes me unawares'). The person does not feel their own agency in the somatic stimulation.

In this 'compulsion to repeat', the anxiety signal that Freud talks about no longer functions as a defence that prepares the person for flight or fright, but is faulty – triggered, often by an associative process, regardless of whether the situation is threatening or not. Rather than the traumatic memory feeling one's own, the trauma lives on as if an alien entity disrupting any sense of bodily integrity or personal identity. Freud (1920) in describing the experience that lives on after the event compares its action to a foreign body that continues as an agent long after its entry, taking the ego by surprise, attacking unexpectedly before the experience can be integrated into a coherent perception.

The trauma as a bodily memory exists as an alien entity disrupting any sense of agency. Laplanche (1985) describes how the alien entity lives on, likening it to a spine living under the skin. In the interpersonal language of Ferenczi (see Stanton, 1990) or Laplanche (1989), we could say that unassimilated somatic experience that cannot be processed lives on as intrusive messages from the other. In the language of psychobiology we should say that there is a state of affective and somatic dysregulation (Schore, 1994).

Freud in his paper on the uncanny (1925) refers to the state of unheimlich – not being at home with oneself, the sense of disorientation, estrangement, and depersonalization as an experience of the most unfamiliar in the most familiar. Freud observes that unheimlich/heimlich are not in fact opposite states but exist on a continuum. What will be suggested is that the experience of the body in trauma as both one's own and simultaneously alien can be likened to an extreme state of unheimlich.

Descriptions of brain–body processes provide us with the neurobiological basis for experience. As noted, these descriptions alone do not capture the quality of the perceptual experience itself, which is why we also require phenomenology. I shall thus also explore the phenomenological nature of the bodily perception in the following clinical illustration.

A clinical illustration

The case of sexual abuse we are to explore took place between two brothers, Martin and Sam. Martin, seven years older than his brother, was the abuser. He began to abuse Sam when Sam was 6.

What happens between siblings has to be viewed in the family context. In this case the failure of boundaries and intrusion in the family reflects a fundamental disturbance in its dynamics and in parental care.

The case illustrates the way trauma lived on in the body of Sam and how the intrusion from the other threatens his sense of bodily and subjective integrity. The way the invasion by the other lives on in reoccurring bodily states, bodily memories and perceptions is experienced as unintegrated. Sam suffered from a fundamental disturbance of bodily being. He did not feel his body and his memories as his own. He experienced them as alien to the self. We shall see how Sam felt that he had no control over his feelings and body sensations, and how the memory of the abuse took somatic form and was experienced as an alien entity that does things to him against his will. The sensory fragments were relived as an invasion, threatening bodily fragmentation.

Sam was described as 'tied to his mother's apron strings', as he refused to go to school and leave his mum. Mother told us how she would be worried to death when the boys left the house, especially with little Sam. Mother explained that she had had three sons. There was one before Sam. This was the family secret, which the parents had kept from the children. The second child had died because the umbilical chord was wrapped around his neck. The parents normalized the abuse and protected Martin. They said that 'Martin had been fooling around and had gone too far'. Being close in this family meant being tied together without boundaries. What was noticeable is the way the parents and grandparents regularly confused the boys' names, suggesting an intergenerational difficulty with self/other differentiation.

Sam had been born to assuage his mother's loss of a baby. Anxious attachment and unresolved bereavement in the family resulted in clinging relationships, which blurred boundaries. Strangulation and adhesive attachment characterized the family's style of relating.

The lack of boundaries and differentiation between family members influenced Martin's course of development. He put into action a perverse sexualized version of boundary confusion with his abusive behaviour. Sam brought his experience of enmeshment with his mother into the abusive encounter with his brother, making him susceptible to fusion with the other.

Sam was my patient. When he first arrived on the unit where I worked as a psychotherapist he was a withdrawn 12-year-old who would sit huddled up with his face buried. No one knew what the problem was. Prior to his admission to our unit, Sam had a medical assessment on account of his physical symptoms. There had been a brain scan to check for a tumour and an investigation into middle ear problems. All proved negative. He had been suffering, since age 11, from severe dizzy spells that would result in a loss of balance and a tendency to topple over. The symptom of dizziness almost brought about a loss of consciousness, leading him to collapse. This could be viewed as a form of temporary disassociation with a definite somatic manifestation, a state of cutting off from his surroundings and from himself by losing consciousness and awareness.

When I met with him, he began to complain of feeling removed from things, of feeling strange. He was very agitated, was sweating and had palpitations. He was not at all at ease in himself. As we have mentioned in the review of the attachment-informed neurobiological findings, extreme states of agitation and hyperarousal can be accompanied by states of hypoarousal (the latter leading to a state of withdrawal and disconnection). In Perry's account, the alterations in autonomic nervous system functioning are described as a bodily reaction to the abusive situation. What we are observing was a highly agitated state intertwined with a disconnected disassociated experience. This state continued to exist in the aftermath of the abuse, many years later. Sam felt estranged from himself and his environment.

After beginning therapy, Sam began to articulate his experience into some sense, describing the 'dizzy spells' as a 'fuzzy interference that would stop him thinking'. However, he could not remember anything about the abuse. He did not even know that there was an abuse. There was no conscious recall, no declarative memory to help describe any event. As Yovell (2000) points out, the hippocampus responsible for conscious memory is not where traumatic memory is stored. Traumatic memory is registered in the amygdala, where it remains unconscious. The subject can feel anxiety and fear, as in the case of Sam, but without any knowledge of what these affects relate to. The memory can remain unconscious until reawakened. When I met Sam, he was in a state of amnesia in respect to the trauma.

Some months after Sam started therapy, he watched a programme on AIDS and experienced a flashback: his brother 'buggering him'. The programme on AIDS had referred to homosexuality. Sam had a thought about what homosexual men might do together. He then came to the associated flashback. The content of the television programme acted as a trigger. In this context he made a preconscious association between the meaning of the programme and his underlying memories, which he could not yet consciously recall. In trying to integrate neurobiology with attachment theory, the meaning of the memory and the neurobiological correlates have to be considered as different expressions of the same process. Meaning is held in the patterning of neural relations.

As he was able to remember the episodes of abuse, the whole story began to unfold. Martin was given the role of surrogate parent, and was asked to 'baby-sit' whilst the parents went out. The abuse would then take place. Sam looked up to Martin as a surrogate caretaker and took him as a model to emulate. All this was shattered by the experience of Martin as the abuser. Sam's mother and father had failed him. They had not protected him and had failed to pick up the signs.

Anal intercourse and fellatio would take place repeatedly. The abuse was more sinister since the brother sometimes invited some of his 'friends' to join in. He got Sam to perform fellatio on him in front of them and they were allowed to touch Sam. Therefore, Martin's enactments acquired a quality of *mise en scène*, an articulated structure. Sam as a protagonist in these humiliating and exhibitionist rituals entered into his brother's world and had to contend with the further elaboration of his brother's practices. I stress this because the narration of an abusive relationship provides a language that construes experience, gives it specific meanings and positions the protagonists in particular ways.

Abuse is always about power, not only the abuser's power to dominate sexually and physically, but also the power to dictate the way reality is perceived. Abuse that occurs to a younger child, before the young child has had the opportunity to develop an articulated and active relation to his own sexual and bodily experiences, intrudes by creating a dominant discourse over the abused child's sexuality and perception of self.

As Bowlby has indicated throughout his writings, the abuse does not take place in a vacuum. It takes place in the context of a dysfunctional family, where the system of communications does not allow the child to own and legitimize his own feelings and knowledge of what is going on in the interaction. As I have further emphasized, the child's cognitive states are then organized in terms of the abuser's fantasies and perceptions. Although Martin was not the primary caretaker, he intervened fundamentally on Sam's emotional, sexual and bodily experience and development.

Sam described the way these awful memories emerged suddenly and unexpectedly. He would then feel as if he was going to fall apart and explode into pieces. The memories could not be assimilated and threatened to fragment his sense of bodily integrity. He felt that, when he was sitting in a room with other people, they could get inside him and invade him, breaking in this way any sense of a body boundary.

An altered experience of the skin boundary is common in adolescents who have been abused. There is, as we have noted, the experience of the porous skin, which too readily lets others in and lets the self in a likewise fashion seep out. Sexually abused children commonly have an altered experience of touch, in which there is a failure to differentiate between an affectionate touch and a sexual one. Affection and sexuality become confounded, 'a confusion of tongues' as Ferenczi would put it. Didier Anzieu (1989) and Paul Federn (1952) have explored the way there can be emotionally induced alterations in the skin experience and perception. What is interesting for us here is the way the perception is an embodied skin experience. The confounded boundary between self and other is experienced as sensory phenomena at the skin surface.

Didier Anzieu (1989) talks of a collapse of a distinction of self and other, using the metaphor of a Möbius strip, twisting on itself, so that the inside becomes the same as the outside and vice versa. He refers to this to describe a borderline experience of the skin envelope. In cases of abuse, the differentiation between my skin and the other's skin has also broken down or failed to develop in skin experience. The other has invaded skin barriers and orifices physically, sexually and emotionally; the abused cannot feel his own skin, feel his own feelings, or think his own thoughts. The abuser has supplanted and annihilated Sam's subjective space and this is re-enacted again and again in the symptom. The protective 'stimulus barrier' in these instances has been truly breached by the other.

Perhaps most significantly, Sam experienced bodily memories as sensations that would simply happen to him, taking him unaware, overwhelming in their effect, experienced as occurring in the now, of the bodily present. We could say these were somatic 'flashbulb' bodily memories in the form of sensory-somatic experiences that could not be assimilated. At times he had sensations in his mouth and anus, which he could not define and understand. He described the sensation in his anus as disconcerting: sad, pleasurable and painful, all at the same time. The pain was like a knife cutting him open, down the middle. Often, when Sam was in a passive position or immobile, for instance when he was sitting, he would suffer a recurrence of the intense sensations in his anus. The sensations did not feel his own, but alien. He also felt as if there was someone taking him over. Sam had no means of regulating these somatic and feeling states. This could also be interpreted in terms of his sense of agency being fundamentally disturbed.

It is as if his active space had been taken over by Martin's sexuality. For Martin imposed his formed sexuality on Sam's very malleable identity. Martin had directed the course of Sam's development before Sam had managed to forge a space to articulate his separateness, interfering in the developmental pathway.

In a more sinister way we could say the other, the abuser, inhabited Sam's body and threatened to take it over. Sam experienced his body, his memories and his disturbing thoughts as alien entities fundamentally disrupting his bodily integrity. The memories lived as somatic states in the present, they happened to him and did not feel his own. In those moments it was as if the other was in his body doing it to him again. The skin could not function as a protective barrier, but felt permeated by the other. In the working model, the other is over-represented and there is an impoverished self-representation.

We could say that the other supplants the bodily self, or even takes possession of it. A state of extreme unheimlich in which Sam does not feel at home in his body, which feels alien and even haunted, controlled, by the other. The idea of a human that is in fact a doll, that on every count appears human but is a mere puppet under another's control, is one kind of experience identified in the exploration of unheimlich. The most familiar has become simultaneously the most unfamiliar, and peculiar.

Sam often looked in the mirror and saw his brother's face, not his own. Freud (1925) described unheimlich as linked to the experience of the double. He refers to his own experience:

> I was sitting alone in my wagon-lit compartment when a more than usually violent jolt of the train swung back the door of the adjoining washing cabinet, and an elderly man in a dressing gown and a traveling cap came in. I assumed ... he had taken the wrong direction and come into my compartment by mistake ... Jumping up with the intention of putting him right, I at once realized to my dismay that the intruder was nothing but my own reflection in the looking glass (p. 248).

The experience involves mistaking oneself as other in Freud's case and in Sam's circumstances it is seeing the other, the abusive brother, as himself. In both situations the experience of oneself as other has come about. There is a fundamental disruption of the sense of familiarity with oneself, as that self now involves an irreducible alterity, the other is at the heart of a sense of ownness. In Sam's perception, when he looked in the mirror, it was much more disturbing: he had become the abuser.

Freud commented on what makes the experience uncanny. One contributory factor is the 'harking back to particular phases in the evolution of the self ... a regression to a time when the ego had not yet marked itself off sharply from the external world and other people' (1925, p. 236). Although contemporary developmental findings question views like Mahler's that propose an original state of undifferentiation of self and other and instead suggest a state of differentiation from birth, it is nevertheless the case that the specific and subtle discriminations between self and other emerge developmentally and are dependent on the quality of relationship provided by the caretaker. Certainly in Sam's experience the confusion of himself with the abuser related to a developmental disturbance, whereby his own agency, sexuality and sense of identity were not yet sufficiently forged and were developmentally directed by the abusive relationship.

In the formation of our body-self image, there is some form of self–other confusion. For all of us, the image of the bodily self is derived from the way others see us and the mirror image is situated outside us.

When the other consumes any subjective space to be, when the 'between being a subject and an object for another' is completely tipped in the direction of becoming the object, then there is a fundamental perturbation of a sense of bodily self. For Sam it was not a matter of feeling as if he was his brother. There was no space for the 'as if' or for reflection. In his inner experience, Sam almost literally became his brother. There was an eclipse of the self as 'I'. The 'I' was conflated with the 'you' (the other, the object). Because he was treated as an object, he experienced himself as an object.

Sam felt he was really going mad when he was compelled to re-enact the abusive acts in relation to inanimate objects. In his words, he 'wanted to do it to objects', to 'fuck walls and bottles'. There was no discrimination between self, object and things. At these times we could say he was on the borders of the human, where all boundaries seem to have collapsed. He became an object pursuing objects. We could see this as the height of disintegration in the destruction of subjectivity. The experience of unheimlich can extend into the realms of ambiguity, as to whether something is animate, inanimate, alive or dead, human or not human, object or machine. What I am suggesting is something much more than identification with the aggressor. In these moments the very experience of having a sense of subjectivity and of a body as something 'belonging to me' was no longer in existence.

The feeling of unheimlich, of not being at home in oneself, also relates to depersonalization. Depersonalization is a dissociative state, the function of which is to split off parts of oneself when one feels the victim of interpersonal trauma. It is as if the individual said, 'It is intolerable to be the subject of abuse', all that can be done is to take any conscious awareness of the self outside the realm of direct experience.

Disorganized attachment and susceptibility to trauma and dissociation

Sam had been highly susceptible to his brother's intrusions, which had resulted in a fundamental disturbance in the experience of the embodied self. Sam's vulnerability had already been put into place by the 'clingy' enmeshed relationship with his mother. Mother could not let her miracle baby Sam 'go', for he was the compensatory child to assuage her unresolved loss for her former baby strangulated by the umbilical chord at birth. She metaphorically strangulates Sam, unconsciously denying a separation from him. Sam expressed all this by being 'tied to mother's apron strings' – playing truant from school rather than leaving his mother's side during the pre-latency years. Mother had been all too obliging in keeping her son at home.

Liotti (1995) points out how 'unresolved parental mourning' (p. 346) has been associated with dissociative disturbances in children (see Chapter 15 by Liotti and Intreccialagli on the relationship between disorganized attachment and trauma and Chapter 11 by Juri and Marrone on the relationship between trauma and loss). It is clear that unresolved mourning that could not be thought about lay at the root of Sam's birth and positioned him in a certain way in relation to his mother's desire. Sam developed dissociative symptoms expressed in dizzy spells that stopped him thinking and states of ego fragmentation that led to feelings of falling apart, exploding, being invaded, seeing himself as his brother and in the acting out of abusive acts with objects in the room.

The findings by Main and her collaborators, replicated also by Ainsworth and Eichberg (1991), note that: 'unresolved parental mourning linked to a major loss through death may be considered a significant risk factor for the development of disorganized attachment in the child' (Liotti, 1995, p. 346). In clinical reality the categories of attachment are not found in pure form; they overlap, or aspects of an attachment category may be present in a combined form with other attachment styles. In reality, attachment categories are more useful for the researcher than for the clinician. For the clinician, attachment styles can be viewed as based on the organization of defence mechanisms and attachment strategies of any given individual. From this perspective, we could say that there were features of a disorganized/disorientated attachment both in Sam's disturbed dissociative and fragmented states and in the oscillation between enmeshed/ intrusive parenting on the one hand and neglect on the other. Intrusiveness characterized familial relations and a lack of separation between Sam and Mum, whilst on the other hand, the parents frequently left the brothers alone and thus allowed the repeated abuse to take place.

Final words

My intention is to highlight the way trauma and, more specifically, sexual abuse, impinge on the experience of the body. I am trying to explain that this impingement shows on two interrelated levels. One is the neuropsychological level. The other is the level of the subjective experience of oneself with a body. I try to demonstrate that psychoanalysis, attachment theory and recent developments in the neurosciences can together help us understand such complex phenomena.

Sexual abuse impacts on the body, on the psychobiological regulation of feeling states and on the neuropsychology of memory storage. It also creates a fundamental disturbance in the sense of agency and identity. The experience of abuse acts as an implanted foreign body, which continues to exist long after its entry. Trauma lives on well after the event or series of experiences, as a wound re-inscribing itself again and again, which is overwhelming in its negative effects. Trauma cannot be assimilated; it resists being tamed into sense. Trauma lives on in unintegrated somatic-sensory states and memories.

References to the neurophysiological components of the damage that a traumatized person experiences may seem to be mechanistic and reductionistic. This would be a misunderstanding of the neurobiology of brain–body processes, These processes are fundamentally informed by interpersonal interactions. In this context, the quality of the interchange and the affective communication influence bodily processes and brain development. We are looking at the relation of affect and meaning in the traumatizing relationship to the emotional and somatic experiences of the traumatized individual.

In optimal circumstances, memory involves an active and constructive process. Remembering involves a creative reworking through of past experiences. Instead, traumatic memory exists in the form of disassociated sensory-perceptual fragments and bodily effects, which are not spontaneously available for self-exploratory and reflective processes. The experience remains unassimilated and unprocessed, as somatized with no linguistic components. As such, a true speechless terror becomes dominant.

References

Ainsworth MDS and Eichberg CG (1991) Effects on infant–mother attachment of mother's experience related to loss of attachment figure. In: CM Parkes, J Stevenson-Hinde and P Marris (eds) Attachment across the Life Cycle. New York: Routledge, pp. 160–83.

Ainsworth MDS, Blehar M, Waters E and Wall S (1978) Patterns of Attachment. Hillsdale, NJ: Erlbaum.

Anzieu D (1989) The Skin Envelope. London: Yale University Press.

Bessel and Van der Kolk B (1996) In: B Van der Kolk, A Mcfarlane and L Weisaeth, Traumatic Stress. The Effects of Overwhelming Experience on Mind, Body and Society. New York: Guilford Press.

Bowlby J (1969) Attachment and Loss, vol. 1: Attachment. New York: Basic Books.
Bowlby J (1988) A Secure Base. London: Routledge.
Brunori L (1996) Gruppo di fratelli, di gruppo. Rome: Borla.
Diamond N (1998) On Bowlby's legacy: Further explorations. In: M Marrone, Attachment and Interaction. London: Jessica Kingsley.
Diamond N (2001) Towards an interpersonal understanding of bodily experience. Psychodynamic Counseling 7.1, February.
Federn P (1952) Ego Psychology and the Psychosis. New York: Basic Books.
Fonagy P and Target M (1997) Attachment and reflective function: their role in self-organization. Development and Psychopathology 9: 679–700.
Fonagy P, Steele M, Steele H, Leigh T, Kennedy R, Matton G, Target M et al. (1995) Attachment, The reflective self, and borderline states: The predictive specificity of the Adult Attachment Interview and pathological emotional development. In: S Goldberg, R Muir and J Kerr (eds) Attachment Theory Social, Developmental and Clinical Perspectives. Hillsdale, NJ: Analytic Press.
Freud S (1919) The Uncanny. Standard Edition 17: 217–53. London: Hogarth Press.
Freud S (1920) Beyond the pleasure principle. Standard Edition 18: 1–65. London: Hogarth Press.
Freud S (1923) The ego and the id. Standard Edition 18: 1–59. London: Hogarth Press.
Garland C (1998) Understanding Trauma. London: Duckworth.
Hoffman M (1994) Le rôle de l'initiative dans le développement emotionnel précoce. Psychiatrie de L'enfant 37(1): 179–213.
Laplanche J (1985) Life and Death in Psychoanalysis. Baltimore: Johns Hopkins University Press.
Laplanche J (1989) New Foundations for Psychoanalysis, D Macey, trans. Oxford: Blackwell.
Le Doux J (1998) The Emotional Brain. London: Weidenfeld & Nicolson.
Liotti G (1995) Disorganized/Disorientated attachment in the psychotherapy of the dissociative disorders. In: S Goldberg, R Muir and J Kerr (eds) Attachment Theory: Social, Developmental and Clinical Perspectives. Hillsdale, NJ: Analytic Press.
Main M (1991) Metacognitive knowledge, metacognitive monitoring, and singular (coherent) versus multiple (incoherent) model of attachment: findings and directions for future research. In: CM Parkes, J Stevenson-Hinde and P Marris (eds) Attachment Across the Life Cycle. London: Routledge.
Main M and Hesse E (1990) Parents' Unresolved traumatic experiences are related to infant disorganized attachment status: is frightened and/or frightening parental behaviour the linking mechanism? In: M Greenberg, D Cicchetti and EM Cummings (eds) Attachment in the Preschool Years. Chicago: University of Chicago Press.
Mitchell J (2000) Mad Men and Medusas. London: Allen Lane/The Penguin Press.
Mollon P (1996) Multiple Selves, Multiple Voices. Working with Trauma, Violation and Dissociation. Chichester: Wiley.

Mollon P (1998) Remembering Trauma. A Psychotherapist's Guide to Memory and Illusion. Chichester: Wiley.

Perry BD (1994) Neurobiological sequelae of childhood trauma: PTSD in children. In: MM Murburg (ed.) Catecholamine Function in Post Traumatic Stress Disorder. Washington, DC: American Psychiatric Press, pp. 233–55.

Perry BD, Pollard RA, Blakley TL, Baker WL and Vigilante D (1995) Childhood trauma, the neurobiology of adaptation, and 'use-dependent' development of the brain: how 'states' become 'traits'. Infant Mental Health Journal 16: 271–89.

Schore AN (1994) Affect Regulation and the Origin of the Self. Mahwah, NJ: Erlbaum.

Schore A (2001) The effects of relational trauma on right brain development. Infant Mental Health Journal 22: 201–19.

Schore AN (2002) Affect Regulation and the Repair of the Self. New York: Norton.

Sgoifo A, Koolhaas J, De Boer S, Musso E, Stilli D, Buwalda B and Meerlo P (1999) Social stress, autonomic neural activation, and cardiac activity in rats. Neuroscience and Biobehavioral Reviews 23: 915–23.

Sroufe LA (1996) Emotional Development. Cambridge: Cambridge University Press.

Sroufe LA, Egeland B and Carlson EA (1999) One social world: the integrated development of parent–child and peer relations. In: WA Collins and B Laursen (eds) Relationships as Developmental Contexts. Minnesota Symposia on Child Psychology, vol. 30. Mahwah, NJ: Lawrence Erlbaum, pp. 241–62.

Stanton M (1990) Sandor Ferenczi: Reconsidering Active Intervention. London: Free Association Books.

Stanton M (1993) Psychic contusion: Remarks on Ferenczi and trauma. British Journal of Psychotherapy, summer. London: Artisan Press.

Stern D (1977) The First Relationship. Cambridge: Cambridge University Press.

Stern D (1985) The Interpersonal World of the Infant. New York: Basic Books.

Trevarthen C (1980) The foundations of intersubjectivity: development of interpersonal and cooperative understanding in infants. In: D Olson (ed.) The Social Foundations of Language and Thought: Essays in Honor of J.S. Bruner. New York: Norton, pp. 316–42.

Trevarthen C (1993) The self born in intersubjectivity: an infant communicating. In: U Neisser (ed.) The Perceived Self. New York: Cambridge University Press, pp. 121–73.

Van der Kolk BA, Greenberg MS, Orr SP and Pitman RK (1989). Endogenous opioids, stress induced analgesia, and posttraumatic stress disorder. Psychopharmacology Bulletin 25: 417–20.

Van der Kolk B, Mcfarlane A and Weisaeth L (1996) Traumatic Stress. The Effects of Overwhelming Experience on Mind, Body and Society. New York: Guilford Press.

Yovell Y (2000) From hysteria to post traumatic stress disorder; psychoanalysis and the neurobiology of traumatic memories. Journal of Neuropsychoanalysis 171–83.

CHAPTER 18

Sexual disorder and attachment: a developmental systems approach

MARY GALES SHANE, MORTON SHANE AND ESTELLE SHANE

In this chapter we shall describe how our developmental systems model integrates selected aspects of attachment theory and of self psychology. It is our hope that this integration will facilitate further investigation and understanding of complex clinical problems, including dissociative disorder, obsessive compulsive disorder, addiction, depression, anxiety and sexual disorder. We shall first present our model and then present a specific instance of this integrative approach to one complex clinical problem, that of sexual disorder.

Common values between attachment theory and self psychology

In our approach, the analytic interchange is categorized on specific values that have been integrated, altered and expanded from the various self psychologies and from attachment theory. By values we mean what one believes is good for human beings. All analysts have values that inform their preferred clinical theory. In fact, change in clinical theory can be understood as a change, subtle or profound, in the values analysts hold as they listen to patients and consider their own responses. Arguably, then, the widely recognized paradigm shift in our field is a reflection of a change in values regarding how analysis cures. Although we recognize that the concept of values can be defined broadly and neutrally to include both positive and negative, we are choosing to define values along the lines of Gerald Edelman's concept where values originate in built-in biases of perception, action and organization that have evolutionary survival value. These, by their nature, are positive in their functioning (Edelman, 1992).

We turn first to a consideration of how values inherent in attachment theory (e.g. Bowlby, 1988; Ainsworth, 1985) are reflected in the various self psychologies. Attachment theory delineates patterns of connection between self and other that first form in the context of the real-life, lived experience of the developing infant and child in relationship with the caregiver. Such attachment patterns are postulated to endure throughout life unless extraordinary life experiences interfere, a postulate supported by robust research. A secure attachment relationship and three distinct varieties of insecure attachment relationships are identified and described through the application of research methods that span over half a century. As applied to the therapeutic situation, the analyst using an attachment perspective is encouraged to view the patient–analyst relationship as a form of attachment relationship, attending to the patient in accordance with specific values inherent in that theory. These values include the importance of fostering a secure base, emphasizing safety, security and exploration.

Using this same attachment lens, Kohut's (1977; 1984) self psychology can be appreciated as having made significant contributions to an understanding of attachment needs in the normal development of the self by identifying three universally experienced attachment requirements – mirroring, idealizing, and alter ego – which, when unmet in childhood, become realized as archaic selfobject transferences in the analytic situation. Mirroring is the self's experience of being admired by the caregiver. Idealizing is looking up to the caregiver as one who can protect and offer ideals and standards to which to aspire. An alterego experience is feeling a closeness and kinship to the other, experienced as someone human like oneself. These are emotional self-regulating functions in which parents take a leading role in development. These selfobject needs contribute significantly to the establishment and maintenance of the attachment relationship. Other self psychologists, notably Lichtenberg, (1989), Stolorow et al. (1987) and Wolf (1988), have added additional selfobject manifestations based on other developmental strivings believed to be present in the clinical situation, which one could see as patterns of attachment. In addition, using intersubjectivity's concept of dimensions of transference, Brandchaft (1994) identifies a pattern he terms pathological accommodation that can be seen, using an attachment perspective, as a description of insecure attachment. An important, shifting emphasis brought to psychoanalysis from both attachment theory and self psychology, then, is the significance of real-life, lived experience in laying down enduring patterns of self- and self-with-other relatedness. This is not to dismiss the role of fantasy, but instead to place fantasy in the context of actual happenings and their influence in self-development.

We identify another significant contribution of attachment theory discernible in, and compatible with, self psychology. In self psychology, autonomy and independence are not conceptualized as developmental goals or values, in and of themselves. Rather, it is a secure interdependence that is the goal and value, an interdependence occurring in the context of mature selfobject relatedness. This is similar to the attachment pioneer Mary Ainsworth's (1985) concept of exploration from a secure base. In both theories, true, authentic independence, as contrasted with pseudo-, defensive independence, is a function of and arises only in the context of secure and ongoing connection with others and such relational needs are conceptualized as life-long.

Another shared set of values discernible in both attachment theory and self psychology concerns human motivational systems. Bowlby identified five motivational systems, including attachment, exploration, sexuality, parenting, and a physiological regulation system focused on the motive of eating. Lichtenberg, like Bowlby, identified five motivational systems, including attachment/affiliation, exploration/assertion, physiological regulation, sensuality/sexuality, and aversion. Both Bowlby and Lichtenberg focus on the importance of motivational systems in the clinical setting, and on the value of meeting these motivational needs in the developing individual.

The importance of real-life events in normal and pathological development

We turn now to a consideration of the values common to attachment theory and self psychology, which we have incorporated in our own model. First, we acknowledge the importance of real-life, lived experience, and the concomitant significance of unmet needs and other traumas occurring in development, which are then laid down and expressed in particular relational patterns of insecure attachment, or of archaic self–selfobject relatedness. Our understanding of pathology recognizes a broad definition of trauma as an etiological factor. As this concerns attachment, we are in agreement with Sroufe (1996) who sees the A (Avoidant) and C (Anxious/Ambivalent) insecure attachments as possible risk factors for later pathology. The D (Disorganized/Disoriented) group is correlated with the more blatant and severe traumas, which have clearly correlated with later pathology (Sroufe, 1996). This understanding of pathology as deriving from trauma is also in contrast to the more mainstream psychoanalytic approach of placing strong emphasis on the pathogenic effect of the patient's fantasies.

To illustrate, a patient came into a second analysis with persistent feelings of depression, lack of self-worth, and a chronic sense of obligation to others. The lifelong pattern of obligation to others was enacted through his continuing to take care of and indeed be preoccupied with their needs, at his own expense. This patient's brother had died prior to the patient's birth. His first analyst, who had placed value on the central etiological significance of fantasy in creating pathology, had developed a narrative, apparently essentially useless to this patient, in which the patient had as a child the pathogenic belief that he had killed his brother in order to be born, and that this attendant guilt had caused the patient's lifelong depression. The patient experienced this narrative as placing the source of difficulty solely within himself, a confusing construction given his subjective view of life within his family, but one that confirmed his sense that he was, somehow, to blame. In contrast, in the second analysis, a narrative was constructed in which value was placed on the patient's subjective experience of being of little value unless he served the needs of others. The narrative that evolved was of the patient having been treated by his mother as a replacement for her dead child, with his own purpose being to soothe and console her in her bereavement. His current depression was understood as stemming in no small part from the sacrifice of his importance as a person in his own right, with a hypertrophied sense of obligation to his family.

In summary, then, an important value for us is to attend to and acknowledge the reality of the patient's lived experience, as well as attempting to understand the meanings inherent in the patient's fantasized elaborations of that experience. We believe such an approach enhances the secure base phenomenon so central in treatment, which, in turn, facilitates the development of a capacity for self-reflective awareness. The narrative constructed in the second analysis is a better narrative in our view than that constructed in the first. It more fully and more accurately reflects the patient's lived experience, encompassing his subjective view of himself and his self-sacrificing actions vis-à-vis others. The achievement of this more comprehensive narrative, reflecting as it did both the internal and the external events of the patient's life as he had experienced it, correlated clinically with the patient's increased self-consolidation and increased capacities for secure relatedness, primary goals of both development and treatment in our model.

Returning now to values in our model, we apply in the clinical situation a specific model of normal development, with analysis conceptualized as a developmental experience dependent on the relationship between the analyst and the patient. We recognize the motivational systems described by both Bowlby and Lichtenberg as basic to development, with the exception of the motive of aversion. Here we are in agreement with Bowlby, who does not elevate aversion to a motivational system but sees aversion as reactive rather than primary. In addition, we believe that not all activities of the self are motivated. Some activity, the brain's organizing activity, for example, just *is*, a given of the self. Thus, clinically, motivational systems and self-development are intertwined. Therapeutic goals will encompass secure attachment and consolidation of selfhood with the self's capacities for self-regulation, mutual regulation, secure interactions with others, self-reflective awareness, and the ability to tell a coherent life narrative. Inconsistency or incoherence in the telling of a narrative has been correlated by attachment researchers with insecure attachment experience in development, this important research being validated by predictive and postdictive studies with impressive statistical significance (van IJzendoorn, 1995). Not all narratives are equal, then, or equally correlated with optimal outcome. As we illustrated above, this is an important matter in therapy: some narratives are correlated with consolidated selfhood and some are not. In addition, the distinction to be made between what really happened to the patient in the past, and what the patient defensively creates in fantasy out of what really happened, is often of compelling significance to both patient and therapist in their efforts to co-create the patient's life story. This is especially true in cases where the patient may have been abused, because experiences of abuse impair the capacity to make distinctions between what was done and what was imagined, but we believe it is always of great import. That is, it is obviously important for the patient who as a child has been sexually abused by her father, and who has learned to dissociate that experience but is invaded as an adult by disabling fugue states or flashback experiences, to have a therapist who will acknowledge the lived reality of that abuse, to the extent that it can be known, as well as exploring with the patient the fantasized elaborations of that experience. But it may be less obvious when a patient has not been a victim of such sexual or physical abuse and does not dissociate.

In terms of our model of normal development, then, we see attachment theory as helping us to understand what facilitates such an achievement. First, as we have said, the relationship in itself is the central vehicle for change. Second, the analyst's reflection upon and response to the patient's attachment needs are *both* essential. That is, the role of the analyst may expand beyond understanding and explaining to include interactions and actions, both verbal and nonverbal, that go beyond interpretation in order to facilitate the development goals addressed above.

We regard as central to development, then, the meeting of attachment needs. When such needs are not met, other motives may be recruited silently by it, or may not manifest at all. For example, exploration may become either truncated or exaggerated, presenting as obsessional, phobic, or counterphobic behavior, in the service of compensating for unmet attachment needs. As another example, eating may become an addictive pattern. And, especially important to the topic of this chapter, sexual behavior may become co-opted by attachment needs, and may be expressed as sexualized activity, sexual addiction, or as behavior that only appears to be sexual, but is not really sexual at all.

We have found Bowlby's parenting motivational system to be an especially useful and not adequately appreciated motivational system in the conceptualization of both theoretical and clinical concepts and guidelines for work with patients (see Chapter 1 by Marrone and Cortina for further discussion of the need for multimotivational systems models in psychoanalysis). We see the value of parenting as a distinct motivational system. Parenting can be metaphorically extended to comprehend the non-defensive, altruistic pleasure inherent in the model of successful caregiving, expressed, from time to time, in friendship, mentorship, marriage, collegial relationships, and, indeed, in the therapeutic relationship. This represents a departure from the selfobject concept of self psychology wherein the selfobject function provided by the parent *for* the child is matched in kind by the parent being provided selfobject functions *from* the child. The selfobject concept is then metaphorically extended to many other relationships, including, again, the therapeutic relationship. Thus, in our view, self psychology leaves no avenue for understanding the parent's wish to take care of the child, and the satisfaction and pleasure gained in that context, other than the selfobject gratification obtained from the child. What attachment theory emphasizes, then, is the parenting motive, the motive that describes the parent's healthy, non-defensive altruistic desire to match and meet the child's attachment needs, not to rely on the child to meet the parent's needs. This theory contributes a different and to us a more persuasive way to explain parental satisfaction and pleasure than is ordinarily found in self psychology. It allows us to distinguish conceptually between children who can comfortably focus on their own self needs, trusting their parents to take care of themselves rather than being preoccupied with meeting the attachment needs of that parent, or heightening their own attachment demands, or disavowing their own needs.

Referring again to the example of the patient who was seen by his mother as a replacement for his dead brother, the case exemplifies such an insecure attachment. The patient could not trust his mother to care for herself, much less to parent him, and so became preoccupied with meeting her needs, and, by extension, the needs of others, at the expense of his own.

Continuing with the parenting motive as an important metaphor for therapeutic action, we shall introduce the concept of contingent responsiveness (Sander, 1962), a responsiveness that takes into consideration the interaction in the dyad between the different and unequal needs of both participants. Our definition of contingent responsiveness is an appropriate, sensitive response to the child's signals that meets the child's attachment needs or, by analogy, the patient's attachment needs, while considering at the same time the requirements of both participants (see also Chapter 3 by Marrone and Pines). In the therapeutic situation, when a contingent response is offered, it is from the perspective of the patient's perceived developmental requirements. Hence it is offered from the perspective of the analyst's parenting motive; it is not offered from the perspective of the analyst's attachment motive. Thus, we have in the patient–analyst system bidirectionality but not equality of need or motivation. For example, a patient who requires a connection on weekends to sustain self-cohesion may need more than a brief connection. The analyst may or may not be able to both respect his or her own personal needs and at the same time fulfill that need. For example, one analyst contending with such a patient may offer to call the patient at the weekend. Another analyst may offer to call for a specified number of minutes. Yet another analyst may feel that his or her own needs make weekend contact impossible, thus leaving the dyad to try to find other ways to keep a connection. On the other hand, where it is the analyst who desires a connection, missing the patient and feeling lonely at the weekend, this represents an attachment need of the analyst that has no legitimate place in the therapeutic relationship.

These two concepts, contingent responsiveness and the parenting motive, help us to address the role of the analyst in establishing a secure base. It helps as well to wrestle with the difficult questions raised in Kohut's model of optimal frustration, in Bacal's (1985) model of optimal responsiveness, and in Orange, Atwood and Stolorow's (1997) model of antidotal function, the addictive potential conceptualized by them as inherent in gratifying selfobject longings (see Chapters 2, 3 and 4). From the analyst's perspective, if a patient seems to be bogged down in repetitive, insatiable demands, or the patient just seems stuck in the relationship, the concept of contingent responsiveness can provide some clues to the reasons for the difficulties in the therapy. Often the problem is that the patient is not being responded to contingently, that is, the right balance has not yet been discovered between what the patient needs and what the analyst feels ready, able, or simply right in giving. While at times it is a limit that best meets a need, we believe that at most times, it is the need itself that must be met.

Pertinent to our topic of sexual disorder, one signal of failed contingency in the relationship, as we have said, can be detected by the analyst who experiences wanting a connection for his or her *own* attachment requirements. The analyst who becomes physically sexual with a patient fits this description. In such a case, the analyst may be organized by his or her sexual need predominantly or by a sexualization of an attachment need of the analyst's self that has gone unmet and which likely remains out of the analyst's awareness; but, in any case, the analyst is not operating contingently, out of a meliorative parenting motive.

We have emphasized in both attachment theory and self psychology that attachment needs persist throughout life, forming familiar patterns that last. We believe that these enduring patterns represent the child's, or the patient's, best effort at achieving needed connections with the caregiver. Such a pattern may be either positive, as in the mirroring selfobject relationship and the secure attachment category of relatedness, or negative, as in pathological accommodation and the insecure categories of relatedness. Attachment theory has identified three categories of insecure attachment, in addition to the secure relatedness category (Attachment Category B). These insecure patterns include: Category A, Avoidant Attachment; Category C, Anxious/Ambivalent Attachment; and Category D, Disorganized/Disoriented Attachment (see Appendix). Based on clinical experience and consistent with our theory, we would introduce a fourth pattern of insecure attachment relatedness, which we term Category RP, Reverse Parenting. This category is derived from Bowlby's work on role reversal patterns and the compulsive caregiver personality type (Bowlby, 1969, 1980). This pattern has also been elaborated by Main (1995) and has been incorporated as a possible outcome of the D pattern. We are emphasizing this pattern as a separate clinical entity because of its presence in patients who exhibit more than D pattern pathology but in A and C patterns as well. Because of its prevalence and importance, we have chosen to elevate it to a pattern in its own right, although we are aware that this pattern as a separate entity does not arise from the attachment research data. Category RP describes a situation in which the child, using the normal childhood attainments of empathy and altruism, extends parental care to the parent. The parent in this instance responds by co-opting these now hypertrophied capacities in the child in order to address and fulfill that parent's own attachment longings.

Attachment and sexuality

At this point, we shall apply our integration to an investigation of sexual experience. We speculate that such integration makes possible a greater understanding of this important, much written about, and yet still mysterious topic. Kohut had lifted out of the broad category of sexuality the concept of sexualization. However, the distinctions that must be made among the varieties of sexual experiences, and specifically, how the relationship between love and sex can be understood, remains an open question, one that we address now (see Silverman, Chapter 19, for another approach to the problem of developing an integrated view between attachment and sexuality).

Specifically, we shall address three types of sexual experience. The first type is the experience of sexual pleasure, per se, which we believe involves the qualities and capacities of a securely attached, B Category, individual, including the potential to be in a satisfying and loving relationship with the self and with others.

In this first type of sexual experience, pleasurable sexual intimacy is used for its own sake and for the sake of sexual intimacy with the other. We believe, quite simply, that children who are loved in a secure attachment relationship are more likely to grow up with the capacity to be in loving relations with others. As a part of such an intimate connection, sexual experience is enjoyable, largely unfraught with conflict, and can be anticipated without marked dysphoria. When such an intimate connection is not available, secure individuals can provide sexual pleasure for themselves, again without significant conflict or dysphoria. Kohut and other self psychologists, too, see nonconflictual sexual experience as a manifestation of a healthy self, one whose experience with selfobject responsiveness in childhood has added up to a sufficiently balanced, harmonious and cohesive self-development. What an attachment paradigm adds to this selfobject experience in development is the back and forth recognition of and sharing with, the other in an atmosphere of positive, pleasurable intimacy. This balance can be described as 'I am there *with* you and you with me,' and 'I am there *for* you and you for me.' We believe it is precisely these emphases that are required to delineate this first type of sexual experience, a sexual experience that is based on secure attachment.

The second type of sexual experience is the experience of sexualization, in Kohut's definition of the term, in which the person uses sexual experience to substitute for other important, unfulfilled, nonsexual, self- and self-with-other needs.

Specifically, we connect sexualization with three of the four insecure attachment patterns recognized in our theory. Categories C (Anxious/Ambivalent), A (Avoidant), and RP (Reverse Parenting). The fourth insecure attachment category, Category D (Disorganized/Disoriented), we see as characterized by a different sexuality, the *third* type of sexual experience, which we shall take up shortly.

We postulate that absence of mutuality in sexual experience is likely to be characteristic of all insecure attachment patterns. Such individuals are lacking a consolidated self, have difficulties in self-integration, and have difficulties in establishing a full and mutually gratifying sexual intimacy with a partner. As such, sexualization, the recruitment of nonsexual motives by sexuality, represents a broad category that often helps us to understand diverse symptom manifestations, including, for example, sexual addiction, sexual obsessions, sexual compulsions, counterphobic sexual fantasies, and counterphobic enactments. Sexualization in sexual experience serves as one avenue through which the individual attempts to achieve the feeling of self-comfort, self-protection, self-regulation, self-preservation, and alleviation of the sense of being alone. Sexual experience becomes a way to serve unmet needs of various types which needs supersede, take precedence over, and substitute for, sexual intimacy.

The use of sexualization as a means of meeting self- and self-with-other needs can be clinically correlated with a particular developmental history, which is unique to the particular insecure attachment pattern involved.

The child who is anxiously/ambivalently attached (Category C) is focused on the parent, attempting to maintain a connection despite the child's experience of the parent as unreliable, alternately responsive and unresponsive in an ambivalent mode. The experience of unpredictability erodes the child's sense of security, leaving the child open to chronic anxiety about being abandoned by the other. The behavioral manifestations are most often an alternation of anxious clinging and angry rejecting behavior, with ongoing strife being characteristic. To exemplify the connection with sexuality in the adult, a patient with an anxious/ambivalent attachment presented clinically with a form of sexualization characterized by sexual addiction in which sex with multiple partners served as a futile effort to assuage anxieties over loss of the indispensable other. This pattern was understood as a response to the dangers he had felt as a child in attempting to rely on his mother, who could suddenly and inexplicably reject him, leaving him alone and feeling bereft.

In contrast to this anxious/ambivalent category, the child who is avoidantly attached attempts to maintain as close a connection as possible with a parent who is hostile to manifestations of that child's attachment needs, again threatening the child's sense of security. This child appears on observation to be distant from the parent, attempting to reveal neither attachment needs nor anger at being unresponded to, but rather diverting himself in active exploration of the environment and/or attempting to show a cool indifference to such needs in order to maintain what he or she can of the parent's limited interest. To exemplify the connection with sexuality in the adult, a patient who presented with an avoidant attachment pattern revealed in therapy a need for behavioral enactment in a counterphobic way by having oral sex performed on him while driving on the freeway. It was discovered in treatment that he used such an enactment because he was unable to feel connected and sexually alive with a partner who was truly intimate. With his counterphobic enactment, the patient could avoid such experiences of intimacy, allowing him to remain unaware of his own attachment needs and vulnerabilities.

In the RP (reverse parenting) pattern, the child maintains greater responsivity to the parent, to the parent's mental state, and to the parent's needs, than does the parent to that child. The balance of contingent responsiveness is thus reversed, and accommodation to the parent is all that remains possible. As this is so, we do not consider the accommodation itself a pathological accommodation, but rather the only means available to the child for healthy adaptation. Such adaptation does lead, of course, to less than successful adaptations later in life. But in childhood, to the extent that the accommodation is successful, the child does receive some measure of connection to the parent, as well as that parent's approval and hence some enhancement of sense of self. The child learns that he or she is of value, but only to the extent that the needs of the other are met. Of course, there are many aspects of the child's self that are then left underdeveloped, unresponded to, and unintegrated, including a sense of being worthy as a person in his or her own right, and not just by virtue of serving the requirements of others.

To exemplify this insecure attachment pattern in the sexual realm of the adult, we can again refer back to our patient whose brother had died before the patient was born for an illustration of sexuality as it might manifest in Category RP, reverse parenting insecure attachment. This man could not assert himself in an intimate sexual relationship in terms of his own sexual need; he had to await the expression of sexual need from his partner. His excessive attention to the other, the imperative to know what she wanted, created in the woman a sense that he was missing, that he was not present as himself, as a fully functioning partner, with desires of his own. He could feel pleasure in sexual experience only if and when he had created pleasure for the other.

At this point we come to the *third* type of sexual experience, an experience that we maintain is not sexual at all. Here one's self- and self-with-other needs are not met, and there is neither love nor intimacy nor sexual pleasure. Moreover, there is neither an integrated nor a consolidated self nor a consolidated tie to the other. This is the experience of sexual abuse and its sequelae. We connect it to individuals who have had such a history of abuse, and who fall into the D Category, Disorganized/Disoriented Attachment pattern. Their experience does involve the genitals, to be sure, but the paradox is that it is not sexually pleasurable; rather it is, most often, genitally uncomfortable or painful, or it is genitally anesthetic because of the self's efforts at dissociative self-protection or dissociation secondary to self-fragmentation. In this situation, one which, as we have said, pertains in sexual abuse, there are experiences of pain, torment, fear, shame, humiliation, anger and rage, in any combination, with, most often, a sense of betrayal. The symptom picture in this type of sexual experience may include post-traumatic stress disorder, dissociative disorders, major depression, sexual avoidance, joyless promiscuity and genital pain.

This third category of (so-called) sexual experience, which has a developmental history of physical and sexual maltreatment as a child or adolescent, causes the patient's self to become damaged as a consequence, shattered, fragmented, or dissociated, with anything good in the connection to the parent being preserved only at the cost of dissociating large segments of painful lived experience. Where the parents themselves were the abusers, they become perceived as dangerous, overpowering and unpredictable. Where the abusers were not the parents themselves, but were others entrusted with the child's care, the parental figures may often be perceived as helpless, non-protective, and neglectful, so that caregivers are experienced as powerless to provide safety. The predominant affect characterizing all of these individuals who have suffered active abuse is ongoing and pervasive fear, manifesting in a wide variety of intensely dysregulated self-states.

We shall provide an example addressing this third form of sexual experience, which, as we have said, is not sexual. A woman sought treatment for chronic pelvic pain and pain on intercourse. In treatment the pelvic pain turned out to be a somatic memory of actual genital torture. This flashback state of pelvic pain resolved when it was recognized as dissociated from the patient's ordinary, day-to-day experience and connected to the patient's actual, lived childhood experience suffered at the hands of her psychotic mother. This patient, as is typical of many D Category adults, had been engaged in repetitive, painful, sexual activity with her partner without knowing why she continued to engage in that activity despite the ongoing pain. No genital pleasure had been possible, even though occasional orgasm occurred in the context of extreme fear, a phenomenon we have termed 'feargasm' (see Shane, Shane and Gales, 1997).

In closing, we have presented what we hope will be a useful integration of attachment theory and self psychology, showing the value of a developmental systems approach as applied to the complex clinical issues surrounding sex and love. Work with each of these patients entailed use of the clinical and theoretical concepts we have outlined. These include (1) the establishment of a secure base leading in the direction of a secure attachment with the therapist, and where possible with others in the patient's life, and (2) the establishment of a consolidated self capable of self-reflection and self and mutual regulation.

References

Ainsworth M (1985) I. Patterns of infant–mother attachment: antecedents and effects on development; II. Attachments across the lifespan. Bulletin of the New York Academy of Medicine 61: 771–91; 791–812.

Bacal H (1985) Optimal responsiveness and the therapeutic process. In: A Goldberg (ed.) Progress in Self Psychology, vol. 1. New York: Guilford Press, pp. 202–27.

Bowlby J (1969) Attachment, vol. 1 of Attachment and Loss (2nd edn, 1982). London: Hogarth Press; New York: Basic Books; Harmondsworth: Penguin (1971).

Bowlby J (1980) Loss: Sadness and Depression, vol. 3: Attachment and Loss. London: Hogarth Press; New York: Basic Books; Harmondsworth: Penguin (1981).

Bowlby J (1988) A Secure Base. New York: Basic Books.

Brandchaft B (1994) Structures of Pathological Accommodation. Unpublished manuscript.

Edelman G (1992) Bright Air, Brilliant Fire: On the Matter of the Mind. New York: Basic Books.

Kohut H (1977) The Restoration of the Self. New York: International Universities Press.

Kohut H (1984) In: A Goldberg and P Stepansky (eds) How Does Analysis Cure? Chicago: University of Chicago Press.

Lichtenberg J (1989) Psychoanalysis and Motivation. Hillsdale, NJ: Analytic Press.

Main M (1995) Attachment: Overview with implications for clinical work. In: S Goldberg, M Muir and J Kerr (eds) Attachment Theory: Social, Developmental and Clinical Perspectives. Hillsdale, NJ: Analytic Press, pp. 407–74.

Orange D, Atwood G and Stolorow R (1997) Working Intersubjectively. Hillsdale, NJ: Analytic Press.

Sander LW (1962) Issues in early mother–child interaction. Journal of the American Academy of Child Psychiatry I: 141–66.

Shane M, Shane E and Gales M (1997) Intimate Attachments: Toward a New Self Psychology. New York and London: Guilford Press.

Sroufe LA (1996) Emotional Development: The Organization of Emotional Life in the Early Years. New York: Cambridge University Press.

Stolorow R, Brandchaft B and Atwood G (1987) Psychoanalytic Treatment: An Intersubjective Approach. Hillsdale, NJ: Analytic Press.

van IJzendoorn MH (1995) Adult attachment representations, parental responsiveness, and infant attachment: A meta-analysis on the predictive validity of the Adult Attachment Interview. Psychological Bulletin 117: 387–403.

Wolf ES (1988) Treating the Self: Elements of Clinical Self Psychology. New York: Guilford Press.

CHAPTER 19

Sexuality and attachment: a passionate relationship or a marriage of convenience?

DORIS K. SILVERMAN

Freud's legacy is our important heritage. There is a great deal in Freudian theory that informs our contemporary outlook. However, I believe the theory can be enriched and enhanced by current information from developmental research. Here I have in mind the affective-regulating function of the attachment system. I wish to illustrate the complex relationship between sexuality and attachment, highlighting the resultant fecundity that emerges from such syntheses. I use clinical and non-clinical vignettes to demonstrate the plasticity of sexuality and its interlacing with the modulating function of the attachment system and their variable outcomes. Acknowledging such linkages in these two systems raises questions about the traditional conception of psychosexual stages. The interconnections between the affect-regulating feature of the attachment system and sexuality are explored for an understanding of some features of transference and countertransference. Sexuality's protean nature allows for a reassessment of the case of Little Hans with the emphasis on the unique interrelationship between sexuality and attachment (for another effort to understand the relationship between attachment and sexuality, see Chapter 18 in this volume).

The attachment system and its affect-regulating function

Bowlby was focused on the infant's and young child's experience of separation, loss, grief and mourning. He studied and observed the infant's early connection to his or her caregiver and recognized the disruption wrought when this tie was ruptured, even temporarily. He was referring to the need of the infant to maintain proximity to the caregiver in times of stress. For example, when the child is 'frightened, fatigued, or sick' (Bowlby, 1988, pp. 26–7), the child is helped by the secure and safe presence of the caregiver.

Ainsworth, a developmental researcher, set out to systematically investigate the attachment system that Bowlby described as occurring naturally over the course of the first year of life. When distress or fear is stirred in the young child, it activates the attachment system in order to provide felt security. Ainsworth and her co-workers developed the Strange Situation, which consists of episodes of departures and reunions between mothers and their infants under tolerable conditions of stress for the infants. The majority of infants are securely attached. They can use their mothers as a base of exploration when stress is minimal and actively work to reconnect when briefly separated. They seek out contact and comfort when needed and then can easily return to play.

Ainsworth discerned two categories of insecure attachment, one she labeled as ambivalent-resistant and the other as avoidant. Ambivalent attachments ensure the mother's tolerance for connection and proximity at the same time that the child experiences some degree of stress and a low level of anxiety. These children tend to be criers according to Bell and Ainsworth (1972). They cried a great deal when separated and when reunited with their mothers. The avoidant attachment children tend to be hostile and display unprovoked aggression (Kobak and Shaver, 1987), 'biting or hitting their mothers without any overt expression of anger' (Ainsworth et al., 1978, p. 159). Thus, such a child permits a bearable connection for mother with some possible loss of feeling in the child.[1]

The ambivalent and avoidant categories are not considered pathological. They are styles of relating and only at their extremes do they flag potential maladaptive relational styles. Attachment system researchers continue to explore these categorical designations. There is constant refinement to the system and other sub-categories within the three categories – secure, ambivalent and avoidant – have been detailed. In addition, there is a group labeled as disorganized-disoriented. This group does reflect a maladaptive style of relating. This category of children displays 'contradictory behavior patterns' (Main and Solomon, 1990, p. 135), seeking out and immediately avoiding an attachment figure. They often are frightened, confused, sometimes apathetic children who can exhibit dazed, frozen or trance-like behavior (for an extensive discussion of the attachment system, see Silverman, 1981, 1991, 1992, 1994, 1995, 1998a, 1998b). Whereas I am describing an interactive behavioral system, it is one that becomes internalized. Such patterns of relating over time are established as mental models or what psychoanalysis refers to as psychic representations. These internal models demonstrate adaptive and defensive features (Silverman, 1998a).

This interactive attachment system is established through mutual emotionally-expressive responses of mother and her infant. It is an affect-regulating system. (I shall be spelling out more specific aspects of this system shortly.) Here, let me say that although affect regulation is tacit in Bowlby's understanding of the attachment system, he did not explicate it with an emphasis on affect regulation, as I am. He was more focused on the need of the infant for proximity to the caregiver. His view is similar to Main's, a major contemporary attachment researcher. She described the biological functions of the attachment behavior system (Main, 1993, p. 213) '... (the system) was primarily protection from predation ... In addition ... proximity provides the protection from unfavorable temperature changes, from natural disasters, from the attacks of conspecifics, and from the risk of separation from the group.' Thus, from Bowlby's explicit view and that of subsequent researchers, the emphasis is on the importance of proximity to ensure safety. However, for Bowlby and others it is also the psychological experience of felt safety that is important. I am building on this idea. The attachment system may have evolved as a protective adaptation in primates. I believe, however, that the same system now serves an important, perhaps related role in affect regulation.

Affect regulation in the attachment system

The initial interactional system between mother and child is dominated by the infant's homeostatic needs. Researchers currently maintain that this system is coordinated between mother and child, so that such infant physiological needs as temperature regulation, level of activation, heart rate, sleep–wake cycles, etc., are regulated interactively. These homeostatic features have a psychological component, that of affect-regulation. Early on, a variety of signals and negotiations develop between the mother and her infant. The infant is pre-programmed to discriminate a range of expressive behaviors in the caretaker and to respond with utterances, gestures, lip and tongue movements, and full-body reactivity (Trevarthen, 1980). During the course of dyadic interactions a great deal of infant learning occurs. Such learning and communication has been referred to as 'implicit relational knowing' (Stark, 1997; Tronick, 1997) or procedural memory – the non-conscious, non-verbal communicative signals that reciprocally flow between the two and lead to increasingly complex dyadic regulation. Such a feedback system offers infants opportunities for both interactive and self-regulation (Sander, 1977; Gianino and Tronick, 1985; Jaffe et al., 2001; Silverman, 1998a; Emde, 1999). These are simultaneously evolving internal experiences. Adequate mutual cueing and reasonably adaptive maternal responsiveness provides the infant with opportunities for regulating the self and intuiting further ways to maintain optimal experiences of security. Researchers (Stern, 1974; Condon and Sander, 1974; Schaffer, 1977; Trevarthen, 1980, 1993; Gianino and Tronick, 1985) carefully analyzing such interactions, report on the cycles of reactivity and complementarity that develop. From this joint self and interactive system there emerges a unique regulatory pattern characteristic of this particular dyad (the developed interactive pattern) and a particular form of self-regulation characteristic of the infant. Thus, the infant learns and develops forms of interactive and self-regulation that are tolerable for both mother and child. The developing attachment system has this affect-regulating feature as an important cementing ingredient, leading to a mental model of dyadic interaction that is internalized.

Whereas felt safety is a distinctive and necessary psychological feature of infancy, it can induce, interact with and reciprocally function with sensual-sexual experiences. I acknowledge and stress the importance of drives; in the context of this chapter, I mean libidinal wishes. The adaptive or pathological features of the attachment system entwine with conflicts generated by libidinal wishes. The result is a complex emergent system unique to each individual that has at least dual motivational components. I leave open, as did Freud, the possibility of including other relevant motivational issues.[2] The nature and relevance of the attachment relationship, I believe, is of such power and significance that it transforms the way we can understand psychosexual stages, which I shall discuss later.

Of course, it is the rich and varied symbolic meanings that we are capable of that allow for the plasticity of sexual responsiveness. What is interesting about sexuality is the varied means by which sexual responsiveness can be stirred. This facilitates sexuality's plasticity. There exists a complicated relationship between 'meanings associated with sexuality and the varied behavioral modes and accompanying range of affective reactions for sexuality's expression' (Klein, 1976). As George Klein suggests, sexuality is 'intrinsically motivational' because of the pleasure it provides; however, it is also an accompaniment of this pleasure that other aims are achieved, if not necessarily acknowledged (Klein, 1976, p. 92).

Because sexuality has the capacity to be such a protean experience, its function can mask a host of other sources of need. This may be especially true with compulsive sexuality and sado-masochistic sexuality. On the other hand, sensual-sexual experiences can achieve full gratifying expression, as well as become inhibited, overlaid, or in general be constrained by non-libidinal needs. The following are some themes and variations on the interaction of desire and attachment relationships. I shall be presenting some short and rather extended vignettes to capture the variable interrelationship between sensual and attachment needs.

Sensual sexuality

Think of the following interaction. A baby is born with a particularly keen sensitivity to sensual experiences. There is intense pleasure in his being stroked, fondled, hugged and kissed. The sensual warmth of being held firmly in a bath of warm water that caresses him, the intense, delightful responsiveness to the subsequent massaging of his bare skin, the mutual titillation in looking and being looked at, the blandishments heaped on a responsive and receptive reactor-baby, the appreciation of skin-to-skin holding and touching, the enjoyment of the odors and kinesthetic sensations that pervade his senses when in contact with his mother.

Using Stern's (1985) idea of cross-modal experiences, we can expect that the sensual pleasures in one zone stimulate the non-conscious analogous bodily experiences in another sensory modality. Freud (1905) had his own idea about the spurring of bodily sexuality. He described a variety of intense, emotional responses tripping a spread of sexual excitation across the body. The child's experience of sensual sensations, seductions, erotic feelings, within reasonable affective bounds, allows him to be seduced by the mother's bodily ministrations, its mystery, its gratifying intensity, and its pleasure The opportunity for the eventual full-flowering of hearty, lustful, fleshy, erotic sexuality can be observed in its incipient stages.

On the mother's part, all of these keen and exquisite excitements and pleasures can occur if she can enjoy her own sublimated eroticism, and she unconsciously sanctions their communication to her infant. Thus, her own experience of sensuality in her caring for her baby is kept within a modulated emotional responsiveness. Using traditional conceptualizations we can say she is sufficiently aim-inhibited or is able to sublimate her own erotic needs, yet appreciate the gratification it offers to both in the caregiving setting. The mother can enjoy the seduction of her child into the realm of sensuality (Freud, 1905). In this context, one also can think about Laplanche's (1997) idea of the unconscious and enigmatic in the mother's sexuality being communicated to her infant. The baby's sexual history is initiated by his awakening to this secret, curious conundrum of her sensuality. (For a rich description of Laplanche's ideas on the enigmatic sexuality of the mother's unconscious implanted in her baby, see Stein, 1998.)

One might ask, how does the mother's sexuality get communicated to her infant? Here, procedural knowledge or implicit relational knowing, which I discussed earlier, is relevant. I am pointing to the non-symbolic system that characterizes not only initial infant–parent interactions, but a coding system that continues unabated throughout our lives. A great deal of emotional signaling and cueing takes place outside of our conscious awareness. Much of our social interactions, which include our use of space with others, our leaning toward or away from the other in discourse, our expressive body, face and hand movements, head shaking, gazing, etc., are governed by our implicit knowledge. It is through such a medium that the mother is able to communicate a tapestry of her rich imagistic-phantasy life as well as her emotional and physiological sensations, both constitutive of her sexuality. These provide complex, quizzical, unconscious sexual messages for her baby.

Now, for a contrasting position, consider a similarly temperamentally endowed child, one who is especially responsive to sensual experiences with a mother who cannot tolerate physical closeness. She manages the physical care of the child with little capacity for sensual enjoyment because the physical proximity is distressing to her. When her infant approaches, you can see her avoidant behavior. (Such an interaction was demonstrated in Tronick's (1997) videotaped parent–infant observation.) However, the infant detects such information through the mutual-regulating process of sensing mother's lessened anxiety through the abridgement of their physical proximity. When mother and infant are seen together by 6 months of age, the baby has already developed a defensive style of non-physical contact with the mother (Gianino and Tronick, 1985). Here the possibility for passionate, erotic sensuality will be completely overridden by the establishment of an avoidant attachment system. If nothing alters in the initial caregiving relationship it can become fixed and enduring. Such an attachment is necessary for the survival and development of the infant and the reduced anxiety of the mother. Here sensual, pleasurable experiences are defensively hidden by the avoidance of intimacy in order to maintain contact that is requisite for a sense of security and safety.

Psychosexuality and attachment

Considering my integrative view of libido and attachment, we need an emendation to the way Freud (1915) thought about psychosexual stages. He maintained that the oral, anal and genital drives are under the 'preponderating dominance of erotogenic zones' (pp. 191–2). Freud understood the erotogenic zones as part of our biological heritage, and they unfold in a linear fashion and are each heightened at the time of its ascendancy. Freud conceptualized these stages as biologically rooted, and phylogenetically unfolding, unlinked to objects.

From my perspective, such a view fails to consider the emergent properties of experience for each individual. Rather than the unfolding of psychosexual stages, development proceeds in a non-linear, erratic and inconsistent pattern, although on a macroscopic level it may appear less than the case (Emde, 1999; Sameroff, 1976; Silverman, 1981, 1991, 1992; Thelen and Smith, 1995).

Second, traditionally we think of the infant's first stage of life as dominated by oral needs. Paramount for baby watchers is the newborn's primitive state system, which includes homeostatic stability and psychological safety and the early entrainment of the mother and infant to achieve these ends (Sander, 1977; Emde, 1999). Whereas feeding is an essential element in the system, it must always be paired with the unique physiological, emotional and social-psychological needs of the infant.

Third, acknowledging the broad framework of the intertwining of libidinal wishes and attachment, we need to look at the specific ways these two features emerge for an individual. A particular zonal emphasis can be elevated to importance depending on the combination of a number of factors: the unique conjunction of a particular caregiver–infant dyad, their consistent or inconsistent temperamental features, personalities, bodily illness, special needs and their unique sensitivities as well as the emotional-cognitive meanings each brings to his/her comprehension of the interaction. Here I am emphasizing the embeddedness of the dyad in a unique field, which of course needs to account for the inputs from the social surround as well. This is in contrast to an emphasis on biological givens in development.

Thus, one needs to focus not on the unfolding of psychosexual stages, but on the contextualization of multiple factors that shape maladaptive infant–parent attachments. Such a troubling relationship has been ongoing and sometimes finds particular expression in some phase of caregiving activity or psychosexual stage. Then, there can be a heightening and distortion of a particular zone, which becomes prominent in the individual.

Clinical examples of psychosexuality and attachment

A compulsive over-eater can remember tugging on his mother's skirts, pulling at her sleeve, pestering her with a whiney insistence sometimes reaching temper-tantrum proportions when he needed her attention. His early memories were of her giving him bread when he was upset. A variant of her behavior, when he was somewhat older and she did not want to be bothered by his demands, was her 'throwing money at him', which he would spend on sweets and treats. One could posit that when he is anxious there is a retreat to an earlier form of oral gratification seemingly unconnected to objects. I should see this as an insufficient explanation, one that does not account for the meanings of recurrent patterned inter-actions in his daily life.[3]

For example, the patient described his current behavior with his well-intentioned nutritionist trainer. She is involved in meticulous formulations of programs and advice to control his dietary excesses. She lectures, emails and calls him frequently. He tells me he 'tunes her out, turns her off' and discards her. In his relationship to me as well he will indicate that although he knows we were talking about something important in a prior session, he typically cannot remember what I was saying. Thus, both with his train-er and transferentially, he becomes the indifferent, deaf mother who disregards the persistent insistent analyst- and trainer-child.

The eating conflict that he describes within himself has some of the ear-marks of his earlier relationship with his mother as well. He argues, complains and battles within himself about eating compulsively until the internal feeling escalates to the point where he must eat. He maintains he wanted his mother's attention, acknowledgment, and awareness of him, which he could not accomplish. He substituted an almost dissociated state of eating until bursting. Then there is disgust with the amount con-sumed and with his appearance, which is similar to his corpulent mother. Through his eating he maintains his battling, insistent, unhappy connec-tion to her, solidified by their mutual obesity.

Such an experience, from an exclusive drive perspective, can be under-stood as the regressive retreat to an earlier zone of oral gratification. Simultaneously there is an unconscious gratification of his sado-masochism (see A. Freud's analysis, Silverman, 1998a). Whereas the former two may be relevant for this patient, a more comprehensive under-standing of all the meanings of his fantasies and interactions would include an attachment perspective. We can posit the reactivation of an old repetitive interactive experience that provided an important though frus-trating attachment relationship. Speculating, one could say that an inconsistent interactive regulatory experience was internalized with a greater tilt toward self-regulation. A sometime responsive early interac-tion allowed for continued hope of engagement with an early recognition of the need to become self-reliant. An analyst's focus on the pathological attachment relationship and the quality of affect-regulatory needs pro-vides increased tailoring of the patient's current psychic and social experiences to earlier patterns of interactions that became internalized.

The following vignette is another example of the reliance on self-regu-lation and the substitution of oral sexuality as an attachment replacement. Another patient talks about food preparation as a sensuous activity, one he likes to engage in completely alone and he does not like to be inter-rupted. His association to this was masturbatory activity. Behavior he hopes will not be interrupted or discovered. We understood the latter as a retreat to an isolated, lonely experience, devoid of a need to rely on a disappointing love object, Here sensuality and pleasure was divorced from intimacy and replaced by an isolated oral-masturbatory fantasy. A disabling attachment connection was substituted with his valorization of isolation and self-gratification.

Anality, too, has potentially diverse motivational features. I do not wish to minimize those steeped in anality as an organizing discourse. This pre-occupation with all aspects of toileting can be powerful. For example, there can be an investment in anal smells, their size, form and consistency; ideas about being clean, orderly, neat, or dirty, smelly, messy and chaotic; the experience of pleasure in holding on to or letting go, or the shame, disgust and moral rectitude about such interests; the experience of accommodation, acquiescence, compliance or the stubbornly aggressive, combative, destructive aspects of excretion. Of course, these ideas in varying degrees exist in all of us. For some, however, it becomes absorbingly conflicted.

However, even traditional conceptualizations that have been clinically useful may not tell the whole story. For example, obsessional behavior related to anal control/struggles around toilet training can in many instances be traced to earlier parent–child interactions. Thus isolation of affect, especially around strong, angry feelings that are displaced away from key relationships on to things and objects in the world, also reflects important early relational configurations. A number of researchers (Lyons-Ruth, 1999; Main, Tomasini, and Tolan, 1979; Malatesta et al., 1989; van IJzendoorn, 1995) have described the distancing from emotional involvement with parents and the displacement on to object and things demonstrated by children at 12 months of age. It is related to the parent–child interaction over the first year of life, including parental suppressed anger and discomfort with close physical contact. It is confirmed as well in the independent assessment of parents in their own attachment interviews (van IJzendoorn, 1995).

The theoretical investment by the analyst in anal-aggressive issues may obscure the sometimes-potent need to emphasize the problematic features of attachment. When this latter is the pertinent issue then aggression should be considered as reactive to the pathological ambivalent or avoidant attachments established between mother and her infant.

In these examples I am also describing what Freud (1905) discussed in his 'Three essays' – 'the pathways of mutual influence'. Freud also described the traversible pathways of sexuality, how a non-sexual need like food preparation (fulfilling nutritional needs) can take on sexual meaning through particular symbolic connections via a seemingly similar pathway, sometimes adaptively and other times pathologically. On the other side, apparent sexual behavior – as demonstrated by the unrelenting pursuit of sexual activity, becomes inculcated with meanings devoid of tenderness, attachment, connection and intimacy, important needs that are indirectly served and mostly submerged in sexual experiences of power and possession. Thus, erotic inclinations and non-sexual needs easily get entangled.

In the next sections of the chapter I discuss different kinds of self and interactive regulation that have emerged from the attachment relationship. Such regulatory patterns flag concern when they tilt too much in one direction or another. As I have suggested in the clinical examples above, the infant can rely too heavily on a self-regulating pattern, on more internal cues, because of problematic experiences in the nature of the interaction. I am particularly interested in how such different regulatory patterns interact with sexuality. I address this idea with clinical examples of the overstimulating mother and its effects. The other extreme is the understimulating mother characteristic, for example, of depressed and withdrawn mothers. I also speculate on the effects of different kinds of regulatory patterns as they may exist within the analysand and/or the analyst. On the other side are those who moderate their affective state through interactive regulation. I discuss this as well and its clinical implications.

Errant self-regulation as a function of a maladaptive attachment style: the overstimulating mother

In contrast to mothers who can modulate their own sexuality, so that it is not traumatic or pathological for the child, are mothers who overstimulate, with inappropriate sexual and sometimes physical abuse. In such a child-caregiving relationship, the need for appropriate quieting and arousal by the mother are undermined. Negotiating such problematic interactions the child leans toward self-regulation prematurely. Here, we can see the potential beginnings of a 'narcissistic' solution in the child (Sander, 1983, pp. 30–1).

Abuse induces traumatic anxiety and potential rage reactions. What then occurs to all the possible experiences of sensuality and pleasure? Such experiences can readily become distorted. The traumatic nature of overstimulation from physical or sexual abuse needs a considerable amount of defensive handling to deaden painful experiences (Shengold, 1999). On the other hand, such deadening experiences leave the person feeling numb and non-existent, with the resultant need to enliven themselves. The pursuit of risk-taking and the simultaneous denial of the need for the other as a source of safety and dependency may lead to perverted sexuality. The need for contact-comfort may find expression only in experiences of sexuality. Sexuality can then become heightened. Aggressized sexuality is linked because of the need to deal with rageful internal responses. Escalating panic and traumatic-like repetitive feelings can often be expressed through aggressivized sexuality. Sado-masochistic sexuality can suffuse the adult's sexual functioning, as he/she attempts to deal with unmodulated (especially rageful) feelings via sexual expression. In contrast, Freud (1905) insisted that 'an erotogenic effect attaches even to intensely painful feelings, especially where the pain is toned down or kept at a distance by some accompanying condition' and thus this is one of the important sources of the 'masochistic-sadistic instinct' (p. 204). That is, all painful feelings contain the possibility of pleasure, which the adult is reenacting to achieve unconscious pleasure. The replication of this position can be found in the contemporary 'mainstream position' papers of Glen and Bernstein (1995) and Wiederman (1995).

Clinical example

The patient, a very troubled man, had endured a seriously neglectful, physically abusive and traumatic infancy and childhood. Early in his life he developed a seemingly independent existence, one in which he was contemptuous and suspicious of others who were 'out to scam him or rip him off'. He was proud of 'never letting himself get fucked', a man sophisticated in the ways of a harsh, cruel, 'dog eat dog' world, always anticipating the 'ball-breakers', the 'exploiters', those searching for what he called 'the edge' over him. He never felt much in the way of emotions. Other people's illnesses, and even deaths of family members, left him untouched. He thought of himself as a misogynist, who, in addition, felt disdain and condescension toward people in general. He was a mixture of arrogant pride and command but he was also gregarious, humorous, smart, and facile, and with excellent showmanship convinced others of his power and success.[4] However, this façade masked a frightened and stress-ridden self. Any experience of anxiety rapidly escalated into a panic state.

Consistent with his contempt for women, he acknowledged 'using and exploiting women, treating them like objects'. Employing fabulously fabled tales of his position and affiliation with power brokers, he would seduce women. His fantasies were about sex with a degraded, inferior, powerless victim and he often became sexually engaged with such women.

His early life had a considerable amount of hours of neglect, existing simultaneously with a chaotic household filled with many older siblings fighting, hitting, cursing, and intruding on each other. There was not a consistent place to sleep, never reliable mealtimes and none of his own clothes to wear. His mother's frustration often led to severe beatings. Filth, disorder, poverty, neglect and brutalization by older brothers contributed to his traumatic childhood. Undoubtedly, his mother must have felt overwhelmed by the demands of this huge brood and unable to cope with her newest baby.

He had trouble modulating his emotions. It would not be surprising that such a mother–infant relationship had an insufficient degree of interactive regulation, which might have contributed to increased modulation of his stressed states. Instead, his early experiences must have led to a heavy, but unsatisfactory reliance on self-regulation. This is consistent with the way he managed his emotion; such states rapidly elevated in intensity and frightened and panicked him. He sought a variety of maladaptive channels as self-regulators (alcohol, sex, gambling) and they were temporarily alleviating. Over time, he was able to utilize the analytic relationship to help moderate his feelings and to forgo most of his pathological ways of dealing with stress.

Analytic work about his contempt for others and his defensive privileging of his independence led to occasions in which he felt very close to a woman. They were often young, helpless and dependent on him so the experience of feeling intimate with another felt safe. At times he even thought he felt much more. This occurred in his new marriage. He could feel close to his wife and hug her so fiercely because of his wish to be joined with her.

Increasingly tolerant of some of his neediness, dependency and wishes for physical closeness and care from his wife, he also recognized his inability to share her with children. However, he acquiesced to his wife acquiring a dog.

He began to explore his relationships more closely when he realized he felt more love toward this dog than he did with people. With surprise, he realized he could not stand to be away from his dog. He thought about it all the time. It was so cute and cuddly. He liked to have it rest on his chest and fall asleep that way. When his dog had romped, played and was tired, he loved the feeling of the dog asleep on his body and the dog's face close to his own. The dog was so trusting and felt so safe with him that it could fall asleep that way. He enjoyed feeding, washing, grooming, all the pleasures often associated with caring for a newborn, and he would go on to train the dog in obedience. He reported that when he was caught up in such concentrated warm and nurturing feelings with his dog, he would get sexually aroused. He described this as similar to reactions he used to have when pursuing young, vulnerable women. For example, his occasional tender feelings of friendship and care for a much younger troubled female adolescent suddenly turned sexual. He commented as well that when he hugged these women, and now when he hugged his wife, he wished to be so close that he feared he would squeeze them and her too hard. With his dog, he was aware of his fear of losing this precious animal and he was disturbed by intrusive thoughts of seriously hurting the dog, for example, of tossing it off a balcony ledge.

There is much that could be addressed in this vignette that arose out of analytic work. He was preoccupied with merger needs, as indicated by his intense desire for physical proximity. In this restoration of unity fantasy there is a temporary obliteration of male and female, mother and father, self and other, and reality and fantasy. This vignette reflects as well his unconscious identification with his helpless dog-baby. There is also a growing capacity for warmth and tenderness, even love – a new experience for him – but less available when humans were involved. Note, too, his unconscious contempt and hatred toward such helplessness, as well as his wishes for power, domination, control and potential destruction that were expressed in his form of caregiving.

However, I wish to focus on his description of the shift from compelling affect to sexual excitation. He described feeling filled with tension as a result of such strong feelings for his dog, similar to his past experiences with young, exploitable females. Such powerful emotions would lead to sexual desire. If he was then able to consummate a sexual experience, the excitement and tension was alleviated and he felt great relief.

I believe this brief example illustrates Freud's (1905) and later George Klein's (1976) notion of vital needs that can be expressed through sexual modes. The patient's wish for vehemently felt physical attachment rapidly escalated to peak intensity and he could not tolerate such heightened anxiety states. Sexuality, according to him, felt liberating and ended his tension. He described an unmodulated affect state, which could be acknowledged as suffused with needs for tenderness, caring, holding and stroking. He gradually understood that such experiences could only be accepted as sexual. In this latter form he felt powerful, masculine, autonomous and in control. I suggest that the zone of phallic sexuality functioned as a channel of relief, masking a host of unmet needs associated with impoverished affect regulation.

The understimulating mother

The above vignette focused on overstimulation in the form of early and repeated physical abuse, intrusiveness and in at least one clearly remembered instance of sexual abuse. Both overstimulating and understimulating experiences may be found at the extreme end of the ambivalent-resistant and/or avoidant attachment relationship, and especially in the disorganized/disoriented attachment. With neglect and understimulation, we can also expect another distortion of sexuality.

Clinical example of understimulation

A patient who was a child of a significantly depressed mother describes the importance of intense experiences that she hopes will not be altered by treatment. She searches for intense stimulation almost to a manic degree. Sexuality, when it is at its best for her, is rough, bruising, almost brutal, as though she and her lover are two animals engaged in clashing, thrilling, deeply penetrating, intense almost harsh sexuality. Here, the primal vital, searingly real sexual interaction fills her with a sense of ecstatic aliveness and transforms an understimulating state.

An historical example of understimulation

Deeply religiously imbued saints and mystics often report ecstatic experiences that I believe may compensate for experiences of understimulation. An unusual report of a life of a sixteenth-century nun (Brown, 1986) reflects the pursuit of intense stimulation, which takes the form of passionate, dissociated, religious apparitions. As a child, the nun had a troubled relationship with a reluctant mother who was unsure of her maternal capacities. She directed her child instead 'to take the Madonna (Virgin Mother) as her mother and custodian' (p. 26). Her father, somewhat more involved, was interested in the development of her spiritual and cognitive life. At 9 years of age the child was already in an austere cloistered monastery, underscoring her removal from the stimulation of parents and social life. This was a strict convent, one inspired by the challenge of the corrupt practices found in many nunneries of that time. Daily life was harsh, consisting of fasts, mortification of the flesh, obedience, poverty, much prayer, interrupted sleep for prayer, modest, simple dress and hard labor. Monasteries were often poor and the requisite diet was skimpy (Sobel, 1999).

During the course of her convent life, the nun went into trance-like states, wherein she was visited by heavenly angels and Jesus himself. In one such occurrence Jesus 'tore her heart from her body' and later substituted his own heart within her (p. 61). Self-aggrandizing features in which she was elevated, publicly acknowledged, and fêted invaded her heavenly visions. Her virtues were praised and celebrated. Such elevating, personal accolades were often commented upon by outsiders and church clerics because it was thought that they hardly demonstrate the rectitude and humility expected of fervent nuns (Brown, 1986; Sobel, 1999).

Trance-like or dissociated states may not be so surprising with experiences of repeated fasting, feverish prayers and isolated cloisterhood. Nonetheless, her elaborate, ecstatic visions that involved self-adulation, self-adoration, and oneness with God provisionally suggest that these hallucinated visions represent reparative aspects of her earlier experiences of deprivation. Her frequent recourse to bodily mortification, flagellations and extended caresses, both real (coercively performed by a younger nun) and fantasized, suggests a longing for intense bodily contact and the stimulation such contacts afforded. Such a presumptive notion becomes more tenable when Brown (1986) commented that the nun insisted that her younger sister nun lay under her for hours at a time.

This narrative provides an interesting historical perspective on lesbianism. So unusual was the idea of homosexuality among women that the investigative clerics did not even understand such descriptions. Whereas male homosexuality flourished, there was not even a label for such a practice with regard to women.

Non-clinical example of understimulation

I am also speculating about features that may contribute to pornographic enticement and cross-dressing experiences for those deprived of appropriate interactive regulatory experiences. Whereas currently there is much more tolerance and acceptance of pornography and obscenity, at its extreme it appears to have features in common with the patient discussed earlier and her need to experience powerful, brutal sexuality. Pornographic interest can provide excitement for an understimulated self. The shock value of obscenity travels a dialectic path. On the one hand, it may be sought after because it is novel and forbidden and therefore, enticingly stimulating. On the other hand, the unexpected and the unpredictable can be distressing, frightening and even revolting. Stoller (1985) suggests that typically there is secrecy surrounding the indulgence in obscenity, which involves risk and thus excitement. I believe this feature of risk-taking has much in common with cross-dressing, where part of the thrill and intensity of the experience stems from the possibility of being found out. Such a discovery in both cross-dressing ventures and pornographic indulgence provides for the dual possibility of being humiliated and humiliating the other. In the latter instance, it is the successful parade as the opposite sex that humiliates the fooled one. With regard to obscenity, according to Stoller, the 'meek hope to humble the mighty ... Victim is to become victor by dumping the dark, moist, smelly, hidden, mysterious, swollen, interior's contents onto society's sin-sniffers' (p. 90). The important features of risk-taking, potential threats of humiliation, and aggression arouse excitement in an understimulated self.

Errant mutual regulation as a function of a maladaptive attachment style: 'vigilant' vocal coordination

Researchers (Jaffe et al., 2001) have investigated vocal rhythm coordination as a way of understanding interactive and self-regulatory patterns and their relationship to attachment styles. They studied vocal rhythm patterns (vocalizing and turn taking) during face-to-face interactions between mothers and their infants, and strangers with infants. Different patterns of vocal coordination predicted different patterns of attachment. 'Totally contrary to the idea that the highest degree of rhythm coordination would index the most well "matched" or well "related" dyads, the highest degree of vocal rhythm coordination predicted the most insecure infant attachments (disorganized and anxious-resistant), whereas the lowest degree of coordination predicted the avoidant' (Beebe et al., 2000, p. 11). When there was too close monitoring, too carefully matched, and highly contingent vocal patterns in the dyad, it coordinated with anxious and disorganized attachments.[5]

Thus, it is legitimate to hypothesize (as do Beebe et al., 2000) that too tight, inflexible, highly contingent patterns of vocal interactions or 'high tracking' (an exaggerated response to the vocal cues of the other) showed an inordinate amount of reliance on mutual regulation approaching interactive 'vigilance'. Too much mutual regulation does not allow the child to rely on inner cues and develop an adaptable self-regulatory pattern (see also Gianino and Tronick, 1985; Sander, 1975). Such a pattern is consistent with West and Sheldon's (1988) elucidation of the anxiously attached caregiving style of relating observed in some adults. Here, early in life, the individual has learned to reverse the pattern of caregiving by becoming the maternal figure to a mother who needs a symbiotic relationship (Levy and Blatt, 1999).

In this context, it must be acknowledged, once again, that the relationship between vocal interaction and attachment is but one feature of an interactional system. The nature of vocal interactions or attachment are only aspects of a complex, emergent personality system. Features such as temperament, cognition and dynamic variables also contribute to the shape of our personality organization.

Nevertheless, one can expect that such high vocal tracking children develop more complex systems of interaction that reflect a tight responsiveness to others. If this early form of coordination persists, it is not such a speculative leap to consider that such individuals become exquisite vessels of the other person's needs. We certainly know many such individuals who recognize their dependence on the vicissitudes of others.

Using multiple sense modalities, they scrutinize their interactions for support, information on living, decision-making, acknowledgment and appreciation. Such individuals are highly responsive to external cues so they can shape themselves to accommodate to the other. Such responsiveness to others has much in common with Winnicott's (1965) notion of a false self.

Further conjecture of a continued highly contingent responsiveness can lead us to imagine, for example, such a woman's sexual life. It tends not to include considerations about her own wishes with regard to sex, at least not in her overt behavior. It is the need of the other that powerfully dominates the consciousness of the couple. In addition to her developed unconscious fantasies about the meaning of such other-directed reliance, we must consider the relevance of her cultural context. The dominance of our patriarchal culture has fostered this mutual orientation of the man's sexual needs as acceptable to both. It is feminists such as Duane and Hodges (1992), Mitchell (1974), Elliot (1991), Williams (1989), feminist psychoanalysts such as Mitchell (1974), Irigaray (1985), Kristeva (1999) and the literary feminist theorists such as Butler (1990), Sedgwick (1990) and Moi (1985) who have written extensively about such skewing of sexuality. Benjamin (1988), in particular, has stressed the importance of alterity, which traditional psychoanalytic theorizing has lacked. When discussing mothers and children, the classical focus was on the mother's effect on her child, neglecting the reciprocal effect of the child's impact on the mother. The recognition of the subjectivity of the female in her role both as a woman and a mother has important implications for the theorization of sexuality (Benjamin, 1988, 1995; Silverman (in press)).

We may all experience some aspects of what I have been depicting when I describe various non-secure attachment patterns. When these are potentially maladaptive, I am focusing on the extreme end of non-secure attachment systems and behavior that has been labeled disorganized/disoriented attachments.

Overstimulation, understimulation, sexuality and its effects on transference and countertransference

Can the ideas of overstimulation and understimulation be usefully employed when considering the therapeutic interaction? If the analyst has a tendency toward reactivity to understimulation it may subtly invade the analytic work life. There are, of course, many strands of meaning that may underlie an analyst's wish to excite and dazzle his or her patient with insights. One thematic trope consistent with the prior examples is the need to stimulate and enliven the self and/or the patient, thereby vivifying a depressed or deadened analyst-self or patient experience. On the other hand, the patient's sexuality, especially in its vitality and sensuality, can provide sufficient ebullience for the analyst so that it will enhance and animate an understimulated analyst-self.

Retrospectively, it is difficult to be clear about current behavior reflecting an overstimulating or understimulating early experience because of the interplay of need and defense in subsequent behavior. Thus, a wish to tease and excite in the psychoanalytic situation may reflect recycled patterns of overstimulation or defensively mask the needs of an understimulated self. The analyst who struggles with a less than stable experience of self-regulation needs to be alert to the specific regulating function potentially served when dealing with a patient's sexual issues as well as adjusting to the qualities inherent in the analytic situation, For example, Kernberg (1991) comments on the openness of the psychoanalytic situation which fosters an undoing of repression and its very nature can be experienced as a 'tease' and it has the quality of 'implicit seductiveness' (p. 359). Further, the analyst needs to steer a careful course between his/her inhibition in exploring sexual transferences or the potential for being 'seductively invasive' in the pursuit of the resistances to the awareness of the sexual transference (Kernberg, 1994, p. 1147). Here I am addressing a different way that analysts may think about their therapeutic interactions modified by their understimulating or overstimulating self-regulatory patterns.

Interactive regulation and sexuality and its effects on transference and countertransference

A similar query may be posed about patients and/or analysts who lean toward close tracking and the effects on transference and countertransference. Potentially high tracking patients may closely monitor their analyst's interventions, shaping themselves in accordance with their analyst's subtle wishes. Thus, the so-called 'ideally cooperative patient', responsive to the analyst's interventions, may reflect the patient's significant interactive-regulatory needs masked by agreeableness and understanding. We are all familiar with such patients; however, I am offering another perspective that might contribute to our understanding of this behavior.

It is easy to expect a mismatch between an analyst who tilts toward self-regulation and a patient who relies on interactive regulation. While an analyst's self- regulatory response need not interfere with his/her capacity for listening and attentiveness, however, when there is a tendency toward such a reliance it can impede appropriate interactive responsiveness, especially with a patient who relies on interactive regulation. In such a mismatch, a patient may feel misunderstood, misattuned, or experience the analyst as unavailable and unresponsive, a disembodied voice behind the couch. Heightened self-containment may also lead to a tendency toward projection of wishes/fears of intimacy in the patient when it may exist in the analyst. When shame experiences around sexuality are presented by the patient, minimal engagement may increase shame-prone experiences in the patient. On the other hand, compensatory interaction may unconsciously be experienced as an enactment of sexual intimacy.

The analyst who may rely on interactive-regulatory experiences may be too inclined to closely monitor the patient's experience. Such a response may evolve into a countertransferential orientation if, for example, it can be felt as an impingement, a lack of breathing space, a missed opportunity for the patient to search and uncover features of his/her psychic life or even, in its extreme form, a retraumatization of the patient. Such tendencies on the analyst's part (impingement, lack of breathing space, etc.) can unconsciously be experienced as sexual seductions or a possible experience of the analyst's need for power and possession. Such high tracking analysts also may not allow for the development of different perspectives, with the possibility of the analyst feeling distinct emotions, images from his/her reverie state, new ideas that may emerge and which he/she needs to challenge or confront. Thus, the analyst may have to steer a careful course between 'empathic introspection' (Kohut, 1977) and the internal tolerance of another perspective.

Little Hans and his problematic affect regulation

Earlier, I discussed Freud's (1909) and George Klein's (1976) concept of 'two way traversibility' as well as the plasticity of sexuality. Both of these ideas are relevant to the case of Little Hans (see Chapter 10 by Luis Juri in this volume for another analysis of Little Hans' case from an attachment perspective).

Freud often used his case material as illustrative of the aspect of theory he was developing. So, too, Little Hans was, for Freud, a vivid demonstration of 'a positive paragon of all vices' – a polymorphous perversity found in all young children. In his lucid and engrossing style, Freud leads us through the budding sexuality of Little Hans and its inhibition and subsequent repression, producing a phobia. The case material presented is multilayered and complex. Here I want to highlight what Freud does not stress, Hans' early and conflicted relationship to his mother. (Bowlby (1973) understood Little Hans as demonstrating an anxious attachment relationship to his mother because the boy was preoccupied with worries about her abandoning him. I argue for other considerations as well.)

There are a number of possible reasons for Freud's lack of commentary about the nature of the child's parenting. First, the culture of parenting was quite different at the beginning of the twentieth century. Sound thrashings were often administered as effective, disciplined childcare. Severe and even harsh responses toward young children were accepted as rigorous and competent child rearing (Wolff, 1988). The Victorian attitude toward masturbation was even more ferocious and extreme. All sorts of almost torturous devices were used to insure against the practice of masturbation (e.g. 'binding hands' and 'locking genitals into contraptions that served as underwear'; Wolff, 1988, p. 64). Second, the parents were followers of Freud, which probably biased his judgment about their parenting. Third, Freud was interested in stressing the normality of Little Hans' environment, so that he could demonstrate the pervasive aspect of polymorphous perversity and the oedipal complex. Fourth, although explicitly acknowledging the ubiquity of ambivalence in mental life, nonetheless Freud maintained that there was nothing so powerful as the love of a mother for her son (Freud, 1910). Thus, Freud acknowledged and minimized what he called the mother's 'over-affectionate' behavior toward the boy and her severe, puritanical responses to his sexual interests because Freud insisted that eventually she would become embroiled in his 'predestined' (p. 28) oedipal drama.

However, when Freud (1910) was speculating about the early relationship of Leonardo da Vinci and his mother, he drew parallels between the Little Hans and little Leonardo's questions and surmises about genitals and sexuality. Freud speculated that Leonardo's mother had an 'erotic fixation' (p. 99) which led her to encourage 'too much tenderness' (p. 99) toward the boy. The almost identical language used with regard to both mothers suggests Freud was refraining from alluding to Hans' mother's inappropriate erotic desires toward her child. In da Vinci's case we can see Freud's explicit acknowledgment of the power of the early mother–child relationship in shaping the child's future sexual life, instead of his theorized position of a natural, biological unfolding of the sex drive as preordained. (Freud, with even greater specificity, describes Leonardo's father's early detachment from his illegitimate son and the son's subsequent treatment of his art productions, his symbolic children, with the same indifference that he experienced with his own father. Here we have an example of the father's model of an attachment relationship with his son then, symbolically expressed intergenerationally.)

Freud's insistence on honesty and integrity and his wish to offer collegial loyalty as well as demonstrate his new ideas in the Little Hans case appear similar to what Freud (1900) did when reporting his own associations to the Irma dream. Freud did not acknowledge his sexual wishes when he talked about the 'comparison between the three women', his associations to a dream image. Instead, he commented, it 'would have taken me far afield – There is at least one spot in every dream at which it is unplumbable – a navel as it were, that is its point of contact with the unknown' (p. 111). While asserting that this conundrum cannot be understood any further, in the following chapter he talks about wishes as instigators of dreams. His Leonardo paper, a similar case study, like the subsequent chapter in *The Interpretation of Dreams* (1900) reveals the contents he was loath to communicate in Little Hans.

Clinical example: the case of Little Hans

Freud tells us that the mother frequently threatened the child that she would leave if he did not behave. Hans also mentioned that his mother beat him with a carpet-beater and his father confirmed that the mother frequently threatened Hans with such an action. She was often harsh, critical and judgemental, at the same time offering intense intimacy. (She frequently let him share her bed and he did so, especially when his father was away.) When Little Hans wished to spend time with 'another woman', i.e. visit for the night with his friend Mariedl, his mother angrily threatened him with eviction. The suggestive picture that emerges is of an overstimulating mother, who is, at the same time, harsh and punitive. This can leave the child in a conflicted state. He would need the anxiety-reducing physical presence of his mother. Yet when he was with her she appeared to flame his emotions, producing a state of extreme overexcitement. She, in turn, would get upset and critical when he was manifestly overheated with sexuality (i.e. calling his sexual interests piggish, and relentlessly checking on and forbidding his engagement in masturbation). Freud's early comment on the case was that the 'intensity of emotion was greater than the child could control' (p. 25). In summary, Freud notes that 'one ought perhaps to insist upon the violence of the child's anxiety' (p. 100). Such conflicting maternal messages may well provide the seeds for Little Hans to develop what would today be labeled an ambivalently organized attachment.

The child's over-excitability can be attributed to a number of sources. There was his unacknowledged hostility toward his mother because of the threats of serious disconnection and abandonment. Freud made mention only of the child's unconscious hostility to his father, stemming from his oedipal wishes. Freud granted that there was sadism in Little Hans' maternal fantasies. However, Freud understood it as a construction of erotic desire (i.e. sadistically penetrate his mother in intercourse).

A further source of the child's anxiety may have arisen from his sexual overstimulation, and his mother's seeming inability to be a consciously soothing, calming non-sexual maternal presence for the child. These features can produce an incapacity for Little Hans to effectively modulate his emotional state, that is, to self-regulate.

Freud certainly recognized the extent of the child's anxiety, but maintained that it was stimulated almost exclusively from internal wishes and fantasies. Here we may see an example of two-way traversibility that Klein described. Viewed from this perspective, the non-sensual aspect of the child's emotional regulation was significantly impaired. Instead, Freud understands Little Hans' anxiety only as a product of unconscious sexual and hostile wishes. From my vantage point, Little Hans needed more calming, and soothing and affectionate responses, allowing for the development of age-appropriate active, curious sexuality. Instead, I would posit that a developmentally available 'zone', his curiosity and pleasure with his 'widdler', developed special power, probably, in part, as his attempt to self-regulate his chronically anxious state. At the same time, the overheated home atmosphere suggests a contribution to his intense erotic preoccupations. Today we can benefit from the inclusion of such an attachment model because it will help us not to neglect attachment needs.

Summary

In summary, traditional psychoanalytic theory needs to expand and integrate relevant motivational issues that have emerged from developmental research. The compelling aggregate of empirical data on the attachment system can no longer be overlooked as irrelevant or as dealing only with surface behavior. The internal working model of attachment with its array of needs and defenses can be demonstrated during the first year of life and it has predictive power, in some studies, through adolescence. The internal working models of mothers' attachment to their own mothers show significant correspondence with the attachment status of their infants. Further, I maintain that it is the affect-regulating feature of the attachment system that is a salient issue in the transmission of attachment styles intergenerationally.

Considering both libidinal wishes and attachment allows the clinician to focus on the significant feature that emerges in the clinical setting. When either desire or attachment is eliminated it may lead to an insufficient analysis of the complex intermingling, overlaying, or salience of one or the other.

Notes

1. Some clinicians (Pistole, 1995; Shane, Shane and Gales, 1997; see Silverman, 1995) often conflate the style of attachment, ambivalent and avoidant, with pathology. Such thinking eliminates the variation among attachment styles within the normal range. Some attachment researchers have begun to pathologize these categories as well. I believe that it is only at the extreme ends of these continua that problematic attachments should be considered.
2. Such motivational considerations as novelty, curiosity about the environment, feelings of effectance, as well as others, should be considered.
3. I agree with Inderbitzin and Levy's (2000) questioning of the concept of regression. A major drawback is the 'outmoded linear model' (p. 981) it supports (see also Silverman, 1981). From my point of view such a label as 'regression' obscures the relevance of the patient's problematic regulation of his affective state. It is this feature that needs further exploration, but may be obscured by the label of 'regression'.
4. Recent more carefully refined categories in work dealing with adult attachment styles have delineated a dismissive avoidant category (Bartholomew, 1990; Bartholomew and Horowitz, 1991). Such individuals 'are characterized by a defensive denial of the need and/or desire for relatedness' (Levy and Blatt, 1999, p. 552). In addition, they are 'high in self-esteem, socially self-confident, unemotional, defensive, independent, cynical, critical of others, distant from others, and more interested in achievement than in relationships' (Levy and Blatt, 1999, p. 552). The patient I am describing fits this category of attachment style.
5. The quality of the interactive relationship, as seen in low mother–infant vocal patterns of coordination and the avoidant attachment group, promotes a reliance on solitary self-regulation (e.g. self-touching, self-soothing), and the infrequent use of the other (see also Freedman and Lavender's (1997) discussion of motoric rhythmicity and arrhythmicity in the analyst and their coordinations with countertransference).

References

Ainsworth MDS, Blehar JC, Waters E and Wall S (1978) Patterns of Attachment: A Psychological Study of the Strange Situation. Hillsdale, NJ: Erlbaum.

Bartholomew K (1990) Avoidance of intimacy: An attachment perspective. Journal of Social and Personal Relationships 7: 147–78.

Bartholomew K and Horowitz L (1991) Attachment styles among young adults: A four category model of attachment. Journal of Personality and Social Psychology 61: 226–41.

Beebe B, Jaffe J, Lachmann F, Feldstein S, Crown C and Jassow M (2000) Systems models in development and psychoanalysis: The case of vocal rhythm coordination and attachment. Infant Mental Health Journal 2: 1–24.

Bell SM and Ainsworth MDS (1972) Infant crying and maternal responsiveness. Child Development 41: 291–311.

Benjamin J (1988) The Bonds of Love. New York: Pantheon Books.

Benjamin J (1995) Like Subjects, Love Objects. New Haven: Yale University Press.

Bowlby J (1973) Separation Anxiety and Anger New York: Basic Books.

Bowlby J (1988) A Secure Base. New York: Basic Books

Brown JC (1986) Immodest Acts. Oxford: Oxford University Press.

Butler J (1990) Gender Trouble. New York: Routledge.

Condon WS and Sander LS (1974) neonate movements is synchronized with adult speech. Science 183: 99–101.

Duane J and Hodges D (1992) From Klein to Kristeva Psychoanalytic Feminism and the Search for the 'Good Enough' Mother. Ann Arbor: The University of Michigan Press.

Elliot P (1991) From Mastery to Analysis Theories of Gender in Psychoanalytic Feminism. Ithaca: Cornell University Press.

Emde R (1999) Moving ahead: Integrating influences of affective processes for development and for psychoanalysis. International Journal of Psychoanalysis 80: 317–40.

Freedman N and Lavender J (1997) On receiving the patient's transference: The symbolizing and desymbolizing countertransference. Journal of the American Psychoanalytic Association 45: 79–103.

Freud S (1900) The interpretation of dreams. Standard Edition 4 and 5.

Freud S (1905) Three essays on the theory of sexuality. Standard Edition 7: 125–43.

Freud, S (1909) Analysis of a phobia in a five-year old boy. Standard Edition 10: 5–149.

Freud S (1910) Leonardo Da Vinci and a memory of his childhood. Standard Edition 11: 59–139.

Freud S (1915) Instincts and their vicissitudes. Standard Edition 14: 111–40.

Gianino A and Tronick EZ (1985) The mutual regulation model: The infant's self and interactive regulation and coping and defensive capacities. In: T Field, P McCabe and N Schneiderman (eds) Stress and Coping Across the Life Development. Hillsdale, NJ: Erlbaum, pp. 47–68.

Glen J and Bernstein I (1995) Sadomasochism. In: BB Moore and BD Fine (eds) Psycho-Analysis: The Major Concepts. New Haven: Yale University Press, pp. 252–70.

Inderbitzin LB and Levy ST (2000) Regression and psychoanalytic technique: The concretization of a concept. Psychoanalytic Quarterly LXIX: 195–224.

Irigaray L (1985) Speculum of the Other Woman. Ithaca: Cornell University Press.

Jaffe J, Beebe B, Feldstein F, Crown C and Janow M (2001) Rhythms of dialogue in infancy. Monograph of the Society for Research in Child Development 66(2), Serial # 264, pp. 1–132.

Kernberg OF (1991) Sado-masochism, sexual excitement, and perversion. Journal of the American Psychoanalytic Association 39: 333–62.

Kernberg OF (1994) Love in the analytic setting. Journal of the American Psychoanalytic Association 42: 1137–57.

Klein GS (1976) Psychoanalytic Theory. New York: International Universities Press.

Kobak R and Shaver P (1987, June) Strategies for maintaining self security: a theoretical analysis of continuity and change in styles of social adaptation. Conference in honor of John Bowlby's 80th birthday, Bayswater, London, England.

Kohut H (1977) The Restoration of the Self. New York: International Universities Press.

Kristeva J (1997) The Portable Kristeva. New York: Columbia University Press.

Laplanche J (1997) The theory of seduction and the problem of the other. International Journal of Psycho-analysis 78: 653–66.

Levy KN and Blatt SJ (1999) Attachment theory and psychoanalysis: Further differentiation with insecure attachment patterns. Psychoanalytic Inquiry 19: 541–75.

Lyons-Ruth K (1999) Two Person Unconscious: Intersubjective dialogue, enactive relational representation and the emergence of new forms of relational organization. Psychoanalytic Inquiry 19: 576–617.

Main M (1993) Discourse prediction, and recent studies in attachment: Implications for psychoanalysis. Journal of the American Psychoanalytic Association 41: 209–43.

Main M and Solomon J (1990) Procedures for identifying infants as disorganized/disoriented during Ainsworth strange situation. In: MT Greenburg, D Cicchetti and EM Cummings (eds) Theory, Research, and Intervention. Chicago: University of Chicago Press, pp. 121–60.

Main M, Tomasini L and Tolan W (1979) Differences among mothers judged to differ in security of attachment. Developmental Psychology 15: 472–3.

Malatesta CZ, Culber C, Tessman JR and Shepherde B (1989) The development of emotional expression during the first two years of life. Monograph of the Society for Social Research in Child Development, 54.

Mitchell J (1974) Psychoanalysis and Feminism. New York: Pantheon.

Moi T (1985) Sexual Textual Politics Feminist Literary Theory. London: Routledge.

Pistole MC (1995) Adult attachment style and narcissistic vulnerability. Psychoanalytic Psychology 12: 115–26.

Sameroff A (1976) Early influences on development. Fact or fantasy? In S Chess and A Thomas (eds) Annual Progress in Child Psychiatry and Child Development. New York: Brunner/Mazel.

Sander LW (1975) Infant and caretaking environment: investigation and conceptualization of adaptive behavior in a system of increasing complexity. In: EJ
Anthony (ed.) Explorations in Child Psychiatry. New York: Plenum Press.

Sander LW (1977) The regulation of exchange in the infant-caretaker system and
some aspects of context-content relationship. Conversation and the
Development of Language. New York: Wiley.

Sander LW (1983) Toward a logic of organization in psychobiological development. In: H Klar and L Siever (eds) Biological Response Styles: Clinical
Implications. Washington, DC: American Psychiatric Association, pp. 20–36.

Schaffer HR (1977) Studies in Mother–Infant Interaction. London and New York:
Academic Press.

Sedgwick EK (1990) Epistemology of the Closet. Berkeley: University of
California.

Shane M, Shane E and Gales M (1997) Intimate Attachments. Toward a New Self
Psychology. New York: Guilford Press.

Shengold L (1999) Soul Murder Revisited. New Haven: Yale University Press.

Silverman DK (1981, Spring) Some proposed modifications of psychoanalytic theories. of early childhood development. Paper presented at IPTAR, New York.
Also in J Masling (ed.) (1986) Empirical Studies of Psychoanalytic Theories,
vol. 2. Hillsdale: Analytic Press, pp. 49–71.

Silverman DK (1991) Attachment patterns and Freudian theory: An integrative
proposal. Psychoanalytic Psychology 8: 169–93.

Silverman DK (1992) Attachment research: An approach to a developmental relational perspective. In: NJ Skolnick and SO Warshaw (eds) Relational
Perspectives in Psychoanalysis. Hillsdale: Analytic Press, pp. 195–216.

Silverman DK (1994) Attachment themes: Theory, empirical research, psychoanalytic implications, and future directions. Bulletin of the Psychoanalytic
Research Society (Section VI) of APA's Division of Psychoanalysis 3(1): 9–11.

Silverman DK (1995) Problems with linking concepts from different domains:
Commentary on Pistole's Adult Attachment Style and Narcissistic Vulnerability.
Psychoanalytic Psychology 12: 151–8.

Silverman DK (1998a) The tie that binds affect regulation, attachment, and psychoanalysis. Psychoanalytic Psychology 15: 187–212.

Silverman DK (1998b, June) Procedural knowledge, affect-regulation and the
attachment system. Discussion of Mary Main's work at the Rapaport-Klein
Study Group. Stockbridge, Mass.

Silverman DK (2003) Theorizing in the shadow of Foucault: Facets of female sexuality. Psychoanalytic Dialogue.

Sobel D (1999) Galileo's Daughter. New York: Walker and Co.

Stark M (1977, March) Welcome and opening remarks. Paper presented at the
Developmental Process and the Enigma of Change in Psychodynamic Therapy
Conference, Boston, Mass.

Stein R (1998) The enigmatic dimension of sexual experience: The 'otherness' of
sexuality and primal seduction. Psychoanalytic Quarterly LXV: 594–625.

Stern DN (1974) Mother and infant at play: The dyadic interaction involving
facial, vocal and gaze behaviors. In: M Lewis and L Rosenblum (eds) The Effects
of the Infant on the Caregiver.

Stern DN (1985) The Interpersonal World of the Infant. New York: Basic Books.

Stoller RJ (1985) Observing the Erotic Imagination. New Haven: Yale University Press.

Thelen E and Smith LB (1995) A Dynamic Systems Approach to the Development of Cognition and Action. Cambridge, Mass: MIT Press.

Trevarthen C (1980) The foundations of intersubjectivity: Development of interpersonal and cooperative understanding in infants. In: DR Olsen (ed.) The Social Foundations of Language and Thought. New York: Norton, pp. 316–42.

Trevarthen C (1993) The function of emotions in early infant communication and development. In: J Nadel and L Camaioni (eds) New Perspectives in Early Communicative Development. London: Routledge, pp. 48–81.

Tronick EZ (1997, March) Relevant videotape vignettes from infant observational research. Paper presented at the Developmental Process and the Enigma of Change in Psychodynamic Therapy conference, Boston, Mass.

Van IJzendoorn MH (1995) Adult attachment representations, parental responsiveness, and infant attachment: A meta-analysis on the predictability of the Adult Attachment Interview. Psychological Bulletin 117: 383–403.

West M and Sheldon AER (1988) Classification of pathological attachment patterns in adults. Journal of Personality Disorders 2: 153–9.

Wiederman GH (1995) Sexuality. In: BB Moore and BD Fine (eds) Psycho-Analysis: The Major Concepts. New Haven: Yale University Press, pp. 334–45.

Williams L (1989) Hard Core Power, Pleasure, and the Frenzy of the Visible. Berkeley: University of California Press.

Winnicott DW (1965) The Maturational Processes and the Facilitating Environment. New York: International Universities Press.

Wolff L (1988) Child Abuse in Freud's Vienna. New York: New York University Press.

The infant and adult attachment categories

JUNE W. SROUFE

The Strange Situation

Starting from the attachment theory of John Bowlby, Mary Ainsworth developed a system for assessing the quality of infant–caregiver relationships (Ainsworth et al., 1978). After hundreds of hours of home observation both in Uganda (Ainsworth, 1967) and in Baltimore, Ainsworth observed important variation in how the mother–infant pairs managed secure base behavior and how they coped with stress.

In one large group, which she termed the secure group, the children were able to confidently explore their world and effectively use the caregiver as a secure base of support if any need arose. When they were upset, they were able to seek and receive the comfort they needed. Within this group, Ainsworth saw further variation. Some of the children were able to explore while having relatively little interaction with the mother, and others were likely to remain closer to her and frequently interact through verbalizations, contact seeking and so on. When stressed, some of the secure children were more easily upset and required somewhat longer periods of contact to be settled than others. Nonetheless, what the children in this group had in common was that they did exhibit productive exploration and, if upset, were well able to use the caregiver as an effective source of care.

In order to explore further these observed differences in attachment style, Ainsworth created a laboratory procedure that would stress the infant, enabling her to observe in greater detail how well the infant–caregiver couple would cope with the situation. In this 20-minute laboratory procedure, the 12- to 18-month-old infant is twice separated from its attachment figure for a brief period of time. Virtually all infants will experience arousal and some distress during these separations. A stranger may serve to aid a distressed child, but a stranger rarely substitutes for what the child has come to know as its final source of comfort. How the infant expresses its need for comfort to the caregiver and the effectiveness of the caregiver's response to that expression reveal enduring qualities of the relationship.

Instead of the two patterns of attachment that she had seen in the home, secure and insecure, Ainsworth was surprised to discover three distinct patterns of attachment, one secure and two insecure patterns. A fourth group, the disorganized-disoriented pattern, was discovered some years later by Mary Main and her research team. The following is a brief description of the four attachment patterns:

1. *The secure (B) pattern.* The first and largest group is the secure (B) pattern. As she had observed in the home, the parent–child relationship provides a secure base from which the child explores the world in an enthusiastic, trusting way. While exhibiting differences in exploration and response to threat, generally the child showing this pattern clearly expresses its distress when upset, differentially seeks care from its caregiver, and is able to be fully settled by that caregiver.

2. *The resistant or ambivalent (C) pattern.* The ambivalent or resistant pattern is characterized by a heightened display of attachment behavior. Before separation, the children in this group are often immature in their behavior and play, and also may be preoccupied with the caregiver. Notably less attention is paid to exploration. Like some of the children in the secure pattern, upon separation the children in this resistant pattern become very upset and cannot be settled by the stranger. Unlike the secure children, however, even when they are reunited with their caregiver, they are not easily settled and may alternate contact seeking with angry resistance. It was hypothesized that these children had experienced an unpredictable pattern of care in which the child is supported at some times and not at others. This leaves the child frustrated and unable to trust that care is consistently available. They are required to adopt a 'strategy' in which they maximize the expression of attachment behaviors, being vigilantly attentive to their caregivers and signaling needs at the slightest provocation (Main and Hesse, 1990).

3. *The avoidant (A) pattern.* As with children in the secure group, the children who are avoidant in their interaction with attachment figures play well alone, interact less with the caregiver, show less wariness of the stranger and perhaps even engage the stranger in play. When aroused by separations, this group of infants behaves very differently to the secure group. Upon reunion, they turn away from the caregiver and do not seek comfort. Indeed, Ainsworth found that the infants in the avoidant group were less likely to seek care as the stress is increased.

Ainsworth had observed in the home that when these infants had sought to be picked up, they were rebuffed. Their mothers hold them as much, in general, but they turned the infants away when they signaled a need (Ainsworth et al., 1978). It is hypothesized that children in this group have experienced rejection when they have revealed their needs. As a result, they have learned to hide their needs for care at relevant moments. As stress increases, their efforts to remain aloof are redoubled. Main has suggested that, in contrast to the anxious/resistant group, these children have adopted a 'strategy' of *minimizing* the expression of attachment. While this protects them from the pain of rejection and may serve to keep the caregiver from being further alienated from them, a price may be paid in subsequent adaptation.

4. *The disorganized/disoriented (D) pattern.* Certain experiences can be overwhelming to a child's adaptation. When this occurs, the normal pattern of coping may break down. Mary Main noted that some of the children in Ainsworth's Strange Situation Procedure exhibited contradictory behavior or an otherwise incoherent strategy for coping with the separation experience (Main and Hesse, 1990). In the presence of the caregiver, these children exhibited anomalous behaviors suggestive of contradictory urges (approaching a parent with head averted) or behaviors that involved apprehension either directly (fearful facial expressions) or indirectly (disoriented behaviors, including dazed and trance-like expressions). She hypothesized that the child was in conflict, even afraid, and unable to maintain a coherent strategy. One situation that could lead to this problem is when the caregiver becomes a source of fear due to child abuse. In this case, when aroused, the child would experience contradictory impulses, since human evolutionary history disposes the child both to run *to* the attachment figure when frightened, and to run *from* the source of the fright. When the parent is both, the child is placed in an unresolvable paradox. Being unable to hold these simultaneous contradictory impulses, the child experiences a breakdown in the usual way of coping and shows signs of disorganization. Indeed, it has been found that the disorganized/disoriented (D) pattern, as it is called, is associated with risk factors such as parental child maltreatment (George and Main, 1979; Carlson et al., 1989; Lyons-Ruth et al., 1991). However, other disruptive experiences can also lead to signs of disorganization. Any frightening experience from which there is no escape may serve as the catalyst for a breakdown in coherent functioning. Some additional risk factors found to be associated with disorganized attachment include parental bipolar disorder (DeMulder and Radke-Yarrow, 1991), and parental alcohol intake (O'Connor, Sigman and Brill, 1987). Recent research has focused on the prevalence of unresolved losses in the history of the caregiver and its effect on the infant. Unresolved losses in the

history of the parent, assessed prenatally, were found to be predictive of frightened or frightening behavior with the infant (Jacobvitz, Hazen and Riggs, 1997). Frightening or frightened behavior, while in the presence of the infant, has also been shown to be associated with disorganized attachment status (Schuengel et al., 1997).

Table A1 offers a summary of the criteria used to assess attachment patterns in the Strange Situation.

The Adult Attachment Interview

This interview is semi-structured and takes about one to one and a half hours to administer. In the interview, individuals are asked to describe their early relationships with important caregivers and to provide specific incidents whenever possible. They also are asked more in-depth questions regarding their current understanding of the quality of their childhood relationships and also about important losses. The interview is transcribed and then scored for state of mind with regard to attachment. As with the child attachment categories, there are four adult attachment groups:

1. *The autonomous group* is an adult parallel to the secure child pattern. This group is characterized by a lively and spontaneous report of childhood experiences, good recall of those experiences and a balanced description of any difficulties that occurred. The two non-autonomous groups are the dismissing and the preoccupied groups, which parallel the avoidant and resistant child groups, respectively.
2. *The dismissing transcript* is characterized by an idealized presentation of childhood, a lack of recall for childhood, and if difficulties are reported, effects are denied or minimized. For example, when asked to give five adjectives that describe his relationship with his father, a man might describe him in very positive terms, such as 'very, very loving'. When asked to recount an incident that illustrates very, very loving behavior, he first restates that he has few memories of his childhood. He then goes on to say that he sometimes drove him to school when he had missed the bus even though he was angry with him and it disrupted his day to do so. This response fails to provide a clear example of very loving behavior, and also fails to persuade the reader that the father acted from love.
3. *The preoccupied transcript* is often characterized by lengthy passages that may be either confused and vague or angry and conflicted. It is as though the preoccupied individual is unable to step back from childhood and present a coherent summary of their experiences. In response

Table A1. Patterns of attachment observed in the Strange Situation

Secure attachment pattern
A. Before mother's departure
   1. Readily separate to explore toys
   2. Share in their play with their mothers
   3. Friendly to stranger
B. Upon reunion
   1. Immediately seek and maintain contact
   2. Are happy to see caregiver
   3. Contact is effective in terminating distress
   4. Are able to return to play

Anxious/resistant attachment pattern
A. Before departure
   1. Difficulty in separating to explore toys
   2. Wary of stranger
B. Upon reunion
   1. Mix contact seeking with contact resisting
   2. May continue to cry and fuss
   3. Are not able to return to play
   4. May show striking passivity

Anxious/avoidant attachment pattern
A. Before departure
   1. Readily separates to play with toys
   2. Very little sharing of play with mother
   3. Interacts with stranger (little preference)
B. Upon reunion
   1. Active avoidance (turning away to toys, looking away, moving away, ignoring)
   2. May mix avoidance with a tendency toward proximity
   3. Avoidance more extreme in second reunion
   4. No avoidance of stranger

Disorganized/disoriented attachment pattern
A. Before departure
   1. Might exhibit signs of disorientation
   2. May interact with stranger (little preference) or appear unduly frightened
   3. Poor quality of play
B. Upon reunion
   1. May appear momentarily dazed or confused or show extensive or intensive expressions of fear, particularly in the presence of the parent
   2. Freezing, stilling or slowed movements and expressions
   3. Mixture of contradictory behaviors. For instance, may mix avoidant and resistant behaviors
   4. Stereotypies, asymmetrical movements, anomalous postures
   5. Seemingly undirected, misdirected or incomplete movements (e.g. moves away from parent), exceptionally slow or limp movement ('underwater' approach movements, falls prone in 'depressed' huddled posture)

to the probe for adjectives to describe her relationship with her mother, a woman might say 'selfish'. When asked to recount an incident from childhood, she might go on to say, 'She always put herself first, never wanted to see things my way ... just ... always! always! Why just last week she made me go to a restaurant that she wanted to instead of my favorite just because ... she's selfish!' This response may go on at some length and still fail to answer the question; that is, provide an example from childhood. Moreover, this individual is unable to step back from the difficult aspects of her relationship and describe it in an understandable way without getting swept up in the preoccupying emotion.

4. *The unresolved group* is parallel to the disorganized group of infancy. Individuals are seen to be unresolved if they show signs of disorientation and disorganization when questioned about traumatic events or important losses. Lack of resolution can result from trauma or from unresolved loss and is assessed by noting lapses in the monitoring of reason or discourse. One of the many possible ways this can be observed in a transcript is when the speaker talks about a dead loved one as though they were still alive. This is an example of lack of monitoring of reason. Most interestingly, unresolved status on the AAI is predictive of the disorganized pattern in the infants of those subjects.

Table A2 summarizes the key elements of the AAI classification system.

Table A2. Adult attachment classifications

Secure-autonomous (F). Dialogue is fresh and thoughtful. Collaborative and coherent when discussing attachment-related experiences. May have positive or negative childhood experiences but are perceptive in understanding their contributions (45–55% in normative samples).

Dismissing (Ds). Transcripts may be short. Attachment concerns are not an active part of the discourse. Lack of recall ('I can't remember') is frequent. Speakers may idealize attachment relationships but cannot support idealizations (20–25% of normative samples).

Preoccupied (E). Transcripts are often long and incoherent. Confused, preoccupied enmeshed or actively angry in describing relationships about attachment figures. May also by passive or vague (10–15% in normative samples).

Unresolved/disorganized (U). Lapses in the monitoring of reasoning when discussing traumatic events or unresolved losses ('mislocations' of the dead person, sudden changes of tense form, confused or incomplete statements). Also assigned alternative F, Ds, E classifications (15–20% in normative samples).

Cannot Classify (CC). No single narrative strategy is evident, often alternating Ds passages with F or E passages.

References

Ainsworth M (1967) Infancy in Uganda. Baltimore: Johns Hopkins University Press.

Ainsworth M, Blehar M, Waters E and Wall S (1978) Patterns of Attachment. Hillsdale, NJ: Erlbaum.

Carlson V, Cicchetti D, Barnett D and Braunwald K (1989) Disorganized/disoriented attachment relationships in maltreated infants. Developmental Psychology 25: 525–31.

DeMulder EK and Radke-Yarrow M (1991) Attachment with affectively ill and well mothers: Concurrent behavioral correlates. Development and Psychopathology 3: 227–42.

George C and Main M (1979) Social interaction of young abused children: Approach, avoidance, and aggression. Child Development 50: 306–18.

Jacobvitz D, Hazen N and Riggs S (1997, April) Disorganized mental processes in mothers, frightening/frightened caregiving, and disoriented/disorganized behavior in infancy. In: D Jacobvitz (Chair), Caregiving Correlates and Longitudinal Outcomes of Disorganized Attachments in Infants. Symposium conducted at the biennial meeting of the Society for Research in Child Development, Washington, DC.

Lyons-Ruth K, Repacholi B, McLeod S and Silva E (1991) Disorganized attachment behavior in infancy: Short-term stability, maternal and infant correlates, and risk-related subtypes. Development and Psychopathology 3: 377–96.

Main M and Hesse E (1990) Parents' unresolved traumatic experiences are related to infant disorganized attachment status: Is frightened and/or frightening parental behavior the linking mechanism? In: MT Greenberg, D Cicchetti and EM Cummings (eds), Attachment in the Preschool Years: Theory, Research, and Intervention. Chicago: University of Chicago Press, pp. 161–82.

O'Connor MJ, Sigman M and Brill N (1987) Disorganization of attachment in relation to maternal alcohol consumption. Journal of Consulting and Clinical Psychology 55: 831–6.

Schuengel C, van IJzendoorn M, Bakermans-Kranenburg M and Blom M (1997, April). Frightening, frightened and/or dissociated behavior, unresolved loss, and infant disorganization. In: D Jacobvitz (Chair), Caregiving correlates and longitudinal outcomes of disorganized attachments in infants. Symposium conducted at the biennial meeting of the Society for Research in Child Development, Washington, DC.

Index